Salt of the Earth

Salt of the Earth

*The Political Origins of Peasant Protest
and Communist Revolution in China*

Ralph A. Thaxton, Jr.

UNIVERSITY OF CALIFORNIA PRESS

Berkeley   Los Angeles   London

University of California Press
Berkeley and Los Angeles, California

University of California Press, Ltd.
London, England

© 1997 by the Regents of the University of California

An earlier version of Chapter 2 of this book was published as "State Making and State Terror: The Formation of the Revenue Police and the Origins of Collective Protest in Rural North China during the Republican Period," *Theory and Society* 19(1990): 335–76.

Library of Congress Cataloging-in-Publication Data

Thaxton, Ralph, 1944–
  Salt of the earth : the political origins of peasant protest and communist revolution in China / Ralph A. Thaxton, Jr.
    p.   cm.
  Includes bibliographical references and index.
  ISBN 0–520–20318–6 (alk. paper)
    1. Communism—China—History—20th century.   2. Peasant uprisings—China—History—20th century.   3. China—Politics and government—20th century.   I. Title.
  HX417.5.T48   1997
  322.4'4'095109041—dc20   96-20359
                                                                 CIP

Manufactured in the United States of America
9 8 7 6 5 4 3 2 1

The paper used in this publication meets the minimum requirements of American National Standard for Information Sciences—Permanence of Paper for Printed Library Materials, ANSI Z39.48-1984.

To Janet, with affection and admiration

CONTENTS

TABLES, MAPS, AND FIGURE

ACKNOWLEDGMENTS

Many wonderful colleagues have given me wise counsel and stimulated me to try to live up to their high standards. Vivienne Shue and Sherman Cochran arranged for me to give a talk on the topic of this book at Cornell University when the project was just beginning to take shape. The helpful criticisms on that talk proved inspirational.

I am especially grateful to those who offered their critical reflections on the early drafts of the manuscript. Mark Selden, Mary Backus Rankin, and Kenneth Pomeranz all read the manuscript in its entirety, and each gave invaluable advice on how to sharpen the focus of the argument. David D. Buck, James Reardon-Anderson, Kwan Manbun, Edward Friedman, Ramon H. Myers, Peter J. Seybolt, James C. Scott, Benedict J. Tria Kerkvliet, Prasenjit Duara, and Daniel Little all commented on several chapters at one stage or another. I am much indebted to my good colleagues Edward Friedman and Ramon Myers for making this a better scholarly work and to my good colleagues Charles Tilly and Frederick Wakeman, Jr., for guiding me to my wonderfully supportive editor, Sheila Levine. The two anonymous readers who reviewed the manuscript for U.C. Press were tough but fair critics whose insights helped me improve this work in countless ways. Their detailed comments and suggestions helped me enrich the historical narrative of my case and contrast its contribution with that of several other scholarly works on the emergence of revolution in rural pre-1949 China. Thanks also to Lucien Bianco and Elizabeth J. Perry, for they were kind enough to read the work right before it went into page proofs. Fortunately, I was able to benefit from some, though not all, of their wise counsel.

Last but not least I would like to pay homage to some of my colleagues in the Brandeis Politics Department. R. Shep Melnick, Ruth Schachter Morgenthau, Seyom Brown, Robert J. Art, Donald Hindley, and Mark Hulliung all have provided helpful advice and criticism. I am especially thankful to Ruth for steering me to the book's title and to Seyom and Robert for helping me better telegraph the reader on usage of oral history sources. But it is to Jeffrey Abramson that I am most indebted, for Jeffrey's advice ultimately stimulated the last critical paragraph in the section on oral history methodology. In short, many good colleagues have helped me improve this work, but of course I alone am responsible for any and all of its shortcomings.

Several institutions have provided generous fellowship support for this project. A grant from the National Endowment for the Humanities helped me launch this field research in 1985, and I also received an NEH Summer Fellowship in 1990. The Social Science Research Council, American Council of Learned Societies, and the Academy of Sciences provided the opportunity for me to study in China under the CSCPRC for more than five months in the period 1989–91. Pam Peirce and Anthony Hutchinson provided helpful guidance in the difficult year following the Tiananmen incident, supporting my return to China for fieldwork in a more restrained research environment. A summer 1991 grant from ACLS gave me the chance to return to rural China for additional field research and to spend time at the Hoover Archives at Stanford University. On two occasions, Brandeis University's Mazer Fellowship Committee awarded travel and research grants, enabling me to carry on this project in rural China in 1987 and 1988. The Yale University East Asian Library and the Stanford University East Asian Library both provided travel grants, permitting me to survey their holdings in 1984 and 1988. To the librarians of Yale, Cornell, Stanford, and the Hoover Institution, I am grateful for invaluable assistance.

Without Professor Wei Hongyun of the Nankai University History Department this field research would not have been possible. I wish to thank him for having enabled me to enter the world of China's village people and for arranging my interviews of Wang Congwu and Nie Zhen in particular. Professor Ding Changqing of the Nankai University Economics Research Institute was kind and helpful, giving me some special materials that resolved some long unanswered questions about the finance ministry's revenue police. Professors Xu Youli and Guo Chuanxi of the Zhengzhou University History Department and Professor Mao Xixue of the Henan Province Academy of Social Sciences made the arrangements for me to conduct field research in Puyang, Nanle, and Hua counties. Zhong Dalu, my research assistant, and I struggled for the freedom we needed to dig up local history. With the help of Mr. Shi Guoqiang, and our village contacts, we moved a step closer to the paradigm of China's country people.

PEASANT MEMORY AND ORAL HISTORY:
A NOTE ON METHODOLOGY

The oral history data for this book were derived mainly from the library of peasant memory. Most of them are from field research focused on three counties (Puyang, Hua*xian*, and Nanle) and three towns (Puyang, Dao Kou, and Nanle) in the section of the North China plain just north of the Yellow River, where the provinces of Hebei, Shandong, and Henan converge. Building on Anne L. Craig's work,[1] I have tapped the remembered life histories of some two hundred participants in a major protest movement and drawn on one thousand hours of interviews between 1985 and 1993 in the rural villages of Qian Kou, Qi Ji, Fanzhuang, and Qian Foji and in Cheng Guan and San Huang, both located within county towns. Borrowing from Paul R. Connerton's *How Societies Remember*,[2] I have recorded peasant "habit-memory," that is, remembrances of performances associated with habitual practices, to illuminate popular forms of resistance that became entangled with CCP-led revolution.

Western scholarship on the origins and nature of the pre-1949 revolution in rural China relies upon inscription, but this process is *verbal*, not inscribed. The peasant saltmakers in *Salt of the Earth* speak to us from brains stockpiled with information on how they performed socially and politically in Republican times. Yet why, if the memory of habitual practice is so prevalent in the countryside, is study of the October 1 revolution via this form of memory virtually nonexistent? The answer—which supersedes both the cold war loss of access to rural China and the Communist Party's ideological representation of the place of the country people in the modern revolution—is so fundamental that it has eluded us. Many of the politicians who played leading parts in the CCP-led revolutionary struggle were themselves country folk who simply were not accustomed to recording their deeds and thoughts: their popularity and political credibility in folk society were acknowledged mainly within the framework of local oral tradition. At the same time, many of the CCP leaders were too busy seeking ways to speed the development of China after 1949, too caught up in the crises of the Korean War, the Great Leap Forward, and the Sino-Soviet split, to write of the interplay between their party's revolutionary history and folk political tradition. *Salt of the Earth* is an attempt to retrieve this interplay.

Peasant memory is an important source of historical information about the unknown cast of folk characters who played a role in the pre-1949 revolution—their relations with local community, their lifestyles, their religious traditions and political sentiments, and especially the extent to which they aligned with the CCP.[3] The justification for rediscovering the October 1 revolution through peasant memory goes beyond well-founded skepticism about the doctrinaire slant of CCP history to the cultural gap between the peasantry and the ruling national elite, which is composed in part of party-trained intellectuals living in cities and capitals far removed from villages in the remote areas where the revolution was based. Socially and culturally distanced from peasant life, these party scholars carry a host of biases. Indeed, such historians have little predisposition to explore the pre-1949 participation of the peasantry from the standpoint of the folk societies and folk cultures that helped shape and define popular commitments to the CCP and its revolutionary program. Perceiving country folk as illiterate, dirty, impulsive, mentally incompetent, and ridden with ridiculous fairy tales, these historians are repulsed by the notion that folk interests and ideas both inspired and invigorated the CCP-orchestrated revolutionary process. Most of them, ignoring peasant memory, delight in consulting written party records and party materials on revolutionary history, seldom questioning whether these are in accord with the remembered history of village people.

Inasmuch as peasant memory reflects the habitual interest-serving performance of a common group of country people, it is a form of memory that usually is retrieved within a localized framework of community history[4] and thus has a logic that is not merely the product of the national historical moments or international political events that have framed the recollections of the October 1 revolution for the regional and national leaders of the Communist Party. As Connerton points out in reference to Carlo Levi's 1935 political exile to an Italian village, members of two separate groups who participate in the same event often place their memory of that event in significantly different frameworks.[5] Levi took special note of the inscribed commemoratives to the local martyrs of World War I, but he also discovered that peasants did not even speak of the Great War and had no memory of it as a critical event. The war they did remember was "the war of the brigands" with the government.[6] This previous war, in comparison to World War I, had left a permanent imprint on their collective identity. Similarly, I found that peasants did not assign the same importance to the definitive historical event that shaped the political identity of many of the CCP leaders who formed the revolutionary Hebei-Shandong-Henan border area government during WWII: the Japanese invasion and the War of Resistance. To be sure, the War of Resistance was important to many village people; but for the great majority its significance paled in comparison to the remembrances of a war against the police instrument of Kuomintang fiscal order. This latter war preceded, intersected with, and persisted beyond the CCP-led War of Resistance and, in many respects, posed a greater challenge to the permanency of peasant life and culture.

The politicization of the peasantry by the CCP, and of the historiography of the October 1 revolution by centrally placed party theoreticians who became the guardians of popular revolutionary history after 1949, both diminished and debased the ways in which pre-1949 local Communist leaders acted in accordance with folk ideas and initiatives. Once the Marxist-Leninist theoreticians began to establish their hegemony within the party-state, and perfected their ideologically neat representations of the revolutionary epoch, it became politically dangerous for the local Communist leaders of the pre-1949 regional and national revolutionary process to write down their insights into how the rural folk had influenced, and sometimes invigorated, the CCP-led insurgency. Local popular memory of everyday revolutionary politics gave way to distortion, silence, and hesitancy to publish oral history findings that were not in harmony with correct party history lines. In myriad ways, this kind of party hegemony has worked to prevent us from entering the pre-1949 revolution via peasant memory. I encountered three examples of this phenomenon. (1) In interviewing peasants in Hua County I discovered that the provincial-level party historians presented the local popular struggle over salt as having been staged under the leadership of the CCP, when in peasant memory, it was clearly the product of local village leaders who were the allies of, but not members of, the party. (2) While interviewing Beijing-based CCP leaders who formerly had been intimately connected with the peasant saltmakers in Puyang, I learned that not only had they not discussed their pre-1949 history with foreigners, but they had not even discussed it with homegrown Chinese historians from Puyang itself, fearing that their reminiscences would not resonate with post-1949 Central Committee historiography. (3) In interviewing peasants in Nanle County I found that the most knowledgeable local historian of the popular struggle I was studying had begun his own village oral history project on this topic, but only in 1979, after the CCP reformers had defeated the antimarket radicals in the party hierarchy. He had yet to publish his voluminous raw notes, partly because the peasant memory they contained did not fit neatly into the categories of high-level party historians.

In collecting data for *Salt of the Earth* I have followed several method-ological procedures, each undertaken to depoliticize the interviews and to maximize the reliability of information derived from them. First, in order to avoid ending up with an extremely biased sample of preselected villages where the CCP was firmly entrenched and where the party leaders could recast local social history and revise the political history of the pre-1949 period, I insisted on the right to choose the "protest villages" in which I con-ducted oral history research. I selected Qian Kou village in Puyang in con-sultation with my hosts; I chose Qi Ji, Fanzhuang, and Qian Foji and the other village interview sites after reading about them in internally restrict-ed CCP documents or after picking up information about them from peas-ants in other border area villages. As a rule, my hosts did not go to these vil-lages with me, especially after my second trip in June, 1987, for they were not interested in learning the revolutionary history of the rural people and did not want to endure the hardships of research in the outlying villages. Usually, no PRC authorities (university hosts, foreign affairs bureau offi-cials, or local county historians) accompanied me to monitor my interviews. Nor did my hosts call villagers, or village leaders, to party offices to "pre-pare" them to give politically correct answers to my questions. At my invita-tion, Mr. Shi Guoqiang of the Nanle County Local History Office accompa-nied me to Fanzhuang once, to San Huang twice, and to Qian Foji once. My Chinese research assistant was with me 70 percent of the time; otherwise, I was alone with local people.

A second ticklish question arose: how could one be confident that the momentary "party line" did not shape the stories peasants thought an inter-viewer should hear? To avoid relying on a biased sample of preselected and pretutored individuals who gained political credit either by parroting the CCP pro-market line of the 1980s or by recalling more bitter suffering under the Kuomintang than their neighbors, I got permission to select my own respondents without interference from my university hosts or village party leaders. For the most part, I chose interview subjects by the technique of "snowball sampling" outlined by Earl R. Babbie.[7] My previously inter-viewed informants helped me build up a network of local people who had participated in, witnessed, or somehow knew about antistate protest at the village, market, and county levels in the 1930s. This technique permitted me to comprehend past changes from the perspective of villagers from all walks of life and from different lineages and to build up a data base that avoided the pitfalls of CCP-controlled sampling. In eight different trips to the countryside, I interviewed two hundred rural people through in-depth household talks and small-group discussions. Approximately half had par-ticipated directly in the saltmakers' struggle of the 1930s, and another 25 percent were from households whose members had supported, or sympathized with, that struggle. Approximately 22 percent of the peasant salt producers, peddlers, and purchase agents interviewed had become members of the Chinese Communist Party prior to 1949; 78 percent had no history of party involvement. Furthermore, many of these peasant interviewees had resisted the post-1949 antimarket campaigns of the CCP-directed state, so that they hardly needed a party line to structure their preferences for market freedom.

I interviewed the majority of respondents in their homes, either alone or with a few family members present. In talking with individual peasants about their relations with the protest movement under study, I placed them within the framework of family memory, for as Maurice Halbwachs has pointed out,[8] peasants are inclined to remember their individual history as part of a pattern of interaction with family. I wanted to see if the struggle with the Kuomintang state was, at bottom, a struggle of members of kinship groups sharing habits that the state was harming, and I wanted to elicit responses anchored in the interior of peasant memory, which I believe is to a significant extent walled off from the propaganda of the party. In all of these household interviews, therefore, I went to great lengths to detect, avoid, and get beyond the "stilted responses" of peasants skilled in the rituals of Maoist recall and attempted to create a climate in which CCP-prepared scripts did not structure responses. The dialogue was, following David W. Sabean,[9] objectively focused on a balanced search for how villagers themselves perceived and defined their proprietary rights and market prerogatives and how they created a discourse among themselves over the attempts of state revenue forces to sacrifice these rights and prerogatives to the fiscal drives of top-level policy makers in Chiang Kai-shek's central government.

Approximately 70 percent of my interviews were conducted in peasant households, and I had permission to go to any household I chose. Of course some of the older peasants misremembered. Thus, I used a fourth, group-oriented interview method in order to better jog peasant memory, interviewing the same aged peasants I already had interviewed privately in a group context, with three to six villagers. I focused on the political life history of only one person among those present, drilling him and asking him and his fellow villagers questions about his past. The logic of this strategy is obvious: many old peasants have not thought about, or talked with others about, their pre-1949 protest activities for fifty years. By bringing old friends together in group interviews, I could nudge one man to help another think harder about hazy memories, thereby frequently stimulating individual memory through a free-wheeling group discussion and exchange.

This group interview method had to be carried out in a way that allowed me to comprehend the relationship between family memory and small-group memory. In bringing peasants of different households together to access their collective group memory, I was careful to note whether they were independently translating group remembrances of local history into images, terms, and insights that lifted them to consonance.[10] I paid special attention to whether they, as individuals, identified with and embraced a pattern of group remembrances without tutoring from local party leaders and took precautions not to interview peasants for the first time in a group context and not to permit a handful of party ideologues to take over and dominate the group interviews. Also, I was careful to avoid arranging group interviews solely in the household or courtyard of the CCP village secretaries (though in the immediate aftermath of the Tiananmen Square incident this proved to be a delicate and difficult task in one village where I had not previously interviewed).

Finally, I employed a number of procedures to control for lying. I made it a point to interview about 10 percent of the peasants with good memories two, three, and four times, so that I could check their original stories as well as collect new information. I also cross-checked, and attempted to corroborate, information gleaned from villagers against three different sources: other peasants interviewed in the same village unit; former CCP leaders who had grown up in the villages but who had left the countryside to take up positions in the PRC government in Beijing, Zhengzhou, and Tianjin after 1949; and documents, manuscripts, and handwritten notes.

Another aide to detecting lying or wild exaggeration involved nonverbal political communication among villagers participating in small-group interview sessions. The animated reactions of the older peasant saltmakers to the overblown melodrama being mouthed by some of the interviewees—raised eyebrows, mutual glances of disbelief, and contemptuous head shaking— signaled a respondent had departed substantially from reality. This was another advantage of intensive, long-term group interviewing.

When a footnote to the text takes a form that reads "Liu Chaoyang, Qi Ji, 8/9/90," such a note is telegraphing the reader that I am relying on an oral interview conducted during my trips to China—Qi Ji village on August 9, 1990. Such a reference is a signal to the reader that peasants are speaking their own history and that something other than the censored Chinese publications that govern so much of Western scholarship on rural life is at work. This system of footnoting, along with signals in the text itself, is what disaggregates the oral from the written documentation underlying the argument, and the reader is encouraged to consult the endnotes in order to ascertain when the oral history is coming into play.

The dictates of length required that I cut vast portions of the oral history materials from the final version of the manuscript; further, a lot of oral history evidence I have gathered did not find its way into the original longer version of *Salt of the Earth,* so that an even greater evidentiary oral history data base underlies the narrative and interpretation presented here. This oral history evidence is composed of handwritten interviews that are stored in my home library. At some point these data will be deposited in an appropriate American university library and will be accessible to other scholars who are serious students of China's agrarian politics and history.

The process of oral interviewing underwent a gradual transformation during the tenure of my project. Essentially, I began with a set of rather stilted printed Chinese questionnaires about peasant life and village economy; moved to a second, more flexible mode of printed Chinese interviews that asked villagers to place their everyday life experiences, including forms of resistance and protest, in the context of political events and processes unfolding in the border area between 1915 and 1949; and then graduated to a mode of informal, open-ended interviewing that often abandoned structured printed Chinese questions and patiently allowed village respondents to rework questions in ways that took me down paths I had not intended to explore and brought me into new, unanticipated streams of local knowledge about politics, society, and economy. Each of these different interview modes was grounded in and/or generated hundreds of questions, so it would be impossible to print them in an appendix. Nevertheless, I am willing to share the oral history questionnaires as well as the oral history raw notes with other specialists, many of whom have not had the privilege of interacting with rural people who helped shape the pre-1949 revolutionary process.

ONE

Bureaucratic Capitalism and the Emergence of Popular Antistate Protest

Day by day, the peasants make the economists sigh, the politicians sweat and the strategists swear, defeating their plans and prophecies all over the world.
TEODOR SHANIN, "PEASANTRY AS A POLITICAL FACTOR"

Anyone seeking to understand the development of agrarian-based political upheaval must first understand peasant China's modern history, for it was in China that peasants first defeated the plans of twentieth-century state makers through insurgency and revolution. Western scholars have overcome great obstacles in reconstructing the authentic political role of rural people in the agrarian-based insurgency that ushered in the PRC, but the "peasantry" often remains an abstract, elusive social group. Until a decade ago, the constraints imposed by the cold war, combined with the horrendous living conditions in the Chinese countryside, made it virtually impossible for anyone from the pasteurized, democratic zones of the planet to conduct sustained scientific field research in the remote seedbeds of the Communist-led insurgency. Moreover, as Barrington Moore, Jr., emphasizes, written materials on the peasantry, filtered as they were through the prism of Communist Party or Kuomintang politicians, interlopers, or academics with political axes to grind, are "sparse and their authenticity often doubtful."[1]

Salt of the Earth explores a long-running dispute between village people and state power holders in Republican China. It reveals how the attempt of top rank Kuomintang state officials to resolve this dispute produced unanticipated political woes for Chiang Kai-shek's central government and examines how the formation and placement of a secret police force in rural society became a chronic, systemic problem in village dwellers' quest for a livelihood and how the Communist Party aligned with, and eventually profited from, their collective resistance. And it shows why, and how, a seemingly unimportant subgroup of rural people in one part of the North China region gave up on Kuomintang governance and threw its support to the Chinese Communist Party and its armed forces in the crisis moments of the civil war.

This book revises previous Western scholarly works on protest and revolution in pre-1949 China in several ways. My anatomy of peasant economy springs from the experience of village people who had mastered the art of survival in early Republican times, reconstructing the formation of long-term popular resistance from the memory of rural people who actually created it. Susan Naquin, Joseph W. Esherick, Elizabeth J. Perry, and Kathryn Bernhardt all present important representations of durable patterns of peasant resistance and rebellion against internal political enemies in the pre-1949 countryside.[2] In several important respects, however, *Salt of the Earth* breaks with conventional Western scholarly approaches to the Communist-led revolution; particularly as to the nature of Communist Party appeals to rural people and the relationship of CCP organization to local struggle and revolutionary mobilization. Although other scholars recognized that peasant struggles to achieve market access were important in twentieth-century China,[3] the present study empirically shows that *the popular struggle for the market was a central issue in Communist Party efforts to elicit mass support for the party's revolutionary mission.* The work places CCP appeals in a complex set of local popular grievances while tracing these grievances to national and international political developments that predated the Great Pacific War. It transcends the thirty-year debate between Chalmers Johnson[4] and Mark Selden[5] over whether the Chinese Communists built up a base of support by appealing to war-induced peasant grievances or to social issues visited on village people by landlords and warlords.

Moreover, this volume also presents the CCP's organizational relationship with peasant mobilization in a way that differs from the approaches of Western scholars who have claimed, as Ordoric Y. K. Wou does in *Mobilizing the Masses,* that "the Chinese revolution must be perceived as a movement deliberately and systematically fomented, organized, and built by the Chinese Communist Party. It was the outcome of purposive actions taken by the party and the party, in fact, stage-managed the revolution."[6] This study gets beyond arguments about whether the CCP-led victory was crafted by outside Leninist organizers or was the product of internal peasant social mobilization. The catalytic role of the Communist Party is beyond dispute; no one questions that CCP elites played a crucial role in revolutionary mobilization. *Salt of the Earth* goes further, showing that such elites were schoolteachers, doctors, and students who were seen by village people as insiders. Their role in fostering revolution is best understood in terms of their intimate connections with local structures of collective action and with existing modes of local protest, both of which were the product of a specific subgroup of rural people acting on their own grievances, interests, and goals. Hard-pressed to freely and fully stage-manage this process of popular mobilization, the Communists won by grasping its relationship to the politics of Kuomintang state making, by accommodating the community impulses and institutions behind it, and by resonating with its cultural transcript, which justified insurgent removal of state-level oppressors.

The interviews with peasants comprise firsthand accounts of conflict with Republican power holders and are backed up by archives, letters, personal manuscripts, and restricted Communist Party publications and Kuomintang Finance Ministry documents. Relying on these sources, I address the seminal question: Why did peasants turn to protest, and how did their protest become entwined with revolution?

Years before organizing anti-Japanese resistance in remote territories, the Chinese Communists were discovering the importance of aligning with a politically aroused peasantry, an experience that later enabled them to defend China against Japanese aggression and ultimately to topple the Central government of Chiang Kai-shek. During World War II the Chinese Communists gained a massive popular following, building up a resilient counterpolity based on communitywide resistance in rural localities coming under the protective umbrella of their anti-Japanese armies.[7] But the Japanese invasion and war itself did not drive China's country people to collective resistance or prompt them to rally to the armed struggle forged by the Chinese Communists during World War II. In some rural North China localities where the CCP organized the war of resistance against Japan a durable form of popular concerted resistance had developed prior to WWII, the persistence of which, in conjunction with the damage inflicted on the Kuomintang state by the Japanese during the great war, gave the Chinese Communists the opportunity to vault themselves to national power.

The Hebei-Shandong-Henan border area was such a place (see Maps 1 and 2). In the Republican era it incorporated thirty to forty counties and approximately twenty million inhabitants. *Salt of the Earth* is based on oral and written sources about pre-1949 politics in five counties—Puyang, Neihuang, Hua*xian*, Qingfeng, and Nanle—half a day's rail journey from Beijing to Anyang and another four hours by automobile on kidney-jarring roads heading east to the Wei River, which flows northward from Dao Kou town in Henan to Yuancunji in Nanle, in Hebei, and then on to Shandong where it joins the Grand Canal at Linqing. Along with Daming, Changyuan, and Dongming, this five-county area makes up the southern cone of Hebei, the western rim of Shandong, and the northern tip of Henan Province.

During the Nationalist decade, 1928–37, this inner part of the border area was, largely, politically subordinate to Daming Prefecture, which the Chiang Kai-shek–led Kuomintang administered between 1931 and 1935. In the period of the War of Resistance, 1937–45, 70 percent of its population came under the influence of the Fourth District of the CCP-led Hebei-Shandong-Henan border region government.[8] The other 30 percent was ruled by the Kuomintang until 1939–40, after which they, along with half of

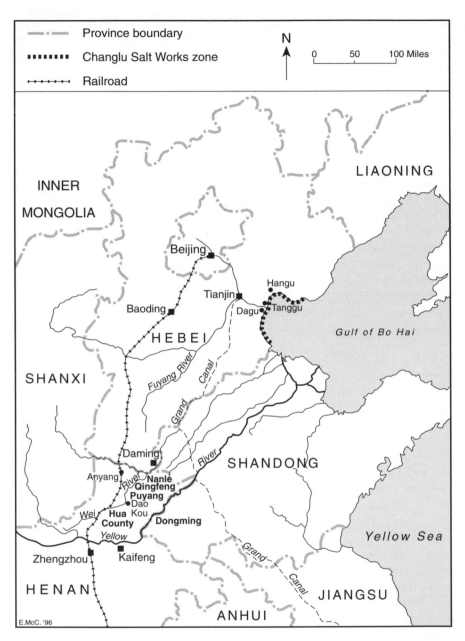

Map 1. North China, showing the Changlu salt works

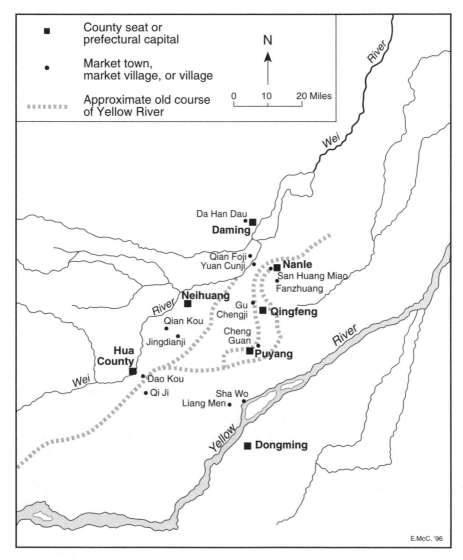

Map 2. The lower North China plain and the old course of the Yellow River

their counterparts in the CCP-influenced localities, were at the mercy of the Japanese army and its quisling military administration. During the civil war of 1946–49 the Kuomintang army attempted to take back this border area. Shortly thereafter, the early round of military struggle for state power between the Nationalists and the Communists was decided around this border area.

CCP interaction with the inhabitants of these core rural places was so crucial to the way in which the Communists gained control of the border region that their story provides the main thread of the larger revolutionary process. These five counties were typical in two important respects: the existence of large amounts of very saline land provided a means of entrepreneurial survival, threatened by agents of the Republican state; and the CCP's ability to build a popular base in these five counties as in many surrounding border region counties by promoting collective resistance to Kuomintang state interference.

In the late Qing, the physical environment of the border area posed a dilemma for the peasantry. Puyang, Neihuang, Hua*xian*, Qingfeng, and Nanle all were situated along the old course of the Yellow River, which, on bolting its bed, had saturated thirty to forty *li* stretches of good land with salt, nitre, and silt. Tillers were left with declining grain crop yields, a chronic problem intensified by the Imperial government's default on the upkeep of the Yellow River conservancy. Doubtless, the diversion of commercial traffic from the Wei River to the Beijing-Hankow railway dealt a blow to the economy of once prosperous river towns like Dao Kou in Hua County.[9] Warlord surtaxes for Yellow River maintenance, collected incessantly between 1923 and 1928, did not help. Nor did the Nationalist government, whose officials transferred funds needed for this inland area's hydraulic upkeep to projects in the advanced coastal sector, leaving the local people to find their own way out of poverty.[10]

The northern gateway to the Central Plain, the area was a strategic point that military strategists of each dynasty attempted to occupy and that rebel contenders had seized in pursuit of the Mandate of Heaven. Its importance increased in the modern period, for it was located only a hundred kilometers from the Beijing-Hankow and Tianjin-Pukou railways. Further, the region's inhabitants had a reputation for rebellion, and legends of the great uprisings led by Zhai Rang at the end of the Sui dynasty and by Huang Chao at the close of the Tang were still alive.

By the Republican period, the average peasant family in the border area numbered about five, with an average landholding about five *mu* per capita, which conforms to the standard picture of approximately twenty-two *mu* per household on the plains of Hebei, Shandong, and Henan around 1930.[11] Because the land was increasingly saline, many peasant families were facing a serious decline in fertile cropland. Although there was little variation from village to village in the average per capita landholding, some noticeable variations existed at the subvillage level. In Qian Foji in Nanle County, for example, the average per capita landholding for peasant households was one to two *mu,* owing partly to the concentration of land in the hands of a few landlords. In Fanzhuang, a village without landlordism, the households in the smallest, poorest lineages often held only one *mu* per capita of bad land. Land salinization, coupled with land inequalities, meant that villagers lived a precarious existence.

A host of premodern social relations characterized rural life. The lesser gentry, bearing titles from the Imperial past, were still active in local politics and business; many a Kuomintang-appointed magistrate sought them out to manage subcounty affairs, and villagers were still inclined to solicit gentry assistance in disputes with county authorities. Few landlords owned more than five hundred *mu* and most held only a hundred or so. Prior to the Kuomintang ascent in 1928 they performed largely as patrons, treating most of their tenants and hired hands fairly. Landlordism usually was subsumed within lineage relations, so that conflicts over class issues often were precluded by lineage ties, and most landlords were careful not to offend the poor folks in any lineage. To violate the "subsistence ethic" of the poor was to invite retaliation, retribution, and possibly the ruin of one's household reputation.

The majority of peasants owned the land they farmed and lived alongside others in their lineages. Most villages were made up of two, three, or four lineages interconnected by settlement myths, by ties of marriage, and by patterns of marketing. All of the villages in this study were allegedly started by migrants from Hong Tong County in Shanxi Province; peasants shared this uniform foundation myth with their counterparts across the border area. Most villages were dominated by one or two prominent families in the most wealthy and powerful lineage, but marriages and other joint activities with other lineages were not uncommon. A shared interest in small trade and a mutual connection to the same local market system bound peasants in a wider community.

In Republican times, most peasants in the Hebei-Shandong-Henan border area tilled grain crops, dealt in livestock, and marketed a host of nonfarm products. Virtually every village had its marshlands, supplying reeds for mats, baskets, grain containers (*dun*), and thatch. On the semibarren sandy soils deposited by the Yellow River floods peasants planted date trees and peanuts; on the marginal saline lands they made common salt and sold it in local market networks. The early chapters of *Salt of the Earth* examine the process whereby peasants came into conflict with Kuomintang state makers over the use of this poor environment, particularly the poor salt lands, and how this conflict drew the attention of a Communist movement looking to mobilize the rural poor.

Several excellent studies, particularly those of Ramon H. Myers,[12] Philip C. C. Huang,[13] Edward Friedman, Paul G. Pickowicz, Mark Selden,[14] and

Kenneth Pomeranz,[15] have furthered our knowledge of the complex nature of the peasant economy of pre-1949 North China. Huang alludes to survival-driven peasant market production; Friedman et al. stress the importance of marketing to peasant subsistence. *Salt of the Earth* provides a detailed, worm's-eye view of the importance country people assigned to market endeavors and shows how the Republican state threatened to snuff out a vital market choice. Borrowing from G. William Skinner's insights,[16] I attempt to extend his logic (though not his grand paradigm) by sketching out the myriad ways in which village people fashioned small, and then big, protest movements against state controls on essential markets.

The four prewar case studies of village protest (Cheng Guan, Qian Kou, Qi Ji, and Fanzhuang) in Chapters 3–6 were chosen for several reasons. First, each was a prewar stronghold of collective protest. The literature on pre-1949 China has little to say about the "protest history" of villages prior to the entry of the Communists or the Japanese invasion. Many studies of peasant mobilization have tended to focus on CCP-instigated mass movements and strategies of party building for brief episodes that are taken as incidents that served the purpose of CCP "base area" development and the seizure of state power. Hence, we have only rudimentary knowledge of how collective protest followed its own rhythm, form, and path. Without such knowledge how can we possibly begin to discern the ways in which the evolving history of village people intersected with, and shaped the course of, the large-scale political change that placed the Communists in power in Beijing on 1 October 1949? To grasp the impact of village protest on the course of the Chinese revolution, it seems logical first to study protest on its own terms where it took place and then bring in the political actors who sought to link that protest with revolution.

Second, the four villages were selected because their economic, religious, geographical, and political differences permit an understanding of why and how collective protest formed across a spectrum of rural communities. In the Republican period, for example, Qian Kou's economy was diversified, prosperous, and only partly dependent on salt making. The economy of Qi Ji was virtually submarginal and was heavily dependent on salt trade; Fanzhuang's inhabitants relied mainly on crop production until they discovered the salt market big time in the early 1920s; Cheng Guan, with its salt-impregnated soils and land scarcity, apparently was almost entirely dependent on market activity for livelihood.

Village religious ties also varied. Qi Ji's strong Catholic affiliations set it apart from the other three villages. Catholic priests made some inroads in Cheng Guan, too, but they never developed a stable of converts who became the leaders of protest, as was the case with Qi Ji. Though Qian Kou's Communist Party activists evicted Protestant missionaries around 1933–34, the Protestants were treated with tolerance, and even appreciation, by the peasant saltmakers of Fanzhuang and Qian Foji (see Chapter 8). In any event, people in all four villages showed devotion to a range of indigenous religious deities, one of which was the war god—a deity the Communists could not afford to attack.

The varied political geography of these villages encouraged inhabitants to openly pursue collective action and influenced the ability of the CCP to gain the security needed to win allies, establish its presence, and promote its programs. Qian Kou, Qi Ji, and Qian Foji all were located a long way from Kuomintang national police forces and provincial power holders. The people of these villages were more inclined to come together to openly protest state intrusion—Cheng Guan, within Puyang town, and Fanzhuang, only a short distance from Nanle County town, were places where villagers had to pursue less risky forms of protest, though, as Chapters 3 and 6 make clear, there were limits to such a strategy, and these geographically insecure people eventually joined in highly visible collective protest with their rebellious counterparts from the countryside.

There were sharp political differences also. Qian Kou's esteemed and educated families had served as advisors to late Qing and early Republican local government, and the prominent families of both Cheng Guan and Fanzhuang also had connections with the influential lesser gentry. If Qian Kou's college-educated youth turned to the CCP in the late 1920s, prior to involvement with the saltmakers' protest, Fanzhuang's elites were committed to the Kuomintang before, during, and even after the rebellion of the mid-1930s. The young protest leaders in Qi Ji were not college educated, so in this poorest of the four villages the Communists had to interact with people who apparently had neither close affiliations with the minor gentry nor modern education. If, as Chapters 3 and 4 suggest, the CCP was better able to fuse with collective protest and build its presence in protest villages with elite connections and modern educational links to prefectural capitals, then what was the fate of the party, and of the protest movement it sought to develop regionally, in the other villages?

A third objective of this probe was to find out if collective action in different villages produced a distinctively similar form of protest. Beyond any doubt, collective action in all four villages corresponded with a form of protest aimed at thwarting the attempts of police agents of top-level Kuomintang state officials to impose taxes on items of necessity and to eliminate a popular avenue of trade. The book also examines why rural people who favored modes of protest that fell short of revolutionary contention eventually were drawn to contentious political activities, and to the CCP. Was the contentious face of popular protest, and its consonance with CCP's political mission, primarily a function of the accent of Kuomintang state making, or did the Communists somehow manage to set the rural people firmly against the Kuomintang government in the 1930s?

Finally, I chose these four villages in order to explicate the relationship between the formation of collective protest and the success or failure of the CCP in linking up with popular mobilization at the village level and bringing country people from different places into a regional political coalition. Focusing on four different villages whose inhabitants all more or less shared alarm over Kuomintang state fiscal expansion presented a way of grasping whether the Communists were able to gain credibility by resonating with the contextual reality of relations between rural people and the agents of top-level political authorities and, further, whether in cultivating local allies they paid sufficient attention to the market community in which protestors from different villages found common interest and solidarity.

In the four village studies we enter a locally nuanced, empirically grounded understanding of why one subgroup of rural people came over to the CCP-led struggle against the Kuomintang state, collectively asserting interest in a sphere of the domestic market economy that reduced the perils of everyday life while holding out the promise of prosperity.[17] Participation in this informal market economy helped peasant families persevere throughout the Republican period. When it came to political behavior, the country people were not "single-issue voters," of course, but they were baseline "market voters," for their participation in protest, war, and CCP-led insurgency was structured by their interest in the informal market economy through which they turned bad earth into glad seasons. The dynamics of this market factor help us comprehend why the Chinese Communists were able to elicit popular support and how conditional that support was.

Chapter 2 deepens our knowledge of change and conflict in the pre-1949 countryside by bringing political institutions into the analysis of societal-state relations.[18] Drawing from Charles Tilly's scholarship on "state making,"[19] I ask how, if at all, the Republican fiscal state impinged on long-standing economic freedoms. The concept of state making, as used in the study, refers to the efforts of national power holders to extract resources from rural people, using these to construct a central government capable of financing its program for political development and to subdue opposition to its administrative preemption of economies crucial to everyday life. Via oral history and written materials, I document a durable pattern of protest against the intrusion of Kuomintang fiscal dictatorship, showing how the central government's attempt to realize state revenue claims in rural villages and markets ignited collective protest.

Adapting Tilly's state-making paradigm to state-societal conflict in Republican China necessitates several caveats. For one thing, Kuomintang state making was convulsed and complicated by imperialism. Kuomintang state leaders unquestionably made serious policy mistakes that eventually ruined them; but the notion of Nationalist officials acting *freely* to raise tax revenue to strengthen national security and support modernization programs is presumptuous, for international pressures precluded total autonomy. The protest movement was linked, at least indirectly, to the external debt crisis enveloping the modern Republican state, fostered by the repeated interventions of the global maritime powers into Chinese domestic fiscal matters. Antifiscal protest against the Chiang Kai-shek–led central government cannot be understood through single-factor causality. Rather, as John Walton has taught us, the causes of protest in the countryside "must be sought within a field of forces that converge on the state."[20] Although it is enlightening to ask how the logic of state making evoked this particular episode of protest, I have taken Sidney Tarrow's[21] advice and eschewed a mode of analysis that moves directly from macrolevel state making to microlevel collective protest. Although Tilly's concept helps flush out the process whereby the recentralization of revenue collection brought tax agents of Chiang Kai-shek's government face to face with village dwellers, this study also shows how Kuomintang state leaders pressed intermediate sociopolitical actors (regional merchants, county magistrates, and subcounty gentry) to facilitate operationalization of their fiscal transcript in the deep countryside. Because until recently many China scholars approached Republican politics as if the central state were missing in peasant society, the function of state-making theory here is to further reveal the nexus between the penetrative actions of central government tax agents and the progression of peasant collective actions aimed at impeding this penetration.

To what extent did the servicing of international debt and internal military buildup contribute to the subsistence crisis? Why did the Kuomintang fiscal elite fail to elicit mass support for its revenue seeking? And why, in turn, did these operations incite popular resistance to the Kuomintang state-building experiment?[22] Following Lucien Bianco and Prasenjit Duara,[23] I illuminate some of the ways in which the Kuomintang fiscal elite pursued revenue seeking to the point of fostering political instability in the North China countryside, producing its own crisis of legitimacy among rural people who, in many cases, were only barely touched by the Communist Party and its formal political doctrines. In this crisis lay the deep root system of popular support for the CCP-led insurgency.

Further, this book explores how rural dwellers resisted the actual intrusion of the fiscal center, defying and in some instances defeating the institutional presence of high-flying Kuomintang central government officials. I have undertaken to study the unfolding of peasant-initiated protest over a long period,[24] tracing the development of three modes of popular antistate protest over a thirty-year span: "everyday peasant resistance"[25] to the key Kuomintang political institution charged with raising taxes for monetary debts, modernization, and army maintenance; direct confrontation with

Kuomintang county officials; and large-scale, increasingly violent resistance and retaliation. A crucial question is whether these three modes of protest, none of which constituted radical challenges to Kuomintang state authority,[26] gave way to more contentious, offensive strategies, while preparing the rural people to respond to the CCP and its insurgent quest for state power.[27] This work brings new evidence to bear on this question, breaking it down in the context of peasant conceptions of the state drive for local resources and the fast-paced changes in rural power relations.

Does the fact that peasants had moved to direct retaliatory protest against the fiscal arm of the Kuomintang necessarily mean they had moved to revolutionary contention? I do not believe that the rural people actually wanted a violent showdown with the Nationalist government at the end of the Second World War. But how are we to explain the swift and startling shift from largely nonviolent protest in the mid-1930s to violent contention and civil war in the late 1940s? The oral history evidence warns us against assuming that the CCP's anti-Kuomintang propaganda by itself turned the country people against the Nationalist state. Their deep-seated resentment against Kuomintang revenue agents, and their hopes for lowering the level of Kuomintang state repression—hopes created both by their own prewar antistate collective protest victories and by the CCP taking advantage of the wartime blow dealt to the Kuomintang by the Japanese army—combined to convince villagers they could counteract the expansion of the state.

That rural people were fairly effective in opposing the march of central government money men, confounding the Kuomintang state attempt to wipe out their market way of life, will surprise few students of modern China. But what role, if any, did prewar protest leaders play in facilitating the formation of the CCP-led anti-Japanese base in the border area? What precisely was the relationship between antistate protest, the Japanese invasion and the War of Resistance, and the development of popular-based CCP power? To what extent did the wartime political success of the Chinese Communists hinge on their alignment with country people involved in a long-running war against the internal revenue army of the central government? Did the Japanese invasion prolong the internal peasant war against the Kuomintang revenue state, allowing its participants to strengthen their position vis-à-vis the Kuomintang army and making them more likely candidates for contentious, violent antistate activity?[28] This study furthers our understanding of whether the Japanese invasion was both a necessary and a sufficient condition for CCP-led success. It suggests that the Japanese intervention was indeed a critical factor contributing to the collapse of the Kuomintang state and hence was a necessary condition for the reemergence of the battered Communist Party. By the same token, however, the persistence of a disbanded but undefeated popular-based protest movement, with its leadership still intact and still on fairly good terms with local Communist leaders, was the critical sufficient condition assuring the Chinese Communists a competent mass base of support.

Before WWII the Chinese Communists had forged a strong bond of political trust with the local leaders of antistate protest in village after village, and during the war these liaisons helped them to get their anti-Japanese message across. If we ignore this unaltered popular internal antistate war, we miss a critical factor drawing the country people to the CCP-led defense of the countryside against external aggression. Worse, we miss the historical experience of the rural people who made it possible for the Chinese Communists to successfully organize mass-based resistance to the Japanese intruders.

Chapter 7 presents a political history of the Anti-Japanese War in the Hebei-Shandong-Henan border area, and it reveals that the injuries people suffered at the hands of the Kuomintang fiscal state in the prewar years predisposed some of them to contribute to the political economy of the CCP-led wartime resistance. Chapter 8 expands on this theme, highlighting the prewar struggle of a market village to preserve its network of exchange and illustrating how its inhabitants became involved with CCP-led resistance during the Second World War. In these chapters we discover that local CCP leaders organized anti-Japanese activities, and moved rural people to assist their resistance army, by placing their patriotic message within an indigenous political-cultural narrative that encouraged popular martial opposition to both internal and external predatory forces. The closing chapter shows how the Kuomintang-CCP struggle for the salt market, and not merely the Communist-directed struggle to redistribute landlord wealth via land revolution, exploded into a civil war in 1946–47, and it taps popular memory to shed light on why the semipeasants of this border zone risked their lives to lift the CCP and its army to national power.

As Gabriel A. Almond and Stephen J. Genco remind us, "the actors in politics have memories."[29] *Salt of the Earth* taps peasant memory to help us understand why and how rural people chose to intervene between the projections of Kuomintang state policymakers and the calculations of the Chinese Communists.[30] It shows that without peasant memory the history of how the Kuomintang state infringed on the market economy of rural people and of how the Communist Party interacted with the popular struggle to preserve the market would be lost to Western preconceptions of why the Nationalists lost and the Communists won.

This book deals with a great, persistent obstacle to comparative political inquiry in the China field: the dearth of locally derived empirical information about how the relationship between the Republican state and rural society affected the genesis of popular participation in the CCP-led revolution. Selecting one case and studying its development through oral history interviews, guided (but not straitjacketed) by the "state-making" paradigm of Tilly, permits us to discover a theoretically relevant answer to the question of why one geographical part of rural China was such a rebellious place in the twentieth century: plainly, there was a positive relationship between the Kuomintang state-making strategy and rural instability.

The purpose of this study, therefore, is to get us involved in what Arend Lijphardt has called "conscious thinking" about the value of case study research based substantially on oral history.[31] In and of itself, as Lijphardt cautions, a case study research strategy cannot produce a new, valid theoretical generalization; nor can it negate a well-established general theory of the rise of revolution in the Chinese countryside.[32] It can, however, offer new insights into the process whereby some rural people became involved in protest and insurgency and offer a tentative answer to a seminal question: what went on when the CCP interacted with the rural people during the pre-1949 revolution?[33]

One advantage of this case study is to provide richly textured empirical evidence that enables us to extend its premises and hypothesis to a larger range of regional systems within China, comparing those areas in which the phenomenon of popular protest was linked to the violent penetration of the countryside by the revenue forces of the Republican state.[34] To achieve comparability, we must first trace the formation of Kuomintang fiscal police forces charged with enforcing state extraction locally, especially in agriculturally poor areas where the production of marginalized peasants for the local market posed a structural dilemma for Kuomintang efforts to raise more revenue by imposing monopoly. We must also explore whether the reach of the Kuomintang revenue forces roused people in these poor-soil areas to resist taxes on salt, opium, alcohol, and other items produced for off-farm income, to see if a process similar to those uncovered in this salt making case was operating elsewhere in China as well. Further, we must pay special attention to one vital question: to what extent did government taxation, or suppression, of production for the market enable the CCP to lead rural people experienced in collective protest to checkmate the Kuomintang? As scholars of pre-1949 China have long known, many Communist base areas were positioned along the junctions of the administrative boundaries of agriculturally unproductive areas, far removed from the main fist of the Kuomintang central army. The question is whether such base areas formed along the axis of microsocial resistance to Kuomintang efforts to squelch popular trade. Does the state-society struggle documented in *Salt of the Earth* exemplify processes of Kuomintang state-induced mobilization and popular contributions to the CCP-led revolution found among similar types of popular struggle in other regions, or regional "base areas"?

A full appreciation of what actually transpired in the interaction among the Kuomintang, the CCP, and the country people in the islands of inland communism will be achieved only by intense scrupulous field research. To achieve comparability for the case I present in this book would require tracing the formation of the Kuomintang Finance Ministry and the implementation of its revenue projects in several other spheres of peasant manufacturing during the same period, examining whether the reach of its revenue forces roused local people to resistance and connected them with the Chinese Communists to see whether the selected key variables produced a similar pattern of popular contribution to the CCP-led revolution, or some variant thereof, in different regions. If this can be accomplished, we can then judge whether the key political variables in the case study lead us into a larger cross-regional, national understanding.

In an important sense, therefore, this case study is a *"hypothesis-generating study,"*[35] paving the way toward a theoretical generalization in a field where few political scientists have trod. *Salt of the Earth* makes the previously missing empirical connection between the reach of the mobilizing Kuomintang revenue center and the emergence of popular antistate protest taking the form of revengeful insurgency and fueling CCP-led revolution in North China. *It does not, however, claim* that such a pattern developed, or became the main current, in the CCP-led agrarian revolution only or merely in comparable "salt regions" of Republican China. The larger issue at stake is not simply "salt," or state control of salt production and consumption areas, but rather whether the Kuomintang attempt to generate revenue by obliterating the competition of country people whose quest to escape agricultural poverty mandated greater participation in other popular market arenas played into the hands of the CCP.

In the section of the North China plain under our microscope, the two uprisings—that of the market-bound country people and that of the Communist Party—intersected and were driven into a tactical political alliance by Republican state repression, enabling the Communists to legitimate their cause by supporting the protest acts of the people who championed market informality, and by convincing them that Communist-led revolution was the only way they could escape the economic consequences of Kuomintang state making.[36] The Kuomintang campaign for state monopoly, which mandated the removal of massive numbers of rural people from the market economy in which they were ensconced, far more than the organizational push of outside Communist agitators, prepared the ground for the October 1 revolution in this part of rural China.

COLLECTIVE PROTEST IN THE HEBEI-SHANDONG-HENAN BORDER AREA DURING THE REPUBLICAN PERIOD

By the early 1930s, scores of rural people had been roused to collective action by a constellation of political forces, the most intrusive of which was the revenue arm of the central government in Nanjing. Chiang Kai-shek and his Western-educated advisors sought to create a modern, centralized administrative state that would wipe out the regional, provincial, and local popular traditions they perceived as obstacles to growth and development and to spread its formal revenue forces into rural areas. In the decade prior to World War II, the spread of the Republican fiscal state posed a serious threat to the peasants, peddlers, and purchase agents, who responded with collective protest.

Environmental downturns, exploitation by factory-owning capitalist labor contractors, and warlord army demands had also stimulated country people to collective protest prior to World War II. Such movements, however, were for the most part small, isolated, and/or relatively short-term affairs, and state authorities were able to restrain them. The central government's growing interference in popular market initiatives, however, precipitated a widespread, long-lasting, community-based protest movement that gave the Chinese Communists a golden opportunity to spread their struggle for power beyond cities and towns.

The creation of a CCP-led anti-Japanese base area along the old course of the Yellow River in southern Hebei, western Shandong, and northern Henan during World War II can be traced to the intimate connections of local Communist leaders with quasi peasants whose community-based anti-state defensive arrangements offered a framework for antiforeign resistance. By borrowing from and building on pre-WWII forms of popular collective action, the Chinese Communists were able to persevere against the Japanese army and its Chinese quisling regime between 1937 and 1945 and successfully prepare for the armed struggle that erupted with the Kuomintang during the civil war.

Several factors prompted a vast subgroup of the peasantry in the Hebei-Shandong-Henan border region to act collectively against the fiscal arm of the Republican state and to adjust their political behavior to the changing promises and practices of Kuomintang and ultimately Communist actors contending for state power. The first was the destabilizing impact of the Kuomintang fiscal apparatus on the peasant economy. Peasants in scores of villages relied on the trinity of cereal production, livestock, and small trade in specialized household-manufactured products to make ends meet. Typically, over half of peasant-owned land was poor, infertile alkaline earth, laced with salt and sand deposits that inhibited the flow of nitrogen and stunted the growth of cereals. A household with twenty-one *mu* might plant only eight or nine to June wheat and fall sorghum. Even in a fairly good harvest year, the grain crop rarely provided more than 60–70 percent of the family's subsistence needs. Late spring drought shriveled the June wheat, which averaged only ninety to a hundred *jin* per *mu*. Red sorghum, the October crop, often fell short of this figure when the wet gale winds of September lashed away the stalks.

Therefore livestock was important. In the Ming dynasty, Qian Kou village in Puyang County, Hebei Province, had been a village of horse traders,[37] and over the centuries peasants in other villages supplemented their income by working as animal purchase agents and hide dealers.[38] In Republican times, villagers carried horse hides, sheep skins, and rabbit furs to small leather-processing factories in Puyang and Handan. At best, however, small livestock accounted for 10–20 percent of household income, and even this pittance declined with the seizure of plow animals during warlord and Japanese army plunder.[39]

During the Republican period, peasants engaged in specialized off-farm vocations—alkali making, leather processing, straw hat making, nitrate manufacturing, and salt making for the domestic regional market[40]—and used the income to purchase grain and other essentials. By 1930, salt making had become the principal means of peasant adaptation to the decline in cereal output brought on by long-term agricultural degradation and, more directly, by the searing droughts of the early 1920s. Many peasants spent half or more of the year plying the salt market trails of the border area, deriving up to 60 or 70 percent of their total household income from this enterprise.[41]

The initial government suppression of the earth salt trade prompted some one hundred thousand peasants in the border area to fight for their market[42] in the very years when Chiang Kai-shek claimed to be replacing the chaos of the warlord decade with peace and public order. It was in the most fundamental sense a popular movement against the centrally directed process of "state making," and it foreshadowed the long march toward Communist-led revolution.

Nearly every rural social group consumed the locally manufactured earth salt, which was far cheaper than the state's salt, and shared an interest in keeping the Kuomintang state from driving up the price. Village-based purchase agents, market-dwelling landlords, and town-based lower gentry figures who spoke for the larger market community[43] joined the protest movement to maintain their own, less-visible position in the earth salt market and frequently mediated between the semipeasants and the Kuomintang county magistrates.[44] Through connections to this active elite, the peasants of the salt market increased their influence in county and transcounty politics. As the news of their collective outbursts in one county inspired their counterparts in another, their ranks swelled. This multiple-class coalition provided a paradigm of associational politics to which local CCP leaders would return during the War of Resistance against Japan.

The use of state force was a third factor mushrooming antistate protest. The violent onslaught of the central government's tax revenue force galvanized people in backward villages to join in protest activities that took them into the political conflagrations in the bigger markets, county towns, and prefectural capitals. There they developed a greater sense of the political significance of their involvement in a growing confederation of market-community actors.

From Avoidance Protest, to Confrontational Protest, to Retaliatory Protest

After more than a decade of resistance that avoided direct confrontations and clashes, a repertoire of popular collective protest activities began to develop across many counties of the Hebei-Shandong-Henan border area. The most common entailed small groups banding together to block the salt tax police from invading a village and destroying its salt production facilities. Peasants gradually began to enlist local teachers, landlords, and lesser gentry figures in settling conflicts with the police and engaged in peaceful marches to present government-sanctioned petitions to county-level courts. As they lost these legal appeals, villagers increasingly resorted to skirmishes with police and abduction of police officers. Organized marches on county towns often culminated in the sacking of salt bureaus and/or physical attacks on the salt police stations and, concomitantly, massive rallies aimed at expelling the police.

Such marches on county towns usually occurred only after a long period of repeated police reprisals, and the protest targets in the early 1930s were nearly always salt police stations—rarely did they spill over to the Kuomintang magistracy or the public security forces. Clashes usually occurred in highly charged local settings where the Kuomintang officials had resorted to force. In July, 1932, a few days *after* the Kuomintang magistrate had dispatched the tax police to suppress a popular assembly of saltmakers in Dongming town, two thousand peasant saltmakers from the vicinity of Zhi Zhai village rushed into Dongming to evict the police.[45]

These repertories of collective protest were not the product of the Communist Party; the peasant saltmakers often organized their own village- and county-level actions and associations. These market-bound people who remembered local party leaders as their staunch allies played a critical role in both anti-Japanese resistance and the defeat of the Chiang Kai-shek center in the civil war.

Prior to World War II, the peasants of the salt market were seeking an accommodation with the representatives of the central government. The politicians in Nanjing, however, pressed the magistrates in distant counties to resolve the conflict by repression. As the protest movement spread to scores of counties where the Kuomintang magistrates could not repress it, peasants formed an empowering idea: their collective resistance had been the key factor compelling the Kuomintang to a compromise; should they give it up, reprisals would replace short-term "concessions."

Only in this political context can we grasp why so many peasant saltmakers saw themselves involved in a long-term struggle with the Kuomintang state and why they worried about letting down their guard. Their protest movement against Kuomintang state making in the pre–World War II period was only a tremor, but the *tsunami* it set off would slam the Nationalist government during the civil war and help the Chinese Communists set China on a new course.

As John Wilson Lewis asserts, the peasants living on the plains of Hebei, Shandong, and Henan were heirs of a centuries-old tradition of collective resistance against unrighteous rulers.[46] The symbolic centerpiece of popular antistate consciousness was Guandi, or Guangong, the god of war. The Imperial government sponsored the Guangong cult because of the god's association with valor and "loyalty to established authority,"[47] and the local people took Guangong as a hero committed to protecting a larger polity to which the fate of local communities was linked.[48] However, villagers had their own understanding of Guangong, and worshipped the god in ways that were shaped by survival needs and notions of justice that ran counter to the prevalent myths of the Imperial polity.[49] Some of their Guangong folksongs, operas, and fertility rituals fell outside of what James C. Scott has called the "symbolic ambit of great-tradition religion."[50]

For the May 13 festival known as *Guanyeh Mo Dao,* the peasants of Fanzhuang in Nanle, of Luo Tun in Qingfeng, and of Qian Foji in Nanle prepared a "family reunion dinner" in honor of Guangong and sent gifts to the Guangong temple.[51] *Guanyeh Mo Dao* literally means "the war god sharpens his knife." To sharpen his knife, Guangong needed water, and because Guangong was in heaven, the water used in sharpening the blade would fall on peasant fields; hence, the knife-sharpening festival was certain to bring the rain needed for a good harvest. Elderly villagers say that their ancestors created this ritual because they had no faith in the Imperial state giving rainfall or irrigation. In the myth of Guangong, villagers found the hope of attaining food security and of protecting their communities from external predators. The Guangong cult permeated much of peasant life and culture and was associated with various forms of popular opposition to state injustice well into the Republican period.

Thus it is important to emphasize that in this part of rural North China peasant beliefs about the war god were formed substantially out of interaction with rulers whose activities occasionally enveloped routines of livelihood and not simply, or mainly, from the Imperial government's promotion of state-legitimating Guandi myths.[52] Implicit in their Guangong worship, which continues to this day, was the idea that Guangong would be on their side in struggles against unjust rulers. Historically, this folk deity stood for the right of the rural people to organize community-based opposition to oppressive state officials. When the Nationalist ruling elite asserted its fiscal policy and attacked the institutional bases of the popular Guangong cult during the early 1930s, local protest leaders drew on the symbolism of this folk deity to rally peasants to resist. It was through the martial activism of the war god tradition, not the doctrines of Marx, Engels, or Lenin, that the

Chinese Communists mounted a shocking counteroffensive against Kuomintang field forces during the civil war and put central government officials to flight.

THE FORMATION OF DIFFERENT TYPES
OF COLLECTIVE PROTEST MOVEMENTS

Although several well-established China scholars have shown that peasants in North China acted collectively in their common interests,[53] others presented a peasantry passively awaiting mobilization by CCP politicians.[54] The disparity between this image of a politically dormant peasantry and the verifiable upheavals in the Hebei-Shandong-Henan border area in the middle years of the Republic of China is striking—but also understandable. None of the previous studies focused specifically on the peasant villages, markets, and towns in which collective protest formed. None pursued a strategy of political analysis that distinguished between different peasant subgroups or different types of peasant economies[55] and explored the ways in which state policy drew such peasant subgroups together to protest against Kuomintang state making. And none traced the formation of collective protest via the memory of village people. From these starting points, we discover that the CCP-led revolution sprang from people living in poor salt land villages, wedded to a market network for critical nonfarm income, and lined up in a collective struggle against revived central state revenue claims.

As Tetsuya Kataoka reminds us, we should be skeptical of CCP propaganda linking the origins of the October 1 revolution to the power of "undifferentiated peasant masses"[56] or, for that matter, to simply any and all peasant-based movements. There were four different types of collective protest movements in the Hebei-Shandong-Henan border area prior to World War II. In surveying them, several points stand out. The first is that the CCP had little to do with mobilizing village dwellers to take part in these movements; they were started by country people organizing their own associations to uphold local interests. Second, the grievances, goals, and gestation of each type of protest movement were different, and not necessarily supportive of the other types. Third, although the Chinese Communists attempted during the early 1930s to merge the four types of protest into a massive insurgency against the Kuomintang, they failed to do so. Finally, the Chinese Communists were able to strike up a potent alliance with only one type of protest movement—one that reflected an ongoing popular struggle with a formal agency of the national state and that lasted over a long time.

One highly visible form of collective protest was undertaken by peasants in search of relief from a sudden, extreme collapse in the physical environment, such as the loss of agricultural crop lands to the Yellow River floods raging along the Puyang-Hua county border. During times of great dearth, many peasants were forced to vacate their villages and join the swelling tide of human traffic that filled the earthen trails.[57] There was an alternative to leaving home ground, however—joining together to acquire enough grain to relieve the hunger at hand by appealing to landlords to share their surplus grains. The goal of these *chi dahu douzheng*, as the struggles were called,[58] was not to take all the landlords' grains, or to level the differences between rich and poor, but simply to redistribute enough grain to get through the time of hunger.

The scope of these antidisaster struggles was limited to several counties or to a string of villages hit especially hard by the Yellow River floods of 1933 and 1935—Liangmen and Yaojia in Puyang;[59] Fengying, Gecun, Biancun, and Xi Gaoping in Hua County;[60] and Taipingzhuang in Neihuang.[61] Those who participated rarely assembled in groups larger than three or four hundred and seldom joined with their counterparts in neighboring counties; the total number of participants was less than ten thousand. With the severity of damage inflicted on cropland confined to several districts in a few counties, and with local Kuomintang governments providing some flood relief, most peasants managed to return to agricultural production within a few weeks or months.

A second kind of popular collective struggle was taken up by village people whose marginal soils often left little choice but to supplement meager harvests with income derived from work in rural protoindustries controlled by merchant capitalists.[62] Peasants in villages linked to the rural towns of Peng Cheng and Guanglu in Ci*xian*, Hebei worked during the summer in porcelain factories and/or pushed small carts (*xiao tuiche*) filled with chinaware to the prosperous market town of Ma Tou, where it was loaded onto junks for shipment to Tianjin and metropolitan China. By the early 1930s income from this work often spelled the difference between subsistence and food insecurity.[63]

Taking advantage of the increased demand for long distance transport work after the disappointing harvest of 1931, however, porcelain merchants in Peng Cheng came up with three new, exploitative contractual measures: a cut in wages; a requirement that each pushcart operator pay to the factory owner a fixed amount of his net profit; and a deposit of two coppers for insurance on each load of chinaware.

In April, 1932, the independent Ci*xian* Pushcart Association launched a general strike for a salary adjustment. The strike lasted for less than a year. At its peak, the number of peasant carters taking part was five to seven thousand. The crucial season for the continental porcelain trade was summer, when the rains swelled the Fuyang River to a point where the junks could sail for Tianjin. When a June rainstorm broke the dikes of the Fuyang River and ruined the main road to Ma Tou wharf, the strike paid off. A delay in the repair of the primitive earthen roads over which the porcelain had to pass posed a serious threat to the merchants—and the pushcarters refused to repair them. Panicked, the Peng Cheng merchants sent representatives to negotiate a settlement.

A third type of protest movement developed out of a self-protective response to the rise of banditry and warlordism in Daming County, a prefectural hub and a strategic military point, and consequently a prime target of bandit armies and warlord troops.[64] In 1925–32, it was plundered repeatedly by rival militarists.[65] Beginning in 1924–25, warlord soldiers pillaged town granaries and imposed tax and surtax levies. Peasants, landlords, and merchants in the better-off villages suffered from the imposition of the land surtax, the stamp tax, the pig slaughter tax, the manpower tax (*corvée*), the horse cart tax, and the fodder tax, all of which went to the supply bureaus of the rival militarists. The local people banded together in a rural self-defense unit known as the Red Spear Society (originally named the Yellow Sand Society) along the back reaches of the Wei River.[66] The society grew into an antitax association whose mainstream units organized tax rebellions against Xie Yutian, the warlord ruler of the Hebei-Shandong-Henan border area in the mid-1920s.[67]

By 1927, the antitax movement of the Red Spears had spread from Daming to two-thirds of the counties of the border area, with active branches in Nanle, Hua*xian*, Dongming, Chengan, and Nangong.[68] This protest movement lasted as long as the warlord tax demands in any given county. The Red Spears remained active in some counties into the early 1930s and disbanded only after the new Kuomintang-appointed magistrates altered the terms of taxation and began to grant their self-defense forces a role in the county militia system.[69]

With the waning of Red Spear activity, the saltmakers' protest movement gathered momentum, ignited by the revenue policies of high-ranking, centrally placed Kuomintang officials who were resorting to increasingly repressive measures to collect the salt tax. The most feared agency was the Salt Inspectorate, which by the early 1930s had developed into a full-fledged tax police force that engaged in anticontraband activities.

Within less than a decade the peasant saltmakers' struggle spread to virtually every county in the border area.[70] By World War II, it had left its mark in twenty-one Hebei counties, twelve in Shandong, and four in Henan. Participants ranged from three thousand to fifteen thousand per county. During the Nationalist decade, the transcounty movement's size mushroomed to one hundred thousand , then nearly five hundred thousand.

The struggle of the peasant saltmakers was not the product of short-term subnational factors that fostered antidisaster, anticapitalist, or antiwarlord struggles; rather, it reflected the long-term growth of central state interference in market routines. This continuing state-societal conflict could not be resolved by soliciting or seizing grain from landlords in richer villages, by bargaining collectively with rural labor bosses, by protesting against warlord tax abuses, or by entreating revenue agents to relax the Kuomintang ban on selling common salt; it required protracted collective actions to stop the penetration of the countryside by tax agents of the state. It was a mass movement that posed a dilemma for the fiscal plan of the central government of Chiang Kai-shek.

As Lucien Bianco has observed, the peasant leaders of antifiscal protest movements did not rush to take up arms against the Kuomintang political order—theirs was essentially a strategy of self-defense.[71] By relentlessly pressing their fiscal demands on the country people, however, Chiang Kai-shek's finance ministry cadres drove them to participate in a marathon protest movement that prepared them for an insurgency aimed at ending the fiscal aggrandizement of the Nationalist government.

THE CCP'S ENCOUNTERS WITH COLLECTIVE PROTEST IN THE EARLY 1930s

In the early 1930s, local Communist Party leaders, who had to contend with the left-wing radicalism of the CCP Central Committee and the right-wing repression of the Kuomintang center, recognized that in this particular region[72] only the protest movement of the peasant saltmakers could serve as a vehicle for long-lasting collective struggle. Although the CCP was not altogether unsuccessful in organizing the other three types of popular struggle, a number of factors combined to curtail its influence among them. By siding with village dwellers who shared their interest in opposing the spread of the Kuomintang central state, local party leaders began to counteract many of the political factors contributing to their powerlessness. By 1932 they had linked their political future with the one protest movement aimed at slowing down the development of Kuomintang state power on the North China plain.

As Stephen Averill has noted,[73] many leaders of the CCP were from well-to-do local elite families with educational and economic connections to elaborate county-level political networks. In the years 1923–35,[74] they began attending the newly developing middle schools and normal colleges in the Hebei-Shandong-Henan border area. They first forged transcounty friendships in the Number Seven Normal School, or Teacher's College, in Daming County, Hebei Province, founded in 1923 by Principal Xie Taichen.[75] A native of Puyang County, Xie taught Chinese history in Baoding, where he had been exposed to the May Fourth Movement. Rejecting the textbook prescribed by the central government ministry of education, Xie introduced his students to history through the works of such modern Chinese writers as Li Dazhao, Lu Xun, and Guo Moro and Chinese classics like *The Water Margin* and *The Stories of Scholars,* and through the works of Gorky and Tolstoy.[76] Xie's own *Teaching Materials on Chinese History* presented analyses of historical episodes from the vantage point of historical materialism.

Under Xie's mentorship, the Seventh Normal School carried out a number of bold educational reforms, and by 1925 some two hundred students from seven border region counties were attending this progressive school. Many were swept up into the first of a number of spontaneous protest movements that increased their consciousness of national politics when, in the wake of the May 30 Massacre, workers in China's major cities went on strike, students boycotted classes, and merchants closed shops. As this movement against imperialism gradually spread to the smaller rural towns in Hebei, the faculty and students of the Seventh Normal School organized a student union and sponsored a Federation of Student Unions in Daming prefecture.[77] Its main leaders were Wang Congwu of Neihuang; Zhao Jibin, Wang Peizhi, and Ping Jiesan of Puyang; Liu Dafeng of Nanle; and Wang Weigang of Ci County (none of whom were yet members of the CCP). With merchants they sponsored a mass rally in the war god temple to denounce the killings by the Japanese, organized an anti-Japanese propaganda troupe, and organized a boycott of Japanese goods. By late 1925 the students had made headway in driving Japanese goods from the rural markets of Daming and had collected over two hundred dollars to send to Shanghai trade unions, in support of the strike.

The CCP was founded in Daming the following year by Feng Pinyi and the leaders of the May 30 Student Union Movement in the Seventh Normal School.[78] A native of Fengzhuang village in Daming, and a graduate of the Foreign Language Department of Beijing Teacher's University, Feng Pinyi was director of the Peasant Department of the CCP Henan Provincial Committee and secretary of the Provincial Communist Youth League Committee. A CCP delegate to the 1924 Kuomintang Congress in Canton, Feng had returned to Daming in August of 1926, when he was recruited as an English teacher in the Daming Normal School. Propagandizing the Three Principles of Sun Yat-sen—nationalism, democracy, and livelihood—Feng sponsored a Study Society for Revolutionary Theory and recruited into it about a dozen students. Three of them—Liu Dafeng, Zhao Jibin, and Li Shiwei— joined the CCP and began publishing *Dawn,* a journal carrying articles against warlords and despots.[79] In November, 1926, these three young Communists went to Beijing to get in touch with the North China Bureau of the CCP,[80] and Liu Dafeng subsequently went to Wuhan via Shanghai to study in the Peasant Movement Institute.[81] On returning to the Daming-Nanle area in 1927, Liu Dafeng and other student activists set up CCP committees in Daming, Nanle, and Puyang counties. Throughout the late 1920s Liu Dafeng, Zhao Jibin, Wang Congwu, Li Shiwei, Ping Jiesan, and the youth of the Daming Normal School strove to link the student movement with the popular struggles erupting in the villages and towns of southern Hebei, northern Henan, and western Shandong.

Between 1927 and 1930, these young firebrands began cooperating with the *Zhinan Tewei* (the Southern Hebei Special Committee of the CCP) and established a number of CCP branches in Puyang County primary schools. Wang Congwu, the secretary of the Puyang CCP, took a position as a primary school teacher in Liangmen village and thereafter led local teachers to help the CCP spread its influence via the primary schools.[82] By utilizing the legal organization of the Kuomintang National Salvation Association, the primary school teachers, and some of the principals as well, launched an anti-Japanese propaganda campaign in Liangmen, Sangcun, and Wuxing villages along the Puyang-Hua county line. Over the next two years, 1931–33, these young Communists struck up liaisons with ninety-nine villages in the border area.[83] Their main tactic was the "*graffito* war," in which Liu Yanchun, a teacher in the Puyang town First Primary School, led small chalk groups to scribble propaganda slogans such as "Resist the Non-Resistance of Chiang Kai-shek" on the stone tablets, trees, and walls of market villages beyond Puyang town.[84] (Liu subsequently became the CCP propaganda chief in Puyang.) Under the leadership of Wang Congwu and Liu Yanchun, the Daming Normal Schoolers expanded into Neihuang, Hua County, Dongming, and Changyuan and began to touch base with various groups of country people involved in collective struggles.

The first round of struggle focused on teachers' salaries. Led by Liu Yanchun, the teachers petitioned the Puyang County Kuomintang Education Bureau for a pay increase, and when this was denied in late 1931, they launched a strike,[85] supported by a semester-long student boycott of classes. This strike encountered stiff resistance from education bureau officials and fell short of its goal; but several months later Wang Congwu led several of his CCP companions to join in one of the first mass protest movements to erupt in the Hebei-Shandong-Henan border area—the struggle of the peasant saltmakers.[86] Throughout 1930–31, the Tianjin-based Changlu Salt Inspectorate sent in armed salt tax police units to prevent the peasants of Daming, Qingfeng, and Puyang counties from making earth salt for the market. On observing that the Kuomintang state ban on private salt production was arousing popular indignation, Wang Congwu, Liu Yanchun, and the schoolteachers began spreading CCP propaganda among the salt-producing villages, some of which had nascent party branches in their schools. Between 1932 and 1935, the CCP successfully forged political alliances with saltmakers in Puyang, Qingfeng, Nanle, Dongming, and Hua counties, and many others.

The Chinese Communists did not directly organize the saltmakers' struggle, but rather orchestrated it through local nonpartisan activists like Yang Jingcai, a saltmaker in Cheng Guan, Puyang. As early as 1930 Wang Congwu and local CCP leaders were in touch with the non-Communist village cadres of this antistate protest movement. The protest motif of these pro-market semipeasants was revealed in the nonviolent collective actions they undertook in the early 1930s, some of which were fairly widespread.

The country people who organized protests did not seek vendettas against the police or the Kuomintang officials—even though in several instances the police had killed some of the saltmakers. In the 1932 spring-time march on Puyang town, for example, violence was directed against the institutions of Nationalist fiscal order—salt bureaus and salt police stations. The peasant saltmakers who marched together into Puyang town from Qian Kou, Sha Wo, and Xi Shuipo expressed their anger mainly by imploring the Kuomintang magistrate to curtail police violence, recognize their right to the market, and order the police out of the county.[87]

Because their peaceful, legal means[88] often resulted in the withdrawal of the salt tax police from the county seats, Wang Congwu and CCP leaders were able to claim a political victory and portray their party as a vehicle through which the peasant saltmakers could pursue legitimate protest channels. This popular association of the CCP with legally sanctioned collective protest might seem strange, for the CCP was outlawed in this period, and any open flaunting of its role in stoking popular resistance to Kuomintang revenue policy would have resulted in the arrest of its leadership. However, in the Puyang area the Nationalist Party headquarters actually was controlled by underground CCP sympathizers, and local Kuomintang leaders shielded the CCP from Kuomintang security forces and magistrates.[89] Moreover, the young Communists revealed their political affiliations to only a limited number of local salt protest leaders, such as Yang Jingcai in Puyang and Liu Chaode in Huaxian.

Buoyed by their 1932 success in Puyang, the Chinese Communists geared up for a second protest movement the next summer.[90] On June 23, 1933, the Yellow River burst its banks at Stone village in Hua County and inundated sixty li along the Puyang-Hua County-Changyuan border.[91] For the next two years, the CCP, led by Wang Congwu, Zhang Jinhai, and Tian Yuan, the principal of the primary school of Liangmen village,[92] helped disaster victims borrow food grains from grain-rich landlords with whom local folk had good relations (hau guanxi).[93] A more belligerent strategy emerged during the Hua County chi dahu struggle of 1935, when under the cover of darkness groups of ten and twenty people cut the June wheat crop of several "stingy landlords" who had turned their backs on the grain-borrowing delegations.[94] For the most part, however, the protest movement avoided plunder. Some looting occurred around Nan Hu village in Hua County,[95] but for most landlords the threat of riot was enough. Following the cue of Zhao Shanzhang, a charitable landlord of Bian village,[96] they complied with requests for loans; some even boiled grain in huge caldrons to feed disaster victims.

Local Kuomintang leaders also provided relief. In 1933 the Puyang County Kuomintang suspended the land tax and began mobilizing local people to buttress the Yellow River dikes. This flood relief, in combination with the charity of landlords, helped the disaster victims survive.[97] Local people were grateful that no one died in this time of hunger,[98] and although by October, 1933, Wang Congwu had spread the influence of the CCP among the peasant disaster victims in the vicinity of Yaojia and Liangmen villages in Puyang,[99] the CCP failed to gain the upper hand against the Kuomintang government.

In 1932 the Chinese Communists connected with the strike activities of the pushcart operators in Cixian.[100] In April, when the pushcarters were organizing the general strike, Liu Dafeng, the CCP secretary in Ci County, and Wang Weigang organized rallies, parades, and speeches to spread news of the strike. Village primary school teachers helped coordinate the strike in eighteen villages and set up small resistance networks. By May eighty-five villages within the Peng Cheng porcelain market network had organized pushcart associations, most of them connected to a countywide pushcart association headquartered at Li Bingzhuang. The association issued permits for pushcart operators from Cixian, then established a twenty-four-hour checkpoint at Zhifang, a key market road village, to impound the carts of nonlicensed transporters of porcelain.[101] To prevent village-by-village settlements with individual factory owners, strike leaders convened mass rallies near Peng Cheng, led the peasant carters in parades throughout the countryside, and ultimately demonstrated at the porcelain factories in Peng Cheng.[102]

The merchant capitalists eventually recognized the independent Pushcart Association and gave in to the strikers' basic demands, restoring the primary contractual terms of rural transport work. With the Kuomintang-sponsored "yellow unions" in Peng Cheng supporting their demands, the strike leaders won small job benefits such as low-interest loans and unemployment compensation.[103] These settlements with the strikers took the wind out of the CCP's sails.

The young Communist Party members in the Daming Normal School also had pinned their hopes on the Red Spear Society,[104] which they perceived as the vanguard of a massive peasant movement against the regional militarists;[105] but ultimately they failed to anchor their party in this popular struggle.[106]

After the Daming Red Spears and their counterparts in Guangping, Chengan, Yongnian, and Nanle drove warlord Xie Yutian out of the border region,[107] Red Spear chieftains Zhang Zhihe and Song Lianqing asked the CCP leader Zhao Jibin to serve as their liaison to the Northern Expeditionary Army so that they could acquire the modern weaponry to effectively fight the warlord tax regimes.[108] Zhao journeyed to Dongming County to meet with the Third Army of the Kuomintang Northern Expeditionary Force, under Kuomintang commanders Liang Shoukai and Zhang Fakui and CCP commissar Wang Jinghan.[109] Within months, Zhao Jibin, Liu Dafeng, and Wang Congwu were enjoining mass Red Spear rallies in Daming, Nanle, Qingfeng, and Dongming to welcome the Kuomintang army's antiwarlord campaign. Throughout the late 1920s Liu Dafeng worked among the Red Spears in Nanle,[110] and in the early 1930s Wang Congwu served as an advisor to the Golden Mean Society, a Red Spear branch under Zhao Dehuai in Daming.[111] Thus some CCP advisors were able to join in struggles to eliminate the militarists' surtaxes in a few villages in Daming and Hua*xian*,[112] where peasants were willing to abide by the comparatively fair land tax regulations that had prevailed prior to the warlord invasion.[113] The Communists scored most of these small antitax victories in places where the Red Spear battle with the warlords had created a temporary power vacuum—which was about to be filled by the arrival of the Kuomintang's Northern Expeditionary Army.

Powerless to prevent the minor warlords from making peace with Kuomintang commanders and from using patronage to integrate some Red Spear chieftains,[114] the young party members from the Daming Normal School lost their access to some of the Red Spear leaders after 1927–28. When Zhao Jibin first served as staff advisor to Zhang Zihe and Song Liangqing, for example, the two Red Spear chieftains promised not to cut any deals with regional militarists; but in 1927, while Zhao was away from Daming, both men became officers in the bandit suppression force of Sun Tianying, a warlord who soon became the pro-Kuomintang pacification commander of the northern Henan plain.[115] These new pacification forces placated Red Spear followers by curtailing surtaxes and collecting only the regular land tax from village people who could afford to pay (a pattern that held long enough to prompt peasants to return to their homes and resume agricultural production).

The CCP fared equally badly in the Kuomintang-CCP competition for Red Spear loyalties. Between 1931 and 1935 Song Zheyuan and Ding Shuben, the Kuomintang Twenty-Ninth Army magicians, placed many big, rich landlords in a privileged tax bracket and clamped down on banditry.[116] In return, the landlords surrendered their rank-and-file Red Spear followerships into Kuomintang-controlled militias.[117] Zhao Jibin, Liu Dafeng, and Wang Congwu were left facing a partially divided Red Spear movement, one that was pro-Kuomintang at the upper end. The petty landlords and minipeasants, embittered over being left out of this accommodation, occasionally sponsored their own Red Spear units to fight against the Kuomintang and its affluent landlord allies; but the fight often ended in tragedy for them and frustration for the Communists. In 1935, to take but one example, the Kuomintang Twenty-Ninth Army, in collusion with affluent landlords in

Daming, wiped out scores of unjustly taxed country people fighting under the banner of the Golden Mean Society.[118]

By 1935, Wang Congwu and local CCP leaders began to see that they were far more successful in organizing the ongoing struggles of the peasant salt producers than the three other protest movements. Peasant saltmakers and CCP leaders shared an interest in preserving their long-standing freedom to participate in rural markets,[119] and CCP leaders who joined with the saltmakers clearly gained access to this protest movement through kinship, school, and market connections. Wang Peili of Sha Wo village, in Puyang, recalls, "My brother, Wang Peizhi, was a student leader at the Daming Seventh Normal School and a classmate of Wang Congwu. Together they organized the saltmakers in this area to fight the salt police. Our family was fairly well off. We produced earth salt and sold it in Wu Xingji and other market villages in Puyang. Seventy percent of our household income was from selling earth salt, 30 percent from crops. Wang Peizhi used some of the salt proceeds for his school expenses."[120]

Many petty landlords and lower gentry figures were also offended by Kuomintang state intervention in the market. They were alarmed that the fiscal pressure from central government power holders would drive ordinary villagers to borrow, beg, or steal grain and money. The Communists drew on their cautious cooperation to forge a political alliance in defense of community interest in the market. For example, Zhang Youwen, a Daming Normal School comrade of Wang Congwu and a native of Cheng Guan in Puyang, was the nephew of a lower gentry leader who sanctioned the collective action in Puyang town in the spring of 1932.[121]

Placing family, occupation, and friendship above the instructions of the leftists who intervened in county-level committees, local CCP leaders insulated their relationship with the saltmakers from the radical influences of the CCP Shanghai Central Committee and the *Zhinan Tewei* after 1930. They brought to the saltmakers' struggle a full understanding of its significance for solidarity and were open to uniting with the conservative propertied classes to protect their interest against the spread of the fiscal state. It was this great popular union, not the struggles of poor dispossessed peasants against the propertied rich, that carried the promise of a revolution against the Kuomintang state.

The Challenge from the Left

The political line of the party leftists (Li Yu, Gao Kelin, and Li Huasheng)[122] in the Special Committee ran counter to the community-supported struggle in which Wang Congwu and the local Communists developed a mass following. Of course Wang Congwu and the Daming Normal School CCP activists were in touch with this committee, but they had not read Marx or

Lenin, they had little knowledge of revolutionary theory,[123] and they turned
a deaf ear on committee instructions to arm the saltmakers to fight the
Kuomintang army.

Around 1930, the *Zhinan Tewei* dispatched several agents to Puyang to
urge the young party stalwarts to challenge the Kuomintang and seize the
bigger "cities" of the Hebei-Shandong-Henan border area by armed struggle.[124] The strategy underlying this approach to mass mobilization owed its
origins to Li Lisan, the general secretary of the CCP in Shanghai. The Li
Lisan line was "a policy which encourages acts of organized violence at a
time when objective conditions preclude such acts."[125] The peasant saltmakers had no intention of jeopardizing the "concessions" they had won
through legally sanctioned forms of collective protest. Wang Congwu and
the local Communists were establishing the credibility of the CCP by
endorsing this political logic. The *Zhinan Tewei* agents' attempt to transform
the county-level CCP committees into "military action committees" was
defeated by Wang Congwu, Liu Dafeng, and the Daming Normal School
CCP members in November, 1930,[126] and little came of the Li Lisan line in
the Puyang area.

To be sure, CCP leaders in a few counties north of Daming apparently
embraced the premises of this *putschist* line, disregarding the moderate
discourse established between the Wang Congwu-Liu Dafeng "native faction" of the CCP and the country people and damaging the party's good
relationship with the peasant saltmakers. Initially, these Communist insiders had maneuvered amidst the contradictions that riddled the relations between the Kuomintang tax police and county political actors. The
lower gentry, the public security forces, and lower government officials in
the small towns of the border area secretly collaborated with the saltmakers and this faction against the police. This "united front from below"
helped to preserve the market access of the village people in the early
1930s. Missing this pluralist complexity, and taking small skirmishes as a
sign that the "broad peasant masses" were ready for armed rebellion, the Li
Lisanists insisted that the peasant saltmakers join them in a *jacquerie* against
the Kuomintang county officials, the gentry, the landlords, and even the
village chiefs, all of whom were said to be in collusion with the tax
police.[127] They stressed the importance of violently assaulting Kuomintang
state authority at the police stations and the *yamens* inside the fortified
walls of the county towns. Where this strategy prevailed—in Nangong, Julu,
and Wei County [128]—the saltmakers were exposed to police gunfire from
well-guarded positions[129] and survivors were hunted down by Kuomintang
garrison forces. This *putschist* formula alarmed Kuomintang officials; it
also frightened the lower gentry and resulted in a silent popular vote of no
confidence.

The specter of leftism appeared again in 1933, in the Wang Ming line,[130] which emphasized the revolutionary prowess of the rural proletariat. Oblivious to the political logic of cooperating with the intermediate social forces—peasant traders, primary school teachers, and petty landlords who fueled the vertical protest of the saltmakers—and of uniting with people from across the entire spectrum of society against the police,[131] the Special Committee pressed to convert the saltmakers' independent associations into a labor union composed mainly of poor peasants and hired hands, who in turn were to form a Poor Peasants' League to lead the saltmakers' struggle after 1932.[132]

This class warfare strategy was advanced when the prosperous quasi peasants and petty landlords of the salt land villages were committing to a communitywide struggle against Kuomintang state interference, and the poorest village people were looking across class lines for counsel. The ascendance of Wang Ming and the Twenty-Eight Bolsheviks in the CCP from 1933 to 1935 complicated, and occasionally undermined, the political work of Wang Congwu and his associates, as relations between local people and the party soured. In the winter of 1933 Tian Yuan temporarily replaced Wang Congwu as the secretary of the CCP Puyang committee. Under the influence of the Wang Ming line, Tian Yuan attempted to transform the grain-borrowing *chi dahu* campaign of flood disaster victims into an armed struggle against so-called "criminal landlords" and to seize guns of the Kuomintang Civil Corps in the vicinity of Liangmen village.[133] Contemporary CCP propaganda to the contrary, there was little popular enthusiasm for the party's effort to destroy the power of "feudalism" by this "struggle from below." When the landlords in Yaojia and Zhen Xiaoqiu in Puyang and of Biancun and Fengying in Hua County reported the attempt of the leftists to seize their weapons, a Kuomintang army regiment under Shun Yide gathered the civil defense corps of *previously immobilized landlords* to suppress the CCP.[134] The civil defense corps killed sixteen CCP members and arrested dozens of party activists in Puyang and Hua County.[135] By 1935 the Wang Congwu CCP-faction had lost the opportunity to use antidisaster struggle to build up a broad mass base.

The Wang Ming line also contributed to the decline of CCP fortunes in the porcelain carters' strike. The Special Committee urged the pushcarters to strike down the capitalist chinaware merchants, smash the Ci County Kuomintang Civil Corps, and redistribute the land; but the carters were focused on basic salary justice.[136] In late 1932 the Southern Hebei Special Committee put out a call for the formation of a North China workers' and peasants' guerrilla army and proceeded to launch guerrilla warfare. Predictably, however, Liu Dafeng was hard pressed to rally them to the cause.[137] Most of them refused to engage in armed insurgency; some even fled.[138]

The Kuomintang army easily suppressed this madcap guerrilla action. By late 1933 the CCP had recruited no more than sixty pushcarters; by 1935 the party activists could point to progress in party branch work in only four villages of Ci County.[139]

The methods used by the CCP in promoting the protest activities of the Red Spears in Daming were also colored by the Wang Ming line after 1933, so alarming some of the privileged landlords that they appealed to the Kuomintang for assistance. In early 1935, for instance, the Red Spear off-shoot formed by Zhao Dehuai and his gentry brother, Zhao Degui,[140] developed a militant following of five thousand in the villages of Xi Daigu, Dong Guan, and Anzhuang in Weixian, Xinji and Yezhuan in Chengan, and Dong Xiaotun in Daming.[141] The Special Committee pressed local party leaders to persuade the Golden Mean Society to help them build up the Revolutionary Twenty-Seventh Peasants' and Workers' Red Army in order to oppose the affluent landlord allies of the Kuomintang army and to organize the Anti-Japanese National Salvation Association.[142] Zhao Dehuai assembled a thousand members of the Golden Mean Society to spring a surprise attack on Daming town, making it unsafe for Kuomintang troops to venture beyond its walls after dusk.[143] A year later Zhao was captured by landlord-supported Kuomintang forces at Long Wang Temple in Daming and was buried alive outside of Puyang County town by Ding Shuben's twenty-ninth army.[144]

In 1932–33, Zhang Linzhi, the young CCP secretary of Nangong County, Hebei Province, turned his attention to the protest movement of the peasant saltmakers, working with them to turn away the salt tax police through "legal protest."[145] But in the two years to follow, the Special Committee operatives established their headquarters in Nangong itself and issued strict orders to focus on guerrilla warfare against the Kuomintang government.[146] In mid-1935 Zhang Linzhi acquiesced in a plan to arm the saltmakers and encouraged them to enlist in a guerrilla army.[147] Song Zheyuan, commander of the Kuomintang twenty-ninth garrisons in Nangong and Daming, and Sang Zhou, the Kuomintang thirty-second army commander in Xingtai, joined forces to encircle this five-hundred-man guerrilla force in Nangong, Julu, and Pingxiang.[148] In the course of an unplanned, confused, and pitifully led retreat in the early winter of 1936, three hundred members of the CCP were slaughtered, along with a smaller number of saltmakers.[149] The prestige of the CCP was badly damaged, and the thousands of peasant saltmakers who were to make up the backbone of this guerrilla army quickly vanished into the villages. Referring to this impetuosity, Zhang Linzhi later wrote, "At the time, the peasant saltmakers. . . actually did not have any demand to overthrow the system of [Kuomintang] state power."[150]

The Central Committee operatives stimulated Kuomintang repression and shattered CCP hopes for combining all four protest movements, but they did not gain any lasting political influence in the border area counties where the Wang Congwu–led CCP teamed up with respected community leaders to consolidate popular opposition to the spread of bureaucratic state monopoly. The CCP's greatest achievement in mass political work during the early 1930s occurred in the fifteen to twenty counties where the pattern of popularly conceived legal, or quasi-legal, concerted resistance to Kuomintang state interference in the earth salt market was not seriously disrupted by the leftism of the *Zhinan Tewei*. Wang Congwu, Liu Dafeng, and Nie Zhen looked askance at the attempts of Special Committee radicals to draw the peasant saltmakers into impetuous, violent actions and opposed the idea that the property of the rich should be sacked.[151] It was especially important, as Wang Congwu said, to unite with all the social forces that could be joined together, because the class makeup of the saltmakers was very complex and because the struggle was fundamentally a struggle "to resist the oppression of the *ruling political class*."[152] Most of the local party leaders of this protest movement professed loyalty to the Mao Zedong-Zhu De Red Army—and it was they, not their orthodox Marxist rivals, who advanced to high levels of the PRC hierarchy in Beijing on victory in the post-WWII period. Wang Congwu, the supreme local CCP leader and patron of this prewar struggle with the Kuomintang state, rose to become the head of the Central CCP Discipline and Inspection Committee in Beijing, a post he held into the period of the Great Leap Forward.

Yet another factor pointed to the possibility of this subgroup of rural people being drawn into CCP-led insurgency. The Chiang Kai-shek fiscal center failed to come up with a set of peaceful reforms capable of defusing their collective protests. Rather, the Kuomintang fiscal policy makers' mode of conflict resolution played into the hands of the CCP. Beginning in the early 1930s, the finance ministry ordered Kuomintang-appointed magistrates to assist the salt tax police in pressing the claims of state monopoly. Although not steadfastly contentious, the country people were aware that the major factor prompting the magistrates to call off the salt police was the power of their own collective actions. Grasping this political reality, CCP leaders repeatedly warned them that the magistrates' compromises and concessions were false and cautioned against relaxing vigilance. The Kuomintang salt revenue police, they insisted, would return as soon as central government rulers could strengthen their position in the North China interior. To the peasant saltmakers, who had seen magistrates give in to the demand to get rid of the salt tax police only when faced with massive protest, this political message made great sense.

In sum, the Chinese Communists derived their popularity by siding with rural people who knew their interests could not be preserved through political accommodation with the Kuomintang central state. Their political activities in the cultural realm, particularly their support for the war god plays and operas, allowed them to assimilate their party into a tradition of antistate politics that legitimated a nonaccommodationist position. Wang Congwu recalls that the local CCP leaders attending the war god operas in Puyang villages celebrating the 1932 victory over the salt police invariably urged local people to continue their struggle against the Kuomintang state.[153] Taking this subaltern variant of antistate action seriously allowed the CCP to assume leadership of a protest movement that would provide a springboard to national power during World War II.

Despite its growing power, the Kuomintang was not capable of crushing the waves of popular collective resistance to its revenue claims in every county of the border area. The uneven development between the strength of Kuomintang state power and its scope created a political contradiction: not all of the rural counties where the tax police agents of the Kuomintang center provoked a confrontation with the peasant salt producers were firmly linked to the main force of the Daming-based Kuomintang twenty-ninth field army under Song Zheyuan, who was from the rival Guominchun of Feng Yuxiang,[154] who was not firmly committed to advancing the fiscal interest of Nanjing. To the south of Daming, the southernmost garrison stronghold in Hebei Province, the Kuomintang-appointed magistrates and tax police units operated without state army forces to back them up until 1935, or later. The Chinese Communists thus were able to find sanctuary in rural "protest counties" where Kuomintang state power was still relatively weak and to survive the first waves of Kuomintang repression prior to the war; here they had time to cultivate friendships with country people whose collective actions stalemated the antimarket policy of the Kuomintang center.

The Challenge from the Right

While coping with the crisis of inner-party ideological sterility, the Wang Congwu-led Communists encountered a far more dangerous threat. In the summer of 1932, at the peak of Wang Congwu's progress in forging the CCP's alliance with the peasant saltmakers, Guo Minghe, a member of the Kuomintang Blue Shirts, became the principal of the Daming Seventh Normal School, with the backing of a pro-Kuomintang faction in the Beijing Teacher's University.[155] Sent to Daming to consolidate the Nationalist government takeover of southern Hebei, Guo quickly organized a Kuomintang Blue Shirt faction within the normal school faculty to crack down on the school-based Communist student movement and to conduct a purge of its leaders. Among these Blue Shirts were Wang Ruzhuang, a member of the Consolidation Committee of the Kuomintang Daming headquarters; and Ji Guodong, a member of the Executive Committee of the Kuomintang District Daming Committee.[156]

Blue Shirt members exalted the Chiang Kai-shek central state and promoted a "nation-first-ism culture," pointing toward a state-controlled economy and educational system.[157] Indeed, the first thing Guo Minghe did was to launch a New Life Movement within the school in order to instill a military spirit among the students and to promote new rules of punishment for unauthorized student meetings.[158] In the autumn of 1932, the Blue Shirts prohibited the printing of Xie Taichen's *Teaching Materials on Chinese History* and colluded with the Kuomintang military police to suppress student protest against this censorship. More than one hundred seventy CCP members and Communist Youth League activists were expelled, and a new educational philosophy was put in place.[159] It essentially legitimated the process whereby Chiang Kai-shek's clique was expanding authoritarian controls over the border area economy, especially over the private market in earth salt, which was portrayed as being in conflict with the national interest and as the product of criminality.

Driven from college, most of the pro-CCP students returned to their villages and some became primary and middle school teachers in market villages and rural towns. Many of these young Communists, who had taken to heart the three principles of Sun Yat-sen, experienced their training at the Daming Normal School as preparation for entry into a regional political elite that would advise and assist the Nationalist government in overcoming China's internal decay and international impotence. Ironically, in dashing their career aspirations, the Blue Shirts drove these progressive students back into a rural milieu in which they were to discover networks of collective protest through which they would create an alternative polity. In the months immediately following the Blue Shirt crackdown they intensified their interaction with the saltmakers' struggle.

Interacting with local protest leaders, the young Communists were able to associate their purpose with the demands of the saltmakers in an increasing number of counties. Through local friendships and united front tactics, Wang Congwu emerged in late 1932 as the chairman of the headquarters of the General Saltmakers' Association of Thirteen Counties,[160] and thereafter the Communist Party derived its legitimacy from leading a regional struggle of salt-marketing communities. The sudden heady success of local Communist leaders within a legal, contagious regional protest movement that was in opposition to Kuomintang state interest was taken as a challenge to the Nationalist government by the Daming Kuomintang authorities.

Kuomintang officials in Daming, an old center of political administration and military affairs in southern Hebei, were alarmed by the CCP alignment with the saltmakers' struggle. In February, 1934, the Blue Shirt faction in Daming organized a spy unit to infiltrate the CCP. Within six months, the Blue Shirts, in collaboration with the military police, uncovered CCP county-level committees in Daming, Nanle, and Qingfeng. All through 1934 arrest warrants for local Communist leaders were issued— and a third round of repression followed. Reluctant to attack the Wang

Congwu–led CCP for invigorating this *independent* protest movement, with its community-inspired forms of legal dissent, Kuomintang officials issued arrest warrants for CCP leaders involved in the three other protest movements, and in late 1934, 1935, and early 1936 numerous CCP leaders were incarcerated. Wang Congwu was thrown into Daming Prison;[161] Wang Tongxing, a CCP leader with ties to the saltmakers in Nanle, was arrested and jailed in Nanle town;[162] Wang Guanru, the CCP secretary of Qingfeng and a liaison to the peasant saltmakers, was locked up in Qingfeng, transferred to Nanjing Penitentiary, and taken to Hangzhou Prison.[163] With the assistance of Song Zheyuan's twenty-ninth army in Daming and the Puyang public security forces under Ding Shuben, the Daming Kuomintang establishment separated the local Communist leaders from their semipeasant allies and from their superiors in the *Zhinan Tewei* and the CCP North China Bureau, leaving a few frightened party members in Nanle, Qingfeng, and Puyang in a state of political depression.[164] CCP membership in the Hebei-Shandong-Henan border area fell from five thousand in early 1934 to one thousand by the Japanese invasion in 1937,[165] and the Kuomintang had either preempted or put down three of the four protest movements in which members had been involved.

If the CCP had been all but crushed, and if the other three protest movements were no longer of political consequence at the inception of the Japanese invasion, how were local party leaders like Wang Congwu and Nie Zhen able to cultivate popular support for anti-Japanese resistance during WWII and rise from the ashes of their prewar defeat to successfully checkmate the Kuomintang ruling group at the end of the war? The answer, in part, is stored in the informal "habit-memory"[166] of the country people.

This prewar protest movement of the peasant saltmakers was sufficiently independent, massive, and widespread to (1) compel the Kuomintang-appointed magistrates in fifteen to twenty counties to withdraw the revenue machinery of the center and (2) withstand its segregation from the CCP, so that it was not seriously jeopardized by the Kuomintang defeat of local Communist leaders. According to Wang Congwu, massive numbers mobilized to protest the tax police interference in their salt production in Daming in late 1934, after the Kuomintang had taken out the CCP.[167] The Chinese Communists, therefore, rose to national power in part by taking advantage of the war-induced crisis of the Kuomintang state to realign with, and to assume the armed extraprovincial leadership of, this protest movement, which was expressive of the state-society conflict that had been building in this border area for several decades. The source of rural solidarity remained the market community,[168] through which peasant saltmakers mounted collective opposition to the course of Kuomintang state fiscal development. Once the Japanese army ripped away the Kuomintang center's repressive controls and the leaders of the CCP returned from captivity, they could rekindle an alliance with undefeated rural people who had created their own repertoire of fighting skills and strategies. At the outset of World War II, they did not play to a Marxist-inspired mobilization of rural paupers or to a Japanese-induced movement of brutalized peasants. The Chinese Communists rebuilt their power base by catering to the interest of village people with whom they previously had joined in collective resistance to violent state intruders.

STATE MAKING AND BUREAUCRATIC CAPITALISM

The protest movement in which the Communist Party linked mass participation with its conquest of state power was a popular struggle against the ambitions of the national state. Provoked by the attempt of central rulers to impose strengthened controls over a critical source of peasant market income, this species of struggle reflected popular resentment over the state attempt to raise money from rural society for modernization. The protest movement of the peasant saltmakers should be seen *in part* through the prism of "state making,"[169] for it was a popular mobilization against centrally placed rulers attempting to take resources away from rural dwellers who had claims on them.

Although this state-making theme does not seem to square with the theme of Republican state disintegration and political devolution, we do not need to recast our view of the entire Republican period to grasp the sociopolitical significance of the Kuomintang state penetration of this border region.[170] Here the seizure of state power by the Chiang Kai-shek–led Nationalist government intensified an ongoing externally stimulated central state conflict with country people who placed the well-being of their local communities before the fiscal health of the Kuomintang state. The conflict not only upset local county elites; it also spilled beyond the county towns to disrupt the life-sustaining routines of tens of thousands of ordinary village dwellers. Their participation in collective protest can be understood fully only in reference to the centralized attempt during the Nationalist decade to increase the "wealth of the state."[171]

What drew these country people into antistate political activities was the particularly militant nature of the state-making process pushed by the "bureaucratic capitalists" at the helm of the central government of Chiang Kai-shek after 1928. Bureaucratic capitalism, Marie-Claire Bergere points out in reference to the period of Chiang Kai-shek's ascendance, "more often than not was merely the capitalism of the higher officials."[172] In speaking of bureaucratic capitalism, I refer specifically to the seizure of national state power by these same officials, especially to the usage of ministerial office to promote the interest of "national community"—a term that was virtually synonymous with their personal fortunes and power goals. The leaders of the "bureaucratic capitalists" in Republican China were the top officials in the central government—Chiang Kai-shek, T. V. Song, H. H. Kong, and Chen Lifu. In their quest to gain political supremacy and to create a powerful, unified national political order, these Kuomintang state leaders relied on the presidency, and particularly on the ministry of finance, to pursue a set of economic policies conducive to the bureaucratic production of state wealth.[173]

With the establishment of the Nationalist government in Nanjing in 1928, the ministry of finance was placed in the hands of T. V. Song, H. H. Kong, and other leaders connected to Chiang Kai-shek by a web of kinship, patron-client, and Kuomintang party ties. The bureaucratic capitalists in Chiang Kai-shek's national political network concealed some of the ministry's most important fiscal practices,[174] but under their tutelage it became the primary instrument of national power during the twenty-two years of Nationalist political dominance. The Kuomintang exchequer assumed responsibility for collecting revenue from the countryside, both to settle foreign debts and to strengthen Chiang Kai-shek's administrative dictatorship.

State making in Kuomintang China gained momentum from the renovation of the revenue-gathering bureaucracy under the ministry of finance. The real power base of Chiang Kai-shek's central government was not the Kuomintang as a mass party, nor the Kuomintang Central Army, nor pro-Kuomintang landlords as a social class, but rather the bureaucratic apparatus charged with resolving the fiscal crisis and developing the economic foundation of the Republican state. Through utilizing the ministry of finance, the bureaucratic capitalists were able to create, maintain, and command field armies, police forces, and propaganda corps and to fend off "social disorder."

In considering bureaucratic capitalism, we must note the interventionist tendencies of the Kuomintang officials seeking to create central state controls over private enterprise in the countryside and, following Etienne Balazs,[175] acknowledge the persistent tendency of Chinese power holders to extend the reach of their political apparatus into rural towns and villages. If the creation of such an interventionist bureaucratic political system was a key aspect of Kuomintang state making, why have we so seldom witnessed the resulting social ramifications? The bureaucratic capitalists at the apex of the Nationalist government in Nanjing worked their way into the countryside by capturing intermediate-level regional institutions and by projecting their fiscal claims into peasant villages through such institutions.[176] The seizure by the Nationalist fiscal elite of the Changlu Salt Company, a regional-level merchant-run salt business firm that historically had been the indirect state instrument for collecting the salt tax in North China, reflected a renewed state attempt to transform salt tax collection into a big profitable business at the expense of the semipeasants of this triprovincial border world.

The logic of this transformation involved Kuomintang state makers in the politics of imposing a rigid monopoly over rural salt markets in order to bolster state revenue intake. Certainly Kuomintang dependence on the salt monopoly was not without precedent; but the way in which the Kuomintang fiscal elite attempted to operationalize monopoly was a distinctive and disjunctive feature of the modern state-making process. Under the salt monopoly regulations drawn up by the Chiang Kai-shek center, the day-to-day operations of the Tianjin-based Changlu salt merchants were increasingly militarized, and an interventionist tax police unit emerged to enforce the central government's fiscal claims. Although this tax police force had been inaugurated by Yuan Shikai, the scale of its operations was increased by Chiang Kai-shek's bureaucratic capitalist order, and its development after 1928 posed a growing threat to the subsistence and security of the peasant saltmakers, many of whom were more heavily armed than in late Qing. Kuomintang state progress in fortifying the formal enforcement agency of its Changlu Salt Division in markets previously free of tight bureaucratic controls threatened the market link to homemade earth salt and significantly increased the tensions between Chiang Kai-shek's money-seeking officials and the country people who relied on that salt for their livelihood. Herein lie the origins of a neglected popular struggle for liberty from Nationalist government penetration and a piece of the puzzle of why the Kuomintang failed to successfully form a popular foundation for state legitimacy in the countryside.

Another feature of bureaucratic capitalism, as I conceive it, has to do with the independent political activity of the bureaucracy. In creating a framework for effective fiscal reform, and in reforming the bureaucracy in charge of salt tax collection, senior officials under Chiang Kai-shek forged a far-reaching fiscal apparatus to extract money from rural people by setting the price of government salt as high as possible. They attempted to extend this centralized bureaucratic search for revenue through the police cadres of national *cum* regional officials personally beholden to them. To a significant extent, the Kuomintang officials in charge of the salt tax collection process in North China acted without consulting members of the rural society from which they sought to mobilize capital, disrupting the symphonic relationship between Kuomintang-appointed magistrates and local subcounty leaders. Ignoring local influential leaders, and ignoring the popular dissent generated by government salt tax policy, they pursued a strategy of *state making* that was independent of rural society. It was, in short, the fiscal policy of a handful of privileged Kuomintang state leaders, political men who were "rising above society,"[177] that engendered "social chaos" during the 1930s.

The nature of the state-making process that took shape under Chiang Kai-shek's "fiscal family" was itself a factor arousing popular resistance to the center's penetration of the countryside and contributed ultimately to the defeat of the Nationalist government. The growing tendency of the Kuomintang national leadership to impose its fiscal claims on the country-side by *deadly force* triggered a massive anti-state movement that mush-roomed into a great regional rebellion during the 1930s.[178] While much of this popular resentment took the form of open collective protest against the dreaded tax gendarmes, such a development usually was preceded by a pattern of less visible, low-key, nonviolent resistance. The decision of Chiang Kai-shek, T. V. Song, and H. H. Kong to repress this popular oppo-sition was the critical factor moving the country people to participate in col-lective protests characterized increasingly by confrontation, bloodshed, and bitterness.

The persistence of fiscal authorities in their ill-conceived scheme to col-lect revenue via the salt monopoly, in conjunction with the political aper-ture provided by the Japanese invasion, gave the CCP an opportunity to anchor its struggle to restore the sovereignty of China within the interna-tional system of nation-states in a broad united front of country people who had an active record of protest against Kuomintang state making. The vio-lent process whereby the Kuomintang center had extended its revenue machinery into village society had delegitimated its rule prior to the Japan-ese invasion; Kuomintang state making misfired, giving the Chinese Com-munists a chance to develop a common political bond with the country peo-ple. This episode of collective protest seemed but a pebble tossed against the larger system of Kuomintang state power, but it shook the foundations of Kuomintang-directed state building in scores of counties and led grow-ing numbers of country people to *believe* they could shape the course of national politics. This popular oppositionist tradition, along with the failure of the Kuomintang leadership to create a system of fair taxes and free mar-kets, permitted the Chinese Communists to conduct the political work that would, over the course of several decades, encourage and equip the coun-try people to support resistance and revolution.

Comprehending the Antistate Protest Movement of the Peasant Saltmakers

Arthur N. Holcombe, C. Martin Wilbur, and others portray the central gov-ernment as a "state blown apart" by military separatism.[179] While acknowl-edging that Chiang Kai-shek led the Nationalist government to defeat most of the aristocratic warlord armies of the 1927–30 period, still other scholars represent the center as lacking the bureaucratic machinery necessary to penetrate the vast rural interior and halt the devolution of state power. According to their analysis, the devolutionary process played into the hands of entrenched local elites who were against state building or who, as Duara has shown,[180] acted as brokers to alter Nationalist government claims in order to serve their own interest. Lloyd Eastman presents the central government of Chiang Kai-shek as real enough, but the plans of its policymakers to create economic wealth and expand controls over rural society presumably were confounded by intensive factional infighting and cut short by the Japanese invasion of North China.[181]

Each of these models enriches our understanding of the relationship of the Republican polity to rural society. Indeed, within the Hebei-Shandong-Henan border area, there were examples of the devolution of Kuomintang state power into warlord hands, of local elite obstacles to the Nationalist government overtaking subcounty formations of power and interest, and of Kuomintang factionalism impeding the center's plan for placing county-level politics under its control. The Kuomintang-appointed magistrates in Daming Prefecture still had to share the land tax with Ding Shuben, the warlord in charge of the twenty-ninth army after 1935;[182] the Kuomintang civil defense corps was based on the armed retainers of four big landlord families in the Puyang-Neihuang-Hua *xian* area, and the magistrates relied on it to pacify banditry and put down CCP-led peasant struggles over surtaxes throughout the early 1930s.[183] In Puyang and Hua*xian* there were a few instances of the centrally sponsored revenue police relying on local tax farmers—Duara's tax brokers—to facilitate the collection of Kuomintang taxes on salt lands, especially in the 1928–31 period.[184] Factional infighting was serious enough to complicate the Kuomintang center's attempt to establish total political control in the border area, for in early 1936 the Kuomintang Blue Shirt faction in Daming was replaced by a Kuomintang faction subservient to Zhang Mutao, a powerful twenty-ninth army figure in the patronage of Fen Zhian, the chairman of the Hebei Province Kuomintang. This prevented the Blue Shirt faction from completing its crackdown on all of the pro-CCP students and teachers in the Daming Normal School.[185]

Although highly accurate, this subnational parapolitical history has little to say about *how* Kuomintang state making produced a dialectic that eventually drew the country people into the CCP-led revolution, for it omits the process whereby central government revenue claims impacted on the immediate life interests of rural dwellers and contributed to the rise of collective action and Communist involvement with popular rebelliousness. Hence a common and influential representation of the CCP-led revolution: the country people, so the story goes, proved receptive to the CCP's message only at the last moment, when the party led them in class struggles against landlords in liberated areas beyond the reach of the weak Kuomintang state.[186]

In the above paradigm, key reasons accounted for the passivity of the peasantry: the alleged weakness of the peasant community, plus the incapacity, and disinclination, of the Nationalist government to penetrate the countryside below the county level.[187] The picture of the Kuomintang state that emerges, however, differs significantly from the existing literature on state penetration of Republican society. The salt administration was a vertically integrated bureaucracy in which orders from the Nationalist capital were passed all the way down to police operatives. If the line of Kuomintang state administration was still fragmented, the case at hand nonetheless argues for a modification of the previous notion of a Republican state without a vertical reach into the habitats of rural people and suggests that the state attempt to reconstruct central administrative controls and overcome the disorder of political devolution was itself a critical factor in the emergence of resistance, protest, and rebellion in the hinterland.

To grasp what prompted rural people to rebel, a deeper knowledge of the politics of Kuomintang state development is necessary.[188] The politics of Kuomintang state making was focused on the collection of salt-based revenue, which led prominent senior officials to pursue a war against semipeasants who made their living by local market initiatives. Although the Kuomintang state was weak vis-à-vis the subcounty gentry and the global powers, it was strong and predatory vis-à-vis its more ordinary village subjects, in part because of the tremendous international pressures to raise tax revenue after 1928. In attempting to maximize salt tax revenue in the short run, the Nationalist government began to destroy a section of the North China peasant economy and turned rural people against its long-run goals of stability and development. Unable to adapt their lives to the central government attempt to create a political economy based on monopoly and state-organized violence, the peasant saltmakers opted for collective antistate protest, which eventually became entwined with CCP-led insurgency.

TWO

State Making and the Intrusion of the *Shuijingtuan* into the Peasants' Salt Market

The scholarship on state making and peasant resistance to it permits us to explicate the origins of protest in the Hebei-Shandong-Henan border area during the Nationalist period.[1] The impact of the Chiang Kai-shek–led central government attempt to generate the resources needed to promote military growth, pay foreign debt, and push ahead with modern reforms stirred up resentment and resistance, giving rise to a popular movement to stop the spread of the Kuomintang state into the counties of the border area during the 1930s. Increased taxation, stemming from the Kuomintang effort to recentralize salt revenue collection, was a major precipitant of collective protest in the countryside.

In attempting to acquire the fiscal means to hold on to national power, Republican state makers from Yuan Shikai to Chiang Kai-shek got mixed up in the daily survival routines of the market-bound village people on the lower periphery of the North China plain. The mobilizing dictatorship of the Chiang Kai-shek Kuomintang created a dangerous conflict between the monetary goals of its own "big structures" and the life-enhancing market activities of the peasantry.[2] State making,[3] the central government effort to extract local resources, threatened the irreplaceable market sphere of the peasant economy and proved to be the critical factor alienating rural people and moving them into anti-state collective protest activities. This growing, largely hidden conflict between country dwellers and the Kuomintang tax state presented local Communist leaders with the opportunity to strike up a political alliance with nonparty village-level protest leaders who were determined to substitute "market justice" for rural misery and move on to a more promising life.

The causal link between state making and the ability of the Chinese Communists to find popular support in border villages is reflected in the rise of the peasant saltmakers' struggles against the Kuomintang state takeover and transformation of the salt administration—specifically the attempt to monopolize salt trade after 1928. The Kuomintang enforcement of the salt monopoly was not strictly a part of the modern state-making process. Taxes from salt monopolized by the state, and marketed by state-licensed merchants, had, of course, been a traditional source of revenue. Yet as Tien Hung-mao has pointed out, the salt administration remained a critical instrument for state revenue accumulation in the Republican era, and the salt tax became even more central to Kuomintang state development as the lack of central government control over the land tax made the recentralization of *gabelle* revenue all the more imperative.[4] But the Kuomintang state effort to reestablish the salt monopoly, driven by the pressures of international debt, endangered the market performance of village people, whose protest against state intrusion into the space of habitual market routines became closely associated with their participation in the Communist-led revolution.

STATE MAKING AND THE PROTESTS OF THE SALT PEOPLE

One of the major concerns of the Kuomintang-appointed magistrates during the Nationalist era was the "disturbances" of the "salt people" (*yanmin*), reported to have converged in protest marches on the towns of the countryside. The disturbances were often interterritorial, involving hundreds of thousands of rural dwellers in different salt production and consumption areas of the Republic of China after 1915. A macrohistorical map of the salt people's protests would illustrate three themes. First, five of China's salt production and salt consumption areas witnessed the development of a high incidence of state-society conflict over salt-related issues: Changlu (North China), Tung (East China, mainly Shandong), Liang Huai (the areas just north and south of the Huai River), Sichuan, and Zhejiang. Second, the Changlu area saw the growth of concerted popular reactions to central government salt policy initiatives during the post-1928 decade, when the Kuomintang was establishing its presence at the county level. Third, persistent collective resistance to central state claims on salt formed mainly in regions far removed from the garrisoned city base of the Kuomintang, and the CCP eventually connected with the popular reaction to this aspect of state making. In some cases, the location of the saltmakers' struggles correlated with the development of the Communist bases—the CCP base along the Hebei-Shandong-Henan border is one example.[5] Here the protest of quasi peasants against the Kuomintang salt monopoly took the form of a struggle to preserve the right to make earth salt for the market, providing the Chinese Communists with an issue in communal history that facilitated the formation of an alternative political order capable of eliciting mass support.

Because the Nationalist fiscal elite interacted with a host of intermediate actors (the Changlu salt merchants, Kuomintang magistrates, and local public security forces) in order to impress central state revenue policy on the village people, it is important to describe and analyze how the evolving competition between central government power holders and actors in the relatively advanced economic sector produced unprecedented political turbulence, giving rise to a mode of rule that deepened the rift between rural society and the state.[6] This specific episode of anti-state protest was largely a popular movement against the attempt of Republican state makers to integrate the Changlu salt merchants into a tight centrist monopoly, which offered the rural people an "irrational public choice," creating artificial scarcity and constricting personal economic freedoms. It is no accident that the thunder bombs of popular antistate protest first exploded in the borderland villages in the year 1932. This was the year in which the central government finance ministry brought maximum pressure to bear on the Changlu salt merchants[7] and replaced their impotent antismuggling constabularies with a modern revenue force that imperiled the life chances of rural dwellers.

Protest against the Nationalist Salt Administration was widespread in the deep interior counties of Hebei, Shandong, and Henan provinces. Many were situated along the old course of the Yellow River, a long way from Tianjin and metropolitan North China. From 1931 until 1935, the people in these rural inland counties joined in collective protest and through petitions, demonstrations, and fights with the tax agents of the salt administration were able to draw Republican magistrates into a discourse over central government salt policy. Their protests did not always gain them much, but they did create a moral agenda with which both the Kuomintang and the CCP had to come to terms.

By failing to recognize the defensive purpose of this subgroup of peasants, the Nationalist government allowed the Communist Party to legitimate its purpose by emphasizing the righteousness of collective resistance against the state assault on traditional market practices. This popular moral claim on the marketplace was strikingly evident in all of the protests of the salt people in the Hebei-Shandong-Henan border region—in the March 19, 1932, march of three thousand on the Kuomintang magistracy in Puyang town, in Hebei;[8] in the 13 May 1932 procession of fifteen thousand protestors in Hua County, Henan;[9] in the 28 July 1933 gathering of twenty thousand people in Dongming, Shandong Province;[10] in the 8 August 1934 struggle of several thousand peasant saltmakers in Hebei's Daming County;[11] in the 12 April 1935 assembly of six thousand salt people on the outskirts of Nanle County town, in Hebei Province.[12] All these protest groups were angrily imploring the Kuomintang magistrates to prevent state tax forces from interfering with the production of earth salt (*xiaoyan*) for the market.

Occurring beyond the bright new world of Nanjing, some of these showdowns turned into bloody tragedies, shattering the hope for political accommodation. Foreigners in the Republic of China—including the American advisors to Chiang Kai-shek's Salt Administration—equated the central government with enlightenment, civility, and the end of Communist-led insurgency and seldom traced the rise of rural protest to its efforts to expand its "taking powers" over the countryside.[13] Reports filed by high-level state revenue officials, however, remind us that protest arose within a pattern of interaction introduced to society by the agents of the foreign-impacted Republican center, and that the pattern threatened land-use rights and market pursuits.

The Question of Earth Salt, or Nitrate Salt

Who were these "salt people," and how did earth salt become such a serious problem? What was its place in the agrarian economy of this part of the North China plain in late Qing and early Republican times? *Xiaoyan* included all of the salt made from alkaline earth deposits, including nitrate, or saltpeter, which was produced in smaller quantity. In the last years of the Qing, more than half of the country people in the Hebei-Shandong-Henan border region used this salt for daily consumption and for culinary purposes, in pickling and preserving foods, and for medicinal powders. In the Republican period, city dwellers referred to *xiaoyan* as nitrate salt, while it had a variety of names in the countryside. Peasants in Shaanxi and Gansu called it private salt; those in Caodong called it wild salt; Hebei, Shandong, and Henan folk called it earth salt. The peasants of the border area still produced *xiaoyan* decades after the founding of the People's Republic, and marketing it remained a popular strategy of coping with disappointing harvests and state-induced dearth.

The greatest quantity of earth salt came from scraping the crust of alkaline soil and drawing it in solarized ponds or decocting it in scalded caldrons. Alkaline earth shows up as a white crusty substance intermixed with yellow earth, so heavily concentrated that the land itself appears to be blanketed by a light efflorescent snowfall.[14] It consists of sodium chloride, potassium, magnesium, and calcium, plus other chemical substances such as acidic salts (*swanyan*) or nitric acid (*xiaoyan*), which make the soil unsuitable for grain crops. Many who resided on these salt lands depended on this small-grained tartish salt both for their household needs and for purchasing grain in the local markets to which they pushed their wheelbarrows of salt.[15] Because *xiaoyan* was also used in making local foods, firecrackers, fertilizer, leather, glass, tea, medicine, tinfoil, and paint, the salt-making villages were connected to a variety of transcounty market networks in the North China plain. There is little doubt of the importance of earth salt, nitrate, and alkali in popular market networks of the seventy to one hundred counties south of Baoding in Hebei, north of Kaifeng in Henan, and southwest of Pingyuan in Shandong in the Republican period.[16] Although the number of country people involved in salt production varied from county to county, in many counties the peasant saltmakers composed the majority of rural households. In 1930, for example, over three-quarters of Pingxiang's village people relied on earth salt production for their livelihood;[17] in Daming, where the salt land occupied half of the land surface, half the villagers were involved in salt making or salt trade by 1934.[18] By contrast, only one-quarter of Puyang's population were salt-makers in 1932.[19]

Within the Hebei-Shandong-Henan border area, the demographic core of this subgroup was located in Puyang, Qingfeng, Nanle, Daming, Nei-huang, and Hua*xian*—all counties lying in what Daniel Hillel has called the "scars of no fewer than fifteen ancient river beds,"[20] created largely by the Yellow River bolting to a new course once a century. The ancient history of "China's Sorrow" combined with the geography of the twentieth-century floodplain to create these salt land villages. Up until the Ming period, the peasant villages of Daming, Nanle, and Wei County were subjected frequently to floods on the two main branches of the Yellow River, so that saline earth deposits from these pre-Ming floods were layered five meters deep in village fields long before the twentieth century.[21] On the other hand, many villages were located near the gradients of the Wei, Zhang, and Xiao rivers or near minor branches of the Yellow, all of which periodically flooded these low-lying peasant settlements into the 1930s. Lacking adequate drainage facilities, the village people made the most of the process whereby the solar evaporation of floodwaters both drew up old and deposited new salt to the top layer of the earth.[22] Hence, peasants could freely gather all the saline earth they could manage well before state policy and agricultural distress made salt manufacturing extremely popular in the Republican period.

Peasants extracted the salt by pouring water into soil-filled ponds, then allowed solar evaporation to draw up the salt. The process, although simple, required backbreaking labor and luck. The saltmakers first had to dig, harrow, and scrape the saline earth from the topsoil, preferably on sunny days just after a light rain in late spring, midsummer, or early autumn. They then constructed a salt pond about fifteen by seven feet, which they packed with more than a hundred wheelbarrows full of damp, heavy surface soil. Each peasant family then lugged several hundred buckets of water to fill its salt pond. The evaporation process took about three days, yielding a solution that was made up of 70 percent bitter salt crystals.[23]

How did popular earth salt making and the crisis of the Republican government in Hebei, Shandong, and Henan counties enter a collision course in the 1930s? From the end of the Qing into the Republican era, agricultural land that originally was free of alkali was subjected to swift-spreading river deposits of sand, mud, and soluble salts. The spread of these alkaline substances into prime croplands was due largely to the decline in upkeep of the Yellow River Water Works in late Qing and to the lack of a comprehensive Republican government program of interior canal building and maintenance. The digging of canals and ditches to wash away the alkali and salt in the soil had long been the key to preventing, or reversing, the alkaline takeover of fertile croplands in North China, but by the late 1920s the spread of alkaline dirt had created scores of semibarren salt land villages and engendered an enormous agricultural crisis, threatening rural communities historically dependent on lands sown to grain crops. At least 30 to 50 percent of the agricultural land in Hebei Province reportedly had become alkaline by 1930.[24] Facing a decline in grain production, many peasants who lost land to salinization started up salt-making operations, scratching out an existence by producing "earth salt" in privately built ponds and peddling the salt locally. The problem of acute salinity, coupled with poor handicrafts, prompted the marginalized peasants of Jinxiang County, in western Shandong, to pursue salt production of this sort in late Qing and early Republican years, selling their salt at the fringe of the official salt monopoly, and with marginal profits.[25]

The other side of the earth salt issue—increased production for the market—was the result of warlord chaos and Kuomintang fiscal drive. The warlord clashes over Changlu salt in Dao Kou around 1923–24, and the ensuing disruption of sea salt supplies, signaled a breakdown in the local enforcement of the salt monopoly in Puyang, Hua*xian,* and other counties and made it easier for peasant earth salt producers to seize the opportunity to meet popular market demand,[26] engendering a new prosperity in villages with previously unproductive salt land between 1923 and 1928. The increased Nationalist government taxes on Changlu salt gave saltmakers greater impetus because the subsequent price increases on maritime salt permitted them to take advantage of state greed and accentuate earth salt production for consumers who could not afford government salt. In Daming, Nanle, and Puyang, earth salt production, legal or illegal, became a big household industry of the village people during the Republican period.[27] The extension of this boom brought forth a large group of rich peasants who were part-time saltmakers within villages and counties where growing numbers of poor marginalized peasants had turned into full-time salt producers and traders.

The history of this development, and the rising expectations it engendered, sheds light on peasant market participation in this part of the North China plain. To be sure, in the Imperial period, when the salt administration was operating fairly efficiently, the peasants of the border villages produced limited amounts of salt for the local market, so that their pre-1920s marketing, geared to cover subsistence costs, constituted a form of what Philip C. C. Huang has called "survival-driven commercialization."[28] The salt market took on additional importance in the 1920s and 1930s, as warlord chaos and Kuomintang state demands prompted the peasants who previously had marketed for sheer survival to increasingly enjoy new economic prosperity via the market. Thus, the salt marketing of the Kuomintang decade surely reflected the rise of new rural entrepreneurs, but by the same token, many peasant saltmakers associated their economic ascent with customary market conduct and justified their protests as a defense of a traditional prerogative.

THE GROWTH OF THE CHINESE STATE AND THE ADMINISTRATION OF THE *GABELLE*

The earth salt economy, connecting the interests of poor and rich country people, was bound to clash with the fiscal interest of the Nationalist government, whose officials set out to monopolize salt-related matters. This is readily apparent in the politics enveloping the Kuomintang state administration of Changlu salt affairs. But long before 1928, the state administration of salt matters had become coupled with the interests of the world powers and the makers of a global fiscal order.

A Brief History of the Salt Monopoly and the Salt Tax of the Old Regime

The Kuomintang state resurrection of the salt monopoly was not a new revenue-making scheme. The Imperial state had monopolized salt production for several hundred years, and, along with the land tax and customs duties, salt was a critical source of revenue.[29] As the studies of Adshead, Zelin, and Rowe show, the late Qing saw a gradual shift from monopoly salt to licensing and reliance on the market[30] as officials enlisted salt merchants to help generate taxes collected on salt production in the Tianjin salterns. Still, the salt tax had made up one-quarter to one-half of the annual dynastic treasure in the Qing, as well as the Ming,[31] and down to the twentieth century it remained one of the three pillars of the political economy of the old regime. State revenue traditionally came from a levy on maritime salt,[32] not on earth salt, the production of which persisted on in distant, poor rural border counties where late Qing and early Republican salt patrols operated with neither the authority nor the force to prevent it for more than short intervals.

The Imperial government salt monopoly was mainly a monopoly over sea salt and for most of Chinese history did not include earth salt. Because 80 percent of the salt produced for North China consumer markets came from the government's coastal salt industry, the salt administration was focused on operating fairly efficiently in the densely settled cities, towns, and counties of maritime China. Before the late Qing period, this "official salt" was consumed mainly by people in such places. When it did reach the country people living along the Hebei-Shandong-Henan border, it was costly and mainly found its way into the diets of gentry, merchants, officials, and artisans. Peasants, and even landlords, relied heavily on earth salt for daily consumption.

Beginning with the Sui dynasty, the Imperial government had pursued a laissez-faire policy toward production of earth salt, allowing rural people in the counties along the old path of the Yellow River to manufacture it for the market.[33] In the Tang period, thousands of peasant saltmakers had followed Wang Xianzhi and Xiang Junzheng in Puyang to support Huang Chao's rebellion, thwarting a dynastic attempt to reinstitute a total monopoly on salt and preventing the central state from boosting revenue by placing a ban on earth salt.[34] To be sure, conflict between the Imperial authorities and village dwellers persisted into the Qing period. In the Guangxu era (1875–1908), there occasionally were inspectorate raids on salt ponds in this border area, and folktales reflect sporadic popular resistance. But the level of this conflict remained fairly low, partly because there was no compelling reason for Imperial officials to force the issue. Hence there had been no major ramified popular explosion over state impingement on this informal economy since Tang.[35] By the mid-1890s a tenuous compromise had evolved between commoners and Qing officials. After meeting a small tax quota, Qing magistrates left peasants to sell earth salt locally, regulating trade very loosely. This pattern of charged peaceful coexistence came under attack in the Republican period, when centrally placed rulers intensified the policing of this "small-time economy."

International Politics and the Transformation of the Administration of Chinese Salt Affairs

From 1895 on, state development was heavily dependent on salt-based revenues and inextricably bound up with the demands of the global economic powers in East Asia. The major world powers, especially England, Germany, and Japan, were expanding their economic interest into Qing China via gunboat diplomacy. The indemnity payments imposed by Japan in the aftermath of the 1894–95 Sino-Japanese War, coupled with the massive indemnity deriving from the Boxer Protocol of 1901, paved the way for the foreign seizure of Chinese political finances. The Imperial Chinese government was obliged to pledge salt revenues to pay for indemnity reparation and foreign loans. The foreign powers, with England and Japan leading the way, used the controls they established over the indemnity repayment process to take over some of the important managerial and financial aspects of the Chinese salt industry, which in the last years of the Qing was still subject to Imperial government supervision.

Over the three decades following the Sino-Japanese War, new foreign claims on salt revenues and new foreign competition for salt-related markets in China brought about a transformation of both the state management of salt affairs and the salt industry itself and gave rise to a Republican government that attempted both to meet debt and indemnity payments and to finance its own expansion by a host of salt-based revenue-making schemes. The first phase of this great transformation, from 1895 to 1912, led up to the eclipse of the Qing order. The second phase, signaled by the formation of the Republic of China and by Yuan Shikai's collaboration with the foreign powers, commenced in 1913, the year of the Reorganization Loan Agreement, and ended with the ascent of the Nationalist government in 1928. The third phase saw the takeover of the salt administration by the fiscal elite of the Chiang Kai-shek center. All three phases were marked by renewed central government efforts to capture salt-related resources and by an intensified drive for salt-based revenues to be delivered to foreign banks and to finance Chinese state growth.

In the first phase the world powers established the premises for control over the salt industry of late Qing China. The Qing government still owned and managed the salt industry, but the salt-related monies now went to pay indemnity and interest payments.[36] Prior to 1895 the Qing government had borrowed money from foreign banks for the purpose of suppressing the Taiping Rebellion and a host of minority uprisings, but the amount borrowed was small, and repayments usually were made on schedule by dynastic officials drawing from various customs duty funds. This state of affairs changed with the defeat of China by Japan in the war of 1894–95. The Treaty of Shimonoseki included a war indemnity payment of 230 million silver *liang*, the first half of which was to be paid within one year.[37] The second part was to be paid in six installments, over the period 1897–1902. There was a second indemnity: 30 million silver *liang* was to be paid to Japan in exchange for its promise to return the Liaodong Peninsula to Chinese rule.[38] Taken together, these two indemnities came to 230 million *liang* without interest. Because the Qing government's total annual income was only 80 million *liang*, there was no way for the old regime to pay this indemnity.

The Qing officials thus faced a cruel choice: declare bankruptcy or borrow huge sums of money from foreign powers. By opting for the second choice, they opened the door to foreign investment in China and committed the salt industry and the salt tax to guarantee the loans from abroad. Between 1895 and 1939, sixteen kinds of government loans were guaranteed by salt taxation (see Table 1).[39] The Qing government was under great pressure to improve on the efficiency of the traditional salt revenue collection process in order to service debts to the world powers, as well as fund state development.

TABLE 1   Salt-Related Loans from World Powers, 1895–1939

Date of Loan	Name of Loan	Borrower	Creditor	Amount In Principal	Guaranteed Item	Scheduled Date of Redemption
1895	Ruiji loan	Qing gov't.	Austria	1,000,000 English pounds	Salt tax and likin	
1898	British and German continuous loan	Qing gov't.	Great Britain, Germany	16,000,000 English pounds	Customs duty, likin, and salt	1943
1908	Anglo-French loan	Qing gov't. (refinanced by the Nationalist gov't. in 1929)	Great Britain, France	5,000,000 English pounds	Increased salt prices, tobacco and liquor taxes, estate taxes, salt, and likin	1938
1911	Hunan-Guangdong (Hukuang railway loan)	Qing gov't. (refinanced by the Nationalist gov't. in 1929)	Great Britain, USA	6,000,000 English pounds	Salt and likin	1975
1912	Crisp gold loan	Beiyang warlord gov't. (refinanced by the Nationalist gov't. in 1929)	Great Britain	5,000,000 English pounds	Salt and likin	1952
1913	Reorganization loan	Beiyang warlord gov't.	Great Britain, France, Germany, Russia and Japan	25,000,000 English pounds	Salt tax and customs duty	1960

Year	Loan	Government	Country	Amount	Security	End
1917	Bank of Japan	Beiyang warlord gov't.	Japan	25,000,000 Japanese yen	Salt tax	
1918–19	Vickers and Marconi	Warlord gov't.		2,403,200	Salt tax	1975
1923	Qingdao Public Authority	Warlord gov't.	Japan	14,000,000 Japanese yen	Salt tax	
1936	Marconi loan	Nationalist gov't.	Great Britain	2,403,200 English pounds	Salt tax	
1919 and 1937	Bank of Chicago loan	Nationalist gov't.	USA	5,500,000 US dollars	Salt tax	1954
1919 and 1937	Pacific Development Enterprise loan	Nationalist gov't.	USA	4,900,000 US dollars	Salt tax	1954
1937	Guang Mei railway loan	Nationalist gov't.	Great Britain	3,000,000 English pounds	Salt tax and railway income	
1937	Puxin railway	Nationalist gov't.	Great Britain	4,000,000 English pounds	Salt tax and railway income	
1938	Xianggui railway	Nationalist gov't.	France	150,000,000 French francs & 140,000 English pounds	Salt tax and railway income	
1939	Same as above	Nationalist gov't.	France	30,000,000 French francs	Salt tax and railway income	
1939	Xuhun railway	Nationalist gov't.	France	480,000,000 French francs	Salt tax and railway income	

Commencing with the defeat of the bourgeois democratic Revolution of 1911 by Yuan Shikai's Beiyang warlord government, a succession of centrist military groups entered into new dealings with foreign powers, each fostering new international controls on the state administration of salt affairs and promising military supremacy. Salt was a crucial factor in Yuan's ascendance over Sun Yat-sen. In order to obtain money and military assistance to check the democratic revolution in South China and to put down banditry in North China, Yuan Shikai agreed to pay back overdue debts and negotiate a number of small cash loans from the Four Country Banking Consortium, representing Great Britain, the United States, Germany, and France.[40] These cash loans, issued in the early part of 1912, permitted Yuan Shikai's clique to establish its presence and stabilize its order in Beijing.

These loans were issued against the salt tax and presented in return for Yuan Shikai's promise that the banking consortium alone would have the privilege of providing a futuristic gigantic loan to be guaranteed by salt tax revenues, which would be collected by the central government.[41] Subsequently, when Yuan Shikai attempted to obtain a bilateral loan from Belgium, the banking consortium—recently joined by Japan and Russia—pressured the Beiyang government to borrow only from the members of what was now the Six Power Banking Consortium. Yuan Shikai officially acknowledged the cartel's loan privileges in May of 1912, when his government received the cash advances that were used to defeat the military forces loyal to Sun Yat-sen and the southern revolution. From this time forth, international banking and state making were inseparable in Republican China, and the entanglement of the central state with foreign banking forces fueled the search for salt-based revenues in many counties of the North China plain.

The May 12 Loan Accords stated that representatives of the Six Power Banking Consortium were to help the central government to reform the salt tax administration. The reformist measures forged by the consortium struck at the sovereignty of modern China's political economy and instituted the beginnings of a centralizing state revolution in the administration of virtually all salt-related matters. On 18 September 1912 the minister of finance, Zhou Xuexi, was informed by the banking consortium that the great loan would be issued on four conditions.[42] (1) The loan would be guaranteed by the national salt tax, which would be managed by the customs house. (2) The income from this salt tax would be deposited to banks selected by the banking consortium, which would supervise the use of the loan. (3) The enterprises of the Republic of China would appoint foreigners as technicians. The office of auditor would take on a foreign director, who would supervise the use of money by Chinese enterprises. (4) All financial reforms were to be negotiated with the banking consortium, which was to be run by financial managers from outside of China.

In March of 1913 the loan was delayed by the withdrawal of the Americans from the consortium. Following this, the representatives of the Five Power Cartel[43] (Great Britain, France, Germany, Japan, and Russia) signed the loan contract, known as the Grande Reorganization Loan, with Yuan Shikai's Beiyang regime. And *grande* it was. It totaled twenty-five million pounds, and it was received at a staggering political cost to the new Republic of China.[44]

The original agreement had called for the customs to take charge of China's salt administration, but the final reorganization loan replaced this clause with an order that *the Republican central government establish a National Salt Administration Bureau in Beijing, which would be supervised by the ministry of finance.* The catch was that this national-level salt bureau was to include an auditing office with one Chinese inspector and one foreign inspector, both of whom were responsible to a foreign director.

The final reorganization loan mandated that the Chinese government establish a branch auditing office within each salt production and consumption area of the Republic of China, that is, in Changlu, Liang Huai, and the other salt areas. The British (the major power in the consortium) were to appoint one Chinese and one foreign manager for each salt area. They shared the task of collecting, reporting, and depositing salt income. The foreign directorate of the "national" salt bureau, along with its provincial contacts, was empowered to issue banknotes and collect salt revenues in each of China's salt areas.[45] The tax revenues from salt in the Changlu area, and each of the other salt areas, were to be deposited in the banks of the international banking consortium, *or in banks appointed by the consortium.* The administration of China's national-level salt affairs was now indirectly controlled by the world powers.

The third phase of the state crisis with the salt-based revenue system began on 4 October 1928, when Chiang Kai-shek led the Nationalist army to take power in the cities of Republican China and moved the capital of the Nationalist government from Beijing to Nanjing, the political base of the Central Executive Committee of the Kuomintang. During this phase of Kuomintang ascendancy the Salt Inspectorate was taken over by the ministry of finance under T. V. Song. There was growing central government dominance of the salt industry in general and increasing ministry of finance interference in the affairs of regional salt firms. By 1931–32 the finance ministry in Beijing was firmly in the hands of Chiang Kai-shek's "fiscal family,"[46] and its brain trust had begun to rely heavily on the Tianjin-based Changlu Inspectorate to collect salt revenue in Hebei, Shandong, and Henan.

Many of the adjustments made by the Chiang Kai-shek central government often were only more sharpened projections of earlier salt revenue policy measures. However, several of them signified discontinuity with previous state practice and resulted in a revenue-gathering process that was not in accord with the attempt of the Kuomintang national leadership to legitimate its purpose locally.

Although the collection of loans secured by the *gabelle* had fallen into arrears in the 1924–27 warlord period,[47] the Chiang Kai-shek center resurrected the salt tax as the guaranteed source of revenue for servicing external debt and making up foreign exchange deficits. Acting on the advice of Arthur N. Young, the American financial advisor to the Nationalist government,* Kuomintang Finance Minister T. V. Song agreed in September, 1929, to resume payment of the required amounts due on the salt loans in order to restore the central government's credit with the foreign banking community.[48] This new pledge included payment of the arrears of interest as well as principal on three major foreign loans—the Anglo-French loan of 1908, which was rescheduled for payment between 1929 and 1932; the Crisp loan of 1912, which was to be paid in arrears of principal between 1932 and 1934, with regular installments restored to schedule by 1940; and the Hukuang railway loan of 1911.[49] With the re-funding of these loans, Republic of China securities were said to have steadied on the British market. The London correspondent of the *North China Daily News* reported that "the Chinese Minister of Finance deserves every credit for the success of his efforts in re-establishing the salt revenue."[50] Such world news roundups failed to mention, of course, that the Kuomintang fiscal elite had predicated the development of its political economy on a strategy of foreign debt service that brought ever greater state pressure to bear on the market side of the triangular peasant economy of the North China plain, especially after 1931.

Comparatively speaking, even in North China, where the Kuomintang was relatively weaker, the central government elite was making the kind of progress in the realm of macrofiscal policy that had eluded its warlord predecessors, especially with respect to recovering salt revenue and retaining the salt receipts. After 1928 the ministry of finance took custody of the revenues collected from the salt tax away from the Sino-Foreign Inspectorate and achieved more autonomy vis-à-vis foreign banking forces in dispensing this revenue—though surely not as much as desired. When the finance ministry announced which particular banks would be entrusted with the salt funds,[51] for example, British, French, and Japanese inspectors protested to no avail, as T. V. Song stuck by his decision to place the funds in only a few

---

*Born in Los Angeles, 1890, Arthur N. Young earned an A.B. at Occidental College (1910) and then took his Ph.D. at Princeton (1914) and his LL. B. at George Washington University (1927), after which he served as an economic advisor to the Chinese Nationalist government, the director of China National Aviation Corporation, and chairman of the American Relief and Red Cross in China. Young also was a member of the Chinese delegation to the 1944 Bretton Woods Financial Conference. From the "Biographicals" in the *Register to the Arthur N. Young Collection*, 1–2.

banks—banks where he and other men who controlled the Central Bank of China had lucrative accounts. The funds for the Crisp loan were entrusted to the Chase Bank in London; those for the Anglo-French loan were placed in the National City Bank of New York, a move that drew a strong letter of protest from the French ambassador to China and from the representatives of the Banque de l'Indo-Chine and the Bank of Hong Kong.[52] Additionally, between 1928 and 1931 T. V. Song took measures to promote the most talented experts available in the Salt Inspectorate in order "to produce an efficient and fully effective collection and control agency for the obtaining of revenues from this source."[53] Thus in 1935 Y. S. Tsao praised ex-Minister of Finance T. V. Song for building up "a very creditable revenue-collecting machinery within a short period of time" and pointed out that after the Northern Revolutionary Expedition, the receipts from salt *gabelle* had "improved very appreciably."[54]

With Kuomintang state ascendancy, the salt tax was, in the words of Thomas G. Rawski, "remitted to the center with greater regularity than before 1927."[55] Rawski is correct, but the regularization of salt revenue from the Changlu area after the Kuomintang center took over seems to have reflected a longer pattern of state economic growth. The sporadic, sometimes paltry remittances of the warlord decade were serious, and yet, by 1936 Changlu salt receipts totaled approximately twenty-nine million dollars annually—ten times more revenue than had been given over to the center prior to the reorganization loan of 1913.[56]

The third adjustment in the administration of the *gabelle* involved the increasing reliance of the Chiang Kai-shek government on the Changlu salt area for monies to *simultaneously* pay off foreign debt and promote internal military development after 1928, 1931, and 1935. The Changlu Salt Inspectorate bore an inordinate burden of this new round of revenue seeking, for several reasons. First, on 16 November 1928 T. V. Song appointed Liu Tsungyi, a native of Hebei and a longtime Changlu district inspector, as chief inspector of the National Salt Revenue Administration.[57] A close associate of Hussey-Freke, the foreign associate chief inspector, and Dr. F. A. Cleveland, the American successor to Hussey-Freke, Liu placed the greatest burden of re-funding the Anglo-French, Crisp and Hukuang loans on the Changlu salt area, and by 1929 the annual quota for this area was significantly higher than for any other area in China.[58] Second, beginning in 1930 the ministry of finance ordered the Changlu Salt Inspectorate to increase its quotas in order to make up for the losses incurred from declining exchange rates, linked to the fall in world silver prices.[59] Third, and very important, was the increasing Kuomintang state pressure for salt tax results in the Changlu area to offset the salt revenue losses stemming from the Japanese seizure of Manchuria in September, 1931.[60] All of these fast-breaking developments gave new urgency to central government efforts to tighten controls over the salt tax receipts of the Changlu area, giving rise to more frequent antifiscal protest movements in the acutely salinized rural areas of Hebei, Shandong, and Henan.

Responsive to foreign pressures to pay back China's foreign debts, the Western-trained officials in the fiscal cockpit of the Nationalist government, particularly T. V. Song and H. H. Kong, increasingly pushed for strong enforcement measures to expand the Kuomintang state's revenue base. The pursuit of this policy brought a growing number of newly trained state tax police units into the Hebei-Shandong-Henan border area in the early 1930s, upsetting relations between peasant salt producers and magistrates. Traditionally, in places like Puyang, it had been the county magistrate's responsibility to see that a centrally assigned quota of Changlu salt was sold locally and that the tax collected was given to the center, with the assistance of the old-style inspectorate. The magistrate was also responsible for supervising the salt tax forces stationed locally. During the late Qing and early Republican periods, the salt tax inspectorate was largely local and, to some extent, merchant funded, even though it was technically subject to a national control office. With the Chiang Kai-shek fiscal elite intensifying the state quest for money, however, the enforcement arm of the *gabelle* became more and more a national paramilitary tax police force, which proved far more responsive to the center's demand for more salt revenue and far less tolerant of the controls of county magistrates, who usually were preoccupied with local political stability.

Following the advice of Dr. F. A. Cleveland, the American-appointed associate chief inspector of salt revenue in the Republic of China after 1930, T.V. Song and his administration moved to do something about the magistrates known for "assuming that local interests are superior to national law, and asserting that the salt locally produced and marketed is necessary to the livelihood of the people."[61] Under the guidance of T. V. Song, the American-educated (B.A., Harvard, 1915) finance minister in the Nationalist government, the Kuomintang Finance Ministry proceeded to transform the old-style salt inspectorate into a disciplined, mobile, armed police force—the centerpiece of the Nanjing government's general plan to utilize "any and every means of preventing the production of earth salt"[62] so as to increase revenues from "licit salt."

Between 1929 and 1933, when T. V. Song was placing the Changlu Salt Inspectorate under the ministry of finance, the *Shuijingtuan,* as this national revenue force was called, built up to forty-five thousand men nationwide, including a twenty-five-thousand-man revenue guard unit.[63] The *Shuijingtuan* was essentially the army of the Kuomintang exchequer, comparing favorably with all regular combat-efficient Kuomintang army units in China.[64] Partly because it was armed with modern weaponry and partly because its subunits were concentrated mainly in places where earth salt production was escalating, this police force caused havoc in scores of poor-soil counties of the North China plain during the 1930s.[65] Between 1931 and 1934, its repressive activities in Hebei, Shandong, and Henan gave rise to more frequent, sharper quarrels between peasant saltmakers and the police, making it difficult for local magistrates to mediate and transforming the Kuomintang center's fiscal crisis in border region settings into a genuine political crisis from which Chiang Kai-shek's government never recovered.

REPUBLICAN STATE INNOVATIONS IN THE REVENUE COLLECTION PROCESS: THE POLITICAL CONTEXT OF POPULAR PROTEST

Republican state makers introduced a whole set of innovations in the realm of revenue collection between 1913 and 1945, igniting repeated protests in the Hebei-Shandong-Henan border area between 1931 and 1935. The protests of the early 1930s can be traced back to state-induced changes in the collecting of taxes, price setting, and the policing of production.

Taxes and Money

With Republican officials relying on the salt tax to pay foreign loans, the world powers sent their officers to oversee the process of collection, to protect their advantages as creditor nations. Once the reorganization loan was in place, the British dispatched Sir Richard Dane, the former chief inspector of salt revenue in India, to Beijing to establish a salt auditing office within the Chinese Ministry of Finance.[66] In the Changlu salt area, the auditing office, run by Japanese and Chinese managers, set up branches in the Feng Cai and Lu Tai areas of Hebei Province.

Between 1913 and 1933—the two decades between the package of salt-secured loans and the outbreak of the saltmakers' protest—Republican state makers improved on salt tax collection in several ways. In order to institute a monopoly in salt distribution and sale, thereby ensuring a maximum flow of revenue, they began issuing special licenses to market sea salt to a handful of Tianjin-based merchant families. For all practical purposes, these were the tax agents of the Republican state, for both the Beiyang government of Yuan Shikai and the Nationalist government of Chiang Kai-shek granted the licenses only to merchants who paid the tax in advance—the big merchants with substantial capital—in return for the right to sell government sea salt in the rural interior.[67]

On the face of it, the Republican license system merely reflected the resumption of a traditional government practice that had prevailed in rural Hebei, Shandong, and Henan during late Qing.[68] The politicians who made the Republican state perverted this previous system, however, appointing to the National Salt Bureau political clients who pressed the Changlu salt merchants to squeeze more tax revenue from the rural people via the sale of salt, and from the reign of Yuan Shikai into the Nationalist decade state-level abuse combined with international plunder to compound the salt tax burden. The Changlu salt merchants did not look favorably on the attempt of the Qing authorities to raise additional revenue via the *gabelle,* and they opposed the rise of a foreign-indebted fiscal regime. They lost ground in 1911, however, when Zhang Zengfang, a Yuan Shikai aide, seized their properties and placed their firms within the Changlu Salt Company, requiring them to operate as a debt-servicing monopoly.[69]

This pinch continued into the 1920s, as evidenced by the career of Zhang Hu, the head of the National Salt Bureau under Yuan Shikai. A key actor in Changlu salt affairs, Zhang threatened the Tianjin merchants with the suggestion that salt be sold freely and that their license privileges be terminated, retracting it only after receiving an under-the-table payment of a million *yuan.* Just as Zhang Hu, according to Richard Dane, devised imaginative methods to implement the fiscal transcript of the reorganization loan, greatly increasing the salt revenue of the Beiyang warlord regime,[70] so the salt bureau officials of the warlord era repeatedly announced guidelines for abolishing the privileges of the Changlu merchants, prompting them to petition the state council and implore the central government to reestablish their traditional role in the *gabelle.* And after 1928 the "new" Kuomintang government continued to threaten the privileges of the Changlu merchants.

This "strained collusion" between the Kuomintang state and the Changlu salt merchants was doubtless behind the salt tax increases and, in turn, the price hikes of the Nationalist decade. After 1930 the Changlu merchants were permitted to raise the price of salt to offset the salt tax increases announced by the Kuomintang authorities.[71] However, the continuing attempt to compel local people to purchase only the salt of the state monopoly, at skyrocketing prices, gave rise to a spate of riots against the salt shops and salt bureaus in the Hebei-Shandong-Henan border area during the early 1930s. The riots in Puyang, Hua County, and Dongming all were presaged by sharp increases in the price of official sea salt[72]—one dimension of the Kuomintang state quest for salt-based revenue.

Another dimension was the new wave of taxes on the production and sale of earth salt. The finance ministry ordered each county government in the border area to assign a land tax quota for villages within its jurisdiction. Originally, this quota applied only to land sown to grain, exempting the people who worked the poor saline soils; but after 1923–24 the county governments in Puyang, Neihuang, and Hua*xian* proclaimed a new salt land tax, which they attempted to collect through brash tax farmers. The gouging by such tax collectors roused popular hostility and occasionally intensified the conflict with the police agents of the Kuomintang salt administration. On top of this, the local county salt bureaus often imposed a tax of one silver dollar per salt pond, as was the case in Puyang and Dongming around 1930.[73]

For the most part, the peasant saltmakers paid such taxes as long as county authorities permitted them to continue producing and selling earth salt. But increasing pressure on Kuomintang magistrates to collaborate with the Changlu tax police in stifling production foreclosed this possibility. In 1931 Gao Junbao, the magistrate of Shandong's Dongming County, declared the production of earth salt illegal and sent Changlu anticontraband forces to shut down production in the villages of Zhi Zhai, Liu Li, and Huang Zhai. A year later, the saltmakers of Zhi Zhai led three hundred people to petition Gao to revive production, but salt bureau officials demanded the saltmakers pay a ten thousand dollar extra tax in order to produce earth salt. Returning to their villages, the saltmakers organized a fifteen-thousand-member confederation of self-defense forces. By the summer of 1932 they had forced Gao Junbao's resignation and driven the tax police from the countryside.[74]

Price Hikes and More Revenue

As the Nationalist government moved ahead with the monopolization of salt affairs, the price of official salt shot up, sometimes very suddenly. Throughout the late 1920s and the early 1930s the Kuomintang Ministry of Finance ordered the Changlu salt merchants to pay increased taxes on the salt in storage and in transit to market catchment areas and permitted them to offset the increases by raising the price of sea salt.[75] After 1928, Chiang Kai-shek's Nanjing government used this tax money to pay back foreign debt.[76]

These price upswings cut across class lines and created the potential for communitywide confrontations with the agents of the Kuomintang center. The salt price hike operated much like a head tax, for each member of every rural household had a certain minimum physical need for salt.[77] Peasants were especially hurt. When the Changlu merchants transported government maritime salt from Tianjin to the distant provincial border counties of Hebei, Shandong, and Henan, they invariably attempted to offset the cost of shipping it along the Wei River and carting it over rugged terrain by raising the price.[78] Thus, peasants in these comparatively poor counties suffered the greatest price increases (see Table 2)[79] and, in effect, shouldered a disproportionate burden of state debt. By the 1930s even shop owners, schoolteachers, and lower government functionaries in Puyang, Dongming, and Nanle were suffering.[80] Hence, peasant riots against Kuomintang salt bureaus and Changlu salt shops drew sympathy from crowds of people from various social backgrounds.[81] They shared a heightened concern that the Kuomintang enforcement of monopoly threatened the cheaper earth salt.

As the price of state maritime salt increased, so did popular demand for lower-priced earth salt in the primordial markets of Daming, Nanle, Puyang, and other southern Hebei counties. Depicting this marketing of

TABLE 2   Salt Prices in Hebei Counties

Hebei Counties	Price Increase per Jin, 1931–32
Inner Core: Tianjin and Metropolitan Zone	
Cang*xian*, Yanshan	9.7 cents
Wuqing, Ninghe, Dacheng Qing*xian*, Jinghai, Wingyun, Nanpi, Jinghai, Fuchang, Gucheng, and Fengrun	9.9 cents
Outer Core: Intermediate Metropolitan Zone	
Lutong, Fu Ning, Lingyu, Changli, Leting	10 cents
Zhou*xian*, Liangxiang, Fangshan, Miyun, Changping, Shunji, Miyun, Huiarou, Penggu, Tong*xian*, Shanshe, Baoding, Su*xian*, Xiange, Xingzhen, Wenan, Guan, Yongging, Cushui, Ding*xian*, Qingcheng, Boye, Rongcheng, Anguo, Jian Lu, An xin, Gaoyang, Le xian, Jin*xian*, Su Ning, Wuji, Haocheng, Hejian, Xian*xian*, Jiaohe, Dongguang, Fengiou, Mingjin, Wuqiao, Guangzuo, Feixiang, Guanpeng, Qinghe, Zunhua, Chen*xian*, Wuqiang, Raoyang, Anping, Shenze, Ningjin, Ji*xian*, Nangong, Xinhe, Zaoqian, Wuji, Weishui	10.1 cents
Deep Rural Interior: Lower Perimeter of the North China Plain	
Daming, Yuancheng, Nanle, Qingfeng, Puyang, Dongming, and Changyuan	10.3 cents
Daxing, Wangping, Changping, Anci, Yi*xian*, Yanqing	10.3 cents
Lincheng, Fan*xian*, Wangdong, Wan*xian*, Zhenwan, Huo Lu, Jingjing, Fuping, Xiangtong, Lingshou, Pengshou, Pengshan, Yuanshi, Xinrong, Xintai, Renxiang, Nanhe, Neiqiu, Raoshan, Julu, Ping*xian*, Quyang, Zhaoxian, Buoxiang, Longping, Gaoui, Lincheng	10.7 cents
Shahe, Yongnian, Quzhou, Jize, Handan, Zhengan, Ci*xian*	10.9 cents

terrestrial salt as a mode of survival fashioned by marginal peasants dealing in illegal economic activities, central government officials called it "smuggling."[82] While the peasants were producing for what high Kuomintang officials termed the black market, circumventing state controls on their country markets, they were making their livelihood without seizing resources from the state (e.g., salt from government salt fields). Before encountering the new Kuomintang center, they had no reputation for criminal behavior.[83] Prior to the onset of Republican government they had carried on earth salt trade in daily village markets and periodic marketplaces like Gu Chengji, a small market town in Hebei's Qingfeng County. This common salt was sold outside of the official economy, but the practice was permitted, apparently with minimal censure, even into the first decade of the Republic. Thus, in reflecting on a 1915 petition by Fan Shouming—a Hebei official who had cautioned against strengthening the state economy without planning for the livelihood of the peasant saltmakers—a Neihuang County gazateerist worried that placing this popular trade in the criminal category was only a rationalization for Kuomintang revenue goals and warned that peasants would continue to ignore the prohibitions on salt trade or perish.

Kuomintang Finance Ministry officials taking over Changlu salt affairs after 1931 were oblivious to such logic, however. Their concern was with increasing the revenue of the *gabelle,* and they apparently convinced themselves that the peasant saltmakers posed a threat to their goal. The problem, according to the Kuomintang money men, was that the earth salt trade had decreased the Changlu Salt Bureau revenue income.[84] The spurious nature of the policy logic of Kuomintang state leaders inevitably provoked a popular outcry against the long arm of the Nationalist government's salt administration in the early 1930s.

By 1930 there was a booming clandestine trade in terrestrial salt, led by peasants in the remote counties of southern Hebei, western Shandong, and northern Henan. In 1932, for example, the same *yuan* that purchased ten *jin* of Changlu sea salt could buy three times as much earth salt in the markets of Puyang.[85] In such places, it would seem, the production of earth salt was slowing down the increase in central government revenue. This slowdown—which the center's finance cadres called a *decline*—had been under way for at least a decade before the outbreak of the popular struggles in Daming, Puyang, Qingfeng, and other counties. The reports of the Changlu salt transportation officials linked the "decline" to the long-term fiscal crisis of the Nationalist government. To take one example, "in the nitrate salt production area of southern Hebei," we are informed, "the sale of official salt in the twelfth year of the Republic (1923) was fifty-two percent of the amount of the salt consumed by the population, and in the twenty-second year of the Republic (1933) it fell to forty percent, so that within ten years the official salt lost 12 percent of its volume of sales."[86]

The Kuomintang Finance Ministry officials had assumed that the salt manufactured in the comparatively modernized Tianjin-centered maritime salt industry would easily capture old markets and create new ones, replacing the primitive, hygienically inferior earth salt. Basing their revenue income calculations partly on this premise, the Kuomintang officials governing Changlu salt affairs quite naturally linked the decrease in salt tax returns in the highly saline counties of the Hebei, Shandong, and Henan countryside with the loss of millions of *yuan* in revenue. Increasingly after 1931, the pro–Chiang Kai-shek policy makers in Hebei and Henan spoke with alarm about the "terrifying invasion" of national income by nitrate salt.[87]

Interpreting this allegedly cascading revenue loss as cause for political alarm, T. V. Song and the foreign advisors to the Kuomintang center increasingly perceived earth salt as a threat to national economic security. The logic behind their perception was based on a statistical mirage, however, for the factual reports on the revenue of the Changlu Salt Bureau during the Kuomintang decade tell a different story.

To be sure, the rise of earth salt trade did influence the spread of the Kuomintang revenue state, but not in the critically serious way set forth by the alarmists in the finance ministry. Once the Changlu salt area came under Kuomintang control, there was a significant increase in salt revenue flowing into the Kuomintang exchequer. Revenue more than doubled between 1929 and 1936. The increase dipped only in the year following the outbreak of the saltmakers' struggle (1933), then leapt back up in the 1934–36 period,[88] when the Chiang Kai-shek center resorted to coercive methods of collection. Much of this increase is explained by the increase in the volume of government salt pumped into the counties of the Hebei-Shandong-Henan border area, as the history of Nanle suggests.[89] In 1903, thirty-two hundred bags of maritime salt, each weighing fourteen hundred *jin*, an amount that long had been fixed by Qing regulators, were sent to Nanle from Tianjin. After the Republic of China was established, however, Yuan Shikai increased the volume of Changlu salt coming into Nanle, depending almost solely on how much his regime sought in taxes. With the capture of the county by Chiang Kai-shek's Nationalist forces in 1931, the volume of Changlu salt recovered from its low points in the years of "warlord disorder" and rose substantially.

Why, given that *gabelle* revenue was going up, did the Kuomintang Finance Ministry leaders insist that the production of earth salt was contributing to a decrease in Changlu salt revenue? We can answer this question through the statistical data on salt income for the year 1934,[90] when the finance ministry took in 22,539,000 *yuan* in salt taxes. This was a substantial increase over fiscal year 1933, but the ministry still reported a loss of 7,775,000 *yuan* to earth salt. Figuring that the peasant saltmakers in the counties falling under Changlu had produced 956,000 *dan* of earth salt, the salt bureau officials in Tianjin reasoned that the tax on that salt would have boosted their revenue by 7,775,000, that is, from 22 million to 30 million *yuan*. They reported this *projected revenue* as being lost to earth salt production and, through conjecture, associated it with the cause of a decline in central state revenue. Thus, although earth salt production detracted from the *projected revenue* to the Kuomintang fiscal center in 1934, the earth salt actually did not pose a serious threat to the long-term growth of Nationalist government revenue in the North China interior. To make this point another way, when the finance ministry officials supervising the Changlu salt area spoke of a decline in income, they surely were not speaking of an empirically demonstrated drop below achieved levels

In short, the Kuomintang fiscal center was not losing revenue to the peasant earth salt producers, and *gabelle* income had not been set back. Any reported setback was a loss only if measured against the insatiable monetary desires of Kuomintang state makers, who simply were unable to raise more and more revenue. If anything, the earth salt production of the country people only slowed down the relatively steady increase in Kuomintang Changlu salt revenue during most of the Nanjing decade. Nevertheless, in order to overcome the politically fabricated loss, the Nationalist government sent increasing numbers of Changlu tax police units into the rural counties and markets of Hebei, Shandong, and Henan to curtail the sale of privately circulated earth salt—a major political spark igniting collective protest.

THE POLITICS OF FORCE: THE STATE ATTACK ON PRODUCTION FOR THE MARKET

In 1913–16, the Beiyang government of Yuan Shikai established an investigative agency within the salt administration, which gradually took on the characteristics of a police force within the National Salt Bureau and its area branches.[91] The prototype of this emergent police force in North China can be traced to the revenue-raising schemes of the late Qing military governor of Zhili (Hebei Province), who was none other than Yuan Shikai himself. Yuan's rise to provincial and national power was predicated significantly on his complicitous relationship with the British, Japanese, and Germans and on his performance in resolving the foreign-induced fiscal crisis pressing the Qing officials.[92]

As Stephen R. MacKinnon tells us in his impressive study, *Power and Politics in Late Imperial China,* although Yuan Shikai became adept at turning up new levies on tobacco, alcohol, and stamps, his administration eventually fell back on the Changlu salt monopoly, which he began to revamp "so as to maximize its contribution to his provincial treasury."[93] By negotiating a loan from a Japanese bank, Yuan Shikai rehabilitated the privileged Tianjin salt merchants who had suffered losses in the Boxer Uprising, then proceeded to cultivate relations with them to ensure more control over Changlu maritime salt and to increase the revenue of the *gabelle*,[94] which became the major source of revenue for his regime.[95]

A significant part of Yuan Shikai's reform of Changlu salt affairs involved the formation of the Salt Investigation Office, an investigative agency charged with cutting the loss of provincial salt revenues to smugglers in Tianjin, Jin County, Cang County, and the Xiao River area.[96] Within a few years this office had established sixteen branches throughout North China, most of them in Hebei. Under the stewardship of Zhang Zhengfeng, a cousin of Yuan Shikai, it became the anticontraband Changlu Salt Investigation Force, composed of five battalions,[97] which pursued peasants and peddlers in the counties abutting metropolitan Tianjin from 1913 to 1915, apprehending smugglers who were selling salt from coastal salterns.

When it came to the issue of earth salt trade, however, the salt investigation force was not all that effective.[98] Manpower was limited, partly because the battalion chiefs collected irregular official pay by keeping each unit up to 70 percent empty. For another thing, anticontraband patrols could not possibly track down the dealings of thousands of salt peddlers scattered over hundreds of miles of primitive roads and rugged terrain. Moreover, the anticontraband units often were in league with local people, a lucrative relationship that lingered on into the Nationalist period. Thus, prior to 1930, the Changlu anticontraband squads mainly carried out sting operations, rounding up a few peasant saltmakers now and then but doing little to stem the tide of "smuggling." Worse, from the standpoint of early Republican state makers, the inspectors often sold the confiscated salt for a profit and after a short time let peasants go back to their "illicit" trades.

Republican China's state makers eventually combined these sting operations with a police campaign to prohibit the production and marketing of earth salt in numerous counties. The development of the Changlu tax police and the crisis its presence engendered in the villages, markets, and towns of the Hebei-Shandong-Henan border area peaked after 1928, when the central government embarked on massive state violence. The transformation of the salt investigation force into a revenue police force came in two separate bursts, in 1913–28 and 1928–35. Both were the brainstorm of finance ministry policy makers.

Beginning in 1915, Zhou Xuexi, the minister of finance under Yuan Shikai, announced a program to abolish earth salt production by transforming the nitre-blanketed alkaline soils of North China into productive agricultural lands.[99] The problem with this program was that it predicated the progress of reform on the destruction of the private salt ponds, leaving the rehabilitation of the alkaline lands to other government agencies. Animosity between the village people and the salt inspectorate was immediate. In 1915 Song Mingshan, the chief of the salt investigation force, led a battalion to destroy peasant salt ponds and prohibit the sale of earth salt in the Neihuang-Lin Zhang area of Henan Province.* The peasant saltmakers in Neihuang resisted, and the police killed one of them, whereupon several thousand peasants surrounded and detained the investigation force. The governor of Henan Province, Tian Wenlie, dispatched mediators to Neihuang County to placate the protestors and simultaneously petitioned Yuan Shikai himself to defuse the crisis, which Yuan did by temporarily relieving Song Mingshan of his post.[100] Such clashes continued in many border area counties up until Chiang Kai-shek established his central government in Nanjing in 1928.

The most striking transformation in the process of salt revenue collection within North China was carried out between 1928 and 1935 under Chiang Kai-shek.[101] After taking Nanjing, Chiang relied on T. V. Song to bolster Kuomintang state revenue. Beginning in 1930, T. V. Song changed the salt investigation force conceived under Yuan Shikai into a full-fledged national tax police force, the *Shuijingtuan*.[102] First established in the Shanghai area, this centrist police force began replacing the old-style merchant-run Changlu Salt Inspectorate around 1931 and subsequently extended the reach of the Kuomintang-controlled Changlu Salt Tax Bureau from Tianjin deep into the remote, highly saline zone of southern Hebei, western Shandong, and northern Henan.

The *Shuijingtuan* was the independent 45,000-man police instrument of the Kuomintang fiscal center—a fact that is borne out by its political operations in the Changlu salt area.[103] Formed out of state power, the Changlu branch of this salt police army numbered 6,350 policemen. It was divided into nine separate districts. Under each district were three subdistricts, and within each subdistrict were three 45-man police teams, usually one team per rural county. Armed with handguns, modern rifles, and one machine gun and riding horses or bicycles, these police teams began positioning themselves in the county seats and large market towns of Daming, Puyang, Nanle, and other southern Hebei localities. The Kuomintang officials in charge of the Changlu division of the *Shuijingtuan* were responsible *only* to the finance ministry and determined to impose the will of the center on the salt merchants, the county magistrates, and the peasant saltmakers.[104] This state tax force brought the revenue scheme of the Kuomintang fiscal center into the lives of the peasant earth salt producers.

*Perhaps the image of a radical break in 1915 is overdrawn, but 1915 is an important benchmark in the evolution of this societal-state conflict because it was in this year that central government forces first resorted to using systematic violence against the peasant saltmakers.

Under the direction of Shen Fan, the *Shuijingtuan* worked hand in hand with the newly established general salt bureau within the Kuomintang Finance Ministry to strengthen the competitive position of government sea salt in North China.[105] This was to be done by enforcing a strict ban on the production of homemade salts and nitrates in the alkaline-plagued counties north of Kaifeng and south of Baoding. In order to increase its tax income, Chiang Kai-shek's debt-ridden center set out to close down the salt production of tens of thousands of peasant households in the agriculturally troubled villages along the old course of the Yellow River. The Kuomintang fiscal group, which had taken over the Tianjin Changlu Salt Company by early 1932, made no bones about this matter. "It must be made known," read ministry of finance order 2407 to the administrative, military, and police departments of Henan Province, "that the purpose of the ban on low quality and unhygienic salt is to remove the obstacle to the sale of government-owned salt."[106] On 15 June 1932, the Kuomintang Beijing Ministry of Finance, in consultation with the Changlu Salt Office, ordered every county magistrate in Hebei, Shandong, and Henan to remove the "illegal salt makers" from their lands and to arrest all who resisted.[107]

Central government orders like this one were passed down rapidly into the provinces and counties through the newly created ministry of finance and its revenue police, who, in the Hebei-Shandong-Henan border area, were known as the salt police. Beginning in 1932 the ministry of finance transferred provincial salt affairs to the National Salt Bureau, then placed relentless pressure on provincial and county-level Kuomintang officials to collaborate with the Changlu salt tax police in the destruction of salt ponds.[108] Repeated quarrels and scuffles with the police, such as occurred in Puyang's Cheng Guan village in 1929–30 and Changyuan's Guan Shang in 1933–34,[109] stemmed from peasant alarm over growing police interference in the making and marketing of earth salt.

STATE MAKING AND THE CENTRAL GOVERNMENT PENETRATION OF THE COUNTRYSIDE

The small gallery of central government actors involved in expanding the state's tax machinery into the countryside and launching a preemptive attack on the economy of the peasant saltmakers was appointed by Chiang Kai-shek and his political family. At the pinnacle of the Nationalist government's salt revenue army was T. V. Song himself. Known in the West as Chiang Kai-shek's personal representative to President Franklin D. Roosevelt during WWII and as the Kuomintang confidante of Henry R. Luce, Walter Judd, and Pearl S. Buck, Song conveyed the Nanjing government's commitment to a gradual, nonviolent political solution to the problems facing peasant China to the global community. Yet, in reality, T. V. Song was the pivot man of a centrally placed Kuomintang state fiscal unit with a reputation for pursuing revenue collection methods that endangered the market life of the peasant saltmakers. The former chief of the Guangdong Salt Bureau and Ministry of Finance for three years before Chiang Kai-shek took power,[110] Song Siwen was the prince linking the formation of the *Shuijingtuan* with the growth of Kuomintang state power.

Whether T. V. Song and his family derived substantial privileges from this political instrument is unclear, though a Chinese journalist, commenting on the return of a salt tax police unit from turbulent Jiangxi Province to Nanjing in the mid-1930s, noted that the soldiers from this special military apparatus of the finance ministry often escorted Mr. Song on national rail tours and accompanied Mrs. Song on the Shanghai restaurant circuit.[111] Officially, the modernizing Kuomintang state had no place for such "family soldiers." Unofficially, the rumor was that T. V. Song, acknowledging the advantages of Japan's warrior past, wanted to develop a sizable contingent of loyal fiscal guards for his own power domain, independent of all other domestic political forces, and yet advancing the growth of the Chiang Kai-shek–led Nanjing government. Nonetheless, the salt tax expansion of the Nationalist government was not merely, or mainly, the product of personal venality or corruption by high Kuomintang leaders. T. V. Song and his associates were responding primarily to international financial pressures.

The choices of Kuomintang Finance Ministry leaders still were limited by exogenous fiscal constraints, and the workings of its police instrument were guided in part by foreign advisors and foreign-trained actors. Wen Yingxing, a graduate of West Point, was appointed chief of the Changlu wing of the *Shuijingtuan* and received his marching orders from T. V. Song in the early 1930s.[112] Zeng Yangfeng, the Kuomintang-appointed chief of the Changlu Salt Office after 1933, was, along with T. V. Song and H. H. Kong, constantly in consultation with F. A. Cleveland, the American associate chief of the Salt Inspectorate, about the earth salt "problem" in the Changlu salt area.[113] In early 1934, Finance Minister H. H. Kong called on Colonel R. M. C. Ruxton to commence a police remolding campaign in the Changlu area.[114] A German ex-soldier who had conducted police training workshops in the Huaibei salt area,[115] Ruxton was appointed the cotravelling salt inspector in Changlu. He clearly was in close touch with Kong, Cleveland, and Zeng Yangfeng between 1934 and 1937.[116] Known for beating and dismissing salt tax police officers who did not meet German military standards, Colonel Ruxton was seen as an iron-hearted tiger by the officers of the Changlu tax police, who often panicked on hearing their districts were scheduled to be inspected by Ruxton.[117]

Seeing the *Shuijintuan* as a legitimate instrument for increasing revenue and moving the peasant saltmakers out of public fiscal terrain, T. V. Song and the fiscal leadership of the Nationalist government labeled the country people who did not bind to its mission dangerous obstacles to state order and development. The viewpoint of the rural people in the border region, few of whom fully understood international debt payments or internal army-building plans driving Kuomintang state makers to infringe on their local market interests, was substantially different. They saw the so-called reformist tax agenda of the Kuomintang state as a threat to everyday survival.

Thus, although the standard Western scholarly paradigm stresses the breakdown of the state bureaucracy, the logic of our data points in the other direction: the central government, and its rejuvenated salt bureaucracy, was overcoming rival warlord regimes and reaching deep into the North China countryside to initiate a new round of revenue seeking. To be sure, the central government's new wave of bureaucratic plunder spread unevenly over the North China plain during the early 1930s, partly because of its pre-occupation with suppressing rural "disturbances" and Communist-led insurgency in South China. Nonetheless, as the map of the Inspectorate of Salt Revenue indicates (see map 3), the Kuomintang Ministry of Finance already had targeted the earth salt production areas of the Hebei-Shandong-Henan border for penetration and suppression by its Changlu salt tax corps in 1934–35.[118]

As Tilly suggests, the logic of state making often is "three-faced," involving competition between central power holders and rival contenders for territory and assets, competition among political units nominally subservient to a national government for material resources supposedly in the hands of the center, and competition between centrally placed officials and local people for resources to which the latter have established a previous claim.[119] Using coercion to capture the market areas of the North China plain and to regiment local society in order to create a political economy yielding greater revenue, the progress of the Kuomintang fiscal center turned the counties of the border area into powder kegs.

The central government of Chiang Kai-shek had by late 1931 wrested control of the Changlu Salt Administration from its provincial warlord rivals and was making progress in creating a centralized framework that buffered the state institutions charged with establishing a monopoly over salt.[120] To be sure, the North China salt industry had been adversely affected by warlordism between 1923 and 1928, and rival militarists fought over the *gabelle* in Hebei, Shandong, Henan, and Anhui well into the autumn of 1930. However, this infighting was significantly curtailed when Chiang Kai-shek's troops took over Kaifeng, in 1930, and proceeded over the next two years to check the ambitions of the northwest army and the Shanxi militarist Yan Xishan. Despite occasional battles with rival warlords over salt revenue, therefore, the central government of Chiang Kai-shek and T. V. Song reportedly had restored the Changlu Salt Inspectorate to "normalcy" and by 1932–33 had resumed salt traffic along both the Wei River and the Beijing-Hankow railway into Hebei and Henan.[121] With these changes, the ministry

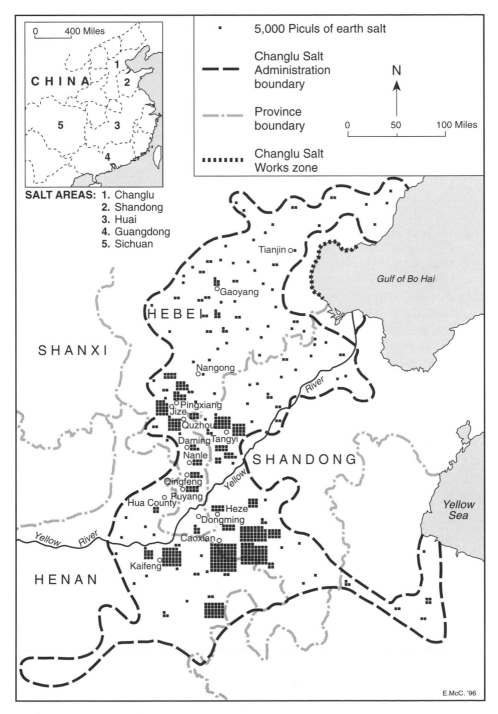

Map 3. Earth salt production areas targeted for suppression by the Nationalist government's chief inspectorate of salt revenue, 6 March 1935. The inset shows selected areas of salt production and consumption in China.

of finance consolidated the former warlord surtaxes on maritime salt and began moving to make lower government units comply with its revenue goals.

The agents of the Chiang Kai-shek government also used their power to challenge a host of "government" competitors for salt revenue. At the county level, the most serious competitors were the Kuomintang magistracy itself, the Kuomintang education bureaus, and the public security forces. In the Qing period, the county magistrates in Puyang and Neihuang had permitted local people to produce salt and had tolerated the existence of "illicit" earth salt trade. Some of this locally made salt had been sold to petty officials in the county governments for various purposes, a practice that prevailed into the 1920s. Challenging this premodern laxity, the central government attempted to supplant locally issued permits with licenses issued by the Changlu Salt Inspectorate and the Kuomintang Salt Tax Bureau. Similarly, in 1934, the Henan inspectorate compelled Kuomintang Education Bureau leaders in northern Henan to abolish educational surtaxes taken on Changlu salt.[122] The inspectorate, following strict guidelines set by the central government salt bureau, challenged the "protection fees" charged on Changlu salt by public security forces stationed along the Wei River checkpoints in 1934–35.[123] If the security forces let go of such fees, they were far less willing to cooperate with the Kuomintang *Shuijingtuan* when it came to confiscating earth salt. In the summer of 1935, for example, Ren Chengxian, a public security leader in Chu Wang town, Neihuang, asked the salt tax police to turn over confiscated earth salt to his men so they could sell it locally, firing on the tax police when he saw the latter had elected to destroy the salt.[124] The Neihuang magistracy subsequently was inundated with telegrams from Henan Salt Bureau officials, warning of the consequences of such a departure from high state policy.

In the third face of Kuomintang state making the features of a centrally directed administrative revolution come vividly to the fore. At least three specific popular groups actively resisted central government agents imposing claims on the resources of rural North China society. The Chiang Kai-shek center attempted to place new state controls on each, achieving considerable success vis-à-vis only the Changlu salt merchants, who were more easily subordinated than the lower gentry and local peasant salt producers.

Perturbed by the Kuomintang pressure on the *gabelle*, in 1934 a lot of Changlu salt merchants sent telegrams to the finance ministry opposing the Kuomintang salt tax increases,[125] and, later in the same year, some criticized the slaughter of peasant salt producers by government tax police units in Daming.[126] Soothing this opposition by small concessions of "tax-free salt," the finance ministry officials turned up the pressure on the Changlu merchants to go along with state efforts to more efficiently police the illicit earth salt operations in Hebei, Shandong, and Henan. This was not the *modus vivendi* the Changlu merchants were seeking, for it drew them into the emerging conflict between the market-focused peasantry and the Kuomintang state.

As many China scholars have shown, in the Nationalist period the gentry presided over subcounty politics and often stifled the attempt of the Kuomintang state bureaucracy to directly mobilize rural society and its surpluses.[127] To be sure, some of the small gentry who possessed the capital to purchase salt from the Changlu merchants became shop operators selling at the county level, so that they were, in a sense, part of the salt tax scheme of the finance ministry.[128] Nevertheless, they did not readily collaborate with the salt tax corps. Because they did not own alkaline lands, they often had to rely on the peasant saltmakers for supply when government salt was scarce. They also stood to lose business if the protests over police suppression engulfed their shops, so that they often preferred to mediate a peaceful solution to the conflict.

Members of the minor gentry, who had a direct interest in the local production of *xiaoyan,* more adamantly opposed the push of the Nationalist government's salt bureau. Residing in the vicinity of rural county towns, they often owned outlying alkaline lands, which they had committed to the underground earth salt economy during the boom of the middle 1920s. Naturally, they wanted to maintain production, avoid government salt land taxes, and resist the efforts of the Tianjin merchants to flood local markets with higher-priced sea salt. Displeased by their behavior, the Changlu tax police issued orders to punish members of the lesser gentry who were harboring the "illegal saltmakers."[129]

The decisive struggle over the salt market, however, erupted from Kuomintang state incursion into the household economies of the peasant earth salt producers. The capital-seeking power holders in the Nanjing government polarized Kuomintang relations with these market-dependent peasants of the North China plain. Of course the peasants of the salt-decocting villages had long been apprehensive of salt intendants occasionally sent from county administrative points to harass popular trade in locally made salt,[130] but such harassment seldom impeded the microeconomy of earth salt production. On taking over Hebei and Henan after 1931, the Chiang Kai-shek fiscal center sought to improve on the ineffective policing of these remote villages. This policy led to a break with past state practice. In challenging the claims of peasants to a share of the salt market, the men behind the Kuomintang exchequer magnified the old divisions between local people and state authorities and fostered the conditions for a bloody conflict.

The most important aspect of Kuomintang state making involved the progressive formation of the salt tax police and their entry into the villages of the Hebei-Shandong-Henan border region. After 1931 central government finance ministry officials in charge of the Changlu Salt Inspectorate developed a coherent plan of reform focused on the proliferation and professionalization of the police forces charged with enforcing the new salt regulations in village society. The reconstruction and redeployment of this tax revenue force—the *Shuijingtuan*—amounted to an unconditional declaration of war against the informal earth salt economy of the quasi peasantry. Among the finance ministry reforms undertaken to transform the old-style salt inspection forces into a modern efficient police force, five stand out.

First, the Kuomintang officials brought the Changlu salt tax police up to strength, adding manpower and ordering the district inspectors to issue pay by roll call so as to prevent commanders from padding employment rolls to pocket extra pay.[131] The thousand new tax police who began pouring into southern Hebei in the spring of 1934 were placed under the supervision of high-level police inspectors responsible for increasing the salaries of the police and providing them with a permanent career, complete with merit pay for outstanding achievements. This, it was assumed, would help the police avoid the "corrupt traps" of the salt peddlers and salt dealers.[132]

Second, in April, 1932, the chief salt inspectorate, by order of the Kuomintang Ministry of Finance, moved to establish a revenue guards unit within the Changlu salt area, the purpose being to rapidly supplant the early Republican anticontraband units and to make the salt police directly accountable to a crack modern police unit. Trained in the Liang Huai salt area, officers from the revenue guards with a reputation for boosting salt revenue collection to an "unexpectedly high mark"[133] by improvements carried out in Liang Huai, Hunan-Hubei, and Shandong were placed on loan to the Changlu Salt Inspectorate. At first confined to anticontraband activities in counties immediately adjacent to the Beijing-Wuhan railway, by 1934 the revenue guards had begun to penetrate Daming and the counties of the Hebei-Shandong-Henan border area.[134]

A third measure involved the creation of "preventive stations" and of new roads and telephonic communications, all aimed at upgrading police surveillance and suppression of village salt production.[135] To accomplish this, in 1933 the salt bureau established a Triprovincial Hebei-Shandong-Henan Salt Suppression Committee headed by Jiang Shouyi, the chief of the Henan Province Salt Tax Bureau. Two other key committee members, the chief inspector of the Changlu (North China) and Tung (Shandong) salt areas, assisted Jiang Shouyi in coordinating the police campaign to destroy earth salt production and to close down earth salt markets from the "preventive stations," usually located in the towns.[136]

The scope of the Salt Suppression Committee's activities was rather wide. From early winter of 1932 to 1935, Jiang Shouyi spent much of his time reporting on progress made in suppressing earth salt production to the a Salt Reform Conference sponsored by the Tianjin Changlu Salt Office of the Chiang Kai-shek central government. In early 1932, acting on the instructions of the ministry of finance, Jiang Shouyi led Henan Salt Bureau officials to set up the *Shuijingtuan* in rural Henan.[137] The first branch of the salt tax corps was deployed in Sanhejian (Three Rivers' Point) in Gushi County; the second in Hui County town; the third in Shang Qiu; and the fourth in Fengle town in Anyang. Between March, 1933, and July, 1935, Jiang Shouyi personally led units of this independent state tax force to Neihuang in northern Henan to patrol remote villages seldom inspected because of the inconvenience of poor transportation, banditry, and the resistance of peasant saltmakers.[138] The goal was to expand police controls into places beyond the coverage of the early Republican anticontraband units and to place a specific number of police within striking distance of the primary earth salt markets of a given territory.[139]

This expanding police campaign produced a plethora of new tactics. One of the most dreaded was the surprise arrest in the marketplace, engineered by secret investigators. Gu Chengji, a bustling border area market town in Qingfeng County, drawing peasants and peddlers from Hui County in Henan, Yuancheng in Shanxi, and Qingfeng in Hebei, was the target of this police tactic just prior to the saltmakers' struggle.[140] Many of its victims were peasants residing in rural satellite villages only a few *li* away from Gu Chengji. Like Luo Shoucheng, a onetime peasant saltmaker from Luo Tun village, in Qingfeng, they apparently were unprepared for the new tactics of the Nationalist government's *Shuijingtuan:*[141]

> I did not take part in the struggle of 1932 and 1933, but I once was taken away by the salt tax police while I was selling earth salt at Gu Chengji. On that occasion the salt police played a trick on us. They did not wear police uniforms. Instead, they came to Gu Chengji in plain clothes. Acting under cover, they went to the fairgrounds and asked the price of salt from the sellers. After they got a response, they suddenly told us they were the salt tax police, and then they ordered some hidden tax police troops to come to arrest all of the sellers. So no one could escape, as there were about twenty police. I was about nineteen when this happened. It was in the early summer of 1933, when the wheat harvest was upon us.

Within the border area the re-energized salt tax force also took the lead in imposing the Kuomintang center's multifaceted campaign for revenue collection at the village level. Hence the police attempt to transform a pivotal set of local village leaders into the "administrative fingers" of the centralizing tax state, which began as early as 1932. The head of the Changlu Salt Tax Bureau, Zhang Zhongli, outlined this fourth dimension of police work to the Kuomintang magistrates attending the multicounty Magistrates' Conference in Shijiazhuang, Hebei, in mid-September, 1934.[142] The Kuomintang magistrates in attendance approved a proposal that required all magistrates to summon village chiefs to town-based meetings to explain the urgency of banning "illegal salt making," then send them back to their respective villages to order the peasant saltmakers to give up production and to purchase salt from the official shops.[143]

Village chiefs were to notify peasants of their "obligation" to turn over their salt harvests to the police, with the promise that they would be reimbursed at a rate of three *jiao* per hundred *jin* of salt. They were to assist a special police inspection brigade whose task was to uncover the prevalence of clandestine production. And they were to inform local people that the police would be wearing yellow armbands inscribed with the characters "salt tax police" and instruct them not to resist the police, as if the latter were bandits.[144]

None of these measures significantly curtailed the production and sale of earth salt. Peasants ignored the Kuomintang state ban on production and initiated a number of nonviolent protests against the police campaign to wipe out the market. The police responded by arresting thousands of peasant salt producers and by suppressing their protests, demonstrations, and marches.

This growing police repression was highlighted by a fifth central government reform of the salt administration, affecting the legal code governing police behavior. The reform was a 1934 edict sanctioning the use of deadly force by the tax police against the peasant saltmakers and exempting the police from personal liability for killing people who resisted them. This *state policy* was conveyed by the following proclamation of the Hebei Province Kuomintang Department of Civil Administration:

> It is spring time, the season when saline earth is gathered. . . . Many peasants are scraping the land and collecting saline earth to make salt. This has hindered government sales of salt. To stop this is the duty of the tax police. Although the peasants are cognizant of the government regulations, some of them often organize resistance against the police.
>
> Our investigations reveal that when the tax police and the National Salt Control Organizations carried out their duties, peasants openly obstructed their efforts. Such actions are obstacles to government operations. They should be punished severely in accordance with the law.
>
> According to the effective regulations on the use of police weaponry recently approved by the National Administrative Council, and according to the anti-contraband regulations, any member of the tax police force is entitled to use his weapon against those who dare to organize collective resistance, or those who plan to seize weapons. In such cases, no policeman will be held responsible for any injuries or killings that occur.[145]

This draconian political change, giving rise to a veritable state of siege in the earth salt-producing counties of the plains, spurred a significant upturn in Kuomintang state revenue in the mid-1930s. The Chief Inspectorate of Salt Revenue reported steady increases in the amount of revenue gathered in the Changlu area for the years 1930, 1931, and 1932. The inspectorate attributed the increased effectiveness of the *gabelle* to the growing centralization of Kuomintang power,[146] and this interpretation was echoed in the provinces. By July, 1935, the chief of the Henan Province Salt Tax Bureau was reporting that with the destruction of the salt ponds, the banning of private salt, and the crackdown on illicit peasant traders, the government sales of salt had picked up, and Changlu tax revenue had increased greatly over 1934,[147] the year in which the center gave the police sweeping powers.

The Popular Response to Police Violence: Collective Protest

Although more political force produced more wealth for the Chiang Kai-shek fiscal center, it also produced great insecurity within the decomposed agricultural villages along the Hebei-Shandong-Henan border, prompting an outburst of popular resistance. The history of the Kuomintang salt tax police activities in Daming County, Hebei Province, suggests that central state "progress" in policing rural society is precisely what triggered collective protest in the countryside. Up until 1920 earth salt had coexisted peacefully with government salt, but after 1928 the Nationalist government increased the volume of maritime salt sent to this area and ordered the local people to purchase only the salt distributed through the Changlu salt shops.[148] By 1930 there were two of these shops in Daming town, which received their salt from the Tianjin Changlu salt merchants and sold it at a price so high that the local people turned to earth salt markets, which mushroomed throughout 1931–32. Responding to the Kuomintang attempt to enforce monopoly, the peasant leaders in Daming's salt-making villages organized a protest movement along the lines of their local salt market community, eventually winning student, merchant, and gentry support.

To suppress the earth salt market, the Tianjin Changlu officials sent a company of salt police to Daming in early 1931.[149] In the same year, the Daming magistracy organized a special police unit with modern weaponry to supplement the Changlu salt police. By 1932 these forces had destroyed the ponds, broken the tools, and confiscated the harvests of hundreds of peasant saltmakers. This destruction of village ponds was accompanied by police raids on rural markets and by the arrest of peasants and peddlers said to be "smuggling" earth salt. A two-phased struggle ensued.

The first phase began in Da Han Dau, a village of about three hundred households seven *li* west of Daming town.[150] Besides a few landlords and well-off peasants, 90 percent of the villagers were peasant smallholders involved in making earth salt. In the spring of 1933 one hundred salt police arrived in Da Han Dau with orders to stop the production of earth salt.[151] They destroyed ponds and confiscated wheelbarrows. Shortly thereafter, Gao Zantang, the Da Han Dau village chief, called on each peasant household to join in collective resistance. Several hundred peasants, armed with spears, iron shovels, manure poles, primitive handguns, and rabbit-hunting muskets, surrounded the police to detain them. Following this, Gao Zantang ordered the sounding of the tocsin, the signal to peasants in other villages to come support their counterparts. The police seized Gao and threatened to kill anyone who sounded the tocsin. But two peasants, Wang Ren and Wang Zhibang, secretly dispatched several villagers with "chicken feather letters" (*jimaoxin*) to summon peasant saltmakers in surrounding villages to Da Han Dau (a chicken feather pasted on a letter has long signified a come-at-once emergency in rural China).

Within several hours, peasants arrived from Zhao Gu, Qi Li Dian, Xiao Tun, Da Jie, and Jiu Zhi villages and from several salt land villages in Nanle County. When the police saw the situation turning against them, they attempted to leave, but they were trapped by a ring of red-faced peasants in the east part of the village. A long, heated verbal battle ensued. The police threatened to open fire; the saltmakers demanded that the police give up their weapons. At nightfall, a Daming-based cavalry unit arrived to rescue the police, but the saltmakers turned the unit back with gunfire. Later, the Kuomintang-appointed Daming magistrate secured the release of the police by promising to keep them away and to recognize the legality of earth salt production and trade.[152]

This little victory strengthened the connections and communications among earth salt villages. By mid-summer of 1933 each village had chosen a few locally respected protest leaders. They relied on family, village, and market ties to forewarn one another of police attacks and to coordinate antipolice resistance.[153]

In the second phase, however, the peasant saltmakers in Daming suffered a setback. In the fall of 1934 a squad of fifty police struck Zhao Gu village while its peasants were busy gathering the autumn harvest.[154] Peasants in Qi Li Dian, Xiao Tun, and Da Han Dau organized confederates from twenty villages to come to Zhao Gu to support the peasant saltmakers. Several thousand peasants carrying spears, shovels, and sticks surrounded the salt police in the southern part of Zhao Gu, and once again an intense verbal war raged.

This was not a rerun of Da Han Dau, however. When the Daming Public Security Bureau chief was sent to rescue the salt police, the saltmakers demanded that he promise that the police would not return, but he refused. Tempers flared. When the county government sent meals by bicycle couriers to the public security bureau personnel and the salt police, the saltmakers intercepted the food. Finally, when the peasants threatened to beat the police if they should destroy the salt ponds again, an auxiliary police detachment opened fire on them, killing twenty saltmakers and wounding another thirty.[155] The police then retreated to Daming town.

The day following the slaughter, five hundred saltmakers organized a protest march on the Daming magistracy. Leading the procession were the family members, including tearful children, of the dead victims. They were received by the magistrate's special ambassador on the outskirts of the Daming town walls and promised 120 silver dollars compensation per family. Cheng Tingheng, the Daming magistrate, however, could not promise an end to police violence.

Subsequently, various public associations, including students of the Seventh Normal School, merchants, and gentry figures of Daming, sent formal messages to the Hebei provincial government protesting the police action and petitioning the authorities to address the public outcry brought against the *Shuijingtuan* with impartial justice.[156] A November, 1934, internal Nationalist government report on the conflict stonewalled any official indictment of the police, however. The report stated that the salt peddlers in Zhao Gu village "took action against the police" and that the investigation into whether the Changlu police had acted in accordance with the law *should be made public only after long internal review.*[157]

A year later the Kuomintang magistrate in Daming was reporting both the spread of transvillage salt people's leagues and the growth of central army involvement in police attempts to "persuade" these "bandit gangs" to disband—one of the popular leagues was based in Matou village, the first big market village northeast of Zhao Gu village in Daming. In responding to the Daming magistracy's reports, the Kuomintang Hebei provincial authorities suggested that the growing regional protest movement might be de-escalated by slowing down the institutional development of the Changlu salt police forces.[158]

Ignoring this advice, the leadership of the Kuomintang fiscal center resorted to more repression. In October of 1935, Liu He, a high official in the Nanjing-based ministry of finance, accompanied Zeng Yangfeng, the Kuomintang-appointed chief of the Changlu Salt Transport Office, to Daming, Nanle, Qingfeng, Pingxiang, and Quzhou to investigate the matter of nitrate salt, returning to Tianjin with a plan to establish the Committee on Alkaline Land Improvement for Southern Hebei. While the finance ministry was "considering" this idea, a conflict broke out between the peasant saltmakers and a five-hundred-man Changlu tax police force in Quzhou, Jize, and Pingxiang, with the tax police using machine guns and mortar fire to raze the homes of the saltmakers. Central government administrators, anxious to restore public order (and revenue flow), authorized the eighty-second company of the salt tax police in Daming and the Kuomintang Fifty-Third Army in Baoding to jointly repress the "*xiaofei*" (nitrate brigands), giving rise to growing trouble in southern Hebei.[159]

The crux of the trouble was that state force triumphed over reforms to rehabilitate the soil for peasant crop production. Even while claiming results in alkaline land reclamation, the Kuomintang Finance Ministry vigorously pursued its violent approach to "the gravity of the 'earth salt' problem," which by late 1934 had spread from 6 counties in the Daming-Puyang area to more than 158 counties, half of which were in southern Hebei,[160] "where the production of earth salt was rampant."[161] The Changlu Salt Inspectorate reported taking effective measures to eliminate this enduring menace to state revenue. By the end of 1935 its police cadres were reporting that "over 200,000 earth salt ponds and 300,000 [salt] pans had been destroyed within the past two years."[162] *On the same page* of the finance ministry report bearing news of this progress we are informed that "the payment of interest and principal of foreign loans receiving service from the salt revenue was duly effected,"[163] with the payment of arrears on the Anglo-French loan of 1908 and the Crisp loan of 1912 receiving priority in 1934 and 1935.[164] Clearly, on the underside of this wave of progress were the peasant salt producers, who had little choice but to resist the Nationalist government.

When Nanjing's fiscal policy is placed in the context of evolving state power, the Chiang Kai-shek—led central government appears less anemic than is usually assumed. We need not deny that a condition of multiple sovereignty persisted in Republican China or that Chiang Kai-shek's government was not fully effective in its attempted expansion. But neither can it be denied that the Chiang Kai-shek regime was attempting to reconstruct the salt inspectorate as an efficient tax arm of its centralizing order[165] and that its policy misfired and triggered collective protest in the countryside. Such an ill-conceived policy, along with the popular resistance to police efforts to enforce it, placed a major constraint on the Kuomintang state-making experiment.

The center's attempt to transform China's long-established system of tax collection into a big profitable business was of course undertaken to pay war indemnities and foreign debts and to underwrite state development. The problem was that progress in this sphere came at the expense of untold thousands of village dwellers. The revved-up salt revenue collection machinery of the Nationalist government's finance ministry drew the country people into confrontations and clashes with agents of the state. At the heart of this little-known story is the resistance of numerous clusters of salt land villages along the Hebei-Shandong-Henan border to a system of bureaucratic police controls supportive of the expansion of central state power. Warlord politics, local elite inputs, and the factional intrigues of the Chiang Kai-shek Kuomintang all played their role, but the fundamental problem facing the country people was the state-making process itself.

The struggles of the peasant saltmakers and their allies underscore the prevalence of the deeply structured market forces of which G. William Skinner has written,[166] reminding us that rural protest sometimes took the form of a broad popular statement against state market regimentation. The story of this struggle to preserve market access also sheds light on Skinner's classic account of the oscillation between "open" and "shut" stances of Chinese villages[167]—which links openness, market access, and upward mobility with periods of stability—and the modification of Skinner's model suggested by Kenneth Pomeranz:[168] in this poor inland swatch of the North China plain, the instability of the Republic offered an unusual combination of external economic opportunities (and thus incentives for peasants to pursue markets beyond home villages) associated by Skinner with eras of dynastic stability and extreme predatory tendencies (and thus incentives for villagers not to receive outsiders) that Skinner associates with political decline. This struggle against state monopoly was, at bottom, waged by externally oriented peasant insiders looking to prevent revenue police agents from eliminating production for the market.

One point stands out: Kuomintang state interference in popular market prerogatives produced a cast of resentful characters who gained experience in organizing collective actions that transcended village politics, and their actions attracted the attention of local Communist leaders who also were suffering from the repression of the Nationalist government. It is into this remembered peasant history that we now venture.

The ensuing four chapters present case studies of instances of prewar protest in four different villages. These cases have been chosen to convey an important point: no matter what the level of village economic security, the issue of making salt for the market became a political issue for village people who did not know much about the Kuomintang or the CCP. Resistance to the central government suppression of the salt market between 1931 and 1935—in which the peasant saltmakers took the lead—was the school in which the people of this region learned that the Kuomintang state was their enemy and that the Communists supported their struggle to stay in the market. These case studies show that people in different villages with diverse political orientations, educational levels, and religious beliefs were opposed to central state intervention in the market. The Communists had to work patiently with such people, respecting their differences, to discover the main story line behind their mobilizations and to tie their village-based protests into a regional political movement under party leadership. The events in Cheng Guan, Qian Kou, Qi Ji, and Fanzhuang underscore the role played by educated local Communist leaders in linking up the salt protests in different villages and counties, and they also inform us that the CCP initially gained credibility among village people who were not equally attracted to party ideology or equally in need of party guidance. The peasant saltmakers appreciated CCP support for their market struggle, but the success of their mobilization prior to the Japanese arrival was predicated more on membership in a market community than on joining the Communist Party.

THREE

The Peasant Saltmakers'
Struggle in Puyang

The most significant of the salt people's struggles erupted in March of 1932 in Puyang County,[1] Hebei Province, north of the Yellow River. The protest movement in Puyang spawned the first popular victory over the newly formed *Shuijingtuan* of the Kuomintang Ministry of Finance and, further, set a contagious precedent for collective struggle in scores of other counties.

Subordinate to Daming Prefecture, Puyang was a major revenue target of the central government of Chiang Kai-Shek. The largest town in the Hebei-Shandong-Henan border area, it was a central market and a crossroads of commercial activity in the Republican period.[2] Its twenty-four big market streets and seventy-two small alleyways drew merchants and peddlers from Anyang, Wei*xian,* and Nanle and other counties. Historically, Puyang was also a cultural mecca. Known as Kaizhou from the Jin dynasty to the Republican era, Puyang was a favored location for popular temple fairs and opera festivities; it was here that the epic stories of *Shui Hu Zhuan* (The Water Margin) and the "Combustible Puyang" opera script from the *Sanguo Yanyi* (The Romance of the Three Kingdoms) evolved.[3] Puyang's temple fairs, revolving around the Cheng Huang, Fire God, and Guandi temples, drew people from Beijing, Tianjin, and Kaifeng as well as from counties of the border area. The Kuomintang state could hardly have picked a worse place to lose its war on peasant earth salt producers. Any storm brewing here quickly became transcounty news; and the Kuomintang Finance Ministry officials were unable to prevent the spread of popular testimonials to the victory of Puyang's peasant saltmakers over the Changlu salt tax police units.

Some three thousand people took part in the Puyang County protest movement of 1932. Most worked the alkaline lands influenced by the Yellow, Wei, and Xiao rivers. The protestors were full-time saltmakers, many of whose occupational histories extended back into late Qing years; landholding peasants who still derived their livelihood partly from agricultural production (mainly grain, peanuts, and vegetables) but temporarily relied on salt production to supplement their incomes; and peddlers, who purchased earth salt from the first two groups and hawked it in local county markets.

One-quarter of the people in Puyang County relied on salt making. Generally speaking, they lived in villages situated near lowland areas that, owing to a century of sporadic flooding, could no longer bear sufficient crops. By 1930, there were three specific types of salt-making villages in Puyang. The majority of the salt people were mainly peasant smallholders who owned five to fifteen *mu* of grain cropland and supplemented their agricultural income by making and marketing earth salt without the assistance of landlords or local government. In villages like Jingdian, Qian Kou, and Huacun salt making became an important branch of production for peasants with fifteen, twenty, and even thirty *mu* of cropland after 1920.[4]

A second kind of village was composed mainly of former peasants who owned little if any good cropland but did own two to five *mu* of salt land, often supplemented by a small patch of reed land. At best, a family of five averaged about one *mu* per capita of the least productive land in all of North China. These marginal peasants were full-time saltmakers, who escaped outright destitution by engaging in other petty trades. In late Qing times they had sold cloth and nitrate in regional market circuits. Most of these full-time saltmakers, such as those around Xi Shuipo and Cheng Guan, were just barely able to avoid impoverishment in the years before the agents of the Nationalist government's salt administration entered Puyang with force.

A third type of salt-making village was composed of people who possessed only one or two *mu* of bad salt land at best. The fate of these virtually landless people, many of them part-time hired hands and manure collectors, was intricately bound up with the market. They were peddlers who had to sell basic items of everyday necessity, including earth salt, just to make enough income to feed their families. Many of them traded salt for grain in local single-link exchanges, avoiding the monetization of higher-level market hierarchies. These peddlers comprised a significant minority of the rural people in villages like Dudian and Yaojia. Their trade carried them hundreds of *li* across various counties of Hebei, Shandong, and Henan and made them a veritable travelling news agency for reports on unequal competition, price constraints, and market controls.

The saltmakers of Cheng Guan village made up the majority of active participants in the protest of 1932. Located just inside the outer wall of double-walled Puyang town, Cheng Guan was a sprawling community of three thousand immigrants from Hong Tong County in Shanxi Province. By 1920, these migrants, who had lived in Cheng Guan for over five generations, numbered four hundred fifty households of about six to seven members. The average family owned one to three *mu* of salt land, one *mu* of reed land, and virtually no cropland. No longer peasants, they still had kinship ties to peasants beyond the town. By 1930 this particular subgroup was exceedingly vulnerable to any meddlings in the salt market.

Most of the salt-bearing land in Puyang was to be found in the dark soils around the county seat and toward the northwest and southeast, along the county's borders with Neihuang and Hua*xian*. Each family drew up the salt by the old process of solar evaporation. Throughout the summertime peak of the salt-making season, villagers rose before dawn to work the salt ponds off and on until midnight. In a sunny, sweltering summer, a family could earn enough income from sieving and selling its salt harvest to purchase most of its annual food grain supply—usually sorghum in villages as poor as Cheng Guan and Sha Wo—and still have a little salt to exchange for a few other needs. But a rainy and cloudy summer threatened the harvest and obliged the saltmakers to switch to boiling salt in cauldrons, or to give up salt making for vending, or to take out usurious loans.[5]

STATE PENETRATION AND THE ORIGINS OF PROTEST

During the first fifteen years of the Republic of China, the Tianjin Changlu Salt Company had gradually extended its reach down the Wei River into southern Hebei and northern Henan. As we learned in Chapter 2, this extension was undertaken in order to obtain a ready market for Changlu maritime salt, which was in competition with the earth salt produced by the country people in the interior. By the early 1930s, the merchants were transporting great quantities of sea salt from the Tianjin maritime salterns into the older earth salt markets of Puyang and other border counties, where undeveloped transport facilities had, until the twentieth century, inhibited the import of coastal salt and raised its price beyond the means of ordinary folk.[6]

Government sea salt was now in direct competition with the locally produced earth salt, and the Kuomintang Changlu Salt Bureau sought to create a larger market by reducing the amount of earth salt produced and consumed in Puyang and elsewhere. Its agents linked up with the Puyang County government to establish "official" salt shops in Puyang town and several outlying market places, such as Jingdian and Liangmen, from 1929 to 1931. In 1930 the Kuomintang-appointed magistrate issued a verbal warning against the production of earth salt and from then on collaborated with the salt tax police to press local people to buy the official salt. Those who were caught "smuggling" earth salt were arrested and imprisoned by the tax police corps created by the Kuomintang Finance Ministry.

The Beiyang government of Yuan Shikai had dispatched an anticontra-band unit to Puyang, but this force was not formidable. Numbering about twelve people, its personnel operated like the old-style Qing inspectors, stay-ing mainly inside Puyang town, making rounds on foot, and seldom inter-fering vigorously with production.[7] Prior to the late 1920s the inspectors had not strictly enforced the central government prohibition on the sale of earth salt in local markets. The warlord vestige of this anticontraband unit had fled Puyang for Tianjin with the arrival of the Northern Expeditionary Army in 1928, and the leaders of the expedition had posted notices pro-claiming earth salt trade to be legal.[8] With the Kuomintang takeover of Bei-jing, however, the Changlu salt tax police returned to Puyang, and by 1930–31 there were more than forty armed, mounted tax police in Puyang.[9] These "horse teams," as the peasant saltmakers called them, were the spear-head of the *Shuijingtuan*. From their headquarters in Puyang town, the salt tax police rode out to patrol the salt-making villages and began to enforce the Nationalist government restrictions on private earth salt production and trade.

The protest movement of 1932 was an expression of popular resentment against the actions of this new tax police force. Within Puyang the police swiftly earned a reputation for their raids, breaking open the salt ponds, rak-ing dirt and sand into them, and confiscating the salt harvest. They also impounded tools, smashed cauldrons, and destroyed scales and confiscated wheelbarrows used to carry the salt-encrusted soil to the ponds and to trans-port the salt harvest to market. By 1931 the police were routinely arresting people who sold salt. In the more active markets of Puyang they shouted warnings of the penalties for selling earth salt and publicly admonished buy-ers who preferred earth salt over the state's maritime salt.[10]

More than any other factor, the violence of the *Shuijingtuan* set off Puyang's protest. In the course of their attempt to destroy the salt ponds in Xi Shuipo, Tan Zhoupo, and Xiao Hepo, the police killed six saltmakers and seriously wounded ten others in the summer of 1931.[11] These salt-making communities, which included Cheng Guan, Qian Kou, and Sha Wo, all had a history of collective resistance to police violence. Countless salt-makers adopted desperate strategies of survival, including crop theft, beg-ging, and banditry; when these proved futile, they turned to open resis-tance. In November, following the lead of Yang Jingcai, a saltmaker from Cheng Guan, the saltmakers in Puyang formed the All-Puyang Association for the Salt People's Livelihood. Nearly half a year before the young CCP activists in Puyang went to the countryside to persuade the saltmakers to join in a common struggle against the tax police, the saltmakers devised a "whistle system" to warn others of imminent police raids so they could quickly join together to fight against the police.[12] The successful defense of the ponds by Yang Jingcai in Cheng Guan triggered antipolice actions by people in other parts of the county. When the news of the victory spread, for example, the saltmakers of Xinzhuang and Nanhu villages also established their own associations and fought the police.[13]

Environmental Crisis and State Intervention

Environmental disaster itself was not always the direct stimulus to popular struggle. Puyang County was stricken by drought several times in the 1920s, and the severe droughts that ushered in the North China famine of 1921 hurt peasant grain producers. But most droughts were minor and temporary and did not seriously impede earth salt production. Many of Puyang's saltmakers recorded average salt harvests for the five years preceding the 1932 protest movement.[14] Puyang and neighboring Neihuang County were inundated by floods in the early 1930s, but they devastated mainly *peasant* agricultural fields and grain harvests and did not seriously damage Puyang's main salt-producing villages. In August of 1931 the Yellow River overflowed its banks, and many Puyang villages were left knee deep in water.[15] The peasants near the overflow points faced a bleak winter, and the rising price of food the following spring caused new anxiety. The majority of salt people who filled the ranks of the March, 1932, protest movement, however, hailed from parts of the county spared by the dikes.

The history of Sha Wo village in southern Puyang sheds light on this complex phenomenon.[16] Located in a basin, Sha Wo's land base was vulnerable to the runoff of rainfall from comparatively elevated surrounding villages. In a major flood, the Yellow River swept away virtually all of the salt deposits, preempting salt production; but after local *minor* floods, large deposits of salt appeared along the highest line of the village's land base, and salt making often flourished. After such a flood in 1931, the output of earth salt went up, whereupon the salt tax police stepped up their attacks on Sha Wo's ponds. The problem for Sha Wo peasants, therefore, was not an environmental downswing but central state interference in their *adjustment* to the downswing.

This political trigger is clearly evidenced in the saltmakers' struggle in Handan,[17] in southern Hebei. In the summer of 1935 minor floods swept over the fields of northeast Handan, leaving scores of peasants short of food and tillable lands. The flood victims of Matai village, located in a zone of saline deposits, turned to producing and peddling earth salt for survival. On October 18, thirty-four armed police were sent to Matai to level the salt ponds and smash the cauldrons. The desperate saltmakers' attempts to stop them ended in a standoff, mediation, and a temporary retreat by the police. But after several days, a four-man police unit arrested a Matai saltmaker. In a protest march on the police station, the saltmakers took back the prisoner. Again, protest was prompted not by environmental disaster but by police interference in an evolving market strategy of coping with environmentally induced food shortages. If the spread of natural disaster was making the border region as a whole more dependent on nonagricultural production, then government suppression of the market only intensified the rural crisis.

The CCP and the Question of Outside Political Organization

Although the protest of the marginalized peasant saltmakers drew the attention of a Communist Party looking to mobilize the rural poor, the notion of CCP organizers instigating protest seems dubious. Over the years 1925–32, the outbreak of protest correlated more with the growing conflict between the Changlu salt police and the people in the earth salt villages. By the spring of 1932 the CCP had linked up with saltmakers in many of these "core" villages[18] in three subzones in the northwest, south, and central parts of Puyang County. In the northwest were Qian Kou, Jingdian, Hua village, and approximately eighteen other villages in adjacent Neihuang County.[19] The villages of Sha Wo, Qucun, and Da Han made up the southern zone, in which Liangmen also played a minor role. In the central part of the county were the Xi Shuipo salt lands, near Cheng Guan. Although Central Committee history holds that the CCP mobilized the poor salters of these villages,[20] their protests often predated the presence of the party, and the Communists were merely spreading the logic of protest—as when party leaders in Cheng Guan collected stories from the saltmakers who had suffered at the hands of the police and disseminated them to warn other saltmakers they would suffer a similar fate if they did not organize to oppose the police.[21] The police, not the CCP, stirred the rural people to protest.

The Japanese Invasion and the Catalyst to Protest

The rural people in these out-of-the-way counties were not oblivious to Japanese economic and political influences—inhabitants of Puyang and Neihuang and Anyang voiced grievances over the growing number of Japanese items entering their market economies and were particularly perturbed by the Japanese-linked traffic in opium and heroin. After the Japanese invasion of Manchuria in September of 1931, teachers and students from the Daming Seventh Normal School attempted to *mobilize* both town and country folk by spreading anti-Japanese "national salvation" propaganda in Puyang.[22] This propagandizing, however, did not override the importance of the threat posed by the regional salt tax force of the Kuomintang central government, and it was linked to the interest of the peasant saltmakers only after their struggles proved successful.

TARGETS AND REPERTORIES OF PROTEST

Avoidance Protest

Within Puyang, the peasant saltmakers pursued several forms of resistance to police encroachment. More often than not, the pursuit of each form initially was characterized by a nonviolent adaptation to the police occupation.

Unlike peasants who performed labor for landlords in exchange for a share of the harvest, the salt producers were not able to profit from "productivity strikes."[23] The most common form of resistance prior to March, 1932, was deliberate avoidance of police efforts to stop production. Many families displayed ingenuity in evading police efforts to level the ponds, concealing household production, and accentuating it in the intervals between bouts of police surveillance. When the police came to destroy the salt ponds, the peasants of Sha Wo, for example, covered their ponds with corn stalks. "Every family disguised its ponds in this way," recalls Wang Choulin, "and sometimes it worked. Nearly half of the ponds went undetected, but eventually the police discovered many ponds and destroyed them."[24]

Similarly, peasants often converted family courtyards into miniature salt evaporation pools. Zhang Youren, a Cheng Guan[25] salt producer who participated in the protest movement of 1932, recalls:

> Before the 1932 rebellion we relied on salt making for our livelihood. But the salt police began to prohibit our salt production. If the police discovered us making salt they would beat us.
>
> In the old days each family went out to dig its own salt land and construct its own salt pond. The women and children from each saltmaker household went to keep watch on the salt fields. This was one of the ways we avoided the salt police in the beginning. The women and children would warn us in advance if the salt police were coming. I remember the police came to our Xi Shuipo fields at a specific time—right after breakfast. And they usually came once every third day, so that we adjusted our production to their arrivals and departures.
>
> If the police came more often, then we faced difficulty. Especially if they were destructive. At that point we had to find another way to avoid them. Hence we moved the salt-bearing soil from the vast open Xi Shuipo fields, where most of the ponds were located, into our household courtyards to secretly make salt at night or, whenever possible, by day. We were able to do this for extended periods, since the police generally checked the households of individual saltmakers only twice a month.

Former saltmakers recall yet another way of resisting the pressures of the Nationalist government's salt administration—the adjustment of marketing activities. In early Republican years the saltmakers of Cheng Guan had transported salt by wheelbarrow to the markets and fairs of Wu Xingji (eighteen *li* to the southeast from Cheng Guan, meeting on 1, 3, 6, 8 every ten days); to Xin Xiji (eighteen *li* to the west from Cheng Guan, meeting on 2, 5, 8 every ten days); to Zhai Hongji (eight *li* west from Cheng Guan, meeting on 2, 4, 6—and still operating today); and Wang Juji (twelve *li* west of Cheng Guan, meeting every day two hours after sunrise). In the late 1920s the saltmakers began shifting to various marketplaces in other counties, including Hua County, Qingfeng, Fan County, Neihuang, and Daming. Recalls Yang Feng, a longtime Puyang saltmaker, "We had to find other markets, because our Cheng Guan village was very near Puyang county town where the salt police were stationed. In many of the distant markets of other counties the police had less control, so we could sell our salt there."[26]

Until the police arrived in greater numbers, the retreat to hidden household production and the search for alternative markets served saltmakers well. The saltmakers supplemented these forms of resistance with others. One alternative to confronting the salt tax police directly was flight; temporary migration (which in time became intermixed with beggary) became alternative resistance activity. Though a small number of saltmakers joined in the long-term migrations to Manchuria, most followed the old trails into parts of Shanxi, Hebei, and Shandong. Yang Xingan, for example, went to Fan County in Shandong, where he hawked various items and eventually had to sell his two daughters.[27] Thus Puyang's saltmakers managed to survive via temporary migration that was local in scope; they left to become peddlers, day laborers, and beggars in other border area counties for a few weeks or months, then returned home.

Not every saltmaker could afford to resume salt production immediately on returning home, of course, for the cost of rebuilding a courtyard pond was several silver dollars. Those who could not make ends meet through a combination of the "working migration" and borrowing from neighbors turned to beggary. "Some of the beggars starved to death," recalls Ren Hailong, a Cheng Guan saltmaker. "Some went out to the Northeast (Manchuria), and some went to Shandong. Those who went to Shandong stayed a while and then returned several days or weeks later. Others begged locally around Puyang town and the markets of the county, going out daily, and sometimes finding work for daily meal wages. When the salt police came here they stopped the saltmakers from producing salt, so the saltmakers went begging and then secretly returned to make salt."[28]

If short-term in-region migration was the norm, a slight countertendency was at work that alarmed the majority of peasant saltmakers. During 1931–32, when the intensity of police repression was reaching its zenith in Puyang, a small but highly visible number of peasant saltmakers who had clashed with the police near the town evaded arrest by entering into temporary migration, but were compelled to flee to distant Guangxi Province, never to return during the Republican period.

Thus, along with the peasant victims of the poor grain harvests of 1920–21 and 1926–27, scores of saltmakers in Puyang turned to petty theft and banditry to avoid hunger and the hardships of long-term migration. By 1927 a bandit force of six hundred roamed the territory beyond Puyang town walls. On one occasion they boldly went after a wealthy landlord who resided inside Puyang town itself. According to Geng Xinyuan, "Li Heizu, a landlord, was kidnapped by the bandits. He refused to go with them, and they killed him with a pistol. He lived on South Street, inside the town. He had about 400–500 *mu* of land outside the town walls."[29]

A number of dispossessed peasant saltmakers opted for military service and even police work. Thus, from 1928 to 1931 a handful of saltmakers gave up their sojourns into banditry to serve as Kuomintang soldiers, hoping that the Puyang County government would provide them with pay, patronage, and protection; but this hope went unfilled. The Kuomintang government was facing a severe financial crisis, and the bandit soldiers were not inclined to obey government orders, so the Kuomintang sent them out of the county to Anyang and other garrison points. (Such a strategy did not prevent them from returning to Puyang and reverting to banditry.) A few saltmakers even served temporarily with the salt tax police. The dialectic of local struggle made this police duty a dangerous occupation, one that was short-lived in Puyang. Yang Dongan joined the police "because he had nothing to eat and his children were starving,"[30] but he was beaten severely by his uncle for having joined and did not return to duty.

Direct Confrontation: Altercations, Threats, and Beatings

Saltmakers who fled their native villages faced an extremely precarious future, and great numbers stayed on to confront the salt tax police. From the spring of 1929 on, the police found themselves embroiled in altercations, threats, and beatings at the hands of saltmakers in different parts of Puyang. After pleading with the police not to destroy the salt ponds, to no avail, saltmakers threatened them with physical harm, then, when the police dismounted their horses to level the ponds, grabbed their shovels and beat them back. This action seems to have worked in Puyang's Qian Kou village during the melee of 1930.[31]

The defense of the ponds sometimes brought together various saltmakers in groups capable of waging small-scale collective resistance. Now, when the salt police came to fill in the pond of a vulnerable family, neighboring saltmakers summoned others to drive the police away. In 1929 and 1930, for example, Cheng Guan saltmakers mobilized whole neighborhoods to march with salt spades and rakes to confront the salt police. In 1929, they joined the local saltmaker Yang Jingcai to gather about three hundred people to oppose the police. After a short while, more than twice as many showed up.[32] The Cheng Guan saltmakers gained special notoriety in 1930, when they successfully fought off a four-man police squad in the act of destroying the salt pond of Zhang Paogou.[33] Although they were not actually beaten, the police did not return. The news of this little victory buoyed up saltmakers elsewhere, and the grapevine hummed with stories of Cheng Guan's saltmakers combining to fight the police.

The saltmakers were also quick to avoid police arrest and to struggle against the imprisonment of fellow salters. In Puyang, where the police had roused the local people by administering bloody punishments for producing and selling earth salt, the Cheng Guan saltmakers posted lookouts in markets who engaged the police in conversation, allowing their counterparts to finish up a fast sale and leave the marketplace. The saltmakers also leaked information on the seizure of people from various parts of the county back to home villages, which quickly sent small delegations to Puyang town to plead for their release. The salt tax police were baffled by the quick response of these popular delegations. Apparently they never found out that Yang Jingcai, the leader of the Puyang saltmakers' struggle, was doubling as a petty jailer in the county seat, enabling him to pass on the news of arrests through his friends in Cheng Guan and his contacts along the market circuit.

Fear of imprisonment drove the peasant saltmakers to barrage the police constantly with inquiries, demands, and offers to release their captives. In 1929, recalls Yang Baozeng, a onetime Cheng Guan saltmaker, "Li Xingqi was arrested by the Changlu salt police, but when he resisted arrest they beat him so hard that he was paralyzed. So the saltmakers collected fifty silver dollars for his bail, and gave this sum to his family for his release from jail. Not long afterwards, our Saltmakers' Association also donated money to help Li Xingqi get by."[34]

Such resistance left the police frustrated and frazzled and provided a rich harvest of protest experiences from which the saltmakers would draw as they moved to sustained collective action against the police and then, in the case of Puyang, took aim at the Kuomintang county government's collaboration with the police in the spring of 1932.

Negotiationist Protest and Republican Government

Puyang's saltmakers occasionally pleaded their cases before the nonofficial local elite and the Kuomintang magistrates. Around 1930 a small delegation of saltmakers petitioned Wang Tianying, a gentry figure with whom they had a close relationship and on whom past magistrates had relied to resolve many problems, to persuade the Kuomintang magistrate to issue a government decree in support of their demand to resume making salt. Yang Laoren, who led a delegation of four saltmakers to the county *yamen*, recalls:[35] "Wang Tianying was the boss of the Puyang town salt shop, which had a connection to the Changlu Salt Company. . . . Wang conveyed our offer to the Kuomintang magistrate, but the magistrate refused it."

Although their shops could show a handsome profit, operators like Wang usually were leveraged and often went bankrupt. They did not, therefore, hesitate to use their gentry reputations and their legitimate sta-

tus as subcontractors to the Changlu salt merchants to run sideline businesses to increase supply from other sources—and their major source was
the adulterated earth salt of the rural people. Precisely because these gentry operators were not directly responsible to the Kuomintang state, they
had some room for maneuver on behalf of peasant salt producers locally;
and because they could not ask the government for additional salt but
could go to the saltmakers to increase their supplies, petitioning for the
economic interest of the quasi peasants was not uncommon in the Nanjing
decade.[36]

This negotiationist protest was also manifest on the issue of land taxation. The high-level spokesmen of the Nationalist government accused the
peasant saltmakers of being opposed to paying the salt land tax.[37] But a delegation of Puyang saltmakers made a secret attempt to negotiate a different
understanding on taxation before the protest escalated into an armed
parade against the town-based police in 1932.[38] Because the Puyang County government had attempted to tax the salt lands, the saltmakers took this
to mean that the Kuomintang recognized their right to produce earth salt
legally and paid the tax until the salt police drove production underground,
around 1929–30.[39] Even after 1930, they engaged in entreaties to pay the
tax to gain support of the Kuomintang magistracy, whose interest on this
issue was not in complete harmony with that of the Changlu Salt Inspectorate. The officials of the inspectorate, who worked closely with the finance
bureau inside the Puyang government, pressured each Kuomintang-
appointed magistrate to turn a deaf ear to this offer.

PROTEST OBJECTIVES AND THE STAGES OF PROTEST

The Kuomintang's refusal to mediate conflicts between the saltmakers and
the police and to return to the *status quo ante* underscored the logic of alternative modes of collective action. In the third month of 1932, the leaders
of the saltmakers launched a protest parade, which generated plenty of fireworks in the town.[40] Their main objective was to garner support from the
magistrate for their demand to remove the enforcement machinery of the
Changlu Salt Bureau from *their* county and to allow them to resume the production and sale of earth salt. The enemy was the Kuomintang Salt Administration, whose police agents were hurting the poor, and the peasants of the
salt lands were coming to town to do something about it.

The Kuomintang finance officials and the salt police had feared the
protest movement would develop multiple-plebeian branches in the town
along with peasant roots in the countryside—and the expansion of participation on March 19 raised the possibility of just such a coalition. What happened in Puyang County town in mid-March of 1932 occurred mainly
because a significant cross-section of society could no longer find an open

legitimate channel for airing grievances.[41] Joining up with the protest movement were saltmakers, peddlers, purchase agents, beggars, and even landlords, and sympathetic members of the small gentry, who were represented by stand-ins.

The saltmakers thought of themselves as respectable, law-abiding citizens; few were Communist Party members, but they had to market salt to make ends meet. The main force of salters numbered almost twenty-five hundred, at least one thousand of them from Cheng Guan and inside the town.[42] Others came from Xi Shuipo and Tan Zhoupo, from Qian Kou, Hua village, and Maji, and from Sha Wo.

The protest in Puyang town attracted a number of volatile elements who, it seems, engaged in actions not well planned by the leaders. Among them were beggars whose initiatives threw the police into a panic and elicited a roar of approval from the crowd. Although the beggars do not figure prominently in the published Communist Party accounts of the struggle in Puyang town,[43] their incendiary actions added bravado to the protest movement.

Liu Xishou was directly involved in the struggle in Puyang (he paraded with a spade, helped tear down the walls of police quarters, and put a white paper hat on the salt police chief) and thereafter became a representative of the Cheng Guan Saltmakers Association. His memory of the role of the beggars in the struggle is sharp:[44]

> There were beggars during the period of the saltmakers' struggle. I remember seeing the beggars take part in the rebellion. They were in the town street. They clapped on the sidelines for *us*. At first they did not take part. They followed along and went where we went during the demonstrations and struggles. At times, though, they even ran to the front of our parade, and took the lead in a disorganized way. The number of beggars decreased after the rebellion because some of them were able to return to making salt, and earn a lot of money.

The beggars were inseparably connected to the saltmakers, for they had been deeply involved in antipolice actions years before. Many had been saltmakers before the police had driven them into a "state of alms," and they had a prior record of active resistance to the police in the vicinity of Puyang. Yang Jingcai, the leader of the 1932 saltmakers' struggle in Puyang, is an example. Born in 1891 to parents who were saltmakers and cloth dealers in Cheng Guan, Yang had only two *mu* of salt land and depended heavily on salt making for his income by 1925. He sold his earth salt in Puyang markets until the police banned production in 1928. Between 1930 and 1932 Yang occasionally listened to Wang Congwu and Gao Kelin talk with Puyang saltmakers about oppression, for these young party members sometimes lived in Cheng Guan, residing in the house of Zhang Youwen, a Daming Normal School classmate of Wang Congwu. "But even before that time," relates Yang Baozeng, the son of Yang Jingcai, "my father had gathered the saltmakers to argue with the Changlu salt police when they came to destroy our ponds. He and others enlisted scouts to alert us beforehand of police attacks, so that people could gather to fight the police. The first time he did this was in 1928, when he gathered three to four hundred people."[45]

In 1928 the salt police attempted to prevent Yang Jingcai and the salters from holding meetings at the Puyang Elementary School. At first Yang led a delegation of ten saltmakers to argue with the police, turning them away. But an armed forty-man police unit returned, only to be surrounded by four hundred people who shouted they had no right to interfere with the meetings and sent them packing. Describing Yang Jingcai's part in the 19 March 1932 struggle, Yang Baozeng sheds further light on the role of the beggars:[46]

> The police were from Tianjin and Daming. When they arrived we implored them to spare the ponds. Our neighbors came to help us plead, but still the police ignored us. Thus we had no choice but to struggle against them.
>
> My father, Yang Jingcai, was the leader of this struggle. Before the police came here he sold his salt in Wang Zhu market to the southwest and in Qing Hetou market to the northeast. When they first came we went to Liangmen to sell our salt there. Later, when they curtailed our summer production and disrupted our salt trade, we had to turn to begging for part of the year. My mother took me begging to Jinzhai and Wang Gu village, four li away. This was in 1928.
>
> Of the nearly five hundred salt-making households on this section of West Street, about half went begging in the years 1928 to 1930. Li Zhaoming was one of those who went begging before the 1932 struggle. On March 19, 1932, Li and the Cheng Guan beggars who were saltmakers went to the struggle. There were more than two hundred of these begging households on our street, and each sent at least one person to the town to participate in the struggle. They all knew Yang Jingcai well. Yang did not know how to ride a bicycle, so that day Li Zhaoming carried Yang Jingcai on his bicycle to each of the saltmakers' homes to tell them it was time for the rising. Li and his friend, Li Yicheng, followed Yang to the salt police headquarters, and they led an attack on the police. Along with my father, all of them swore an oath to fight to the death, and they proceeded to pull down the wall of the police station and then drag two policemen towards North Street to confront the magistrate.

Peddlers also joined the struggle. Fan Renbang, who like his father was a landless grain miller and a small peddler, had peddled salt in the markets of Qing Zu and Shagudui before 1932. When the Changlu Salt Inspectorate sent its anticontraband squad into Puyang, the police prevented Fan from selling his salt openly in these markets. Hence, he engaged in clandestine trade and was a witness to the struggle in Puyang town. According to Fan, "A lot of small peddlers sympathized with the saltmakers, and some of them participated in the rebellion. I did not participate directly, but I did benefit from the rebellion. As soon as we peddlers heard the salt police had been driven away we began to sell our salt again."[47]

There was more to this peddler involvement than meets the eye. Li Zhaoming remembers that the peddlers "encouraged us to fight the police because they were hard up too, and had difficulty making a living."[48] In the preceding two years the police—the same police who heedlessly interrupted selling in the countryside—had collected bribes in return for not checking the peddlers who wanted to leave Puyang town with earth salt to be sold on rural market circuits.[49]

Puyang landlords who rented out salt lands often shared interests with their tenants, and their relations were characterized by reciprocity. As late as 1932 many of the salt land tenants in Cheng Guan, for example, still depended on a form of share rent wherein the landlord bore part of the burden of a poor harvest yield.[50] Because landlords and tenants shared an interest in maintaining production, the landlord as well as tenant lost his share of the salt harvest if the ponds were filled in by the police. In the years leading up to the struggle, family members of jailed salt tenants implored their landlords to put up bail money so they could return to work the salt ponds. Although CCP documents hardly mention the issue,[51] it is clear that some of the landlords who owned salt-bearing lands in Puyang cheered on the saltmakers' protest and participated in subsequent meetings. From Zhang Youren, a former Cheng Guan saltmaker, we learn: "Most of the salt field landlords of Cheng Guan made sure they were not overly active in the rebellion. But the ordinary saltmakers did try to align with them, and did appeal to them to join. In fact a minority of the landlords did join us. Zao Maicheng did not participate, but his brother, who owned 250 *mu* of land, did participate in the rebellion of 1932."[52]

Even landlords with substantial croplands, such as Zhou Haibang with his six hundred *mu*, did not want to see local people reduced to desperation, beggary, and crop theft. They had nothing to gain by opposing the protest and a lot to preserve by not criticizing it.[53] And these same landlords stood to reap a bonanza from the harvests of the early 1930s.

Among the three thousand in the March 19 street crowd were students, teachers, and various Puyang townspeople. Several of the active student elements had the support of members of Puyang's minor gentry. Relations among the salters, the students, and the small gentry were complex and politically significant. Zhang Youren, for example, was a Cheng Guan saltmaker whose family owned just two *mu* of salt land and several of reed land. They could barely make ends meet. But his brother, Zhang Youwen, had attended the Daming Seventh Normal School, courtesy of an uncle who was a well-to-do member of the small gentry. In the month before the saltmakers' march, Zhang Youwen, now a local student activist, won his uncle's sympathy for the idea of a general mobilization against the police.[54] Other students and teachers residing within Puyang County town had gone to Cheng Guan, Jingdian, and Sha Wo to urge the saltmakers to join in a countywide struggle against the police, and they made clear that members of the upper stratum were sympathetic to their intentions of publicizing the salt-makers' grievances. Graduates of the Puyang Model Primary School, several of these students had followed Liu Yanchun, the school's respected principal, and his teaching staff into the Wang Congwu–led CCP, and in 1931 they had joined school teachers in Puyang in a strike for higher wages.[55] The strike had failed, and the rising cost of government salt further strained their meager wages—they too had a pressing interest in maintaining the marketability of earth salt. Their cheers for the saltmakers constituted a vital symbolic link in the cross-class unity of the popular struggle.

In mid-March of 1932 the outlying core salt-making villages sent contingents of three or four saltmakers into Puyang town. Disguised as peddlers, they arrived on the evening of the eighteenth and stayed in the town overnight, boarding with fellow saltmakers in Cheng Guan. With the assistance of town-dwelling friends and local schoolteachers they kept an eye on the actions of the Kuomintang county government and the Changlu salt tax police station. At dawn on March 19, they sent a messenger to the several thousand saltmakers who had gathered at the Xi Shuipo salt fields, instructing them to invade the town at once. The village squad leaders blew their whistles, summoning hundreds upon hundreds of saltmakers from Qian Kou, Sha Wo, and Cheng Guan. Carrying a triangular red flag and brandishing spades and rakes, several thousand protestors raced up North Street to surround the tax police headquarters.

The plan was to capture the chief of the salt tax police and to compel the local Kuomintang authorities to accept the demand stated in their petition of grievance: *the police were to be expelled from Puyang at once.* But most of the police had fled.[56]

Yang Jingcai urged the crowd of three thousand to rush the police headquarters, which was located in the Wang family courtyard. Saltmakers smashed doors and windows, broke pots and bowls, and tore down the walls to the inner court, where they discovered two salt policemen hiding under their beds. These policemen were beaten and kicked. Their lives were spared in return for revealing that the police chief had gone to report the attack to the Kuomintang county authorities.

The Puyang County magistrate, Sun Peiji, was stunned on hearing the news of the demonstration, or so he said. He was in a dilemma. If this protest got out of hand—and from the standpoint of high-level authority, it already had—he would lose his position. He took swift action, ordering the peace preservation corps to rush from several nearby districts into the town and directing the head of the public security bureau, Chao Yushe, to deploy his men to protect the remaining salt police and disperse the crowd. By the time the public security forces appeared, however, the leaders of the protest had turned the crowd of angry saltmakers up North Street, dragging along the two salt policemen. Cries of "Bury them alive!" and "Drive out the salt police!" filled the air. The saltmakers' leaders were not cowed by the arrival of the public security forces. They turned over their police captives to Chao Yushe only on condition that he acknowledge their demands to get rid of the police and support their request to return to the normalcy of production. With a crowd of jeering protestors surrounding him, Chao agreed to relay their demands to Magistrate Sun Peiji.[57]

The protest coalition occupied Puyang town and neutralized the security organs of the Kuomintang county government around 1:00 p.m. The saltmakers regrouped and set off for the *yamen,* collecting sympathizers as they marched. As they arrived at Xi Xin Street, they learned that Sun Peiji and three hundred armed members of the Puyang County Peace Preservation Corps were rushing to meet them. The saltmakers forged ahead to form a ring around the magistrate and the corps. Outnumbered thirty to one, the corps members did not draw their weapons. Many of them actually sympathized with the saltmakers and holstered their arms, for a good number of them were native sons of Puyang and had made earth salt in their home villages over the preceding decade. Magistrate Sun was left virtually alone to contain the protest crowd, whose leaders had worked their way up through the salt police, the public security forces, and now the peace preservation corps to declare war on the Kuomintang salt monopoly.

The protest movement now held Puyang town and had Sun Peiji trapped in his own headquarters. The spokesmen for the saltmakers knew their rights, and they insisted they had been driven to protest and that the police were the ones violating the customs governing salt making. Scarcely had Magistrate Sun begun to admonish the leaders when several protestors cut him off: "We are expelling the salt police in order to preserve our livelihood. We have done nothing illegal towards the government. So why do you say we are making trouble and disturbing the peace?"[58] They went on to argue that the police were destroying the public order and that the magistrate should prevent them from killing taxpayers.[59]

By about three o'clock, Yang Jingcai and those who led the protest movement had extracted a promise from Sun Peiji to evict the salt tax police and to recognize their right to produce salt. Having put the police on the run, the salt people extended their challenge to the entire institutional framework of the Changlu Salt Inspectorate and its repressive operations in Puyang. First, they demanded that the Kuomintang authorities acknowledge their right to sell earth salt at prices subject to free and fair competition in local markets, which of course struck at the heart of the central government's revenue-producing scheme. Second, they demanded that the Changlu salt shops beyond the confines of Puyang town be closed. The main Changlu salt shop inside the town would be permitted to keep its doors open only on condition that it include locally produced earth salt. These negotiations dealt a small but significant economic blow to the salt revenue machinery of the fiscal center. Li Xuanxi, a former saltmaker in Liangmen village, a five-hour walk from the county seat, recalls that "after the struggle in Puyang town, the local salt sold flourishingly again, and it beat out the sea salt. The Tianjin sea salt lost its market in Puyang."[60]

To the chagrin of the Puyang magistrate, another demand popped up. The protestors informed Sun Peiji that they would no longer pay the government salt land tax, which they had faithfully paid since its imposition in the 1920s. Interestingly, they did not raise the issue of the Kuomintang government tax on peasant grain lands; they simply declared a tax on their salt lands to be out of the question.[61]

After the first round of street-level negotiations with Sun Peiji, the protestors returned to their early morning gathering point near the war god temple in Cheng Guan, where many of them began to worry that the magistrate might not keep his promise. Several hundred protestors, including several members of the CCP, returned to the *yamen* to insist that Sun guarantee his promise and to enter into additional agreements with him.

Without directly challenging the legitimacy of the Kuomintang county government, these renewed negotiations raised the protest to a distinctively political level. The Puyang government was to issue twenty cards[62] bearing the words "Saltmaker. A Permit to Produce Salt. No One May Arrest Him" to Yang Jingcai, who was to issue the cards to members of the Puyang Saltmakers' Association. The cards were transferrable, so that the leaders could make them available to any salt producer who sought protection from the police.

Further, the Kuomintang government was to guarantee that neither the salt police nor the public security forces would interfere with the saltmakers while the latter were staging operas in Cheng Guan and the outlying villages to celebrate their victory. Lastly, the delegation demanded that Sun give official recognition to their salt league, the Puyang Saltmakers' Association, to acknowledge their sovereignty over matters of local salt production and trade and to display loyalty to the local Puyang community.

To a considerable extent, the CCP built its rural political base along the axis of this antistate protest. According to Liu Cun, the personal secretary of Wang Congwu, the number of Communist Party members increased three times in Puyang's villages during the year following the struggle of 1932. More than 90 percent of the new party members were poor peasants and saltmakers.[63] Clearly the protest movement was the horse pulling the cart of party-building fortunes.

The Communists organized the peasant salters for further collective political action, as evidenced in the party role in promoting the growth of the Puyang Saltmakers' Association, which proved a key vehicle of prewar Communist influence. Within a year of the 1932 uprising the village saltmakers' associations had chosen delegates to attend the Puyang County

Saltmakers' Congress. But local party leaders first had to find the activists mobilizing the saltmakers. In Puyang, Wang Congwu and the leaders of the county CCP discovered that Yang Jingcai was the "natural leader" of the peasant saltmakers when Yang was leading hundreds of them to push down the walls of the police headquarters.[64] The congress elected Yang Jingcai as the head of the Puyang Saltmakers' Association.[65]

This association became a mass organization under the leadership of the Communist Party in Puyang. Nevertheless, it remained substantially in the hands of locally respected non-Communist protest leaders. CCP members made up only one-quarter of the association's leadership. At both the village and county levels, the record of participation in the protest apparently was as important as party affiliation in determining leadership of the association. The unaffiliated non-Communists stayed on, and they often decided when and how to mobilize against the Kuomintang salt police. Their major leader, Yang Jingcai, held his position as chairman of the Puyang Saltmakers' Association for a year before joining the party in 1933.

There is no denying the crucial role of the CCP in linking up locally generated collective resistance with county and regional associations and in sharpening the political focus of the big protest incidents in the county towns. CCP leaders Wang Congwu and Liu Yufeng worked closely with Yang Jingcai to link and coordinate the protest movement in Puyang with its counterparts in other counties of the Hebei-Shandong-Henan border area after 1932. When it came to giving the local protests a more ramified and regional political voice and to transforming the sporadic, locally grounded economic struggles of the saltmakers into a more permanent political movement, therefore, these young Communists clearly made a difference.

The CCP influenced Puyang Saltmakers' Association, which traced its origins to the autonomous village leagues that had formed spontaneously over the years 1929–32, thus served as a political umbrella for the salters, making its services available to all members who sought freedom and protection from the interference of the tax police. The services included sending groups armed with salt spades and pitchforks to contest police attempts to level the ponds, petitioning the Kuomintang magistrates to allow salt production, coordinating mass assemblies, parades, and demonstrations, and sponsoring operas in town and country.

The association collected dues and in return helped its members obtain the protection and dignity they were powerless to achieve alone. Two of the most important services were protection from police arrest and detainment, and funeral support, such as burial clothing and coffins.[66] These services were made available to the plebeian allies of saltmakers and delivered by independent community-based collective action. When the movement began in Puyang, for example, the association sold "protection contracts" for one silver dollar, and the peddlers who purchased these contracts received protection from the police. Thus Zhang Youren remembers that Er Frei, who had a contract, was arrested by the salt police when he travelled from Xi Shuipo in Puyang to Hua County's Wang Gu village to sell his salt. However, according to Zhang, "When our Saltmakers' Association got word of the arrest we sent a strong delegation to the police to demand that they return his wheelbarrow and salt and set him free. The police did in fact give it back, and he was let go. They knew that if they did not heed our request we would take action."[67] This was in 1931, *before* the CCP led the big struggle in Puyang town; afterwards the party built up the association, and its political controls, by furthering such protective services.

The provision of such associational services, *coupled with the protest victory itself*—far more than the mere presence of the CCP—played a crucial role in solidifying the popular movement in Puyang, where the saltmakers' association swelled from under one thousand in late March, 1932, to three thousand by December.[68] Its leadership was active in spreading the rebellion to villages and markets in other counties. In early summer of 1932 a series of traditional operas staged in the villages of Cheng Guan, Qian Kou, Sha Wo, and Da Han drew saltmakers and peddlers engaged in evasive actions and small brush wars with the salt tax police in surrounding counties, some of them deputies of nascent salt leagues. They listened to speeches, absorbed news from a "salt people's newspaper," and exchanged stories with fellow saltmakers about struggles with the salt tax police. Inevitably, they took some of the lessons of Puyang's successful collective political action back to their local communities. In the ensuing three years, this struggle was replicated in Daming, Nanle, Qingfeng, Hua*xian,* Neihuang, Changyuan, Dongming, Chaocheng, Pu*xian,* Guancheng, and Fan County, all in the southern part of the Changlu salt area and the North China plain.

By mid-1932 saltmakers' associations had sprung up in thirteen counties of the Hebei-Shandong-Henan border area. In July the saltmakers of ten counties selected deputies to the General Association of Saltmakers, representing approximately eighty thousand saltmakers, which subsequently held a congress in Gu Chengji,[69] the largest salt market in Qingfeng County, to study production, sales, and the process of collective struggle with the police. The headquarters for the congress was the Guangong temple, where Qingfeng's peasant saltmakers had come together to organize collective antipolice activities in 1931 and 1932.[70] Within a year the general association moved its headquarters to Puyang town and in 1933 began receiving delegations of saltmakers into what came to be known as the Liang He Saltmakers' Association.

This triprovincial saltmakers' association coordinated an expanding popular struggle against the police. In the spring of 1933 the Tianjin

Kuomintang Changlu Salt Bureau officials sent a battalion of cavalry police to the Hebei-Shandong-Henan border area to suppress the saltmakers' popular leagues.[71] The main force established its base in Daming County, and the vanguard reached Nanle to prepare an attack on the general association's headquarters. The association, however, organized a surprise counterattack on the advance Changlu police units in Nanle. There the saltmakers dealt a severe blow to the police, then pressed the Nanle Kuomintang magistrate to sanction their actions and to compensate them for damages.

Objectively, this was a popular struggle against the taxation methods of the Nationalist elite, with local Kuomintang officials caught between the peasant saltmakers and the police arm of the central government's salt administration. However, the question remains: did the peasant saltmakers themselves see their protest as "antistate"? Although many simply hated the salt police and did not reflect deeply on the politics behind their coming, a few who participated in the 1932 protest had begun to develop a political awareness of the police, linking them with high-level politics. Wang Decheng, a veteran of Puyang's struggle, recalls that he and his father often had discussed the origins of police intervention in the seclusion of their home during the years of siege: "We guessed the Changlu salt police came from the Central government, but we were not sure. We knew they were from Tianjin and were supported by the Kuomintang."[72]

THE REJECTION OF KMT PATRONAGE AND RETREATIST TENDENCIES

The Kuomintang-appointed Puyang magistrate did not want the salt tax police to drive the marginal peasantry to starvation, for that would bring him real problems. Moreover, he was aware that the saltmakers, in consultation with the CCP, had decided to fight mainly against the finance ministry's police and not against the Puyang County government. Why, then, did the Kuomintang magistracy not co-opt the popular salt league and demobilize the saltmakers by combining preemptive reforms with "soft forms" of police control?[73]

In the case of Puyang, the political ideology and resources of the Kuomintang combined to inhibit co-optation. The top-rank Nationalist officials were more concerned about prosperous landowning peasants, landlords, and big merchants than about the marginal poor. Moreover, they could neither transform the poor alkaline soils into productive grain lands nor make available an alternative means of subsistence for the saltmakers. The salt people therefore remained fearful that any reforms propagandized by the Kuomintang state were part of the police scheme to expropriate their means of production and self-employment and drive them from home villages.[74] This fear was well founded.

Rejectionist tendencies in the popular movement were also at work. Despite the Kuomintang willingness to recognize the popular salt leagues, and despite a modest Kuomintang county government reform program, Puyang's rebel activists[75] sought to retreat from the modern revenue state by finding political fellowship mainly in the confederation of market forces emerging in the border area. The dealings of the peasant saltmakers with the Puyang County government in the aftermath of the 1932 protest movement illustrate this point.

In the summer of 1933, more than a year after the peasant saltmakers had stormed Puyang town, the Yellow River swept over the southeastern part of Puyang County, and by July the flood waters threatened the town itself. The Kuomintang county government, still based primarily inside the town, called upon the local people to help fight the flood. According to Xu Jinshan, most of those who went to Wu Jiandikou and Feng Yutang to build up the embankment were peasant saltmakers,[76] who took their salt wheelbarrows and battled the flood for a whole day and night. Their flood relief work was led by the leaders of the saltmakers' association, Yang Jingcai, Chou Fuhai, Li Yunling, and others. Although the Kuomintang government did not compensate those who risked their lives in this antiflood work, it did send food to them, which they refused. Guo Xinhai, a participant in the embankment work, explains: "If we ate the government food then we would have been obligated to obey the government. We saltmakers were obligated to obey only the Saltmakers' Association. The Kuomintang had to ask our Saltmakers' Association to coordinate the embankment work."[77]

A Kuomintang attempt to institute agricultural reform in Puyang several years after the upheaval of 1932 met similar rejection. Ding Shuben, the Kuomintang magistrate in charge of Puyang from 1935 to 1940, formed a local salt patrol to publicly discourage villagers from producing salt[78] and gave them cotton seeds to sow on their salt lands. Cotton did not flourish in the poor saline fields. Xu Jinshan, a Puyang saltmaker, recalls that those who agreed to grow cotton "sold most of the seeds, and when the local salt police came to inspect the lands they let the police see a little bit of cotton, but all the while they secretly produced salt in their ponds and inside their household courtyards."[79] This localized salt patrol seldom provoked confrontations with Puyang's "cotton producers," so that its halfhearted crop substitution effort was yet another factor inflecting Kuomintang state making in the early phase of Ding Shuben's tenure.[80]

TWO FACES OF POPULAR PROTEST IN PUYANG

The struggles of Puyang's saltmakers evolved, through the collective actions of market-driven community associations, into a loosely integrated transcounty mass movement. Erupting in the major town of the border region, the rebellion temporarily united town and country, local elites and village leaders, landlords and peasants, and stoked identical struggles in surrounding counties, some of which combined with Puyang's rebels and some of which pursued an independent course of collective action.[81]

The antistate protest movement centering on Puyang town was also related to the rise of "peasant" resistance in the border region after 1932. The Puyang saltmakers' victory acted as a catalyst to peasant antidisaster and antisurtax movements in Puyang and Neihuang in 1933 and 1934.[82] The social networks linking the leaders of the antifiscal protest movement in Puyang to the village world, coupled with the convergence of interest among townsfolk and countryfolk on prices and taxes, provided them with the political alliances needed to develop a peasant clientele in rural Puyang and nearby counties. Here was the CCP's link to the village world. No wonder, then, that by 1935 Kuomintang officials considered the peasant saltmakers' protest a serious threat to Republican authority.

But was it?

The face the movement presented to the *local* Kuomintang authorities in Puyang was noncontentious. Clearly, the country people made a deferential attempt to settle disputes over salt with the gentry and Kuomintang magistrates. They consciously sought to persuade the Kuomintang county officials to stand by the interests of local society and displayed no intention of challenging Chiang Kai-shek, T. V. Song, and the Kuomintang provincial governors who had selected the magistrates. For the most part, they carried out their protest activities within certain well-understood rules of politics. In confronting the Kuomintang magistrate and his local allies with their antipolice anger, they carefully avoided attacking the Puyang County government or its local public security forces. This cautious and civil face of popular disobedience enabled them to draw the Kuomintang magistrate to their side in the confrontation with the army of the fiscal center.

As F. G. Bailey has pointed out, confrontation "is a process of communication between competitors; communication implies that both sides are using the same language. They agree not only about the meaning of symbolic action but also about permissible tactics. In other words, when confrontation is the principle mode of interaction between opponents, they are playing a game and both are interested in keeping the structure of that game (i.e., the rules) intact."[83] To the peasant saltmakers, confrontation was a way of working out a settlement with the Kuomintang magistrate that was to envelop two principles, both compatible with traditional politics. To begin with, the Kuomintang was to return the administration of county affairs to a past in which "financial administration" did not exist, that is, to a world in which the central state did not usurp the kingdom of the local market to expand its own wealth and power. Moreover, the Kuomintang magistrate should behave righteously, rural people said, and recognize the

sovereignty of their market community. They urged that he give considera-
tion to both the local people's livelihood and the national economy and tol-
erate trade in locally made salt.

Sun Peiji embraced this logic. While pointing out that he had to obey
orders, he also stated that he knew the people had to make salt for a living
and that he sympathized with their situation.[84] He demonstrated his sympathy by sponsoring a theatrical performance celebrating the exit of the salt
tax police;[85] his counterpart in Dongming County later gave the saltmakers
an apology banquet, complete with ten thousand strings of firecrackers and
one hundred tables of food.[86] All of this was part of a complex process of
local politics in which many of the Kuomintang magistrates were trying desperately to prevent the revenue policy of Nanjing state makers from alienating local peasant groups and pushing them into the arms of the Communist Party.

The movement's other face was one of contention, of the local people
openly pledging themselves to a combative antistate defense of their collective interest in the marketplace. The saltmakers reserved this face for the tax
police, who stood for the belligerent revenue scheme of the alien state (and,
ultimately, its international financial entanglements) and who posed an
immediate threat to the dependency of their households on the salt market.

Contention implied that communication between the peasant saltmakers and the police arm of the Kuomintang fiscal center had broken
down. Ringleaders of the protest movement stressed that the police had
broken the fundamental rules of confrontation. They were not competitors. They were *predators* who were not held accountable for their actions
by the Nanjing-based government. They searched households without warrants; they arrested people for defending their salt ponds, their implements, and their harvests; and they combined illegal imprisonment with
unusually cruel punishments. Expelling them and ending the salt monopoly hardly seemed a radical course. Hence the ease whereby the language
of spades, cudgels, and spears replaced the language of common peaceful
discourse.

It is important to ask whether we are dealing with a local versus center
struggle that was different from anything that might be described as "antistate" protest. Appealing to the local authorities was, in one sense, a way of
keeping alive a tradition of political discourse that was being lost to Kuomintang state making. The leaders of the protest knew that the magistrates
and salt police saw themselves as being on the side of the Nationalist government, but they also recalled the Imperial past, when the magistrate was
responsible for the well-being of the local community as well as the center.
Appealing to this dual responsibility was a way of splitting the Kuomintang
magistrates away from the police arm of Chiang Kai-shek's administrative
dictatorship. This appeal also created the appearance of a peaceful local
versus center struggle, while permitting the protest leaders to promote a

movement that was, fundamentally, a struggle against the fiscal policy of the Kuomintang state. This movement was characterized by more contentious antistate actions, which the saltmakers pursued locally with familiar cultural weapons.

The popular consciousness that formed this contentious face of protest was evident in the celebrations of the Puyang saltmakers' victory over the police. The Communist role in structuring these celebrations sheds further light on the reasons for party success in building a base among the peasant saltmakers. After the establishment of the Puyang Saltmakers' Association, Yang Jingcai informed the CCP county committee that the saltmakers wanted to celebrate the victory with three days of plays and dramas in Puyang town.[87] Wang Congwu and Liu Yanchun approved these plays, the first of which was *Uprising in Xuzhou*. This play was about Gu Guanqiong, a heroic saltmaker in the declining Yuan dynasty. Arrested by the government for selling salt, Gu was punished by forty whips and thrown into jail. The play emphasized the evil of such punishments, but, more significantly, it was aimed at promoting divisions between county government and the national Kuomintang ruling group, for its central message was that Gu Guanqiong had persuaded Magistrate Xuda to rebel against the Yuan dynasty—just as Wang Congwu and the saltmakers' association had, implicitly, persuaded the Puyang magistrate to break away from Nanjing. Of course Magistrate Sun was not willing to go this far, but the message of the play was that he had done just that by accepting the demands of the protest movement.

The contentious operas further alarmed the Kuomintang magistrates, who could not muster the means to control them. Sun Peiji is said to have warned the Puyang saltmakers not to use the operas to attack the police, but his warning fell on deaf ears. In the summer of 1932 Yang Jingcai and the saltmakers' association arranged for a Puyang opera troupe to stage *The Romance of the Three Kingdoms* on the grounds of the Fire God temple near Cheng Guan.[88] They instructed the players to adapt the skits of several Guangong operas, incorporating wickedly humorous anecdotes ridiculing and shaming the police as unfilial sons who had deprived their fathers of their daily salt needs.[89] These performances electrified the crowds in Puyang town. During the biggest of such rowdy, police-bashing operas, a ripsnorting satiric performance from *The Romance of the Three Kingdoms* held in the spring of 1935 at the Three Emperors' Temple in Nanle town, Magistrate Zhang Yongheng delivered a speech criticizing the salt tax police and condoning the celebration itself.[90] Twenty thousand people, including massive numbers of saltmakers from the thirteen border area counties, attended this spirited event.

These popular operas, with their burlesque mockery of police assailants, were repeated in some of the remote village strongholds of the peasant saltmakers. Wang Yuxi of Sha Wo remembers the opera celebrations in June, 1932, when ten thousand people came to his village to celebrate the defeat of the salt police. The opera players were from Puyang town and had taken part in the celebration in Cheng Guan. They performed several operas from *The Romance of the Three Kingdoms*. Yang Jingcai, Wang Congwu, and Wang Peizhi, the leaders of the saltmakers' struggle, all came to speak about the victory and led the crowds in shouting antipolice slogans.[91]

It was in villages like Sha Wo and Qian Kou—villages to which the Kuomintang magistrates did not come to converse with the country people—that the Communist Party members from the Daming Seventh Normal School politicized this popular movement. To be sure, most peasant salt-makers only knew Wang Congwu and his cohorts as returned college students who were siding with the home folks.[92] Nevertheless, these local party leaders utilized the opera celebrations to damage the reputation of Nationalist state makers in the consciousness of the local folk.

To begin with, the Communists simply tried to make local people aware of the "partners of the police," telling them the police were under a ministry within the central government, the creature of Nanjing and not the local Kuomintang. Those who manipulated the police were political outsiders looking to maximize state revenue by cutting the lifeline of local folk. Why, asked Wang Congwu and his associates, should the saltmakers contribute to central government money-making schemes to pay off foreign debts that benefitted *only* the new rulers in Nanjing?

The young CCP activists were dealing with village people already aware of police links to some type of extralocal political unit. "We knew that the Kuomintang magistrate in Puyang was not responsible for sending the salt police to repress us," says Wang Yuxi, "and that the police were under different leadership. If the magistrate had . . . posted a notice, we would have known the production of earth salt was against the law of the county, and we would not have produced the salt openly."[93] In denouncing the police, the Communists had only to reveal the names of centrally placed officials who had ordered the police to use violence against the poor. Carefully distinguishing the national Kuomintang elite from small, local Kuomintang fish, they portrayed the finance ministry officials in charge of the salt tax police as shamelessly out of step with Sun Yat-sen's three principles—which included the right to produce one's livelihood. If the police did not respect the right of the peasant saltmakers to live, the young CCP leaders told the opera audiences, "it is only reasonable for *us* to oppose them."[94]

CCP leaders also drew on comparative political logic to sustain popular outrage at Kuomintang fiscality, going one step further to portray the police as contributing to China's humiliation. In the Sha Wo opera celebrations, for example, Wang Congwu delivered a stinging criticism of the Nationalist government's policy of allowing the Japanese army to take over the Northeast without any fight.[95] How was it, he asked, that Generalissimo Chiang Kai-shek, whose Kuomintang armed forces outnumbered the Japanese army ten to one, failed to contest the takeover of 18 September 1931, in the meantime finding ways to wage a war against poor country people like the peasant saltmakers in Puyang and Sha Wo? The police were represented as harming the interests of rural citizens in a time of national emergency, as the "running dogs" of Japanese imperialism. Operating in the context of the *Three Kingdoms* operas, with their praise of Guangong, the Communists did not have to spell out their national salvation message to the local people, for the operas reminded them that Chiang Kai-shek's men had attacked their conception of national sovereignty. The peasant saltmakers detested the secular cadres of the Kuomintang center's New Life Movement for their sacrilegious campaigns against Guangong, the folk deity who was remembered for saving the Han dynasty and, in time, for protecting the common people from predatory rulers.[96] Just as these semipeasants had drawn on their own forms of community defense to resist fiscal despotism, so they had organized secret resistance to Kuomintang attacks on the Guangong statues in the village temples between 1929 and 1932.[97] They still paid homage to Guangong before private household altars and in public temple ceremonies, knowing that Guangong was a threat to Kuomintang power.[98] By comparing the Kuomintang's appeasement with Guangong's defense of the Han state and its rural subjects, the returned Communist students utilized the temple-based operas in Sha Wo and elsewhere to effectively refute Chiang Kai-shek's claim to national political legitimacy.

Of course, the Chiang Kai-shek central government had only begun to establish its presence in the rural counties of this triprovincial border world. And in attempting to expand the reach of its revenue apparatus into the villages, the Kuomintang stirred up a firestorm of popular opposition. Non-Communist and nonrevolutionary, the participants in this protest movement were looking to end the infringement of a critical segment of the Kuomintang state on their customary market rights. The peasant saltmakers, to use Lucien Bianco's terminology, "almost never took up arms with a view to conquering new rights."[99] They were out to preserve a treasured market right that was being threatened by modern state force. By the same token, however, this was not simply a peasant movement whose participants were mobilizing to merely redress local grievances, for the grievances had been generated by distant Nationalist government officials whose search for revenue was charted by their connections with international financial institutions and, further, had alarmed rural people strung together by their mutual dependence on the marketplace.[100] The popular movement spanned town and country, cut across rich and poor villages and nearly all social classes, drew in peasants, peddlers, and purchase agents, and appealed to locally educated people who were candidates for the Kuomintang as well as the CCP.

Looking back on Cheng Guan's protest history, we learn something important about the location and nature of the popular movement in which the CCP was making headway during the early 1930s: the Communists worked in villages located inside of county towns—the place of San Huang in Chapter 6 further corroborates this understudied phenomenon—and the town-based protest activists had kinship and market connections with peasant saltmakers living in distant villages, so that the protest movement in which the CCP made headway was the creature of mutually enhancing interaction between country towns and rural villages *within the same market system*. The outbreak of the 1932 Cheng Guan collective action followed the intervention of the Kuomintang tax police, and the formation of collective protest inside the town was based on the participation of rural villages that already were mobilizing to defend the market against state envelopment. For the CCP, the case of Cheng Guan also underscores the political importance of aligning with rich folk as well as poor, for some of the protesting saltmakers were bringing their struggles in rural Puyang to the county town in order to maintain prosperity recently derived from the salt market. (The case of Qian Kou drives home this point.)

In this political complexity, particularly in villages politicized by the violent intrusion of the salt tax police, Wang Congwu and the small band of CCP students from the Seventh Normal School began to make political capital from the "little mistake" of Kuomintang state making. The points scored by these young Communists with the country people would play to their advantage during the tumultuous years of the Second World War. Thus it is important to grasp the CCP's emerging relationship with antistate protest in the villages where the peasant saltmakers were rising against the Kuomintang revenue state before the Japanese army occupied the border area and tipped the scales toward the CCP and its popular constituency.

FOUR

Qian Kou Village:
The Police Attack on Prosperity

Qian Kou (Thousand Crossings) village had accentuated earth salt production in the decade prior to the formation of the *Shuijingtuan*. The emergence of popular collective protest within Qian Kou was directly related to
the role of earth salt in the overall development of its economy and to the
changed relationship of the salt revenue machinery of the Kuomintang
state (and, to a lesser extent, of the Puyang County government) to the market community in which the village was situated. The CCP gained a foothold
in this southern Hebei village by resonating with the politics of earth salt,
placing its cadres in the eye of the storm of antistate protest.

QIAN KOU'S ECONOMY IN REPUBLICAN TIMES

According to the standard Chinese Communist version, Qian Kou's "poor
peasants" were rescued from landlord exploitation by the redistributive justice of the 1947 land revolution.[1] In reality, however, before the Japanese
introduced murder, chaos, and misery, Qian Kou had become a prosperous
village, and most of its peasants managed to withstand economic disintegration.[2] Situated at the intersection of Puyang, Hua, and Neihuang counties, along the border of Hebei and Henan, Qian Kou is fifty *li* from Puyang
County town. Here the forty-five-*li* Nitrate River (*Xiao He*)[3] flows from Hua
County in Henan into the areas north and east of Qian Kou and remains a
five-minute walk from its outskirts. Qian Kou was named "Thousand Crossings" by the long-dominant Liu lineage, whose ancestors crossed a thousand
rivers en route to this area from Hong Tong County in Shanxi Province during the reign of the Yan emperor in the Ming dynasty.[4]

The Nitrate River, whose sole water source is the rains of July and August, often dries up in spring, and was dry even when I visited Qian Kou during a torrential rainstorm in June of 1987. In the middle of the river is a strip of reed land, from which the villagers obtained fuel and reed materials for making mats. Reed land was taxed at half the rate of cropland and throughout Ming and Qing times had a variety of owners. The barren river bank land remained wild, unclaimed land. This vast expanse of public land, open to anyone who could find a way to develop its saline, alkaline soil, remained a potential source of fallback income in hard times and became an important factor in Qian Kou's buoyant development.

Wheat Land and Peanuts

The best village land was, and is, west of the village, a zone of black, fertile, sandy land between the river and the date tree lands to the southwest. From the end of the Qing until the early Republican period this area had about sixty *qing*, or 6,000 *mu*, of farmland, with a high yield per *mu*, and early on became Qian Kou's granary.[5] About half has always been planted to wheat in November, then, following the June harvest, resown to sorghum. Just before the saltmakers' struggle of 1932, Qian Kou had approximately 240 households and a population of about 1,250. There was enough grain cropland alone to give each person approximately 5 (4.8) *mu*—which means that Qian Kou peasants held as much, or more, land per household than most of their counterparts in the North China plain.[6]

At the end of the Ming dynasty many date trees were planted in the powdery, sandy land south of Qian Kou. The peasants still pride themselves on the big, sweet dates from these trees. This sandy land spreads into the old course of the Yellow River and a zone of sand and tall cogon grass that in the Republican period was ten times as large as Qian Kou's farmland. Much of it was ownerless. Like the sandy farmland of southern Hebei, it was good for growing peanuts. Before 1920, when peanut oil suddenly became an international commodity, peanut fields occupied only a few *mu* of Qian Kou's land surface. The peanut growers were mainly small peddlers, who grew minute peanuts on patches of sandy land by village roads or at the edges of the date groves.[7] They roasted the peanuts and sold them and occasionally extracted peanut oil and carried it around on shoulder poles within a three-*li* radius of the village, to exchange for articles of daily use. Traditionally, Qian Kou's landlords were not involved in peanut culture even on a small scale.

In 1920, however, the price for peanuts rose to nine cents of a silver dollar per *jin*, up from twenty-four *wen* per *jin*.[8] The world demand for peanut oil was coupled with the introduction of a new "miracle peanut seed" into North China, and the planting of peanuts became popular in the sandy villages of southern Hebei and northern Henan. In Qian Kou, rich landlords rushed into production. They were joined by landowning peasants, who used about half of their sandy farmland to grow peanuts, and some, after a year or two of cautious experimentation with the new peanut seeds, helped engineer a veritable explosion in production for the world market.

Liu Yufeng, the leader of the saltmakers' struggle in Qian Kou, recalls:[9]

> In my grandfather's time we were poor and deeply in debt. We often mixed cotton seed oil with corn for the Spring Festival. When I was about ten years old, however, we began to make salt and gradually we saved enough money to buy some land. By the time I was twenty-two, in 1924, we had acquired ten *mu* of sandy land. On six *mu* of this land I had begun to plant nuts. I bought other land too, little by little. The money to buy the land came from three channels: salt making, date production, and growing peanuts.
>
> Before 1922 we had planted red beans on our sandy land. In 1922 a new kind of peanut was introduced into our village. We were not sure from which country it came, but we knew it was foreign. Our local peanuts were exceedingly small, and we could only produce 100 to 200 *jin* per *mu*. But the new kind of peanut yielded 800 to 1,000 *jin* per *mu*. One *mu* produced at least twenty-two bags, and one bag equalled forty *jin*. In the first year, we planted only half a *mu* to this new peanut seed. After we saw the results, we planted six *mu* the next year. Thereafter we continued planting these bigger peanuts, and nearly all of the village's sandy land was given over to peanut production. The oil from our peanuts, and from the nuts grown in the surrounding villages, went to Chu Wang town in Neihuang county and to Wu Ling in Tangyin, and from these places passed on to Tianjin *via* the Wei River, and abroad.

After 1923, Qian Kou blossomed into a new marketplace for the peanut trade. Peasant families sold their peanuts directly to peddlers from outlying villages[10] or, for a slightly higher price, at Jingdian market.[11] Within a year Qian Kou's peanut boom brought a new group of middle-level business agents into the market,[12] purchase agents and brokers who introduced peasant sellers to merchants for various oil shops.[13] After 1924, Qian Kou's old general store and grain shop was transformed into a purchasing center. By 1925 the village's rich peasants and landlords had also established a few centers, and the purchase agents were doing a brisk business.

Zhao Jibin, the founder of the CCP in Qian Kou, claims that the purchasing agents were thrown out of work or compelled to work for landlords who bought up the harvest at low prices in late autumn and sold it in spring for a killing to merchants from afar.[14] If anything, however, purchase agents proliferated in Qian Kou during the late 1920s.[15] Purchasing centers financed by landlord capital by no means absorbed all the peanuts produced, and they did not displace the small entrepreneurs.

More and more, the peanuts these centers purchased were pressed in oil mills, which in 1925 became closely allied with the purchasing centers. The oil was carted to Chu Wang, Dao Kou, and Daming, then taken downriver by barge to Tianjin. By 1930 the managers of the four oil mills had sold their operations to landlords Liu Yaobin, Zhao Shaofu, and others,[16] who amassed small fortunes.[17] About 70 percent of their income came from selling oil to Chu Wang and Tianjin, and ultimately the world market; 20 percent from producing *dou bing*, (pressed oil cakes), used for fertilizer; and 10 percent from renting out the tools to press oil and produce *dou bing*.[18]

The landlords did *not* monopolize the peanut business;[19] peasants could sell to oil shops in Jingdian anytime Qian Kou prices displeased them. The landlords were barely able to compete with the purchase agents.

Before the saltmakers' struggle most Qian Kou peasants benefitted from peanut cultivation. Some peasants who ten years previously had been poor now owned horses and stately houses. By 1930 a few had become rich.

Several factors made for this ascendance. About 1925, Qian Kou peasants began opening up the ownerless sandy land near the old course of the Yellow River.[20] First they planted a few bushes to prevent the sandy soil from shifting away; then they applied fertilizer. The Puyang County government tax on peanut land remained low even into the late 1920s, enabling dozens of peasant families to prosper. Increasingly, grain land was given over to the "peanut rush." By 1935, Ma Xinxi remembers, "most of the peanuts were planted not on the newly opened up riverland, but on lands that had formerly been used for grain production."[21] This prosperity was bolstered by the popularity of peanut-oil lamps in North China until 1937, when American kerosene purchased in Jingdian began replacing peanut oil.[22]

For fifteen years, following the big droughts of 1920–21, atmospheric conditions and solar activity favored peanut cultivation in Qian Kou. Harvests were average to abundant. "No serious drought affected our peanut harvest in Qian Kou between 1922 and 1932," Liu Yufeng states. "The harvest was average in 1931, and we had no substantial fall off in production in the year before the saltmakers' struggle."[23] We cannot attribute Qian Kou's involvement in the struggle of 1932 to an environmentally induced decline in agriculture, for there was a countertrend at play—and peasants were making the most of it.

The market price for peanuts remained buoyant well into the world depression of 1929–32,[24] when prices dropped from nine cents to five cents (of a silver dollar per *jin*). For a few years peasants in Qian Kou could only get four cents per *jin*. Nevertheless the market for peanuts was not seriously jeopardized. Liu Yufeng, a producer and purchase agent in these years, explains:[25] "The price we received for peanuts from 1922 to 1934 was fairly steady and did not drop much. Sometimes we could not sell our dates. But we never failed to sell our peanuts. We seldom produced too many. After all, China itself provided us with a great domestic market for our new variety of peanut, so we were able to make up for foreign influences." Even with the impact of the depression, the price of peanuts per *jin* more than doubled for Qian Kou's producers in 1920–35.[26] The number of families cultivating peanuts nearly doubled, and half of Qian Kou's tillable cropland was given over to peanut production. The sphere of exchange was extended from border area market towns to foreign market points, and the ownership of the village oil mills was assumed by fairly prosperous "live-in landlords." Small peanut tillers, middlemen, and landlord shop operators all continued to rake in gains over and above their 1920 incomes.

Earth Salt

A visitor to Qian Kou around 1917 would have found only a handful of peasant saltmakers. Ten years later, and until the outbreak of WWII, earth salt production was booming, involving more than 90 percent of Qian Kou's families.

What turned Qian Kou's peasants into part-time saltmakers? Part of the answer lies in the fate of native alkali. Before 1920 peasants worked the indigenous alkali-bearing land stretching along the slope of the Nitrate River to extract alkali.[27] While grain, animal dealing, and dates were the mainstay of Qian Kou's economy in late Qing, for ten to twenty households alkali production was an important side occupation. In early Republican years, Qian Kou, along with Xing village, Yaocun, and Pukou, was one of several key villages where alkali was made.[28] Much of it was sold locally, as a soap powder for washing clothes. Old-fashioned dye houses and mills in Dao Kou, Daming, Nangong, and Handan all used it in the cloth-dyeing process,[29] and Qian Kou peasants sometimes went farther north to Baoding in Hebei and to Linqing in Shandong, where they could get a better price.[30]

In the last year of the Qing dynasty Qian Kou's alkali makers could name their prices, for their market had been protected by the old regime and by the absence of Western scientific advances. After 1920, however, all this changed. Just as Republican state makers had busied themselves with internationalizing the salt industry for greater production and profit, so they yielded to foreign pressures to open China's gates to new products that posed a threat to rural alkali industries. After 1913 the Chinese central government allowed the importation of British industrial alkali, and its spectacular advances contributed to the decline of the old agrarian economy and the growth of a subclass of marginalized peasants who came to rely on salt making for their income. Much of southern Hebei was subjected to this history, Qian Kou in particular.

A new world alkali market was maturing in the years 1890–1920. By mastering and monopolizing the development of the soda industry in the 1890s, the English firm of Brunner & Mond had begun to promote a new international trade in synthetic alkali.[31] The potential demand for alkali in China, where it was used in washing soda and for small industry, was especially appealing.[32] Between 1900 and 1920 Brunner & Mond recruited

Henry Glendinning and a host of other Protestant missionaries to proselytize the miraculous usages of its alkali products in rural China. By 1915 China was taking more of B&M's alkali trade than Mexico, Latin America and the Caribbean, and all of South America combined; the rapid annual rate of increase placed the Chinese Republic second only to Japan.[33] After 1920 B&M alkali poured into China free of any tariff restrictions and was disseminated through British branch firms dealing directly with local customers and setting prices to their own liking.[34]

By 1926–27 alkali makers in Qian Kou and scores of villages along the old course of the Yellow River had lost at least half of their former customers.[35] Being a monopoly, B&M was in a position to defeat native competition—a practice it had perfected in the 1921–22 price wars with Kenya-Magadi, the major competitor for the East Asian market.[36] Moreover, the purified chemical properties of synthetic alkali made it more efficient than natural alkali; and it was cheaper. Thus by the mid-1920s, many peasants were switching to producing earth salt to offset their income losses.

Zhao Wangni, one of Qian Kou's peasant alkali producers in the 1920s, recalls how the intrusion of foreign alkali prompted him to pursue earth salt production:[37]

> Before the struggle of 1932 my family also had produced alkali. . . . Prior to 1927 we had sold alkali in the markets of Handan. I remember we also sold it at Bei Guantou and Nan Guantou, about three hundred *li* from our village. We had no trouble selling the alkali. We did not need the buyers to pay immediately. We just took our payments at the end of each year
>
> But in time the alkali from England became more and more popular in this area. On my trips to Handan, I heard that the foreign alkali had the same function as our alkali—people used it to prepare food and wash and dye clothes. Our locally made alkali was in a big block size; so it was not easy to use it. The purchaser had to break it up, and this was inconvenient. People therefore bought the imported alkali more and more. Gradually we had trouble selling our alkali, and [in 1927] many people in Qian Kou gave up making it. . . . All of us . . . lost some income from the invasion of foreign alkali.
>
> Before the foreign alkali came here, I earned twelve silver dollars per year from my alkali sales, but after the foreign alkali came I could earn less than one silver dollar annually. . . . Of the more than ten families in our village many eventually gave up alkali making and began making *xiaoyan* [earth salt].

By shifting into earth salt production, Zhao and his companions more than recovered the income they had lost to foreign alkali.

The boom in earth salt production actually began in the early 1920s, when the price of government salt rose to a point beyond the peasants' means. Even Qian Kou's comparatively wealthy landlord households purchased only earth salt in the middle decades of the Republic.[38] Another political factor drove up the demand for earth salt: The 1923–28 warlord struggles along the northern Henan–southern Hebei border interrupted the flow of maritime salt into Puyang County and skyrocketed the price of Changlu salt, giving further impetus to a rising market for earth salt along the Nitrate River.[39]

Although defined as illegal by the central government, salt making became enormously popular in Qian Kou. Before 1920 only three families were involved in earth salt production; by 1930, nearly the entire village was linked to this underground economy. This adaptation in Qian Kou can be separated into three periods.

In late Qing and early Republican times, roughly from 1895 to 1919, the production of terrestrial salt was largely a temporary side occupation of the marginal poor. Between the end of the June harvest and the end of July, rather than competing for work as hired hands in other southern Hebei counties, villagers developed the wild land at the slope of the Nitrate River to produce earth salt, which they sold door to door in Qian Kou and near-by villages. By 1919 the price for one *jin* of this earth salt was about twelve *wen* of Hebei money (less than one cent of a silver dollar), so the main purpose of salt production was obviously to restabilize household income when the crop was disappointing. This, plus the fact that most peasants owned their own grain and date tree lands, explains why Qian Kou had only a handful of salt-making households in this early period.[40]

As the price of Changlu salt rose, during the second period, 1920 to 1927, earth salt came into great demand, and scores of landowning peasant families took up production.[41] The price climbed to six cents of a silver dollar per *jin,* six times as high as its pre-1920 price. The bulk of the village's landowning tillers took up salt making for the summer months and into September.

The enlargement of the underground salt economy was also the result of the terrible drought of 1920,[42] precursor of the North China famine of 1921, which seared Qian Kou's fields and threatened the wheat harvest. Thirty to forty families in dire need of fallback income took up salt making, which soon became the principle means whereby half of the village avoided long-term migration. By 1927 previously threatened peasant families were claiming that "from one day's salt production we can produce a pot of gold!"[43]

The salt making took place along a six-to-seven-*li* stretch of the barren white banks of Nitrate River. Liu Gongchen, who was born in 1913, recalls that "the salt land had been there in my father's and grandfather's time. They had produced the salt freely. They did not need a license. There were no government regulations on this *xiaoyan* land."[44] The salt land along the Nitrate River was common land, open to anyone, and not subject to any government tax. "Whoever opened it up thereby claimed ownership to it," explained Zhao Tianbao, the village head from 1952 until 1983.[45]

For three silver dollars one could purchase a wheelbarrow, two spades, a basket to carry soil, and several dozen *jin* of lime to line the salt pond. The peasants who opened up common land were able to generate a great surge in salt production very quickly. By 1927 approximately two hundred households had entered earth salt production and trade. Many earned twenty to thirty silver dollars per year and expanded production by adding a second pond.[46] Between 1920 and 1927, peasant income from salt making increased 320 times, and most families were freed of the fear of hunger by late 1923. So prosperous was Qian Kou that bandits considered the village a major prize, and crop theft within the village was virtually unheard of for the year 1927.

The third phase lasted into the twilight of the Republic, encompassing the interruption of the Kuomintang salt tax police.[47] In this phase, Qian Kou's salt industry was characterized by consolidation and upsurge in circulation, by internal conflict, and by the expansion of earth salt production facilities. By 1930 Qian Kou had blossomed into one of the newly emergent interior salt markets to which southern Hebei people flocked.

Qian Kou's marketing behavior suggests an ingenious duality. On the one hand, peasants engaged in most of their exchanges in the large market town of Jingdian. Products such as peanut oil and red dates then went on to Chu Wang town or other intermediate markets, up to the city of Tianjin, and into the world economy—the red dates from the Qian Kou area were the talk of the 1914 Panama World Trade Exposition.[48] On the other hand, they were selling some of their salt-based products to peasants and peddlers from other villages who made direct purchases in peasant homes, village streets, and under the tents of the Xiao River salt market, which had burst on the scene after 1927. This "minor" salt market had begun to attract thousands of peasants and peddlers, possibly illustrating what Skinner has termed an "incipient standard market."[49] This emergent earth salt market was in competition with the government-controlled salt markets in Jingdian and Puyang town, and its popular clientele was expanding. The remarks of Liu Gongchen underscore this point and reveal the complexities of commodity production and exchange in this section of the North China plain:[50]

> The salt we produced in Qian Kou was of comparatively poor quality. And it was cheaper. Thus peddlers from many different villages came here to buy it from as far as thirty *li* away, from a village called Du Dian. They possessed salt that was better to eat in part because their salt was taken from land that had different chemical elements. These peddlers mixed our salt with the higher quality *xiaoyan,* and then resold it in various markets. We Qian Kou saltmakers seldom if ever sold our earth salt in the local markets beyond our village. For the most part, we sold it to the peddlers who came to . . . the Xiao River

Salt Market. . . . The peddlers who bought our salt took it to the big market in Jingdian, and they also sold it in the highland areas to poor families who could not get sea salt.

Rich peasants and landlords began to look with envy on the earth salt business and to entertain thoughts of capturing it for themselves. A few began to rent small plots of reed land and salt land to tenants and to issue grain loans to peasants in the spring, when the price of grain was high, so they could be repaid in earth salt in late summer. One or two purchased earth salt from village saltmakers when the price of earth salt was low, stored it until the price rose in late winter, then sold it in Neihuang, Anyang, and Lin Zhang at a 100 percent profit.[51]

The smallholding peasant saltmakers actually grew in number and countered the landlord attempt to absorb the profits of *xiaoyan* business. Perhaps Qian Kou's landlords preferred not to invest this income in tenants and hired hands, who were few and far between in Qian Kou.[52] Perhaps they were not prepared to compete with the new group of salt purchase agents, weighers, and peddlers who were gaining a niche in the earth salt economy. Just prior to the Northern Revolutionary Expedition one *mu* of Qian Kou's reed land, which abutted the salt land, was taxed at a rate of thirty coppers per *mu*. The landlord families who owned this reed land, burdened by a string of tax increases after 1927,[53] began selling their lands in order to escape the tax. A new wave of Republican government taxes on salt lands prompted them to sell their salt lands as well. The land given over to peasants in the third phase was invariably converted to earth salt production. Clearly, the landowning peasant majority, whose landholdings were *increasing*, was in command of Qian Kou's salt economy by 1930.

The Kuomintang salt tax corps struck Qian Kou in a period of prosperity, when its peasant saltmakers were lifting their households above subsistence. On the eve of the invasion by the salt police, many salt-making families were making fifty to sixty silver dollars annually, and were expanding production. Peasant families opened up three, four, and even more salt ponds during the first decade of Kuomintang rule, sometimes earning more than thirty silver dollars per pond.[54] In good years, old-timers told me, they made as much as two hundred silver dollars per salt pond annually. The leader of the Qian Kou saltmakers' protest, Liu Yufeng, insisted this was the case for his salt pond operation in the harvest years of 1932–34.[55]

If each member of a 7-member household (the average comprised 5.2 persons) needed five hundred *jin* of grain per year to survive,[56] the family needed enough income to purchase thirty-five hundred to four thousand *jin* of good wheat or four thousand to six thousand *jin* of sorghum, husks, and coarse grains and still have money for salt (which they now produced themselves), clothing, farm implements, medicine, and other necessities for themselves and their farm animals. With approximately sixty silver dollars income from two salt ponds, after spending thirty to thirty-five silver dollars on grain, this larger-than-average household had twenty-five left. (One silver dollar could buy two hundred *jin* of sorghum, or thirty to fifty *jin* of wheat, in the Jingdian market in 1930.)[57]

NITRATE

Another mainstay of peasant livelihood was nitrate. Derived from the bottom layer soil deposits of the Nitrate River land, nitrate was relatively easy to produce.[58] Like earth salt, it required the construction of a pond. Alkaline earth was placed in the pond and the nitrate drawn to the top; the next day the surface nitrate was scraped from the top of the water; and a day later, the accumulated nitrate was boiled down in order to get refined nitrate. Peasants usually made nitrate in the winter and increased production when the harvests were poor. Thus nitrate production came into vogue around 1920, when drought parched the village grain fields.[59]

Qian Kou's peasant nitrate producers were involved in a regional market economy. Peasants in Puyang and in Anyang used the nitrate both as a fertilizer for hard lands and as a medicinal additive for animal fodder.[60] Many peddlers also purchased the nitrate at a low price and took it to marketplaces along the Wei River.[61] In the late 1920s some peddlers went as far as Hankou in Hubei Province, where they resold the nitrate at a still higher price. Whereas other nearby villages produced the nitrate for fireworks, Qian Kou's nitrate market was linked to the in-region leather factories of Puyang, Dao Kou, and Handan, where hides of horses, mules, sheep, and rabbits were treated and turned into leather products, and to more distant glass factories.

THE NEW REVENUE SCHEME OF THE REPUBLICAN CENTER

Although the Republican state took a number of taxes, the crucial question is whether its tax agents were appropriating profits to a point where peasants were unable to sustain their recently achieved standard of living and where their production for the market was placed in jeopardy. Except for the new state pressure on earth salt production, the answer is a resounding "no." The familiar Republican county government taxes, provincial warlord taxes, and semiofficial entrepreneurial tax broker fees constituted a burden, to be sure; but prior to the peasant saltmakers' protest nine-tenths of the people in Qian Kou were earning income sufficient to pay them.

Year in and year out, peasants coped with the four kinds of tax placed on Qian Kou's resources by the Puyang County government: the grain land tax (historically the most important), the sandy peanut land tax, the salt land tax, and the reed land tax. The tax on grain land amounted to one silver dollar per *mu* for good wheat land and one-half silver dollar per *mu* for average (sandy) grain cropland. Because few peasant families owned more than five *mu* of average grain land (which brought only two *yuan* when sown to wheat and about three to four *yuan* when planted to peanuts)[62] by 1930, the most they paid in taxes was about two silver dollars. The tax on sandy peanut land amounted to no more than thirty coppers per *mu*, or considerably less than one-half silver dollar per every ten *mu*. Some peasants say that the tax amounted to almost nothing.[63]

There was no tax on Qian Kou's salt lands prior to 1920. After 1923, however, the Puyang County government consistently attempted to collect such a tax on the land along the Nitrate River. Liu Gongchen recalls: "The Puyang county government tax on salt land was about one silver dollar on every two *mu*, and this was twice the tax on our grain crop lands. This tax started around 1923, and there was an attempt to increase it around 1929, by which time it had become clear that peasants were earning money from the salt lands."[64]

The reed land tax was about one-half of the good grain land tax.[65] (This tax became burdensome after 1927, but sporadic warlord pressures mainly account for increases.) Reed land remained the most insignificant source of income for Qian Kou peasants, so the tax was paid without complaint.

Qian Kou's peasants faithfully paid their land taxes every year, even when the grain harvest was poor. Most walked the long distance to Puyang town to deposit their silver with the county tax office.[66] They were committed to upholding the village's reputation for responsible citizenship with county government. According to Liu Shiyin,[67] "In 1928 Zhao Baoyu did not pay his taxes. The Puyang Kuomintang government sent an official to arrest him. At that point, Liu Haiyun, the head of our village, came out to speak good words on Zhao's behalf, and also paid for his release. Landlord Liu Yaobin had helped to appoint Liu Haiyun."

This moderately prosperous village was entering into mutual reciprocity with Puyang County government and was maintaining a fairly good relationship with local authorities prior to the impact of the Chiang Kai-shek Kuomintang. The peasants of Qian Kou were allowed to postpone their taxes when the harvest was meager and were afforded protection from bandits and other outside predators. Several, Liu Yunxing among them, harbor fond memories of the local Kuomintang's antibandit accomplishments during the early 1930s:[68]

> In those years we were receiving government protection from the bandits who were after village resources. There were bandits who took our oxen and kidnapped people for ransom. Magistrate Ding Shuben was successful at killing

bandits. His effort to kill the bandits and keep them out of the village was seen as a good thing by us.

In Qian Kou [too] there was a bandit group known as the Two Lius [Liu Errui and Liu Youni]. These two people lived in Qian Kou. They were not professional bandits, but they were troublemakers. In the daytime they farmed their fields, but at night they secretly left our village and stole oxen from other villages. When Ding heard about this matter he sent a regiment to Qian Kou to seize these two people. Liu Youni was apprehended and killed by the Kuomintang troops.

What about warlord taxation? Armies passing by villages in various parts of Puyang sometimes issued demands for food and transport taxes. A crisis of this nature arose during the southern Hebei warlord brawls of 1927–28, when the rival militarists Zhang Zuolin, Yen Xishan, and Tan Fuchu ordered the Puyang County government to collect a surtax for troop support (the hated *tanpai*) from the villages. Qian Kou itself suffered no substantial losses from this warlord incursion. "The warlords actually never came to Qian Kou. They came only to parts of this sandy area,"[69] declares Liu Yufeng. The village was never occupied by the armies of rival militarists, and its peasant saltmakers did not have to repeatedly pay the cost of troop support, partly because it was located a long way from warlord power bases in Puyang and Daming.

Qian Kou's peasants were subject to entrepreneurial fees by tax brokers and tax farmers. Purchase agents and oil shop operators often had to pay a small tax on peanut transactions. This tax was paid to someone (peasants call him a hooligan) in the hire of Kuomintang government, who kept any extra money he collected.[70] This fee made a barely perceptible dent in household budgets, however, and was accepted without complaint.

In the autumn of l927, the Puyang government declared its intention of imposing a land surtax for the latest band of militarists to descend on the county[71] and charged the landlords in various districts with collecting this tax and turning it over to the authorities in Wen Xinggu. This tax, and the rumors about the corrupt fee practices surrounding its collection, displeased everyone in Qian Kou. Landlord Liu Yaobin had to pay the heaviest tax of all, as the surtax was to be levied on each *mu* of land and then, after a spate of peasant refusals, was taken on eight *mu* of grain land.[72] He and Zhao Shaofu were the tax collectors in Qian Kou.[73] Like the other landlords, they were in no hurry to place the surplus of the village in the hands of the Kuomintang group, for they had a large share of this surplus themselves, besides which, the goods, services, and exchanges of their fellow villagers were contributing to their advancement. When the peasants and saltmakers refused to pay the surtax, they looked the other way and had to be goaded into collecting it. "We felt it was unjust," says Zhao Wangni, "so in Qian Kou we never paid it."[74]

Many peasant saltmakers possess sharp memories of the mundane details of their daily elementary production and its role in enabling them to eke out their existence in the 1920s. They know whether the spate of local tax levies substituted penury for prosperity, and they can recall their household earnings in the years leading up to the outbreak of protest against the Changlu salt tax police. Liu Guoju, who was about twenty at the time of the saltmakers' struggle, gives an account of his annual household production at the time:[75]

In 1927 I had five *mu* of land. Three *mu* was sandy land. The other two were occupied by date trees. On the sandy land I grew both peanuts and sorghum. At that time, I also had twenty *mu* of salt land.

I started growing the peanuts around 1930. I got 150 *jin* of peanuts per *mu*, or 450 *jin* altogether. Some of the richer sandy lands in the village yielded 300 to 400 *jin* of peanuts per *mu*. We planted the peanuts mainly on the sandy lands.

For my 450 *jin* of peanuts I got a lot of money. I received one silver dollar for every fifteen *jin* of peanuts in 1930. I sold the peanuts to the landlords who owned the oil shops in our village. I also sold my peanuts in the markets of this area, especially Jingdian, where I got three cents more per *jin* than I got from Qian Kou's landlords. I sold the peanuts to marketgoers, and to peddlers. The peddlers baked the peanuts and resold them to people on the streets. Still, I had to pay a small travel fee for myself to go to Jingdian, so this cut into my three cent profit. This is why I sold seventy percent of my peanuts to the oil shops here in Qian Kou. I did this freely. It was my own choice. The landlords did not compel us to sell here. We just wanted to do it. The landlord oil shop operators paid us in silver, and sometimes in copper coins. Altogether I got about thirty silver dollars per year.

I also cultivated three *mu* of sorghum on the poor-quality land. I got 150 *jin* per *mu* on the average, and 200 *jin* per *mu* in a good harvest year. The sorghum crop yield was about average in the years 1927 to 1932. The sorghum sold for twenty coppers per *jin* in the market around 1930. So for one silver dollar you could purchase about 200 *jin* of sorghum. Hence we needed at least eighteen silver dollars for our yearly grain supply.

In 1930 my two brothers and I still had the twenty *mu* of salt land. On this land, we had four small salt ponds, and one huge pond. We put earth into the big pond to mix it with water. Then we let the salt water pass into the smaller ponds. When the water evaporated, the salt was left over. This is how we produced earth salt.

I remember that we worked the ponds in June and July, and we shared the salt harvest from these months. We got 200 *jin* per day per pond. The four ponds could produce 800 to 1,000 *jin* of salt per day and we got about 50,000 *jin* per year from the four in all. In fact I got 25,000 *jin* because only my elder brother and I worked these ponds.

We got two cents per *jin* for our earth salt. We could get one silver dollar for about 300 to 400 *jin* of salt. On the average we earned fifty silver dollars a year, and in some years I got as many as thirty silver dollars for myself from our salt harvest.

I sold this salt in Qian Kou to peddlers who came here from Du Dian village and Jingdian market.

My parents were the proprietors of a clothing business in Jingdian market town. . . . They earned about one hundred silver dollars a year from this business. My parents lived in Qian Kou, but they rented a house in Jingdian to carry on their trade. My grandfather had this business ever since the Qing dynasty.

I also had two *mu* of date tree land in 1930, with fifty date trees. I got 800 *jin* of dates per year. I sold the dates in the village street markets . . . I was too busy to sell in the big market in Jingdian. So I began to run a wholesale business from my home in Qian Kou, and I sold the dates to peddlers who retailed them in Jingdian, Liangmen, and other places around here. The date merchants drove big carts full of dates to these markets.

I got forty cents per *jin* for the dates. On the average I was able to make about fifteen silver dollars per year before the War of Resistance. Date production was good then, and harvests were above average, even better than now [1987].

When I was fifteen there was a small drought here in Qian Kou. This was in 1927. But we still could produce the earth salt that year. At that time, I also produced nitrate on my salt land. I made it in the cold weather months.

In the winter months the nitrate harvest was very high. I got 500 *jin* per day, and 10,000 *jin* per year. My elder brother and I shared one pond, and we sold our nitrate harvest to peddlers. The nitrate we produced and sold was used for leather treatment, and as an additive to animal foods. It was also used to produce an eye medicine for people. But most of it went to the leather factories in Puyang, Neihuang, and Hua county.

The nitrate sold at 3,000 coppers per five hundred *jin*. We got seventy silver dollars each year for it. I split it with my brother, so each of us got thirty-five silver dollars. The income from nitrate production was steady before the salt-makers' struggle, and before the arrival of the Japanese.

On the twenty *mu* of salt land there was some reed land. I cultivated this reed land to get the materials to build house roofs and mats. Both of my brothers and I cooperated in this endeavor, and we [each] got ten silver dollars a year.

Virtually everybody in this village managed to pay the land tax. We paid the tax directly to the Kuomintang county government, though sometimes a tax collector came here.

Liu Guoju paid the following taxes:

LAND AND PRODUCTION	TAX
3 *mu* of peanut land	1/2 silver dollar
3 *mu* of sorghum land	2–3 silver dollars
20 *mu* of salt land	10 silver dollars
2 *mu* of date tree land	none

| nitrate land | none (because it is same as salt land) |
| reed land | none (same as salt land) |

Total tax liability: at most 14 silver dollars

The essential requirements for the yearly welfare of Liu Guoju's family were as follows:

ITEMS OF NECESSITY	COST
1. Basic food grains: 2,000 *jin* of good-quality wheat, or 4,000 to 6,000 *jin* of sorghum and husks (they rarely purchased wheat grains)	30–35 silver dollars
2. Salt	0
3. Oil	1
4. Vegetables	6
5. Matches	1
6. Clothes	2
7. Pond construction and repair	3
8. Implements and fertilizer	3
9. Emergency grain storage and medical needs	4
Total	55 silver dollars

The 55 silver dollars Liu needed to stay at subsistence level includes an additional 4 silver dollars to provide basic grain reserves (as a cushion against unexpected rottage while in storage, upward price swings, warlord requisitions, and against sickness). All in all, Liu needed 69 silver dollars to cover both taxes and survival needs. The yearly income from Liu's production came to about 117.25 silver dollars:

ITEMS OF PRODUCTION	
Peanuts	30 silver dollars
Grain 450 *jin*	2.25
Earth salt	25
Nitrate	35
Date trees	15
Reed land	10
Total	117.25 silver dollars
	−69
	48.25 silver dollars

Liu Guoju's yearly income was considerably above what he needed to keep his family of four at a tolerable level of existence in the early 1930s. Actually, the Liu household enjoyed a substantial profit.

Born in 1904, in the last years of the Qing dynasty, Liu Shiyin was a participant in the Puyang saltmakers' struggle of March, 1932. He has reconstructed his family's economic history:[76]

When I was fifteen we had fifteen *mu* of land. There were eight persons in my family then: father, mother, grandfather and grandmother, three sisters, and me. Of this fifteen *mu* of land, three *mu* was crop land, and sown to wheat. Twelve *mu* was sandy land and sown to red beans, peanuts, and millet.

I got 200 *jin* per *mu* on the wheat land. On the twelve *mu* of sandy land I got 150 *jin* of peanuts per *mu,* and I usually planted at least five *mu* to peanuts. Ever since I had been young we had grown peanuts. In a bumper year my peanut harvest yield was 250 *jin.* The average yearly harvest yield was about 150 *jin.* I sold my peanuts in the village oil shops, or in the markets outside of Qian Kou. The peanut oil went to Chu Wang. I sometimes sold directly to the oil shops, but the purchase agents more often brought the buyers to my home to buy the peanuts. A lot of buyers for oil shops came to my home through the introduction of the purchase agents. They came from Lu village, Huai Di, and Wen Xinggu. In one year I could earn thirty to forty silver dollars from these sales.

We also had two salt ponds. I worked the salt ponds while my father tilled the croplands. We did not *fenjia.* I had no brothers, so there was no reason to separate and divide the property. I started making salt when I was about fifteen or sixteen, in the ninth year of the Republic. In that year we did not have enough crop land to carry us through. There was a big drought that year, and the crops were affected. Since our family was expanding we had more people to work. So we began working the salt lands, and opened up two ponds near the reed land. This land originally belonged to us. Our salt production fluctuated year by year. In a good year we could earn thirty to forty silver dollars.

Our salt ponds were far away from the village. The salt police never came this far, and did not destroy our ponds. Still, in 1932 I went to Puyang town to fight them because they would not permit us to make earth salt. The salt sold well before the police arrived in Qian Kou, and we still found ways to sell it after they attacked our market. The peddlers came to my ponds to buy the salt. There were also purchase agents for the earth salt, and some were from our village. Zhao Dekun and Liu Sandi were agents. Both were landless. They spent their time introducing others to buy our salt.

I also produced nitrate. I earned thirty silver dollars per year on the nitrate. I produced about 5,000 *jin* per year. I sold it to peddlers and they carried it to Handan, Lin county and places to the west. It was used to treat leather. In Lin county they also used it as a fertilizer and an animal food additive.

On our 12 *mu* of sandy land there stood many date trees. We earned about forty silver dollars per year from our date sales. There were petty thieves who pilfered our dates. Most of them were from our village. I watched my trees closely. But when I could not watch and turned my back the little thieves got them. I did not mind if the thieves only stole a little. They had no date trees of their own, and they were poor people.

On our reed land I made about ten silver dollars each year. I also had a few small oxen. Most of the poor peasants had oxen to plow their lands, and we cooperated in raising the oxen. Our oxen could eat the grass near the wild land by the Nitrate River.

Liu Shiyin's taxes totaled fourteen silver dollars (three on three *mu* of wheat land; five to six on the twelve *mu* of sandy land; none on the salt land, which was so far to the south that the Kuomintang county government had not detected it; none on the nitrate or date production; and about five silver dollars on ten *mu* of reed land). With an annual income of approximately 145 silver dollars, Liu and his father had 131 silver dollars left for basic family necessities, which for their family of eight required no more than 94—leaving a profit of about 37 silver dollars.

These two respondents were typical of Qian Kou's "poor peasants," *not* the 25 percent of the peasantry categorized as middle peasant and rich peasant in the 1947 land revolution. From their economic histories, it seems reasonable to surmise that the majority of Qian Kou's salt-making households were in fine shape before the Changlu tax police infringed on the village.

The economic dynamism of Qian Kou, bringing new benefits to the village majority, was not weakened by the famine of 1921.[77] Its people survived by a combination of short-term in-region migration and salt making. The latter development made emigration to Manchuria unnecessary for all but a few of the poorest villagers and within a few years opened the door to "illicit prosperity" for the majority. Those who did migrate in 1921 returned to Qian Kou to recover in 1922.[78] Until the Henan famine of 1942 compelled eighty-six families to sell 320 *mu* of land and forty-eight families to migrate, mostly to Shanxi,[79] virtually no one in Qian Kou died of starvation.[80]

The only disaster in the northwestern quadrant of Puyang was in 1937, when summer's flood waters damaged the autumn crops, brought salt making to a temporary halt, and turned peasants into beggars and bandits.[81] But salt making in Qian Kou did not cease altogether; half a season of pond work was salvaged, and the salt harvest was only slightly below average. Although some of the poorest saltmakers migrated to Guizifu,* Manshantou, and Zhengzhou, many of them returned to Qian Kou in time to plant the autumn crops.[82]

By 1930 about three-quarters of Qian Kou's peasants had to purchase half of their food grains in Jingdian sorghum markets,[83] and there was a

---

*Peasants coined informal colloquial names for many of the places to which they migrated in the 1930s, so that it is not always possible to find these destinations on formal maps.

great deal of envy of the seven grain-rich landlords, whose wheat harvests went exclusively to their own grain storage facilities or to extravillage markets. The villagers had their squabbles over ownership of the reed lands, land tax rates, and crop pilfering. Liu Yunxing, a smallholder with thirty *mu* of cropland, twelve *mu* of sandy land, and five *mu* of date tree land in 1930, remembers that landlords were the targets of occasional petty theft, especially after 1934. The poor "only stole the grain crops of the landlords. They almost never stole the crops of other poor folk."[84] These crop thieves, according to Liu Shiyin, sometimes were "members of the poor who had been harmed by the landlords and could not retaliate openly. They got even by stealing the crops from landlord fields. Li Liangli once stole Liu Yaobin's grain crops, and was caught by Hua Zhong, Liu's hired hand from Maji village. Li was fined one silver dollar. Li Liangli's family paid this fine by borrowing money from Liu Jituan. Li paid back the loan by income earned from making salt."[85]

For the most part, the landlords in the Liu or the Zhao lineages never squeezed peasants to the point where they could not provide for their families. Most of the smallholding peasants had taken up peanut production and salt making. By 1930 the village had no more than ten hired hands and only a few tenants. So critical was the labor shortage that the wealthy landlords had to hire some ninety men from other villages to help bring in the June wheat harvest and to assist them with small jobs, such as treating date trees and carting peanut oil to market.[86] Qian Kou's landlords did engage in small forms of usury, but peasants used loans wisely and relied on their salt-making and salt-trading activities to free themselves from debt quickly. In the fifteen years following the 1921 famine peasants were able to secure loans on reasonable terms from landlords in their lineages and invariably paid back these loans within a short period.[87]

Landlords honored the old gleaning rights of the landless poor and tolerated a great deal of crop pilfering. Liu Yaobin and Zhao Shaofu both owned guns, but they did not hire armed guards to watch their crops. Disputes over missing crops were settled without violence;[88] outsiders were never asked to intervene, and it was rare for a dispute to develop even to the point of a verbal shouting match or a fine.

In short, Qian Kou was a village in which most people were growing prosperous together. The practical importance of Qian Kou's shared economic advancement overrode the significance of peasant envy of the new streams of landlord wealth or resentment about landlord misdeeds.[89] Despite county government claims on Qian Kou, and despite the fact that landlords still owned the lion's share of premium cropland, most of Qian Kou's peasants were doing better than their parents had. Many peasant saltmakers had money to save and spend, and they spent it on colorful weddings, decent burials, and local festivals and fairs.[90] By 1930 many Qian Kou peasants had become esteemed consumers who used their surpluses to purchase farm implements, foreign clothing, and presents for their children. Here were up-and-coming rural folk enjoying newfound prosperity.

COLLECTIVE PROTEST AND COLLECTIVE ACTION

The catalyst mobilizing Qian Kou's peasant saltmakers for collective protest was the regional arm of the revenue force of the central government—not the claims of local Puyang government, or the warlords, environmental contortions, or landlord injustice. Arriving in Puyang in greater numbers around 1931, the Changlu salt tax police quickly defined Qian Kou as a thorn in the side of the Kuomintang Ministry of Finance. At first the police said they wanted only to tax the ponds, but shortly thereafter they threatened to destroy them. This threat angered villagers more than anything else.

The dry white bed of the Nitrate River was a vast welfare plot that poorer village households could fall back on in hungry years; peasants had also come to regard this land as being bound up with the community's right to get rich. By the outbreak of the Puyang saltmakers' struggle 93 percent of the families in Qian Kou had opened up a few salt ponds on the alkaline common lands along the Nitrate River,[91] and three out of four peasant households were deriving 20 to 50 percent of their income from earth salt.[92] Poor peasants, saltmakers, purchase agents, and rich peasants combined forces to wage a collective defense of their "common interest."

The salt tax police made three assaults on this interest in the years 1927 to 1932. The first came around 1928, when the police rode into Qian Kou on horseback and warned the village chief that they intended to arrest anyone making earth salt. Liu Shiren, a veteran of the 1932 struggle, remembers how the village chief in 1928 established a pattern of community resistance to this intrusion:[93]

> The salt police sometimes came to Qian Kou to arrest someone or to stop us from making salt. At first they did not come often; eventually they came here four or five times a year. In the beginning the police asked the chief of the village, Liu Shigong, to urge us to stop making earth salt. At other times they came to us directly at our salt ponds to warn us against making salt. Although the village chief was on our side, he was forced by the police to agree to stop us from making salt. He promised them he would help them. But after the police left the village, and the village chief realized they were gone, he just turned his head and allowed us to make salt. Liu Shigong was not a landlord, though he had some relationship with the comparatively wealthy households. Liu had fifty *mu* of crop land, and more than twenty *mu* of salt land.

In 1929, saltmaker Zhao Kunni became the village chief.[94] At first Zhao Kunni followed the example of Li Shigong, feigning collaboration with the salt police but refusing to institute a crackdown on his fellow saltmakers. Discovering on several surprise visits that he produced earth salt himself, the police arrested him and took him to Puyang town for arraignment and interrogation, during which he was severely beaten. He died shortly afterwards.[95] This news shocked Qian Kou saltmakers, and for a few months the villge leaders did not dare deal face to face with the police.

Throughout much of 1930 the police sent patrols to Qian Kou, but they seldom found anyone to seize. The villagers pursued several strategies of avoidance. At first, on seeing that the police were coming, they dropped their tools and scattered in all directions. By the summer of 1930 peasants had adopted a more organized, cleverly conceived strategy. Partly in collaboration with peddlers from Du Dian, they positioned spotter teams along the outskirts of the Nitrate River lands and, when signaled the police were coming, promptly abandoned their salt ponds and ran to their peanut and melon fields. "When the salt police came," Ma Xinxi recalls, "we usually pretended to be tilling our croplands. This fooled them, and so they sometimes passed us by."[96] Even so, in this avoidance phase the police destroyed the salt ponds of Zhao Liancheng and Zhao Ermu.

In 1930, a contingent of the Changlu salt police came to enforce a tax of one silver dollar per salt pond in the twenty villages along the edge of the Nitrate River: a tax on top of the Puyang County government's salt land tax.* The police, who had established a beachhead in Jingdian market, enlisted several entrepreneurial tax collectors from Jingdian, who paid the Kuomintang county government for the privilege of collecting the pond tax and in return were allowed to pocket any money they collected in excess of the estimated tax quota. (The power of Duara's model is evident here.) Guo Lanyuan, a salt pond tax collector in 1930, came to Qian Kou often. According to Zhao Tianbao, the saltmakers paid the pond tax to Guo Lanyuan in 1931, then paid it a second time in the same year.[97] But when Guo came around for the third time, Liu Yufeng, Zhao Gaiming, Zhao Heming, Liu Ruiren, and Zhao Hezhu greeted him with an angry refusal. "We did not care if he threatened us," Zhao Tianbao recalls. "The regular Changlu salt police did not accompany him to Qian Kou, so we told him we should not have to pay any tax on the salt ponds. We argued with him, and told him the ponds were made by our own labor."[98]

The five saltmakers led a delegation of their comrades to argue with Guo Lanyuan and threatened to throw him out of Qian Kou if he ever showed

*Strictly speaking, the Changlu police should not have been involved with enforcement of local salt pond taxation because their mission was prohibition of any salt production. But in both Puyang and Hua County they cooperated with the county tax authorities in 1929 and 1930, before the Kuomintang Finance Ministry's prohibition forces took over the policing of salt production in 1931 and 1932.

his face again. Zhao Tianbao, who witnessed this argument, informs us, "The Jingdian tax collector had come here twice. We paid twice. Then we gathered and decided we would not pay again. So the next time the collector came we organized a delegation to confront him. After this, the tax collector went away and was too frightened to come back." At this point the Changlu tax police sent a four-man patrol to Qian Kou, only to find the five saltmakers, led by Liu Yufeng, waiting at the eastern front of the village, flanked by five hundred other Qian Kou saltmakers. Massively outnumbered, the police departed the village.[99]

The first open clash with the salt police came in the salt-making season of 1931, when they commenced raiding exercises to destroy the ponds. Liu Yufeng organized the salt-making households within Qian Kou to join together in groups of ten to prevent the police from filling in their ponds. Liu Shiren remembers, "Each of these groups of ten had a head. It was up to the head of the group to warn us when the police were coming to destroy our salt ponds."[100] These small groups brought their salt spades to do battle with the police at the pond sites, and over several months Qian Kou's saltmakers successfully turned back the police. Although thirty to forty saltmakers suffered pond damage or destruction, more than half the village went unscathed. Many of the old saltmakers boast that the police either damaged their ponds only slightly or did not even touch them, a fact they attribute to their resistance tactics and, in some cases, to their ability to construct ponds far up the back reaches of the Nitrate River, where the police rarely ventured.

Elated with this success, in late 1931 Qian Kou's saltmakers teamed up with their counterparts in Dian Dong to launch a broad-scale counterattack on the police.[101] For over a year, the peddlers from Dian Dong, along with those from Du Dian, had informed the heads of the Qian Kou resistance teams when the police were coming,[102] allowing the saltmakers to flee the village, don their false "peasant faces," or prepare for hand-to-hand combat. Now about one hundred saltmakers gathered to chase the police out of both villages.

Out of the concerted action with Dian Dong's saltmakers grew Qian Kou's struggle against the Kuomintang Changlu salt police in Puyang town in the spring of 1932. Most of the county's saltmakers were not organized to wage sustained collective resistance to tax agents or take the initiative against the police, observes Liu Yufeng, who was in touch with peasants, saltmakers, and peddlers in twenty villages along the Nitrate River and in the various earth salt markets in the vicinity of Puyang town.[103] In contrast, by 1931, Qian Kou's peasant saltmakers gained a countywide reputation for protracted collective action: for organizing the salt-making households one by one, for forming ten-family resistance squads, and finally for forming a village alliance to protect the common lands from police raids—the forerunner of the Qian Kou Saltmakers' Association.

The association was not yet connected to county- or regional-level politics, nor was it truly insurrectionary. But in early 1932, when the central government's finance ministry began applying maximum pressure on the Changlu Salt Inspectorate to generate ever greater revenue, Qian Kou saltmakers began acting with their Puyang counterparts. Increasingly, they sponsored popular rallies, demonstrations, and marches against the police. Less than six months after their successful mobilization with Dian Dong village, the Qian Kou saltmakers were approached by a small delegation from Cheng Guan village in Puyang town,[104] appealing for help against the salt police stationed inside Puyang town. The protest leadership pondered this dangerous proposal with great caution. Liu Yufeng, Zhao Gaiming, and others sent Zhao Ertou from Qian Kou to Cheng Guan, where the saltmakers gave Zhao a banquet and described the strength of their own forces and their contacts with other Puyang saltmakers. The peasants and saltmakers of Qian Kou and Cheng Guan fixed a date on which they would launch a large-scale collective march on the police headquarters in Puyang town and present their demands for police eviction to the Kuomintang magistrate.

On 17 March 1932, two days before the march on the town was scheduled, Liu Yufeng called a meeting of Qian Kou saltmakers at the village's main temple. Ma Xinxi, whose father went to Puyang town to fight the salt police, recalls, "A few days before the march, Liu Yufeng gathered the saltmakers here at the Guanyeh *miao*. The peasants and saltmakers often held their meetings in this temple in those days, and people in Qian Kou went to this temple to enlist the support of the war god."[105]

Liu Yufeng asked the heads of Qian Kou's ten-family self-defense squads to arm their members for the march. The main goal was to attack the Changlu tax police headquarters on North Street—or so it was said. An intriguing rumor swirled along the village grapevine (what Geertz has termed one of the intimacies of local knowledge).[106] Liu Yufeng and Liu Hansheng had secretly obtained permission from the Kuomintang-appointed magistrate for the march and, moreover, had gotten his promise not to intervene.[107]

Two hundred stalwart men, mostly between twenty and forty years old, left the village to march with Liu Yufeng. They were joined by beggars in nearby villages—people recently thrown out of work by police raids on their ponds. But the main *rural* force of "rioters" joining Qian Kou's rebels came from semipeasants and peddlers in Dian Dong, Wen Xinggu, Xinggu, Xi Shuipo, and the string of salt-making villages around Xi Shuipo, along the walls of Puyang town.

This rebel troupe joined with the saltmakers from Cheng Guan and Sha Wo to storm the Changlu police headquarters on 19 March 1932. Armed with spears, spades, and shovels, they followed Liu Yufeng and Yang Jingcai to attack the police station, to face off with the public security forces, and to engage the Kuomintang magistrate. The demonstrators made it clear they had not come to Puyang town to warn the police or to conduct cordial talks with the Kuomintang magistrate. Liu Yufeng shouted to the assembled multitude, "Those of you who fear death should go back!"[108] Joining with beggars from Cheng Guan and West Gate village, Liu Yufeng and the saltmakers destroyed the police living quarters, then charged up North Street to meet the public security forces. They presented the Kuomintang magistrate with a short list of demands. What it called for, instantly and finally, was that those in charge of local government detach Puyang from the state-making scheme of the Kuomintang center. In essence, all three of its demands constituted a challenge to the *modus operandi* of the centralizing Nationalist government:

1: Honor Our Right to Make Earth Salt Without Government Intervention

2: Stand Behind Our Right to Market Salt Freely

3: Send the Changlu Salt Police Out of Our County[109]

So little did the saltmakers trust the local Kuomintang government *on this issue* that they took every precaution to prepare Qian Kou against political retaliation even after the magistrate's announced support for the three basic demands. This proved to be a wise decision.

In the days following the march, Qian Kou's saltmakers returned to the village to celebrate their victory over the police. The saltmakers' association sponsored a series of plays and operas, including a selection from *The Romance of the Three Kingdoms*. Liu Tieyu, one of the long-time saltmakers in Qian Kou, remembers that everyone paid one silver dollar to the association to help cover the cost of the operas performed down by the Xiao River salt market. "Many people came here from Wen Xinggu, Dian Dong, Hua village, and Maji village to attend the opera celebration in 1932. There were about ten thousand people in attendance over the four days of celebration."[110]

The Kuomintang-appointed magistrate sent some seventy armed members of the Puyang Civil Defense Corps to stop the celebration, and he threatened the saltmakers and ordered them to go back into their villages. Zhao Yungfu, who had gone to Puyang town with Liu Yufeng as a Qian Kou delegate, recalls that the saltmakers—many whom were armed with handguns and hunting rifles—defied these local defense forces and dared them to open fire.[111] They did not dare.

The leaders of Qian Kou's Saltmakers' Association had urged its members to bring any weapons they could find to the Xiao River salt market celebration and to borrow weapons if necessary. Zhao Xingzheng, a veteran of the 1932 struggle and a participant in the victory celebration, took this advice to heart. "I borrowed a rifle from a relative," he recalls. "I told him I needed it to hunt rabbits. But I really borrowed it for the purpose of defending our victory celebration against the salt police. Many of us got weapons in this way."[112] Because mainly rich peasant and landlord households could afford to own firearms in the early 1930s, many of the saltmakers borrowed weapons from better-off villagers with whom they shared lineage bonds and friendships.[113]

Although denouncing the "rebellion" to Hebei provincial officials, the Puyang magistrate decided to recall the civil defense corps, leaving Qian Kou to celebrate its independence from the centralizing state.[114] The politics of this small place, plus the national crisis in Kuomintang-CCP relations, combined to make the magistrate refrain from enforcing the ambitions of the Nationalist government's salt administration. The peasant saltmakers' movement in Qian Kou was not only armed but also intermingled with the transcounty collective protest forming in Puyang and the border area. For another thing, Liu Yufeng and Qian Kou's peasant salters were in touch with educated, wealthy, esteemed Daming Normal School graduates like Zhao Jibin, Liu Hansheng, and Wang Congwu, whose connections to elite families and modern education legitimated their role in ordering the ongoing community protest.[115] Moreover, the Puyang County Kuomintang was stacked with local people who knew and sympathized with these local Communist leaders and with the local saltmakers, and they voiced opposition to the use of the civil defense corps to stop the local folk from commemorating their collective performance against the police.[116] Finally, painfully aware that no one, including the local Kuomintang, knew whether the Nationalists or Communists were going to win the struggle for national power, Puyang's Kuomintang power holders prudently cautioned of the potential incrimination from harmful interference in the celebrations.

THE CHINESE COMMUNIST PARTY IN QIAN KOU

Zhao Jibin, the son of a late Qing scholar, was born and raised in Qian Kou. In 1923 he ventured off to Daming County to study in the Eleventh Middle School, and after graduating he went to Beijing, where he was influenced by tides of the May Fourth Movement. His initial conception of revolution came from his early connections with the New Cultural Movement (*Xin Wenhua Huodong*), to which he became attracted in 1924. Two years later Zhao Jibin was introduced to the CCP by Feng Pinyi, in the Daming Seventh Normal School, and from this time he used his summer holidays to carry out village investigations around Qian Kou.[117]

Zhao Jibin's house became the scene of intense discussions about the local agricultural economy. Zhao came to recognize that Qian Kou was not part of an immiserated peasant society. In reference to Qian Kou of 1927, he wrote later, "At that time, within this sandy area, a village such as our Thousand Crossings was not impoverished. On the contrary, it was prosperous. Here grain production was of secondary importance. The middle peasants and poor peasants . . . depended on salt making, nitrate making, alkali production, date trees, and the planting of peanuts on barren land. In this situation, anyone who had labor power could make a living."[118]

It was in this prosperous economic climate that Zhao Jibin began his career in agrarian politics. In the spring of 1927, right after the Northern Expeditionary Army reached Daming, Zhao joined the Kuomintang and became chief of the Puyang Propaganda Bureau.[119] He returned to Qian Kou when the army of the Republic occupied the Puyang Kuomintang headquarters in the county seat. With his Qian Kou associates, Liu Hansheng and Zhao Siyun, along with Wang Jianjian and Wang Congwu and Wang Zhouru of Hua village, Zhao Jibin carried out investigations of local bullies and evil gentry in the area of Jingdian market and Wen Xinggu. They posted their findings on gentry misdeeds on the village walls and reported them to the Puyang County government.

Just at this moment, the July 15 counterrevolution struck Wuhan, shredding the national alliance between the Kuomintang and the CCP. The Communist-oriented members of the Kuomintang in Puyang County were thrown into turmoil. Toward the end of summer Zhao Jibin and Liu Dashan went to Xinxiang, where they encountered Liu Dafeng, a CCP member involved with the Daming Normal School student movement who also was active in peasant politics.

Zhao Jibin, Liu Dashan, and several other young intellectuals formally withdrew from the Puyang Kuomintang and retired to Qian Kou. In October, they set up the Puyang County Committee of the CCP, establishing its first branch in Qian Kou village.[120] Two other branches were established, one in Hua village and one in Jingdian market. The first secretary of the CCP Qian Kou branch was Liu Dafeng. Zhao Jibin was the chief of propaganda, and Liu Hansheng and Liu Dashan were in charge of general affairs, including recruitment. Owing to a CCP Central Committee decision to allow only workers and peasants to serve as local party secretaries, Liu Dafeng stepped down and was replaced by Liu Yufeng, a "poor peasant" who was discovering prosperity through salt making and peanut purchasing.

To some extent, the profile of CCP leadership reflected local prosperity. Zhao Jibin was the son of an important minor gentry figure; Wang Congwu, who was to become the key CCP leader of the Triprovincial Saltmakers League, was from rich peasant stock; Liu Yufeng was a purchase agent involved in multilevel market dealings. Thus, although the CCP's base was made up of peasant saltmakers, its leadership came from the better-off, better-educated members of the local market community, in which Qian Kou was positioned and through which the party leaders would organize collective resistance.

In the two decades ahead, these men attempted to lead the peasants of Qian Kou in class struggle, disaster relief campaigns, the Anti-Japanese War, and land redistribution, but the party's first real success in gaining a village following came in 1932–33, during and after the saltmakers' struggle with the Changlu tax police. Prior to this struggle, they had overlooked the market interest of the country people.

In 1927, the Puyang CCP began its first experiment with class struggle. Zhao Jibin and Liu Hansheng organized a peasants' association in Qian Kou and fifteen other villages[121] to unite poor peasants, tenants, and hired hands to help one another with house repairs and field work and to launch work strikes against landlords. In Qian Kou the peasants' association went further. When landlord Zhao Lanyi died, for example, and no one in the village would help bury him, the association humiliated the family by sending Zhao Retuo, a poor peasant who was looked down on by most of the wealthy households, to take charge of the funeral.[122]

The Qian Kou CCP branch attempted to move the struggle against the rich to a new stage when, in the fall of 1927, the Puyang County government announced a heavy land tax to provision a warlord army and put the county's landlords in charge of collection. Landlords Liu Yaobin and Zhao Shaofu, the tax collectors in Qian Kou, were supposed to work with Cai Hongbin, the chief of the Puyang County Civil Defense Corps in Wen Xinggu. But Liu and Zhao were reluctant to collect the tax from their fellow villagers, for such an act implied that they too were obliged to pay. They called on Cai Hongbin for help. Cai's civil defense corps arrested two villagers, but the peasants' association intercepted them and freed them from custody on the road to Puyang County jail.[123] Somewhat crestfallen, Qian Kou's landlords accepted the small victory this action signified for the CCP.

In the winter of 1927–28, Zhao Jibin, Liu Hansheng, Liu Yufeng, and Zhao Xizheng led a dozen members of the peasant association to audit the accounts of the Wen Xinggu tax office.[124] Their investigation revealed that Cai Hongbin had increased the land tax to cover his personal living expenses. Admitting his guilt, Cai Hongbin agreed to reduce the tax. At the same time, however, he sought out landlord Liu Yunzhi from Liu Xinggu village and landlord Wen Zhenggong from Wen Xinggu, who had affiliations with the Kuomintang, to enlist their assistance in bringing a charge of sedition against the peasants' association. These landlords took the charge to the Kuomintang Puyang government.

Then intrigue followed intrigue. The peasants' association charged Cai with corruption and, with the help of a few secret CCP members who sat on the Puyang County Kuomintang Committee, won the case. Cai Hongbin was arrested and detained for trial. However, Liu Yunzhi and Wen Zhenggong persuaded Cai's nephew, Cai Zhaoling (a CCP member), to betray the party by handing over secret documents on party development in western Puyang.[125] These documents subsequently were presented as evidence of a CCP-planned revolt against the county government, forcing the local

Kuomintang "friends" of the CCP in Puyang to go along with the attack on the peasant association and the subsequent crackdown and arrest of CCP members. This ugly incident notwithstanding, the CCP continued to enjoy the protection of local Kuomintang sympathizers. The incident was an aberration to the larger pattern of secret coexistence and live-and-let-live political relations between the two local groups.[126]

In 1929 the Qian Kou members of the CCP had planned a mass meeting to celebrate the victory against Cai Hongbin and the landlord tax collaborators. This Wen Xinggu Temple meeting was surrounded by rumors of Communist-inspired poor peasant attacks on an infamous gentry figure and by talk of peasants' association mockery of landlords who had lent a hand in county tax collection.

The Puyang magistrate instructed the civil defense corps of Puyang, Neihuang, and Hua counties to join forces with the local guards of Puyang's big landlords for an attack on the Wen Xinggu meeting, set for February 15. This multicounty defense force, led by landlords Liu Yunzhi and Wen Zhiggong, surrounded the temple and ordered the crowd to disperse.[127] Du Jingsheng, the head of the Hua village guards, led his men into the temple grounds and opened fire, killing several people.[128] The civil defense corps rushed to the front and arrested Zhao Jibin, Liu Hansheng, Wang Zhouru, and Li Dashan, all of whom were detained for several months. Only Wang Congwu and Liu Yufeng escaped.

The next day, Wang Congwu led a contingent of peasants from several villages to attack the landlord forces in Hua village,[129] where they seized twelve guns from the local defense corps and took Du Jingsheng's wife hostage. Du led a hundred local guards to surround Hua village. Hand-to-hand fighting began at noon and lasted until nightfall. The result was a massacre of the peasant activists and a setback for the local Communists: Wang Deyun, He Rewai, and He Qingfa and his son, all peasant association cadres, died in the fight.

The Hua village CCP members had no time to summon reinforcements from Qian Kou; and the majority of peasant saltmakers in Qian Kou were reluctant to rally to the cause of the peasant victims of the landlord-supported civil corps massacre. Over the next two years, the CCP Hebei Provincial Committee sent down several party activists to take advantage of the "growing divisions" within rural Puyang society. They invariably failed. Liu Yufeng reflects on the CCP's failure in this period: "Why were the masses so timid that nobody wanted to participate in the rebellion at this time? In this period, the life of the masses was getting better. They could earn several dollars each day by making private salt. It was unrealistic to start a rebellion in this situation."[130]

The violent intervention of the finance ministry's salt police threatened the shared market interest of peasants in Qian Kou and gave the CCP the opportunity to organize their ongoing collective actions to defend a vital community resource. The first happy time for the CCP followed on its alignment with the saltmakers against the police in 1932. Nearly two-thirds of the thirty-three men who joined the party in Qian Kou between 1927 and 1937 were saltmakers who in one way or another had contributed to the struggle of 1932.

No doubt peasants saw their protest as a defense of essential community resources and did not have a grand picture of the CCP's national power goals. Even so, Qian Kou was a village of "rational peasants," to use Popkin's term, and both peasants and party leaders were aware that its multipronged market adaptation, involving the "simple commodity production" of salt and nitrate, boded ill for the Kuomintang Finance Ministry plan to accumulate salt revenues.[131] The CCP gained a foothold in Qian Kou, and scores of other salt land villages, by championing rural people whose fear of losing their newfound prosperity led them to participate in collective antistate action.

By July of 1932 Liu Yufeng and Wang Congwu had become border region celebrities. Over the next year they led saltmakers from Qian Kou, Hua village, and Maji village to join with the salt people of Hua, Dongming, Qingfeng, and Nanle counties against the salt tax police. They attracted so much attention that Liu Chih, the governor of Henan Province, and Pang Bingxun, a Kuomintang army commander, led regiments to Puyang.[132] After killing several people in Jingdian, a small contingent of these Kuomintang forces came to Qian Kou briefly to seal the homes of Liu Hansheng and a few other CCP members. Throughout the next four years, the peasant saltmakers of Qian Kou remained united in their struggle for autonomy and prosperity, and the CCP gained credibility with the majority of villagers by presenting itself as the pro-market party. This movement strengthened the CCP in the larger Nitrate River area, so that in 1933 local party leaders were able to organize tax resistance in Taiping village, where they also compelled landlord Lian Jingbang to lend grain to the poor during the Spring Festival of 1934.[133] The saltmakers' association of Qian Kou developed a number of services, including house repairs, tax resistance information, and burial assistance.[134] This associational mode of politics lasted into the period of the Anti-Japanese War.

By 1930 the peasants of Qian Kou had begun to attain a standard of living that more than satisfied their short-run material needs. Relieved of the constant fear of food scarcity and death,[135] Qian Kou's peasant salt producers were less inclined to perceive market gains of other households as their own losses. It seems that their shared status diluted envy, suspicion, and cutthroat competition enough to provide the CCP with a favorable economic environment in which to organize them for political action.[136] The party activists could point out that the struggle against the salt tax police was to preserve the gains of all families, and the strength of this appeal partly explains why Qian Kou's saltmakers, including those not directly harmed by the police, participated in concerted family-based actions to resist the intrusive centralizing tax state. This modest prosperity also led to an increase in cultural activities (such as operas) promotive of a greater sense of, and pride in, community, making collective popular action with party guidance all the more possible.

The peasants used surpluses to maintain the cross-generational continuity of their families, a process that involved the redistribution of family lands among male offspring.[137] The gains of Qian Kou's peasant saltmakers made it possible for their marriageable sons to stay in the village and start up a "junior line."[138] Brothers, uncles, and cousins participated in plowshare arrangements, started up crop watch associations, and pooled their resources for salt pond development. Qian Kou's peasants' keen interest in associational politics, which continued well into the period of maximum Kuomintang state penetration, enabling the CCP to build up its base in Qian Kou, resulted in village solidarity and provided a convenient social grid for sustaining collective resistance.[139]

Continued activism on behalf of the common interest was also facilitated by the elite-derived educational sophistication of Qian Kou's young communist intellectuals. Zhao Jibin and Liu Hansheng hailed from traditionally rich and refined village families, who now had a stake in the salt market.[140] Qian Kou's school had been around since Qing times; the Liu and Zhao lineages had produced scholars who had been involved in advising Qing state officials. This political training, which could be sustained only by an economy strong enough to underwrite the next generation of advisors, carried over into the Republican era. The young intellectuals of Zhao Jibin's generation were preparing themselves for positions in the Nationalist government before the Seventh Normal School in Daming was temporarily closed down by warlord occupation of 1925,[141] then captured by the Kuomintang Blue Shirts in 1932. These developments prompted Zhao Jibin and Liu Hansheng to leave Daming and go back to Qian Kou village to begin propaganda work among the peasants attending night classes in a "free school."[142]

These young Communists had sacrificed family wealth and risked family status to espouse revolutionary ideas and were committed to using those ideas to liberate Qian Kou from the reach of Kuomintang revenue seekers.[143] They brought to the village people the idea that structural political factors, not scarcity or environmental crisis, shaped chances for survival and that the actions of those who held key positions in national political hierarchies had consequences for peasant well-being. Their central message was clear: the central government power holders sought to subordinate peasant interests to their own revenue goals. What had thrown Qian Kou into crisis was *national politics.*To the peasants who attended the night school, Liu Han-sheng spoke of oppressors and the oppressed and explained how the poor became poor and the rich became rich.[144] "What he said touched our hearts," says Liu Yufeng. "After we had listened to his talks for several days we all put forth a demand to rise up and take action."[145]

Resentment over regulations governing taxation was voiced publicly throughout 1926 and 1927, the years of warlord and civil defense corps taxes. Why, peasants demanded, did they have to pay taxes to feed the civil corps?[146] The four big landlord families of Puyang, Hua County, and Nei-huang, each owning two thousand *mu* of land, did not pay the corps' living expenses[147]—those were to be covered by a land surtax borne mainly by peasant cultivators, a tax so onerous that even landlords like Liu Yaobin despised it. Qian Kou's young CCP activists were determined to put an end to such privilege, and their daring audit of civil defense tax records in Wen Xinggu was the first step toward that end.

The popular movement in Qian Kou drew further strength from the fact that Zhao Jibin and Wang Congwu were eclectic Communists, not deterministic Marxists. While these young Communists remained steadfast in their commitment to the rural poor and their struggle against the minority of "criminal landlords," they quickly learned that they had pushed class struggle too far and brought down the landlord-dominated civil corps on the peasant movement, which did not attract the prosperous majority of Qian Kou's saltmakers. From 1931 on Zhao Jibin and Wang Congwu came to realize that the major line of conflict in Puyang was between the Republican state bureaucracy and the little proprietors of Qian Kou and the surrounding countryside—peasant saltmakers, purchase agents, and peddlers—and not between landlords and the proletarianized poor.

Perceiving the state as an independent apparatus with new, unreasonable claims on village surplus,[148] these young Communists concluded the salt police were going to strengthen the power of Chiang Kai-shek's government at great cost to Qian Kou's peasant saltmakers. Distrustful of adversarial Marxism, that is, a simplistic class approach to Puyang's agrarian problem, they deepened their involvement with the saltmakers' antistate protest activities in the border area.

The case of Qian Kou shows that Kuomintang state expansion threatened some of the border region's richest salt land villages and reaffirms an important strand of wisdom in the literature on local society and the origins of the CCP: Kuomintang state making alienated potential allies within the local elite, and the CCP was formed by young, educated offspring of this elite—some of whom advised county government and mediated disputes between rural people and the officials of the Nationalist government. Here the CCP was anchored in a protest village that was prospering from both the indigenous salt market and the international market, and the pursuit of elite status in the prefectural normal college brought Qian Kou's youthful CCP activists into contact with well-connected peers from other border area villages. As mentioned in Chapter 1, they, and many of their Daming Normal School peers, were driven back to home base by Kuomintang dictatorship, only to find interest and opportunity in the popular struggle against the salt police. Thus, the CCP first advanced its purpose in progressive, rural salt-trading villages like Qian Kou and initially was able to foster regional collective action from rural places where its well-educated cadres had connections with minor local elites supportive of market protest. However, this border area was a big place, and the young party leaders from the Qian Kou area had to reach out to people in faraway villages where the struggle for the market was a desperate act to halt a slide into unimaginable poverty.

FIVE

The Police Attack on Impoverished Qi Ji

Some forty-five *li* south of Qian Kou is the market town of Bai Dao Kou. Fifteen *li* to the west is Dao Kou town, the capital of Hua County, Henan Province. One of the oldest centers of early lowland peasant settlement on the North China plain, Hua*xian* is a restricted strategic military area. Until my arrival, no Westerner had ever been allowed to visit its villages in the post-1949 era. South of the macadam roads linking Puyang town to Bai Dao Kou is a world of narrow dirt roads, of weary peasants coaxing oxen to cooperate in ageless harvest routines, of land on which the Yellow River has left the indelible stamp of its turbulent history. In ancient times the Yellow River passed through this part of Hua County. When the river changed its channel to Nan Tu, its floodwaters left vast alkaline soil deposits in the fields of villages on its old banks.[1] Gradually, thousands of *mu* of fertile agricultural soil turned into barren land.[2]

Peasants in the villages invaded by this flood dirt had trouble making ends meet. The high concentrations of alkali and sodium left them with salinized lands that demanded great amounts of labor and fertilizer and still did not yield enough grain to get a family through a year. The peasants in poorer districts turned to producing and purveying earth salt and used the income to purchase basic food grains. Even when harvest yields were normal, the earth salt proceeds were critical to their subsistence.

Hua County's salt producers quickly saw the advantages of collective action demonstrated by their counterparts in nearby Puyang. In May, 1932, shortly after the Changlu salt police had been driven out of Puyang, five thousand saltmakers from scores of villages in Ba Li Ying district put on white armbands, armed themselves with knives and salt spades, and convened a mass rally under a banner bearing the inscription "Peasant Salt-makers' Army."[3]

The most celebrated of the villages at the epicenter of the Hua County protest movement, all located along the old course of the Yellow River, was Qi Ji, in Ba Li Ying district.[4] It was in Qi Ji village that the peasant saltmakers first clashed with the Changlu salt tax police, and it was from Qi Ji that they filed a communal protest claim with the Kuomintang Hua County government against the police prior to the rebellion of 1932. Qi Ji became the headquarters of the peasant war against the police in town and countryside.

I entered Qi Ji searching for data that would help differentiate its protest history from that of Qian Kou and help answer a complex set of questions. How important was earth salt production in the peasant economy of Qi Ji village? What was the changing relationship between Qi Ji and Hua County government in Republican times, and how did change affect the life chances of the villagers? Why did Qi Ji peasants play such a pivotal role in organizing protest at the village level, and what contribution did they make to collective action beyond the confines of the village itself? What role did the CCP assume in the formation of protest within Qi Ji? To what extent was the party successful in developing its presence in Qi Ji after the protest was under way?

QI JI'S ECONOMY IN THE REPUBLICAN PERIOD

Since the end of the Qing period, Qi Ji has been one of the poorest villages in peasant China. In 1953 the annual per capita income was one hundred *yuan*, forty of which came from the grain harvest. Following the state-induced poor harvests of 1960–61, per capita income fell to seventy *yuan*. It rose to two hundred *yuan* in 1980, to two hundred fifty in 1985, and to four hundred in 1987. Life has improved since the Great Leap Forward, in part because of a new irrigation system and in part because of the inauguration of the household responsibility system. Even so, before 1987—the first year in half a century when peasants were able to secure their basic food needs via agriculture and animal husbandry—the average peasant family was short of its annual subsistence grain requirement by at least five hundred *jin*.[5]

The signs of dire poverty are everywhere. One sees them in frugal food offerings and in food relationships with peasants. In Qian Kou, when I politely declined the bottle of beer the village chief offered me, he insisted on opening it and accompanied the offering with a bowl of steamy noodle soup, flavored with scrambled eggs and juicy red tomatoes. In Qi Ji, the village chief, Wang Mingdao, and I became good friends—but he never pressed food on me.

Qi Ji is located many rambling, primitive earthen roads away from the rich wheat fields of Bai Dao Kou and its lucrative grain market, and the scrawny body frames of the older inhabitants testify to more than one food-supply crisis. Typhoid, smallpox, and tuberculosis were rampant here in Republican years, leaving many peasants with thin, shrunken torsos and a look of permanent fatigue. Qi Ji's peasants worried constantly lest meager grain harvests fail to withstand locusts, bandits, hail storms, and bad government, and its bad alkaline lands bear the marks of a thousand relentless droughts.

In early Republican times, the economy of this rural Henan village was very different from that of prosperous Qian Kou. The peasants of Qian Kou relied on a tripartite land system to escape poverty: the nonalkaline wheat lands; the sandy peanut soils; and the salt-bearing lands of Nitrate River gradient. With only one land system, its soils laced with salt and blanketed with nitre, Qi Ji peasants had no choice but to grow all of their grain crops in this seemingly dead saline earth.

Qi Ji was and is composed of three lineages. The Duan lineage occupied the back part of the village, known as Huo Qi Ji. The Li lineage occupied front Qi Ji. Western Qi Ji was occupied by the Liu lineage, the poorest of the three up to the 1920s. The serious impairment of agriculture was reflected in the existential dilemma of the Duan lineage, which for nearly five generations has occupied Qi Ji's richer, fertile, grain-yielding lands. In the Republican period, there were about twenty-two hundred *mu* of land in back Qi Ji.[6] About 20 percent was lost to acute salinization. The remaining eighteen hundred *mu* were unsuitable for cotton, and only a tiny portion nourished wheat, so peasants grew mainly sorghum and black beans. The average sorghum yield was about eighty *jin* per *mu*. There were 720 people in back Qi Ji in 1920, each with approximately two and a half *mu*, giving an average family of four ten *mu,* with a harvest yield of about eight hundred *jin.* Each individual needed about five hundred *jin* of grain to survive—so even in the Duan lineage, a family of four lacked half its basic grain requirement.

The deep impoverishment of Qi Ji was not the result of big landlordism, the unequal distribution of landholdings, or surplus appropriation by a parasitic landlord class. Before the Anti-Japanese War there were only three "landlords" in the village, all in back Qi Ji. Duan Baotian owned 120 *mu,* Duan Guantian owned 150 *mu,* and Duan Jiongshun owned 200 *mu.*[7] Of these 470 *mu,* 190 were inferior salt land. The combined annual yield from the remaining wheat land was twenty-five thousand *jin,* barely enough to bring their three families plus an additional eighty persons in Qi Ji up to subsistence grain levels.

"Landlord" Duan Baotian sowed eighty *mu* to wheat, bringing a yield of five thousand *jin* per year. On the face of it, his family of five (his three sisters, his daughter, and himself) could easily make ends meet. After deduct-

ing wages for hired hands and taxes for the Hua County government, however, Duan Baotian was only a shaky step above subsistence. He too could be
forced to purchase grain for survival and be driven to ruin in a year of long
drought.[8] "Duan Baotian worked the fields side-by-side with us hired
hands," Duan Zhouqing recalls. "He worked at all kinds of light jobs, such
as cutting sorghum. We also cut the sorghum, and Duan came and gathered
the sorghum heads and loaded the cart. We drove it to the grain storage
area. In August the landlords here also plowed the fields to prepare for the
autumn planting. Duan Baotian and other landlords worked the fields to
save money and to avoid hiring hands."[9]

Lacking fertile sandy land and adequate transport, Qi Ji's tillers could
not take advantage of the transplantation of New World peanut seeds. They
had no pigs, vegetables, fruit, or nitrate. Profitable animal husbandry was
virtually nonexistent in the 1920s and 1930s, so that villagers were always
short on fertilizer supply and consequently grew few vegetable crops. The
back roads to Qian Kou are bordered by flurries of China aster and red date
trees; Qi Ji is surrounded by barren waves of used-up, pale yellow dirt land.
The river bed, a short walk south, is bone dry and barren.

Salt making in Qi Ji spelled the difference between life and death. In
1920, income from salt making comprised 60 percent of the total income
of 162 of the 180 households in the Duan lineage—the lineage with the
most productive grain land in the village.[10] They used this income to purchase grain in Ba Li Ying market, eight *li* away. Without this salt-based
income, the peasants of Qi Ji had no way to make up for meager harvests.

THE NEW REVENUE NEEDS OF THE REPUBLICAN CENTRAL GOVERNMENT, THE CRISIS OF ENVIRONMENT, AND THE CLAIMS OF WARLORD RULE

In 1922, when Qian Kou's peasants began to put new world market forces
to their advantage, Qi Ji's peasants were having difficulty keeping their
households at subsistence level. A decade later, Qian Kou was composed
largely of small proprietors, purchase agents, and small traders maximizing
profits through commercial pursuits;[11] Qi Ji was a backward village of
impoverished peasants, still decimated by the famine of 1921. Its inhabitants were preoccupied with belt tightening, seasonal begging, and internal
migration, which had been crucial strategies of survival since early Republican times. To a significant extent, the social dilemma of Qi Ji reflected the
condition of peasants suggested in Mats Lundahl's model of peasant economy:[12] here were poor, smallholding peasants who had fallen below subsistence, severely conditioned by their inability to produce enough food crops
to feed their families from one season to the next.

Thus, whether the post-1928 assertion of central state fiscal claims
imperiled the ability of peasants to restore the viability of their household

economies is a crucial issue. Was Qi Ji threatened solely by the fiscal demands of the central government, or did such demands combine with other, more local crises? How did the Kuomintang state figure in the decline of Qi Ji's economy and in the outbreak of collective protest?

The terrible drought of 1920 burned up most of the June wheat harvest and made it exceedingly difficult for many peasants even to sow a sorghum crop. By late spring, agriculture in Qi Ji all but came to a halt, and the village was caught in the grip of hunger. Two-thirds of its inhabitants could not meet their food requirements. Almost all of the peasants in the Liu and Li lineages turned to begging. Members of the Liu lineage, which had the least land in the village (and the worst), became vagabonds begging throughout Hua County and other border area counties. "I first went begging when I was seven," Liu Guoxing recalls. "That was in 1920. We begged most every year afterwards."[13] Most of the Lius went begging in Dongming County, Shandong Province, in late autumn after the sorghum harvest and stayed on through the Spring Festival. They stayed in the Dai Wang Temple, a river bank shrine to a legendary emperor, where they encountered many beggars from unfamiliar places.[14]

The famine intensified in 1921, plunging nearly 70 percent of Qi Ji's peasant households further into crisis. Peasants who had relied on begging in better-off local market villages and temples began taking the migration trails into Shanxi. Liu Chaoqing, who went with his parents to beg in Lu Cheng County, Shanxi Province, in 1921, was one of the few to return to Qi Ji after the famine. "In Lu Cheng we encountered many beggars. About forty families from West Qi Ji went to this place in Shanxi to beg. More than twenty families perished in Lu Cheng that year."[15]

The famine of 1921 left most of the peasants who managed to survive "standing permanently up to the neck in water," to use Tawney's famous metaphor.[16] This desperate situation pertained all through the age of warlordism, into the Nanjing decade, and on through the struggles with the salt tax police. There were minor droughts in 1924 and 1926, and 1931 saw yet another in the vicinity of Qi Ji. The harvest was poor, and a climate of hysteria prevailed for part of the year. Many of the strongest peasants were emaciated.

The tax disorders of the Republican period further jeopardized peasant attempts to regain security. In the decade prior to the saltmakers' struggle, the taxes on the salt-encrusted lands were piled on top of other taxes: county government land taxes, provincial warlord taxes, entrepreneurial taxes. Prior to 1915 Qi Ji's peasants had paid little if any land tax to the Hua County government, for the village had been viewed as hopelessly poor.[17] Shortly after 1920, however, the Hua County government announced a land tax of about ten *jin* of grain for each *mu* of land, to be paid semiannually.[18] The magistracy let it be known that peasants were to pay this land tax in silver.[19]

Most peasants still paid in grain and strove to pay on time; villagers remember walking to the Hua County seat to pay. They also recall that they made this trip less frequently following the 1921 famine. Peasants could no longer make ends meet, and Qi Ji acquired the reputation with the Hua County tax officials as a tax-evasion village. There were quarrels with the land tax collectors, and the magistracy began sending in armed collectors to arrest villagers who did not pay on time.[20] Some peasants stayed out of jail by entreating their kinsmen to pay the land tax for them, but only those in the better-off Duan lineage had that option. A few others managed to avoid jail by appealing for a one-year postponement of taxes, but the following year they had to pay a double tax.[21]

On top of the Hua County land tax came endless warlord taxes. Here there was a peasant explosion over the new claims of provincial militarists. In 1926, after another minor drought and a disappointing June wheat harvest, the Hua County government still attempted to collect the land tax from Qi Ji and the surrounding villages.[22] Three months later, in September, General Feng Yuxiang led Guominjun units of the Northern Expeditionary Army north of the Yellow River and into Hua County. General Feng's troops allied with the Hua County government to press for peasant taxes and added an autumn harvest surcharge on top of the regular land tax. Many Qi Ji peasants from all three lineages joined the Red Spear Association, a league of rural people who declared they would pay no taxes and who drew from a common fund to sustain their antitax protest. As Slawinski, Perry, and other scholars have pointed out, the Red Spears formed mainly to fight against abusive banditry and warlord taxation.[23]

The militant core of Red Spear participants hailed from the better-off Duan lineage and from the recently imperiled Liu lineage. "About one hundred people from Qi Ji joined the Red Spear Association in 1926 and 1927," says Liu Chaoyang. "The Red Spears came here from other counties, and their members lived in Liu An village temple, about three *li* away. There were at least thirty thousand people in the Red Spears, and almost all of them were poor peasants. As a member of the Red Spears, I did not have to pay a tax and I could have my meals free in the Liu An temple."[24]

The Red Spear tax revolt was underwritten in part by the wealthiest Duan lineage member, whose grain lands made him a major target of warlord tax injustice.[25] The revolt was a community tax strike, and from the autumn of 1926 until the Spring Festival of 1927 Qi Ji did not pay any tax. But then came the crash of the Great Revolution, of which this tax strike had been an important part. In September of 1927 Feng Yuxiang's troops defeated the Red Spears in Hua*xian*. Liu Wen Zhuang, Liu Xuan, Liu Wenhe, and Duan Gang, all four Red Spear peasants from Qi Ji, were massacred by Feng's army in the battle of Jian village, just south of Dao Kou town.[26] After the slaughter, the Hua County tax collectors began creeping back into the countryside to make the autumn harvest assessment.[27] Unable to cope with poor harvests and tax pillage, Qi Ji's Red Spear activists fled. By October, many peasants from the poorest lineages were making their way into Shanxi, where they sought work as hired hands or once again took up begging.

Chiang Kai-shek's troops established their own government in Hua County in 1930, and the "new Kuomintang" revived the land tax. In the vicinity of Qi Ji the tax was calculated at approximately one *jin* of grain per *mu* for better cropland and one-half *jin* for the poor saline land. County officials insisted that peasants pay the wheat land tax in silver and the sorghum land tax in grain. The Duan lineage was overwhelmed with requests to help pay the taxes of the poorer members of the community. Facing growing tax resistance in the villages of Ba Li Ying district, the Hua County government resorted to tax farming. Duan Fatian, who worked both croplands and salt pond lands, recalls that the Ba Li Ying authorities employed a private tax farmer, named Zhang, from Wu Fang village. He showed up in Qi Ji to collect the autumn harvest tax. If Qi Ji peasants failed to pay on Zhang's first trip, they had to pay him the tax plus a personal travel fee when he returned. In 1930, according to Duan Fatian, "Duan Weixuan quarreled with the collector, and beat him. The Kuomintang sent five or six county policemen here to arrest him, and his family had to pay to get him back."[28]

The Hua County Kuomintang did not reduce the land tax when the harvest was poor[29]—and it was poor in 1931. A tax on land, rather than on the harvest, ruled out underreporting, and peasants had to pay or be imprisoned.[30]

Around 1929–30 the Kuomintang Hua County government announced a tax on Qi Ji's *xiaoyan* lands, similar to the salt land tax in neighboring Puyang.[31] For every ten *mu* of salt land previously exempted from taxation, peasants had to pay the tax equivalent of three *mu* of crop land, regardless of whether they had reaped any harvest.[32] A showdown was in sight. Qi Ji's peasants already had clashed with a contingent of the salt tax police when the police attacked their salt ponds in 1928 and 1929.

Were the peasants of this poor, submarginal Henan village able to regain a minimally acceptable standard of living in the decade prior to the struggle with the Kuomintang state? Did the tax claims of pre-1928 Republican county and provincial rulers accelerate Qi Ji's economic decline? Was the protest movement of May, 1932 solely the product of the new revenue needs of the centrally directed salt police?

Only one thing stood in the way of massive village migration to Northeast China and the permanent breakup of village families: the peasants of Qi Ji still possessed salt lands, and they used these lands to produce earth salt, which they sold in the markets of Ba Li Ying, Bai Dao Kou, and Dao Kou and of adjacent counties. The salt harvest was at least average after 1927. The minor droughts actually favored earth salt production, enabling villagers to take one tiny step toward subsistence in the period 1927 to 1932. "The way we survived was to produce more salt, but even then we went begging in the winter time and during the spring hunger,"[33] Duan Fatian declares.

Duan Fatian, a participant in the 1932 struggle against the salt police, held more land than most of his counterparts.[34] Before 1932 he had twenty *mu* of poor saline land, but with nine people in his household, his family size was way above average. The family had no wheat land, but they did manage to plant five *mu* of the saline land to sorghum and five to black beans. The average sorghum crop was one hundred *jin* per *mu* for much of the Republican period, but in the five years before 1932 the harvest was poor. (Between 1921 and 1931, sorghum crop yields fell from one hundred *jin* to twenty *jin* per *mu* and never returned to normal.)[35] Peasants from the Li lineage constantly stole the crop, and the Duans took in only twenty to thirty *jin* of sorghum per *mu*. After taxes, they needed at least four thousand to forty-five hundred *jin* of good-quality grain to feed the family. All of this additional grain had to come from salt-based income from the harvest of its one salt pond. The Duans produced several thousand *jin* of salt each year, which they sold in the markets of Ba Li Ying and Bai Dao Kou. After 1927 they began travelling to markets in Hui County, some two hundred *li* from Qi Ji, where the same amount of earth salt that brought only five or six *jin* of grain in Hua County could be sold for proceeds used to purchase nearly two hundred *jin*. To the Duan family, this long-distance salt market activity was synonymous with survival.

Liu Chaodong, one of the peasant saltmakers in the Liu lineage,[36] had ten members in his family in 1915—Liu, his father and mother, four sisters, and three brothers. Altogether they owned three *mu* of poor salt land and virtually no cropland. Seventy percent of their income derived from earth salt production, though occasionally they might wring a few hundred *jin* of sorghum from the saline land. By working the salt ponds from June to September they could bring in 3,000 *jin* of salt, which bought them 1,500 *jin* of sorghum in the Ba Li Ying market. If they were fortunate, they could supplement this sum with 210 *jin* of sorghum in the June–October term, bringing their annual grain total to 1,710. The Hua County salt land tax was 60 *jin* of grain per year, which left them with 1,650 *jin*, or enough to provide only three family members with the minimum of 500 *jin* of grain annually—*providing* that they lost no grain to rottage, had no medical expenses, and none of their salt harvest was confiscated.

Unable to make ends meet, Liu Chaodong's parents sold his youngest sister to a child peddler in 1918. The following year his two brothers died of smallpox. During the famine of 1921, his parents sold his youngest brother. The family survived the next decade through a combination of summertime salt trade, wintertime begging, and year-round belt tightening. Liu Chaodong himself produced salt in the summer and purchased grain with the money obtained from the sales. Liu and two of his sisters went to Dong-ming County to beg after the sorghum harvest and returned to Qi Ji only in late spring. Liu's father worked as both a porter and a cook for a Catholic priest who resided in Hua County town and travelled to rural parishes. The marriage of his two younger sisters helped to alleviate hunger at home—a little. Even after they were married, Liu Chaodong recalls, his sisters took their meals in their husbands' households for several days, then rotated to their parents' household for a few days. "Even with earth salt income," he says, "we still had only 275 *jin* of grain per person and we sometimes had to forgo meals and eat wild plants to survive."[37]

Thus, even before the salt tax police entered the picture, Qi Ji was a time bomb. All but a few of its inhabitants had suffered from terrible famine and endured chronic nutritional stress. The few people who counted them-selves among the fortunate minority plowed their own fields, worked along-side their hired hands, and were constantly preoccupied by day-to-day sur-vival concerns.[38] The Republican fiscal center's tax claims, coming in a decade of relentless drought, threatened to perpetuate this economic decline, which peasants sought to reverse by salt production for the market.

The warlord surcharges on Changlu salt distributed by Dao Kou–based merchants, and the subsequent drop in demand for the overpriced and pol-luted official salt, triggered a rise in popular demand for earth salt in Hua County and Puyang between 1923 and 1928,[39] and by the late 1920s salt making had taken on a frantic pace in Qi Ji. In the five years before 1932, peasants stepped back from the abyss of death by stepping up their salt trade. In reality, Qi Ji's recovery was reflective of an extremely precarious adaptation vis-à-vis a one-sided market activity that raised a few peasant households (ironically, those in possession of the largest amounts of poor saline land) above subsistence while renewing the hope of the majority for a return to some basic economic guarantees.

PEASANT ANGER AND COLLECTIVE PROTEST

As we have seen, the government of Chiang Kai-shek placed great pressure on the Changlu Salt Inspectorate to increase sales of maritime salt; and in early 1932 the finance ministry ordered the magistrates in Henan to assist the newly formed *Shuijingtuan* in the suppression of earth salt production. The logic of state economic interest predicted the arrival of the Kuomin-tang *Shuijingtuan* in Hua County, whose 180-man police force was nearly five times greater than in neighboring Puyang, for this county was a key ter-minus on the transport route for Changlu maritime salt. The boat from Tianjin along the Wei River made two important stops, one at the Long Wang Temple in Daming County and the other at Dao Kou town,[40] the main salt distribution center for all of rural Hua County, Xun County, Puyang, Neihuang, and Dongming County.

The Changlu salt tax police first appeared in Hua County in 1915, when Song Mingshan, an ex-member of Yuan Shikai's Beiyang Army and the commander of the Changlu Anticontraband Force for North China, established an anticontraband headquarters in Dao Kou town. By 1924 this Dao Kou anticontraband unit, consisting of thirty police on horseback, had begun to patrol the poor rural districts of Hua County.[41]

In the pre-1928 phase of police activity, there was great confusion in Qi Ji about just who the salt police were.[42] Bandits frequently impersonated the Changlu salt police and pressed the villagers to pay a "protection fee" for not destroying the ponds. After several run-ins with these bandits, who had no real police uniforms,[43] villagers paid a visit to the Hua County magistrate, who denied that local government had anything to do with them. Thereafter, Qi Ji's saltmakers struggled with these "hooligans" on the assumption that the county government would not reprimand them for defending the village from bandits.

The authentic Changlu salt police struck Qi Ji repeatedly. "Three salt policemen came here to destroy our ponds in 1928," recalls Liu Guoxing. "At first we ran away, and then returned to repair the ponds they had damaged. The police came to Qi Ji about once a week. They never called on the village chief. They just rushed in and destroyed our ponds without warning."[44]

The locus of conflict was the market system, not just the village proper. For one thing, the police were out to seize control of the market. The important markets of the twelve districts of Hua County—Dao Kou, Bai Dao Kou, Ba Li Ying, Hongji—received far more police attention than peripheral villages like Qi Ji because the Changlu Salt Bureau had established its salt shops in such places to promote the "tide water economics" of the Kuomintang state, and because the police were to help these shops achieve dominance locally. Unlike the rural dwellers in Qian Kou, the peasants in Qi Ji had no significant market of their own, so that they had no choice but to sell their salt in markets far beyond home territory. Within this overland market world, in which salt trade was taken as an integral part of the pressing routine of survival, the peasants of Qi Ji came into contact with the commandism of the fiscal police.[45]

The Police Attack on the Market

A native of Qi Ji village, and a participant in the 1932 struggle, Liu Xingquan was born in 1894. He was ninety-three when I spent a day with him in the summer of 1987 and ninety-six when we talked again in 1990. The historical narrative of old-timers like Liu helps us to see that the rebellion of 1932 was a popular response to a deepening stage of state penetration that dated back to early Republican politics:[46]

I had two *mu* of land on which I produced earth salt for a living. I sold the salt in the markets of Hua county and in the markets near the river in Tangyin county. I often went to Bai Dao Kou and to Ba Li Ying to trade in the market fair. I went to the market fairs in Liangmen only occasionally. I used the money I got from selling the salt to purchase grain.

The Changlu salt police first came to Hua county around 1921. They stayed in Dao Kou town and Ba Li Ying. There were about twenty police living in Ba Li Ying, and they had big horses. When the salt police came to Qi Ji people here shouted warnings to one another and ran away. Then the police rode in and destroyed the ponds. The police caught some saltmakers here and beat them severely. They caught Niu Xing, a saltmaker from our village, and they whipped him three hundred times.

When the salt police occupied Ba Li Ying we did not dare go there any more. So we altered our market pattern. It was also more difficult to go to Bai Dao Kou to sell salt because the Ba Li Ying police often patrolled Bai Dao Kou and other big markets. So we started going to the countryside to sell our salt to individual villages. We went north of Bai Dao Kou to Shang village and Gaozhuang. We also went to Liangmen in Puyang more often. Later on, I sold the salt in the markets of Taicon and Hui county.

The police seized many people who were selling earth salt. Liu Changzhu was seized at San Li Zhang. There the police seized about ten wheelbarrows of salt. This Liu Changzhu had only twenty *mu* of salt land, and no other way to make a living. The salt police beat him, and then damaged his salt wheelbarrow. They threw his salt into the water.

This long passage of market-based conflict with the police educated the saltmakers of Qi Ji to the fact that the police were a group apart form the working poor and alerted them to the growth of widespread popular antagonism over police behavior. Born in 1901, Liu Chaoqing still has a sharp memory of how the police disrupted his extravillage market routines before 1932. His testimony is a powerful reminder that even the marginalized peasants of one of Henan's poorest villages were still connected to market networks through their own self-reliant selling endeavors and that in the Republican period peasants often were introduced to the discipline of Kuomintang state making within the wider parameters of the marketing world sketched out by G. William Skinner:[47]

> I went to Bai Dao Kou to sell my salt. But the markets I most often went to were in Ji county and Hui county. I always went to Dong Gao, Xi Gao and Ma Liu villages, about one hundred *li* from Qi Ji. I pushed a wheelbarrow full of salt from Qi Ji to these places. It took at least three days to get there, and three days to get back, and I stayed over in these places for one or two days. I lived in the homes of peasants. I lived in this village today and that village tomorrow, just like a beggar.
>
> The government salt shops would not permit us to sell our salt. The anti-contraband forces chased us and when they caught us they confiscated our carts and salt. Once my cart was seized by the anti-contraband police. This was

in Xun county; I asked my friends and acquaintances to plead with the anti-contraband squad for me. I finally got back my cart after some of my fellow peddlers did me a favor. They helped me implore some local merchants to use their influence with the salt police to return our salt carts.

Later I witnessed the saltmakers' struggle against the police in Xiao He village market, Xun county. This was in 1931. At that time, about twenty salt-makers fought with the police, making them retreat. I did not say much about this incident when I returned to Qi Ji, but I took part in the struggle against the police in Hua county shortly thereafter.

Legal Protest and the Development of Collective Action

The peasants of Qi Ji pursued several different protest strategies. Their initial response to state interference was not violent. Rather, they pursued what they thought to be a peaceful, government-sanctioned form of protest to reaffirm their right to sell earth salt at a fair market price—the petitioning of the Hua County court.

This legal protest was launched in 1925 by Liu Chaode, the young leader of the peasant saltmakers in Hua*xian*. A smallholder in Qi Ji, Liu Chaode relied on the sale of earth salt for nearly four-fifths of his income and was becoming prosperous from the salt trade. In 1925 the Changlu salt police destroyed Liu's salt pond and salt tools and took Li Yenniu, Li Youhe, and Li Yousen to Dao Kou jail, where they were tortured.[48]

A graduate of the Ming Yuan primary school run by the Catholic Church in Hua County town, Liu Chaode was qualified to do land tax assessment and to register land deeds for the Hua County Kuomintang Land Tax Bureau.[49] Prior to the peasant saltmakers' protest, he had conducted surveys to grade village soils and adjust tax levels according to the quality of land. Acquainted with many peasant leaders in the salt land villages of Ba Li Ying district, including those surrounding Qi Ji (Dingxian, Yuancun, Liu Liyan, and so on), Liu called on village chiefs to persuade scores of peasant saltmakers to join together to file a lawsuit in the Hua County court (*xianya konggao*) against the police. In mid-1925, he led a small group of saltmakers to Hua County town to present a legal petition to the magistrate, demanding that the government punish Sergeant Cui Qinghan, the police sergeant who had led the attacks on Qi Ji, Tan village, Caopo, and Shang Guan village.[50] Magistrate Liu Zhenzhong threatened the saltmakers with a countersuit if their claims proved unfounded[51] and tried to frighten Liu Chaode and his counterparts into withdrawing their claim by summoning court marshals to punish Liu for making trouble. However, the delegation stood its ground.[52]

Magistrate Liu prolonged the review process by persuading an ally in the Hua County Finance Bureau to inform the plaintiffs that he was away on official business each time they came to petition the court. Liu Chaode petitioned the court five times in 1925, once in 1926, and once each year until the protest rally of 1932, filing ten legal briefs with four different county magistrates (with Liu Zhenzhong in 1925, Yue Wei in 1926–27, Wang Congde in 1928, and Xie Suian in 1932).[53]

In 1927 the peasants took their case to the Henan provincial court in Kaifeng.[54] Magistrate Yue Wei insisted that the case had to be handled at either the provincial or central government level, yet the Henan authorities informed Liu Chaode that the case was to be handled by the local court. Once again, the peasants petitioned Yue Wei, who said they could rely on him. But they waited and waited—and Yue Wei was gone, and yet another magistrate, oblivious to their case, was on the scene.

Kung-Chuan Hsiao reminds us that the unwillingness of the magistrate to "settle litigations satisfactorily" often brought on popular demonstrations and riots in rural China.[55] The case at hand illustrates this insight. From 1928 to 1932 Liu Chaode persisted in his lawsuit, and in this period the Changlu salt police twice attempted to arrest him during attacks on Qi Ji.[56] In the spring of 1928 Sergeant Cui Qinghan, with ten unarmed police, came to arrest Liu and two other saltmakers. Several dozen saltmakers surrounded them, gave them a beating, and threw them out of the village. Ten days later Cui Qinghan brought thirty armed men on horseback to capture Liu Chaode. The local people were ready for them—sixty young saltmakers were hiding by the village entrance, armed with rabbit-hunting shotguns, choppers, and spears. After the salt police entered west Qi Ji and dismounted, the saltmakers blasted them with buckshot, then rushed them with choppers. Once again, the police were driven from the village, nine of them suffering from shrapnel wounds.

The police came less often after this second clash, but the peasants were fearful of a reprisal. Liu Chaode pushed on with the legal petition, but his life was constantly in danger. He is said to have stayed with friends in different villages, returning home only under the cover of darkness.[57]

With the growth of police repression, Qi Ji's saltmakers pressed the Kuomintang to give undivided attention to their lawsuit. In 1932, after several years of police siege, the peasants took their case before the central government in Nanjing. By this time, the Hua County magistrates were in the service of the "new Kuomintang" of Chiang Kai-shek and T. V. Song.[58] They were appointed by Liu Chih, the governor of Henan Province, and approved by Chiang Kai-shek and his central government. Because the police now were known to be under the central government's salt bureau, Liu Chaode and his confederates decided to approach the local Kuomintang. In April, the Hua County magistrate, Xie Suian, paid an official visit to the Ba Li Ying district government. Liu led a group of thirty Qi Ji saltmakers to Ba Li Ying to entreat the magistrate to review the saltmakers' grievances and support their case with the high court.[59]

Xie had falsely accused the saltmakers' association in the vicinity of Qi Ji of being infiltrated by Communist sympathizers, Liu Chaode said, and had allowed the security forces to seize ordinary folk—small peddlers who had nothing whatsoever to do with the Communist Party. "I am here to tell you that I am the head of this Association. Do I look like a Communist? If I do, then go ahead and seize me! If not, then from now on be sure you do not ever again say our Saltmakers' Association has Communist sympathizers in it!"[60] He demanded that Magistrate Xie release the incarcerated saltmakers or supply proof of their Communist affiliations.

Their fellow saltmakers had been illegally detained, the peasants declared, and they insisted that the magistrate release them if they were not going to be interrogated within a reasonable period of time. Xie took this insistence on the right to *habeas corpus* as an insult to his authority. The timing of the interrogation was none of their business, he told Liu Chaode and his delegation. Liu Chaode insisted the matter *was* their affair because the families of the incarcerated saltmakers were in dire straits. "If it is your affair, what are you going to do about it?" the magistrate demanded.

"I will lead the members of the Saltmakers' Association to destroy your county government," Liu Chaode retorted.[61] This was going too far. Magistrate Xie summoned ten policemen, but Liu Chaode drew a knife from his waistband and rushed him, shouting to the police that he would kill the magistrate if they took one step forward. The police did not move, for the thirty saltmakers waiting outside of the Ba Li Ying district government had entered the grounds brandishing spears. Now the police backed off, and Liu Chaode released Xie Suian. Peasant and magistrate began another round of heated discourse.

Finally, having received a report of growing numbers of saltmakers arriving to surround Ba Li Ying district, Xie Suian accepted Liu's request to release the peasant salters, and he was allowed to return unharmed to Dao Kou town.

In the month following Xie's promise to get Liu Chaode's petition a hearing in Nanjing, the salt police pressed ahead to wrest control of the salt trade in Hua County and Xun County. The situation reached a crisis in early May, when the peasants of Qi Ji staged an armed rebellion against the rural-based salt police, then marched to the outskirts of Dao Kou town to demand the removal of the police from Hua County.

The uprising of 13 May 1932 was the outgrowth of several years of popular resistance to the Changlu salt police, which took on a collective dimension at both the village and county level.[62] The first collective action was prompted by a police attack on Qi Ji's salt ponds in the late summer of 1929. Before then, the peasant saltmakers had pursued a number of now familiar avoidance strategies, including hidden production inside household courtyards. This latter strategy had its limits in Qi Ji, for most households had only one salt pond and lacked the water resources needed to engineer a retreat to sustained courtyard production, which is why they were enraged over the police invasion of their courtyards in August. The villagers were in a panic over how to pay the upcoming autumn land tax, so Liu Chaode and Liu Chadong had no difficulty in gathering antipolice resistance.

The twenty mounted police who descended on Qi Ji were greeted by Liu Chaode and several dozen saltmakers from the Liu lineage. About a hundred saltmakers from all three Qi Ji lineages fought the police to a standoff. "When the outcome was still in doubt," recalls Liu Chaodong, "many more people came to aid us, and we defeated the police. The police then retreated to Ba Li Ying. . . . Half of the people involved in this struggle were named Liu. But nearly all of the people in Qi Ji made earth salt, and so people from all quarters supported us."[63]

A fortnight later the Qi Ji saltmakers struck back. The weapon they chose was *Henan Bangzi Yuzhu,* an old popular folk opera that attracted several thousand people from the salt land villages of Caopo, Gangzhuang, Wangzhuang, Xingzhuang, and Gong Xizhuang. They were greeted by Liu Chaode and the saltmakers, who informed them of a newly organized association called the *Dayanhui* (Association to Fight the Salt Police). Liu Chaode, the head of the association, urged his fellow saltmakers to follow the example of collective resistance set by Qi Ji's skirmish with the police two weeks earlier. Joined by nearly one thousand other peasants, Qi Ji's saltmakers marched to Hongji market village, about twenty-five *li* from Qi Ji, where they destroyed the outpost of the Changlu salt police and chased off a government salt inspector who had taken up residence there. They tore the roofs off the police headquarters, but they harmed no one.[64] After this victory, they saw less of the police.

By early 1931 the news about Qi Ji's antipolice initiatives had spread to many villages, and in October the leaders of Caopo, Caoying, Shang Guan, and other salt land villages joined with Liu Chaode to establish the Hua County Saltmakers' Association.[65] Between November, 1931, and February, 1932, the leaders of this nonpartisan saltmakers' league, along with several members of the Hua County CCP, expanded its membership to eight thousand, with roots in more than one hundred villages of Hua County. A general headquarters was set up in Qi Ji village under the leadership of Liu Chaode, who was elected the head of the association in early 1932.[66]

The association notified T. V. Song's *Shuijingtuan* of its intention of reclaiming the market. In mid-March a twenty-man anticontraband squad arrested about ten peasant salt peddlers from Xu Ying village who were pushing their wheelbarrows to market, ordered them to pay a fine of ten silver dollars to secure the return of each wheelbarrow, and detained them in the Golden Buddhist Temple, just south of Song Lin village. One of the peddlers, Zhang Masan, was sent back to Xu Ying village to raise the fine money; but the peasants of Xu Ying sent him to Liu Chaode, who summoned more than thirty members of Qi Ji's saltmakers' association to prepare to attack the police at the temple. A chicken-feather letter was sent by special courier to Hou Xusheng, the leader of the saltmakers in Zhangzhuang, to bring another thirty. While the police were sleeping, the sixty peasants surprised the two police temple guards, released their brothers from Xu Ying and recovered the salt carts, then rapidly withdrew. The Changlu salt police were shaken by this silent concerted action, which shattered the assumption of any sanctuary beyond the walls of Hua County town.[67]

The saltmakers' association created its own militia, divided into seven "regiments."[68] The first was based in Bian Ying and led by Yao Quanzhi; the second in Caopo and Gao Qian Ying and led by Zhang Gubang; the third in Qi Ji, headed by Liu Chaode. Equipped with primitive muskets and explosives, each regiment appointed a few sentries to warn of oncoming mounted police and to summon their respective villages. The third regiment turned the tables on the salt police, arresting them, jailing them, and administering various punishments. Now there were two systems of authority in Hua County, one in the town, the other in the villages. The countryside was becoming a dangerous place for the police. In early 1932 a rumor circulated about a policeman who had been apprehended by Qi Ji's saltmakers near Wang village: the third regiment had cut off his ear as a warning to other intruders.[69]

Several months later, the intrepid third regiment carried out an antipolice action that threw Hua County into an uproar. Cai Qinghan, the vice-director of the Dao Kou–based Kuomintang salt police, ordered Cheng Erduan to lead an attack on Shang Guan, halfway between Ba Li Ying and Qi Ji. As soon as Cheng's squad entered Shang Guan, however, they ran into Zhang Pengyu, a leader of the seventh regiment, along with ten sentries.[70] Cutting off Cheng Erduan's escape route, the seventh regiment seized him and escorted him to Qi Ji village, the unofficial headquarters of the salt peasants' war.[71] Liu Chaode and the third regiment escorted him to the Xiao Han temple fair and ushered him onto a stage to receive public condemnation. As Liu Chaode recited his misdeeds, twenty angry peasant saltmakers denounced him. The crowd began to chant "Kill him! Kill him!" Kowtowing before Liu Chaode, Cheng begged for mercy. The leaders of the saltmakers' association tattooed the Chinese characters *huai zhong* (bad seed) onto his forehead.[72] For several days they paraded him along Hua County's village roads, through Caopo, Bai Dao Kou, and even into Neihuang County town, then set him free on the promise of not making trouble again.[73]

This protest action alarmed the Kuomintang Hua County government and T. V. Song's salt revenue police. From this point on, local plots to capture the salt police multiplied. The saltmakers in the vicinity of Bai Dao Kou captured Men Ni, a notorious salt policeman in Xun County, rushed him onto a temple stage, and tattooed the characters for "bad seed" on his face as well.[74]

Regaining the Market

In the previous two years, the salt tax corps had stepped up its efforts to prevent illicit private trade in earth salt in Hua County, erecting toll stations along the roads connecting Bai Dao Kou and the big markets to the remote salt land villages and seizing the popular earth salt cargo in the higher-level markets.[75] This police blitz especially hurt sellers from the marginal salt land villages in the vicinity of Qi Ji. Liu Xiaoxing recalls, [76] "After my father died, we had five mouths to feed. We had no crop land. We made our living by selling salt produced on fifteen *mu* of salt land, and from spinning cloth bought in the markets. I made earth salt with my brother in Qi Ji. We went to sell the salt, and I was arrested near Dao Kou by the salt police. The police jailed me in Dao Kou town for seven days. There were eight others who were arrested. Six were from Li Family village and two were from Qi Ji village. I borrowed five silver dollars from a landlord to get out of jail. I was able to pay back the loan to the landlord by making earth salt and selling it."

The struggle came to a head on May 13—the Festival of *Guanyeh*. In contrast to Puyang, where there was advance planning and the Communists were involved in the plot, the mobilization against the salt police and the march on the Hua County magistracy was spontaneous, taking the entire county by surprise; even party members were pressed to keep pace with its development.

On May 10, the salt police in Hongji seized a group of salt-making peasants from Xie Zhai village who had gone on the road to sell their salt and confiscated their carts.[77] Xie Erliao escaped and ran to Qi Ji, where he was taken to Liu Chaode. Liu and the third regiment spent the rest of the day contacting saltmakers from Caopo, Kang Zhuan, Zhaozhuang, Zhang village, Wen village, Xing village, East and West Zhongtou villages, and Luo Ying village. Within hours, five thousand armed people from some twenty villages assembled near Qi Ji. "When we arrived at Hong market village," recalls Liu Chaodong, "we went to the salt police station and confronted ten policemen. They had locked the saltmakers from Xie Zhai inside a makeshift jail, so we broke inside and linked up with the captive saltmakers to smash in the head of the police squadron leader. We also tore apart the jail, and we destroyed the buildings where the police were housed. At that point, someone shouted: 'Let's go to Dao Kou town to attack their headquarters!'"[78]

Liu Chaode concurred, and the uprising was on. Within a few days the peasant regiments destroyed the Changlu salt shops in all twelve districts of Hua County.[79] Just before sunrise on May 12 ten thousand protestors left Hongji village for Dao Kou, where the police were stationed. As they marched to Da Pu village, on the eastern outskirts of Dao Kou, their ranks swelled to fifteen thousand. When they arrived at sunset, they were greeted by Xie Suian.

Magistrate Xie knew what had happened in Puyang town, and here he faced five times as many saltmakers. Moreover, on learning of the armed protest march of fifteen thousand, most of the salt tax police had fled. Left with two hundred local county police,[80] Xie was unable to turn back the popular movement.

Liu Chaode and the saltmakers informed Xie they had come to fight the salt police, who had persecuted them and deprived them of their livelihood. "We are going to Dao Kou to fight them to the death!"[81] Magistrate Xie pointed out that the salt police already had taken the train to Xinxiang. Moreover, he argued, because Dao Kou town actually belonged to Xun County, there was nothing to be gained by going there. Assuring the protest leaders he wanted to avoid a war between them and the police, Xie Suian invited them to join him in a mediation dinner back in Hua County.[82]

The discussions in Da Pu lasted well into the morning of May 13. The village was surrounded by saltmakers armed with spades, swords, spears, and hunting guns and brandishing the red flags of the saltmakers' association. Liu Chaode came directly to the point. The leaders wanted the Hua County government to honor their original petition to the court and grant four requests: withdraw the salt police from Hua County and guarantee they would never return, acknowledge the saltmakers' inalienable right to market salt, abolish the Kuomintang Salt Bureau and exempt earth salt from taxation, and instigate legal proceedings to make the police compensate the saltmakers for their losses.[83] Xie signed a statement agreeing to Liu's demands, and Qi Ji's third regiment returned to the villages.

Strictly speaking, the Hua County Saltmakers' Association disbanded its regiments and suspended the war against the Kuomintang police state after this May 13 protest victory. But in the ensuing years Liu Chaode and a few members from the third regiment continued to take up various forms of resistance to police infringement. In the summer of 1932 they sponsored a big open-air opera to celebrate Qi Ji's victory, and Yang Jingcai and Wang Congwu, the leaders of Puyang's saltmakers' association, came to express their solidarity with Liu Chaode and the saltmakers of Hua*xian*.[84] In 1933 and 1934, Liu and his fellow saltmakers filed yet another lawsuit against the police unit under Cui Qinghan and pressed the Hua County government to arrest and punish Cui.[85] And in the spring of 1935, after joining the Thirteen County Saltmakers' League, a small contingent of Hua County's peasant saltmakers teamed up with their counterparts from Puyang, Neihuang, and Dongming in an armed march on Nanle County town, entering the struggle to evict the salt police from the wider border area.[86]

THE CCP IN QI JI: A PARADOX OF BACKWARDNESS

Here was a village that had successfully stood in the way of Kuomintang state makers whose involvement with international lending and infatuation with national army building had advanced them along the road to tyranny. Not surprisingly, the CCP had great expectations for Qi Ji's contribution to the revolution. By late 1932, however, party leaders had come to realize that Qi Ji was not fertile ground for party recruitment. Nevertheless, several CCP leaders did strike up a close relationship with the saltmakers who spearheaded the popular struggle in Qi Ji. Wang Congwu, the secretary of the Puyang County CCP, forged a strong bond with Liu Chaode. In 1930 Wang heard through the Daming Normal School grapevine of a Hua County saltmaker who had led peasants in a legal struggle against the Kuomintang salt police[87]—several of Liu Chaode's classmates had gone to Daming to study and had spread the news of Liu's protest activities.[88] On a rainy autumn evening, dressed in peasant garb and armed with an umbrella, Wang Congwu paid a visit to Liu Chaode. The two men talked until midnight. Wang Congwu came directly to the point. "If they were to defeat the salt police, they had to unite not only the salt making peasants of their own villages but also those of each county, and bind them up like a 'bundle of chopsticks.'"[89]

Since late 1929, several leaders of the Hua County CCP, including the county secretary, Nie Zhen, had worked alongside peasant saltmakers in the vicinity of Shang Guan, Lanjicun (Blue Chicken village), Jian, and Cheng Guan villages. On hearing of Qi Ji's successful fight with the police, Nie Zhen came here from Jian village, a salt-making community about ten *li* to the south.[90] A part-time saltmaker himself, Nie Zhen was hardly a cerebral Marxist interloper. Along with CCP member He Zichen, who hailed from Hua Family village about thirty *li* away, Nie occasionally stayed in Qi Ji to advise Liu Chaode on the state of the countywide struggle.[91]

In the spring of 1932 these underground CCP activists linked up with the Hua County Saltmakers' Association.[92] They mainly assisted the members in building up a legal war chest and in filing written complaints with the Hua County court to defend the right to sell earth salt, thereby broadening the base of legal protest begun by Liu Chaode.[93] The association began using membership fees to purchase small arms to distribute to various salt-making villages undertaking a defense of their ponds.[94] A few party members joined with saltmakers in the May 13 march.

CCP documents claim that the Hua*xian* party was borne along the axis of the salt protest,[95] but this clearly was not the case for Qi Ji. No one in the village joined the CCP until 1942,[96] and Liu Chaode rejected a formal request to join by Yang Yufeng, the CCP secretary of the prefecture of which Hua County was a part.[97] "When we were asked to join the party, we went to consult Liu Chaode about it," recalls Liu Chaoyang. "Liu said, 'The CCP has nothing to offer us. Do not join it.'"[98]

Wang Congwu and Nie Zhen remained on friendly terms with Liu Chaode throughout the 1930s, and Liu cooperated with them to conduct anti-Japanese guerrilla warfare along the Hua*xian*-Puyang border in early

1938. This resistance, which is sometimes equated with the return of Zhao Ziyang from the regional Anti-Japanese Training School of the CCP Northern Bureau,[99] was far more the product of the early credibility of local party leaders who had supported the peasant saltmakers. Thus, in comparison to Qian Kou, the CCP struck out when it came to recruitment of party members; but the record of locally esteemed Communist leaders in siding with local village leaders in their fight with the Kuomintang fiscal police still would later serve the party well.

A combination of factors converged to undercut the party's chances for institutional success in Qi Ji. The first was poverty. A year after the 13 May 1932 struggle most Qi Ji residents abandoned their community-based actions and began to behave in ways that precluded the pursuit of the kind of durable interest group politics on which the CCP had thrived. The fear of dearth made it exceedingly difficult to sustain participation in the associational politics that facilitated party building in Qian Kou.[100] Qi Ji's economy deteriorated throughout the decade following the 1932 struggle, and unity gave way to individual household fears of premature death from scarcity, to suspiciousness of others, and to widespread unwillingness to share and cooperate.[101] The CCP was unable to overcome this state of *miseria* and build up a party branch.

After 1932 the environmental crisis actually worsened, making it more difficult to produce grain crops or earth salt. On 23 June 1933 the Yellow River overspilled its banks and invaded villages in the vicinity of Qi Ji.[102] This disaster recurred in 1935, when Qi Ji's fields were flooded one meter deep. Many peasants could not make salt and had to leave the village.[103] Most of them migrated to Shanxi's Lu Cheng and Hong Tong counties, not to return until 1940 or later. They were the wise ones. In 1938 a severe drought settled over Hua County, and Qi Ji saw no harvest that year. The spring of 1942 brought another severe drought, and both the June and October harvests failed. Even Duan Baotian, with his 120 *mu* of cropland, had to use his skimpy savings to buy grain.[104] Seventy percent of the peasants, including 40 percent of those in the Duan "wheat lineage," had to go begging.[105] Without any specialized products for the world market— peanuts, cotton, pig bristles—without the little extra trades for country and town markets, this forlorn Henan village was reduced to wretchedness, and many of its inhabitants resorted to scavenging and stealing in Hua*xian* or to begging or becoming hired hands in faraway counties.

Compounding their anguish, at least half of the peasants who stayed in Qi Ji after 1932 could not even afford to bury their dead. When his father and other family members died, Duan Fatian recalls, "We just buried the corpses without a coffin. We buried them in our lineage burial ground. Our neighbors were named Duan, and they helped us bury our corpses."[106] The saltmakers' association had no resources to help with funeral services, as was the case in Qian Kou.[107] Some peasants kept the corpses of their loved ones in their homes for several months, or years, in the 1932–38 period.[108] Preoccupied with death, many peasants displayed an aversion toward CCP appeals to "join the revolution," and few peasants saw any reason to stay in the saltmakers' association.

The critical food shortages created competition for village-grown cereals, with increasing squabbles over crop theft. Even before the communal protest movement of 1932 most peasants had begun to engage in crop-watching vigils. Some members of the desperate poor considered pilfering a morally defensible act.[109] "My father once was forced to pilfer grain from the fields of landlord Duan Baotian," recalls Liu Jingjiao. "This was not gleaning. We went out early to cut his crops before he could instruct his hired hands to harvest the wheat. We did it secretly. We often waited until the hired hands were beyond the fields, and once they were away from the fields they could do nothing to stop us. Eventually, the landlord hired field guards to watch the crops, but we knew he did not have enough guards to watch all of his fields. If they stood to the west we entered from the east."[110]

Until the Yellow River flood of 1933 dealt a new round of hunger, the thieves were able to avoid retaliation. When Duan Fatian and his brother caught Li Dongchuan from Front Qi Ji stealing their sorghum crop in the year of a minor drought, they only made him pay back what he had pilfered.[111] With the floods of 1933 and 1935, those who possessed grain crops were more and more inclined to seek what J. K. Campbell has called "retaliation with interest."[112]

After the June 1933 flood relations in Qi Ji were increasingly characterized by mistrust and noncooperation. "Before Liberation," says Mi Jingjiang, "no one trusted anyone, and we were hesitant to share with each other."[113] After the flood no one would lend grain for fear that the loans would not be paid back.[114] Few peasants, if any, formed mutual-aid groups aimed at sharing food or goods or overcoming the economic decline of the village. One is struck by the absence of joint family efforts to expand the number of salt ponds beyond one per household. With family breakup replacing the solidarity of the protest movement, associated economic activities withered—and so did the CCP's chance to sustain collective peasant actions.

A few villagers transcended this Hobbesian mentality, in part because they were able to re-enter the marketplace. Their leader was Liu Chaode. On quadrupling his earth salt production through cheap land purchases between 1932 and 1935, Liu pursued the market with gusto, reaping profits second only to Liu Xiangfeng, who produced more earth salt than anyone in Qi Ji.[115] Between 1932 and 1938, therefore, Liu's family was able to sustain small improvements in its living standard via the earth salt trade. Its newfound prosperity from salt market profits placed the Liu household in the upper 5 percent of the village in income.[116]

Liu Chaode's market success was catapulting him into a position of leadership during and after the 1932 saltmakers' protest. His reputation for turning bad land into big profits made him a prince of prosperity in the eyes of the poor;[117] his escape from poverty held out the hope others might do the same. On the other hand, Liu demonstrated that profit from the market offered villagers a way out of "amoral familism." Of course, profits went mainly to the Liu household, but some of the gains were distributed to the poorest members of the Liu lineage and the larger village by way of small loans to start up small businesses, charity loans to stave off hunger, and cash contributions to help pay police fines. The salt loans of Liu Chaode and Liu Xiangfeng, Qi Ji's two most successful market dealers, permitted one-third of its families to survive the worst months of the 1942 Henan famine. Still, such goodwill could not reverse the misfortune of the great majority of peasant households, and CCP influence was limited to liaisons with the small number of peasant saltmakers who were able to stay in the market.

The impoverishment of Qi Ji weakened many peasant families to a point where they could no longer reproduce their family lines and strengthen their kinship bonds via participation in associational economic activities. Few peasants could depend on their parents to help them accumulate the little material gains they needed to start up their own households, and many were too old to produce children by the time they found the means to marry. The intensification of dearth did not necessarily reduce the number of persons living under one roof. Peasants say the number of persons living in each household in 1930 was far larger than half a century later, in 1980, and the number of persons in each one of their extended families has increased greatly since the founding of the PRC. Mi Jingjiang recalls:[118] "Before Liberation people in Front Qi Ji could not afford to live separately. We could not reproduce our families, or multiply our family households, or expand our family resources. We could not *fenjia*." Thus, the CCP was able to maintain its political association with Liu Chaode partly because the market-bound peasants in his lineage were able to cope with the crisis of *fenjia* and rely on extended family to free up for participation in extra-village political activities.

A low educational level was another important factor making Qi Ji unfit for the CCP's recruitment designs. Before 1949, Qi Ji's rudimentary educational system consisted solely of a private elementary school, run by Duan Pingtian, which served only a few of the comparatively well-off Duan lineage members. Enrollment was limited to about ten children, half of them Duans. A village teacher and doctor had gotten their starts in this school, but the "Duan graduates" were mostly semiliterate villagers, who had no involvement in affairs of state and who seldom sent their children to the postprimary schools of Hua County or the prefecture.

Even had they aspired to do so, they could not have pursued an education beyond the village after 1920, when tuition fees shot up to the point of provoking student protest.[119] From 1923 on, the offspring of peasant, landlord, and merchant families in the better-off villages of Hua County went to Ji County for elementary and normal school training.[120] Few in Qi Ji had the resources for this exit. Few young people came into contact with the CCP in the prefectural normal school, and no Marxist firebrands returned to the village with political ideas, resources, and connections to help peasants translate protest into CCP-led insurgency.

Qi Ji peasants turned to popular religion for guidance in the politics of protest: to the folk Christianity of Liu Chaode and the Liu pauper lineage. At the time of the saltmakers' struggle, Liu Chaode and 80 percent of the peasants in the Liu lineage were Catholic,[121] and the local church evidently provided a locus for organizing on the salt market issue.

Qi Ji had been a center of Catholic influence in Hua County for some time. Approximately ten Catholic missionaries had come to Hua*xian* from Italy around 1895–96.[122] After the Boxer uprising they went into hiding in Lin County, then returned to Hua County to purchase land and build a church in Xiao Zhai village, Liu Gu township, thirty-five *li* east of Hua County town. Through providing food relief and charity money, the missionaries Bai Yuhua, Ai Wenhua, and Pei Chengzhang amassed a following of several thousand people by 1912. By 1929 they had persuaded thirteen thousand people to join the Catholic Church.[123] Most of their earliest converts were peasants from the poor salt land villages in southeast Hua County—Guan Chaoying, Zhong Xinzhuang, Caopo, and Qi Ji.[124]

By the outbreak of the struggle against the salt police there were some four thousand Catholic peasants in Qi Ji and its sister villages.[125] One of the earliest converts to Catholicism in Qi Ji was Liu Benxing, the uncle of Liu Chaode.[126] In 1923 Liu Benxing became a priest and converted Liu Chaode.[127] Liu Chaode was able to use these connections to Catholicism to resist the Kuomintang fiscal center in the years 1925–32. In 1925–27 Liu Benxing and his former fiancée, now a nun, encouraged Liu Chaode to file his legal petition in the Hua County court.[128] From 1928 until 1931, the assembly hall of the Catholic church in Qi Ji became a meeting point for the peasants' deliberations on how to fight the salt police. The third regiment's recruits were from the predominantly Catholic lineage, of which Liu Chaode was an eminent member.

When it came to mobilizing Qi Ji against the revenue force of Kuomintang state makers, therefore, Liu Chaode was able to call on the Catholic peasants of the salt market. Most interestingly, although the saltmakers in Qi Ji's third regiment were converts to Catholicism, their political activism also resonated with older folk religious precepts that prescribed community opposition to oppressive governance. Throughout 1929–32 Liu Chaode had organized antipolice assemblies on Catholic church grounds and then gathered the saltmakers in these assemblies to prepare for combat with the police at the adjacent Guangong Temple.[129]

Clearly, Liu Chaode was able to utilize his ties to folk Catholicism to foster popular support for the anti-police action of 1932 in Qi Ji itself and within the twelve-district area in which the countywide May 13 movement formed.[130] For one thing, the geography of the movement correlated positively with the poorest salt land villages, which figured prominently in Catholic lay organization. The Mingyuan Primary School, from which Liu Chaode had graduated, had been established by the missionary Pei Chengzhang, and its admissions policy was aimed at accepting primarily the poor children from the agriculturally distressed villages. For another, after 1923–24, when Ai Wenhua became the bishop in Hua*xian,* this primary school became a center for teaching students the logic of collective action, and young people like Liu Chaode were instructed to unite their villages to defend the interest of the Church and its peasant followings against warlordism. On returning to their villages, many of these students became the self-appointed protectors of local folk against the salt police. By 1923 the Catholic Church was deeply involved in Hua County politics. The local priests in Caopo and Qi Ji were in close touch with town-based Italian priests who, owing to their privileged foreign status and their followerships in the villages, had assumed the role of advisors to the Hua County magistrates. From 1917 on they mediated disputes between the Hua County government and peasants; from 1921 on they pressed the Hua County magistracy to arrest and punish bandits who took the mission villages as their targets; from 1925 on they sanctioned peasant enlistment in local self-defense forces—and in 1928 they welcomed the Northern Expeditionary Army to Hua County. Liu Chaode's championing of peasant resistance to the police invasion of the salt market reflected this post-1911 Catholic political activity on behalf of the country people.

Many scholars have documented a process whereby foreign Catholic missionaries interfered in Chinese state relations with local society,[131] supporting lawsuits of local converts and protecting their religious clientele from the rule of the magistracy. This Catholic hegemony aroused great anger in county-level officials and eventually gave rise to a spate of antiforeign campaigns against missions in western Shandong during the Boxer Uprising.[132] The Chinese Communists also were dubious of the religiopolitical activities of Catholic missionaries and feared competition for peasant followerships from priests. One CCP source claims that the Catholic peasant saltmakers played a passive role in the 1932 rebellion, meekly submitting to the police in the Christian belief that the Superior Being would punish evil power holders in the afterlife;[133] and a party rendition of Liu Chaode's reminiscences on the Hua County saltmakers' struggle does not even mention the Catholic affiliations of Liu and his associates.[134] Contrary to this CCP caricature, the Catholic peasants of Qi Ji were the vanguards of the popular struggle to reject Kuomintang state development in Hua County. They mobilized their religious network to reinforce their collective protest to chase the market opportunity presented to them between 1923 and 1928;[135] they found protection from the fiscal arm of Chiang Kai-shek's police state in the indigenous Catholic priests who had developed considerable political clout in the Hua*xian* prior to 1928.[136] The native Wang Congwu–led faction of the CCP thus gained popularity by acknowledging the authority of the local Catholic leaders of this collective opposition to Kuomintang state making and enhanced its reputation by assigning Liu Chaode, and his priestly advisors, a significant place in the Thirteen County Peasant Saltmakers' Association that formed in the wake of the 1932 anti-state protest actions in Puyang, Hua*xian,* and Dongming.

The CCP's frangible organizational presence also presented a problem. The party had established its organization in Hua County in 1931, when Nie Zhen, Hu Jingyi, and Wei Bocai founded party branches in Sancun and Cheng Guan village.[137] The half-year before the 1932 rebellion saw these local party leaders advising peasant saltmakers on how to proceed with collective action, and they also participated in a few antisurtax struggles around Sancun in late 1931.[138] But in the year following the May 13 protest movement they could not even carry out propaganda work in the villages around Qi Ji, for in October, 1932, Liu Chih, the pro–Chiang Kai-shek governor of Henan, led Kuomintang troops to Hua County to arrest Nie Zhen and smash the CCP, whose stalwarts had organized a premature autumn harvest uprising. By late 1932 Nie Zhen was forced to flee to Beijing via the party's underground network in Hebei, and the Hua*xian* CCP had collapsed.[139]

In the postrebellion decade, the peasants of Qi Ji relied not on the CCP, but rather on the generosity of their market-based leaders, Liu Chaode and Liu Xianfeng, to cope with disaster.[140] A few families obtained relief grain from Tianjin Relief Missions, placed their sons in the tuition-free Ming Yuan Primary School,[141] and sent "surplus daughters" to the Catholic Mission School in Ji County.[142] They also relied on the goodwill of local Kuomintang leaders to avoid the political fate of the Hua County CCP, as Yang Rui, the sympathetic Kuomintang chief of Ba Li Ying district, repeatedly warned Liu Chaode to hide from the spies of the Nanjing government's Salt Inspectorate.[143]

When it came to mobilizing Qi Ji, therefore, the Communists had to go through local Catholic peasant leaders who already had established themselves as the champions of the antistate movement of the poor. Qi Ji's peasant saltmakers had taken on the police with the counsel of a few local party leaders, but they had started and sustained the struggle by their own initiatives. Poverty, popular Catholic allegiances, and the political insecurity prevalent in Hua*xian* after May of 1932 ruled out the kind of party building that was occurring in Qian Kou. The Wang Congwu–led CCP was connected to Qi Ji's peasant saltmakers by the barely visible thread of its brief contribution to their collective struggle to maintain the salt market. It is this shared interest in the struggle for the market that is remembered by the older peasants, and this memory would prove critical to the party's quest to organize popular resistance against the Japanese army during WWII.

The case of Qi Ji reveals that the role of the CCP in village protest was not as central as is often presumed in party-dominant models of mass mobilization. The people of this village organized their own collective defense of the salt market, which offered the only escape from debilitating poverty, without significant CCP guidance—Liu Chaode had been orchestrating peaceful, legal protest against intensifying police interventions for many years before the Wang Congwu–led CCP approached him, and the Communists did little to alter the mode of such protest. Here they were obliged to consider the particular economic, religious, and political features of village life conditioning peasant responses to the general process of Kuomintang state making. If there was to be any chance of linking village protest with the popular union of border area peasant saltmakers, then such particulars had to be respected rather than reshaped or replaced by Communist ideology and organization. The case of Qi Ji informs us that the CCP sometimes drew its poor village allies into regional struggle through a process of reinforcing community economic protest that did not automatically build up the party's administrative base locally.

SIX

The Battle with the Bicycle Cops in Subsistence-Level Fanzhuang

The struggles of the peasant saltmakers in the Hebei-Shandong-Henan border region extended from 1915 to 1935 and even up to the eve of the Japanese invasion, so that it was not just a matter of a few big protest incidents breaking out for a year or two in the county towns (Puyang, Dao Kou, etc.) on which most of this narrative is focused. The 1932 protest movement in Puyang was but one important part of a coherent pattern of regional collective action. In the ensuing years saltmakers in scores of counties took part in similar mobilizations. In August of 1934 the Changlu salt tax police destroyed salt ponds around Zhao Gu village, north of Daming, provoking a confrontation that swelled the ranks of the salters to several thousand, many of whom joined in a protest march on Daming town.[1] A year later, on October 15, several hundred saltmakers in Quzhou County resisted the police ban on production; when the salt police, now joined by hundreds of other police units, attempted to enforce the ban with machine gun fire, several thousand saltmakers appeared at Zhangzhuang village, where the two sides engaged in a violent fight that lasted a whole day and night.[2] The Quzhou uprising, which involved saltmakers from Pingxiang, extended into early 1936, when the peasant saltmakers and nitrate producers of Qi village attempted to bomb the Pingxiang headquarters of the salt police,[3] who beat the protestors back and who stalked their leaders into late 1936.

Six months before the Quzhou uprising on 12 April 1935, six thousand people surrounded Nanle County town and let the Kuomintang-appointed magistrate know they were in solidarity with the Transcounty Saltmakers' Association.[4] This big town-focused protest event, which reflected popular indignation over the aggression of the finance ministry's salt police in

Nanle town, grew out of many smaller, low-profile protests against salt police incursions over the previous several years.[5] In the fall of 1931 salt-makers from west Nanle had gathered against the police in Yuancun market. For the next four years crowds of county people in different villages and markets followed suit, their protests culminating in the 1935 springtime protest.

The Nanle saltmakers also were linked with the forms of regional political resistance promoted by their counterparts in nearby Puyang. In July, 1932, for example, they sent several representatives, including CCP activist Guo Shukui, to join the General Union, which grew out of the 1932 struggle in Puyang town.[6] When a Changlu salt police cavalry battalion attacked the General Union in the spring of 1933, killing four saltmakers at Qi Li Dian on the Daming-Nanle border, Wang Congwu, joined by Yang Qixiang, the head of the Daming Saltmakers' Association, led people from thirteen counties to fight the police battalion in Nanle, and some of Nanle's salters joined in this fight.[7] In mid-1934, months after the destruction of the Nanle CCP, Zhang Ziyou and a small delegation of Nanle saltmakers secretly went to Bei Wangzhuang in Qingfeng to request help from Wang Shanyi, the leader of the Qingfeng County saltmakers; and in early 1935 they travelled to Puyang's Cheng Guan to seek advice from saltmakers Guo Fengxiang and Huang Decheng, two leaders of the 1932 rebellion in Puyang town.[8] Clearly there were linkages back to the big protest action in Puyang; just as clearly these linkages were not solely or simply the product of CCP activity.

The leaders of the regional CCP-led Transcounty Saltmakers' Association actually did not control the popular movement in the towns or villages of Nanle. At the county level, CCP controls were minimal: Wang Tongxing, a Nanle party activist, was part of the leadership of the Nanle Association for the Salt People's Livelihood, and some of the savvy village-based leaders were aware of party support for their struggle. The saltmakers' movement was based in the villages of Liangcun, Liancunpo, Yuancunji, San Huang, Fanzhuang, and Nan Qing Dian, all in the western and southern parts of Nanle, where the soil was impregnated with salt. The popular movement was largely independent of the CCP, and the influence of the CCP-led saltmakers' association was indirect until 1933–35. Prior to the protest explosion of early 1935, the movement was limited to an elementary, cautious form of resistance, involving verbal battles and brawls with the fiscal police and appeals to the county Kuomintang authorities.

In Fanzhuang, which became the headquarters of the 1935 springtime upheaval, protest was characterized by low-profile civil disobedience, and prior to 1935 it was only loosely integrated with the main storm front of the saltmakers' movement in Puyang. Agriculture in Fanzhuang still took precedence over earth salt production into the early phase of Nationalist rule, and few peasants were inclined to leap into antistate protest. Nevertheless, because of its proximity to the county seat, Fanzhuang became a crucial spot in the saltmakers' movement. By focusing on Fanzhuang, one can more fully appreciate the way in which the popular struggle over the market created splits in the state. Where Kuomintang county government did not totally become the instrument of the centralizing state and its Salt Inspectorate, peasants often gave up their produce and labor power in hope of enlisting the help of local authorities. They treated the local Kuomintang and CCP activists according to their own rules of self-initiated protest and counted among their friends those who helped them settle the conflict with the national state in favor of their market prerogatives, even if such allies had strong Kuomintang connections.

EARTH SALT PRODUCTION IN FANZHUANG'S ECONOMY, 1921–35

Production of earth salt was about the only thing enabling Qi Ji's people to keep body and soul together prior to WWII. Strictly speaking, Fanzhuang was in a different category. Still landowning minitillers, its inhabitants relied mainly on cropland production for survival up until the onset of Nationalist rule. They neither produced cash crops for the world market nor depended overwhelmingly on selling earth salt for long-distance internal markets.

Located in southern Nanle, Fanzhuang is one of thousands of wheat land villages on the North China plain. Even in 1930, nine-tenths of the village land was devoted to grain and vegetable production. Cotton occupied less than one hundred *mu* of the land. Except for a tiny minority of land-short households, peasants grew three successive grain crops over two years— wheat, Indian corn, and sorghum—supplemented by red turnips, pumpkins, sweet potatoes, and melons. Wei Yinshun recalls, "Prior to the Anti-Japanese War we could eke out an existence and survive mainly by eating grain and the many vegetables we planted."[9]

Prior to 1930 there were 105 peasant households and 500 people in Fanzhuang. Most had migrated to Nanle from Hong Tong County in Shanxi during the Ming period. From the Qing dynasty until today there have been seven lineages in this village—Wang, Song, Zhai, Yao, Zhang, and two Weis. Fanzhuang was a bastion of peasant smallholders before the struggle with the salt tax police.[10] There were no landlords in the village during the Republican era. Four out of five peasant households among those designated as poor after liberation in 1945 had been plowing and planting their own fields prior to 1930.

In Fanzhuang, the average peasant household numbered five persons, and its average landholding was in the range of sixteen to twenty-three *mu;* three-quarters of the peasant households in five of the main lineages owned

TABLE 3   Zhang Lineage Landholdings
in Fanzhuang, 1930

Name	Number of Mu of Land
1. Zhang Xuan	12.0
2. Zhang Xianghui	20.0
3. Zhang Haishan	13.0
4. Zhang Tongtang	12.0
5. Zhang Lanxiang	40.0
6. Zhang Bin	32.0
7. Zhang Jun	30.0
8. Zhang Tingjun	30.0
9. Zhang Xin	27.0
10. Zhang Cheng	25.0
11. Zhang Shongshen	22.0
12. Zhang Xiaoshun	23.0
Total land owned by Zhang lineage	291
Mu per lineage member	23.8

upwards of twenty-three *mu*. Most peasants were in roughly the same economic position—they had just enough cropland to earn a livelihood.

This is not to say there was absolute equality, or that peasants had equal access to the material resources of the village. The Wang lineage owned more than one-fifth of the village land, and three Wang families possessed one hundred *mu* each in the western quarter. The Wangs possessed the best wheat land in Fanzhuang (also partially salinized), with an average of twenty-three *mu;* those in the poorest Zhai lineage averaged ten and a half *mu* of acutely salinized land.

The landholdings of the Zhai lineage illustrate the economic gaps among lineages and vulnerability of poor tillers prior to the arrival of the police. Before 1935 there were fifteen households in the Zhai lineage, averaging six persons. The households of Zhai Zuolin, Zhai Yuangao, Zhai Feng, Zhai Jinyan, and Zhai Zhen possessed twenty-five, twenty, eighteen, sixteen, and fourteen *mu*, respectively. The remaining ten—including that of Zhai Peng, one of Fanzhuang's protest leaders—all possessed less than twelve *mu*, and five of them possessed less than seven. People in these land-poor, marginalized lineages survived in part by making earth salt for the market, a routine that preceded the establishment of the Nanjing government and its *Shuijingtuan*.[11] (See also Tables 3 and 4.)

Fanzhuang was not a strife-torn village. The peasants in lineages with greater landholdings did not exploit land-poor peasants. Leaders worked through a common village chief to provide services for villagers of various

TABLE 4   Yao Lineage Landholdings
in Fanzhuang, 1930

Name	Number of Mu of Land
1. Yao Wuxu	14.0
2. Yao Juiwen	30.0
3. Yao Tongluo	25.0
4. Yao Tongtang	43.0
5. Yao Jianli	34.0
6. Yao Juihui	22.0
7. Yao Shiying	23.0
8. Yao Hesheng	19.0
9. Yao Tengmao	25.0
10. Yao Song She	11.0
Total land owned by Yao lineage	296
Mu per lineage member	29.6

lineages and to protect the village's resource base from outside claims. And peasants from every lineage came together to celebrate the Spring Festival, which centered on the Guandi, or war god, temple.

Although Fanzhuang had some of the poorest soils in Nanle County, its peasants by and large managed to scratch out a living following the famine of 1921.[12] They made several adaptations to cope with grain scarcity in the years 1922–35. The first involved purchasing tiny strips of land in nearby villages to increase the number of *mu* planted to wheat and Indian corn, using income earned from selling straw hats (the village's specialty) in Nanle town, steam buns in Anyang, and cloth grain bags along the Nanle-Daming border. Through purchases of land in Yuangzhuang, Huzhuang, and Wenzhuang, all within one *li* of Fanzhuang, the village increased its landholdings from fifteen hundred *mu* to two thousand *mu* between 1929 and 1939,[13] enabling 80 percent of its peasant households to meet their minimum food requirements for over half the year when rainfall was adequate and the harvest was fairly good.

Still, grain harvests could not keep pace with subsistence needs. The harvest all but failed in 1927, was poor in 1928, and for the next five years was at best average. Red turnips, pumpkins, and sweet potatoes thrived in the alkaline soils of Fanzhuang, however, and vegetable crop production became very popular. "We could manage half a year with our grain yields," recalls Wang Wenxun, "but the rest of the year we ate vegetables, especially salt turnips."[14]

But even the richest peasants could not count on grains and vegetables alone.[15] Their second, and by far the more significant, adaptation was salt making. Compared with Qian Kou's experiment with earth salt production, theirs initially was a cautious means of restabilizing food supply. Fanzhuang peasants used the salt proceeds to purchase food grains in Nanle markets, thereby avoiding working as hired hands in other villages or migrating every time there was a drought.[16] Most villagers say that salt making did not commence until around 1923, when the grandfather of Zhai Zhongchun introduced the technique of boiling salt from Da Han Dao village in Daming County.[17] Before that time, Zhai recalls, "We made our living by cultivating the land."[18]

The technique of salt making in Fanzhuang differed from the solar evaporation method used in most villages of Puyang and Hua County. In Nanle County, peasants gathered salt earth from the poor alkaline lands and carried it back to their villages, where they placed it in small water basins, scooped up the liquid salt water in pails, and then poured the water into cauldrons, often shared by several families. They boiled it to yield a form of salt purer and more desirable than the salt produced by the solar pond system.[19]

During the Zhou dynasty this part of Nanle had been in the bed of the Yellow River, and up until the Ming period the villages of Nanle, Daming, and Wei*xian* were frequently subjected to floods. Although there were no major floods in this area during the century before 1930, the saline earth deposits still were five meters (sixteen feet) deep in the villages of southeast Nanle. Fanzhuang's peasants could freely gather all the saline earth they could manage.[20] They made trips to villages such as Xuzhuang and Huangzhuang to collect saline earth.[21] Moreover, Fanzhuang was rich in sorghum stalk and tree leaves, which cut fuel costs tremendously. In comparison to many other villages in Nanle County, salt making here was lucrative.

Selling earth salt prior to 1935 enabled Fanzhuang's peasants to stay in the village and maintain their agricultural routines. Zhang Yun describes economics in his household:[22]

There were eight people in my family when I was ten years old, around 1929. We owned twenty-six *mu* of land. We planted twenty *mu* to wheat, and after the wheat harvest we planted this same twenty *mu* to Indian corn. Another two *mu* was planted to sorghum, and two *mu* was sown to millet. We planted one *mu* to beans and one *mu* to cotton. We also planted two *mu* of red turnips in May, and one-half *mu* of pumpkin in March.

The wheat crop yield was one hundred *jin* per *mu* on the average. The Indian corn . . . averaged one hundred fifty *jin* per *mu*. We got one hundred *jin* of sorghum per *mu* and seventy *jin* of millet per *mu*. We got two thousand *jin* of wheat, three thousand *jin* of Indian corn, two hundred *jin* of sorghum, and one hundred forty *jin* of millet. All in all, therefore, we got about 5,340 *jin* of millet. Each person needed at least 500 to 600 *jin* of grain per year, so we were able to get by on our grain crops and vegetables. We did not sell any of the food we grew. We ate all of it.

But after the drought of 1927 we sometimes did not have enough food. We had to buy food grains to make up for the shortfalls. There were two ways we got the money to purchase grain.

We peddled grain and charcoal balls in Hebi, a distant market town. My father started doing this around 1929. We borrowed the money to do this peddling from Wang Jun, the teacher in our village. He did not charge us interest. We used these loans to purchase millet in Nanle markets, which we sold for a higher price in Hebi. We could earn a profit of sixty *jin* of grain per week in the slack agricultural season. While in Hebi we bought charcoal balls at one cent per *jin*, and then resold them back in Nanle for two cents per *jin*.

My father started making salt when I was about twelve years old, around 1931. . . . We owned one cauldron and shared it with [three] other Zhang households. Each family paid one silver dollar towards the cauldron. Since my third brother was in school and my second brother was a soldier in Nanle town, I was the one who made the earth salt.

We boiled the salt and got one hundred fifty *jin* in one day. We also had two ponds. If the weather was sunny and hot we could get fifty *jin* per day from the two ponds. Relying on these two methods, in one month we could produce about 2,050 *jin* of salt.*

We sold the salt near the King of Hell temple and in Wu village market. We also went to Yuancunji, but only if we could not sell all of it elsewhere. Our Fanzhuang salt was very famous for its superior quality and desirable taste. It was not like the bad tasting *xiaoyan* from Neihuang; some people said it tasted as good as the sea salt.

For every forty *jin* of salt we sold we got about one silver dollar. In 1932 one silver dollar could buy twenty-eight to forty-five *jin* of red sorghum grain. So we could get about fifty silver dollars for our salt per year, and we could purchase at least fifteen hundred *jin* of grain with this income.

A third adaptation was migration. When the harvest withered in the drought of 1927, Song Shanguan recalls, "I went to Tong Guan county in Shanxi to stay with my uncle, who was a Buddhist monk in the Golden Bell temple. I worked in a private steam bun factory and earned three silver dollars per month. I stayed there about five months, from November through the Spring Festival and returned to Fanzhuang in March 1928."[23]

Approximately 10 percent of Fanzhuang's families had to migrate. The Wei and Zhai lineages, whose lands were located in the acutely salinized eastern quarter, said to be the worst salt land in Fanzhuang, began to migrate to Da Ning, Pu*xian*, and Tong Guan in Shanxi in the late 1920s.

---

*They did not produce the salt every day of the month.

When drought increased the difficulty of wringing a crop from the land, the young males from these lineages often followed the old migration trails that led to Shanxi and worked as hired hands, porters, and shepherds. Most of their migrations were temporary, however, for the possibility of making salt in Fanzhuang occasionally allowed them to return home to Hebei, rejoining their families to help with farming.

Wei Qingyuan, who first began migrating to Shanxi in 1928 when he was fourteen, says that returning to Fanzhuang became a normal routine:[24]

> Around the seventeenth year of the Republic [in 1928] there was a flood in Fanzhuang. My third brother and I fled to Shanxi. Father, Mother, and my elder brother stayed on in Fanzhuang. I returned to the village permanently only in 1935.
>
> We went to Shanxi because people from about ten other Fanzhuang households went there. Some . . . had established themselves in Pu county. We begged our way to Pu county, and once there we saw a lot of untilled land. We began to cultivate wheat and Indian corn. We got at least one harvest each year. For the first three years we did not pay anything to the landowners, but afterwards we paid them for allowing us to till the land. We paid the money to the chief of Lu Ziyan village in Pu county.
>
> I came back to Fanzhuang many times, and I was here at the time of the saltmakers' struggle in 1935. I helped to boil the water for the several thousand saltmakers who came to Fanzhuang and lived and ate in our village for a few days. My father and brother joined the saltmakers who came here to drive the police away. They had made salt in the years before the struggle, and the salt harvest was good in these years.

REVENUE DEMANDS AND PEASANT LIVELIHOOD

From the fall of the Qing to the outbreak of the saltmakers' struggle in the early 1930s, the peasants of Fanzhuang were dutiful political actors, and no major conflict occurred between its residents and the Nanle magistracy prior to 1935. There was trouble over land tax payments around 1931, but things returned to normal in 1932, after the Nanle tax officials taught peasants the importance of prompt tax payments. The crisis in peasant-state relations occurred only when the central government's revenue police refused to heed the village plea to halt the attack on earth salt production.

The county government collected only two kinds of taxes in Fanzhuang. One was the land tax. Fanzhuang's peasant paid one silver dollar per every eight *mu* of land sown to grain or vegetable crops, about average for the county. Peasants usually paid this tax to the village head, or *touyi*, who was chosen by the better-off households to deal with taxation. Most paid the land tax on time, and the village head was rather successful in persuading tax assessors to make reasonable adjustments. Prior to 1930, Zhai Zuolin remembers, "those who could not pay the precise land tax could get it reduced."[25] A family could postpone payment if the crop was poor, on the promise of paying double the following year. In actual practice, recalls Yao Zhixian, "the poorest members of the village seldom had to pay a double tax in the second year."[26]

The county government also took an "animal labor tax" on peasant households with over sixteen *mu* of land. In lieu of cash, those affected could deploy their horses, mules, or donkeys to work for the Kuomintang county government. Wei Yinchun and others often used their animals to transport grain, bricks, and firewood for Kuomintang troops in town and countryside.[27]

From the death of Yuan Shikai in 1916 until the ascent of Chiang Kai-shek in 1931, Nanle County was a stomping ground for various militarists, and Fanzhuang itself was given an introduction to warlord politics around 1930. Late in this period of multiple sovereignty, Feng Yuxiang's National People's Army held Nanle County. Between 1928 and 1930, however, Zhang Xueliang's northern army challenged General Feng and captured the county in the Great War for the North China plain, and thereafter appointed the magistrates and assessed the taxes in Nanle. In 1929, a contingent of Zhang's northern army took up residence in Fanzhuang, and stayed for a fortnight, but brought their own food and provisions.[28]

For the most part, the land tax was paid directly to officials appointed by the Kuomintang government tax bureau, and paid on time.[29] The county tax authorities occasionally sent a person from the jail, as opposed to the tax bureau, to collect the land tax. According to Wei Yinshun, "this person was corrupt, and did not give all of the collected tax to the Nanle government."[30] This seems to have been the extent of political entrepreneurship in Fanzhuang. There was little or no broker activity in the realm of trade.

Fanzhuang's old-timers mention only two surtaxes: one on selling pigs and another on building the foundation for a new house. The pig tax was shrewdly avoided, and complaints over the building tax were voiced mainly in the Wang lineage, whose fertile wheat fields and educational skills gave its leaders the means to negotiate such matters with the local Kuomintang government.[31] The real significance of Fanzhuang's surtax history was in what did *not* transpire: the county government never slated the village for a land or harvest surtax.

Although relations with the Nanle Kuomintang Tax Bureau worsened somewhat after 1928, taxation produced only one minor conflict, around 1929, which grew out of the fear that the tax officials were going to eliminate the land tax exemption of the poorest households whose fields were situated in the acutely salinized eastern outskirts of the village. Peasants who owned less than sixteen *mu* of poor salt land in the east had been exempted from the land tax when the harvest was poor.[32] About 1928, however, the

Nanle tax authorities decided to assess according to the amount of land sown, rather than the quality of the land or the amount of the harvest. Peasants saw this political development as a threat to their security, especially because they were looking to salt-generated income to purchase grain and to offset land taxes.

Around 1930–31 Fanzhuang's peasants began to choose two village tax representatives, one for the "rich" western part of the village and one for the poor eastern half. Both representatives reported to the Fanzhuang village chief, who in turn dealt with the Nanle tax authorities.[33] If the *touyi* failed to turn in the designated tax quota on time, the Nanle Kuomintang tax officials took him to the county jail. In the years of disappointing harvests the Nanle tax officials never apprehended the west side tax representative, but they repeatedly arrested the representatives of the salinized east.[34]

For more than a year, the village was thrown into a minor crisis with the Nanle County government. The Nanle tax officials pressed the representatives to pay any land tax deficit, but this scheme proved counterproductive: no one then dared to become the tax representative for east Fanzhuang.[35] Peasants sought tax relief via a combination of nonviolent stratagems: by taking one-month turns as tax representatives, by borrowing money to pay the land tax in the autumn, and by increasing their earth salt production.

Fortunately, the peasants of Fanzhuang could generate the income they needed to stay at subsistence and satisfy the Nanle County tax officials. They were able to use their earth salt proceeds to restabilize family income. Zhai Zuolin's family, for example, had eighteen *mu* of land in the alkaline eastern half of the village;* and his household was producing earth salt at a rate equivalent to the average yearly maximum output for Fanzhuang in the 1930s.[36]

> I was born in 1909, and I grew up in Fanzhuang. After the *fenjia* [in 1927] my father received twelve and one-half *mu*. Thereafter, my father's household acquired four *mu* of poor land, and purchased yet another two *mu* of land. . . . From 1927 until 1942 I lived with my parents, my sister and my brother. The five of us depended on the eighteen and one-half *mu* of land. Sixteen *mu* was crop land. But eight of the sixteen *mu* was salt land and hardly suitable for grain crops.
>
> In 1930 one person could eat only 200 to 300 *jin* of grain, but this was not enough to get by on, so we ate a lot of vegetables. We grew red turnips, pumpkins and sweet melons.
>
> In 1931, when I was twenty-two, we could produce 80 to 90 *jin* of wheat per *mu* in an average year. (A good year could bring 120 *jin*.) So we got about 720 *jin* per year. On this same land, we grew Indian corn at 100 *jin* per *mu*, and got

---

*Better off than other peasants in the Zhai lineage, Zhai Zoulin's household was in the lower half of village income brackets.

800 *jin* per year. The Indian corn was planted right after the June wheat harvest. But in some years we devoted four *mu* of this land to yellow beans.

In addition, on the other ten *mu* we planted five *mu* of sorghum, three *mu* of red turnips, and two *mu* of pumpkin. The sorghum brought 100 *jin* per *mu,* the turnips 300 *jin,* and the pumpkins 100 *jin.*

We also had one salt cauldron and one salt basin. I helped father make salt. I pulled the wheelbarrow full of salt earth from the fields to the basin. This earth came from our fields and from waste land near Fanzhuang. We produced earth salt three to four months of the year. We could get 100 *jin* of salt for every three days, or about 1,000 *jin* per month. The output was 3,000 *jin* per year.

I sold the salt at the King of Hell temple market fairs and in the Wucun market. Prior to the struggle with the police the price was four to five *fen* per *jin* of salt, that is, half the price of the Tianjin sea salt. We could get about sixty to seventy-five silver dollars earnings for the 3,000 *jin* of salt.

We used the earnings to buy sorghum. At the time one silver dollar could buy at least twenty-eight *jin* of sorghum in local grain markets. But we also had to use a portion of the proceeds from salt sales to buy the firewood for firing the cauldron, and this was a lot of money. We had to use two *jin* of firewood for every one *jin* of salt we produced. The market price of firewood was 2 *fen* (cents) per *jin,* so that this factor reduced the earnings from salt making by as much as half.

Here are the annual earnings of Zhai Zuolin household juxtaposed with basic subsistence requirements and the claims of the Nanle County government, circa 1931:

LAND AND SALT PRODUCTION	TAX (*In Silver Dollars*)
8 *mu* of wheat land	1
8 *mu* of sorghum/vegetable land	1
2 *mu* of grain land	1
animal corvée	1
one salt cauldron	1
Total	5

ITEMS OF NECESSITY	COST (*In Silver Dollars*)
1. Basic food grain (3,000 *jin*)	107
2. Salt	0
3. Oil/firewood (for stoking cauldron and decocting salt)	37.50
4. Vegetables	0
5. Matches	1
6. Clothes	0
7. Cauldron, pond construction, wheelbarrow	3
8. Emergency grain storage and medical needs	4
Total	152.50

ITEMS OF PRODUCTION AND INCOME	TOTAL
Land planted to grain (2,020)	72
Wheat—720	
Indian corn—800	
Sorghum—500	
Vegetables (equivalent to one-half year grain supply)	53.50
Earth salt production (3,000 *jin* per year, at 75 silver dollars)	75
Total	200.50
	−157.50
	43.00 silver dollars above subsistence

Zhai Zuolin's family was able to care for its livelihood and its tax obligations, but it is clear that the family could not do both without engaging in salt production. Zhao Zuolin says, "We were a little better off than other poor peasant families. In three out of ten years, the yield from our land could just about provide our family with all of its food. The rest of the time, however, we depended on salt making."[37]

SALT MAKING AND PEASANT RESISTANCE TO THE BICYCLE POLICE

Salt production for the market apparently took off between 1923 and 1928, for several reasons:[38] the warlord struggles over, and surtaxes on, maritime salt coming into the border area; the difficulty of producing a good harvest in the drought-ridden 1920s; the soaring price of Changlu maritime salt.

Protest within Fanzhuang had only a little in common with the resistance to the salt tax police in Qian Kou and Qi Ji, however. There were no fist-fights, no defenses of production with shovels and spades, no pellet-gun clashes with the police. Nor did the village spawn a saltmakers' association. Contrary to what CCP documents tell us,[39] peasant resistance to the police was not simply the product of the formally organized Thirteen County Salt-makers' League in which the party members were politically active, and Fanzhuang did not become a stronghold of the saltmakers' movement in Nanle County until the wild happenings of 12 April 1935.

Fanzhuang's location put it at a marked disadvantage (see Map 4). It was immediately adjacent to a flat macadamized highway that linked the surrounding countryside with Nanle town, the main gate to which was only four *li* from the village. Moreover, the Tianjin-based Changlu salt police, stationed in Nanle town after 1931, grew to company size by 1933 and were

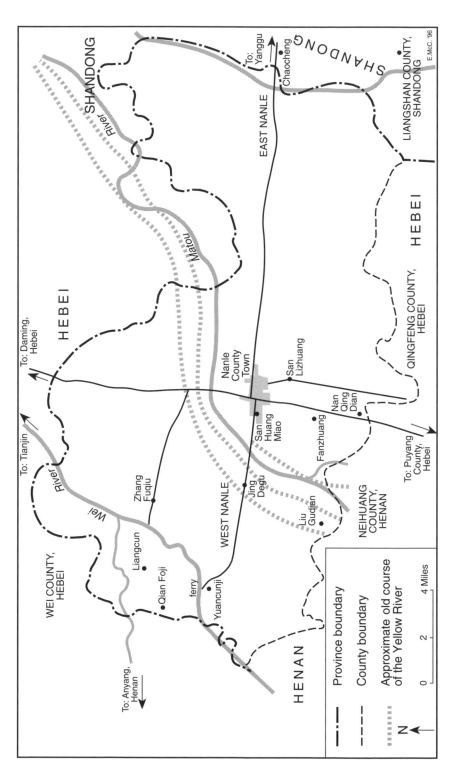

Map 4. Nanle County, Hebei Province, 1935

SHANDONG

SHANDONG

Matou River

HEBEI

Wei River

To: Daming, Hebei

To: Tianjin

To: Anyang, Henan

WEI COUNTY, HEBEI

Liangcun

Qian Foji

ferry

Yuancunji

Zhang Fuqiu

WEST NANLE

Jing Degu

Liu Gudian

Fanzhuang

NEIHUANG COUNTY, HENAN

HENAN

San Huang Miao

Nanle County Town

San Lizhuang

Nan Qing Dian

To: Puyang County, Hebei

EAST NANLE

To: Yanggu

Chaocheng

Chaocheng

LIANGSHAN COUNTY, SHANDONG

HEBEI

QINGFENG COUNTY, HEBEI

E.McC. '96

Province boundary

County boundary

Approximate old course of the Yellow River

N

0   2   4 Miles

backed up by several battalions in nearby Daming and Handan by 1935.[40] The forty-seven tax police stationed in Nanle town also were armed with modern Czechoslovakian-made firearms that surpassed the advanced weaponry of Zhang Xueliang's warlord troops.

The Changlu tax police came to Fanzhuang not on foot or horseback but on the modern bicycle. The bicycle, which the police introduced to Nanle in 1931, put Fanzhuang within only fifteen minutes of the forty-seven armed police, thirty of whom sometimes made daily raids on the village. The presence of this armed, mobile police force, coupled with reports of police killings of saltmakers along the Nanle-Daming border in September, 1934,[41] struck fear into the peasants of Fanzhuang, who chose to wage a war of passive noncompliance, while attempting to preserve the village's reputation of a law-abiding community of conservative tillers.[42]

From the standpoint of the tax police, Fanzhuang posed a serious problem. On the one hand, its salt was of superior quality and outsold the state's maritime salt. On the other hand, the people of this village were setting a dangerous precedent for other *peasants* who might contemplate salt production for the popular market.

Beginning in 1931 bicycle police rode into Fanzhuang with steel bayonets fastened on their rifles and used them to destroy the cauldrons along the main village streets.[43] The police also seized peasants who were in the fields gathering earth to be taken back to the courtyards for boiling[44] and took them to Nanle town, where they were detained in a makeshift jail and fined three silver dollars per head.[45]

The police attempted to restrict Fanzhuang's market participation in several ways, seizing and throwing the salt into small rivers and confiscating the peasants' wheelbarrows, to be returned only upon payment of a stiff fine.[46] There were police raids on peasant markets all across Nanle, with alarming consequences for Fanzhuang. By fall, 1931, they were disrupting the sale of earth salt in the village's three important primary markets: Yuancunji, Yan Wang Temple, and Wucunji. The raids on Yuancun market discouraged Fanzhuang peasants from trading there, but poor road conditions and the lack of allies for the bicycle police in the far countryside made strict enforcement in the Yan Wang (King of Hell) Temple market difficult.[47]

The first line of resistance to the police attack on production was a nearly universal retreat to nocturnal household production. Yao Shixuan remembers, "When the police first came to Fanzhuang to stop us from making salt we pretended to obey them. But actually we continued making salt. We carried the salt earth back from the fields to our courtyards at night, and we secretly made the salt. . . . I was afraid of the police, but I had no other way to make ends meet."[48] By the autumn of 1932 Fanzhuang at midnight looked as if it were burning down, as the women of countless households stoked the bonfires beneath the cauldrons. Peasants in surrounding villages knew the reason for the "flaming village," but the police never came at night, it was said.[49]

Peasants remember another aspect of resistance—the anonymous seizure of police bicycles. Around 1931, villagers formed small "police watch groups" that took away bicycles while the police were searching for cauldrons or chasing those who were gathering the saline earth from the fields. Yao Zhixian, whose father's cauldron was destroyed by the police, recalls,[50] "Once when I was playing in the fields the police came to our village. There were many more saltmakers than police. Some ran and some stayed. A few of the saltmakers who stayed seized the police bicycles and hid them in the fields. The police became very angry, because they had to walk back to the town. Later they sent a person to talk to us about the disappearance of their bicycles, and to ask us to get back the bicycles for them. Our village chief, Wang Xisan, sometimes arranged to have them returned to the police."

Going to jail became another form of popular resistance. Of course peasants pleaded with the police not to jail them, and throughout 1931–33 the Fanzhuang village chief went to Nanle town to implore the authorities to release many who had been unjustly jailed. A few peasants were released, and the fines imposed for the return of their salt wheelbarrows were reduced.[51] To some extent, these practices were attributable to the fact the police could not afford to feed their prisoners, but the significant point is that the saltmakers were able to rely on their relations (*guanxi*) with native Fanzhuang villagers who had lower positions in the Nanle County government to arrange such releases. Only in 1934, when Yao Zhisan took over as the Kuomintang party secretary of Nanle County,[52] did the releases cease.

Peasant resistance remained within the bounds of permissible disobedience. Some of the villagers greased the hands of the police and paid fines to retrieve wheelbarrows. But this form of resistance was too costly for the marginal poor. "My father and I once had our wheelbarrow taken by [the police] and we had to pay three silver dollars to get it back," Zhai Zhongchun relates. "We borrowed the money from a landlord named Yan Shuangde. He lived in another village. We paid off the loan in half a year. A lot of people borrowed money from this landlord. They had to pledge land as security for the loan. Most were able to repay the loan, but a few lost their land to Yan Shuangde."[53] Those "few" harbored bitter feelings toward the police, not toward landlord Yan.

Hoping to move beyond the reach of the police, peasants reduced their salt trade in Yuancunji and Nanle town market and shifted to the more rural markets of the King of Hell Temple and Wucunji. These traditional fairs enjoyed a pronounced surge in participation after the police besieged sellers in Yuancunji and Nanle town, with Fanzhuang's peasant saltmakers joining hundreds of their Nanle counterparts in searching out peddlers and purchase agents.[54] In resisting the police after 1932, Fanzhuang's peasants made the most of two great advantages—familiarity with territory and friendships with peasant buyers. Aware that the police were overextended, the saltmakers turned the King of Hell market into the main earth salt market in Nanle in this period. The police could send no more than twenty to thirty men to patrol each country market, and they were afraid of being physically abused if they converged on such markets with limited force. They simply could not mount the physical energy to effectively regulate clandestine salt trade coming into the Yan Wang Temple market from the surrounding villages.[55] According to Wei Qingyuan, who sold salt in this market area, the police sometimes made no appearance in such distant markets for many days.[56] When they did pedal into the King of Hell Temple market, they seldom apprehended more than a few people, for the market goers spotted them in the distance and signaled sellers to prepare for rapid dispersal.[57] Their flight was facilitated by widespread popular mistrust of the police and by market-based friendships between the quasi-peasant sellers and peasant buyers. According to Zhang Yun, "We avoided the police by running to the houses of peasants near the temple fair who hid us because we had traded with them many times, and they had purchased our salt. The police did not chase us into the houses, because they only wanted to disperse us."[58]

Having failed to halt marketing, the police renewed their efforts to stop production. In early 1933[59] they came to Fanzhuang again and again to destroy cauldrons and ponds. Rather than open retaliation, scores of peasants sought alternatives, the most common of which was seasonal work in the smaller towns of Nanle County.[60] Wei Chunyun left Fanzhuang to work in a winery in Can Gu town,[61] Wang Wenxun worked in a brick factory in He Xi,[62] and Zhai Zuolin went to work in a straw hat factory in Nanle town.[63] The young peasants who left the village for these jobs always returned to help their families with the spring harvest and summer planting and to produce salt on the sly. Along with those who stayed in Fanzhuang, they sometimes played a role in the next round of "struggle," which began and ended with the verbal battle of 1933.

By 1933 the police had begun to threaten even the better-off peasants in Fanzhuang, giving the poorest saltmakers the chance to associate their interest with the dominant actors in the village. The rich peasants and respected patrons of the Wang family lineage provided a political conduit for opposition to the police, and the development of the saltmakers' struggle in Fanzhuang must be understood in the context of their support for the poor Zhai lineage, whose members the police had driven to desperation.

During the winter of 1933 the grandson of Wang Jun, the primary school teacher of Fanzhuang, returned to the village on holiday from the Seventh Normal School in Daming. Wang Jian had been a Daming Seventh Normal School student for several years, but throughout his youth, he had produced earth salt for income. On learning of the police attack on Fanzhuang's salt production, Wang Jian became the key advisor to the peasant saltmakers, many of whom had attended his grandfather's school. He told them the story of *The Water Margin,* the epic tale of a "just" peasant uprising in Shandong during the Song dynasty.[64] The message apparently struck home, for in the following summer a delegation of saltmakers solicited his assistance in repelling the police.

The police were now confronted by a growing peasant counteroffensive. Each time they came to the village office they were received by a hostile gathering of about fifty peasants who, on Wang Jian's advice, shouted that salt making was not illegal. Their demand for the police to leave was supported by Wang Jian himself, now the counsel to the village office *in situ.* His message to the police was clear: *If you forbid the villagers from making a living, if you cut off their livelihood, then they will rebel and you, good fellows, will be held responsible.* There was a prolonged verbal war in which this message was reinforced by the vociferous popular assembly outside of the village office, and on this occasion, the salt tax police returned to Nanle County town without destroying the cauldrons and ponds.[65]

The police came back many times, however. Wang Jian returned to Daming without having established a formal saltmakers' association in the village, and although the verbal battles with the police continued, they were on a smaller scale. Fanzhuang peasants did not rush impulsively into anti-state rebellion. By 1934 they had gotten word of the police killings of peasant saltmakers in neighboring Daming. Fanzhuang quieted down for a time, and throughout the early 1930s protest remained nonviolent.

Nonetheless, in April of 1935 the village threw open its gates to several thousand armed saltmakers from Puyang, Hua*xian,* Neihuang, and Dongming—the vanguard of the Triprovincial Saltmakers' Association formed in Puyang and Qingfeng counties in 1932–33.[66] This protest league declared its support for the struggle to liberate Nanle County from the Changlu police. Armed with spears and shotguns, plus a few cannons, its militant volunteers (Dongming alone sent two thousand) marched up the main road from Puyang, through Qingfeng, and into Nanle. They intended to surround Nanle town and wallop the Tianjin-based salt police, who in the preceding six months had killed twenty peasant saltmakers and wounded many others in clashes near Da Han Dao, Qi Li Dian, and Zhao Gu village, just over the Daming-Nanle county line.[67] Fanzhuang, on the main line of this march, served as a rural staging area. Here the militants pitched camp, positioned their cannons to shell the town, and issued a call to arms. Overnight the village became a base for the rebellion. Many villagers helped out by boiling water, preparing tea, and arranging housing.[68]

Within a matter of days Fanzhuang's political fate was linked with that of the protest movement that was spreading across Nanle County. Responding to an April 10 request by the representatives of the Thirteen County Saltmakers' Association, one person from each household went to confront the police, so that, recalls Zang Ke, "about one hundred people joined the struggle; they all sat down in the town in protest for half a day and then came back to Fanzhuang."[69] The influential leaders of the Wang lineage played a role in negotiations that enabled the Nanle magistrate to settle the conflict over earth salt and to shorten the war that was breaking out between police and saltmakers.

One policeman and three saltmakers were killed, and scores of others wounded, in a battle to keep the police from exiting Nanle town to level salt ponds to the south.[70] The next afternoon Zhang Yongheng, the Nanle magistrate, led a delegation of local notables to Fanzhuang to negotiate a peace with several thousand saltmakers. The assembly included a gathering from Fanzhuang itself, headed by Zhai Peng, Zhang Lantai, and Zhai Hongliang, the leaders of the saltmakers.[71] The magistrate agreed to three demands: withdraw the salt police from the county; allow people to make and market private salt; and reimburse the families of the slaughtered protestors.[72] The Nanle magistracy thereby avoided a war that most likely would have toppled the local county government and acknowledged the legitimacy of peasant grievances against the central state.[73]

Kuomintang central government history holds that peasants were dragged into protest by the Communists; and CCP Central Committee history claims that primitive rebels could not have conceived or achieved any significant political goals without the party's assistance.[74] By understanding the hidden ways in which Fanzhuang was drawn into the county-level struggle, however, we can gain some perspective on the deep structure of the divergent popular forces in the countywide protest movement; and by focusing on the interplay between Fanzhuang's guarded resistance and the politics surrounding the changing process of protest in Nanle County, we can see that the threads connecting Fanzhuang's day-to-day resistance to collective protest were to be found in both country and town.

The big market village of Yuancunji quickly became the place where peasant crowds gathered to resist the police. In the spring of 1931, the Tianjin Changlu salt police came to Nanle town. They were commanded by Shao Qiyin, a college-educated salt inspector who promoted the use of bicycle police squads to suppress the earth salt markets in Yuancunji and surrounding villages. For several months, groups of ten bicycle police raided Yuancunji on market days. In the fall of 1931 the first struggle in Nanle started in this marketplace.[75] The peasant saltmakers of Yuancunji, Qian

Foji, and several other villages organized an ambush of strong men with carrying poles, knives, and bricks.[76] When the police entered the Yuancunji market, they were surrounded by several hundred, who seized the bicycles. After an hour of rough treatment, the police were released on the promise of never returning to Yuancunji and beat a hasty retreat back to Nanle town—on foot.

For twenty days Yuancunji peasants used the police bicycles to collect and transport saline earth to their salt ponds, only a short distance from the market. This was a blow to police prestige. Moreover, the bicycle was a novelty in Nanle, and many curious market fairgoers took a side tour to see the saltmakers ride the bicycles along the roads abutting their fields.[77] The story of how the saltmakers had acquired these contraptions, and extracted a promise that the police would not interfere in *xiaoyan* market transactions again, spread on Nanle market circuits.[78] The spate of bicycle disappearances in Fanzhuang in late 1931 was an echo of solidarity with the Yuancunji rebels.[79]

By mid-1932 the people of Yuancunji had formed a secret club of thirty people to watch the marketplace and inform people of impending police raids. This club received help from secret agents in the Nanle County Public Security Bureau, enabling its scouts to prepare the village well in advance of police arrival.[80] (The scouts were free-floating groups of three and four young men known for their pranks; in 1934 they gained notoriety by deflating the bicycle tires of a police squad.)[81] The police found an all-but-deserted salt market, as the scouts were quick to forewarn peasants and peddlers to flee the marketplace and hide in nearby houses, selling on back roads.[82] This same pattern of resistance surfaced in Fanzhuang's main salt market around 1933, just after villagers had learned of its practical value during market trips to Yuancunji, which explains in part why they took up market scouting and evasive selling in the King of Hell Temple fairs in 1933–34.[83]

The decisive influence in the peasant war in Nanle, however, came from salt producers and purchase agents living within the county town itself. Their village, San Huang, was located near the San Huang Miao (Three Emperors Temple). Its inhabitants were extremely poor, landless people who relied almost wholly on salt making, supplementing this activity with an assortment of small, town-based occupations.[84] Their material world was simple, but they were members of a very complex local economy that put them in touch with people in town and country. Before the police arrived, they sold earth salt in Nanle town marketplace, Yuancunji, the King of Hell Temple fair, and Wucunji. They made nitrate and sold it to private firecracker producers and to the Nanle County government Nitrate Bureau. They picked up manure from the town streets and sold it to peasants for fertilizer. They worked in the local straw hat factory or in the public security bureau of Nanle County. A few even worked as purchase agents for the Changlu Salt Company, simultaneously peddling earth salt!

Having overrun these marginalized people, the police discovered they could not control them. San Huang's rebels were prepared to do perpetual battle with the police, whom they repeatedly outwitted. Their daring conduct eventually ignited the popular imagination for collective action in Fanzhuang and other villages.

When the salt police first came to Nanle town, they set up headquarters in the Changlu Salt Shop and proceeded to attack three of the village's old markets—including the market in Nanle town, only a ten-minute walk from San Huang. The police seized a number of San Huang saltmakers. Several young saltmakers moved quickly to counter the police seizures, triggering a sensational rumble that had countywide ramifications.[85] In the spring of 1932 the police seized the uncle of Xu Chun. In a rage, Xu Chun challenged the police single-handedly. Taking a bag of earth salt to the Changlu Salt Shop, he began "selling" it openly, daring the police to lay a hand on him. The Changlu salt tax police were thunderstruck (just as they were in neighboring Daming County, when, in this very spring, a hot-tempered saltmaker from Wang village armed himself with a sharp knife and began selling his earth salt in front of the government salt shop near Da Han Dao village.)[86] The central government had not yet authorized them to use deadly force in dealing with the saltmakers—that was two years away. In the days ahead Xu Chun repeatedly carried his earth salt to the salt shop, distributing it free of charge to any "customers" who came to the scene. He then assembled six of his fellow saltmakers, all skilled in *gongfu,* who went to the salt shop and beat up several police. Additional salt police units came to the scene and locked the protestors inside the shop. Wei Zhouchao, an influential member of the Nanle gentry and San Huang's most illustrious resident, petitioned the police for release of their prisoners.[87] Reluctant to offend the nobility of the town where they resided, the police released the young turks.

The episode bore a significant message for the peasant saltmakers who were hauled into jail or forced to substitute work in the straw hat factory for salt making: the police were no match for the collective power of the poor. This was the unrecorded history of Fanzhuang, as well.[88]

The police campaign to suppress the salt market drove San Huang's people to join up with popular anti-police actions in the countryside, where they spread the idea of market sentry groups (as in Yuancunji) and of seizing the police in besieged marketplaces (as in Qi Li Yao). During early 1932 the police arrested four people in Qi Li Yao village and brought them to the detention center in Nanle town, where they held them for arraignment in Daming. Thirty villagers in San Huang and Qi Li Yao abducted several policemen, then demanded an exchange of prisoners. The saltmakers gave up their captives plus fifty silver dollars, borrowed from many neighbors, to get back their confederates, and San Huang thereby gained the reputation of being a magnanimous village.[89]

Such popular abductions were combined with parades of the captives through the villages of the countryside. The people of San Huang played a leading part in the most famous procession, which took place just south of Fanzhuang in the autumn of 1932.[90] Xue Jiaofa led a hundred people, including thirty from San Huang and fifty from Huayuan village, to Nan Qing Dian to capture Shao Qingyi, the chief of the salt police, during a police raid on Nan Qing Dian market, then paraded him through Qi Li Yao, Yaodong and Yaonan, and Nan Qing Dian itself, "making him promise peasants in each village he would not interfere with salt making,"[91] recalls Xiao Jianchao (the nephew of Xie Jiaofa). Li Chunchuan, the leader of the San Huang saltmakers, persuaded the troupe to release Chief Shao and gave him a safe personal escort back to town, past Fanzhuang, whose silent rebels did not miss the counterattack by the people of the town.

Protestors sometimes achieved their goals without physically engaging the police. The Wu Li Bei incident of 1935 is a case in point. The people of San Huang, learning that the salt police in Nanle town were preparing to conduct a raid on a market near Qingfeng, gathered a hundred people to surprise a thirty-man bicycle squad at Wu Li Bei. Outnumbered and without reinforcements, police let it be known they did not want a violent confrontation and returned to Nanle town. The recent history of conflict resolution in Daming and other protest counties had shown that they might have to compensate the families of saltmakers killed in street fighting. Many of them were poor; and they were not persuaded that the Kuomintang center would keep its promise to insure them against personal liability.

Within twenty-four hours, however, the police struck back at San Huang, sending a massive force to destroy salt tools and cauldrons and to proclaim a state of siege in San Huang and other salt-making villages inside Nanle town. Li Chunchuan and the saltmakers' association of San Huang began contacting salt producers in Nanle, Puyang, and Neihuang to join in a collective action to run the police out of Nanle town.[92] In March, about seventy people from San Huang came secretly to Fanzhuang along the back roads and through the fields to ask the peasant saltmakers to align with them in an open struggle against the police.[93] The peasants of Fanzhuang agreed and informally elected Zhai Peng, Zhang Lantai, and Zhai Hongliang to lead them in the struggle.[94] Subsequently, men from Fanzhuang and San Huang travelled to solicit help from counterparts in counties where the struggle was more advanced and in the hands of the Thirteen County Saltmakers' Association. Fanzhuang had been drawn into the vortex of regional antistate rebellion.

The 1935 protest movement in Nanle turned up an interesting array of actors, alerting the Kuomintang center to the persistent strength of its societal rivals on the North China plain and reminding its officials in the Hebei provincial government that the misuse of state force, and not simply the concentrated influence of the CCP, was fostering political mobilization and collective protest.[95]

As the saltmakers in San Huang broadened the base of the rebellion, a new cast of characters entered the struggle against state market controls. First came the little army of the Transcounty Saltmakers' Association, whose leadership authorized a march to Fanzhuang, where it prepared to bombard the ramparts of the town and storm the police headquarters. Its 3,007 members came from nearly ten counties and put on a show of strength that compelled the Nanle magistrate to reconsider the wisdom of harboring the revenue police. The association's demonstration of force drew in 3,000 peasant saltmakers from the rural salt land villages surrounding Nanle town—from Xinyuan, Cangu, San Lizhuang, Huangzhuang, Miaozhuang, Xuzhuang, Ji Lo, Wu Litun, Lizhuang, Nan Qing Dian, and from Fanzhuang. The popular force doubled as the political balance of power began to shift.[96]

Numbers and banners were not enough, however, to do battle with the Kuomintang center's revenue police. The leaders of the San Huang saltmakers reached out for new allies. In the second week of April bandits were brought into the struggle.[97] Their lair was in western Shandong, only fifty *li* from Nanle town. Wang Pengzhao, a San Huang resistance leader, had served with their leaders, Zhi Ergang and Zhang Shidong, in Yuan Shikai's Qing army, and all three were skilled in the use of weaponry. Now the popular movement had added a quasi-military element, whose leaders were assured first pick of the weapons garnered from the police and, it was rumored, the public security bureau.

The movement now stood at 6,207. Six hundred members of the Red Spear Society rallied to join the rebels, who were in the process of ringing the town. The Nanle Red Spears were mainly from Wucunji, Zhang Fuqiu, and San Huang,[98] with allies in Wei*xian*, Daming, and ten other counties.[99] As we have seen, this secret society had a history of incendiary political activity in the small towns of the Hebei-Shandong-Henan border area. The appearance of its members on the outskirts of Nanle town, taking common ground with the saltmakers, portended a political crisis of great magnitude.

The Red Spear Society was a carryover from the Boxer Movement, which had gone underground in late Qing and spread from Shandong's Tangyi County to Nanle County in 1919.[100] In Nanle this society was led by Yang Yan,[101] whose unit served the interest of landlords and small peasant landowners and even protected the property rights of poor marginal peasants.[102]

In the spring of 1924, Yang Yan launched a campaign to spread the influence of the Red Spears in the vicinity of Ma market, along the Wei County border,[103] bringing his branch into open conflict with Shandong warlord forces.[104] Yang's five thousand followers staged armed struggles with warlord power holders in the small towns of Nanle, Wei County, Daming, and Qingfeng in Hebei, Neihuang, in Henan, and Fan*xian* and Dongming in Shandong[105] and did battle with the Nanle County government from 1924 onward.[106] The inability of the Kuomintang county militia to defeat this Red Spear force led to the dismissal of Bu Hengxu, the Nanle magistrate, around 1928, after which the militias of surrounding counties struck up a tenuous alliance with the Red Spears.[107]

The contingent of Red Spears who helped the saltmakers seal the Changlu salt tax police in Nanle town in April, 1935, was led by Yang Yuming, one of Yang Yan's trusted lieutenants.[108] This contingent was an electrifying force. Its leaders had been fighting the Nanle County government for over a decade, and its presence delivered a clear message: if you want to escalate this political conflict, we will oblige you.[109]

The Red Spears had established a foothold inside Nanle town in San Huang itself. Worse, from the standpoint of the Nanle County government, some Red Spears in San Huang had come to play a critical role in the Association for the Salt People's Livelihood, formed in Nanle just before the June wheat harvest of 1932. By 1934 this association had six hundred members, including a few local CCP leaders.[110] Many of the key leaders of the association lived in San Huang, and half of the association's leadership in San Huang was composed of Red Spear participants.[111]

In the protest of April, 1935, more than thirty members of this San Huang contingent of Red Spears led several hundred saltmakers to link up with the salt league army, peasants, bandits, and the other *ad hoc* Nanle Red Spears on the outskirts of the town.[112] They were not organized by the landlord-sponsored Red Spears of Zhang Fuqiu. Nor were they mobilized by the CCP, for the Communist Party had been all but destroyed by the Daming-Nanle Kuomintang in January, 1934, and its cadres had lost the limited influence they had exercised over the protest movement from late 1932 until early 1934.[113]

The Kuomintang-appointed magistrate realized that further police intervention would result in civil war. Unable to mobilize local force to guarantee the safety, not to mention the mission, of the police, he gave up on the finance ministry's scheme to siphon off salt revenue from the countryside by violence. Clearly, it was only after the popular movement checkmated the Nanle County government's ability to maintain the salt police by the deployment of collective force that the magistrate entered into "active discourse" with the country people.[114]

As his role as a central government spokesman diminished and popular access to him broadened, Zhang Yongheng embraced community protest by endorsing the "just dissent" against the Kuomintang center's salt revenue policy and by entertaining the popular request to rid the countryside of police. Many in the formidable crowd had invisible connections to the county government and their local elite—as did Zhang himself. This *internal* political situation tilted the outcome toward a favorable agreement on April 12.

The first ally was to be found in the Nanle Public Security Bureau. Many members came out of the village world, had blood ties to peasant salt producers, and were not prepared to subordinate their loyalties to high-level Kuomintang state makers. In Nanle County, for example, Xu Chaojing, Guozhang, and Li Si, all members of public security,[115] were also planted agents of the Association for the Salt People's Livelihood who constantly forewarned the country people of police raids on rural markets. When the crisis peaked, Magistrate Zhang knew he could not count them as reliable allies. He had only a hundred-man Kuomintang militia plus a harried contingent of bicycle cops, and he was not a foolish man.

Nanle was a gentry stronghold, and prominent minor gentry figures were unhappy with the police attempt to alter the structure of the local earth salt trade, turning peasants into crop thieves and bandits. Moreover, the gentry themselves had an economic interest in the earth salt trade. In Yuancun market village, for example, they secretly purchased earth salt wholesale from local peasants and peddlers and mixed it with the Tianjin sea salt, which they received at the wharf linking Yuancunji to the Wei River, and then sold the "sea salt" at a price below that of the maritime salt sold through the Changlu Salt Shop in Nanle town.[116] Similarly, the gentry in San Huang were involved in a web of relations with earth salt peddlers and purchase agents, such as Guo Shukui and Li Chunchuan, two of the leaders of the Association for the Salt People's Livelihood.[117] Wei Zhouchao, the gentry leader of San Huang, had placed himself on the side of the saltmakers as early as 1931, pressing the police for their release and preventing the saltmakers from undercutting deliberations with the magistrate.[118] A descendant of Wei Guangwei, an Imperial government advisor in the Ming dynasty, Wei Zhouchao had obtained *gongsheng* status in the late Qing period [119] and was far more influential locally than the Kuomintang-appointed magistrate.

When faced with political danger, therefore, the Kuomintang newcomer to Nanle County turned the governance of the county over to Wei and his associates.[120] On 12 April 1935, Magistrate Zhang called on the Nanle gentry to ask them to mediate the conflict and accompanied them to a number of villages where the mediations took place. He first went with Wei Zhouchao to San Huang and San Lizhuang, past the red flags of the popular assemblies; he then went with Wan Nianhe, another member of the Nanle gentry, to Fanzhuang, where the leaders of the small army of the peasant saltmakers were camped. In each village they visited, the Nanle magistrate and his gentry stewards begged the saltmakers not to attack the police, promising that in due course the police would be transferred out of the county.[121]

Zhang Yongheng, the Kuomintang-appointed magistrate, was not a member of the Kuomintang and was not prepared to pursue the interest of the central state to a point of surrounding himself with thousands of angry peasants. Appointed during the crisis years of the Republic, Zhang had not wanted this difficult post.[122] His position on the saltmakers' struggle was simple: the salt police were making it more difficult to collect the land tax, and the land tax with no rebellion was preferable to rebellion with no tax. The country people who greeted Zhang when he entered Fanzhuang to announce that the police were on their way out of Nanle were in agreement with this logic.

THE CCP IN FANZHUANG

Unlike Qian Kou, Fanzhuang had only a small CCP presence in the period of the saltmakers' protest; and unlike Qi Ji, where the party failed to build its base from liaisons with the popular movement, the CCP was able to make some headway among peasants who had been "reluctant rebels." Ironically, however, the strength of the CCP, whose members operated underground from 1934 until 1944, was derived in part from its supportive liaisons with a political form that has eluded many Western scholars of CCP-peasant relations: the Kuomintang.

On the face of it, the same combination of factors that facilitated the rise of the CCP in Qian Kou seems to have been at work in Fanzhuang. Its peasants were not locked into massive poverty, either before or after the 1935 rebellion. The loss of income derived from salt making was offset in the pre-1935 period by other avenues of employment and in the postrebellion phase by a return to normalcy in agriculture and salt production—right up until the Henan famine of 1942. Fanzhuang peasants were never reduced to the point where the amoral pursuit of material gain dominated interpersonal relations, and they regularly helped one another minimize the dangers of scarcity. The CCP was able to enter the village through the leadership of the families who assisted others in obtaining resources needed to resolve subsistence dilemmas.

The economy of Fanzhuang stabilized in the aftermath of the 1935 rebellion. The grain crop was about average. In 1937, when the Zhang River overspilled its banks and flooded village fields, the Indian corn was damaged, but the sorghum crop was fairly good.[123] The price of sorghum went up, in fact, enabling the peasants to rely on sorghum, profits from grain sales, and fish caught in their fields to make it through until the next harvest. The flood left the land richer, preparing it for a rich harvest the following year. Locusts threatened in 1938, but peasants beat them back, and

Fanzhuang enjoyed a bumper wheat harvest in that year. Salt making came back in these years. Peasants recovered income lost to state repression and began to reduce their dependency on supplemental wages in the town-based factories. When poor peasant families ran short of food, they sent a son to Baoding or Guangping in Hebei, or to Da Ning or Pu*xian* in Shanxi, where he worked as a hired hand, cattle herder, or shepherd for half a year.[124] This restabilization was reflected in the fact that no one died from starvation before 1942. Very few peasants left the village to beg until the 1942 Henan famine, in which forty persons perished.[125] Profits from salt making permitted the expansion of the village's cropland base by one-third and allowed Fanzhuang to cope with inadequate rainfall and to avoid the "hysterical materialism" that had preoccupied households and inhibited community discourse and camaraderie in Qi Ji after 1932.

With this stabilization, Fanzhuang's peasants were able to cope with the crisis of death and avoid the moral desolation that had defined Qi Ji village. Prior to 1942 even the poorest members of the village were able to die in dignity.[126] The rich members of the Wang lineage could afford funeral music,[127] and most Fanzhuang families could pay for proper funeral cere-monies. When there was a death, a family member approached the village chief to make the funeral arrangements. The family purchased a thin coffin in Ji Dao village, and eight pallbearers carried it to the burial ground. In short, with their economic condition improving slightly after 1935, most of Fanzhuang's saltmakers were able to ponder the advantages of future col-lective action.

The stability of Fanzhuang's grain harvests and the resumption of salt production for the market allowed peasants to avoid the internal squabbles over food supply that had ruptured the peace of Qi Ji and many other vil-lages. Crops were pilfered in Fanzhuang, too, but rich peasants were seldom pitted against poor, and seldom did this small thievery meet with bitter retal-iation. Wei Qingyuan's recollection of crop theft in Fanzhuang after the 1935 struggle suggests that the peasants of the salt market recognized the right of the poor to subsistence[128] and were capable of helping fellow vil-lagers. "Someone once stole from my sweet potato crop, in 1936. The thief was from Fanzhuang. The fellow had nothing, and his family was hungry. He was caught red-handed by me. I told him 'Do not steal from us. If you want the sweet potatoes, then just come and ask us and I will give them to you. . . .' We too had gone hungry at one point, and we lived in the same vil-lage, so it was reasonable for them to ask us for help."[129]

The first claim on village food resources was augmented by the Crop Watch Association, whose main purpose was to protect Fanzhuang's grain crop from outside predators. The association paid the ten poorest people in Fanzhuang to watch the fields for the entire village day and night. "Sorghum bandits"—sometimes led by the leaders of crop watch groups in other salt land villages—were repeatedly turned away. Wang Wenxun, who once worked for the association, recalls that they generally did not try to catch the crop thieves, but just drove them away.[130] The one or two who were apprehended were asked to find a guarantor from their village to give the victim an "apology dinner" and were then let go on the guarantor's promise that the culprit would not steal Fanzhuang sorghum again. The Crop Watch Association was supplemented after 1936 by family-based night watch groups.

In the years following the protest of 1935,[131] norms of trust and mutual cooperation guided Fanzhuang's peasants. Mutual aid pervaded basic agricultural pursuits. Two peasant households, each having only one traction animal, loaned one another their animals during the busy seasons, enabling both families to take turns using the animals to pull fertilizer carts or transport the harvest, thereby avoiding subhuman forms of labor. Salt making was also facilitated by mutual assistance. Villagers continued to pool funds to purchase cauldrons and shared wheelbarrows to transport salt to market.

To a surprising extent, interlineage reciprocity played a role in the economic recovery. This multilineage cooperation in crop production and salt making also suffused social relations and rituals surrounding death. Poor people often helped one another bury their dead.[132] The Weis and Zhais came to help the Zhangs, and the Zhangs came to help other lineages when it came to providing meals, digging graves, and carrying coffins.

CCP success in this village seems to have fallen halfway between Qian Kou and Qi Ji. Although the CCP eventually was able to take advantage of the existence of the family connections that gave Fanzhuang its propensity for collective action, several factors, in addition to great political insecurity, slowed the party effort to establish a deep and broad political base in Fanzhuang in the mid-1930s.

In Fanzhuang the CCP's recruitment fortunes reflected the diversity of peasant lineage endowments. There was a strong correlation between substantial landholdings, lineage strength, educational status, and CCP fortunes.[133] Thus the party achieved a degree of spotty growth between 1934 and 1938, emerging along a limited axis of extended familism that, in a comparably robust version, had favored associational politics for Qian Kou. The village people who initially came over to the party in 1938 possessed the prime grain lands, received the best education, and produced a junior line via the process of *fenjia*.[134] The earliest cadres of the CCP in Fanzhuang were all from the rich peasant households in the Wang lineage—Wang Xilu, Wang Jian, and Wang Sanxuan all came from a background of "enabling familism."[135] All were able to use the wealth, prestige, and power of their lineage to enlist peasant saltmakers in the party. Conversely, the land-hungry, uneducated, and poorly endowed households residing in the highly saline eastern sector—including Zhai Peng, Zhang Lantai, and Zhai Hongliang, the leaders of the peasant salters—never joined the CCP. Their kinfolk who opted to join stood in stronger socioeconomic positions and were far better equipped to divide property shares in a manner that proved advantageous for marriageable sons and the common descent group.

Migration also seems to have inhibited political contact and collaboration.[136] Many young Fanzhuang peasants were part of a migratory labor force that was away from the village for half-year intervals, or slightly longer, and were not in Fanzhuang long enough to develop relations with underground CCP activists. The pattern of migratory dispersal, a vexing problem for the CCP, is illustrated by the party's missed connection to Wei Jing. In 1934 Wang Xilu, Wei Jing's former primary school mate, returned to Fanzhuang from the Daming Seventh Normal School and invited a few villagers to meet with him secretly in the fields to introduce the CCP and its purpose. Wei Jing attended this meeting and made an informal commitment to the CCP, but in the same year, when the police depressed his salt-based income, he went to Shanxi's Da Ning County to work as a hired hand. Wei Jing recalls, "I lost my contact with the CCP. My father had been hurt by an ox, and I had to migrate to make a living."[137] Wei Jing did not join the CCP until ten years later, after the Eighth Route Army presence in Nanle made it possible for him to give up his semiannual shepherd job in Shanxi and return to Fanzhuang for good. The CCP got its start among villagers who stayed close to home salt markets and struck up school ties with the prosperous Wangs.

Patronage and education powered the CCP's early development. Wang Jian, along with Wang Xilu and Wang Sanxuan, all were Daming Seventh Normal School graduates.[138] The CCP's access to the peasant saltmakers was facilitated by their kinship connections with other educated, influential villagers, many of whom had joined the ranks of the Nanle County Kuomintang, thereby fostering a potentially beneficial link to the lower ranks of town-based officialdom.[139] Excepting the salt tax issue, prior to 1935 the Kuomintang was making progress in integrating Fanzhuang, and Kuomintang power within the village was virtually uncontested.[140]

The limited success of the CCP following the 1935 struggle was facilitated by the defection from this Kuomintang flow by Wang Jian. His family history, and its relationship to the saltmakers' struggle, illustrates how the CCP got its start in this pro-Kuomintang village.

Wang Jian was born in 1912 into a peasant household.[141] Wang's family owned only seven *mu* of land, but during the 1920s his grandmother started buying cotton and sewing grain bags for sale in local markets. With profits the family purchased seventy *mu* of land, including fifty of prime wheat land around Fanzhuang. This, plus income derived from purchasing and then reselling straw ropes in villages and markets across Nanle, made the Wang household one of the better-off peasant households in Fanzhuang by

1930. They also were greatly admired, for Wang Jun, the grandfather of Wang Jian, was the primary school teacher and patron of Fanzhuang.

The Wang household had the connections to allocate resources in the village and to assist peasants with town-based government affairs and provided a host of patronage services to the peasant saltmakers.[142] It offered interest-free loans to peasants in different lineages, provided meals to beggars from surrounding villages, and ran a small health clinic that became renowned for its eye disease treatments—given free of charge, with medicine acquired from Ding County in Hebei, to peasants who were on the verge of blindness.[143] The family also arranged other collective services, such as village defense and, above all, village education, which equipped the peasant saltmakers to enlist members of the local Kuomintang to protect their interest in the salt market.

Even before 1930 Wang Jun had taught in the tuition-free school, which the Wang family sustained partly with its own small surplus and partly with gifts from the pupils. Peasant children from every lineage attended this Wang family school for three to five years prior to the rebellion of 1935.[144] A small number of them, including several from the well-to-do Wang lineage, were able to attend a small middle school in Nanle town in the 1930s. With this training, they were prime candidates for the Kuomintang. At least six of Wang Jun's students had become stars of the Nanle Kuomintang by 1935. Wei Yinghuai and Zhai Pulin, for example, had become county-level Kuomintang members. The Kuomintang militia, in Nanle town, was headed by Wang Huafeng, who lived in Fanzhuang while he directed the militia against the desperate peasants and bandits who took aim at Nanle's big landlords. More important, however, was the career of Yao Zhisan. A graduate of Fanzhuang's primary school, of the Nanle County middle school, and of the Seventh Normal School in Daming, Yao Zhisan took charge of the staff organization department of the Kuomintang in 1933 and a year later became the secretary of the Nanle Kuomintang.[145] He was a powerful political figure in Nanle County, for the Kuomintang Party secretary appointed the Nanle magistrate.

These Kuomintang connections gave Fanzhuang a good deal of leverage with authorities in the town. The postponement of tax payments, protection from banditry, and factory wage jobs all were arranged by the mutual liaisons between the village's educated youth and the Kuomintang government. This web of ties to town-based county government, sanctioned by Wang Jun, served the village well until two interrelated political developments ruptured the evolving pattern of patronage and protection. The first was the alliance of the Nanle Kuomintang, under Yao Zhisan, with the Chiang Kai-shek–led central government. Not only did Yao support the police-induced reversal of salt-based income, but villagers found it increasingly difficult to secure the release of their jailed confederates by appealing to highly positioned comrades in the Nanle County government. Whereas most of the home-grown Kuomintang members remained faithful to their old village community, and its market adaptation, Yao Zhisan went with the machinery of the modern revenue state. This angered many of Fanzhuang's peasant saltmakers, who henceforth had to fall back on ad hoc forms of internal self-help to stave off police repression.[146]

To be sure, the conflict over the salt market had been mediated not in the town by the Kuomintang Party secretary but within Fanzhuang itself by the Nanle gentry and by Wang Jun.[147] In fact, the political resolution of the conflict with the police was accompanied by a Kuomintang attack on peasant culture that angered almost everyone in Fanzhuang—and Yao Zhisan also helped to engineer this attack.

This second development, the Kuomintang state assault on the folk religious symbolism infusing the protest movement of Fanzhaung's peasant saltmakers, began shortly after the settlement of 1935, when Yao Zhisan dismissed Zhang Yongheng and appointed Wang Jiajin to head the magistracy of Nanle County. Within no time, the new magistrate sent a squad of police to Fanzhuang to pull down the Guangong temple.[148]

This folk deity of the Three Kingdoms period symbolized the right of rural people to protect themselves against unjust rulers. As Prasenjit Duara points out, "his worship was particularly intense during periods of war and rebellion."[149] Almost every village around Fanzhuang (Huangzhuang, Mengzhuang, Xuzhang, etc.) had a Guangong temple in the early 1930s, and each year on March 3 a play was performed in one of them.[150] As we have seen in Qian Kou and Qi Ji, the temples had become a rallying point for popular mobilization against the Kuomintang state-backed salt police after 1931. This was also true for Fanzhuang and its sister villages. In 1935 this old temple network became the principle target of the New Life Movement started by Chiang Kai-shek and his central government. This campaign to wipe out peasant superstition was aimed at dismantling a part of popular religious culture that played a critical role in collective protest against the central state itself.[151] The state attack on their Guangong cults and the attempted destruction of the war god temples further alienated villagers from the Kuomintang element aligning itself with the center.[152] Fanzhuang's peasant saltmakers were appalled and angered by the attack, and by Yao Zhisan's support for it.

The CCP was able to take advantage of this political split within the Kuomintang and enter Fanzhuang via the populism of Wang Jian, who had advised the peasant saltmakers to defy the tax police. Like many of his pro-CCP cohorts from the Seventh Normal School, Wang Jian had concluded that the overzealous salt revenue drive of the Kuomintang Finance Ministry was upsetting the peasant society on which the Nationalist government was dependent, and prior to joining the CCP he worked this criticism into an indictment of the Kuomintang center, one that resonated with folk justice found in war god symbolism. By 1935 Wang Jian and his Fanzhuang-based CCP associates all were aware that the 1932 saltmakers' struggle in Puyang had centered in the Guangong temple in Cheng Guan, that the Thirteen County Saltmakers' Association had been founded in the Guangong temple in Qingfeng's Gu Chengji in 1933, and that the April, 1935, peasant salt-makers' gathering at the Three Emperors' Temple in Nanle County town was also a Guangong assembly. (The peasant saltmakers assembled *en masse* near the Three Emperors' Temple only because the huge war god temple complex had burned to the ground accidentally, during a ferocious battle between the Red Spears and the Nanle County warlord government in the previous decade.)[153] While teaching basic chemistry in Nanle Teacher's Training School[154] in Nanle town, Wang Jian brought his indictment of the Kuomintang more fully into line with the mythology of Guangong, and began to pass it on to peasants on many visits to Fanzhuang. Thus, he tells us, "just before the outbreak of the Anti-Japanese War, I was helping the peasant saltmakers to understand that to merely oppose the salt police was not enough. I also told them they had to fight the Kuomintang government, which was behind the salt police."[155]

A member of the Chinese Liberation Vanguards, a local unit led by the CCP, Wang Jian was not yet a CCP member in 1936.[156] Nevertheless, the newly appointed Nanle magistrate responded to this indictment by issuing an order for his arrest. But his uncle, a member of the centrifugal Kuo-mintang faction that favored its Fanzhuang roots, warned Wang Jian in advance, allowing him to escape to Liangmen in Puyang. Hunted by the Kuomintang state, Wang Jian changed his name to Wang Jingru, and in the spring of 1938 he formally joined the CCP.[157] During trips to Fanzhuang in that year, he started a secret branch of the CCP, composed of himself, Zhai Zuolin, and Yao Zongdao, the village chief. By the time Wang Jian left Fanzhuang in late 1938 the branch had ten members.

This CCP presence at the outset of the Anti-Japanese War thus was relat-ed to the party's involvement with the prewar salt protest. Many of its mem-bers were peasant saltmakers who followed Wang Jian into the CCP because of his prewar support for their struggle. The nonparty leaders of the prewar struggle shared with these party recruits a perception that the CCP had been on their side in the struggle for the market, for the consonance between the prewar antistate stance of Wang Jian and their contribution to the later competency of the CCP is clear: Wang relied not on one of the ten party recruits but, rather, on Zhai Hongliang, a copilot of Fanzhuang's pre-war protest movement, to act as village chief and to help organize the vil-lagers to curb the infringements of the Japanese during the early stage of the war. Formally, Fanzhuang was ruled by the Kuomintang after 1935, but informally it was in the hands of local village leaders who knew the Wang

Jian–led CCP had championed their protest against the Kuomintang fiscal police.

Fanzhuang's protest history teaches us that even the most conservative tillers with a short-lived interest in the salt market were drawn into collective struggle by the police arm of the Kuomintang Finance Ministry. Given their vulnerable geopolitical position, and given their promising relationship with Kuomintang county government, the people of Fanzhuang pursued low-profile, nonviolent avoidance protest until the police violence of 1933–35 threatened production and extravillage trade. The inflexible revenue-gathering initiatives of the Nanjing government drove a segment of the village's educated local elite away from the local Kuomintang, and these young rural intellectuals utilized their connections with the saltmakers and the small gentry to orchestrate collective resistance to police raids—a familiar pattern. However, the key student advisor to Fanzhuang's cautious saltmakers had not discovered political life in the CCP in the prewar period. Surely the semipeasants of Fanzhuang were aware of Communist support for the struggles of the saltmakers around Nanle town, but it would be incorrect to say that Communist Party politics was the major factor shaping the form and course of the village's participation in collective protest. The major lessons they applied in their own protest were gleaned from knowledge of popular antipolice actions in markets beyond Fanzhuang and from the impromptu advice of the returned student Wang Jian. When the war broke out, and Wang Jian joined the CCP, he clearly was in a position to bring over the protest coalition formed outside of the CCP in the prewar years to Communist-led national resistance.

Thus, despite its differences with the other villages, and despite the fact that it joined the militant antipolice action of mid-April, 1935, only after the transcounty army of peasant saltmakers broadened the protest movement, Fanzhuang shared an important piece of history with the other villages. Prior to the war it had been involved in a broad-based market struggle to bolster community powers against Kuomintang state making. As the following chapter illustrates, during WWII the Chinese Communists were able to rally the carriers of this struggle in many different salt land villages to help them forge a political economy that served the goals of resistance and revolution.

SEVEN

Peasant Resentment, War, and National Resistance

The grievances that had galvanized the peasant saltmakers did not evaporate after the outbreak of WWII. The rise of CCP-led resistance was real enough, but the participation of the village people in the resistance was not solely, or mainly, the product of the brief flash of the Japanese invasion and the CCP rallying peasants to resist the atrocities of the Japanese army, all the while persuading them to participate in a revolution aimed at rejuvenating the national state. Nor was the CCP's wartime resistance predicated on promoting rural socioeconomic reforms pure and simple.

Beyond question, the success of the CCP did coincide significantly with the Japanese invasion of North China, for Communist Party leaders reestablished their institutional presence in the counties of the Hebei-Shandong-Henan border area during the war. They elicited popular support for their wartime resistance, however, from rural people who had been active in the antistate resistance for more than a decade. Because it had supported the peasant saltmakers in the early 1930s, the CCP's political credibility was not in question at the outset of the invasion. Furthermore, local party leaders were able to anchor the War of Resistance, substantially, in the internal war in which they had gained credibility in the first place.

Chalmers A. Johnson pinpoints a meaningful phenomenon in the ability of the CCP to transform peasant anger over Japanese brutality into a national resistance movement.[1] Mark Selden, among others, focuses more on the ways in which the CCP linked its wartime resistance to peasant expectations for redistributive justice and a pattern of mass participation in which the poor stood up to past oppressors.[2] These classical studies constitute significant contributions to our understanding of the origins and process of peasant mobilization during WWII. Surely anti-Japanese patriotic appeals and rural socioeconomic reforms framed by the CCP weighed importantly in the development of Communist power during the war, but in much of the Hebei-Shandong-Henan border area the laurel of the CCP's involvement with the collective protest of the peasant saltmakers provides a major key to understanding the success of Communist-led resistance.

The country people aiding the anti-Japanese resistance were motivated significantly by CCP support for their struggle against centralized state power. In the Japanese invasion, and the collapse of the Kuomintang state, they saw a chance to build up a political order that posed an alternative to "bureaucratic capitalism." Of course the CCP, and its Eighth Route Army, sought to promote antiforeign resistance from the participants of other types of protest movements, but with only limited success. The party was far more successful in assembling a political coalition of the social forces that had rebelled against the central government implementation of salt revenue policy.

Above all else, the Japanese invasion gave the Chinese Communists another opportunity to align with the pro-market people who had been stung by the Chiang Kai-shek center and to bring them into a broad coalition that would challenge both Japanese rule and the resumption of Kuomintang state making at war's end. Although this coalition was pro-Nationalist, it was founded on a local political economy that was antithetical to the strong national state economy promoted by central government policymakers. Spearheading it were local Communists who hailed from some of the newly prosperous, prominent families. They were looking to latch onto popular grievances so they could negotiate their way toward the role of revolutionary patrons—indeed, their leader, Wang Congwu, already had assumed this role as chairman of the Thirteen County Saltmakers' Association prior to the Japanese invasion. During the war, they used it to enlist wealthy and well-educated local county-level elites in national salvation work. More important, they relied on it to reenter the villages through the local protest leaders of the prewar period, working closely with them to persuade the peasant saltmakers to support anti-Japanese struggle. As the war unfolded, the relationship between the larger CCP-led anti-Japanese resistance and the prewar collective movement of the peasant saltmakers proved critical.[3]

THE JAPANESE INVASION OF NORTH CHINA AND THE DISINTEGRATION OF THE KUOMINTANG STATE

The Japanese invasion violently interrupted the revenue campaign of the Kuomintang Ministry of Finance. If Kuomintang county government interaction with the prewar protest movement is taken as a barometer of state-society relations, it might appear that the Kuomintang was pursuing a course of political accommodation with the peasant saltmakers and was on its way to integrating them into its political order. This "accommodation," however, was mainly the product of popular rebel negotiations with the Kuomintang-appointed county magistrates, many of whom recognized that the Nationalist center was creating a dangerous polarization between the village people and its own revenue forces. The Nationalist fiscal elite was largely oblivious to the protest movement its policies had fostered and was formulating an ever more violent solution to "popular disturbances" in the border area before the Japanese penetrated it in late 1937. The persistence of the Kuomintang central government in asserting its fiscal interest further alarmed the country people, so that the Japanese curtailment of Kuomintang repression gave the Chinese Communists a chance to reconnect with the rebels of the prewar period.

The Japanese invasion cut short a renewed Kuomintang state attempt at violent revenue collection after the initial victory of the peasant saltmakers in 1935. In March, 1936, units of the Kuomintang Twenty-Ninth Army under Song Zheyuan were deployed to suppress thousands of peasant saltmakers in Hebei Province, just north of the seedbed of the Puyang-based protest movement.[4] Operating out of Daming, Nangong, and Xingtai, these army units went after the village people who worked the "small saline plots" and made their living from purveying common salt. Shortly thereafter they made preparations to subdue the counties to the south, where the peasant saltmakers were still basking in their recent victory.

The renewal of Kuomintang state violence was unquestionably the doing of high state policymakers. In 1935, only a few months after the Hebei provincial authorities had warned the finance ministry of the dangers of escalating the war to increase salt revenue, Chiang Kai-Shek himself sent a telegram instructing the twenty-ninth army to eliminate the "red peril" in the southern part of Hebei Province.[5] In April, 1937, the Changlu Salt Tax Bureau was reorganized into a salt police army under the leadership of the Nationalist government salt administration,[6] and steps were taken to incorporate it into the twenty-ninth army. All of this was in line with the effort to punish the marginalized peasants, who were seen as standing in the way of state power and development.[7]

This same process was at work, sporadically, in relations between the rural people and the regional militarists, such as Ding Shuben and his twenty-ninth army in Puyang.[8] Ding Shuben had joined Zhang Jingyao's warlord army at age eighteen. Following a promotion to sergeant, he was transferred to Feng Yuxiang's army, then promoted to major. While stationed in Shanxi, he was the supervisor of the salt administration under Zhang Duoguan. In 1935, Ding became chief of Puyang special district, and two years later Ding was promoted to superintendent of the fourth district of Hebei Province. His twenty-seven-thousand-man twenty-ninth army unit was stationed in Daming, Puyang, and Nangong and was credited with successfully dealing with banditry, containing CCP agitation, and restoring law, order, and security. Thus in 1938 Ding became the Kuomintang chief of the public security forces in the Hebei-Shandong-Henan border area.

Ding Shuben also was praised for his commitment to the Kuomintang war on salt traffickers, but in fact he displayed only minor enthusiasm for enforcing the salt monopoly of Chiang Kai-shek's government in greater Puyang district. He did not perceive the peasant saltmakers as a dire threat. His concern was that he not erode the position of the twenty-ninth army by promoting the Kuomintang's drastic solution to the "problem" of earth salt. Thus, at first Ding's locally recruited Puyang salt police unit operated somewhat independently of the Changlu salt police, and his twenty-ninth army did little to improve on the efficiency of the *Shuijingtuan* in the counties south of Daming.[9]

But although Ding Shuben's regime did not immediately launch an attack on the earth salt economy, neither did it close the chapter on this conflict between the Kuomintang state and the peasants of the salt lands.* The saltmakers' struggle had gained momentum and gone on to victory not in Daming, which was a prefectural garrison under the immediate control of the twenty-ninth army, but in Nanle, Qingfeng, Puyang, and Hua counties, where Kuomintang state power was comparatively weaker in the early 1930s. Aware that the twenty-ninth army was not able to overcome this weakness on its own, Ding Shuben began integrating members of the dispersed salt police into his twenty-ninth army in 1936, thereby identifying this force with the interest of the salt moguls in the finance ministry and signaling the country people that Nationalist leaders took Kuomintang county-level accommodations with the Thirteen County Saltmakers' Association as merely a short-term setback. Yao Huibin of Qian Foji village, who was a student in the Nanle County Teachers' Training School, recalls,[10] "During my stay in Nanle town I came into contact with the salt police. Many of them were young people who liked to play basketball, and we often played together in the town. Most of them had received some education, but not enough to be employed by the Kuomintang county government. Some were educated in the primary schools, in the villages and the town. In Nanle the police dispersed after the victory of the peasant saltmakers in 1935. Some went back to the villages; and some joined Ding Shuben's 29th Army."

The Japanese invasion nipped this development in the bud, for as the Kuomintang armies were dislodged from the county towns of the border area in late 1937 and early 1938, the salt police were increasingly cut off

*We must keep in mind that although Ding Shuben wanted to preserve his local power, he also was affiliated with the national Kuomintang and was pressed to prove he was moving to promote the interest of the Kuomintang state over that of local society.

from central state assistance. The Japanese acknowledged neither the authority nor the autonomy of the *Shuijingtuan*. The pressures of the Japanese invasion and the patron-client politics of the Kuomintang "fiscal family" combined to fracture its power in the Hebei-Shandong-Henan border area. At least 60 percent of the salt police, having lost their salaries, defected and became spies, guards, and scouts in the Japanese puppet army in 1938.[11] The Baoding- based special Japanese brigade incorporating the police not only did not reinstitutionalize the police suppression of earth salt production, it never reached the border area counties in which the peasant saltmakers' and their allies in the CCP were based.[12] Consequently, the anti-market operations of the Kuomintang fiscal police were all but jettisoned until after the Japanese surrendered and the central government of Chiang Kai-shek and T. V. Song attempted to recapture the Changlu salt area.[13] Moreover, to the advantage of the CCP and its mass base, the crack patriotic units of the salt tax corps were not to given over to the Ding Shuben Twenty-Ninth Army, but rather increasingly were transferred to Ji County in Henan, uniting with the Kuomintang Twentieth Army under Shang Zhen, who was in the political entourage of H. H. Kong, the Kuomintang finance minister.[14] Preoccupied with fighting the Japanese south of the Yellow River, this Kuomintang tax force no longer posed an immediate threat to the peasant saltmakers in the border region.

The Japanese advancement into the border area in late 1937 threw the Kuomintang Twenty-Ninth Army into confusion and stimulated a retreat south toward the Yellow River. It was at this point, when the Kuomintang army was temporarily paralyzed and the Japanese army had yet to penetrate the remote villages, that the first popular anti-Japanese resistance groups were formed in the Hebei-Shandong-Henan countryside.

The Kuomintang officials, not the Japanese invaders, had interfered with the flurry of peasant market prosperity. The leaders of the CCP saw this situation and maneuvered to unite with country people who were clamoring for market rights. Between autumn 1937 and autumn 1940, the CCP reaffirmed those demands and brought the saltmakers into a broad coalition against the Japanese.

POPULAR MOBILIZATION WITHIN THE ANTI-JAPANESE UNITED FRONT

Chalmers A. Johnson, Lyman P. Van Slyke, and Lloyd E. Eastman all have shown how important the Japanese intervention was in altering the structure and stability of the central government.[15] The intrusion of the Japanese army, and the reaction of the nominally pro-Kuomintang warlord officers who had risen to power in the border area prior to the war, frustrated even further high state efforts to eradicate the saltmakers' protest movement. In developing the anti-Japanese united front, the Chinese Communists drew in people from all walks of life and isolated the regional Kuomintang actors who pursued strengthening the state over strengthening popular forms of antiforeign resistance. As Kuomintang army leaders, few of whom were firmly in the mainline central army of Chiang Kai-shek, set out to resist the Japanese by squeezing the barren salt land villages, the Communists were able to gain an advantage in their efforts to enlist the local people.

Anti-Japanese resistance passed through three stages.[16] The issue of competing Kuomintang and CCP modes of popular mobilization for the Anti-Japanese War came to a head between 1937 and 1940. This first stage, which saw the formation of the united front, was characterized by massive political upheaval and mindboggling political complexity. Its culmination saw the defeat of Kuomintang state dictatorship and the birth of a CCP-led anti-Japanese government with a tenuous foothold in the dispersed villages of the countryside.

In accordance with Chiang Kai-shek's decision to suspend the campaign to crush the Communists and start up a Kuomintang-CCP united front, a number of local CCP leaders were released from prison. As late as the summer of 1937, the main CCP leaders of the saltmakers' struggle in Puyang were still in prisons scattered throughout the country. They were among the more fortunate party members, for the Kuomintang Twenty-Ninth Army and the public security forces had virtually destroyed the Communist Party in Daming, Nanle, and Qingfeng County and had driven Liu Dafeng, Zhang Linzhi, and other leaders underground.

The CCP's wartime success reflected a pattern commonly found in other studies of wartime resistance: the Kuomintang's release of jailed Communist Party members was critical to rebuilding the party apparatus around national salvation, and many local CCP leaders eventually went back to the border region to rally the home folks to anti-Japanese resistance.[17] Still, the Chinese Communists entered the salt land villages, and built up a mass base for wartime resistance, through their prewar connections to local village leaders who took them mainly as allies in their own tradition of collective resistance to outsiders. In October of 1937, Wang Congwu and his returning comrades teamed up with Liu Dafeng to build up a popular army in Liu Gudian village in Nanle County and in Gu Chengji in Qingfeng—a stronghold of the peasant saltmakers' resistance to the Kuomintang revenue police before the Japanese invasion.[18] This popular guerrilla unit became known as the Fourth Branch of the Hebei People's Army.[19] Numbering only fifty at the outset, it expanded to one thousand by year's end and became the first anti-Japanese armed force under the leadership of the Chinese Communist Party in the Hebei-Shandong-Henan border region.[20] In early June of 1938, the fourth branch army assumed the title of the Eastern

Advancement Column of the 129th Division of the Eighth Route Army under Liu Bocheng, and thereafter became a model regiment of the CCP regular army.[21]

Under the leadership of Wang Congwu and Liu Dafeng, returning students from the Daming Seventh Normal School and the Jianyi Normal School of Qing Feng County, many of them village schoolteachers, made up the majority of the first group of soldiers to join the fourth branch army. By late October, 1937, even before the Japanese took Daming, this fourth branch student corps had expanded to a force of two hundred and was receiving weapons, ammunition, and legal currency from Gao Xuxun, the commander of the Hebei People's Army.[22]

The next jump in army growth came in March of 1938. According to the memoir of Peng Yuemei, one of six woman soldiers in the original fourth branch army, the CCP reached out to a bandit army in Puyang led by Liu Xiangyou, who had a reputation for resisting the Japanese, and persuaded him to join the fourth branch army. Bringing over five hundred armed followers, Liu became the fourth branch army's deputy commander.[23]

A new spurt in army development occurred between March, 1938, and March, 1939, when Wang Congwu, Liu Yanchun, and Liu Dafeng led the fourth branch army into the sandy zone of Hua County. To the chagrin of the Northern Henan Public Security Forces under Gong Bailing, the Kuomintang Hua County magistrate, Chen Shuhui, led a county-level battalion in an uprising and brought in some four hundred men armed with modern rifles. Magistrate Chen thereupon became the commander of the second detachment of the fourth branch army, which now had approximately fifteen hundred participants[24] and was soon to be joined by several thousand peasant saltmakers from Hua County. Six months later, Jia Xinzhai, the new Kuomintang magistrate, was persuaded by Zhang Huizeng (an old family friend of Jia Xinzhai and a CCP operative under Liu Yanchun) to change sides, whereupon he established a CCP-controlled government in Hua County.[25]

The fourth branch army's most dramatic expansion took place when it moved to the vicinity of Jingdian, Qian Kou, and Huacun along the Puyang-Neihuang border during the Spring Festival of 1938. Operating along the old course of the Yellow River where the saltmakers' struggle was centered, where the Japanese army had yet to appear, and where the county-level Kuomintang regimes were in chaos, the fourth branch army drew in a massive influx of market-bound quasi peasants. The CCP-led resistance army swelled from fifteen hundred to two thousand, four thousand, and finally seventeen thousand by late 1939.[26] The participation of these quasi peasants, making up more than 80 percent of the resistance army's new blood, was a critical factor in the formation of the Hebei-Shandong-Henan detachment of the Eighth Route Army under Commander Yang Dezhi—*before* the

Japanese unleashed their savagery against this triprovincial anti-Japanese base in 1941 and 1942.

To be sure, the initial survival and growth of the CCP-led fourth branch army was partly the result of co-dependency with Ding Shuben. Following the Marco Polo Bridge incident of 7 July 1937, the twenty-ninth army under Song Zheyuan offered resistance to the Japanese army. After the fall of Beijing on July 29, and of Tianjin on July 30, however, the twenty-ninth army was in full retreat along the main transport lines into southern Hebei, with Japanese troops in hot pursuit.[27] On October 3, the Japanese army took Dezhou, Pingyuan, Yucheng, and Gaotang; Shijiazhuang fell on October 10, followed quickly by Xingtai and Handan. Anyang, the first train stopover on the Henan line, was taken on November 4, giving the Japanese a rail-serviced garrison point from which they prepared to attack the rural county towns of the border area.[28] By the end of autumn they had routed the twenty-ninth army garrison forces in Daming, and in December Japanese gendarmes could be seen marching along the earthen streets of Daming, Nanle, and Puyang towns.[29]

This turn of events left Ding Shuben in charge of national security for the southern tip of Hebei Province. Ding Shuben was shaken so badly by the rapid Japanese success that he moved the headquarters of his twenty-ninth army southward to Changzhuang village on the banks of the Yellow River and then entered into a united front with Liu Dafeng, Wang Congwu, and Ping Jiesan, the CCP's youthful brain trust, and the leaders of the fourth branch army.

In the months following the Japanese invasion, Ping Jiesan, secretary of the Puyang-Neihuang-Hua County CCP Committee and dean of the Qingfeng County Teachers' College, linked up with local college deans and school-teachers to form the National Salvation Association in southern Hebei.[30] Ping and his compatriots entreated Ma Runchang, the subordinate of Song Zheyuan in Daming, to join the fight against Japan, but Ma refused. Persistence paid off, however, for these CCP leaders reached an agreement with Ding Shuben whereby the twenty-ninth army in Puyang would cooperate with the fourth branch army in anti-Japanese resistance. This agreement marked the start of the Kuomintang-CCP anti-Japanese united front. Most important, it allowed the CCP to operate openly within the Kuomintang Twenty-Ninth Army and to recruit village schoolteachers into the National Salvation Association. Beginning in 1938, the director of the twenty-ninth army's political department was Luo Shigao, a CCP member; the director of the civil education department was Ping Jiesan; and the director of the anti-Japanese training class was Zhang Wei, the Eight Route Army representative in the border area.[31]

Up until this point,[32] the twenty-ninth army had operated somewhat independently of the central government. Its dissolution accelerated, ironically, with Ding Shuben's alignment with the Chiang Kai-shek fiscal clique betrayal of the united front and with the authoritarian mobilization of rural civilians for war with Japan.[33] After the twenty-ninth army had teamed up with the CCP-led fourth branch army to route the Japanese in the Battle of Little Puzhou, in Pu County, in March of 1938, Ding Shuben refused to share captured Japanese war materials with the fourth branch army; more, he enlisted porters to send the war booty of canned fish and meat to his former warlord commander, Feng Yuxiang, now a high-ranking official in the central government. When the news of Ding's success at Little Puzhou reached Chiang Kai-shek, the generalissimo promoted him to chief of the defense corps of the Hebei-Shandong-Henan war zone, which was to include Daming, Nanle, Qingfeng, and Puyang in Hebei, Dongming and Fan County in Shandong, and Hua County in Henan. In 1939, on returning to Puyang from the Nationalist Government Conference of Division Commanders in the First War District of the North China Area, Ding Shuben apparently pursued a policy of "single-party resistance" on behalf of Chiang Kai-shek, whose government was now giving him weapons, gunpowder, and communications equipment.[34] All of the CCP staff directors were expelled from the twenty-ninth army and were replaced with pro-Kuomintang agents, who proceeded to transform the political department of the twenty-ninth army into a club for the *San Qing Tuan*—the Three-People's Principles Youth Corps (a vanguard youth corps dedicated to exalting the exclusive dictatorship of Chiang Kai-shek).[35] The CCP cadres and the Eighth Route Army representatives withdrew from the twenty-ninth army and repositioned themselves in the villages of Puyang—Liangmen, Wen Liu, and Qian Kou.

In this stage, the CCP built up an anti-Japanese base area in the ungoverned parts of Puyang, Neihuang, Nanle, and Hua counties, establishing a small power base in the previously mobilized villages of Qian Kou, Taipingzhuang, Qi Ji, Qian Foji, and Liu Gudian; and the rural populace gradually became aware that the CCP-led resistance was committed to a strategy of economic development that favored local market forces over the greater state controls of the Kuomintang.[36]

While the twenty-ninth army resisted the Japanese, Ding Shuben's sub-officers lorded it over the districts where they operated.[37] Expanding the land tax base to cover the expense of war, they compelled the peasants on the poor saline lands to dip even deeper into their off-farm income to purchase grain (usually wheat) for the regular troops. The levy per *mu* was the same for everyone, regardless of the amount or quality of land, so that this wartime tax especially hurt the saltmakers.

Fatally, the twenty-ninth army used the war as a pretext to monopolize various supplies. Ding Shuben's brigade officers requisitioned peasant food grains, horses, and carts and imposed all sorts of extra war levies (*tanpai*) for supplying Ding's swelling army. Ding became notorious for his corruption and cronyism. In 1937, one of Ding's favorites, Guo Shenzhai—the director of the procurement office in charge of procuring grain for the Kuomintang-led resistance—raked in personal gains through his public connections to Wang Zhiyi, the chief of the Puyang *baoandui*. This Guo-Wang clique moved to monopolize the distribution and sale of kerosene, confiscating thousands of barrels from kerosene merchants in Nanle's market towns and selling them in Puyang.[38]

Around 1940, a multicounty grain relief fund entrusted to Ding Shuben disappeared,[39] and a Kuomintang official on his way to a meeting in Chen village, Puyang, to find out the whereabouts of the fund was murdered. The affair was the political backdrop to the famine of 1942.[40]

As the twenty-ninth army retreated and disintegrated, the CCP built up an anti-Japanese regime in the ungoverned rural villages of Puyang, Neihuang, Nanle, Hua County, and Dongming.[41] The first crack in the Kuomintang power structure appeared in early 1940, when Shi Yousan fled south from Japanese attacks near Daming, then surrendered.[42] Shortly thereafter, Ding Shuben made the mistake of moving his twenty-ninth army beyond the sanctuary of the Puyang anti-Japanese resistance base into Hua*xian* and then into Dongming. This panicky retreat sealed the fate of the twenty-ninth army, whose soldiers were mainly from Puyang and did not want to leave home ground. Frequent desertions occurred along the line of retreat. Then Ding made another costly error: The second brigade under Chen Xiaozhen was sent to northwest Changyuan to shield the march, but the Japanese surrounded this brigade and killed hundreds of soldiers. The twenty-ninth army subofficers lost interest in fighting, and morale was shattered. Troop strength fell from twenty-seven thousand in the spring of 1941 to two thousand a few months later. Ding Shuben secretly negotiated a surrender to the Japanese garrison at Changyuan and fled to Lin County.

It was at this critical juncture that CCP leaders obtained weapons from deserting Kuomintang soldiers and patriotic members of the old local elite and established the first official wartime Hebei-Shandong-Henan Party Committee. This regional committee formed the Hebei-Shandong-Henan anti-Japanese base area, which included five counties in southern Hebei (Puyang, Qingfeng, Nanle, Daming, and Changyuan),[43] three in Henan (Hua*xian*, Neihuang, and Xun*xian*), and five in Shandong (Dongming, Pu*xian*, Fan County, Guancheng, and Cao*xian*).[44] These counties had been the center of the saltmakers' struggle, and all of them contained thousands of country people who identified with a warrior tradition that encouraged resistance to outsiders. Wang Congwu, the CCP secretary of the new anti-Japanese base, was keenly aware of the importance of this popular tradition, which may explain why in 1940 the CCP Hebei-Shandong-Henan Regional

Committee set up its headquarters in the war god temple of Wang Shi village in Qingfeng County.[45]

In spreading anti-Japanese resistance beyond their Puyang-Qingfeng base to the wider border region, the Regional Committee members clearly relied on their connections with the mass movement of the prewar period. Liu Yanchun (CCP vice-secretary of Western Shandong and the Regional Committee's delegate to the 1940 Yan'an Conference) had collaborated with Wang Congwu in orchestrating the 1932 saltmakers' struggle in Puyang and had conducted party branch work in the salt land villages of Shandong's Fan*xian*, Guancheng, Yanggu, and Cao*xian* throughout 1936.[46] The guerrilla squads that Liu recruited into the fourth branch army from these marginal rural places between 1938 and 1939 shared the antistate protest history of their counterparts in Puyang. Collaborating with Yang Dezhi's Ji-Lu-Yu detachment, they began to threaten the Japanese hold on the Beijing-Hankow, Jin-Pu, and Longhai railroads in 1940.[47]

The second stage of anti-Japanese resistance, between early 1940 and late 1942,[48] saw the ascendance of Japanese puppet army rule. The Japanese had declared the Hebei-Shandong-Henan border area a low priority, partly because there was no cotton to plunder and no central army counteroffensive.[49] Hence, they assigned only a small garrison force to hold Daming County town and were short on troop strength in the counties to the south. Their attacks on Qingfeng town and Puyang town in 1938 were carried out with only one infantry company and one cavalry squad, and they were roundly defeated by the fourth branch army and the twenty-ninth army at the Battle of Little Puzhou. For the next two years, they could make only feeble incursions into Puyang, a day's march from Daming.

The pattern of Japanese army devastation underscores the logic of G. William Skinner's regional-systems model for predicting the deliquesce of political force in North China.[50] As a rule, the highest Japanese-caused death rates were found in the areas immediately adjacent to the county towns, not in the remote countryside. In the aftermath of the Japanese attack on Qingfeng County town in early 1938, rural people reported seeing more and more new grave mounds, about five *li* away. The number increased as they came closer to the town, where the Japanese damage was worst.[51] Conversely, the CCP-led fourth branch army, far removed from these rural towns, enjoyed a comparatively high level of security.

In this second stage, the Japanese absorbed thousands of deserting Kuomintang army soldiers, bandits, and police into a so-called puppet army. By the time the Japanese attacked Pearl Harbor, there were 39,200 puppet army troops under indirect Japanese army command in the Hebei-Shandong-Henan border area,[52] and by late 1942 this puppet force reportedly stood at 80,000.[53] The predatory puppet army attacked, plundered, sabotaged, and blockaded the CCP-held anti-Japanese base. One of its most notorious leaders was Yang Faxian, a former bandit and a onetime officer in Ding Shuben's twenty-ninth army. In early 1940, with the assistance of Yang Faxian and a host of perfidious puppet army commanders, the Japanese initiated an offensive against the CCP-led resistance.

Only a few months after the CCP had established the Hebei-Shandong-Henan anti-Japanese base area government, the Japanese puppet army launched a drive to crush the Eighth Route Army and capture its village strongholds in the Shaqu area of southern Hebei.[54] The drive was focused on Puyang, Neihuang, and Nanle. The Japanese puppet army combined with the Sharp Knife Society, a secret society in Puyang County, to inflict serious damage on the CCP-led resistance. On June 10 the Japanese sent thirty thousand puppet army soldiers and 170 armored personnel carriers from Kaifeng, Xinxiang, Anyang, Handan, and Zhengzhou against the anti-Japanese base, dividing southern Hebei and stationing puppet army troops at key market towns, such as Jingdian and Liangmen in Puyang and Yuancunji in Nanle. The resistance was caught in a crisis. There were soaring defections from the CCP itself, and its guerrilla army forces repeatedly fled when attacked, leaving civilians at the mercy of Kuomintang turncoats like Shi Yousan, whose troops collaborated with the puppet army and the Sharp Knife Society to take over eastern Puyang and northern Qingfeng and to threaten Neihuang.

CCP officials emphasized the importance of rectifying "leftism." By February, 1941, the elimination of suspected traitors and the arbitrary making of financial decisions had come under critical scrutiny. Steps were taken to institute the three-thirds-system of democratic resistance government at the village level and to improve fourth branch army relations with villagers. But just as this internal-party rehabilitation campaign took off, the Japanese launched another devastating attack, on 12 April 1941.[55] The Eighth Route Army and its guerrilla detachments were caught off guard. The troops of the twenty-fourth puppet army under Yang Zhenlan, and the anti-Communist independent army headed by Sun Buyue, maneuvered eight hundred solders to occupy the city of Anhua (currently Er'an) in Neihuang County, on the western border of the CCP's southern Hebei base. The Eighth Route Army immediately sent three regiments to counterattack, leaving the anti-Japanese base area unprotected. On April 12, Japanese troops of the thirty-fifth division joined with the puppet army forces of Yang Zhenlan and Sun Buyue—a combined force of twenty thousand—to strike at the heart of the triprovincial base. The Japanese puppet army all but wiped out the second battalion of the Eighth Route Army's fourth regiment between Nan Zhang Bao and Sang village. The rear service forces of the CCP-led resistance—hospitals, clothing factories, and arms production factories—were destroyed. And the country people along the Puyang-Neihuang county line were subjected to hideous cruelty in the

Japanese-orchestrated "three all" ("kill all, loot all, and burn all") campaign, the main goal of which was to destroy the foundations of the peasant economy in pro-CCP villages. According to one estimate, the Japanese and the puppet troops razed more than 140 villages, killed four thousand people, and destroyed thousands of *mu* of peanut crops, hawthorne forests, and red date trees in the vicinity of Qian Kou,[56] destroying part of the economy upon which the resistance was based.

Qian Kou and Wen Xinggu, which were at the forefront of the CCP-led resistance, were hit especially hard. On April 12, the Japanese puppet army accomplices slaughtered 1,372 people in Qian Kou and fourteen other villages along the Puyang-Neihuang border.[57] Within a week, they murdered every member of 103 peasant families, plundered 1,700,000 *jin* of grain, 613 carts, and 1,172 farm animals, and felled nearly 17,000 red date trees. When the Japanese withdrew on April 19, a trail of death and destruction stunned even the toughest of the CCP survivors. Members of village burial teams had to place washcloths soaked with liquor over their noses to mask the stench of rotting corpses, which spread for several *li*. The wailing of village people could be heard everywhere.

Next, Japanese forces rounded up everyone suspected of having liaisons with villages where the CCP anti-Japanese resistance was active and slaughtered them.[58] Liu Fengcun, a saltmaker who had joined the fourth branch army in 1937 but returned to Qian Kou just before the April 12 attack, says,[59] "Many of the people killed here in Qian Kou by the Japanese were from Yuan Zhou and Huacun. Yuan Zhou had skillful merchants. They traded in dates and peanuts. They wanted to please the Japanese so they could continue their business. But the Japanese just opened fire on them."

The Japanese army persuaded people in places under its occupation to come with trucks and plunder the recently attacked villages in southern Hebei. The CCP cadres had to contend with a new wave of banditry, plus local infighting over the resources of the villages ripped apart by the Japanese attack. Seldom were they able to build popular antiforeign resistance in these plundered villages. Li Duo, the CCP secretary in Neihuang during this grisly, plunderous stage, has written, "At this time, the main task for the local armed forces was to guard the border area and to resist the disturbances of the puppet army troops and bandits."[60]

From early 1943 to mid-1945, the CCP and its resistance army recovered lost ground in the salt land villages of southern Hebei and set up a strategic military base from which to launch a counterattack.[61] The CCP drew strength from the international war front in this third stage. Beginning in the summer of 1943, Japan withdrew troops from North China to shore up the defense of its home islands in response to its defeats by the United States in the Pacific theater[62] and to participate in the Ichigo campaign in South China. Henceforth the CCP regulars and their guerrilla brethren were able to involve the country people in thwarting the Japanese mopping-up operations more effectively. The CCP-led resistance was also the indirect beneficiary of a round of bloody war between the Kuomintang militarists in the border area during which Gao Xuxun killed the Kuomintang traitor Shi Yousan,[63] who had broken the united front by organizing puppet forces to launch an attack on the CCP-led resistance in Pu County and Fan County in Shandong. A patriotic Nationalist army commander, four years later Gao was to become the first Kuomintang field general to revolt against Chiang Kai-shek and go over to the CCP. Thanks to these power changes, the CCP resistance army was able to recover its former position in Puyang County, and Pu County, and to begin to build toward a military comeback.

The distinction between the War of Resistance as a war fought against the Japanese army and as a war against the puppet army is missing in most treatments of CCP efforts to build up community resistance during WWII. The war with the puppet army was by far the most extreme political conflict taking place in the Hebei-Shandong-Henan border area in the years 1940 to 1945, and it had crisscrossed the CCP's struggle with the Japanese ever since the outbreak of hostilities. The CCP-led resistance had to find a way not only to constrain the puppet forces but to win them over to the anti-Japanese united front.

To neutralize the puppet army and to win its troops over to the "non-communal"[64] war against the Japanese, the CCP relied on methods of struggle that recalled forms of resistance to the salt police. One approach used was the small-scale "cautious attack" on local Chinese who collaborated with the Japanese puppet regime,[65] including character assassination, threatening posters, and abductions of proven collaborators. When the Japanese set up a Peace Preservation Committee after occupying Qingfeng County town in 1938, for example, fourth branch army leader Xiao Hanqing handpicked a few guerrilla soldiers and captured two members of the committee. They followed a familiar pattern of rebel politics: the captives were paraded through rural villages, put on public trial, and executed before a mass rally.[66] This method of resistance recalled that of parading the police around the countryside, though now the larger, institutionalized, violent political framework that the CCP-led resistance was forging threatened to upend the pro-Japanese puppet regime.

Avoiding direct clashes with the well-armed police had been one of the trademarks of the peasant saltmakers, and everyone, including CCP leaders, could remember the setbacks incurred in the impetuous, violent struggles with the Changlu salt police in Daming, Pingxiang, and other Kuomintang strongholds. Peasants who participated in the War of Resistance say CCP leaders took this lesson to heart,[67] shunning open positioned battles that would provoke military retaliation. As Wei Liangke, a veteran of the fourth branch army, put it, "We tried to avoid direct confrontations with the

Japanese. Generally, we attacked only a small Japanese unit, and then we ran away."[68]

The peasant saltmakers in the rural districts where the Japanese puppet army held the upper hand were not opposed to supporting the undercover activities of the CCP-led resistance, but they were opposed to the Eighth Route Army fighting battles and openly drilling, singing songs, and holding public rallies. With the Japanese puppet forces patrolling strategic territory prior to 1943, the CCP was obliged to form small propaganda work units to secretly win popular support. This task was made somewhat easier by enlisting the saltmakers who had joined the fourth branch army and who had longtime relations with local people.

Few of the puppet village chiefs were arrested or executed. CCP leaders were bent on persuading them to participate in multivillage confederations supportive of anti-Japanese resistance and knew that a mistake on one chief was bound to spread fear along the village leadership grapevine. The chiefs were the liaisons to the local Japanese army posts. Winning them over permitted the CCP to secretly investigate the operations of the Japanese within a district and to take advantage of the contradictions between the Japanese and puppet troops. Furthermore, the CCP propaganda units carried out investigations of the families of puppet soldiers, building files on their lineage connections and political backgrounds and informing them of the advantages of aligning with the resistance. The peasant saltmakers in the propaganda units conducted dialogues with puppet soldiers on maneuver in the countryside, beyond the binocular range of their pro-Japanese officers.[69] These activities resembled the small-scale collective resistance to the Kuomintang *Shuijingtuan*—the house-to-house solicitations designed to mobilize small neighborhood groups against the police and the intense "wars of reason" with the police on patrol in distant villages.

A third method was to sow discord between the Japanese and the puppet forces, backing up the slogan "Chinese Should Not Fight Chinese" by sparing puppet troops who were sympathetic to the anti-Japanese cause. The fourth branch army, on scoring a decisive military victory, annihilated only the attacking spearhead of the Japanese puppet army, showing the rank and file that a different set of rules applied to them. Some of the captured soldiers were returned into the puppet army itself. Through them, CCP cadres spread stories of lenient treatment of POWs, adequate medical care to wounded prisoners, and promises of amnesty, luring many puppet troops to defect.[70]

Perhaps the most significant breakthrough in this "second war" began in the summer of 1943, when the CCP successfully recruited a slew of puppet army subofficers who were in conflict with their pro-Japanese superiors, and their armed units, to work for the anti-Japanese resistance. Zhao Baozhen, a former leader of the Ding Shuben Twenty-Ninth Army and a key puppet army commander in the Daming area, along with half of the puppet army subofficers, had secret sympathetic ties to the CCP-led resistance.[71] Zhao led a company to surrender to the CCP at Men Guo village, and after a meeting with Yang Dezhi, the commander of the CCP 115th division, joined the Eighth Route Army. Similarly, Zhang Hongbin, the head of the puppet army cavalry, and Lu Tianzhen, the police chief of Han Zhang town in Nanle, secretly entered into concord with the CCP-led resistance. They helped the fourth branch army units within the Eighth Route Army to mount an offensive against the Japanese and their die-hard puppet allies and to anticipate and thwart puppet attempts to plunder grain in the pro-CCP villages of the base area.[72] Notwithstanding the "second war's" comparatively greater violence, its processes resembled forms of local resistance used in the prewar struggle with the Kuomintang fiscal center. The manual for anti–Japanese puppet army work was prepared partly from the lessons of the conflict with the Kuomintang state, for the CCP and the peasant salt-makers drew on their previous experience in forging hidden political alliances with the local public security forces to enlist the "puppet" forces to foil the designs of regional Japanese commands.

By autumn, 1944, the CCP-led resistance had integrated thousands of puppet forces and was growing in military and political stature. Building on previous victories over the puppet armies of Jin Chengbing, Tang Haiting, and Li Ying,[73] in late 1943 Yang Dezhi's Eighth Route Army went on the offensive. By the summer of 1944 it had conducted 1,272 successful operations, taken eight hundred puppet strongholds, recovered ten counties, killed 10,083 puppet soldiers, and captured another 29,000,[74] thereby reducing the number of collaborationist forces by one-half and enticing thousands of puppet soldiers to become members of the increasingly powerful resistance army. In this period, the CCP-led militias developed a system of underground resistance inside enemy territory that yielded a precise reading of key Japanese *cum* puppet army positions and resulted in the capture and execution of 74 minor Japanese army officers.[75] The Eighth Route Army moved from victory to victory in its battle to liberate scores of towns from Japanese puppet army rule—Puyang, Qingfeng, Nanle in Hebei, Hua County, Ji*xian* in Henan, and Fan*xian* and Caozhou in Shandong. Nearly half a year before the *Enola Gay* climbed over Tinian on its secret run for Hiroshima, red flags were flying from government buildings in many small county towns of the Hebei-Shandong-Henan border area.

THE ROLE OF THE PEASANT SALTMAKERS IN THE FORMATION OF THE HEBEI-SHANDONG-HENAN ANTI-JAPANESE BASE AREA, 1937–45

The telescope of oral history makes the relationship between the prewar protest movement of the peasant salters, CCP power, and anti-Japanese resistance unequivocally clear.[76] The CCP-led resistance was directed by the regional leaders of the saltmakers' struggle, was based in villages with a long history of protest against the Kuomintang tax state, and was joined by the same quasi-peasant proprietors and petty traders who had challenged the militarized state-making process of the central government.

These prewar protest villages were especially attractive to the party because they were not directly targeted by the Japanese army in the early stage of the war. Thus, although the Japanese invasion helped to create the political anarchy in which the Chinese Communists were able to regroup, the early growth in the CCP's national resistance owed its origins to the efforts of local party leaders like Wang Congwu, Liu Dafeng, and Zhang Linzhi to reconnect with rural people who had moved the Kuomintang state out of their market communities but who were not victimized by the Japanese army.

A remarkable conjunction of the right political circumstances fueled the CCP's wartime success, but the party's relationship with the long-term struggle of the peasant saltmakers proved critical to the formation of anti-Japanese resistance in the Hebei-Shandong-Henan border area. The prewar liaisons to the local protest leaders such as Liu Yufeng in Qian Kou, Yang Jingcai in Cheng Guan, and Liu Chaode in Qi Ji enabled Wang Congwu and stalwarts of the CCP to raise the issue of resisting the Japanese among the village people after the autumn of 1937, for these protest leaders were also the advisors to ordinary peasants on matters of politics and livelihood. Of course some of the village narratives suggest the CCP role in the prewar protest was minimal. However, the connection between the salt protests and the CCP's wartime success was a *regional* connection, and the leaders of the peasant saltmakers in villages where the party was not well established still were aware of the political affiliations and protest contributions of the likes of Wang Congwu. As leaders of the Thirteen County Saltmakers' Association, Wang and his party associates had spoken to tens of thousands of peasant saltmakers in transcounty conferences, rallies, and celebrations prior to the war, awakening them to the party's support for their concerted actions. Thus the connection between the CCP leadership of this regional protest movement and the saltmakers' early collective empowerment proved decisive when it came to linking the villages into a regionally based network for national resistance.

At the regional level, Wang Congwu and Liu Dafeng were active in forming the fourth branch of the Hebei People's Army during the opening moments of the Japanese invasion. Made up mainly of several thousand peasant saltmakers, it was led by Wang Tongxing, a leader of the 1934 saltmakers' struggle in Nanle County and a CCP follower of Liu Dafeng.[77] In late 1937, Zhang Linzhi organized the saltmakers' anti-Japanese guerrilla army in Nangong, Hebei, a ten-thousand-man force of young saltmakers who had participated in the 1935 struggle with the Kuomintang revenue police.[78] This guerrilla army linked up with the 129th division of the Eighth Route Army in 1938. A third anti-Japanese force emerged under Liu Zihou, who from 1933 to 1935 had led several thousand saltmakers against the Kuomintang Changlu tax police in Pingxiang County. Liu teamed up with Zhang Linzhi and Li Huasheng to form a "saltmakers' self-salvation association," which they also termed the "Patriotic Saltmakers' Association."[79] In the two years prior to the Japanese invasion, this force had attacked salt police stations and civil defense corps in the big market villages and towns along the Yellow, Zhang, and Fuyang rivers. Its leaders dubbed it "The Pinghan Railway Guerrilla Detachment of the Chinese Workers' and Peasants' Red Army."[80] On 25 January 1936 they renamed it "The North China People's Anti-Japanese National Salvation Army in Denunciation of Chiang Kaishek."[81] Linking up with the CCP-led Eighth Route Army, this army collaborated with the fourth branch army and with Zhang Linzhi's army in the Hebei-Shandong-Henan border area and spread the resistance struggle into southern Henan.

These preinvasion armies of the country people comprised the sociopolitical core of the CCP-led Eighth Route Army in the border area during WWII.[82] Some of their leaders rose to become the paramount CCP authorities in the Hebei-Shandong-Henan anti-Japanese base area government. Zhang Linzhi's career is especially informative. A part-time saltmaker, Zhang had led the saltmakers' struggle in Nangong and had become the salt commissioner of the Special Committee of the Southern Hebei CCP in 1935.[83] While organizing armed struggle against the Kuomintang salt police in Nangong, Pingxiang, and Daming in the mid-1930s, Zhang became a key member of both the Southern Hebei and Western Shandong District Party Committees. During the Anti-Japanese War he became the powerful secretary general of the Hebei-Shandong-Henan CCP Committee[84] and subsequently played a major part in leading rural people to victory in the 1946–49 civil war.

On the village level, a similar process is discernible. The villages from which the CCP-led Eighth Route Army drew popular support were those in which the party's interaction with the peasant saltmakers had forged a foundation for mass collective protest—villages like Qian Kou and Wen Xinggu in Puyang, Qi Ji in Hua County, and Fanzhuang, Liu Gudian, and Qian Foji in Nanle.[85] The semipeasant leaders of the saltmakers' struggles in these villages were among the first country people to reorganize themselves into anti-Japanese guerrilla forces and to align with the CCP's national resistance army. Hence the country people who knew them are the best source for revealing the process whereby the prewar antistate protest movement became a weapon in the CCP's anti-Japanese arsenal.

Let us listen to three old-timers, each hailing from a different "protest village." Wei Liangke of Qian Kou, relates:[86]

> Before the fourth branch army established itself in this area, the leaders held a mass assembly in Qian Kou village around the Spring Festival of 1938. This

meeting drew people from surrounding villages. Liu Dafeng and Liu Hansheng asked the people to contribute whatever they could spare. Those who
had guns were asked to give guns; those who had grain were asked to give
grain; those who had money were asked to give money; those who had virtually nothing were asked to join our fourth branch army.

At the conclusion of this mass gathering, they recruited 400 soldiers. At
least 80 to 90 per cent had been peasant saltmakers from Qian Kou and the
surrounding villages. Almost all of them had participated in the saltmakers'
struggle against the salt police. Nearly all 200 of the Qian Kou saltmakers who
had gone with Liu Yufeng to fight the salt police in Puyang town in 1932
joined the fourth branch army.

Liu Chaoyang, a former participant in the 1932 saltmakers' struggle in
Qi Ji, strikes a similar chord, suggesting that the template of anti-Japanese
resistance was not simply the organizational presence of the CCP, but the
party's interaction with networks under the control of the nonpartisan leaders of this popular struggle:[87]

Liu Chaode was not a member of the CCP. Still, Liu was the head of the
National Salvation Association of Qi Ji, and he ran the underground National Salvation Association of Hua county, which he organized with Du Fengzhai,
a landlord from Linying. Under Liu's influence, about eighty people joined
the Eighth Route Army here during the Anti-Japanese War. People in this village joined the Eighth Route Army earlier and more often than in other villages. Actually, they originally joined the Northern Henan Anti-Japanese
Brigade. There were three regiments of this brigade from this area. Some people from the original Third Regiment of the Hua County Saltmakers' Army
here joined the brigade under the leadership of Liu Chaode around 1938 or
1939. Later this brigade came to be called the Eighth Route Army.

Before the war, Liu Chaode had organized the saltmakers into several regiments. When the Japanese invaded, Wang Congwu, Nie Zhen, Hou Zizhen,
and Yang Yufeng came to Liu Chaode to ask him to help them recruit the saltmakers' pre-war regiments for anti-Japanese resistance. Since the salt police
already had been defeated, the three regiments had been dissolved. However,
Liu Chaode still had contacts with the saltmakers in his old regiments. So after
Wang Congwu and Nie Zhen came, Liu Chaode helped them to organize the
Northern Henan Anti-Japanese Brigade. This anti-Japanese brigade was made
up of saltmakers from the surrounding villages, and eventually grew into a
force of three thousand.

I know this because I was among the first twenty people from Qi Ji to join
the Northern Henan Anti-Japanese Brigade. I also had participated in the saltmakers' struggle, and I was one of the first to do battle with the salt police
when they came to Qi Ji. . . . The situation was different than during the struggle with the salt police, because during the Anti-Japanese War we had more
efficient weapons.

The rise of anti-Japanese resistance in Fanzhuang village was actively
linked with the structure of popular resistance to the Republican state,

which ran all the way back to 1933 and recalled "soft networks" associated with the nonpartisan defense of the salt market. The CCP's stalwarts discovered that success in anti-Japanese mobilization *within local units* was ensured principally by working through local people who had united their villages in defense of the salt market economy. In Fanzhuang, without going through leaders like Zhai Hongliang, whose connections to the miniconfederation of its saltmakers were far better than the CCP's, the party leaders could not have built, or broadened, anti-Japanese resistance. "Zhai Hongliang," recalls Wang Wenxun,[88] "was the leader of the saltmakers' struggle here, and the village chief in the period of the Japanese presence."

> Zhai Hongliang was the village chief from 1938 to 1942. We depended on him to greet the Japanese and to deal with them. If everyone fled when the Japanese came, and no one was here to greet them, they would think we were Communists and burn our village. So we needed a courageous person to deal with them. This Zhai Hongliang had been a soldier in the warlord army of Wu Peifu, and thereafter the leader of our saltmakers' struggle. He had returned to Fanzhuang from serving in Wu Peifu's command before 1933, after Wu had been defeated by Chiang Kai-shek. He had made earth salt and sold it in the local markets of Nanle. He also occasionally sold straw hats with me in those years.
>   Zhai Hongliang was not a member of our Peasant Association or of the National Salvation Association. He was just the village chief. However, he was not looking to serve the Japanese. In fact, when the National Salvation Association held mass meetings, Zhai Hongliang actually helped it. Wang Jingru, the leader of the underground CCP and the National Salvation Association in Fanzhuang after 1938, went through Zhai Hongliang to organize anti-Japanese resistance.

The Return to Market Politics

Over the course of the war, CCP leaders enunciated a number of policies designed to construct a political economy capable of enlisting peasant support, varying from programs of relief from natural disaster, to campaigns to reduce rates of interest and rent, to the construction of protosocialist cooperatives, to the building of the Eighth Route Army itself. Although all of these policies helped the peasantry to cope with wartime dearth and hardship, the appeal of each was limited both to the specific existential situations of different villages, districts, and counties and to the span of time in which the CCP leaders could safely interact with the people of a given village and/or market system.

No one of these four policies, however, spoke to the broad issue facing the village people who depended on the salt-encrusted lands of the border region. Of course, many CCP leaders presumed the particular base area policy experiment they were involved with was the key to mobilization and legitimacy, but the four strategies all had problems. What did work was the rebuilding and protecting of salt trade and market networks.

The Henan famine of 1942 left countless border area villages in a catastrophic situation. Hunger and starvation prevailed, especially in predominantly agricultural counties. The CCP-led anti-Japanese government came up with several methods of famine relief, the most important of which was a "grain-borrowing campaign," calling on the hungry poor to redistribute the grain of rich households. The grain-borrowing movement created social chaos and disrupted the rural economy, causing landlord and rich peasant targets to withdraw from "production for pillage." Once the movement started, it spread quickly and uncontrollably to small proprietors. Many *liu mang* elements exploited the opportunities for plunder, seizing grain from surplus households even when there was only a minor, temporary disaster and even when such households were not hoarding grain for speculation. "Since the *lumpen* elements often bullied the weak and feared the strong [landlords]," writes Zhang Linzhi, "the middle peasants suffered badly. Such actions violated our policy and harmed the interest of the masses, and destabilized our social order." [89] The movement also produced a spate of "free riders" and fostered what the CCP cadres referred to as the "lazy bone mentality."

Zhang Linzhi and CCP leaders moved to limit grain borrowing to the most severely stricken disaster areas. They instructed the party cadres to win broad public sympathy for grain borrowing, to implement it in a legal way, and to give protection to lenders through contracts. The grain-borrowing campaign was to be converted into a normal lending-borrowing business relationship, and landlords were to be given an interest in the process. Moreover, party leaders were to see that those who borrowed the grain did not simply live on it; once they had made a physical recovery, the borrowers were to reengage in production.

In late 1943 CCP leaders admitted that they still did not have a better alternative to grain borrowing, and yet the Eighth Route Army grain supply program and the CCP Financial Bureau grain price stabilization program did not effectively come into play until 1944. How, then, did most of the rural dwellers of this border region pass through the terrible dearth of 1942–43? Indispensable to relief and recovery was the continuous independent popular expansion of earth salt business, for this produced a constant flow of small gains from which charity loans could be made to stave off community tragedy. To be sure, the more prosperous salt-making villages were in a better position to weather the disaster. Yet even Qi Ji, with its terrible poverty, could transform salt trade into charity during the worst years of war and famine. Thus Liu Chaoyang says:[90]

> The demand for earth salt was greater during the war because the flow of sea salt had diminished. So some people made a small fortune *via* their earth salt businesses. Liu Xiangfeng, for example, had more bad salt land than anyone, and there were many laborers in his family. Therefore, the Liu household

could produce and store a lot of salt. They had stored it from three years past when the Big Famine of 1942 struck. At that point, Liu Xiangfeng had over ten thousand *jin* of stored earth salt.

During the Famine many people came to Liu Xiangfeng's house to reason with him. They had less land, and no storage facilities, so when the Famine came they were short of food. They reasoned that since he had so much salt, when others could not make a living, Liu Xiangfeng should be generous and give some salt to them so they could sell it. Liu Chaode asked Liu Xiangfeng to give charity loans of salt to the other people to tide them through the Famine. Liu Xiangfeng redistributed his salt to about sixty households, and helped them market their way through the most difficult months of the Famine. Not only the Liu's received these loans. People from the Wangs, Guos, Nius and Hans also received them. They were among the poorest and smallest families in Qi Ji.

Similarly, the semipeasants of Qian Kou retained their salt-making enterprises and renewed their salt market endeavors during the critical months of the 1942 famine. The first good wheat harvest after the terrible year of 1942 was in June, 1944, but villagers recall they had been on the road to recovery ever since 1943. Following the onset of the famine the income from salt making in most peasant households made up 50 to 70 percent of the total. In combination with sales of dates, saltpeter, and peanuts, this income allowed peasants to purchase the sorghum, black beans, and corn needed to last out the famine and to inch their way back to subsistence.[91]

A number of village dwellers, of course, escaped empty bellies by emphasizing agriculture. Ironically, they were often the indirect beneficiaries of the Japanese slaughter, as in Qian Kou. Liu Zhouchen was born in the last year of the Qing dynasty and was thirty-two years old when the 1942 famine settled over Qian Kou. He got ten *mu* of land from one uncle and fifteen *mu* from another, both of whose families had been killed in the Japanese assault of 12 April 1941. The use of their lands enabled him to get through the famine. But few in his situation stopped making earth salt for the market in this critical period.[92] Most of the peasant saltmakers relied on the market, rather than on CCP famine relief formulas. Moreover, the CCP anchored its national resistance activities in the border area's upscale salt-making villages, whose small proprietors had preserved their market access through a long-term struggle with the Kuomintang state.

CCP leaders were also involved in promoting an experimental land reform movement during the war. In the Hebei-Shandong-Henan anti-Japanese base this movement took the form of a rent and interest reduction campaign. Zhao Ziyang, the deputy secretary of the Northern Henan Prefectural Committee, is said to have gotten his start in national politics partly by leading the tenants of Hua County in the rent reduction drive of 1943–44.[93] These rent reduction campaigns had great moral appeal because the peasant tenants who participated in them were prepared to press landlords to reinstate a set of social guarantees they had withdrawn since the ninth year of the Republic (1920). The CCP supported tenant efforts to make landlords honor long-term land leases, to restore the old fifty-fifty land rent contracts in which both sides shared the harvest equally, and to reduce the crop rent by 25 per-cent when the harvest was poor—the practice before the war broke out.

This "return to traditional morality" in tenant-landlord exchanges was an important part of the CCP's announced repertoire of politics during the Anti-Japanese War.[94] Yet this movement cannot be counted among the vital permanent developments contributing to the CCP's rising wartime fortunes. The passions of "antilandlord struggle" notwithstanding, CCP reliance on rent reduction as a means to mobilize popular support for its national resistance goals posed a number of problems. To begin with, peasants who fell into the category of tenant seldom comprised more than 10 to 20 percent of the rural working population. This border area was still a world of smallholding villagers who by and large were not enmeshed in land tenure relations.

In addition, not all tenants were prepared to question the fundamental right of their landlords to rent the land and receive a share of the harvest. In the villages where the CCP was fairly successful the *ganqing* relationship[95] was still intact, and tenants (who now speak of it somewhat cynically) sometimes derived satisfaction from it.[96] Many landlords labored in their own fields and employed members of their own lineages. It proved virtually impossible for the CCP to persuade tenants of different landlords, and different villages, to close ranks and engage in a sweeping class struggle.

A third obstacle involved a number of complex rental problems.[97]

1. Persuading landlords to divide shares equitably. To plant, cultivate, cut, and market the June wheat crop took fifteen "labor tasks." A tenant who performed ten labor tasks received ten shares of the harvest, and the landlord five; but many tenants had accepted the landlord notion that the harvest was to be shared fifty-fifty. The CCP cadres were at a loss as to how to prove such inequities and to successfully cast the issue in terms of class exploitation.

2. Persuading big, nonworking landlords to reduce rents in cases involving subleasing by secondary managerial landlords. The suggested method was for the primary landlord to reduce the rent to the second landlord by 25 percent and ask the secondary landlord to follow up with a 25 percent reduction to his tenant. This method worked in share tenancy, but proved unrealizable when the secondary landlord took a fixed rent from the tenant.

3. Finding a fair way to reduce the rent payments and increase the salaries of aged villagers, childless families, and widows who leased landlord lands. The issue was even more complicated when these

poor, labor short households had members in the Eighth Route Army and desperately needed the income from leasing land to survive.

4. Arriving at a way to apply rent reduction to cases involving watermelon patches and vegetable gardens. Because there was no fixed rent on melon patches, and production varied greatly, the tenant was authorized to reduce the amount of rent if his crop did not cover his costs. There was to be a 25 percent reduction of rent on vegetable plots, where high fixed rents prevailed. Developing a uniform set of regulations for such thorny rental issues was virtually impossible. Thus CCP cadres often raised false hopes among tenants or provoked landlords to take revenge.

5. Lastly, there was the changing political context of tax obligations.[98] The shifting fortunes of war constrained the ability of the CCP to readjust the tax liability between landlords and tenants. If the Eighth Route Army was able to establish firm controls and implement its reasonable burden tax system, the party cadres could press landlords to pay 80 percent of taxes on rental lands. But if a county was not politically secure, and tax implementation was incomplete, they had to leave the distribution of tax liability unchanged, even if a landlord had illegally shifted the burden of taxes onto tenants.

The initial focus of the cooperative movement, aimed at helping villagers survive the famine of 1942 and increase production for the CCP-led resistance army, was on elevating grain production. By concentrating the cooperative movement in the agricultural sector, however, and by recruiting mainly the disaster victims with depleted resources, the CCP made a serious mistake and promoted irrational forms of economic cooperation that were hopelessly grounded in the poverty of agriculture and only minimally helpful.[99]

The early cooperative experiment left villagers with paltry grain yields and locked them into fragile poverty-sharing arrangements. At the end of 1943 only 130 cooperatives had been set up in the border region—1 to 3 per county. According to CCP Finance Bureau inspectors, few of these were able to carry on production.[100] The basic problem, however, was that the cooperative leaders lacked the knowledge to link production with the market. The cooperative movement had not sufficiently focused on conjoining production with supply, markets, and transport. "Production," one CCP official wrote in March, 1943, "should not be taken in abstract terms. It should be concrete production, such as men digging wells and transporting salt, and women spinning and weaving."[101] To succeed, the local party leaders had to find ways to release people from the poverty of the land into the market, where private exchange could produce the small profits needed to purchase the food supplies that would open up the possibility of household recovery.[102]

The earliest successful cooperative ventures in the Hebei-Shandong-Henan anti-Japanese base area were taken up by people who had capital, resided in comparatively well-off villages, and had engineered their own recovery from the 1942 famine by forming joint self-help market arrangements. The testimony of Liu Zhouchen, a participant in the Qian Kou cooperative, shows how the peasant saltmakers crafted the wartime cooperatives in the image of their own creative market urges:[103]

> In early 1943 a number of us pooled our money, and used it to purchase sea salt, kerosene, cigarettes, candy, thread, and ropes in Jingdian market and then sold these items in the streets of Qian Kou village. . . . The money I used to purchase these items came from the income I generated from selling earth salt, dates, and peanuts on my own. The earth salt income made up 30 per cent of the money I contributed.
>
> In my cooperative, there were fourteen people. We joined voluntarily. This movement had nothing to do with the Soviet Union. No one told us anything about cooperatives in the Soviet Union, or about how Communism worked there. Of course the CCP called on us to start the cooperative, and we answered the call. About 50 percent of the people in Qian Kou participated in this movement, often two or three from the same household. All of them made earth salt. The money from our salt businesses was one of the factors enabling us to found the cooperative here.

The cooperative movement was not based on the protostate management techniques of the CCP, whose cadres had a tendency to think of dispersed, spontaneous private business management as nonprogressive.[104] The movement flourished mainly in villages where the peasant saltmakers utilized their own small capital for private household production and carried on their own private trade.[105] Its leaders agreed to aid one another not only in agricultural production tasks but also in profit-earning side occupations and small trading ventures. Even the "model village cooperatives" ballyhooed in CCP propaganda pamphlets were consumer-oriented retail enterprises aimed at obtaining profits from selling bean curd, straw hats, and salt-based foodstuffs.[106]

The cooperative movement, with its twin goals of rebuilding the peasant economy and beefing up the resistance army, was considered indispensable to the CCP-led resistance. But the Japanese puppet forces made it very difficult for the CCP to transform the cooperatives into war supply factories. People who lived in the path of the puppet army were preoccupied with survival and safety. The joint household mutual aid projects that laid the basis for the cooperative movement were started up in the comparatively secure CCP villages and were not connected to the Great Production Movement itself until June of 1944, the date of the first bumper grain harvest since 1940. Yet CCP descriptions of cooperative arrangements for recovery and resistance in this bumper year do not refer to a classic peasantry tilling its croplands. Instead, we learn that in 1944 the Eighth Route Army units operating in the villages of Neihuang and Gaoling responded to the anti-Japanese border area government's call to mobilize the village people to boost production in the base area by clearing barren land and by "helping the masses boil salt."[107]

During the war many CCP leaders assumed that popular anger over suffering from Japanese military attacks would ensure recruitment of peasants, and many villagers did send their sons to join the Eighth Route Army. The question is whether such popular volunteerism ensured the war-mobilized peasantry a place in the resistance army and, in turn, affected the party-army in ways that expanded the political hold of the CCP.

The hypothesis that by ripping apart the fabric of peasant society the Japanese army played to CCP recruitment for its resistance army is certainly plausible. But the Eighth Route Army could not absorb all who had been uprooted by Japanese force. Food supply was a critical factor. "Even the troops often had nothing to eat," declared Yan Changqing, a CCP leader of the anti-Japanese base. "Thus, the party superiors made a decision that the basic troops could not take in the [war] refugees."[108]

In semi-isolated villages and small market towns, where the war did not seriously disrupt routines of agriculture and trade, the CCP organized grain transport groups to rescue rural people.[109] Time after time during 1942 and 1943, the fourth branch army teamed up with the Eighth Route Army in Puyang and Nanle to carry out rescue missions in Neihuang County, in Henan, and Caoxian in Shandong.

Although some of these CCP policies had considerable appeal, none of them would have gone very far in getting massive numbers of villagers to commit to party-led anti-Japanese resistance without the party supporting the salt market struggle that was going on simultaneously. The party built up broad popular support for its anti-Japanese struggle by reaffirming the rights of villagers to freely pursue household-based manufacturing and marketing routines that had been harmed by the central government revenue drive in the prewar period. The CCP's wartime strategy involved creating a political economy in which the purveyors of salt played a critical role, and the ranks of the party and its army were filled by the peasant salters who had been waging a war to protect their patterns of petty trade in this commodity for several decades.

The link between the peasant salt traders and the CCP-led resistance was forged at the inception of the Japanese invasion. By October of 1937 Wang Congwu, in collaboration with Puyang CCP Secretary Jiang Zhongyue, was leading the restoration of party branches and calling for anti-Japanese resistance in the villages along the Puyang-Hua county border area.[110] He and his associates spent the next three years rallying local guerrilla forces to resonate with the anti-Japanese activities of the 115th division under Yang

Dezhi, units of which penetrated the saline territory along the old line of the Yellow River between September, 1938, and February, 1939.[111] The CCP army commissars surely educated Wang and the local party faithful in the Yan'an line of wartime struggle.[112] But they relied on the likes of Wang Congwu, with his inside knowledge of the salt land question and with the local political connections he had forged in the course of the saltmakers' struggle, to elicit popular support for the army's wartime mission.

The manufacturing of salt-based commodities was inextricably bound up with peasant survival and community benefit; the issue of land use rights *cum* market prerogatives touched the daily life of both peasants and the petit bourgeoisie. As village-dwelling smallholders and petty traders in red sorghum, watermelons, and salt-based products, the saltmakers fell into both categories. According to Wang, the CCP would need to develop a policy supportive of their labor on the saline land and their pursuit of market prosperity.

During the early stage of the war the Chinese Communists stepped back from the land taxation policy of the Kuomintang and virtually eliminated the land tax burden of the salt land peasantry. Nie Zhen, the Hua County CCP secretary in 1932, helped form the Hebei-Shandong-Henan anti-Japanese base during WWII. His testimony suggests that the CCP's effort to cultivate popular support for its anti-Japanese cause was fundamentally an extension of the process whereby the party relied on tax relief to forge a political bond with the peasant saltmakers in the prewar period:[113]

> The first time I mobilized the village people against the salt police was in Blue Chicken village in the winter of 1929. . . . When the Changlu salt police came to enforce the taxes on the salt lands, some people from Blue Chicken village came to me to ask for my help. I advised them not to pay the tax. I said if the Kuomintang government sends someone then just unite and surround him. I told them to fetch their local rifles [*tu qiang*] and shoot the tax collectors if they came, and to beat the Changlu salt police if they came.
>
> In 1932 we had just begun to lead the saltmakers. Later, in the first years of the Anti-Japanese War, we led the saltmakers and peasants and we eliminated the salt land tax. Thereafter, they did not have to pay it.

Encouraged by the Kuomintang army retreat, and heartened by the advancement of the Eighth Route Army into Puyang, Wang Congwu, Liu Dafeng, Nie Zhen, and the CCP leaders of the Hebei-Shandong-Henan Border Region National Salvation Association sent hundreds of young party activists into the villages of Puyang, Hua County, and Nanle. The mass anti-tax movement that ensued, fueled by the same peasant saltmakers who were the victims of the twenty-ninth army's sporadic tax drives in the first years of the war,[114] was a resounding success, sweeping aside nearly all of the prewar Kuomintang levies and permitting the CCP anti-Japanese cadres to disassociate themselves from corrupt Kuomintang officers.[115] By suspending all

taxes up until 1940 the CCP made it impossible for the Japanese to represent themselves as a better "taking regime" than the Communist-led resistance, thus undercutting the Japanese attempt to legitimate the collection
of tribute grain by its quisling puppet troops, which became the practice
around 1940. By the autumn of 1939 the CCP was in a position to elicit
widespread popular support for the creation of an anti-Japanese government, with the promise of a world without Kuomintang state extraction and
Japanese tribute.

The critical factor for the peasants of the border area, however, was the
promise of locally esteemed CCP leaders, such as Wang Congwu and Liu
Dafeng, that the party's political objective was the destruction of the Kuomintang tax state (in party vocabulary, "bureaucratic capitalism") and the
preservation of the medley of salt-related market pursuits. The CCP delivered on this promise in the first stage of the war, *before* its rent reduction
campaigns, natural disaster relief programs, cooperative experiments, and
regular army building got off the ground in the second and third stages.
"After the Eighth Route Army came into the border area in 1938 anyone
could produce earth salt and sell it freely," says Wang Jingru, a member of
the CCP-led resistance and a former "advisor" to the saltmakers of
Fanzhuang in Nanle County. "So from the perspective of the saltmakers, the
contradiction between their livelihood and the Changlu salt police, which
had existed under the Central government, disappeared."[116]

By 1940 private trade in salt-based products manufactured within peasant households was booming. This upsurge was followed by another marked
increase in the second stage, around 1941–42, which lasted until the end of
WWII. The peasant saltmakers had done rather well for themselves alongside the Kuomintang state's imperfect salt monopoly before the Japanese
invasion; during the war they did even better.

The impact of the invasion on the position of Changlu salt favored popular salt making for the market. The Japanese took over the Tianjin Changlu
Salt Company, retaining many of the prewar Changlu officials—including
the chief of the Changlu Salt Administration—whose familiarity with the
industry permitted the Japanese to more easily sustain, or increase, production. However, approximately 70 percent of the salt produced in the Japanese-occupied Tianjin salterns was exported to Japan for industrial use, with
a corresponding drop in the volume of sea salt shipped down the Wei River
into the border area by the Changlu salt merchants.[117] Facing Changlu salt
merchants whose capacity to expand distribution and sale in the rural sector was severely curtailed, the peasant salters took full advantage of this
development.

During the war, controlling the production and flow of common salt
became even more hopeless. The Japanese not only ruined the central government's plan to rebuild its revenue forces and pour more salt police

units into southern Hebei;[118] they did not vigorously support the suppression of the underground earth salt economy.[119] The Nationalist government officials claimed that the center still was in control of Changlu salt revenues. If the truth were known, they feared, it would precipitate desertion from the central army, whose officers and mainline troops were partly dependent on Changlu salt revenue for salary and supplies. The country people took advantage of this additional foreign restraint on Kuomintang state making to manufacture earth salt at a pace that outstripped prewar production.[120]

In the war's middle stage, the puppet army of Yang Faxian attempted to resurrect a miniature version of the Changlu salt monopoly, which apparently shifted the focus of the peasant saltmakers to the Japanese client regime and permitted CCP leaders to recast the issue in simplistic patriotic terms: resistance to the Yang Faxian puppet army would prevent the Japanese from channeling the Changlu salt into the border region and help drive the Japanese out of the country. Whether large numbers of the peasant salt producers were thereby motivated to join the CCP-led resistance is not clear. Many probably did see the Japanese puppet army as the new obstacle, but perhaps they were driven more by the knowledge that the puppet forces reflected the degraded status of the same Kuomintang revenue state they, and not just the Japanese, had damaged and driven out of the countryside.[121] As the war continued, they discovered they could more easily reclaim the market from the Japanese puppet regime than from its centralized predecessor.

For most of the war, Wang Congwu, Zhang Linzhi, and the CCP leaders of the Hebei-Shandong-Henan anti-Japanese base forbore to reintroduce an internally controlled public salt monopoly. This third factor in the wartime expansion of salt commodity markets is of special concern. The young CCP activists who rose to power in the border area during the war years took for granted the righteousness of this petty-trade issue for which the rural people had been fighting. Avoiding the mistake of the overzealous revenue agents of the Kuomintang state, the CCP won over the peasants of the marketplace by forgoing the activity of "public fiscal privilege."[122]*

Martin King Whyte has emphasized that bureaucratization is a process by which the independent self-sustaining activities of families, kin groups, and local communities are captured by huge, impersonal, and hierarchical political organizations that regulate the production, distribution, and consumption of such groups for government ends.[123] The salt land peasants escaped this pattern of Kuomintang bureaucratic dominance during the

---

*The CCP did not reintroduce the salt bureaus to this border area until 1991.

war, and by resonating with their efforts to preserve their marketing liberty, the CCP was able to draw these market-bound rural people into its anti-Japanese struggle and build a political base in the countryside.

The purveyors of earth salt epitomized the spirit of "folk capitalism" in the countryside and exemplified a pattern of development that linked the immediate interests of peasants *cum* petty traders to the emergence of the "bourgeoisie democratic revolution" of which Mao Zedong spoke in his 1940 essay, "New Democracy." In shaping the political economy of the Hebei-Shandong-Henan anti-Japanese base, they assumed a role that was in line with their own "unifying investment logic" (to borrow a phrase from Popkin[124]) and that was consistent with the CCP's goal of creating an inter-regional economy by connecting popular-based market systems among the various anti-Japanese base areas.

The emphasis during the war was on combining agricultural production with the development of handicrafts and sidelines for market entry. This permitted the country people to create material wealth and to rely less on the economy of the Japanese-occupied territories. By late 1943, sidelines previously subordinated to simple grain production had mushroomed. Peanuts, straw hats, and earth salt paved the way to economic prosperity and involved peasants in expanding market exchanges.

The CCP enlisted the support of the peasant saltmakers in reviving the traditional rural market fairs, and some were said to have been even more prosperous than before the war.[125] A few developed into regional fairs in bigger market villages like Gu Chengji in Qingfeng, Hebei. Significantly, the products of these fairs were sold *inside and outside* of the key counties of the Hebei-Shandong-Henan anti-Japanese base. The circulation of specific commodities apparently had its own pattern, order, and pace, which could not be contained by the Japanese and which provided the CCP with a natural instrument for interlocking the interests of peasants in different anti-Japanese strongholds, that is, politically secure economic zones. The millet growers from eastern Shanxi, for example, historically sold in southern Hebei, and the earth salt producers of southern Hebei had peddled in the markets of eastern Shanxi. The Japanese "three all" disrupted this pattern, but within a few years the peasant saltmakers—who were experienced in reopening trade routes that connected seemingly isolated sectors, waging clandestine guerrilla warfare, and establishing legal discourse that upheld the business rights of country dwellers—reestablished it.

SALT AND THE SALTMAKERS IN THE POLITICAL ECONOMY
OF THE WAR OF RESISTANCE

The most obvious wartime contribution of the peasant saltmakers was economic. They helped the Eighth Route Army by provisioning its recruits, selling earth salt to the army and its guerrilla forces in dispersed local markets.

As Robert Multhauf has pointed out, access to salt has been a crucial factor determining the outcome of wars between powerful central states and insurgent counterforces since antiquity.[126] Salt-poor guerrilla armies have fared poorly even in the age of national independence movements. In southern China prior to WWII, Chiang Kai-shek's central army, with the assistance of the salt revenue guards, blockaded the supply lines to the Communist-led guerrilla army and its peasant base, creating a salt famine that left the Jiangxi guerrilla army in a crisis.[127] The popular army of Mao Zedong and Zhu De was deprived of common salt and other items of commerce and consumption, the price of which surpassed the means of its soldiers.[128]

The Japanese attempted to mimic the Nationalist government strategy by imposing a tight economic blockade of coastal salt, but they succeeded in doing little, if any, damage to the inexhaustible salt resources of the CCP-led resistance army in the border area—particularly after 1940, when, as Zhao Chunzhi points out, regional party leaders grasped that pushing earth salt production and breaking the Japanese blockade were two aspects of the same struggle.[129] Obviously, the economic reality of the wartime crisis was a factor in the party's salt policy. Cut off from sea salt, and anxious not to import from Japanese-occupied areas, the CCP embraced the production of local salt partly out of necessity. Still, local Communist Party leaders, such as Wang Congwu and Liu Dafeng, had supported the manufacturing of salt for the market all along, and the war-related economic reality gave them greater reason to embrace it. Dispersed in hundreds of villages, the peasant earth salt producers were well known to the CCP guerrilla army leaders, and their disaggregated salt trade defied virtually all means of direct Japanese control. Thus the party-led fighters could find ample supplies of salt, and salt-based foodstuffs, in the markets through which they passed. Xiao Bianxian, a former leader of the fourth branch army, recalls that he and his ten counterparts who joined the Eighth Route Army in 1938 bought earth salt in Gu Chengji in Qingfeng and near the Yan Wang Temple in Nanle, both of which were "markets near the places where we stayed."[130]

During the first stage of the Japanese invasion, after the Kuomintang commands fled, the peasant saltmakers produced and supplied more and more by way of basic war materials for the CCP and its regular army. The interplay between CCP army supply agents and the country people broadened to include a multitude of villages.

The intriguing question is how the CCP was able to win over this particular constituency so quickly. "Rational choice" theory would suggest that the local people simply knew their economic interests and produced the materials they had always produced, selling them for a premium to a new, ambitious market actor, the CCP. Indeed, sales of salt and nitrate to meet the demands of the CCP-led resistance army soared around 1940. From

1937 until 1939, the saltmakers still sold vast supplies of salt and nitrate to Kuomintang armies, which provided their local guerrilla affiliates (including the CCP-led fourth branch army) with bullets, gunpowder, and horses.[131] Only after Shi Yousan retreated south, and after Ding Shuben exposed his twenty-ninth army to Japanese muscle, both in late 1939,[132] did the CCP-led fourth branch army break off its relationship with the Kuomintang fortieth and twenty-ninth armies and gain salt and gunpowder sources completely independent of official Kuomintang supply lines.[133] From this point on, production for the CCP-led resistance forces exploded in the villages of the border area.

But politics and psychology were at play as well. The popular shift from the Kuomintang to the CCP was also the result of lingering peasant resentment toward the central government's attack on family-based salt production. When Kuomintang state power was all but shattered, many country people decided to support the wartime cause of the CCP, whose cadres promised to preserve the gains for which they had sacrificed in the prewar struggle.

Yang Depu, a saltmaker in San Huang, had produced both earth salt and nitrate (saltpeter) with his father since 1927. They had sold their earth salt to peddlers in Nanle town markets and to peasants in the markets of Yan Wang and Wucunji. Their nitrate, however, was sold to purchase agents with connections to the gunpowder factories of the Kuomintang government. When the Kuomintang Finance Ministry's salt tax police closed down the Nanle town salt market in 1934,[134] they destroyed the Yang family cauldrons, and in 1934 and 1935 the household's income slipped to an all-time low. On the eve of the Japanese invasion, Yang Depu still resented the Kuomintang government suppression of salt making and was offended by the Kuomintang attempt to redefine him, his family, and his village friends as "salt smugglers." When the Japanese army invaded Nanle County in late 1937, Yang Depu got even by curtailing his sale of nitrate to the Ding Shuben Twenty-Ninth Army and switching secretly to a new customer—the CCP resistance army. He tells us,[135] "We had two main customers here before the war: the Kuomintang Government Nitrate Bureau, and the private firecracker makers. Before the war we sold the high quality nitrate to the Kuomintang. But after 1937 we sold the nitrate to peddlers who came here to buy nitrate for the CCP Eighth Route Army gunpowder factories in Nanle villages. Beginning in 1939, our nitrate increasingly went to the 129th Division of the Eighth Route Army."

The surge in nitrate production for CCP-led guerrilla warfare signified another blow to the Kuomintang. By 1941–42 peasants in scores of nitrate-producing villages were boosting profits and bypassing the crumbling "official" nitrate market, which in theory had been accessible mainly to Kuomintang-licensed purchase agents, although a lively black market in nitrate had existed in the shadow of state controls. As the CCP connected its cause to the popular nitrate market, its anti-Japanese resistance government put itself in a position to challenge the Japanese army by the manufacture of gunpowder, land mines, hand grenades, and even primitive machine guns in Qian Kou in Puyang, Liu Xinggu in Neihuang, and Qian Foji, Fo Shan, and Zhang Fuqiu in Nanle County. All of these villages were in the saline zone; all had supported the saltmakers against Republican state makers— and all were now delivering their explosive power into the hands of the CCP-led anti-Japanese resistance army and its guerrilla affiliates. Xiao Bianxian, the leader of the fourth branch guerrilla army unit from Liu Gudian, recalls,[136] "We got most of our gunpowder from Qian Kou and Jingdian in Puyang. We purchased the nitrate through underground CCP cadres who had connections with purchase agents. I personally led our unit to this Shaqu area to fight the Japanese and carry on guerrilla warfare in 1938 and 1939. Ping Jiesan, the CCP Secretary, received us in Jingdian market."

Acting from indignation over Kuomintang state-induced injury, and given to multiple occupational activities, the peasant saltmakers often enabled the CCP-led anti-Japanese resistance to mobilize resources for war from a much larger territorial constituency than might be imagined if one looks only at the villages that were pro-CCP. Liu Jingxiang, the son of a veteran of the saltmakers' struggle in Qi Ji, is from a village universe that diverges significantly from most paradigms of Western scholarly debate about why rural dwellers supported the CCP. His remembrance points to a previously unknown thread that wrapped popular commitments to CCP-led anti-Japanese resistance around an internal war against the Nationalist government of Chiang Kai-shek:[137]

> Ever since I could remember, my father had told me about how Chiang Kai-shek's salt police had tried to stop us from making earth salt. My grandfather, father, and I were animal purchase agents, saltmakers and tillers. We did all three of these things for a living. Before the war, we got 70 percent of our income from salt making, 20 percent from agricultural production, and 10 percent from animal purchase work.
>
> My father often complained about the central government preventing us from improving our livelihood. We still resented the Kuomintang officials even after we won the saltmakers' struggle in 1935, because they had interfered in our salt business and disrupted our livelihood. We did not consider it to be a Kuomintang concession that the central government stopped interfering in our business. After all, *we* made them stop.
>
> During the Anti-Japanese War, we often helped the Eighth Route Army to buy horses and mules. The army men came to the market fairs at Wang Gu village to buy animals, and they went through my father since he was an expert in selecting the best animals. They always paid a fair price. I am not sure where they got their money.
>
> We mainly dealt with Li Cunxian, the commander of the Sixteenth Horse Cavalry Regiment of the Eighth Route Army. He came here to Qi Ji and to

Wang Gu market to purchase from us. This was not dangerous work, because the Eighth Route Army buyers came disguised as common people. No one knew Li was Eighth Route Army. Only my father knew about his political connections. This Li Cunxian originally was from Qi Ji village, so everyone knew him.

Because we still resented the Kuomintang we helped the Eighth Route Army. We wanted to strengthen it against the Kuomintang. Even though it was the Anti-Japanese War, the Eighth Route Army was carrying on a two front struggle, fighting the Japanese and preparing to defeat the Chiang Kai-shek Central Army. So we were committed to strengthening it to defeat both the Japanese and the Kuomintang. Of course the Japanese were the main target then, but we still resented the Kuomintang.[138]*

Clearly, though, the war *was* a boon to many, providing a steady flow of customers for various war-related products—earth salt, nitrate and gunpowder, horses, and weapons. The clandestine armaments factories set up in Qian Kou around 1940 were run by experts employed by the CCP Liucun anti-Japanese district government. The people who made the explosive powder for these armaments were the peasant saltmakers and nitrate producers of Qian Kou, Wen Xinggu, and other villages along the Nitrate River. As long as the Japanese stayed away from their villages, these small-time gunpowder producers and gun runners derived substantial benefits from the war.

This war materials production was one of the factors behind the Japanese army decision to attack Qian Kou and other villages inside the CCP-controlled war districts of Puyang County during the spring of 1941. The village had become a hotbed of anti-Japanese resistance and was supplying men and selling war materials to the Eighth Route Army and the Hebei People's Army, which together had scored a string of minor victories against the Japanese along the Hebei-Shandong border in 1938 and 1939. The Japanese army decimated Qian Kou and knocked out its armaments factory in the bloody "three all," but was not strong enough to bulldoze all of these armaments operations. With the growth of CCP-led resistance between 1942 and 1945, rural arms bazaars sprang up like weeds.[139]

The CCP was able to quickly build up a counterpolity in the broadly based conservative social forces of these tight-knit, premobilized, market-oriented villages. Along with village schoolteachers and doctors, the peasant saltmakers made up one of three significant village-level social groups. Accustomed to travelling through the villages and markets of the border area, they were experienced in winnowing and drafting popular demands. Here was a political force not continuously tied to the land in one particular locality, capable of organizing collective resistance based in, and yet with

---

*Neither Liu Jingxiang nor his father was a member of the CCP during the war years.

the propensity to transcend, this or that isolated village community. Because many of the peasant saltmakers had acquaintances and allies in every nook and cranny of the countryside, the CCP also was able to go through them to mobilize the rooted smallholders who made up the majority of respectable working folk.

For the troubled CCP-led anti-Japanese resistance, these "near peasants" were a source of political stability in this turbulent border area. When CCP leaders surveyed the social circumstances in the countryside at the outset of the war, many concluded that they were caught up in a world of bankrupted peasants who, under pressures of rural unemployment and urban underdevelopment, became vagrants in the countryside or roamed inside the cities. A December, 1942, report delivered by Huang Jing to a meeting of high-ranking CCP leaders says,[140] "This border region has the largest vagrant population in the whole of North China. The emergence of the 'conscript soldiers' in Hebei-Shandong-Henan itself, of the 'bandits' in *Liangshanpo,* of the 'Shandong brothers' and 'Henan folks' who brave the migration trails to Northeast China, of the 'police' in Shanghai, of the 'water boys' and 'night-soil collectors' in Beijing—all are specific manifestations of the problem of unemployment spilling out from this border area."

There was a tendency among party activists to associate the floating population with revolutionary potential, and the CCP attempted to recruit such poor *lumpen* elements for anti-Japanese resistance. In the same year they brought the bandits under Liu Xiangyou into the fourth branch army, Ping Jiesan and local CCP leaders, acting on instructions of the Southern Hebei Special Committee, attempted to bring another bandit force into the anti-Japanese united front. Its leader was Yang Faqiu, who had been a Kuomintang officer before the Japanese invasion and still had connections with landlord figures on the west side of the Wei River. Yang accepted the CCP invitation to fight against the Japanese with the fourth branch army.[141]

The problem was that the peasants and petty landlords on the east side of the Wei River regarded these west side bandits as a predatory force. In the prewar period, villages on the east side had been robbed time and time again, and some of the west side bandits had been killed by the east side landlord forces. In November of 1937, the west side bandits, led by Guo Qing and Zheng He, came across the Wei River to raid Xiao Huai village. Instead of protecting the village, the CCP-led fourth branch army withdrew. While Ping Jiesan and the fourth branch army's third battalion sat comfortably in Jingdian market town, the west side bandits plundered at will, slaughtering three hundred villagers and torching peasant homes. "After this disaster, the local people were very unhappy with us, thinking that we did not want to protect them," Ping admitted. "Some landlords told the local people that we only wanted weapons and refused to fight against the

Japanese. They also said that the Communist Party was not reliable. We were in a difficult situation."[142]

As late as 1942 CCP leaders still clung to the hope of incorporating *liu mang* and bandit forces and attempted to recruit them to raid Japanese-occupied compounds and munitions facilities instead of robbing the common folk.[143] For all practical purposes, however, the local party leaders wisely gave up on this strategy.[144] In the Hebei-Shandong-Henan anti-Japanese base CCP leaders went back to the peasant saltmakers, who were seen by peasants and landlords alike not as untrustworthy drifters or dangerous criminal elements, but as contributors to the vitality of their communities.

Whereas other literature has linked the CCP's success to uniting with either loose bands of dispossessed elements or the solid earthbound peasantry, in the Hebei-Shandong-Henan base it was through quasi peasants whose communities were still intact that the CCP effectively organized popular mass participation in the Anti-Japanese War of Resistance. The majority of these semipeasants stayed in their villages to organize and fight locally, under the leadership of the more prosperous saltmakers and their scions. Because they also travelled a lot, these quasi peasants also provided support for party-army operations locally and rallied to join the regular troops in firefights with the Japanese and the puppet troops.

The powerful role of the prosperous village leaders was evident in various aspects of resistance. Their relationship with the landlord and gentry figures who had supported market struggle was the umbilical cord through which the CCP nurtured multiclass national resistance and brought the local nonofficial elite into the anti-Japanese united front. These leaders had engaged the lower gentry in the early salt protests, and some of them—particularly the purchase agents—were still the invisible business partners of the county elite. Clearly, they shared an interest in minimizing Japanese army damage to their salt-based trade, and many of them attributed the Japanese presence to central government abandonment and abuse. Thus, Wang Congwu, Liu Dafeng, and the returning ex–Daming Normal School students could persuade the unofficial county-level elite that their efforts to link up with the peasant salters for anti-Japanese resistance were not a threat to its interest.

The evidence also suggests a pattern more common to the wartime politics of the CCP: the role played by students and schoolteachers in constructing the anti-Japanese united front.[145] On returning to southern Hebei as the vice-secretary of the Special Committee, Liu Dafeng joined with Wang Congwu to set up an anti-Japanese force that would unite people from all social classes. At the same time, right after establishing the fourth branch army, Liu Dafeng, Ping Jiesan, and Chao Zhepu set up the National Salvation Group of Ten in Qingfeng County. An Fagan, the director of the CCP organization department, led this group in founding an anti-Japanese training center in Liu Da market village. The group recruited eighty school-teachers from border area villages and relied on them to unite with the lesser gentry to establish a mass anti-Japanese defense corps. Made up of three hundred members and based in the bigger market towns of Puyang, Qingfeng, and Nanle, this corps was charged with maintaining public order and supporting the legal rights of all members of society. Its teachers worked with the fourth branch army to involve the armed forces of landlords sympathetic to the resistance,[146] and its gentry figures advised the CCP-appointed magistrates on the local politics of anti-Japanese resistance work for the duration of the war.[147]

In the opening moments of the war, however, the consummation of the anti-Japanese united front was complicated by an ultraleftist approach to politics that had its origins in the Wang Ming line within the circles of the CCP *Zhinan Tewei*. As in the prewar period, this Wang Ming line emphasized "peasant communism" and violent class struggle as the answer to problems that were resolvable by community discourse within a legal framework and stressed the subordination of the CCP's various county-level committees and anti-Japanese guerrilla forces to Kuomintang government commands as the correct way to maintain the united front. These two apparently contradictory policies reinforced one another to produce a serious political dilemma.

The young CCP guerrilla army leaders drew in a substantial number of poor peasants and *liu mang* elements under the command of Lu Wenxin, an unemployed peasant with no sense of discipline. Initially, the fourth branch army was feared as much as the Kuomintang. The absorption of Liu Xiangyou's bandit army in May, 1938, exacerbated tensions. Liu had robbed so many families that some landlords and wealthy peasants had organized armed resistance to him. The better-off villagers could not believe that such an anti-Japanese force could serve their interest.[148] To them, the fourth branch army promised little more than a repeat of the prewar "redistributive justice" dispensed by the wretched poor in the struggles to consume the surplus of rich households. CCP leaders were able to bring the landlords into the wartime coalition only when they replaced the poor riffraff with the peasant saltmakers and established village anti-Japanese governments that imposed democratic checks on poor peasants and bandits seeking to plunder. These moderate semipeasants of the salt market helped to hold the passions over landlordism in check, significantly reducing the number of landlords killed by vigilantism, though of course the fact that landlordism was never a big enough issue to mobilize many people facilitated their success.

The flip side of the Wang Ming line proved harmful to the CCP attempt to build anti-Japanese resistance by cultivating good relations with the country people. On 21 February 1938, acting in accordance with the Wang Ming strategy of subordinating everything to the united front, the CCP *Zhinan*

Tewei ordered the fourth branch army under Liu Dafeng to accept the leadership of Ding Shuben, to reorganize its troops as a detachment of Ding's Puyang public security forces, and to operate jointly with the twenty-ninth army, as opposed to remaining independent of Chiang Kai-shek–affiliated officers, expanding guerrilla warfare by programs aimed at improving popular livelihood, and establishing anti-Japanese governments in territories protected by the Eighth Route Army—all of which Mao Zedong had urged in the Lo Ch'uan Politburo Conference of August, 1937.[149]

The decision to pursue this "second Wang Ming line"[150] was imposed over the objections of Liu Dafeng and the majority of local party leaders by Zhu Zemin, the CCP secretary of the *Zhinan Tewei*. It damaged the image of the CCP and the growth of the fourth branch army, which by the Spring Festival of 1938 had become the main anti-Japanese resistance force in the border area.[151] At this point, the Japanese had launched a second attack on Qingfeng and Puyang, and the Kuomintang officials, public security forces, and a huge fraction of the twenty-ninth army had fled south in panic, leaving Ding Shuben with few reliable followers. The chief of staff of Ding's skeleton army was Chen Mingshao, a warlord army veteran, and most of his soldiers were jobless peasants, ruffians, unemployed police, and *liu mang* elements who had little sense of patriotism and were terrified of the Japanese. By subordinating the fourth branch army to this ragtag army, the CCP Special Committee effectively licensed Ding Shuben to go on raiding villages on the pretext of mobilizing "war provisions." This alarmed the peasant saltmakers in the fourth branch army because it indirectly associated them with Ding's predatory army and shifted the focus away from organizing popular resistance in the villages toward impractical front line combat with superior Japanese forces. Only after February, 1939, when the fourth branch army was combined with the regular troops of the Eighth Route Army in Puyang, Neihuang, Hua*xian*, and Nanle, were these problems overcome. Army strength jumped from twelve hundred in the early spring of 1938 to seventeen thousand in the late autumn of 1939, at which point the popular army outnumbered the Japanese (though not their puppet forces) by more than three to one in the border area.

Popular Culture and Nationalism

There is some merit in the scholarship that has emphasized the CCP exploitation of the Japanese destabilization of Kuomintang state power to recruit a war-mobilized peasantry on the basis of national salvation propaganda or to arouse peasants to join in wartime resistance by promoting economic reform and social revolution from below. But such representations do not fully address the cultural aspects of the CCP relationship with the country people in the Anti-Japanese War period—a topic to which the party leaders in the Hebei-Shandong-Henan border area had to devote careful attention.

Nationalism became a far more effective political tool for the CCP when the struggle against the Japanese was presented in a traditional cultural form in which the country people found identity and interest. According to Joseph Esherick, the open-air theaters of western Shandong disseminated martial ideas that legitimated an armed collective defense of community rights.[152] The leaders of the CCP used these vehicles of popular culture, particularly the war god operas, to draw country dwellers to their anti-Japanese mission. Yao Huibin, the director of the National Salvation Association in Nanle County from 1938 to 1945 and the CCP secretary of Nanle in the same years, reminds us that the anti-Japanese messages of insurgent groups were far more likely to be heeded if presented within what Esherick calls the "narrative context" of daily cultural practices of the country folk:[153]

> In order to save the nation after the Anti-Japanese War broke out, we used the idea of Guangong loyally serving and defending Liu Bei to uplift the national consciousness of the Chinese people. In Nanle we used this concept to elevate peasant consciousness, and to prepare the rural people to resist Japanese imperialist aggression.
>
> Of course some of the peasants had seen the violence of the Japanese invasion up close, but we had to find a way to persuade the people to get together to oppose the Japanese. We used the Guangong tradition to move them to take collective action against the Japanese. The peasants in the border area did not suddenly develop national consciousness just because the Japanese invaded, because the scope of the Japanese invasion was limited to only one county town, a market town, or just a few villages, as was the case in Nanle county.
>
> The use of Guangong theater and operas was only one form, or method, of uplifting the national consciousness of the common people. But it was an important method. The Magistrate of Nanle, Hu Tongsan, and I sponsored Guangong operas and songs in Jing Degu, Nanle, in 1940, 1941, 1942, and 1943. We also put on a lot of modern anti-Japanese plays. But whether we sponsored either traditional or modern plays, we always invited the peasants to come and see the Guangong operas. They emphasized the imagery and expressions of Guangong—the war god. We used *The Romance of the Three Kingdoms* to illustrate how Guangong loved his country, so as to let the peasants learn of Guangong's patriotism [and] to mobilize the villagers to oppose the Japanese. So Guangong was an important bridge to our national salvation propaganda.

An alarmingly high number of CCP cadres in the Hebei-Shandong-Henan base sold out to the Japanese, and the Guangong plays were useful in combatting such capitulation.[154] In Qian Kou, for instance, Zhao Xiuni (the younger brother of the CCP stalwart, Zhao Jibin and a "model" Eighth Route Army member) accepted money from Yang Huaxin (an ex-Kuomintang army leader in the Japanese puppet army) to murder Xu Liansheng, one of the high-ranking members of the CCP-led anti-Japanese base area government. Although he bungled the job, news of this betrayal utterly shocked the CCP-led resistance, for Qian Kou was presumed to have been firmly committed to national salvation.[155] Thereafter, the CCP repeatedly sponsored *Guangong Bei Cao Cao Zhua Zhule,* which stressed that Guangong would not accept bribes or gifts from his enemies and could not be bought off. This became the most popular wartime drama in the base area. According to Yao Huibin, "it allowed us to get the message across that the masses should not capitulate."[156]

The war god was the cultural grid through which the CCP won over scores of poor village people, who otherwise might have become puppet village heads and squad leaders and helped the Japanese plunder the border area. As the evidence on Wu Loucun in Nanle County illustrates,[157] the first step was for an underground CCP member to explain to puppet village chiefs and squad leaders that the Japanese would not take their Chinese accomplices back to Japan. When the leaders passed several tests of their loyalty to the resistance, the CCP enemy affairs department issued an identity card with Guan Yunzhang's (Guanggong's) picture on it, signifying that although this person was in the enemy's camp, his heart was with the anti-Japanese cause. Recipients of this card in the Japanese puppet "stronghold" of Wu Loucun were guaranteed safety in encounters with the Eighth Route Army, the fourth branch army, and the militias. They reciprocated by suspending the anti-Communist activities of their subordinates during the 1941–42 Japanese campaign to root out the CCP and its allies in the salt land villages of Nanle.

The myth of Guangong echoed a popular belief in martial behavior that inspired courageous acts sanctioned by the community.[158] The war god still played a role in the creation of popular identity, and young people still imitated this martial tradition in the 1930s.[159] During the Anti-Japanese War CCP leaders in Qian Foji in Nanle sponsored the play that best illustrated bravery and will, *Guangong Guowuguan Zhan Liu Jiang* (To Pass Five Strongholds and Kill Six Generals), to appeal to the popular admiration of courage in combat, thereby inspiring villagers to join the resistance without fear of death.[160] By appealing to this active warrior tradition, the CCP could successfully mobilize village people facing the possibility of extinction to join in the anti-Japanese struggle.[161]

Guangong was a folk deity of great versatility, and the country people sometimes worshipped him as the god of wealth.[162] A patron saint of professional trades, Guangong was the guardian of the salt trade. By sponsoring Guangong operas around the markets, the CCP was able to expand its anti-Japanese audience.[163] The CCP secretary of Nanle County sponsored Guangong operas at least once annually in sixteen markets (including Yuancunji, Qian Foji, Wucunji, Jing Degu, and Nan Jingdian). After the

Japanese occupation, they moved the operas to unoccupied places. According to Yao Huibin, "The masses did not come to these markets to see or hear the CCP. They only came to burn incense, offer food sacrifices to the gods, pray for prosperity, and observe the operas. Each of the peasant households near these places had its own Guangong altar. Our National Salvation Association used the pilgrimages to the fairs to expand the scope of its anti-Japanese propaganda work, and to reach a greater number of peasants. Each of the temple fairs drew crowds of about 20,000 people."[164]

The Guangong operas enabled the CCP to shift its emphasis away from propaganda that appealed mainly to the victims of Japanese violence and to antiforeign anger,[165] underscoring the local, daily rewards of anti-Japanese resistance. The stubborn perseverance of the peasant saltmakers to recover their markets paralleled and projected itself into the War of Resistance[166] and, at the cultural level, enabled the Chinese Communists to effectively build on the promise of felicity from protracted struggle—symbolized by the war god. The CCP was far more successful in building party branches in villages where the tight-knit, fairly wealthy lineages made up of peddlers, purchase agents, and peasants with one foot in the marketplace took this message to heart. These "resourceful people," wrote Zhang Linzhi, were the "new aristocrats" who disappointed the CCP's plan for establishing "ideal party branches" (with poor peasants and hired hands in the majority), gave the party its political advantage at the village level, and led the common people in the struggle to improve their livelihood during the war.[167]

The symbolism of the Guangong operas, and closely associated forms of popular culture, also interlinked national resistance with antistate politics. Traditionally, the Guangong myth permitted the country people to assert their interest in righteous government and justified insurgency against Imperial rulers who attempted to impose the absolute power of the state.[168] Under Chiang Kai-shek, the central government had waged a war against this popular folk version of Guangong, for its subaltern transcript clearly had provided a symbolic critique that justified resistance to the treasury arm of the Kuomintang state.[169]

The CCP did not abandon this symbolic critique of national state dominance and hegemony in the countryside during WWII. Rather, the Chinese Communists portrayed the Japanese invasion as the product of the Nationalist government's damaging fiscal entanglement with the super military states of the world economy, the most aggressive of which, Japan, was now replacing the Republican state. Filtered through the prism of Guangong symbolism, the CCP's anti-Japanese propaganda was a primal means of urging the people who had risen to oppose the national Kuomintang state to renew their tradition of collective antistate resistance. According to CCP leaders who worked in the Hebei-Shandong-Henan border area during the war, the formation and presentation of their anti-Japanese propaganda was easier, and more effective, after the collapse of Kuomintang Twenty-Ninth Army power in 1940. Thereafter, their national salvation propagandists could go public with the war god operas, which were staged without Kuomintang state interference in the market villages located in the interstices of the Japanese occupation.[170] On presenting these operas, the Chinese Communists often drew a parallel between the logic of defying state rulers and resisting the Japanese.

Certainly the CCP's number one priority remained its national resistance war. The mobilizing of rural people for struggles with domestic adversaries, such as landlords or the local Kuomintang leaders who stayed on in the border area, was suspended throughout the duration of the War of Resistance. In theory, the CCP also put the saltmakers' struggle with the Kuomintang state on the back burner. Nevertheless, when it came to the political myths with which the CCP aligned its purpose, the party leaders pursued a "biaxial" propaganda approach, continuing to claim that the fate of the country people was dependent on their preparation to prevent the Japanese from seizing the resources of the villages. At the same time, they maintained their symbolic affiliation with the antistate impulses of the peasant saltmakers by sponsoring a host of operas, plays, and dramas that reinforced their right to resist the Kuomintang revenue state.[171]

The Guangong operas often were preceded or followed by dramas about the rebellion of Huang Chao (*Huang Chao Zaofan*), a righteous ninth-century popular uprising in Shandong's Caozhou. Precipitated by the attempt of Tang officials to boost state revenue by raising the price of government salt and banning the sale of private salt,[172] the rebellion's legendary folk leader was Huang Chao, a salt peddler from Yuanju in Caozhou,[173] whose profession brought him into frequent dealings with village people seeking to lighten their tax burdens by earth salt trade.[174] Opera units travelling with Yang Dezhi's Eighth Route Army performed this opera in Niu Chao village, in Puyang, between 1943 and 1945.[175] According to Yao Peishan, a CCP member of Yang Dezhi's company, "popular dramas like this one allowed us to attract the villagers to our propaganda grounds, and to present other ideas, such as nationalism, to the village people."[176] The Chinese Communists selected *Huang Chao Zaofan* to assure the peasant saltmakers that their struggle would not be neglected at the end of the Anti-Japanese War. The salient implications of this wartime drama were not lost on the fiscal elite of the Nationalist state; Chiang Kai-shek later declared Huang Chao to have been one of the worst bandits in Chinese history.[177] Kuomintang state making, and its relationship to the earth salt economy, was hardly a back burner issue for the country people during the war years. The issue shaped the course of the war itself.

EIGHT

Community, Culture, and the Persistence of Rural Collective Action: Qian Foji in the CCP-Led War of Resistance

The Japanese invasion engendered the development of at least three different patterns of village politics in the Hebei-Shandong-Henan border area. In one, the Japanese army imposed firm direct controls and all but stifled popular-based national resistance. In a second, the CCP and its Eighth Route Army gained ascendance in villages far removed from any Japanese controls and organized patriotic resistance. The Japanese army was stretched very thin and directly occupied only county seats and a few key market towns and strategically positioned villages in a given county. On the other hand, many of the CCP's unmolested villages were reduced to ashes in the bloody "three all" campaigns. It was in a third type of village that the CCP-led resistance grew and persisted: in leeward villages located just beyond the points of the Japanese danger and held indirectly by the Japanese army through the loose controls of puppet troops, the Chinese Communists developed an empowering relationship with the unsubdued peasants of the salt lands during the Second World War.

Qian Foji, or Thousand Buddhas village, was one of these semicolonized villages. This village, situated in the low marshland of the southern Hebei plain, has been selected for analysis for several reasons. First, many (though not all) of the inhabitants of the previously investigated villages who had been involved in the Anti-Japanese War had died in the 1949–85 period, but in Qian Foji a large number of war participants had survived, permitting a fuller, more accurate reconstruction of its wartime history. Second, Qian Foji had been a stronghold of the peasant saltmakers' struggle against the Kuomintang salt tax police in the pre-1937 period and of CCP-led anti-Japanese resistance during WWII. Its history permitted investigation of the link between prewar protest and the emergence of wartime popular resistance, while illuminating how the earth salt issue was interwoven with the regional political economy championed by the CCP-led resistance. Moreover, like many villages in the Hebei-Shandong-Henan border area, Qian Foji came under the thumb of the Japanese puppet army during the third year of the Japanese invasion, and its history therefore permits us to better grasp how this puppet army regime impacted on party interaction with the peasant saltmakers at the village level. Though its wartime experience was somewhat unique, Qian Foji typified the kinds of semicolonized villages in which the CCP had to carry on underground activities to survive and build up popular anti-Japanese resistance.

Peasant saltmakers in Qian Kou, Qi Ji, and Fanzhuang also sided with the CCP-led resistance during the war. The living testimony of some of them who, like their counterparts in Qian Foji, took part in the War of Resistance, indicates certain commonalities, as well as differences, in wartime participation. In each village the prewar salt protest leaders helped the CCP organize anti-Japanese resistance; in each the issue of salt making (and nitrate making) for the market became linked with the formation of the CCP's wartime political economy; and in each the Communist Party was able to utilize the war god tradition to win popular support for its struggle with the Japanese puppet army. Evidence on the wartime experience of these other three villages, presented toward the end of this chapter, underscores similarities with and differences from Qian Foji and magnifies the political lesson of its wartime history.

What, then, was that lesson? The discussion to follow suggests that anti-Japanese resistance was not just a function of Japanese brutality, CCP stage management, or, for that matter, strategic security. The wartime resistance was organized along the grid of antistate collective action, and the CCP was able to enlist the same militant semipeasant leaders of the prewar struggle by supporting their quest for off-farm income and accentuating their contributions to a united front based on local kin ties and transvillage market habits and connections. Thus, at the microlevel, pre-existing strategies of resistance to Kuomintang suppression taught the semipeasants of this region how to fight against external predatory force, and the CCP alignment with this tradition helped party leaders invigorate, conduct, and sustain anti-Japanese struggle.[1]

At the outbreak of WWII, Qian Foji was located in Zhang Fuqiu district, Nanle County, Hebei Province, on the frontier of three border counties: Neihuang to the southeast, Qingfeng to the southwest, and Wei County to the northwest. This was the dangerous, bandit-infested back country of the Wei River. To reach Qian Foji from their base in Nanle town, the Japanese had to travel fifteen *li* on a semipaved road to Yuancunji, then thirteen *li* on a rugged, broken-brick road to the Wei River, then ferry across the river, and then pass another three *li* along a narrow dirt trail. Qian Foji, however, was not always accessible by road. When the Wei River burst its banks and flooded west Nanle in the autumn of 1937, for example, peasants could travel beyond the village only by boat for several weeks in a row.[2]

QIAN FOJI'S ECONOMY IN THE REPUBLICAN PERIOD

According to folklore, Qian Foji was established by migrants from Hong Tong County in Shanxi Province. After flooding the land on which Qian Foji is located, the Yellow River jumped its track to another course, and the bed of its old course subsequently became uninhabited agricultural land. The Yaos and the Sangs, who led the migrations from Hong Tong, settled here in the first century of Ming rule[3] (see Map 5).

In the Republican period Qian Foji's peasants had less land per capita than their counterparts in Qian Kou, Qi Ji, and Fanzhuang, and they were not engaged with the world market. But Qian Foji was the most prosperous of the peasant villages we have surveyed. Laced with deposits of salt, nitre, and sodium, the land around Qian Foji had lost some of its good soil by late Qing, so that salt making went back a long way. Still, this was a village of fairly successful agriculturalists even into early Republican years. Most of its people were tillers who derived approximately three-quarters of their income from grain, vegetables, and melons and the rest from specialized work skills (like masonry) and from the sale of earth salt and nitrate. After 1920, however, peasants began to emphasize salt-related business enterprises in order to generate off-farm income. This income not only became a crucial factor in peasant survival, it also helped boost many a family a step beyond a mere subsistence. The profits derived from selling earth salt within Qian Foji itself and from peddling or brokering a variety of salt-based products in the villages and market towns of the border area placed at least two-thirds of Qian Foji's inhabitants in a world of gains they had never known from tilling the tiny plots of their pre-Republican ancestors.

In addition to the expanded market opportunity induced by the high price of inspectorate-managed salt, there were two microlevel pressures behind this drive for nonfarm income. For one thing, throughout the late 1920s the Wei River repeatedly overspilled its banks in August and September, inundating the fields of nearby villages. Qian Foji lost much of its autumn grain crop to these small, temporary floods. For another, sharp land inequality combined with a village demographic explosion to leave many peasant households without the amount of land needed to scratch out an existence from agriculture.

The structure of landholdings and demography in the pre-WWII decade underscores this crisis. Before 1930 Qian Foji had 270 households, with an

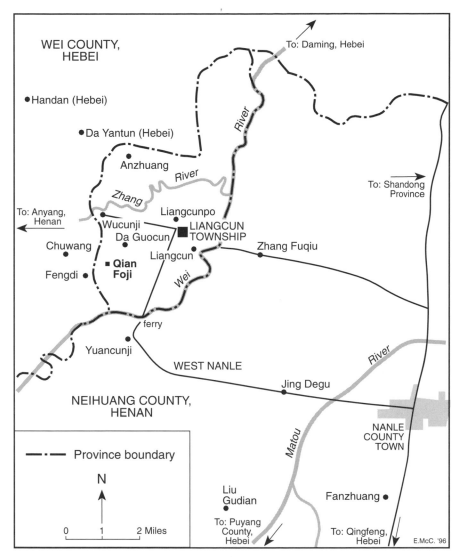

WEI COUNTY,
HEBEI

●Handan (Hebei)

●Da Yantun (Hebei)

To: Daming, Hebei

● Anzhuang

River

Zhang   River

To: Shandong
Province

To: Anyang,
Henan

Liangcunpo

● Wucunji
● Da Guocun   ■ LIANGCUN
TOWNSHIP

● Liangcun   Zhang Fuqiu ●

● Chuwang

■ Qian
Foji   Wei

Fengdi ●

ferry

● Yuancunji

WEST NANLE

River

NEIHUANG COUNTY,
HENAN

Jing Degu ●

NANLE
COUNTY
TOWN

Matou

Province boundary

N

Liu
Gudian
●

Fanzhuang ●

0   1   2 Miles

To: Puyang
County,
Hebei

To: Qingfeng,
Hebei

E.McC. '96

Map 5. Thousand Buddhas Market in West Nanle

average of five members. If Qian Foji's land surface of 4,200 *mu* had been distributed evenly, peasants might have preserved their predominantly agricultural designs for living. By 1930, however, 4 landlord households in the dominant Yao lineage owned at least 1,800 *mu* of the best land. Fifty *mu* was village temple land. For the remaining 266 peasant households, the average per capita landholding was 1.7 *mu*. Thus, from the 1920s on the vast majority of peasant families in all five of the main lineages—Yao, Sang, Feng, Zhang, and Wang—possessed only 7 or 8 *mu* of saline farmland. If a family produced bumper harvests in both the summer and the autumn quarters on this land, the grain output, when combined with vegetable and melon yields, still would have been sufficient, barely, for survival. Bumper harvests were few and far between in the late 1920s, however, and Wei River floods often ruined the fall crops. To compensate for their shortfalls, the village people turned to making earth salt and to related small trade activities, which proved so beneficial that even some of Qian Foji's poorest peasants became fairly prosperous. This trend continued into the war years, when the CCP-led resistance embraced it.

After liberation, the older villagers perfected the art of presenting themselves as "poor peasants." But in fact, before 1949 most of them made earth salt, which pulled them above subsistence. Seventy-one-year-old Yao Zhenbian relates:[4]

> In 1918 when I was five we had eight *mu* of land, and five people in my family. Mother, father, me, my grandmother, and sister. My father was a peasant in Qian Foji. He tilled the fields, and my mother helped him plant pumpkins and grind the wheat after the harvest. My father also made earth salt and nitrate.
>
> We planted seven *mu* of crop land to wheat, and one *mu* to pumpkin. After the June wheat harvest, we also planted two *mu* of corn and two *mu* of millet and two *mu* of green beans. In ordinary years, we could barely get by on these crops. In this area, however, the Wei River repeatedly flooded, and thus for many years the autumn corn and millet crops were lost, and the beans also were damaged. The first Wei River flood was in 1927. In that year we did not have enough grain to eat. At that time, we survived by selling four *mu* of our land, and by making nitrate at home. Since the floods washed the salt from the fields, salt making in the autumn and winter quarters was more difficult.
>
> Over the next decade the Wei River floods often harmed the autumn crops. In the flood years, we had to depend even more on earth salt production. We collected the alkaline earth right after the Spring Festival, before the rains came. We used a cauldron to make earth salt. We could gather the earth from all of the fields of our village. Because taking the salt from the fields helped the wheat to grow, anyone in Qian Foji would allow us to collect the salty earth.
>
> After 1927 we shared a cauldron with Yao Xishi. In an average year we could get 300 silver dollars from our salt production, but in a good year we could earn 500 silver dollars. We used the 300 silver dollars to buy grain, firewood,

oil and other essentials. We bought vegetables such as eggplant, turnips, and cabbage at Yuancun market. We also relied on part of this income to pay for a doctor if someone in our family got sick, or if there was a funeral and we had to help out. The 300 silver dollars was used to prepare for next years' agricultural production and for salt production too. At that time, we also had to pay a land tax of four silver dollars to the Nanle County government.

We also made nitrate each year before the Anti-Japanese War, and we earned about 200 silver dollars from our nitrate sales. We spent the 200 silver dollars on good food and nice clothing, and occasionally on new furniture. My father had made nitrate. Our nitrate was of very high quality. Yao Laoliu was a very successful nitrate maker here, and he passed on his skill to me.

Many local purchase agents and peddlers came to Qian Foji to purchase our nitrate. I also sold it in the surrounding villages, places like Da Yantun in Wei County and Zhaozhuang in Nanle County, where there were firecracker makers and gunpowder producers. Since the nitrate of our village was famous, we got a higher price for it if we took it to Da Yantun, or to Yuancun market.

The earth salt produced in Qian Foji was of much higher quality than the salt produced in surrounding counties and was in great demand in the early 1930s. At that time, one silver dollar earned from the earth salt trade could purchase thirty *jin* of wheat. Therefore, a family of five could rely on its nonfarm income to purchase its basic grain supplies and still make a modest savings. This rising salt business, when coupled with sales of pumpkins and melons and nitrate and noodles in local markets, explains why few people in Qian Foji had to beg, migrate, or borrow grain prior to the Henan famine of 1942.

The production of earth salt, and its by-products, stimulated a robust market economy in Qian Foji, turning many people into specialists in petty trade and strengthening the economic position of the village before World War II. Qian Foji was also one the most famous nitrate-producing villages in Hebei Province. The technology and skills for making nitrate, or saltpeter, were closely guarded family secrets. Only 40 percent of the village households made nitrate. Most of them produced far less nitrate than earth salt, but in the 1930s nitrate was in great demand and was ten times more expensive than earth salt; even a small yield meant eighty to one hundred silver dollars annually to a household.[5]

This upsurge in the nitrate market in Qian Foji and scores of other villages was partly the result of the downturn in German exports of high-quality nitrate into the Republic of China after the commencement of World War One.[6] Well into the 1930s, native merchants, eager to supply the state with native saltpeter for armaments factories and fireworks shops, placed orders for *tuxiao* (local nitrate) with rural purchase agents operating out of villages like Qian Foji in Nanle and Liu Xinggu in Neihuang County. Thus, apparently, the village people who produced the old, inferior quality nitrate from the salt-encrusted lands of the border area captured a small slice of the growing internal market.

Qian Foji's nitrate trade, a three-season affair that spanned village and town, was only loosely supervised by Republican county officials. Peasants sold 70 percent of their nitrate directly to individual buyers who came to their homes and who dealt with them face to face or indirectly through friends who were purchase agents. The purchase agents and petty traders, including Feng Yuqing and Yao Wusheng, arranged contracts with buyers from villages like Da Yantun in Wei County and Zhaozhuang in Nanle to purchase nitrate for their fireworks factories and gunpowder plants. Beyond Qian Foji, peasants occasionally took the nitrate to agents in surrounding villages and markets, including Da Yantun and Yuancunji. This comprised about 20 percent of their trade. A few sold to purchase agents presumably licensed to obtain nitrate for public gunpowder plants under the control of the Kuomintang, like the one in Puyang County town.[7] Much of the nitrate trade was conducted in the shadows of state regulation.

Other Qian Foji residents gained a reputation for selling dried noodles, the mainstay of noodle soup (*min tang*). For many households, the noodle business spelled the difference between borderline dearth and economic success—and here, too, making earth salt was the basic conduit to peasant market entry. Feng Cunshan, for example, was from a family of seven with only five *mu* of land in 1936. Feng, his father, and three brothers made earth salt in the spring and then stored the salt until "we used it to make the noodles." "Earth salt," Feng continues,[8]

> was the ingredient that turned the noodles into fine sticks, and salt was what hardened the noodles as they dried. Making the noodles at that time was a special skill. I was the one who made the flour for the noodles, and my father added the earth salt. My father and brothers then prepared the noodles by adding water and more salt with the flour, and by kneading the flour onto a thin stick, and then stretching it into a long thin thread.
>
> Thereafter, we went outside of Qian Foji to sell our noodles in other villages, such as Wucunji, Anzhuang, Liangcun, Sungzhuang, and Yuancunji. All of these places were in Nanle. My father was the one who went out to sell to them. At that time, a dried noodle dish was itself a meal for poor people around here.

A fourth commodity was bean curd, which the peasant salters manufactured from yellow beans and *lu shui*, a by-product of nitrate production. This trade was limited mainly to those village people who made nitrate.[9] Many of the better-off saltmakers stayed away from it. *Lu shui* was itself slightly poisonous and thus hazardous to work with. Most nitrate makers simply threw away the *lu shui*, but some peddled it for sale locally because it was used in making bean curd and in fertilizing the crops. The process of producing bean curd for profit was complex; it involved mixing ground and soaked beans with the *lu shui*. A few of the peasant saltmakers even sold the bean dregs (the residue from beans used in making bean curd) outside of Qian Foji in Feng Di, Licun, and Gaodi, villages where peasants purchased the product for cheap food or for pig feed.[10]

Many of the small peasant traders invested the savings from their private salt and nitrate market dealings in retail ventures that lifted them to higher-level markets. Such trade was often the springboard to involvement in advanced market town exchanges. Of course villagers relied on salt-related income to obtain food supplies, but in Qian Foji this income also was used increasingly to purchase items for resale in intermediate market towns like Yuancunji, which drew twenty thousand participants per market day before the Japanese army occupied it in 1938. This was the experience of Yao Xiren, who used the earnings from earth salt trade in the markets of Liucun, Shi Gu, and Dong Yanzhao to start up a small business in coloring dyes, threads, and needles purchased in Daming town and then resold in Yuancunji—and also in porcelain items.[11] In this way, ironically, the country people were using their black market connections to make their way into markets subject to Kuomintang licensing and controls and thereby gaining a niche in economic territory previously considered unpenetrable. On the eve of World War II, the income from such "legitimate trade" constituted half of the income of some of Qian Foji's poorest households.[12]

THE REVENUE CLAIMS OF THE REPUBLICAN CENTER, WARLORDISM, BANDITRY, AND OTHER PREDATORY PRESSURES— TRIGGERS TO COLLECTIVE PROTEST

Most of the peasants in Qian Foji paid a land tax of one silver dollar per *mu* to the Nanle County government.[13] A household with fifteen *mu* planted to June wheat would have paid fifteen silver dollars to the tax collectors, which was enough to purchase the annual subsistence grain for one family member. Villagers felt this land tax was unfair,[14] but they paid it anyway. Only once were Qian Foji's inhabitants unable to come through for the Kuomintang county government. In late 1930, San Guozheng and Zhang Guandong, the two village tax representatives, were beaten by the Kuomintang tax authorities.[15] Otherwise, peasants paid the land tax year in and year out and successfully implored the Nanle Kuomintang not to take the tax when the Wei River flooded the crops in autumn.[16]

Qian Foji was also the focus of warlord taxation, a phenomenon peasants recall with hissing or spitting and other contemptuous body language. Yet here too we find a mixed record of attempted warlord rule. The troops of Zhang Zuolin "visited" the village for three days, around 1929, raided a few homes, and disappeared without incident after their defeat by Feng Yuxiang.[17] The soldiers of Song Zheyuan's twenty-ninth army stayed in Qian Foji eight days around 1935 but brought their own flour and firewood. Two years later, Ding Shuben's soldiers demanded *corvée* service, and peasants had to carry firewood, shoes, and quilts to villages and towns as part of their duty to the army commands nominally under the Nationalist government.[18]

After 1931, Nanle County authorities tried to collect a number of taxes on peasant commerce. This was done through tax agents who either came to Qian Foji or descended on peasant market stalls in market towns, such as Yuancunji. Two such taxes stand out in local memory.

One was the pig-killing tax. Sang Puyi's father was Qian Foji's middleman for selling farm animals and, simultaneously, was known for buying black oinkers, butchering them, and selling pork from his small village shop. Although there were no taxes on farm animal sales, the Nanle County government did impose a tax on pigs slaughtered for sale after 1931. Sang found this tax irritating, but paid it without protest and maintained his pork business long enough into the late 1930s to acquire land from his business returns.[19]

Although there were no taxes on the peddling of products like dried noodles and bean curd in small periodic markets, peasants encountered a new tax on their small business activities in the officially supervised intermediate markets of Nanle. Under the Kuomintang, the Nanle County government levied a fee on the market stalls of sellers in Yuancunji. This fee was collected by a tax farmer.[20] Yao Xiren, who purchased items in Daming in order to sell them in Nanle, paid a fee of one silver dollar per month for maintaining his place of business in Yuancunji. In speaking of his relationship with the tax farmer, Yao says, "If I could have avoided him, I would have, but I could not do this because my business stall was there in Yuancun market."[21]

A spate of surtaxes, designed, as Philip Huang has advised us, to build up the fiscal base of Republican county government,[22] fell on Qian Foji in the decade before the Japanese invasion. The *gongzhai* tax was a land surtax requiring households owning fifty *mu* or more to purchase ten silver dollars worth of government debt bonds in the years 1926 to 1931. The bonds were issued by the central government, but in the early 1930s the Nanle County government informed Qian Foji's village chief of the duty to purchase them. This bond tax, collected irregularly over a five-year period, fell on only fifteen peasant households—those who depended almost solely on agriculture.[23]

Although most villagers generally could afford to pay taxes, Yao Zhenbian—whose name was to become a metaphor for Communism in Qian Foji—spoke for the majority when he said, "Because the salt land could produce nothing, it was not right for the Kuomintang government to ask us to pay any taxes. Almost all of our money came from non-farm activities."[24] If Yao and his fellow saltmakers were so expressly against paying taxes to

Republican local government, then why did they pay? One piece of the answer is this: by the Nationalist decade Qian Foji had become the prized target of two different bandit armies, one from Hui County in Henan and another from Daming in Hebei Province. The bandits specialized in kidnapping for ransom, and Qian Foji had more than its share of moneyed folk, so its leadership was anxious to secure the protection of the Nanle County government. In this period the Daming bandit Zhang Jintang kidnapped the brother of Sang Xinshi, whose family sold half of its 120 *mu* of land to help pay a ransom of six hundred silver dollars. But tax reliable Qian Foji's leaders were able to enlist the support of the Kuomintang Nanle County militia in this matter, and Zhang Jintang was hunted down and killed by the Nanle militia.[25]

Another reason they paid is this: thanks to the profits they were gathering in the shadow of the state-regulated salt business, most peasants were enjoying a fairly comfortable standard of living. As long as the central government, and its salt bureau, did not challenge their informal earth salt economy, Yao Zhenbian and his commercial oriented counterparts paid up and had good prospects for household prosperity.

The confraternity of Qian Foji's small entrepreneurs had turned their bad salt lands into a booming salt-based trade and were steadily tracking prosperity. In fact Qian Foji remained a fairly rich village all through the Republican period, mainly because of its earth salt–based enterprises. This is not to say that the salt trade was in and of itself sufficient to carry the village people through every crisis; there were extenuating circumstances, including global history and the moral visions of its village leaders at play.

The innovative spirit of Qian Foji, along with supravillage intervention, saved the people of this village from the starvation and death stalking many other peasant communities in Nanle County during the Republican era. Peasants survived the North China famine of 1921 by making salt and by making the best of missionary generosity. In 1920, after the June wheat crop failure, a Protestant missionary attached to the North China Famine Relief Commission arrived in Qian Foji.[26] This unknown soldier of Christianity was an American—the only person of European heritage to visit Qian Foji before my first visit in 1989. He and his small team of relief workers authorized relief notes that entitled the hungry poor to obtain sorghum grain from a church relief agency in Handan town. This relief grain, which peasants converted to porridge, allowed the most desperate 30 percent of the village to survive the famine year without massive physical degeneration.[27] This, along, with the salt trade, got peasants through the first subsistence crisis of the twentieth century. As Yao Zhenxiang, who was fifteen in 1920, recalls, "Few people in Qian Foji died because they relied on salt making to buy grains to eat and to sell in other places to get through the famine."[28] Thus, only a few peasant families migrated. They went to places like

Yueyang County (Gu*xian*) in Shanxi, where they grew crops on low-grade lands for a brief time and returned home in late 1921 and early 1922.[29]

Qian Foji was a victim of the other great subsistence challenge, the Henan famine of 1942. In 1941 the village lost its fall sorghum crop to drought, and by late October the land was so parched that planting wheat had become impossible. There was no wheat harvest in June of 1942. Although the mild rains of early summer allowed peasants to seed fall sorghum and millet, both crops were reduced by locusts in the autumn. Understandably, the spectre of the Henan famine, which Theodore H. White and Analee Jacoby described in their unforgettable masterpiece, *Thunder Out of China*,[30] is frozen in peasant memory. Sang Binwen, for example, was from a family of accomplished stonecutters and travelled with his father to cut tombstones during the famine. Business, according to Sang, was bad, and there were terrible scenes of children (especially orphans) dying of starvation everywhere.[31] But these scenes were on rural roads outside of Qian Foji. Within Qian Foji few villagers died of starvation. The more than twenty old-timers I interviewed about this issue could recall only ten persons who died in the Henan famine. Of the ten who did, seven were bachelors.[32] With no one to help them, they became emaciated and vulnerable to "little illnesses," such as flues and high fevers,[33] easily complicated by malnutrition. It was mainly this tiny minority of poor unmarried males who succumbed to the worst months of 1942, while peasants in strong families survived by a host of strategies—including the art of selling earth salt.

The history of Qian Foji reveals how important salt trade, which actually picked up in the war years, had become in peasant life chances and how the village people relied on it to slip through the famine. The major strategies of peasant survival in the Hebei-Shandong-Henan border area during the famine were salt making, migration, and grain loans obtained from landlords through fierce redistributable struggles. In Qian Foji the politics of war severely curtailed the second and third strategies. By 1941–42 the Nanle County puppet forces of Yang Faxian, whose headquarters were in Qian Foji itself, were under strict orders to prevent any peasant migration out of Qian Foji. The peasant families with members who repeatedly were missing when Yang's soldiers made their periodic household checks were singled out as Communist Party suspects. Understandably, these peasants were extremely reluctant to migrate even when the famine was forcing the issue. About thirty peasant households, half of them from the poorest lineages[34] (Wangs and Zhangs), finally fled in the desperate months of 1942, going to Puyang County and Fei County in Hebei,[35] but 70 percent of these outbound villagers returned less than one year later to resume salt production and to reap the June wheat harvest of 1943.[36]

In addition, by 1942 the Qian Foji branch of the CCP had been forced underground. The villagers were too frightened to openly engage landlords in struggle over the issue of grains—to which Yang Faxian's puppet forces also staked a claim, so that peasants were forced back on earth salt enterprises for famine survival. Central to this history was the constant maneuvering of markets to match up with the changing politics of the war years, a point made clear by Yao Zhenxiang:[37] "During the 1942 Famine Yang Faxian's puppet army was stationed here, and yet this gave us an opportunity to do small business with them. We made earth salt to buy grain to sell to them. We also sold them cigarettes, *jiaozi* (dumplings), steamed bread, clothes, and cups and bowls. We went to Chu Wang town and Liu Yan to buy some of these items from the Japanese, and we then sold them to the puppet forces." The popular trade in earth salt extended well beyond exchanges with the puppet forces, allowing people to endure the famine and to engage in self-serving forms of resistance to the puppet forces and the Japanese, both within and beyond Thousand Buddhas village.

Although the structure of landlordism clearly was a cause of unequal land distribution, the disagreeable aspects of landlordism in Qian Foji did not produce any sharp peasant repudiation of class exploitation in the decades before the Japanese invasion. Prior to the war, peasant anti-landlord sentiments were not striking. Conflicts were focused on only a few landlords after 1938 and were largely confined within a Yao lineage war over limited violations of the customary grain loan practices by a few big Yao landholders during the famine of 1942.

To be sure, Yao Huibin, who, along with his father, worked as a tenant for landlord Yao Shizhuang, and who joined the CCP in 1938, swears that landlordism was *the* factor producing swells of peasant anger in the village before liberation.[38] There is, however, little in the way of evidence to support this assertion. For wartime CCP Secretary Yao Zhenbian, and for the peasant saltmakers who formed the party during the war years, this interpretation is an unhappy one. As they remember, landlordism became an intolerable problem only during the alarming moments of the 1942 Henan famine and the puppet army lockup, and even then it was not a problem that could be resolved simply by class action.

Prior to the Henan famine, Qian Foji's peasants did not have great difficulty coming to reasonable terms with landlords. For the most part, the latter had effectively upheld a number of old paternalistic norms that more or less legitimated their position. The four Yao landlords employed only a handful of people.[39] Approximately five tenants and ten hired hands, half of whom were from other villages, worked for the Yao landlords as permanent employees, so class exploitation was never an issue. To be sure, as many as thirty people in Qian Foji went to work for landlords for several days during the busy May–June harvest season, but they were paid well and had a say in the decisions on their specific work days. Most tenants were treated fairly, and the evidence suggests that landlords supported them when lawsuits were brought against them by outsiders.[40]

The Yao landlords did not speculate in grain sales beyond the confines of Qian Foji, and, with a couple of exceptions, they issued grain loans at reasonable interest rates in the years before the famine of 1942.[41] Furthermore, they stuck to the time-honored tradition of allowing villagers to glean their fields after the harvests. Many peasants still remember the days when people from other Hebei villages (Feng Di and Licun in Wei County) joined them in waiting at the edge of the Yao landlord wheat fields to glean after the June harvest.[42] They also gleaned other landlord fields along the Zhang River, roving as far as seven and eight *li* away from Qian Foji.[43] Like their counterparts in Qian Kou, over in Puyang, the landlords of Qian Foji posted their hired hands around their fields before the harvest, but there was little crop pilfering, and, according to Sang Puyi, "the guards often turned their heads when people stole the crops at night."[44]

The continuing prosperity of Qian Foji can be seen even in the land rental system in which twenty-five peasant households participated from time to time. There were two land rental arrangements in Qian Foji in the Republican period. Both promised greater food security and even an escape from dependency on landlordism for the peasantry. In one, which was based on an oral contract, peasants rented several *mu* of land for one to five years. The tenant received 75 percent of the June harvest and 50 percent of the crop come October. Sang Mingzhai, who rented three and one-half *mu* from landlord Yao Shizhao, summed up the advantage of this rental arrangement: "We rented the land mainly when things were difficult and when we needed more work to earn more income. We had more laborers than land in our family, so we decided to rent the land. We earned a profit from renting this land, and we were better off because of it. We used the profit to eat more food, and to buy higher quality foods. We rented this land from Yao Shizhao from 1930 to 1935, and then abandoned the rental agreement because we had generated enough savings to pawn some land."[45]

The other rental arrangement was known as *huodi* (living land).[46] Peasants refer to it as pawning land, a version of the pawnshop agreements wherein people deposited land or property in return for cash. In Qian Foji, those who "rented" the land were not required to pay anything to the landowner, himself in need of cash. The prospective "tenant" lent money to the landowner, and in return the tenant could use the land for three years or until the landowner was able to pay back the loan. If the landowner could not pay back the loan for which he had given over his land, ownership rights were automatically transferred to the tenant.[47] Predictably, this "rental" arrangement became rather popular in Qian Foji during the 1930s. About 40 percent of the land-hungry peasant salt producers in the Yao and Sang lineages began purchasing the land provisionally from landlords and peasants in Qian Foji, Da Gutun, and other surrounding villages.[48] Some acquired two, five, and even ten *mu* in this way before 1942. Villagers concur that the *huodi* arrangement was a way of avoiding the demanding loan arrangements of the big Yao landlords.[49]

To sum up, the peasants of Qian Foji were on the road to prosperity throughout much of the Republican period. Their involvement in multiple rural market enterprises meant they could deal with most of the Nanle County government tax claims on agriculture. Although the Yao landlords dominated nearly half of the village's land base, the village people were not the victims of unjust exchange, or death rents. The local folk did not accuse the Yao landlords of having violated their notions of "moral economy" until the old terms of interest on hunger loans were overturned in the terrible famine of 1942, and even then the dynamism of the local economy allowed Qian Foji's inhabitants to make a fairly quick comeback. Here, then, was a village that was halfway to paradise as the world plunged into war in the late 1930s. To give one small example of how firm this hold on prosperity was, the Yao and Sang lineages had always sponsored "redistributive festivals" from the proceeds gotten from leasing out little plots of their lineage temple lands in April and October of each year.[50] During these old festivals, people ate pork balls and paid homage to ancestors. With the exception of 1942, these festivals were still carried on even in the years when the puppet troops of Yang Faxian occupied Qian Foji—1940–45. Moreover, in these same years, the customary journeys to Wucunji, with its market fairs, tempting foods, and temple festivals, continued for the majority of Qian Foji's peasants.[51]

What sustained this material progress was off-farm income, which the village people stood to lose completely when T. V. Song's *Shuijingtuan* drew them into the state history of other peasant salt-making villages in the border region. Of course, the claims of the Nanle Kuomintang, the Yao landlords, and the terrible famine of 1942 were not appreciated by the peasant salters. But what really made their blood boil was the decision of the centrally placed Kuomintang fiscal authorities to root out their very means of livelihood even though they were tax-paying citizens.

COLLECTIVE PROTEST AGAINST THE SALT TAX CORPS

With approximately 90 percent of Qian Foji's households committed to earth salt production, and with two-thirds of the village's inhabitants prospering from nonfarm income, it is not surprising that the Kuomintang Changlu salt tax corps showed up in the village in the early 1930s. The salt police attack of 1930 triggered a united counteraction by the saltmakers. Resistance was two-pronged.

The first round was essentially a defensive effort to keep the police out of the village. In the spring of 1930, the peasant saltmakers and landlords in Qian Foji united to oppose the impending police intervention. The chief of Qian Foji, landlord Yao Jinshan, who also benefitted from the earth salt trade, was rich in real estate and political relations in Yuancun market. Having caught wind of the salt police activities near Yuancunji, Yao placed a carefully planned telephone call to the chief of the Changlu salt police in Nanle County town. The message he conveyed: "If the police come to Qian Foji, then I will be unable to stop the saltmakers from killing them."[52]

The police took up the challenge. Within a month a squad arrived in Qian Foji and ordered Yao Jinshan to inform villagers to refrain from making earth salt. Although Yao agreed to comply with the police order, he secretly told peasants to continue with salt production, and he repeatedly informed them of the arrival time of the police squads, so that they could hide their cauldrons. Moreover, with the police threatening repeated interventions, Yao Jinshan teamed with Feng Yuqing and Yao Zhenbian to prepare the village for battle. When the police entered Qian Foji in the spring of 1930, they were greeted by a crowd of angry peasants. Hailing the police at the front gate, Yao Jinshan warned them that the salters were ready to shed blood. In fact, this was not true—the villagers were armed only with shovels and spears, and they were terribly apprehensive. The police, however, did not know this, and they retreated without a skirmish.[53]

Round two came in the autumn of 1931, when thirty of Qian Foji's peasant saltmakers joined with more than one hundred of their counterparts in the first transvillage collective action against the Kuomintang salt revenue police in Nanle County. This was the wild antipolice action at Yuancun market. Yao Zhenbian, who helped to orchestrate the protest march to Yuancunji, remembers: "I fought the salt police in 1931, and so did Feng Yuqing, the purchase agent. He was the leader. Feng could produce the best nitrate in Qian Foji, and he also was very good at producing earth salt. Many people learned the nitrate and earth salt trade from him. This is why he was the leader of the saltmakers' struggle. Sang Faliang was also involved in the struggle. He made both nitrate and earth salt, as did Yao Wusheng and Yao Peifu, who also were involved. About thirty to forty people from our village were involved. All of these people were among the better-off villagers who were capable of making nitrate and earth salt. They did so because they wanted to earn the money to purchase land."[54]

Clearly, the police had interrupted a market endeavor that kept alive the hope of acquiring good land for these half-peasant people, who were not going to give up that hope without a fight. This is why they marched the sixteen *li* to Yuancun market to beat the police with cudgels and why they joined with their counterparts in hurling bricks at the heads of the police. (Conveniently, there was a small brick factory, with loose bricks strewn everywhere, situated at the intersection of the dirt and semipaved roads over which Qian Foji's protestors had to pass.)

Thus, Qian Foji was never bloodied by the salt police. By undertaking collective protest its "peasants" were able to keep their salt market open and to continue the pursuit of prosperity before the tides of the Great Pacific War ebbed over into village life.

WAR AND RESISTANCE IN QIAN FOJI, 1938–45

Marching down the Daming-Nanle highway in December, 1937, the Japanese first occupied Nanle County town and then dispersed their troops west to occupy Yuancun and Wucun markets; but with no more than three hundred or so Japanese and Korean troops the Japanese army could not directly hold all of the points of strategic and commercial importance in rural Nanle. The solution to this quandary was the Chinese puppet troops (*weijun*) made up of local people who supposedly had no political loyalties to the Kuomintang or the CCP.

In Nanle the Japanese quickly recruited Yang Faxian, a onetime bandit, the boss of a tea house in Yuancun market, and a former commander in the Kuomintang Twenty-Ninth Army under Song Zheyuan and Ding Shuben, to organize and run the puppet army.[55] Composed of desperate peasants, bandits, and deserting Kuomintang soldiers, Yang Faxian's puppet force had grown to a thousand men by late 1939. During the winter of 1940 it commenced maneuvers with the Japanese army against partisan guerrilla fighters in league with the CCP-led national resistance army. The puppet army of Yang Faxian was an ultrarepressive force, the key to instituting Japan's version of political order in the Nanle-Daming-Puyang area. In the early phase of the war, 1938–39, it was camped at Yuancunji, but in late 1939 Yang moved the entire main force sixteen *li* west of Yuancun to fortify the Japanese hold on the strategically important Wei River. The village in which this puppet army entrenched itself for the next five years was Qian Foji. Ostensibly, Qian Foji was chosen only for its proximity to the Wei River, but the Japanese sent Yang Faxian to Qian Foji also because they were alarmed by reports of its support for partisan resistance.

The collapse of Kuomintang power, and the arrival of the puppet army, proved to be a major turning point in the history of Qian Foji, permitting villagers to cast their lot with the CCP-led resistance and providing the CCP activists with the chance to inspire the village people to continue taking up forms of collective resistance that, over the course of the war, further served their interest in the economy of earth salt and swept away the salt revenue plan of Chiang Kai-shek's central government.

Resistance in Qian Foji: The Early Phase of Collective Action

In the early phase of the war, Qian Foji was located in what the Japanese termed an unpacified zone. Located three hours by jeep from the Japanese garrison in Anyang town on the Beijing-Hankow railway, and also a long way from Japanese-held market towns, Qian Foji was not occupied by puppet troops until late 1939. During the early part of the war, therefore, it became one of several Nanle villages where the Chinese Communists were able to draw support for national resistance. Under the leadership of the CCP, Qian Foji established a party branch and entered the fight against the Japanese army.

The early leadership of the wartime resistance in Qian Foji was composed of a coalition of village teachers, purchase agents, and peasant saltmakers, who were eventually joined by enlightened village landlords.[56] Most of these people hailed from the Yao lineage. All had sympathized with and/or actively supported the struggle against the Nationalist government's salt police. The three key leaders in the early years were Yao Chenmei, a graduate of the Daming Seventh Normal School, the village primary school teacher, and its esteemed doctor; Feng Yuqing, Qian Foji's leading purchase agent and the liaison to extravillage salt and nitrate markets; and Yao Zhenbian, who, with Feng, had led fellow saltmakers to pitch out the police in the Yuancunji collective action of 1931.

When a unit of the Eighth Route Army passed by Qian Foji in the spring of 1938, Yao Chenmei and Yao Zhenbian organized an impromptu village militia of ten. To ensure that Qian Foji had a minimum of protection, Yao Chenmei went to the village chief, Wang Guoding, and proposed selling temple land for the purpose of purchasing arms for a militia. Within a matter of days, the sale was approved by an assembly of eight hundred villagers.[57] The land was sold through a purchase agent to peasants from Lucun village and was actually reported to the land registry. Shortly thereafter, Yao Chenmei and Yao Zhenbian purchased the guns to arm the members of the militia, who henceforth presented themselves as the village crop-watching team. Actually, they were defending the CCP branch established in 1938 [58] and the economic benefits won through collective mobilization in the same year.

By late 1938, half a year after Yao Chenmei had introduced the CCP, sixty villagers had joined the party. Over the next six years another thirty joined, bringing membership to ninety by early 1945. The rapid success in CCP recruitment can be explained by its cadres' actions on two familiar problems: taxes on agricultural crop lands and state intervention into nonfarm income.

The first reason why so many village people went over to the CCP had to do with taxation. In 1938 Yao Chenmei, the first CCP secretary of Qian Foji, galvanized villagers to support a proposal to reform the tax system. The reform all but abolished taxes on agriculture and alleviated the miscellaneous tax pressures on the micropeasantry. The CCP tax policy was based on a "reasonable tax burden" (*heli fudan*) payment system.

The advantage of such a system was announced in a villagewide meeting in the Temple of the Tang Emperor during the fall of 1938. At the beginning of the meeting, some five hundred people democratically elected Wang Guoding, a CCP cadre, to the post of village chief. Teaming up with Wang, Yao Chenmei persuaded the crowds of people who came to this village election to implement the reasonable burden system. Not long after this meeting, the party leaders gathered one hundred people to parade throughout the village, so as to spread word of the benefits of the reasonable burden tax system.[59]

What *heli fudan* meant, in practice, was that the peasant saltmakers no longer paid the land tax solely on the basis of how much land they owned. In Qian Foji, each peasant household could possess one *mu* of land per capita tax free.[60] A family of seven with seven *mu* of land, therefore, was totally exempt from any tax payment. Feng Dianchun, the Qian Foji accountant under the CCP, recalls that the percentage of households exempted from taxation under the *heli fudan* was about 30 percent[61]—the same poorest one-third of the village that had received missionary relief grain in the famine of 1921.

Furthermore, those with less than three *mu* per capita paid only ten *jin per mu*, whereas those owning three to five *mu* paid thirty to forty *jin* per *mu*. The great bulk of grain taxes was paid by twenty-four upscale households (including four landlords and fifteen peasants with around fifty *mu*). Indeed, landlords Yao Futang, Yao Shizhao, and Yao Jinshan each paid ten thousand *jin* of wheat and yet another ten thousand *jin* of inferior autumn grains. Because the tax was taken according to the harvest, they, along with the peasants, received a reduction if the crop was disappointing.[62] The reasonable burden payment was made a little more tolerable by lifting the Kuomintang rule that it be paid in silver, which had been a pressure moving peasants further out of agriculture in the preceding decade. In the struggle to simplify taxes, the CCP also swept away the sporadic warlord levies and the land surtaxes that had plagued Qian Foji and taxes on petty trade.

The other issue on which the CCP elicited massive popular support was nonfarm income. Virtually everyone, including the CCP activists, wished to restore the recently threatened prerogative of market participation and cheered the Eighth Route Army's commitment to protect the market exchanges that promised material uplifting. In Qian Foji, as in scores of other salt land villages, popular trade in salt-based products picked up and was even promoted by the antiforeign army of the CCP. This earthshaking political change induced a silent euphoria in peasant relations with the army. The twenty villagers who originally joined the Eighth Route Army in 1938–39 were soon joined by eighty more, and by 1943 the army had become a haven for Qian Foji's popular cartel of salt "smugglers." Here, then, were the country people who committed their flesh and blood to the CCP-led wartime resistance.

The Expansion of the Earth Salt Economy in Wartime Qian Foji

As I have stressed, no one has sufficiently emphasized that the CCP ultimately won over the rural people by upholding their rights to produce homemade products for retail trade.[63] The Qian Foji party branch stood by the principle that villagers had the right to receive an acceptable economic value for the commodities they purveyed in country markets. This principle, coupled with fair taxation, became the cornerstone of the CCP's relationship with the peasant saltmakers during WWII. In 1938 Yao Chenmei, Qian Foji's cherished teacher and doctor, told his fellow villagers that Communism included this principle.[64] To local folk, it signaled a world in which market initiatives would not be impeded by state-level intervention, a chance to firmly recover a way of life unhindered by fiscal injustice. This was the main reason why so many people in Qian Foji joined the CCP.

The CCP's adoption of this principle drew more commerce to the village and pitted the confraternity of semipeasant traders indirectly against the Japanese. The passageways to Qian Foji's old periodic market, which met four days (second, fourth, seventh, and ninth) of every ten-day market cycle, began to throng with buyers, vendors, and brokers from surrounding counties at a rate even more favorable than in the prewar period. Throughout the early phase of the war, peasants continued to sell to the old customers who came to the village from places like Da Yantun, in Wei County. At the same time, the Japanese occupation of Yuancun market caused a rapid decline in trade, sending hundreds of frightened patrons more than sixteen *li* away to Qian Foji [65] to purchase earth salt, nitrate, noodles, and bean curd from the peasant saltmakers. In this period, just before the puppet army occupation, these same peasant chemists were selling earth salt and nitrate to the Eighth Route Army. After 1941, when the Ding Shuben Twenty-Ninth Army disintegrated and left the public gunpowder market to the Eighth Route Army and the Japanese puppet forces,[66] nitrate also became a really hot item of sale. From this point on, Qian Foji's chemists secretly produced nitrate for sale to the CCP-led army, whose purchase agents spirited it off to gunpowder plants. Yao Tianyi, for example, a common saltmaker without any Communist Party affiliation, made nitrate, and even gunpowder, for the eighth routers off and on throughout the war.[67]

Qian Foji also became a pacesetter in the wartime salt market expansion, which bolstered peasant economic power and produced forms of resistance that further undercut the vestiges of the Kuomintang central state in the triprovincial border area, all the while enhancing the credibility of the CCP-led government.

With the collapse of Kuomintang state power, a growing number of peasant salters rushed to fill the void created by the disappearance of state-controlled Changlu sea salt. There is unanimity among the aged peasants in

Qian Foji that after the Japanese arrived in Nanle County it became easier to earn money from selling earth salt. Many set out in pursuit of markets in which they had seldom participated or from which they had been driven by the salt police. Some stopped going to Japanese-occupied Yuancunji and switched their salt trade to the markets of Fengdi, Gaodi, Xinzhuang, and Shigu; others switched to Xi Ji, which was right next to the King of Hell Temple in Nanle County.[68] Xi Ji was very popular, they recall, because it had not been occupied by the Kuomintang army, the Japanese army, or the puppet army—or even by the salt revenue police, who had tried in vain to regulate it before the Japanese invasion.

By 1942–43 this market expansion was beginning to look like an all-out popular usurpation of maritime salt. Yao Zhenbian and little groups of Qian Foji's salt traders were ranging out of Hebei, as far as Shang Chengji, in Henan, where they purchased sea salt from salt shops taken over by the Japanese and carried it back to Nanle to sell for even bigger profit.[69] Whether the Japanese were aware of this popular CCP-linked trade in what had been the salt of the national state is unclear, but the profits from it were clearly flowing into the private hands of Qian Foji's money-minded peasant Communists.

The pursuit of profit was sometimes coupled with a commitment to help other peasant communities and to bring them into the CCP-led struggle to reclaim the market terrain that the Nationalist government had attempted to capture. The conscience of Feng Tianhua, the aged son of Feng Yuqing, allows us to ponder this other side of rural China's wartime resistance:[70]

> After we left Qian Foji in the early war years, we went to Du Jiacun on the Hebei-Shandong border, inside the east Nanle base area. The CCP district leader there employed me as a mail carrier in the Eighth Route Army and I delivered mail and messages to the villages of Du Jiacun, Yancun, Fancun, Wu Huaguai, and Jiangzhuangji. I lived in Dujia village with my mother and brother, for it was too dangerous to return to Qian Foji.
>
> My job was to get messages to the militia in the base area villages which were protected from the Japanese Puppet Army. The peasants in these villages did not make salt before the war. In the past they had to purchase sea salt, and depended on it for all of their supplies. I taught them to make earth salt.
>
> After the sea salt had stopped coming to their markets in the war period, these peasants had tried to make pond-salt. But when I taught them the cauldron method they were elated because the salt from cauldrons was of higher quality and more healthy. The pond-salt was bitter and contained salt brine. In time, I taught 20 percent of the people of this village to make salt, while I made salt for myself and for sale in the market.

Double-Hatted Qian Foji: A Trojan Horse Within the Puppet Army

By the summer of 1939 Qian Foji was a dependable outpost of Communism on the North China plain. Even the CCP secretary of Nanle took comfort in its accomplishments. It was one of the first villages to succeed in implementing the reasonable burden tax payment system in Nanle, and its erstwhile cadres were rising stars in the Nanle County resistance and the CCP-led border area government.[71] Yao Chenmei, the teacher/doctor who had started the Qian Foji CCP, travelled over the Wei County line to establish new party branches among his "patients" in the villages of Li Zhao, Er Zhao, Zhang Dapu, Zigang, Lucun, and Hucun.[72] Knowledge gained from his involvement with the student movement at the Daming Seventh Normal School enabled him to talk about the 1917 October Revolution in Russia, about why Lenin had succeeded and Trotsky had not, and about China's outstanding Communist Party activist—Zhou Enlai. Within Qian Foji, Yao Chenmei, Wang Guoding, and Yao Peishan set up the Anti-Japanese Patriotic Democratic Pioneers[73] whose members contributed money for the anti-Japanese resistance. The leading contributors were the peasant saltmakers who had joined the CCP-led militia. Looking beyond the village, Yao Huibin (the Nanle County CCP secretary in 1941–44, a member of the Hebei-Shandong-Henan CCP Committee in 1949, and the head of a PRC ministry after 1952) set up the National Salvation Association among the village schoolteachers of Zhang Fuqiu district. It quickly reached out to peasants, landlords, merchants, and gentry to form an anti-Japanese united front in Nanle.[74]

An incident in 1938 illustrated the strength of the bond that was forming between Qian Foji and the CCP-led resistance. In late autumn, just after a seventy-man Japanese army patrol had paid a harmless seven-day visit to Qian Foji—one of the few Japanese appearances of the war—Wang Guoding and Yao Chenmei asked their fellow villagers to build a trench line through the fields to make it more convenient for the Eighth Route Army to conduct its war operations and to facilitate village self-defense against future Japanese incursions.[75] One hundred villagers volunteered to dig this trench. But landlord Yao Jinshan, the only landlord to criticize the reasonable burden tax system, tried to stall the "trench-digging movement." Wang Guoding called a meeting of the ten neighborhood heads, who decided to fine Yao Jinshan. Three hundred villagers attended a "struggle meeting" on this matter and were told that Yao Jinshan's fine was to provide an apology dinner for the hundred people who were digging the trench line. Yao reluctantly provided this dinner, which for much of the peasantry signified the first symbolic defeat of landlord rule. Shortly after this incident, Yao Jinshan was abducted by the Eighth Route Army and disappeared from village life forever. Such a fate was not unforeseeable. The local grapevine had been humming with a rumor that several landlords in nearby Songzhuang had been killed by peasants in league with the resistance army when they had stood in the way of the local struggle for national independence, in which Qian Foji was now involved.

The winter of 1939 brought a sudden reversal of political fortunes, however. Yang Faxian moved his one-thousand-man puppet army to the outskirts of Qian Foji, where its troops entrenched themselves. Yang Faxian himself lived in Qian Foji, and hundreds of his soldiers stayed in peasant homes for two- and three-year stints. By 1940 Yang's puppet army had begun to replace the revolutionary experiment that had drawn Qian Foji to the CCP-led resistance and to restructure the village economy to serve the schemes of the Japanese. The reasonable burden tax reforms were dismantled; the production of nonfarm income was regeared to serve the puppet army mission; and the plans for tolerable rates of interest and rent were put on hold. During this period, Yang Faxian set out to harass and harm the villagers who had joined Qian Foji's CCP branch. By the spring of 1940 Yao Chenmei, Yao Huibin, and Yao Peishan had fled the village, and in the fall, six new CCP recruits were rounded up and buried alive in a field west of the village.[76] Terrified by this turn of events, the remaining CCP members went underground.

On taking over west Nanle in 1940, Yang Faxian's army ousted the popular leadership groups in villages like Qian Foji and imposed a tax system that was a stark alternative to the *heli fudan* tax reform of the CCP-led resistance. The puppet army tax was collected according to the amount of land owned. Qian Foji's minitillers lost their tax-exempt status and were forced to pay a fixed sum of grain regardless of harvest yield.[77] This tax system was far worse than anything peasants had experienced in the Republican period because they were told to pay 120 *jin* per *mu* annually, four times as much as the land tax rate they had paid in previous decades.[78] The Yang Faxian puppet regime reduced the grain tax from 120 to 60 *jin* when the harvest was poor,[79] but there was no allowance for a catastrophe. Yao Xiren, the puppet-appointed village head in 1942, bitterly recalls, "They even made us pay the grain tax in the year of the Henan Famine."[80] The Yao landlords now had to pay three times more grain annually than under the CCP and four times more than under the Kuomintang, and they knew that the poorest villagers now would swamp *them* with requests for grain loans when there was great dearth.

By late 1941 Yang Faxian was commanding a puppet army of two thousand men in west Nanle, the main contingent of a collaboration force of three thousand in the county.[81] Yang Faxian also began selling sea salt acquired from the Japanese-controlled Changlu Salt Company for a brief stint around 1941–42, but this posed little threat to peasant salt trade because the Japanese transport of Tianjin maritime salt to Japan left Yang's puppet forces with woefully inadequate supplies and drove the price of sea salt even higher. As far as salt making (and nitrate making) was concerned, the inhabitants of Qian Foji all agree the puppet army was preferable to the central government and its salt revenue commandos because the former did not impose any unduly competitive restrictions on their market-focused earth salt enterprises.[82]

On the other hand, the war duties imposed on Qian Foji after 1940 threatened the capacity of the village people to continue making salt based products for their own benefit. Forced trips to build Japanese blockhouses in Yuancunji took a toll on peasant time, and the loss of time and trade was exacerbated by the fact that Qian Foji's peasants were forced to labor without pay in a number of armaments factories established by the puppet troops in the village circa 1941. The plan was to convert the chemically based cottage industries of Qian Foji to serve the Japanese occupation. By 1941 a team of master gunsmiths and munitions experts from Anyang had arrived in the village to start up several puppet army arsenals. Qian Foji's peasants were compelled to collaborate with them in making hand grenades and gunpowder in the house of landlord Yao Futang,[83] to produce handguns and small bombs in Yao Jinshan's house,[84] and to make primitive machine guns on the premises of landlord Yao Shizhao's home.[85] Every healthy male peasant had to work in these factories for at least two or three days per year without compensation. This particular form of wartime *corvée* would become a hidden weapon in the hands of the weakened CCP village resistance.

The human cost of the Japanese puppet army occupation, however, must be measured in the damage it did to peasant options for relief grain during the radical dearth of 1942. The famine of 1942, when coupled with the plunder of the Japanese and their puppet soldiers, plunged many southern Hebei villages into a terrifying subsistence crisis. Seventeen thousand village people died of starvation in Nanle County alone in the fall of 1942.[86] This was 9 percent of the county's population.[87] One might assume that the triggers to this starvation ignited anti-Japanese resistance, but the party's wartime cadres say that working conditions were very difficult in this period.

This was true for Qian Foji, even though the village was only indirectly occupied. Suspecting Qian Foji of revolutionary agitation, Yang's puppet soldiers attempted to suppress the CCP by severely curtailing movement in and out of the village. "Residence cards" were issued to all peasant households, and there were periodic checks on suspected partisan sympathizers.[88] Households with persons missing for more than one week were fined. The gates of Qian Foji were guarded closely to prevent liaisons between villagers and the resistance army. The older inhabitants recall that relatives found it difficult to visit them around 1941–42.[89] Migration was all but halted until the Henan famine literally forced some of the poorest villagers to flee and risk persecution in the fall of 1942.

Before 1942, migration was hardly necessary because the poorest villagers had, in addition to salt trade, two fallback sources of relief grain.

Beginning in 1939, and going up to the puppet army "lockup" of 1941, the Eighth Route Army had smuggled in small supplies of millet for families with connections to the CCP-led resistance.[90] When the puppet army canopied Qian Foji in 1942, however, this supply dwindled, and marginal peasant families had to turn to the Yao landlords for hunger loans in the famine. Landlord Yao Shizhao, who supplied grain loans to over 50 percent of the village, abandoned the low interest rates of the past and applied the screws to those who sought loans. If a peasant family borrowed thirty *jin* in the spring of 1942, for example, that family had to pay back sixty *jin* right after the June wheat harvest; if they could not, the amount owed doubled.* With labor, property, land, and progeny pledged to these loans, and with many peasants having failed to sow wheat in the preceding autumn, little tragedies followed. Yao He, whose family could not come up with the payment, was forced to join his father in a secret half-family migration to Shanxi; his mother was soon forced to give up the family home to pay back Yao Shizhao.[91] This was not the experience of the majority, but its nearness helped to move the majority to cooperate with the CCP-led underground resistance.

From 1940 to 1945 the CCP movement continued to exist underground and to establish liaisons with the puppet army, which its cadres utilized to carry on various forms of covert resistance against Japanese military occupation. The peasants of Qian Foji wore two hats during the Anti-Japanese War period. Strictly speaking, they were part of the protofascist puppet regime of Yang Faxian and expressed allegiances to the flag of the rising sun. From 1940 on, however, they swore a secret oath of loyalty to the CCP and its resistance army and pledged to kill anyone who betrayed the unity of the party. Thus, Qian Foji's semipeasants became a "Trojan horse" within the puppet army occupation, discreetly forming little groups to defend the lifelines of their local economy against Yang Faxian's puppet force and to assist the Eighth Route Army in its anti-Japanese activities. The importance of the CCP keeping secret its role in antiforeign resistance was driven home in 1942, when Yao Chenmei was seized and murdered by traitorous landlord *min-tuan* forces in Hucun village in Puyang. This event stunned Qian Foji's cadres, who henceforth took extra precautions to carry on resistance in the cloak of outward collaboration.[92]

As the antitax activities of the CCP underground resistance attest, the period of the Japanese puppet army occupation was one of unbelievable deception and defiance. Yao Zhenbian, the CCP secretary after 1942, persuaded his comrades to take up a collection to pay Yao Yiqing to act as the

---

*This was the equivalent of the wheat harvest yield per mu, which seems impossible. But then, the Yang Faxian regime was the brutal instrument of a foreign colonial force.

head of the Qian Foji "Peace Preservation Committee," so that the resistance could have its own liaison to the Japanese army in Yuancun market.[93] Through Yao, the CCP cadres pursued a strategy of feigned cooperation with the Japanese, fecklessly meeting their demands for *corvée*, building materials, and chickens so as to avoid trouble from the puppet army.[94]

It is hard to say just how effective this Janus-faced strategy of resistance was. By late 1940 Yao Yiqing, the head of Qian Foji, was serving on the Forty-Seven Village Working Committee under Yang Faxian, and Yang was heavily dependent on this committee for resolving issues in district grain taxation. Yao Yiqing generally managed to convince the puppet army leadership that Qian Foji deserved a tax reduction when the harvest was poor. Yao also managed to afford some protection to those who quarreled with the puppet troops about taxes or who temporarily fled when taxes proved unbearable. Except during the famine year of 1942, his pleadings actually were ploys to permit Qian Foji's peasant salters to pay a tax rate that allowed them to stay on the road to prosperity. Most household budgets were in the black until late 1941, and Yao Zhenbian tells us that he led a "little war of resistance" against puppet grain taxes, squabbling with the puppet soldiers over tax collection once in 1942 and then pleading to them to reduce the tax in 1943, when there was a good harvest and the salt trade was again booming.[95] That the puppet army needed the peasant salters to help develop its arsenal probably gave Qian Foji's clandestine party branch some leverage in the struggle to keep taxation halfway tolerable. When these ploys faltered, more risky forms of resistance appeared: in late 1942 Yao Kai, the brother of CCP stalwart Yao Huibin, secretly led several villagers to "steal back" millet given over to the puppet army granary.[96] If Qian Foji's little Communists were powerless, certainly they were not helpless.

Ironically, too, the peasants who worked in the arsenals of the puppet army after 1941 converted them into supply depots for the CCP-led resistance army,[97] often smuggling out hand grenades and gunpowder, which they sold to the Eighth Route Army soldiers in their travels beyond Qian Foji or sold for silver dollars later used to buy the bullets needed by the resistance army. The bullets, we are told, were bought from Japanese puppet soldiers in marketplaces far removed from home ground. The safety and success of such was surely guaranteed only by secretly planned cooperation.

By 1942, landlord Yao Futang, the vice-secretary of the Qian Foji CCP, had become the chief of the Zhang Fuqiu district puppet government, reporting directly to his blood brother, Yang Faxian. This move, which Yao Futang made without renouncing his CCP membership, opened the door to grain supply in Qian Foji during the worst moments of the famine. Yao Futang was now in a better position to help the underground party branch secretly ferry in small relief grain supplies though its liaisons with the Eighth Route Army in Xi Tianzhou village over the Wei County line.[98] Yao Futang also issued interest-free hunger loans to about 10 percent of the village households in the spring of 1942.[99] This "kindness toward the poor" was extended selectively to the families of the semipeasants whose sons joined the Eighth Route Army in 1942–43.[100] Yao later was criticized for his liaison with Yang Faxian, but no one laid a hand on him during the land revolution.

By the autumn of 1943 the CCP had gathered enough strength to make villagers feel as if they were shielded from the violence of the Yang Faxian puppet army, whose soldiers included the scattered former members of salt police and the Kuomintang Twenty-Ninth Army. Through the memory of Yao Peiji, we catch a glimpse of how the peasant saltmakers carried on veiled forms of everyday resistance to the predation of the puppet soldiers. In the autumn of 1943 Yao Peiji came into conflict with a soldier over the use of the stone roller. The customary practice was that any villager could use this roller, which belonged to Yao Futang, to mill grain as long as it was not being used by others. On arriving at the threshing ground, Yao started to use the roller. "But just then," recalls Yao,[101]

> One of Yang Faxian's soldiers came to use the roller. I wanted to continue using it, so we got into a fight. The soldier tried to hit me with a brick. I ducked. Then I struck him in the eye with my fist. He went away and got another five soldiers, and they came with belts to beat me. I ran back home and locked the door. Then they came to my house, but they thought I had fled. Later they demanded that I apologize. I thought it advisable, so I went to their company headquarters to give an apology. But I was seized and beaten by Cui Jindou. The beating lasted for a long time. While it was going on Yao Yiliang walked by, and came in to ask the soldiers why they were beating me. Yao Yiliang then rescued me by slapping me in front of the soldiers, as if they were in the right, and by quickly spiriting me out. In this way, he saved my life.

A kindred member of Qian Foji's salt market fraternity, Yao Yiliang had joined the CCP under Yao Chenmei in 1938 and was a secret member of the Anti-Japanese Vanguards. By 1943 his father had departed the village as a member of the Eighth Route Army, after which he worked for the organization department of the Hebei-Shandong-Henan border area government.[102]

Beyond the confines of Qian Foji, the CCP activists mounted a threat to the Japanese army itself, committing themselves to the resistance army's fight against the Japanese occupation in its broader regional context. Perhaps, as some of the following examples suggest, they were playing a double political game, but there is little doubt that they were solidly in the CCP camp and prepared to give the Japanese a dose of the methods of collective resistance used in their war with the Nationalist government's salt revenue police.

By 1941 Qian Foji was a veritable counterintelligence agency for the CCP-led resistance. Feng Yuqing, the purchase agent who had led the saltmakers' struggle, joined the Eighth Route Army in 1941 and thereafter tripled as a chef, a purchase agent, and an intelligence officer. Posing as a peddler, Feng passed by Japanese forts in Nanle, Qingfeng, and Neihuang to ascertain enemy troop strength and reported back to Eighth Route Army intelligence in Nanle, so that the army could attack the Japanese at night and then retreat into hiding.[103]

Wang Qing, one of several villagers who served in Yang Faxian's puppet army around 1940, joined the CCP in the same year and the Eighth Route Army shortly thereafter. An integral member of an anonymous CCP "secret service" within the puppet army, specializing in anti–prisoner of war activities, Wang was twice involved in saving the life of Li Huaming, who later rose to the rank of the CCP Central Committee. In 1940 Li Huaming was an underground CCP activist from Lizhuang village in Wei County. Wang was his kinsman and comrade. On receiving word that the Japanese army was driving south to surround Mo Ding village, where Li Huaming was working, Wang drove a cart ten *li* from Qian Foji to Mo Ding and secretly escorted Li Huaming to safety before the Japanese arrived. Not long after this, Li Huaming was apprehended by the Japanese puppet army at Ma Da market village and taken to a Japanese stronghold in Linzhuang for incarceration. On learning of this through his puppet army connections, Wang Qing says, "I went to the puppet army prison headquarters in Linzhuang and got him out. Since I was a member of the puppet army I could get him out because the leader of the puppet battalion knew me. His name was Cui Jindou, from Nanle's San Huang Temple. I was a message carrier for this Cui Jindou. I served in the puppet army, but I also wore another hat and helped the Eighth Route Army."[104]

The wartime outreach of Qian Foji's underground resistance also included working tirelessly to secure and smuggle weapons for the Eighth Route Army. With their wealth of black market experiences and liaisons, Qian Foji's peasant salt traders were prepared to form a counter-alliance *within* their engagement to the Japanese puppet forces, and undoubtedly this was another of their "gifts" to the CCP-led resistance. Yao Zhenbian, for example, repeatedly risked his life to purchase weapons for the Eighth Route Army from 1941 to 1944. He saved money from the sale of horses in enemy-held territory, then purchased guns and bullets from individual puppet soldiers in Lucun market, where the brother of his good friend, Zhang Fuwen, served as the bodyguard of Chen Daohe, a Kuomintang soldier turned puppet army commander. The money to underwrite this "horse trading" came largely from Qian Foji's salt traders, who made up the nucleus of the CCP. Yao Zhenbian, the head of this confraternity, and a little group of saltmakers routinely visited Lucun in the war years because, he recalls, this was a place where many weapons had been left behind by Kuomintang troops fleeing south in 1937, and Chen Daohe and the Japanese "puppets" were secretly trafficking in these leftover arms.[105]

Qian Foji's peasant saltmakers were moved to join the Eighth Route Army, especially when they were hurt by Yang Faxian's political inquisition and by the Henan famine. Throughout the war, and even in the early years before the puppet occupation took hold, they risked their lives as soldiers operating secretly outside of Qian Foji for short periods. By 1939 some twenty saltmakers had joined the fourth branch army and other guerrilla groups affiliated with the Eighth Route Army. Yao Xizheng, Sang Mingzhai, Yao Zhonghui, and others had undergone a brief Eighth Route Army training course in Zhang Machang village in Puyang County, a stronghold of the CCP-led resistance. Thereafter, they returned to live in Qian Foji, but in fact they were part of a two-thousand-man resistance army. Occasionally they left the village to team up with the army, as when they fought the Japanese at Wu Long village in Hua County in 1939 and Cao*xian* Shandong in 1943— by that year one hundred of Qian Foji's peasant saltmakers were members of the CCP-led Eighth Route Army. Because of the puppet army controls on Qian Foji, many of its soldiers could not afford to allow the demands of war to take them away too often, or too long. They also fought the Japanese indirectly by contributing food, money, shoes, and medicine[106] to the regular army secretly though the Qian Foji "puppet" village chief.[107] These contributions were underwritten by income earned from salt making.[108]

By August of 1943 the Qian Foji CCP, and party branches in a growing number of Nanle villages, had established secret liaisons with key subordinate commanders of Yang Faxian's Japanese puppet army, further strengthening their capacity to resist. Chen Xiufu, the captain of Yang Faxian's troops in Nanle County, and Lu Tianzhen, the chief of police in Nanle's Han Zhang town, were in sympathy with the CCP-led resistance.[109] Through such hidden ties, the CCP underground was able to continuously ambush the Japanese grain transport groups, damage Japanese forts and lines of communication, foil Japanese attacks on villages where the guerrilla *cum* regular army was stationed, and free its members from Japanese-sponsored prisons.[110] In such activities, Qian Foji was a pacesetter.

Clearly, the repertoire of collective protest that resulted from earlier encounters with the *Shuijingtuan* was a factor allowing Qian Foji's Communist Party to mobilize support for prolonged national resistance. Qian Foji's saltmakers had a rich history of collective resistance that had evolved from over a decade of practical antistate protest activity,[111] including the sharing of secretly gathered intelligence about intruders, daring attempts to release fellow villagers from prison, exploitation of seemingly invisible contradictions between local security forces (the public security forces and the puppet army) and the warriors of the outside world, and sudden and short-term bursts of participation in an insurgent army pledged to defend the interest of local folk against military order from above. All of these ways of chipping away at the Japanese occupation bring to mind collective aspects of the popular struggle against the salt police in the previous decade, a struggle in which the rural people had, as with the Japanese *weijun*, for the most part avoided direct and dangerous clashes.

Liberation and Expansion

This in part explains Qian Foji's reaction to the arrival of a unit of the Eighth Route Army during the Spring Festival of 1945, six months before the Allied triumph in the Pacific War. Members of the underground army teamed up with their counterparts, who had been living in base area villages under control of the resistance army, to challenge the puppet army and drive Yang Faxian from Qian Foji and the Wei River area.[112]

The following weeks, Yao Zhenbian, Sang Mingzhai, and Sang Puyi gathered seven hundred people in the threshing ground and called on them to carry out a campaign to reduce interest and rent.[113] All debts incurred to the Yao landlords during the 1942 famine were canceled, they agreed, and landlords had to return all of the interest they had collected on hunger loans since 1942. Tenants were thenceforth exempt from rental payments.

In March of 1945 Qian Foji's acidic Communists shifted their struggle onto a map of larger scale as they prepared to strike the weakened Japanese army with the Eighth Route Army. The group of ten militiamen dug up the arms they had buried when Yang Faxian had taken over the village five years before, put the puppet arsenal to their own advantage, and recruited twenty new members. On April 20 this thirty-man force joined with scores of other village militias to drive sixty Japanese soldiers from their fort at Yuancun market and then marched fifteen kilometers east to support Liu Bocheng's 129th division of the Eighth Route Army in a successful assault on several hundred Japanese soldiers and their puppet accomplices in Nanle County town.[114] According to *Liberation Daily*, on 24 April 1945 this main force launched a second attack on Nanle town from Yuancunji in Nanle and Long Wang temple in Daming, killing thirty-seven Japanese soldiers and capturing all three thousand members of the Yang Faxian puppet army.[115] The thirty-man Qian Foji militia unit assisting in this assault was led by Yao Zhenbian and the saltmakers who had participated in the struggle to kick the salt tax police out of Yuancunji, Guo Xingguo, and Nanle County town a decade past, so that there was a connection between the early anti-state protests and anti-Japanese resistance: clearly, there was a personnel carryover, and the military success of the main resistance army built on the strategy of multivillage collective mobilization used against the *Shuijingtuan*.

Following the liberation of Nanle town on April 27, Qian Foji remained a feeder for the CCP-led army. Its regular army volunteers helped expand the scope of CCP rule in the North China plain, and each of its militia members has a story to tell about how he served as a grain carrier or stretcher bearer in battles to liberate a distant county town—Qingfeng in Hebei or Cao*xian* in Shandong.[116]

In short, Qian Foji was a cloud with silver lining for the CCP-led border area resistance. To be sure, the substantial puppet army presence turned the village into a minimum security prison, compelling its people to comply with many pro-Japanese directives. But to brand Qian Foji a collaborator village, whose peasants some fifty years later put the best face on their collaboration, would be a radical mistake. The semipeasants of Qian Foji were engaging in a form of political sublimation, temporarily diverting their commitment to participate directly in CCP-led anti-Japanese warfare to less detectable forms of resistance. Restrained by the power of the puppet forces, they did what little they could do for the national struggle. Significantly, not one of them betrayed the party-army by giving political secrets for the privileges of collaboration. There was no capitulation here. Compliance, not collaboration, was a cover for sublittoral collective resistance. Hence the great promise: if the CCP-led resistance held in Qian Foji, where there were puppet controls, then imagine the progress the party could make in other market-geared, culturally enabled, and semicolonized salt land villages where there were few, if any, puppet forces present. The Nanle CCP leadership, with its close multiple connections to Qian Foji, was buoyed by the geopolitical implication of Qian Foji's contribution to its cause.

EXPLAINING THE CCP'S WARTIME SUCCESS IN QIAN FOJI

What factor, or set of factors, made it possible for these quasi peasants to play such a tenacious part in the CCP-led mobilization for national defense? To be sure, the absence of the Japanese army and the imperfect structure of puppet surveillance meant that they could test the limits of colonial army controls to undertake hidden forms of resistance during the occupation. By comparing Qian Foji with the wartime fortunes of the party in several differently positioned salt land villages, we can grasp the reasons for the staying power of CCP-led resistance and why peasants in other villages were inclined to orbit Qian Foji and were attracted to the collective actions of its party branch.

One factor facilitating wartime mobilization was the existential state of the village itself. Qian Foji was an island of the blessed. Savoring a better agricultural base than many of its highly saline counterparts, its peasants had a striking range of indigenous food resources. Wheat, yellow beans, watermelons, and pumpkins made for healthy diets and placed the village in a food regime that was a world apart from that of poverty-stricken Qi Ji. The manufacturing output of the multiple salt-based household industries of Qian Foji turned it into a trade surplus village and ensured a food surplus within this historically grain-deficit part of the North China plain. By 1930 Qian Foji clearly was a small trading village whose peasant households were in pursuit of material advancement and whose successes lifted them above the margins of economic safety. The pursuit of prosperity allowed them to avoid sharp intravillage competition, which would have atomized them and driven them against one another. As in prosperous Qian Kou, the CCP discovered that its fortunes were favored in villages where manufacturing diversity and a radiant economic performance enabled peasants to satisfy immediate material needs and then contemplate political action for their common interest.

Released from the strictures of poverty and protein deficiency, which had preoccupied their counterparts in Qi Ji, the peasants of Qian Foji were not overwhelmed by the constant fear of death or the ordeal of dying. They were fairly successful in maintaining the bereavement practices of the past, and they displayed a tendency to adapt these to the national resistance movement in which they were involved.

Within Qian Foji, no one died of starvation before 1942. Those who died a natural death did so within the hospitable framework of their homes, and with dignity. Most families were able to afford a willow-wood coffin, and the upscale members of the Yao lineage often used pine coffins.[117] Throughout the Republican era, Qian Foji had its own pallbearers' association, which was a permanent village group based on interlineage cooperation. Yao Zheng, a victim of salt police violence before the Anti-Japanese War and the head of the pallbearer's association, remembers that when a person died, the family approached the head of the association, and the members assisted with funeral arrangements and proper ceremonies.[118] CCP leaders built on the nodes of this interlineage hospice and converted it into a means for coping with death in war, often donating money to help purchase coffins and provide funerals for the relatives of resistance warriors. When Sang Chunkui, a member of the Eighth Route Army, was buried alive in a pit near Yuancunji after being captured by the puppet army in a mop-up operation in late 1941, for example, the CCP Nanle Committee gave his brother and uncle the money to buy a coffin, after which they secretly went to dig him up and put him in a temporary grave.[119]

The bereavement functions of Qian Foji's party cadres alleviated the fears that no one would respond to family needs during the crises of war and provided a sense of personal worth that sustained patriotic sacrifice. The tradition of dignifying those who sacrificed themselves in the struggle for national power endured beyond the War of Resistance. In 1958 Qian Foji's peasant salters returned Yao Chenmei's corpse from Hucun, where he had been murdered in 1942, and gave him a martyr's funeral and a pine coffin and paid the expenses to rebury the martyr Sang Chunkui along the Wei River.[120]

The Japanese occupation did not reduce Qian Foji to the point of unresolvable intravillage competition over food resources. Having recaptured their income from salt making through the antipolice protest action of 1931 and weathered the minor Wei River floods of the prewar decade, its inhabitants were able to avoid internal war over local crops. Pilfering was largely confined to landlord fields, and in the crop pilfering that took place in the desperate spring hunger of 1942 fewer than twenty of Qian Foji's 270 households were implicated.[121] The family-initiated crop watching that prevailed in submarginal Qi Ji and in subsistence-level Fanzhaung, was replaced by a village crop watch team aimed a preventing theft by outsiders. This so-called crop watch team was made up of six ex-thieves, whom Qian Foji villagers paid so that they would not steal from fellow villagers.[122] It was supplemented by a small militia force, originally formed to cope with the first wave of warlordism and strengthened later in response to the raids that followed the flight of the Kuomintang from the invading Japanese army.[123]

The continuity of peaceful coexistence and the renouncement of internal raiding were undoubtedly underwritten by the fact that the puppet army occupation did not, after all, seriously damage the off-farm market income of Qian Foji's salters. Peasants agree that the war gave them two new sets of customers—those in flight from Japanese-occupied Yuancunji and the soldiers of the puppet army itself—to whom they sold earth salt, pork balls, and watermelons in Qian Foji's enlarged market. With this underlying economic history, Qian Foji's peasants manifested their desire to come together politically to protect their common interest in morally acceptable forms of acquisition. Most interestingly, when the first anti-Japanese militia force was formed in Qian Foji in 1938, the party cadres told villagers they were taking up donations to buttress Qian Foji's two main defense units— the crop watch team and the militia.

With few internal foes and with market-based prosperity, the peasant salt-makers were able to build their party branch on a tradition of social trust and to extend ageless forms of joint self-help and cooperation to repelling the Japanese puppet forces. Allegiances to the CCP-led resistance flowered in old forms of interpersonal trust. Sang Chunji, a well-off nonparty Protestant, says that one of the reasons he and fellow villagers supported the CCP was because its trustworthy leaders gave them grain tax refunds when possible, as in the tax movement of 1939.[124] And Yao Zhenbian, the CCP secretary from late 1942 to late 1944, says that mutual trust helped cement the party's tacit alliance with the Yao landlords, who supported the anti-Japanese united front and even sheltered members of the Eighth Route Army on occasion.[125]

Mutual aid during the war replicated old forms of joint household production, such as the pooling of family funds to purchase salt caldrons, and plow share arrangements involving loans of single oxen by families in need of two plow animals. Some of this cooperation was cross-lineage: Sang Puyi purchased and shared a salt caldron with four other households, two from the Yao lineage and two from the Sang lineage. Thus in comparison to villages where poverty and Japanese power shredded the social fabric, Qian Foji's CCP was able to nurture forms of national resistance based on a strong, living history of social cooperation. The formation of the anti-Japanese militia from the donation of village temple land, the cooperation of local people with a CCP campaign to collect weapons from landlords for the resistance army, and the movement to arrange for substitute laborers to help families with Eighth Route Army dependents plant and bring in the crops—all these mimicked habits of prewar cooperation and collective action.

As illustrated previously, the forms of collective action conceived by the peasant salters in the prewar period gave local CCP leaders a proven repertoire of resistance strategies from which to draw in the Anti-Japanese War. In the case of Qian Foji, this argument cannot be pushed too far because the puppet army forced the party cadres to abandon many forms of open collective resistance after 1940. Nonetheless, some of the collective acts against the national state before the war foreshadowed collective resistance against the Japanese occupation. Although the Japanese never violently invaded Qian Foji, they did march through the village on several occasions between 1938 and 1941. Each time, the local CCP leaders rolled out the prewar strategy of avoiding the salt police: they suspended production and hid their tools and produce; they fled the village until the political situation cleared; and they shifted trade to safer market spots—in this case, literally from the main village street to several impromptu market spots located a few minutes' walk away from Qian Foji. Just as the peasant saltmakers had left the village to participate in a collective struggle against the police ten years past, so they now left to join up with their counterparts from other villages to fight the Japanese, under the shield of the Eighth Route Army.

If Qian Foji proved a resilient base of CCP support, this was facilitated by the fact that its prosperity gave it a crew of peasant activists who relied on family-based enterprises to bolster their own household economies and who were in the habit of cooperating with the people with whom they associated in everyday work life.

To a significant extent, Qian Foji was like Qian Kou. Here too there was a tradition of "associational familism," particularly among the Yao and Sang lineages. Peasants in these lineages were mostly the beneficiaries of "extended familism," and the CCP was able to build its base in the one kinship system that best embodied this phenomenon: the Yao lineage. The peasants in the Yao lineage, along with those in the Sang lineage, had the most land, property, and labor power. They were the most adept at manufacturing and marketing. And they lived in the best houses and had the best educations. By and large, therefore, they were better able to deal with the difficulties surrounding the crisis of *fenjia* and handle the division of estates to sons looking to start up families. Even more than their counterparts in Qian Kou, the peasants of Qian Foji were able to rely on off-farm market-generated income to avoid the pains of family poverty, disintegration, and uprooting. With few exceptions,[126] peasants in these founding lineages pioneered kin-based strategies of prosperity to strengthen local roots and utilized their strong lineage relationships to line up the village for mobilization against predatory outsiders.

This strong peasant familism, which had served Qian Foji's concerted resistance to the Kuomintang Finance Ministry's salt tax police a decade past, also gave the CCP a great advantage in its efforts to organize collective resistance against the Japanese—the CCP itself, the National Salvation Association, and even the Peace Preservation Committee all were linked to a long history of intermittent collective struggle initiated by the leaders of Qian Foji's self-energizing frontline lineages. This history, which facilitated Qian Foji's feigned support for the puppet army, allowed the CCP to avoid the scorched earth tactics by which the Japanese were destroying resistance in the "red core" of the Hebei-Shandong-Henan anti-Japanese base—recalcitrant Qian Kou in Puyang was one such village—and to continue working within an expanding market economy with a resilient social base during the worst years of World War II. Semicolonized, prosperous, close-knit Qian Foji, with its ties to the network of reopened local markets, was a place where the village people *could move together* with the political rhythms of CCP-led patriotic resistance.

Education was a third key to the CCP's impressive record. Of course the authority of the party did not depend on education alone, but its leaders were able to gain esteem because the underlying history of education gave them a hold on peasant minds, if not hearts. Even before the Qing dynasty was blasted away, Qian Foji had a substantial primary school enrollment. Its peasants tell us that in Republican times they paid greater attention to education than most of the surrounding villages in Zhang Fuqiu district. They say, too, that the private tuition fees paid by each family produced real benefits in the realms of business and politics.[127]

The decade linking the saltmakers' struggle with anti-Japanese struggle saw thirty students attending the Qian Foji primary school annually. Half of them hailed from the relatively prosperous Yao lineage. A number of the Yao graduates climbed the ladder of educational success in Nanle County and the triprovincial border area and then went on to concern themselves with affairs of the Republican national government. We can divide them into two distinct groups. One, epitomized in the careers of Yao Huibin, Yao Peishan, and Sang Chunkui, had graduated from the Yuancunji Secondary School and then gone on the Nanle County Teacher's Training School. The graduates in this group returned to rural society to serve as primary school teachers in the villages of the border region—Foshan in Nanle and Er Zhao in Wei County.[128] The second group was headed by Yao Chenmei, who had gone to the Daming Seventh Normal School, where he intermingled with young CCP firebrands, like Wang Congwu and Liu Dafeng.

On returning to teach in Qian Foji's primary school around 1935, Yao Chenmei introduced villagers, including his former classmates, to Sun

Yat-sen's three principles—nationalism, democracy, and livelihood. He knew firsthand the salience of the latter issue, for his father, Yao Mingyuan, was a saltmaker who had been involved in the local struggle against the salt tax police. It is not surprising, therefore, that Yao Chenmei stressed the morality of standing up to the administrative despotism of the Chiang Kai-shek center. Such talk resonated with conceptions of righteousness that Qian Foji's peasants had learned from the *Si Shu*, "the four books" that still formed the Confucian bedrock of the village school curriculum. In the attempt of the Kuomintang salt police to wipe out their livelihood, school-master Yao reasoned, they could see ample proof of the CCP's warning that Chiang Kai-shek's Nationalist government was building its power base in the city world by mistreating country people. Not only had they been right in acting together to resist the police; this little episode of collective protest had involved them in the larger CCP-led struggle to create the framework for revolutionary socialism in China. Reaching this goal, however, required mounting collective resistance *through* a political institution steadfastly opposed to the violent state readjustment of their way of life.[129]

The Japanese invasion of North China had improved the CCP's chances of organizing the village people for this purpose, mainly because of the breakup of the twenty-ninth army and the defection of young intellectuals from the Kuomintang educational system, now in disarray. Yao Huibin, who returned to Qian Foji to be introduced to the CCP by Yao Chenmei in 1938, was one such intellectual. The National Salvation Association that he set up in Qian Foji and the surrounding villages drew in people from all walks of life and united local intellectuals of Kuomintang and CCP persuasion. Yet according to Yao, the peasant saltmakers were among its most active ele-ments. One reason for this was the fact that the Japanese occupation, while damaging the top-level structure of Kuomintang power in Nanle town, brought them face to face with the soldiers and salt police who turned up in the puppet army. The anti-Japanese struggle served as a kind of looking glass that alerted Qian Foji's peasants to the looming danger of the weak-ened Nationalist polity.[130] Thus Yao He, a peasant saltmaker who had been educated by the CCP in his native Qian Foji before he joined the Eighth Route Army in 1942, is speaking of this danger when he tells us that he hated the puppet troops even more than he hated the Japanese because they helped the Japanese kill local people.[131] This "dirty hand" of the Japan-ese army was directly responsible for the deaths of three hundred people in Zhang Fuqiu district alone during WWII.

Of course fighting the Japanese remained the number one priority of Qian Foji's patriotic CCP. Yet the cadres increasingly were concerned about the potential of the Yang Faxian puppet army to develop into a parallel gov-ernment capable of competing with the party's antiforeign propaganda and of bolting to the side of a re-energized central government at war's end.

Qian Foji's villagers caught a glimpse of the former in a sadistic local incident in Zhang Fuqiu district, where Yang's puppet regime exerted its own interest over that of its Japanese masters. Around 1940 the local Nanle Japanese commander ordered Qian Foji to send it several women for sexual use. On going to Wucunji to buy some women for the Japanese, the Qian Foji village chief discovered himself in competition with the male heads of other villages. The resulting tension was relieved when Yang Faxian himself led a squad to Wucun market and killed two Japanese soldiers who were in the process of molesting a local woman. This action stirred a sense of admiration for Yang Faxian in local society, but to the CCP it was a dangerous counterpoint underlying the need to drive home its message that the puppet army had slaughtered its "kindred spirits" with total impunity under the Japanese occupation. Qian Foji's well-schooled Communists were able to grasp this logic and to both carry on concealed resistance to the Japanese and resist integration into the puppet regime—which was not always the case in villages where poverty, ignorance, and Japanese power prevailed.

The data on the wartime experience of the three salt protest villages studied in Chapters 4–6 point up differences from and similarities with Qian Foji during the War of Resistance. If prosperity, a tradition of extended familism, and an educated leadership experienced in defending local market terrain favored the formation of Qian Foji's wartime resistance, the continuity of such resistance was facilitated by the fact that the Japanese army never severely damaged the economic base or the social cohesion that argued for collective political action. In contrast to Qian Foji, Qian Kou was ripped apart by the Japanese and their puppet armies during the savagery of the "three all," so that Qian Kou's peasant saltmakers were pulverized and displaced by war, which made it harder for the Communist Party to organize sustained resistance within the village.[132] In this respect, Qi Ji's wartime experience was similar to that of Qian Foji, for although the Japanese army passed through Qi Ji, they did not attack the village, so that foreign force did not increase the insecurity of the 1942 famine, as was the case in Qian Kou. Yet Qi Ji differed from Qian Foji, too, because the Japanese did not station puppet army soldiers there.[133] Ironically, therefore, because of Qi Ji's safer political environment, the CCP was in a better position to enlist the leaders of the saltmakers for protracted anti-Japanese resistance in this place than in any of the other three villages. Nevertheless, despite its lack of military security, Qian Foji was still a comparatively good candidate for CCP-led resistance, for it was not subjected to the constant Japanese army patrols known to Fanzhuang. Clearly, Fanzhuang's CCP wartime party branch was handicapped by this close Japanese presence. Zhang Ke recalls, "During the war the Japanese built a fort in the east field of our village. Because they were too close to the village no one in Fanzhuang dared to oppose the Japanese openly."[134] In contrast, Qian Foji's party stalwarts were able to develop resistance in the interstices of the puppet army's occupation in part because they were farther removed from direct colonial force.

In drawing out the differences between Qian Foji and the other salt land villages of this border area, we must not overlook the common features of rural society and wartime politics that made it possible for the CCP to mobilize the peasant saltmakers of different villages for anti-Japanese resistance. Three similarities are of vital importance.

To begin with, in each of these villages a substantial number of young peasant saltmakers joined the Eighth Route Army during the war—Qian Kou sent two hundred; Qi Ji, one hundred; Fanzhuang, forty; and Qian Foji, one hundred. This relationship between the salt protest villages and the involvement of their people in the resistance army held up regardless of the size or stature of the CCP branch locally. What explains this shared relationship? Of course some young salters joined the army simply because their families still had trouble wringing a livelihood from the poor salt lands right after the war broke out.[135] There were more decisive factors, however. During the first stage of the war (1937–40) the CCP was no longer operating as a secret political organization, so that many peasant saltmakers who previously knew little about the party became aware that it was aiming to improve their life chances by increasing their political leverage locally. On virtually every issue, from relieving the land tax burden, to checking the corruption of village leaders, to promoting market entry, this party effort to involve villagers in a political community designed to strengthen the economy locally proved magnetic.

For another thing, during the War of Resistance many peasant saltmakers began to grasp that the Eighth Route Army, with their help, possibly could win the struggle with their major enemies in the border region—the Kuomintang, bandits, and the Japanese, all of which were seen as predatory and murderous, especially in comparison to the CCP-led resistance army. By late 1938, even in villages untouched by direct Japanese violence—Qi Ji, Fanzhuang, and Qian Foji—the local grapevine already carried stories about the death of a fellow villager in some distant market arena or war engagement.[136] Furthermore, when the Japanese began to build up their collaborationist forces from bandit and Kuomintang armies between 1939 and 1942, the choice of the peasant saltmakers became crystal clear. They would act together in support of the growing power of the CCP-led resistance army, which was now home to many of their sons and which supported their habit of marketing the salt from the earth. The rising tide of Eighth Route Army victories over puppet forces in the border region between 1938 and 1944 stoked this political logic.[137]

All of the villages studied apparently benfitted from the economic policy of the CCP-led resistance army during the Anti-Japanese War, for its policy fostered salt making for the market. Thus does Liu Xingquan of Qi Ji recall,

"The *balujun* (Eighth Route Army) wanted us to produce salt for them. Its soldiers paid a high price for our salt. Salt-making served two purposes. It allowed us to earn money from trade; and it improved the harvest yields because there was less salt in the land after we made the salt."[138] This dual benefit, which Qian Foji's saltmakers enjoyed too, contrasted starkly with the loss of economic security to the Kuomintang salt police in the decade past.

Finally, and significantly, the cultural tradition that made for a propensity to collectively mobilize for war on a large scale was still intact in virtually all of the villages studied. Just as the peasants of Qian Kou remember that saltmakers who joined the Eighth Route Army often lived in, and gathered at, the war god temple for several days at a time,[139] so peasant memory of the cultural basis of village support for CCP-led national resistance in Qian Foji is significant: the Thousand Buddhas village not only shared in the war god tradition of the Three Kingdoms epoch; it was the mecca for popular religious Guandi, or Guangong, temple pilgrimages in the Nanle-Puyang-Wei tricounty border area.

In the early Republican period the Guandi temple was the largest and most patronized of seventy-two temples in Qian Foji. During the old *Shui Lu* (land and water) fairs that occurred during the Spring Festival and just after the June wheat harvest, peasants from villages in various parts of Hebei, Shandong, and Henan journeyed to Qian Foji's Guandi temple. They carried sacrificial offerings, including food, money, and animals (sheep and pigs), which they deposited in front of the main Guandi temple and the smaller Guangong shrines to cover the expenses of the fair and its operas, the most popular of which was from *The Romance of the Three Kingdoms*.

The Guandi temple gatherings in Qian Foji were raucous events well into the early 1930s. Right after the 1935 peasant saltmakers' struggle in Nanle town, however, the Kuomintang Nanle government ordered Qian Foji to destroy its war god temple. As in Fanzhuang, the peasants here were unwilling to carry out this order, and so, the story goes, the local authorities relied on two "good-for-nothings" in Qian Foji to pull down the temple. Although the Guandi temple itself had disappeared by the outbreak of the Anti-Japanese War, peasants still worshipped Guangong with little statues and pictures in their homes.[140]

During the war, therefore, the CCP could, and did, connect its call to national defense with the old community memories of Guangong. The CCP could take Qian Foji as a cultural beacon for its anti-Japanese resistance, in part because its militant inhabitants were predisposed to arming themselves against external predatory forces and in part because the Eighth Route Army resonated with the political symbolism of this folk religious deity.

That the Nationalist government had orchestrated the destruction of the Guandi temple complex in the prewar period, or that the Japanese puppet forces had prevented the CCP from openly disseminating the political message of Guangong via the open-air operas during the post-1940 occupation, did not necessarily preclude this political-cultural continuity. Peasants remember that the CCP leaders Yao Chenmei and Yao Huibin arranged for local opera players to perform Guangong skits in Qian Foji on several occasions in 1938 and 1939, just after the Kuomintang Twenty-Ninth Army began to collapse and just before the Yang Faxian puppet forces descended on the village and curtailed these performances in late 1940. Thereafter, according to Yao Huibin, "we invited the traditional professional storytellers of Qian Foji to secretly present the message of the war god operas to the local people. For helping us, we provided them with money and meals, and we helped them with household problems. Their message was the same as in the operas, but the form was different."[141]

Similarly, when Qian Foji was liberated by a unit of the 129th division of the Eighth Route Army in February, 1945, the CCP leaders took up a villagewide collection to sponsor five days of operas in celebration of this euphoric moment. Sang Puyi, the CCP secretary and the head of Qian Foji's Opera Selection Committee at that time, says that the most popular of these operas was from a story of the *Three Kingdoms,* one that glorified Guangong.[142] Its performances, before which the CCP eulogized the martyrs of the war, drew virtually everyone in Qian Foji and attracted ten thousand people from surrounding villages. These opera festivities, with their ancient war god precepts for popular action against intolerable political interference, reminded the country people that the CCP and its army stood for their own empowering tradition of resistance and rebellion and that joining with the CCP-led resistance only strengthened their struggle to defend both shared material and spiritual interests.

NINE

The Popular Fear of the Return of the Kuomintang Fiscal Center and the Outbreak of Civil War

An early school of Western scholarship perceived the civil war as a social revolution in which the CCP mobilized peasants to carry out a radical land reform in the counties that fell under the control of the PLA. Under the administrative control of the CCP, a "land-to-the-tiller" movement galvanized peasant resources and recruits for the PLA campaigns against central government commands, transforming a class struggle against landlord dominance into a wider political war against the Kuomintang.[1] Focused almost entirely on the land issue as seen through the written reports of CCP "insiders," Suzanne Pepper's impressive monograph on the civil war portrays such a development in the Hebei-Shandong-Henan base during 1946–47.[2]

In a more recent view, what precipitated the civil war and drew the country people into its vortex was the CCP and its military. Steven I. Levine claims that the critical theater of civil war was not North China, where the old CCP anti-Japanese base areas were, but rather *Northeast* China, where the CCP confronted a quiescent peasantry lacking a tradition of rebellious political activity.[3] With the assistance of the Soviet Union, the CCP rushed PLA soldiers into Manchuria in 1945–46 to attack a local elite whose authority had been diminished by decades of draconian rule and whose central government allies lost out in the race for the resources of the rich Northeast region. The land reform, imposed on the villages by PLA soldiers,[4] was merely a violent means for coping with these shifting international and national circumstances. Through its military superiority, the CCP compelled peasants to bear the burdens of war service against Kuomintang commands,[5] placing the needs of the PLA's war front before peasant desires to reinvest the gains of land redistribution for household prosperity.[6]

To the peasant saltmakers of the Hebei-Shandong-Henan border area, however, the reappearance of Kuomintang government forces was the principal factor precipitating civil war. Shortly after the Japanese surrender, in 1945, the central government reassumed its authority over Tianjin and the production centers of the Changlu salt area, recovering the Changlu Salt Company from the pro-Japanese officials who had run it during the war.[7] From 1 January 1946 to 25 March 1947, the Kuomintang Finance Ministry proceeded with plans to place branches of the national salt bureau in the salt consumption areas falling to government forces—North China, East China, Taiwan, and Liang Huai were the major anticipated prizes. Beginning in January, 1946, H. H. Kong, the head of the finance ministry, began putting in place the financial package necessary to underwrite the rush of maritime salt back into the interior and dispatched a group of capitalist merchants to transport the salt to Hebei, Shandong, and Henan. Over the following year, Kong tripled the price of official sea salt in the markets of Hebei Province.[8]

The problem was, however, that the Kuomintang state, holding only the Tanggu and Hangu salterns, had little control over the transportation and sale of salt beyond metropolitan Tianjin. The majority of the Changlu salt market areas had been taken by CCP forces. By 1 January 1946, much of the inland trade in public maritime salt, not just private earth salt, was in the hands of the CCP, whose troops delivered it to cooperative shops in the bigger market towns of the border area. The price of maritime salt was only a little higher than that of earth salt, which still was legal and in a market surge.

The country people who helped the PLA transport this maritime salt were the very peasant saltmakers who had been targets of the Kuomintang Changlu salt police in the prewar era. In late 1946, Sang Mingzhai of Qian Foji sailed up the Wei River to Linqing County in Shandong Province and brought the sea salt by boat to a CCP-run border area government shop in Yuancun market in Nanle County.[9] The money earned from these public shops went to the PLA for its fight with the Kuomintang, giving the CCP as well as the peasant saltmakers an interest in controlling the distribution and sale of Changlu sea salt.

Now the central government of Chiang Kai-shek faced an even greater revenue-gathering dilemma than before the war. A plan to reconstitute the *Shuijingtuan* and to suppress the production of earth salt in the North China plain was put on paper in 1946–47;[10] but government forces first had to overcome the peasants, peddlers, and purchase agents with connections to the CCP in the hundreds of salt land villages. Otherwise, the Changlu transport merchants and the police could not safely return to the border region.

Thus, behind the central government declaration of war against the CCP was the determination of Chiang Kai-shek's capitalist officials to address the fiscal insecurity of their political order.

To the outside world, the Chiang Kai-shek government presented its counterrevolutionary strike of 1946–47 against CCP positions in Hebei, Shandong, and Henan as an attempt to dislodge predatory Communist forces. The *New York Times* carried stories reinforcing this Kuomintang posture, reporting in one instance that the same Communist forces that had assimilated the peasant saltmakers were "raiding the countryside."[11] Locally, however, the Kuomintang-PLA battles for Dao Kou in Henan, Long Wang Miao in Hebei, and Linqing in Shandong all reflected a growing political struggle for control of key inland salt distribution centers and for the salt market. Seeing that the Nationalist forces wanted to connect up these places with their Tianjin maritime salt monopoly, the peasants of the marketplace took the return of the Kuomintang as a threat to hard-won profit, dignity, and empowerment and sided with the PLA to thwart it.

THE CIVIL WAR AS A PEASANT DEFENSE AGAINST THE REASSERTION OF CENTRALIZED STATE POWER

Peasants in the salt land villages were jubilant on recovering their rights to freely market earth salt at the close of WWII. Such feelings were seldom conveyed in the formal propaganda of the CCP, which emphasized peasant impoverishment stemming from the inequality of landholdings, the peasant outcry for land redistribution, and peasant zeal for settling old scores with landlords. But the country people were far more focused on the vertical struggle against the Kuomintang state. The peasant saltmakers were preparing their own collective defense against the anticipated Kuomintang intervention well before the Chiang Kai-shek government broke off negotiations to include the CCP in a national coalition government in late June of 1946—a move that signaled the destruction of CCP-led local governments protective of popular sovereignty[12] and the start of open hostilities. Yao Zhenbian, a peasant salt trader and party leader from Qian Foji, analyzes the place of the Kuomintang state in the origins of the civil war:[13]

> In the year following the Liberation of March 1945 we continued to boil salt for our own use. If we wanted to sell earth salt we could sell it.
>
> We felt we could fall back on our salt trade whenever the crop failed, or whenever we needed to do so. Our right to make the salt was established through Liberation, and recognized by the CCP-led government because there was no such term as *si yan* (illegal salt) after March of 1945.
>
> At that time, however, we knew the Kuomintang officials still wanted to make money from selling the sea salt. They still did not want us to produce the

earth salt because the sea salt yielded a tax for them. The CCP, on the other hand, encouraged us to produce anything we could, and purchased many of our items to use in constructing the nation—things like nitrate, for example. We knew that if Chiang Kai-shek returned to power through the civil war his armed forces would not allow us to make the earth salt anymore. They would tax us, or punish us, for making it because the revenue obtained from the salt of the state (*guojiade yan*) would be invaded by our earth salt.

If Chiang Kai-shek had won, the salt police would have returned and harmed our livelihood. We would have lost the good life we had gotten. By March of 1945 the CCP had revoked all taxes imposed by the Kuomintang, including the salt tax. Thus we held a mass meeting in the village, and we told villagers that "when Chiang Kai-shek returns he will bring back all the old land taxes, the miscellaneous taxes, and the salt tax, and we will not have a good life." In this mass meeting, we told them that the Kuomintang would not allow us to make earth salt.

This fear was echoed in scores of villages. Implicit in the remembrances of their older inhabitants is the notion that involvement with the CCP, as a political institution dedicated to defending their household economies, had identified them as the enemies of Kuomintang power holders who sought to convert their local marketing communities into "inputs" for the national state. The Kuomintang state drive to take back territory held by the CCP was therefore seen as a form of political integration that portended the extermination of peasant families involved in an independent market community.

Born seven years before the end of the Qing dynasty, Liu Shiyin of Qian Kou village has outlived warlords, Japanese intruders, and Kuomintang state makers. Despite bittersweet memories of the preliberation CCP, he has no doubt of his decision to support the party in the civil war:[14]

In 1945, after I had gotten 12 *mu* of land in the land redistribution, my crop output doubled. At this point, I gave up salt making. Even though I did not produce earth salt, I knew I could turn to making it if the crops were poor.

However, when the Kuomintang New Fifth Army returned to this area, I feared that the salt police would come back again. All of the peasant saltmakers in Qian Kou were concerned about this possibility. When Liu Yufeng, Liu Hansheng, and Wang Congwu returned here after the Anti-Japanese War, they propagandized this matter. They said that because the Kuomintang was still powerful, we should be prepared to fight against the salt police again.

The first meeting about this matter in Qian Kou was secret. Liu Yufeng, leader of the 1932 peasant saltmakers' struggle here, was a member of the CCP. He said the CCP now has weapons and mass power, and that if the Kuomintang were to come here again the salt police would come again, and that we would fight them.

One reason I fought the Kuomintang in the civil war was that I resented their oppression in the past, during the 1920s and 1930s. If the Kuomintang had won, all of the members of my family would have been killed. I had been involved in the saltmakers' struggle with Liu Yufeng, and I had been a member of the Communist Party for twenty years.

By 1945 many of the semipeasants who had been involved in struggles with the salt police during the early 1930s had a clear political consciousness of the relationship between the "bureaucratic capitalist" state of Chiang Kai-shek and the role of the police in spreading the exclusionary political economy of top-level Kuomintang rulers into the countryside. This consciousness was heightened through their active participation in the CCP-led Eighth Route Army during WWII. Partly through informal exchanges about their struggles against the police and partly through army educational sessions about the "dirty hands" behind the police, they became the carriers of a counterideology that saw the central government as an illegitimate force dispossessing peasants and proprietors.

Yao Lishen, a Qian Foji saltmaker, describes how he arrived at his political awareness of the Kuomintang center and its salt moguls:[15]

> Prior to 1937 we had seven *mu* of land and six persons. Our land was some of the poorest in Qian Foji because our land was lowland. The salt was three meters deep, so we got virtually no crop at all.
>
> My father was a tinker. He traveled to Nanle town, to Xinzhuang, and to Cao Maoxi in Nanle to sharpen scissors and knives for local people. My mother was a professional beggar in the surrounding villages. We mostly depended on salt making, and we produced a little nitrate to sell to people who came here to buy it for fireworks. We barely could get by on the combined income from salt making, scissors sharpening, and begging.
>
> In the land revolution of 1947 we got 20 *mu* of land, so now we had 27 *mu* altogether. We planted wheat, sorghum, millet, and corn, and beans and pumpkin. This was enough to get by on, and we had a little surplus. In the years 1945 to 1947, I still produced my own earth salt. Before I had possessed no crop land, so I was a saltmaker. The land revolution of 1947 changed me into a peasant.
>
> Still, I was afraid that if the Kuomintang came back I might be stopped from making earth salt. Of course, I knew that the salt police had been defeated, but I also knew that they were connected with the central government. We could defeat them in this local county, but when Chiang Kai-shek came back he would bring more forces, so the salt police would eventually come with more force too.
>
> I learned about the political connection between Chiang Kai-shek and the salt police after I joined the CCP in the period of the Anti-Japanese War. In this period, I learned there were four big capitalist families at the top of the Chinese Central government. Chiang Kai-shek was one. Song Siwen was one. Kong Xiangxi was another. Also Chen Lifu. Each of them had a bank and issued as much money as he wanted. We had to use their inflated currency notes. When Chiang Kai-shek triumphed in the wars with Feng Yuxiang, Wu Peifu, and Zhang Zuolin we all knew he was the most powerful person in China. Thereafter, we learned about his connection with the four big families.

Perhaps locally this consciousness was limited to a minority of worldly wise party members, or PLA participants, in 1945, and surely there was a later CCP-led process whereby peasants learned to articulate local facts within the framework of national party highlights. Still, the oral history evidence also suggests the prevalence of an older interior mode of peasant memory about life under the Kuomintang, a memory that should not be confused with post-1949 CCP-driven politicization.[16] Thus did Liu Wanli, a 76-year-old (in 1990) former peasant saltmaker with no history of party membership, remember that peasants in Qi Ji supported the Communists during the civil war because village leaders explained their poverty was due to the exploitation of the "four big families," that the Chiang Kai-shek government denial of their salt making was an example of such exploitation, and that the poor had to help the PLA in order to have a good life.[17] Reflecting the shared political fears of many peasant families, this collective memory of the country people made it easier for the CCP to enlist them in its war with the Kuomintang.

THE POLITICS OF LAND REVOLUTION: RESENTMENT OF THE KUOMINTANG STATE VS. PEASANT VIOLENCE AGAINST "CLASS ENEMIES"

Although the civil war in North China has long been portrayed as dominated by a land reform process that ushered in class war, there is little evidence for such a development in the Hebei-Shandong-Henan border area. Although the process of redistributing landholdings generated friction, and sometimes sharp conflict, between peasants and landlords,[18] arousing peasants to carry out violent collective purges of landlords was not a standard practice of CCP village leaders. The village people in this remote border region were alarmed far more by the oppressive forces of the Kuomintang fiscal state than by the immoral deeds of landlords. In most villages, landlords who had acted immorally were subjected to rituals of shame and repentance. Landlords who had assisted central government troops in carrying out the 1946–47 counterrevolution against the CCP and its rebel base were the main local targets of mass rage, and it was they who met violent death by execution.[19] The order of the period was political war against Kuomintang state oppression and not "class war."[20]

The land reform that unfolded in three phases between March, 1945, and October, 1947, was guided by community-generated codes of fairness and justice that had little to do with the upper-level CCP penchant for a radical antilandlord assault. The resourceful and rich semipeasants of the market ran the land reform in "bad earth" villages in a way that shored up their own land ownership positions first, then brought the poor landless peasants into the movement.

The first phase of land reform in the advanced CCP villages within the Hebei-Shandong-Henan liberated area commenced in the spring of 1945, right after the CCP had taken power in Puyang, Nanle, and Hua counties. The Communists had promised land to the peasants in these counties ever since 1926; now the market-bound peasants who had aligned with the CCP against the Kuomintang state were pressing the party to live up to its promise. The local people began this phase against the wishes of CCP higher-ups and had all but finished it before the May 4 land-to-the-tiller directive of 1946 was issued.

This early phase was marked by a mass movement, called *dauzu dauxi*, to persuade landlords to reimburse the peasants who had paid unreasonably high rent and interest following the famine of 1942. In most of the villages where the peasant saltmakers held the upper hand, however, tenancy was hardly an issue because only a few people had rented land from landlords. Such was the history of Qian Foji. Here the local people were so unconcerned with the rent issue that they converted this campaign into a drive to reimburse the hired hands who had been underpaid by their landlord employers since the famine. The landlords willingly consented to this wage adjustment.[21]

The campaign to recover interest on grain loans touched more village people. The peasant association set up a "grain court," where people could register grievances, and assigned go-betweens to verify the amount of interest paid on the loan prior to 1945. If the amount was verified, the association instructed the landlord in question to pay back the loan within a stipulated period. Subsequently, peasant borrowers came to the court to collect the payment.

Nearly half of Qian Foji's households got from three hundred to three thousand *jin* of grain from landlords and well-off peasants. Because about 30 percent of the households had borrowed grain from landlords outside of Qian Foji, the peasant association extended the movement beyond the village. Sang Puyi, for example, had borrowed two *dou* of grain from a landlord in Luo Di village, Wei County, Hebei, and had repaid ten *dou* in 1944. In the spring of 1945 Sang requested the Luo Di Peasant Association to confirm the loan with the Luo Di landlord, who subsequently returned the interest.[22]

In 1946 the CCP sent a batch of young land reform cadres into the Hebei-Shandong-Henan liberated base from Handan to set up poor peasant leagues (*Ping Nong Tuan*) and emancipation committees (*Fanshen Weiyuanhui*) to lead the village people in pouring out mass hatred against landlords.[23] These cadres apparently never showed up in the border villages under our microscope, where land reform was carried out peacefully. Most of the wealthy landlords and rich peasants who stayed in the villages cooperated with the local CCP-led peasant associations in making moderate reforms.

The second phase of land reform saw the actual redistribution of land. Tens of thousands of peasants received land between March, 1946, and early

January, 1947, when the Kuomintang counterrevolution cut short redistribution. CCP documents and *People's Daily* reports stress an upsurge in the participation of the wretched poor in CCP-mobilized land redistribution meetings against landlords in this phase; but local peasant history shows no such development. Although land changed hands on a massive scale, this transfer was brought about through land sales, not simply confiscation. The principal form conceived for ironing out the land problem was the voluntary sale of land at public auction.[24] Although public auction was not the order of the day everywhere, such a tendency prevailed in many salt land villages.[25] (Many landlords, of course, put land up for sale either because they feared it would be confiscated or because they felt they stood a better chance of keeping some of the land if they donated substantial landholdings.)[26]

The sale of prime croplands in this phase primarily benefitted the semipeasants of the marketplace, who were in a position to compete for them.[27] Yao Xixin, a Qian Foji resident who still depended on salt trade for 30 percent of his total income in 1946, bought his land from the boomlet of the salt market.[28] So did most of his fortunate lineage members who, unlike Yao Xixin, were committed to the CCP and entrenched in the peasant association leadership. Yao Zhimin, for example, tells us that "in the 1946 land sale I got the money to purchase my eight *mu* from selling salt and bread. I used my business capital to buy it."[29] *For much of the peasantry, then, the salt market made it possible to purchase land on the "public market."*

The third phase was initiated in response to the Kuomintang army raids on the salt-making villages in early January, 1947, and to violence by government forces against the peasant base of the CCP-led border area government.[30] The semipeasants in the market sector took the lead in redistributing the remaining land and property of landlords to poor peasants, hired hands, and tenants who had been left out of the second phase.

This was a period of rising violence and political chaos in many villages of the Hebei-Shandong-Henan border area, and the CCP lost control of events on the land in more than one village. Affluence-seeking rogues flooded the ranks of the CCP, corrupting the process of land reform by physically abusing peasants and protecting landlords who invited them to savor the rewards of hidden patronage.[31] Some CCP cadres, swept into the storm over the land, harmed the interest of the market peasants, small merchants, and landlords. In Fo Shan village, Nanle County, cadres even led a slaughter of landlords who should have been given a way to reorder their lives and redeem themselves,[32] resulting in the deaths of seven landlords. The sensational incident prompted an investigation by the CCP border region government, whose leadership was distraught by the attempts of the ultraleftist faction of the CCP center to push the land reform into a radical phase by relying on "poor peasant dictatorships."[33] In most of the salt land villages, however, the leadership of land reform still remained largely in the hands of the conservative market-bound peasants. These semipeasants led the local CCP branches to their own resolution of the land problem and were fairly successful in checking the spread of indiscriminate class violence against landlords. They knew the relationship of land and labor was less important than the relationship of the Chiang Kai-shek–led government to their struggle to preserve the market.

In Qian Foji, for example, the peasant association compiled a list of peasant households possessing less than three *mu* per capita, then offered each household enough land to make up the difference. Approximately nine hundred *mu* of landlord lands were divided along these lines. "The rule of three *mu* per capita was not fixed," recalls Sang Puyi. "There were other factors to consider. A family with less than three *mu* per member might have lived quite well if the quality of land was better and if they plowed adeptly. Or, conversely, a family of five with only twelve *mu* of extremely poor crop land and poor agricultural skills was entitled to more than three *mu*."[34] A crude equity, not equality, prevailed, and, consequently, the poorest village people often were recipients of the poorest land. The redistribution of landlord property, houses, and lands was the market peasants' way of placating the poor, reluctant latecomers and small winners, so as to solidify their support for the revolutionary coalition.

Land Revolution and Rural Class Violence vs. Realpolitik

The land revolution documents issued by the CCP Regional Committee in 1947 portray a wave of violent terror against landlords.[35] According to the country people who participated in the land revolution, however, only a tiny minority of landlords were the victims of mass violence, and peasant association leaders were largely opposed to the taking of landlords' lives.[36]

The picture of a peasant-directed pogrom against landlords is not in accord with the remembrance of rural people and is not worthy of belief for four basic reasons. The first has to do with time and place. At the time of the third "radical phase," when landlords were to be denounced in the speak bitterness meetings of 1947, most of the major landlords in Puyang, Neihuang, Hua*xian*, and Nanle had fled with the Kuomintang army to the secondary cities of North China. In Qian Foji, all four of the Yao landlords—Yao Shizhuang, Yao Shizhao, Yao Xingzhai, and Yao Futang—escaped CCP leaders who sought to parade them on stage in the third phase.[37]

Another factor belying the view of massive, CCP-orchestrated violence against landlords had to do with the persistence of patron-client relations, reinforced by lineage relations and market relationships of mutual interest. Far from seeking mastership over peasants, many landlords displayed humane treatment of tillers, whose respect, honor, and goodwill they desired. Some landlords in Qian Kou, Qi Ji, and Qian Foji had provided low-interest loans, sponsored feasts, and preserved gleaning rights. Such landlords were in turn treated with fairness and respect in the third phase of the land reform campaign.

According to Liu Yunxing, the CCP leader of the Qian Kou Peasant Association, several Qian Kou landlords "actually came forward to the Peasant Association and offered their land."[38] One of them was Liu Zhihe, a teacher who taught in Puyang County town. Liu was praised by the peasant association and his students. "On the day of denouncing the landlords Liu's students rushed to find him and protect him."[39] Qian Kou landlords who gave up their land were allowed to keep some land, furniture, and livestock. Although such accounts seem a little too neat and harmonious, the counterevidence for landlord households actively opposing the CCP-led land reform process in this border area is weak.

Educated local people, landlords, and the quasi peasants of the salt lands saw their interest in uniting against the disruptive Kuomintang center. For the most part, landlords had not spoiled the popular united front against the salt police or the Japanese; the peasants of the market were not about to lose their support just as they were coming under attack from the army of the Kuomintang state. Although the acts of certain "immoral landlords" aroused villagewide indignation, the peasant saltmakers were careful to refrain from physical attacks and punitive violence that would have driven wealthy people to side with the Chiang Kai-shek Kuomintang in the civil war.

Yao Xingzhai, a truly misanthropic landlord in Qian Foji, had drawn scathing criticism since 1934, when he demanded that villagers honor him by contributing money to a *bian* (a board on which couplets were carved in commemoration of benevolent deeds). Between 1934 and 1938, Yao Xingzhai punished several people who failed to contribute to his *bian* by destroying their sorghum crops.[40] In the 1942 famine, he refused to make hunger loans at reasonable interest rates, forcing the poorest villagers to go outside the village to beg.[41] Five years earlier, he had discontinued gleaning in his fields and posted guards to apprehend even the poor women who took only a few wheat stalks after the June harvest.[42]

Though landlord Yao had created widespread peasant animosity and set himself up for a painful class-based struggle, the peasant saltmakers refrained from physical attacks on Yao, settling instead for verbal ridicule and for the redistribution of his grain, land, and personal belongings. Whatever his wrongdoings, he had not actively joined the central government counterrevolution to drive them from power and subordinate their market community to state monopoly, and they shunned a course of action that would push him to join ranks with the Kuomintang counterrevolution. Most of the peasant saltmakers wisely perceived the broader political struggle with the central government as paramount to the struggle landlords such as Yao Xingzai had invited in this period of the civil war. This clear political thinking was a third factor negating CCP-guided peasant violence against the "landlord class."

Finally, it should be stressed that the "landlords" who did lose their lives during the land revolution by and large had willfully aided the central government in its attempt to reassert its fiscal interest and root out CCP village cadres. Among sixty men and women with direct social connections to eleven landlord households in Qian Foji and Qian Kou, only two were sentenced to death, and in both cases the evidence of all-out complicity with the Kuomintang army inquisition was especially damaging. Villagers reacted to the role assumed by landlords in the Kuomintang army attack on their recently won market rights and only secondarily, if at all, to the ways in which landlords had subordinated them as "social producers."

Ironically, given that many of the active Kuomintang landlords were hiding in cities, peasants fighting the Kuomintang for political control of their communities often directed their violence against members of pro-Kuomintang landlord households who did not flee with the central army—often the women. Landlord Yao Shizhuang, for example, was a known member of the Nanle County Kuomintang; and yet it was his mother, not he, who paid the price of his political indiscretion. Although Yao Shizhuang had denied the pleas of the Feng lineage beggars for grain handouts in the famine of 1942,[43] he had not wantonly violated the moral precepts of the village poor, as had landlord Yao Xingzhai. When the Kuomintang Fortieth Army returned to raid Qian Foji in 1947, Yao Shizhuang also returned and conspired to undermine the CCP-led revolution. One of the servants in his household informed the Kuomintang troops about the secret grain storage facilities of the pro-CCP peasant saltmakers. This disloyal act was compounded by the fact that Yao accompanied the retreating Kuomintang army to Anyang one month later. In the land revolution that followed, the CCP-led militia seized Yao Shizhuang's mother. In one speak bitterness meeting, several field hands denounced her for oversalting their meals during the 1942 famine so that they would eat less.[44] She was given a chance to repent by confessing her son's complicity with the Kuomintang counterrevolution, but refused and was hanged.[45] By the time the PLA captured him in late 1947, the CCP decree to allow killings had been revoked by the Hebei-Shandong-Henan liberated base area government, and Yao Shizhuang's death sentence was commuted to life imprisonment.

The wife of landlord Liu Huazhu was also hanged. When the Kuomintang New Fifth Army attacked Qian Kou from Jingdian town in late 1946, Liu and his nephew helped the Kuomintang troops to dig up and destroy the grain the peasant salters had stored for the PLA, then drove out the leaders of the Qian Kou Peasant Association. Unable to catch the pair, the Qian Kou militia leaders seized Liu's wife instead. In a speak bitterness meeting, she was abused for "treating the poor terribly," which meant that her household had opposed the peasant salters' war with the Kuomintang state.[46]

Other so-called landlords who lost their lives were really wealthy peasants who had conspired openly with the Kuomintang army in the 1946–47 counterrevolution. Yao Peili of Qian Foji had fled during the first round of the land reform in 1945, when he was asked to return back interest to local borrowers, including his uncle. When the Kuomintang Fortieth Army raided Qian Foji in early 1947, Yao returned to the village and informed the Kuomintang troops of his uncle's CCP membership. The CCP leaders of the peasant association arrested Yao and sent him to the gallows. In peasant minds, this was not the violence of class struggle. "We never would have struggled Yao Peili if he had not returned with the Kuomintang to threaten our cadres," says Sang Puyi. "We agreed that the rich peasants were not the object of our struggle."[47]

Chen Lanxi, a Qian Kou peasant, suffered from a similar political mistake. When the Kuomintang New Fifth Army struck Qian Kou village from Jingdian town at the end of 1946, plundering grain supplies and running the CCP activists out of the village, Chen Lanxi attempted to retrieve some of his redistributed land and, worse, to organize Qian Kou's landlords into a Kuomintang cabal. When the tides of war shifted two months later, Chen was executed by a PLA firing squad.[48] No other "landlords" in Qian Kou, not even members of the Kuomintang, were harmed, for no one else had implicated himself in the politics of state making.

If this was a struggle against the Kuomintang state, why did some landlords choose to collaborate with the Kuomintang? In reality there were three different levels of struggle in the salt land villages. At the highest level, there was a community struggle against the state, supported by many landlords who were unhappy with Kuomintang fiscal policy. At the intermediate level raged the peasant struggle for land, and some landlords sided with the Kuomintang because they feared the Communists would radicalize the peasant demand to distribute their property (interestingly, only a minority pursued this course). And, on a third level, a small number of so-called landlords were killed by peasants for personal reasons. Such acts often were at odds with the CCP-led united front against the Chiang Kai-shek government. Seeking to curtail this personal and class violence, Liu Yanchun, the Puyang-educated director of the Hebei-Shandong-Henan Regional Party Committee, led the border region government to strictly prohibit the killing of landlords without upper party approval, so as to maintain the united front and magnify the struggle with the Kuomintang army.[49]

The Kuomintang State as the Main Enemy: Resentment and Dignity

To focus mainly on landlordism and class struggle, therefore, is to miss noninscribed folk memory of the primary threat to human security in this saline part of the North China plain: the newly formed national revenue state of Chiang Kai-shek. "We fought the Kuomintang in the Civil War," says Liu Shiyin of Qian Kou, "to keep the land we had gotten in the land redistribution and to keep the Chiang Kai-shek government from bringing back its salt police. Moreover, if we had to choose between eliminating the Kuomintang, the bandits or landlords, between eliminating one or the other, then we would have chosen to eliminate the Kuomintang and the bandits."[50] In all of the interviews, villagers concurred that the Chiang Kai-shek government and its army was their major foe. The landlords were a secondary enemy, even a tertiary one, behind the Kuomintang and banditry.

This is not to say land reform was not a welcome, empowering movement for the poor or that it did not draw peasants to support the CCP against the Kuomintang. The point is simply that there was a popular antistate movement paralleling land reform at the outset of the civil war and that in the minds of the peasant salters this movement was both connected to land reform and critical to its lasting success. As Liu Wanli of Qi Ji puts it, "After land reform, the poor were in high spirits and we knew we had to unite to defend the victory of land reform. But defeating Chiang Kai-shek was as important as defeating the landlords, for without defeating Chiang no one dared to divide the landlords' land."[51]

From the summer of 1946, as Van Slyke notes, the CCP increasingly emphasized "an anti-Chiang United Front" in order to prepare the people for a struggle with Chiang Kai-shek government forces, at least within its liberated bases.[52] Within the Hebei-Shandong-Henan base, the peasant militias and PLA were in a position to respond to Kuomintang intervention by severing all ties with landlords and killing every Kuomintang soldier they could. There were very few violent attacks on landlords, however. The united front held, and the mobilized village people spent most of their time and energy chasing down Kuomintang military personnel who had committed crimes against the leaders of the peasant associations.

In early 1947, just after the Kuomintang Fortieth Army stormed Qian Foji, Da Guo, and Liangcun in Nanle and drove hundreds of peasant salt-makers out of southern Hebei into the PLA sanctuaries in western Shandong, Kuomintang officers spread the word that anyone who fled the villages and joined the PLA would be killed. Xun Haide, the head of the Da Guo Peasant Association, was captured and slaughtered by Yang Haiqian, a former squad leader of the Yang Faxian puppet army, whose officers and troops had gone over to the Kuomintang Fortieth Army in Anyang in early 1946. When the PLA captured Yang Haiqian, it delivered him, as was the practice, back to the village where he had killed civilians. The Qian Foji militia escorted the captive to Da Guo village, whose people took him to Liangcunpo, a big salt-making village in west Nanle. A crowd of four thousand people stared in silence as the father of the murdered peasant association chief sliced open the Kuomintang officer's head with a chopper. "It was the policy of the CCP at that time to let the common people settle their debts with their enemies, Yao Zhenbian says, "and this was a way of mobilizing the people to defend their communities."[53]

Other places saw a similar pattern of antistate violence. Lu Jinwen, a regimental officer in the Yang Faxian Kuomintang, was captured in Chu Wang town, taken to Yuancunji, and put on an open stage where the war god plays from *The Romance of the Three Kingdoms* were performed. Here Lu Jinwen confessed to killing his uncle, a CCP member, of Xun Shi village. For three hours the spouse of this party leader shouted her grief in his face, then the militia-led crowd marched him to a trench near the Wei River, where he was shot.[54]

Thus although some violence erupted in the salt land villages during the civil war, the CCP was attempting to legitimate its use only in the struggle against the state and to limit its popular application mainly to the Kuomintang elements who proved they were beyond political redemption. The security of this PLA-held border area, which the Kuomintang recovered only briefly in early 1947, facilitated the CCP realization of this goal, allowing the focus to remain the peaceful construction of a broad anti-Kuomintang united front regionally.

Counterrevolution and Political Relative Deprivation: The Double-J Curve

The peasants of this border area did not voluntarily join the CCP and its liberation army *en masse* against the armies of the Kuomintang until the spring of 1947. Why, if they already were resentful of Kuomintang rule, did they not go on the warpath in 1945 or 1946, when the Kuomintang army began reoccupying county seats? And why did they rally their communities to support the revolutionary cause in the second, "moderate" phase of land reform, even before the CCP issued the radical land directive of October, 1947?

A Hebei-Shandong-Henan CCP Regional Committee report by Xu Yunbei, which claimed that fifty thousand men were recruited into the CCP liberation army in early 1947,[55] helped to create the impression that army recruitment was solely dependent on land reform because a similar campaign had borne little fruit in the previous year, when land reform was not in full swing. Our rich local oral history data allow us to hold on to this hypothesis while entertaining another line of reasoning: the material losses peasants suffered from the violent Kuomintang intrusion of 1946–47 were seen as continuing a disruptive pattern of central government revenue gathering and taken as a grim reminder that Chiang Kai-shek's government posed a constant threat to gains made in the salt market trade, which was sanctioned by the CCP.

What CCP documents on the civil war do not tell us is that these people of the salt market, the longtime enemies of the leading money-making enterprise of Kuomintang state officials, made up the majority of rural war participants in the early phase of the civil war, helping the PLA hold the line against Chiang Kai-shek's efforts to smash the liberated base until the land revolution of 1947 made possible the mobilization of masses of peasants into the PLA. Virtually all of the thirty-five old-timers, CCP members and non-CCP members alike, I interviewed about this matter said their decision to risk death in the civil war was made in response to what social scientists James C. Davies, Ted R. Gurr, and Edward N. Muller have termed "political relative deprivation."[56]

In advancing the "J-curve" hypothesis, Davies and his imaginative disciples argue that people who are suddenly, painfully deprived of recently acquired material resources by repressive government institutions are prime candidates for participation in antistate protest activities. To the market-bound peasants of this backward, state-abused border area, the Kuomintang strike of early 1947 signaled precisely this kind of painful reversal. Hence they considered it rational and reasonable to align with the CCP in a violent insurgency against the Kuomintang army, whose top officials were intent on depriving them of their market.

As of the spring quarter of 1947, the peasant saltmakers still believed the improvement of their living standard was the product of the political struggle through which they had regained the market, and not through the land revolution per se. Further, the livelihood of the majority *was* improving by leaps and bounds between the March, 1945, liberation and the Kuomintang strike of 1946–47. The J-curve theory of a revolt by rural people whose newfound prosperity was being interrupted yet a second time by the Kuomintang seems useful, therefore, in explaining the civil war mobilization of the local peasant leaders who had a niche in the salt market. But what of the poorest villagers? Were they active players, or mere pawns, in this J-curve revolt? Prosperity and poverty had coexisted for many decades in this border area, but the evidence on the string of salt-making villages under scrutiny suggests that the poorest village people also hoped to climb out of poverty via the salt market. Not only were they keenly aware that the newly prosperous local village leaders had been poor themselves before the salt market burst of the previous two decades, but, as will be shown in a moment, the poorest villagers also thought this way because they had to reinvest salt market proceeds to develop lands they were receiving in the land reform. Thus, the J-curve model of revolution also helps us grasp what the majority of rural people were fighting for. The counterrevolutionary thrust of the Kuomintang army signaled Chiang Kai-shek's determination to compel all of them to surrender the market, and thus to give up the one local resource that held out hope for a better life.

Of course land distribution drew peasants into the CCP-led peasant associations, providing them with material benefits for which they subsequently
would fight the Kuomintang. This was doubtless the reality in much of rural
China. But Yao Zhenbian is representative of why so many village political
activists in the Hebei-Shandong-Henan border area rose up to repel the
Kuomintang state in the civil war. Following the 1945 liberation, life was getting better for Yao, especially after he got twenty *mu* in the land reform and
gained the freedom to use the land the way he wanted, producing earth salt
for family consumption and nitrate for sale. Using the proceeds from the
sale of saltpeter, Yao started up a grain trade business and sold grain surpluses for profit in Qian Foji. He recollects, "After the land redistribution
of 1946, many other people had surpluses too. When the Kuomintang
troops struck on New Years day of 1947, they found the stored grain in our
fields and took it with them. I fought the Kuomintang because I was a CCP
member, and because if the Kuomintang returned, we would have lost what
we had acquired. If we did not defeat the Kuomintang, we would have lost
our capacity to strengthen our household economies by production and
marketing." [57]

The fear of the revenue-seeking Kuomintang armies returning was fairly
widespread, even among country people who were not members of the CCP
and were not enriched by the land revolution. Liu Chaoxun, of Qi Ji village,
was not a member of the CCP or a beneficiary of the land division movement, but he shared the great hope and the great fear of the market-bound
peasantry:[58]

> In the land reform, I was seen as being in the "middle," so I did not get any
> land. With my twenty *mu,* I already had about what the average landholding
> was supposed to be. My land, however, was classified as eleventh grade land,
> which was the worst land in the village. It was all salt land, and I could not
> trade any of it for good crop land.
>
> Prior to land reform, more than 60 percent of my household income had
> come from the salt trade, and after I still got about 60 percent of my income
> from my salt business. The other 40 percent came from agriculture. So the
> land reform made virtually no difference in my livelihood. About 30 percent
> of the villagers were in my situation.
>
> My life was improving in the years before the outbreak of the civil war
> because after Liberation . . . I could market my salt freely, and this enriched
> my household. I was afraid that Chiang Kai-shek's Kuomintang Army would
> interrupt this improvement, and this is one reason why I went to help the PLA.
>
> The people of our village had beaten the salt police, and some of us, though
> not members of the CCP, had served in guerrilla army units attached to the
> Eighth Route Army. So if Chiang Kai-shek's soldiers had come back here, they
> would have destroyed our salt ponds and done away with us. When the Kuo-
> mintang troops came back in 1947, for example, I had to hide in the fields
> and forests surrounding the village in order to avoid being apprehended, and

so I joined the militia during the War of Liberation. . . . The main reason I supported the PLA was to protect my right to market the earth salt.

A Qian Foji native, Wang Qing transported millet from Jing Degu in Nanle to Yuncheng in Shandong for the PLA and performed stretcher bearer service in western Shandong's Jinxiang and Juye counties during the civil war. His story is similar to Liu Chaoxun's. In 1945 the Wangs had eleven *mu* of land, yielding barely enough to get by on even in a good year, when there was plenty of rainfall. So they depended on salt making to tide them through the years when the crop faltered. Wang Qing did not get any land in the land auction of 1946, nor in the land revolution of 1947. The only laborer in his four-person household, he needed Wang Han (a relative) to help him work in the fields. At the time of liberation, and after the land revolution, Wang Qing still made earth salt and feared that if Chiang Kai-shek came back, he would bring the salt police. Still remembering when the police had come from Yuancunji to destroy his cauldrons, Wang worried that the police would repeat this repression. Thus he says, "In 1947, the leaders of the Peasant Association shouted the slogans to beat down Chiang Kai-shek, and I shouted too. At that time, the landlords were a threat on the spot, but Chiang Kai-shek was the real source of this threat and the utmost enemy."[59]

This same fear was commonplace in Fanzhuang. Zhang Xiaoxun relates:[60]

> There were eight people in my family. Before the land reform I had fifteen *mu* of poor salt land. I got four *mu* of good land through the reform. Afterwards, we put more effort into agriculture, but I used the income from salt making to purchase farm tools and grain.
>
> In fact, my livelihood had improved after the famine of 1942. Right before the land revolution I sold the earth salt in Yan Wang temple, Wucunji, and in villages within twenty *li* from this village. I made the earth salt for sale right up until the time we dug the wells around 1955. I went to the same markets, and I still got 70 percent of my income from it. All through the period of the land reform I was afraid the Kuomintang would come back and interrupt my progress.
>
> Actually, in the years 1945 to 1947 we did not desire to fight the Kuomintang. We just wanted to live in peace and be left alone. However, we knew that if Chiang Kai-shek returned here with troops, the Kuomintang would reverse the order of things and we would lose what we had gotten.

The discourse between local border government CCP leaders and the semipeasants in these salt land villages touched on an old truth. Were they not the rural people who had suffered the most from the fiscal mandate of the prewar Kuomintang state? Were they not the ones who were in danger of being driven out of the villages into the ranks of the uprooted floating *lumpens,* cut off from family, friends, and fraternity? Were they supposed to risk the good life they had gotten through collective resistance to the chaos of Kuomintang fiscality by discontinuing the revolution?

One school of Western social science later concluded that modern China had a Communist-led revolution because the Kuomintang army had become incoherent and ineffective. The country people saw the predicament of the Kuomintang state a bit differently: their indestructibility was dependent on their self-initiated, persistent collective defense of their market way of life, and so they had no choice but to mobilize to prevent the weakened state from engineering a comeback. The land revolution would be carried to its logical conclusion, but mainly to make sure that the Kuomintang center did not reestablish its salt revenue force in the border region. Like the high-flying politicians in the Nationalist government, macro-minded scholars may tend to underestimate the political significance of these semipeasant rebels in a few counties far away from the Kuomintang power centers. Thus a neglected, important correlation: in Puyang, Neihuang, Hua*xian,* and the counties where the CCP had forged a strong alliance with the peasant saltmakers, the party and its popular army were able to withstand the violent return of the Kuomintang army.[61]

When the Kuomintang center launched its offensive against the Hebei-Shandong-Henan liberated base in the winter of 1946–47, the semipeasants of the salt market stood by the party. They watched in trepidation as the Kuomintang troops slaughtered the men in charge of the local CCP branches, dismantled the peasant associations, and called on the landlords to help run the army campaign of retaliation against Communist leaders. They were alarmed when *peasants* in their native village party branches declared themselves satisfied with their thirty *mu* and one oxen, gave up their party membership, and voiced fears of jeopardizing land reform gains by fighting the Kuomintang. The saltmakers stayed with the CCP, for it was the institution that promised integration into the market life of the emergent nation. Abandoning hope for a reversal of Kuomintang despotism, they threw down the gauntlet to the armies of Chiang Kai-shek.

Fleeing their villages, they connected with district and countywide militias designed to augment the armed power of the PLA and roamed the countryside with guerrilla army units that helped the PLA alternately avoid and attack the Kuomintang. On returning to their villages, they prepared their communities for the final showdown with Chiang Kai-shek.

What precisely was their contribution? To begin with, they shored up their party branches by purging the wavering elements who urged a retreat to peaceful agricultural production and away from the struggle with the Kuomintang state. There were only a few such rattled peasants in each of the villages under study, but they were now out of the CCP forever. Second, they brought with them modern weapons obtained from their participation in the Anti-Japanese War. They convened the peasant associations to denounce Chiang Kai-shek and drive home the logic of maintaining the sovereignty of popular organs of village power, which they declared was the only alternative to the despotism of the central government and its militarized fiscal machinery. These local organs had, in alliance with the CCP-led liberation army, allowed them to both defend and expand their market interests against the centralization of Chiang Kai-shek and his insatiable salt inspectorate. And finally, to make sure they did not end up an isolated minority, the peasant saltmakers announced their intention to redistribute all of the remaining village lands to the poor landless peasants whose poverty and powerlessness had left them out of the early rounds of land reform. Preaching the destruction of the Chiang Kai-shek dictatorship, they politicized the process of transferring land to the poor so as to strengthen internal village solidarity and prepare the way for a massive entry of the poor into the PLA.

When we couple this popular insistence on gains from the internal market with peasant reports of the returning Kuomintang troops seizing salt wheelbarrows, taking salt weighed on the market scale without paying for it,[62] and plundering salt harvests within the villages,[63] the concept of political relative deprivation seems to offer an even surer clue to why this semi-peasant subgroup got involved in the civil war. The template of the salt market network, as opposed to the presence of the CCP itself, was the most accurate guide to the distribution of support for the Communist Party in the civil war. This is why, for example, in Fanzhuang many peasants, while refusing to join the CCP, nevertheless promised the party recruitment agents that they "would do whatever you want us to do."[64] Joining the CCP was risky, but failing to unite against Chiang Kai-shek and his state revenue forces was riskier. The peasant saltmakers who supported the CCP did so from a perspective on the performance of the Kuomintang state that looked like this (see Figure 1).[65] Clearly, a rising crescendo of mass political mobilization followed Kuomintang attempts to eliminate market-related enterprises in the 1932–33 period and then again in 1946–47, after which salt market proceeds surged.

THE SILENT MARKET REVOLUTION AND THE LAND REVOLUTION

The three-phased process of land redistribution turned some marginalized people back into tillers, increasingly dependent on agriculture. As grain production for household subsistence became their preoccupation, they gladly let go of the rigors of rural marketing. One in four villagers interviewed said that tilling the land was better than involvement with the trade and transport activities they had relied on in the Republican era. Yao Zhenbian spoke for many of his counterparts in salt land villages when he said, "Salt making was much harder than tilling the land. We had to get up before sunrise to carry the salt-encrusted earth back to our households, then carry the water, then soak the earth, and then boil the water well into nightfall.

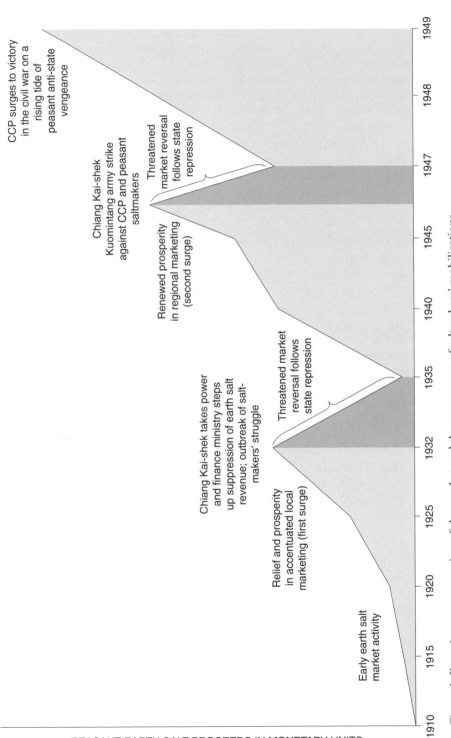

PEASANT EARTH SALT PROCEEDS IN MONETARY UNITS

CCP surges to victory in the civil war on a rising tide of peasant anti-state vengeance

Chiang Kai-shek Kuomintang army strike against CCP and peasant saltmakers

Threatened market reversal follows state repression

Renewed prosperity in regional marketing (second surge)

Chiang Kai-shek takes power and finance ministry steps up suppression of earth salt revenue; outbreak of salt-makers' struggle

Threatened market reversal follows state repression

Relief and prosperity in accentuated local marketing (first surge)

Early earth salt market activity

1910   1915   1920   1925   1932   1935   1940   1945   1947   1948   1949

Figure 1. Kuomintang suppression of the market and the occurrence of saltmakers' mobilizations

From doing this work, we were more tired than when we tilled the good land. When making salt we had to consume more grain in comparison to cultivating the land. So giving up working the bad earth was a good thing."[66]

Nevertheless, it must be pointed out that living purely from agriculture was possible for only a few families, even *after* land reform. Yao Zhenbian's introspection did not reflect the situation of the great majority of village people. Yao could act on his preference for agricultural-based subsistence because he had received twenty *mu* of fertile land. Also, by 1947 Yao was the top CCP leader in Qian Foji. Though Yao occasionally still produced nitrate for sale and invested his proceeds in a grain trade business, he had less and less time for selling earth salt.[67]

In contrast, most common villagers were heavily committed to salt production for the market long after the land revolution. Hawking this product in the markets of the border area was absolutely critical to their survival, and to their pursuit of profit, well into the post-1949 period. We cannot grasp this hidden market dimension of the civil war period by relying solely on the testimony of the quasi peasants who became the CCP leaders of border area villages, both because they were able to use their lineage *cum* party connections to acquire enough of the best land and because, being increasingly dependent on both agricultural-based income and rewards derived from party-based patronage, they were too busy with politics and agriculture to actively pursue the market. The great majority of country people had a different history. They still operated in the world of petty trade, the only way they could develop the land they recently had received in a productive manner.

For most, the risks of relying solely on agriculture for survival were extremely high even after the final stanza of land revolution. For one thing, few families actually received three *mu* per capita. Apart from the fact that CCP leaders of the major lineages often allocated the highest-quality land to themselves and their close kinfolk, many villagers voluntarily declined the land due them because they did not possess the family labor power to cultivate it. For another thing, much of the land designated for redistribution was still highly saline, and thus unproductive. To take on more land, and to try to wring a living from this bad salt land, was far riskier than relying on the steady income from the old routines of the market. Moreover, although the CCP had declared a three-year tax moratorium in the border area circa 1945, the village people still had to worry about the burden of taxes for a civil war they had to win. Profits from the market, far more than grain crop production, assured them they could pay the public grain tax, which went to defeat the Chiang Kai-shek center. Finally, many of the poorest village people lacked the skills needed to become successful cultivators. If the redistributed land was located far beyond the village, this factor posed a particularly serious obstacle to their enthusiastic participation in the party-led land redistribution experiment.

The land revolution history of Qi Ji underscores this point. As the peasant saltmakers saw it, the land in and of itself did not guarantee a better living. In 1947 nearly one-fifth of the villagers in Qi Ji got land from other villages because much of Qi Ji's land was too poor to till. The CCP leaders of Ba Li Ying district arranged for them to receive 310 *mu* of land to work for grain production. One hundred and ten *mu* of this land were located twelve *li* away in Guozhuang village, the other 200 *mu* lay far beyond. The peasants rejected this offer, saying the land was too far away and that they had no tools, carts, or horses with which to make it pay. The CCP district leaders were unhappy with this decision, and a lively argument ensued. The peasants agreed only to work the 110 *mu* in Guozhuang, where the harvest was at hand.[68] The district CCP leaders were obliged to implement land redistribution by a more popular democratic method, one that did not sacrifice peasant market options for the higher interest of the party.

With all this in mind, we begin to rethink the CCP representation of the popular mobilization occurring during 1947 in this old anti-Japanese base area. This was not a land-to-the-tiller movement pure and simple. Most villagers were actively siding with the CCP because its leaders stood for what they most cherished: the chance to reaffirm the permanence of the market and their right to pursue its rewards. The peasant saltmakers led this silent market revolution (a revolution the Communists would later betray, as they proved far more effective than the Kuomintang in curtailing earth salt production for the market in the Great Leap Forward)[69] on the plains of Hebei, Shandong, and Henan during the civil war. This movement was not principally the product of CCP-inspired mutual cooperation or credit given by the CCP liberated area government. Nor was it a secondary "minor commodity movement" within a larger Communist Party–administrated agricultural renaissance in which the peasant majority took grain crop production as the key link in livelihood.[70]

The data on both Qian Foji and Qian Kou clearly and consistently illustrate the central importance of market prerogatives in the goals for which the peasant saltmakers were fighting during the civil war. Table 1 shows how significant the market remained in the lives of village dwellers. Of eighty peasant families surveyed in Qian Foji, nearly all still produced earth salt for their own consumption; fifty-five families, or 69 percent, still made salt for the market even after the final round of the 1947 land revolution. The data only begin to reflect the importance of deeply structured market forces in rural society and the important role of the market community in preparing the ground for the Nationalist government's destruction.

A substantial number of village people felt they had little choice but to continue making salt. The proceeds from their salt trade were essential to survival, they said, and to rising above subsistence, either because they still were working marginal lands or because they did not receive enough land to resume the role of full-time tillers. This was true even for some of those who had committed themselves to the CCP and had taken on leadership roles. Even after receiving twenty *mu* in the land redistribution, 10 percent of Yao Yiliang's yearly income came from producing and selling salt, 20 percent came from selling peanuts, and 70 percent came from grain crops. The profits from salt and peanuts sometimes yielded extra income for household essentials and occasionally for agricultural investments.[71]

Yao Peiji, who had relied on sales of earth salt for 30 percent of his income up to 1945, had fled the Kuomintang salt police with fellow peddlers in the early 1930s and joined the CCP in 1938. A combination of salt trade, grain trade, and rural transport work saw his family through the dearth of 1942. Yao remained a CCP member until 1945, when he "got nothing from the land revolution." "I was angry and could not understand why the party leaders did not redistribute land to me at the time," he says. "I was a middle peasant, but there were people who were poor peasants who were better off than me—even before they got the land."[72]

In fact, Yao Peiji's household had seven *mu less* tillable land after the 1947 land revolution than in 1937. They had sold land and lost land to *fenjia* in the intervening decade. Throughout 1945 Yao had survived by tilling land, peddling grain, and selling salt—now only 10 percent of his income. However, in the period of the civil war, when he became head of village public security, Yao Peiji actually stepped up his salt making. The market for this product enabled him to navigate the turbulent political waters of the period. He recalls:[73]

> At this time, we had only thirteen *mu* of land, and we got by on this land and on the salt we sold in Qian Foji. The market fairs were bustling then. Over ten thousand people came here each market day. Occasionally we could have as many as forty or fifty thousand people here over the course of a market cycle. Of course in the harvest season few people came here. However, in the off season thousands of peasants came to buy our salt. In this period, life was getting better for us. I had less land, but the salt market was booming. The salt was more expensive then, and my son could help me make a little more earth salt than I had produced for the market in the past.

Many of the land-hungry semipeasants who had gained the land needed to provide for their basic living expenses were still reluctant to give up the market and join the ranks of pure tillers. Their progress in food crop production was inextricably linked to their ability to plow small profits derived from marketing back into agriculture. Feng Tianhua, whose family received more land than it could manage in the land reform movement of 1947, clarifies this relationship between the market and the land:[74]

Ever since the time of my grandfather, my family had made earth salt. We were the first saltmakers in Qian Foji. We made salt before Liberation in 1945, and after the land reform of 1947.

Prior to 1945, we had seven people and six *mu* of land. We were among the poorest people in Qian Foji. In the famine of 1942 we had sold our six *mu* of land at the price of twenty *jin* of grain per *mu*.

We returned here from east Nanle in the spring of 1945. In the land reform we got twenty-five *mu* of good land. After receiving the land, however, we still made salt and sold it in Qian Foji market and Yuancun market. We also produced nitrate. We earned nearly one thousand dollars annually from the two. From the new land we got about 3,800 *jin* of grain per year. This was enough for us to survive on as a family.

We had become a family of tillers. But in the winter and spring, when there was little to do in the fields, we produced salt. We were able to save part of the income from the salt trade and use it to buy some bricks to build a house. With it, we paid for the meals of the neighbors who helped us build our home. We also invested our salt market income in farm implements, plow animals, carts, and seeds. These investments enabled us to improve the land, which brought a better life.

Actually, the land reform not only gave land to us poor folk, but also made it possible for us to incorporate our farming activities into our marketing activities, even though this was just taken for granted and not publicly proclaimed. At least 50 percent of the peasants in our village continued to make salt after the land reform.

As Skinner's work suggests,[75] to proprietary folk, agriculture was an integral part of a market world in which small village entrepreneurs freely entered into exchange for profit and, when successful, used the returns to strengthen both the economic security of their households and the political leverage of their village *cum* market communities against the untimely claims of central government fiscality. Whether through the politics of evasion, legal protest and petitionist logic, or armed struggle, the country people had maintained this right to the market over the half-century before the Kuomintang found ways to remove it in the interest of state making.

By the end of WWII they had reestablished this right through their involvement in the CCP-led resistance against the Japanese and the weakened Kuomintang state and were committed to upholding it through supporting the CCP and its popular army against the Chiang Kai-shek center. The Western conception of land reform mobilizing the rural people in civil war is only partially correct,[76] for it misses this important point. That conception was fostered by unsubstantiated land revolution rumors by Kuomintang city folk,[77] by the dramatic tales of college-educated CCP activists who descended on the villages to take over the land revolution work,[78] and by the reports of American relief workers and journalists who visited the Hebei-Shandong-Henan border region under the auspices of the Communist-led government.[79] The spokesmen of Chiang Kai-shek's central government happily embraced this conception, for it helped to conceal their attack on the natural market-based capitalism of the country people. Thus, when the ambassadors and advisors to American leaders Franklin D. Roosevelt and Harry S. Truman met with high-ranking central government officials to facilitate the formation of a national political coalition incorporating the Communists in 1945 and 1946, they were effectively screened off from the popular movement that CCP leaders would be able to rally against Chiang Kai-shek in this part of the North China plain. As Feng Tianhua points out:[80]

> Once we could put the money from the market into the land we were thoroughly committed to the Communist Party. We did not want the CCP to fail because our fate was bound up with that of the party. It was only natural for us to think that if the Chiang Kai-shek Kuomintang had won control of the country, its leaders would have tried again to set up a capitalist state, and still make money from the sea salt. This would not have been good for us, because they would have come back and sent the salt police to repress our salt making.

Virtually all villagers were in agreement on this point. As members of a market community, they had entwined themselves with a native Communist political movement that had further empowered them to keep Kuomintang state makers from enforcing the claims of the fiscal center. They even knew that the Kuomintang used part of the money earned from salt revenue to support its crack central army commands.[81] They were stuck in a dangerous political situation, and there was no turning back because their own long-term collective struggle for the market had projected them into the emerging struggle for state power between the Kuomintang and the CCP.

By the eve of the civil war this subgroup of country people had become the main thrust of the Communist movement in the border region. They were the force that moved the CCP forward, that allowed the party leaders to develop armed power at the village, district, and county levels, and that facilitated party attempts to create alliances with other rural groups against the Kuomintang's shaky fiscal and military system. The pressure of the semi-peasants striving for the market was a major factor enabling the Chinese Communists and their popular army to bring down the Kuomintang center when Chiang Kai-shek and the Four Big Families decided to forgo a coalition government with the CCP and launch an armed offensive against the liberated base in early 1947. In the face of this impending Nationalist government repression—which was indirectly backed economically by the most powerful Western nation*—their contributions to the CCP cause proved vital to the revolutionary victory. Moreover, there is ample evidence that the

---

*According to the United States Information Service, the U.S. provided the Chiang Kai-shek government with $3 billion in loans between August, 1945, and March, 1948. Cf. Mary Austin Endicott, *Five Stars Over China*, 462.

outburst of popular support for the CCP was stimulated by a vision of the party as a partner in a thrust to prevent the Kuomintang state from destroying the melange of political associations the peasant saltmakers had formed to protect their expanding manufacturing and marketing economies—peasant associations, county militias, and the PLA.

These rural people were even more dependent on their market pursuits in bad times. They remember the Republican era as the worst of times if only because the Kuomintang state, in its search for revenue, sought to squelch the market adaptation they were naturally accentuating. Most accounts of the unfolding of the CCP-led mass movement in the North China plain during the civil war ignore this peasant fear of the Kuomintang state threat to the market. Yet this factor was critical in mobilizing the smallholders of these seemingly closed salt land villages to collectively participate in the CCP-led insurgency against the Kuomintang in the crisis moments of the civil war.

Clearly, these semipeasants were desperate to prevent the agents of the Kuomintang state from interfering with their land-use rights, which included the right to decoct salt *within* their villages. Half of their struggle was for closure, that is, for warding off the intrusive armies and police forces of the centralizing dictatorship of Chiang Kai-shek. Yet to convert the salt they teased from the earth's crust into some value, these same village people were obliged to form transvillage associations, whose collective political activities were aimed at securing their access to the market—the alternative to begging, forced migration, and banditry. Regional CCP leaders facilitated their efforts to move these people to support the PLA during the civil war by fastening on the paradox of peasant politics in this particular border area: the same conservative semipeasants who were strengthening the ramparts of village self-defense systems were the vanguards of market anarchy and consequently were prepared to link up with extralocal CCP forces to preserve the prosperity that had prevailed since the early 1930s, when the Communists had consorted with local protest leaders to keep open the earth salt market.[82] Fearing that the Kuomintang army, and its bandit allies, might shut down the market and reinstitute economic insecurity, they held the key to collective antistate action at the district, county, and regional levels. They were even candidates for the growing interregional *cum* national CCP-led war against central government commands.

In 1946–47, the CCP organized this vast subgroup of market-bound village people around the local issue that constantly had strained relations with the Republican administrative state. Following Popkin's wisdom,[83] we can see that these quasi peasants, though initially reluctant to join the CCP insurgency, proved to be some of its most audacious supporters. The affluent leaders of the salters proclaimed their support for the Agrarian Law of 1947, which promised that all of the poorest village people would receive land in a third round of land reform. Their proclamation drew in the land-hungry peasants and solidified the villages against the Kuomintang.

For example, in Qian Foji, the six-person family of Yao Zhangyin had only one *mu* of salt land before land reform and depended almost entirely on the earth salt market to barely make ends meet. The nine *mu* of land received from landlord Yao Jinshan's household in the last round of reform, coupled with exchanging bags of earth salt for grain in the markets of Feng Di, Si Gang, and Er Zhao, permitted Yao's family to achieve basic food security. Thus, Yao recalls, "We feared we might lose what we had gotten if Chiang Kai-shek had returned. This is why, when we held mass meetings for the third round of land reform in the summer of 1947, the Kuomintang was the prevailing topic. We knew that if it was not defeated, Chiang would return and help the landlords take back the land and force us to make salt secretly again."[84]

THE PEASANT SALTMAKERS AND CIVIL WAR

On 26 June 1946, Kuomintang central army commanders began mobilizing 1.6 million troops to surround and attack the CCP base areas on the North China plain.[85] Chiang Kai-shek personally gave the order to concentrate 300,000 Kuomintang soldiers to destroy the Hebei-Shandong-Henan liberated base area.[86] Commanders of the PLA responded by warning the country people of an attack, which began in late June.

In an effort to recapture Puyang and reestablish Kuomintang power north of the Yellow River, Ding Shuben reassembled the twenty-ninth army in Kaifeng and marched ten thousand troops into Dongming County. At the same time, the Kuomintang Fortieth Army was regrouped in Anyang city under Yang Faxian, the former puppet army commander in the Daming-Nanle theater. After absorbing twelve thousand bandits under the leadership of Hui Long in Wei County, Hebei, the fortieth army struck deep into Nanle, Daming, and Puyang. Finally, in late 1946, a third Kuomintang force began advancing on the border area. This was the new fifth army, under commanders Zhou Qingchuan and Wang Sanzhu. The leader of the strongest bandit force in the Hebei-Shandong-Henan border area at the end of the Anti-Japanese War, Wang Sanzhu was the son of a former Kuomintang district leader in Hua County. Summoned to confer with Chiang Kai-shek in Zhengzhou, Wang was made commander-in-chief of the anti-Communist forces in northern Henan. Operating in collaboration with Zhou Qingchuan, he led a bandit force of twenty thousand to attack the CCP in Hua County and assist the central government army units in recapturing the border area.[87]

Although these scattered Kuomintang forces lacked unity, their campaigns were loosely coordinated by the crack central army unit under the command of Ma Fawu, who, in consultation with Chiang Kai-shek, simultaneously launched a drive on Handan County, which had become the headquarters of the CCP-led Border Region Civil Movement and an important military induction center for PLA recruits.[88] The advance of Kuomintang forces against Handan, the northern gateway to the liberated base, and the subsequent battle for Qi Ganzhang, or Flag Pole City, marked the beginning of the civil war on the lower perimeter of the North China plain—a war in which the Kuomintang took no prisoners, sent CCP members scurrying for sanctuary, and slaughtered peasant activists.

CCP base area leaders were pessimistic about their ability to effectively counter this large-scale assault. While the possibility of coalition with the central government elite faded with each new clash of Kuomintang and CCP-led field forces, the CCP magistrates in Puyang, Nanle, Hua County and elsewhere still were frantically convening meetings of students, gentry, and peasant leaders to find ways of forestalling the eruption of civil war.

By early 1947 Chiang Kai-shek's forces had gathered momentum. The Kuomintang Fortieth Army had penetrated some of the vanguard CCP villages in the liberated base. From January 1 to January 23, these Kuomintang army units occupied Nanle County town and prepared to attack Daming and Puyang, which would have given them strategic superiority in this vast border zone of the North China plain.[89] They launched a campaign to seize the grain supplies of the salt-making villages, driving CCP village leaders from home ground into a growing stream of "party transients" in search of PLA protection or putting them to the sword. By March, the border area was engulfed in the swelling war for the lower northern Chinese plain, the gateway to Kaifeng, Xuzhou, and Nanjing. When it came to carrying out war mobilization work, the CCP faced a serious dilemma. Although its agrarian political coalition held, the capacity of the party to mount a quick, unified, and continuous armed counterattack from all of the villages of the countryside was limited. The peasantry—the so-called "main force" of the revolution—did not answer the CCP call for civilian sacrifices in the intensifying clashes with the Kuomintang army; peasant association leaders in many villages were hard pressed to keep the full-time peasants from abandoning their party affiliations or from disappearing from war service assignments altogether. Although some of the rootless poor did find their way into the ranks of the PLA, their numbers did not swell, and the progressive land reform program meant that thousands of previously marginal beggars, migrants, and petty bandits could rediscover a subsistence niche as tillers. Those who did not tended to lend their services to the Kuomintang army and the pro-Kuomintang landlords.

When the Kuomintang army commands stormed the Hebei-Shandong-Henan liberated area in early 1947, the country people who played the critical role in supporting the PLA were the semipeasant traders, peddlers, and purchase agents who had given resistance to the state-building plans of the supreme Nationalist government leaders since the establishment of the Nanjing government in 1928. Until threatened by unconstrained state violence, these alienated market-bound quasi peasants had shunned extremist politics, voicing a strong preference for the moderate, reform-minded agenda of the CCP during the anti-Japanese united front and the first and second phase of land reform.

Why did the quasi peasants who only a decade before had avoided confrontations with the Kuomintang authorities, pursued remedialist protest via legal means, and turned to retaliatory violence only as a last resort suddenly decide to join with the CCP-led PLA in violently bringing down the central government of Chiang Kai-shek? If there was one overarching reason why these country people willingly risked death in revolution, it was the conviction that they would lose what they had acquired through the collective struggles of the past if Chiang Kai-shek and his clique were to reposition their people in county governments and reinsert their tax agents locally. They saw clearly the implications of what Lloyd Eastman pointed out forty years later: The central government had lost a great deal of its revenue base during WWII, including the salt tax, and without immediately recovering this source of revenue, among others, the Kuomintang state leadership faced the prospect of runaway inflation[90] and, worse, runaway soldiers. Peasants also knew that the central government recovery of the Changlu salt area, and the salt tax, figured in the Kuomintang scheme to stabilize the economy of the state and the pay of its soldiers. A resuscitated central government would reimpose state making to recapture this source of revenue. Such a development, to their way of thinking, meant economic deprivation and possibly death.[91]

It is shortsighted, I think, to depict peasants as people without politics, as the unwitting cannon fodder of the CCP-led revolution. The villagers were conscious of the state-making process that had impinged sporadically on their lives throughout the Republican era.[92] They knew what life had been like when the Kuomintang had ruled the border area in the 1930s, what it was like when the CCP and its resistance army had ruled the roost during the War of Resistance, and what it would be like under the Kuomintang again. They knew they would become a "problem" to high-level Kuomintang planners. They listened attentively during the mass rallies of the summer of 1947 when the Communists attempted to convince them that central government money men would use violence to evict them from the salt lands—but they did not need convincing.[93]

All of the antistate resentment expressed in the low-profile collective protest activities of the past welled up and exploded in the form of massive popular vengeance to help the PLA repulse and destroy the Chiang Kai-shek center and its military clients in the civil war. This explains why so many of the peasant saltmakers said they were "getting revenge" when they journeyed beyond their villages on war service assignments for the PLA and why

many of them say they talked mainly about how to beat down the bureaucratic capitalist group in the Chiang Kai-shek government during the mass
meetings of the civil war, and only secondarily about landlordism. It may
also explain why they fought so ferociously against the minority of landlords
who aligned with the Kuomintang in the 1946–47 counterrevolution. If
these landlords had taken back their croplands, these "half-peasants" would
have lost the lands *as well as* the market, and been abandoned to the whims
of landlords, loan sharks, and local government charity. Such was not the
life for which they had struggled.

Peasants from nearly every village I visited said that their participation in
guerrilla warfare during the Anti-Japanese War had taught them the effectiveness of achieving their goals by armed struggle and that this political lesson gave them the idea of overthrowing the central government officials.[94]
The prewar saltmakers had no real army. Militarily weaker than the salt
police and the Kuomintang army units backing up the police, they had
been reluctant to move from more peaceful collective protest means to violent insurgency to overcome the intransigence of the central government
and its *Shuijingtuan*.[95] But now they could fight in or alongside the PLA, and
they were skilled in the use of modern weaponry and force.

These small proprietors and petty traders had not been stripped of their
basic social rights by landlords, and although the Kuomintang army invaded their villages briefly during 1946–47, they actually never lost the social
guarantees they gained from their market ascent. Thus although the pre-
dominant factor motivating them was economic interest,[96] the indignities
suffered when Kuomintang soldiers again violently intruded into their lives
unquestionably added fuel to the fire and turned them toward the CCP in
the civil war.[97]

The larger issue at stake was dignity, which for the peasant saltmakers
meant the right to utilize market rewards to reaffirm the worth of family,
mainly within the circle of close kin but also in the village collectivity. On
returning to the border region, the Kuomintang police, army, and bandit
units rudely violated the right of these semipeasants to conduct their daily
lives in a dignified manner, verbally and physically abusing them in villages
and marketplaces. Illegal seizures, beatings, cursings, and murders heightened popular anger and facilitated the fairly rapid CCP-led mobilization for
the PLA victory in the civil war. Liu Chaoyang, like his counterparts in Qi Ji
and other salt land villages, served as a cook and munitions carrier for the
PLA during the civil war. Why, I asked Liu, if he was not a CCP member, did
he help the PLA? He replied, "I was once beaten by the troops of the New
Fifth Army. I was just carrying my young son in the village streets, and the
Kuomintang troops suddenly entered Qi Ji and seized me. They interrogated me. They asked me if I was a militia member. I told them I was a timid
peasant. But the Kuomintang officer hit me in the face. This happened in
early 1946, right after the Japanese surrender. . . . At that time, the Kuomin-

tang government lost popular support because its local armies were out of control."[98]

Many peasant saltmakers remember the 1946–47 Kuomintang counter-revolution as belonging to the same long-term state-making process that had led to humiliating treatment prior to the civil war. Looked down upon by Kuomintang commanders, Feng Tianhua was still resentful of treatment by Yang Faxian, the subcommander in Ding Shuben's twenty-ninth army and the leader of the puppet army. On returning to Qian Foji in a big army truck during the Japanese occupation, Yang Faxian had kicked over Feng's sweet melon basket and scolded him for daring to sell his "dirty melons" in front of Yang's headquarters, leaving Feng to pick up the scattered melons one by one. "This made me feel as though I were being treated like an animal," recalls Feng.[99] Thus when Yang Faxian developed his forces with Kuomintang help after the Japanese surrender, Feng quickly embraced the CCP mobilization for civil war.

The political notes stored in the memory of Sang Chunhai reveal a similar history. Recalls Sang, "In 1947, when the scale of struggle expanded into a national affair, the people of our village were, in a sense, more determined to fight because through our struggles with the salt police we knew the true nature of the Kuomintang. At this critical point, we knew that the Kuomintang was a powerful state, with more soldiers and better weaponry. But we were confident the Kuomintang could not win."[100] An indignifying experience had taught Sang that the Kuomintang could not count on popular support. In 1939 Sang had been abducted near Qian Foji by Shi Yousan's fortieth Kuomintang army. The soldiers kicked him and pressed him to serve as a guide. Sang led them astray and later escaped. But the affair left a bad impression. "By way of comparison," says Sang, "the CCP-led troops kindly asked us if we would like to be their guides, and they called young men brother and old men uncle when they asked us to guide them."

In short, the civil war derived its savage character in part from peasant vengeance over a process of dehumanization fueled by Kuomintang state oppression. The peasants of the earth salt market equated the PLA counteroffensive of 1947 with their desire to drive on from profit to dignity and power. Although highly politicized by the high stakes of Kuomintang state making, they were not preoccupied with the third phase of the land revolution. Experienced in collective action and armed struggle, they took up the challenge of long-distance, highly mobile war service work and battle for the PLA.

Among the most pressing of war services was food supply. The market-bound peasants, with surplus to spare, took the lead in collecting grain, storing it for the PLA, and shipping it to the front lines. The peasant saltmakers of Fanzhuang contributed and carried grain to the PLA during the battle for Huaying, in Henan and to the Battle of Liangshan, in Shandong. Wang Maiji, who did not join the CCP until 1958, became a runner for the

Hebei-Shandong-Henan liberated area government in 1945.[101] Afterwards, he passed messages to different villages for the government and went to tell them to get the public grain ready for the PLA. His companions, Wang Wenxun and Zhang Xiaoxun, were not CCP members either. Still, they gave of their grain and made sure it got to the troops. Why? With market security and land reform, they all say, both rich and poor could get something to eat and have a good life. Alarmed and angered by the Kuomintang New Fifth Army, which in late 1946 had raided Fanzhuang and threatened their progress, they shuttled grain to the PLA because it had supported their salt making and land redistribution activities.[102] Qian Kou and Qian Foji, with their stronger CCP ties, poured as much grain as could be spared into the PLA.

Liu Yunxing, a peasant saltmaker from Qian Kou, helped the PLA with food supply throughout the civil war. A longtime peasant association leader, Liu had resigned from the CCP in 1947, when the CCP district officials declared him too compassionate to carry out antilandlord work. Disgusted with the CCP and never a member of the PLA, Liu nonetheless supervised the collection of the grain tax for the PLA from each village household throughout the war and personally carted it from Qian Kou to a PLA grain storage facility. When state death squads killed several peasant association leaders and stalked Liu during the 1946–47 Kuomintang strike against Qian Kou, he was forced to flee to the safety of relatives in Lu Zhou village. Liu Yunxing's ability to stay on home ground, to stay in the market, and to survive was from this point on dependent on the defeat of the Kuomintang state—grain flowed to the PLA from such quasi peasants because they knew their political interest.[103]

A second form of support for the PLA was one in which the peasant saltmakers specialized: the mobilization of arms and ammunition. When the civil war broke out, the CCP war provisioning department in each county asked the village people to bring bullets and guns to the battlefields for PLA soldiers. The people of Qian Foji combined in small work groups of four to six to scavenge weapons from crimson-stained battlefields. Yao Zhenbian, who led one such group, recalls,[104] "We went to the battlefields in pairs, and there was one cart for every two persons. After the battle was over, we collected guns from the fields and made sure we got the good ones for the PLA. We also armed ourselves with higher quality weapons. We then took the captured guns to Yanggu county, Shandong province, where there was a base area for the PLA. We regularly transported grain and guns for the PLA."

Without ammunition, the captured arms were of little use against the firepower of foreign-supplied Kuomintang commands. All through 1947, peasants frantically gathered leaves and firewood to produce saltpeter (potassium nitrate),[105] which constituted four-fifths of the chemical base of gunpowder.[106] This material provided the PLA soldiers with loaded shells, but the Kuomintang troops periodically faced a shortage of live ammunition. The salt-manufacturing villages along the Wei and Nitrate rivers, all with a long history of resistance to Kuomintang state making, took the lead in delivering saltpeter to the munitions plants and military command posts of the PLA.[107] This "powder rush" to the PLA was produced by rural people who stood to benefit from bringing down the Kuomintang state.

Auxiliary intelligence work and backup security constituted a third dimension of the saltmakers' contributions. Wang Wenxun and his friends in Fanzhuang gathered intelligence for the PLA during their market routines throughout 1946–47, reporting back to CCP district headquarters on the changing location and strength of Kuomintang forces. The other side of intelligence work, disinformation, sometimes proved to be as hilarious as it was hazardous. Recalling his tour of stretcher-bearer duty to Da Shizhuang for the battle of Chaoyuan, Liu Chaoxun of Qi Ji says that it turned out there were no wounded soldiers to carry: "The PLA asked us to walk around this area for a whole night. We were to leave our footprints in the vicinity of the area in order to mislead Kuomintang intelligence into thinking a big PLA offensive was in the offing. So I walked for a whole night. At dawn I saw that we had walked in circles and travelled a distance of only three *li* all night long."[108]

Though not a CCP member, Liu Chaoxun was a member of the Hua County militia and thus part of the auxiliary security force of the PLA. The militias, in which the peasant saltmakers participated in large numbers, were committed to helping the PLA stave off the first and second strikes of the Kuomintang forces against the liberated base in 1946–47. After recapturing Anyang, for example, the Kuomintang sent two thousand troops to destroy the CCP-PLA in Neihuang. The PLA was outnumbered two to one, but its political commissars were able to line up hundreds of militia members from scores of villages. Yao Zhenbian and thirty members of the Qian Foji militia in Nanle actively engaged the Kuomintang in this battle.[109] Of course the PLA did not always come out on top; but its troops were often able to separate into small groups and disperse into the villages. The peasants of Qian Kou harbored PLA troops throughout 1947 and provided them with the "clothes of the common people" so that they could slip across enemy lines to rendezvous with their regular units.[110]

Stretcher-bearer duty was another important dimension of war service work. This dangerous task was shouldered by the peasant saltmakers. Yao Zhenbian, the co-leader of Qian Foji's saltmakers' struggle and the head of the Qian Foji militia, formed stretcher-bearer groups in 1946–47, leading them to Qi Ganzhang in Handan to fight the first major battle of the civil war.[111] In this battle, they carried the wounded to PLA field hospitals at Bei Gou market in Hebei.

After 1942, Yao Zhenbian had sold his salt south of the Handan battle front, and during the civil war he used market connections to find recruits for stretcher-bearer service. So did Yao Peiji, who also carried stretchers for the PLA just after the Kuomintang Fortieth Army attacked in early 1947. His testimony reminds us that participation in the war was stimulated as much by the return of centralized state violence as by CCP propaganda:[112]

> I left Qian Foji for one month to carry stretchers for the PLA during the War of Liberation. I carried the wounded soldiers to the PLA field hospitals in the Hebei-Shandong-Henan border area. I also went to the Battle for Liangshan town in Liangshan county, Shandong, where I carried the dead bodies on stretchers to a forest. There I buried them. This was a horrific task because many of the soldiers' corpses were decapitated, or without limbs and hands. It was so horrible that when I returned to Qian Foji I could hardly eat for a full month. I knew this battle was to defeat Chiang Kai-shek. My resentment against the Kuomintang soldiers who had beaten me was the most compelling reason why I joined in this mass action to support the PLA against Chiang Kai-shek.

When the civil war escalated, these semipeasants joined the PLA and rushed to die on the battlefronts. As Lucien Bianco suggests, the Chinese Communists raised a "peasant army" from the villages of the North China plain;[113] part of its vanguard came from the "half-peasants" of the salt lands, people with a market outlook, people whose market adaptations to the atrophy of agriculture and the advance of the modern fiscal state had been challenged by the military forces of the Kuomintang center. Their participation in the PLA took them beyond the confines of the border area and into the widening arena of the civil war, making them national political actors. They fought with their own specific goal in mind: to drive Chiang Kai-shek and his salt moguls out of power and capture the National Salt Bureau of the central government in Nanjing.

On 22 March 1947, one hundred thousand peasants from the salt-making villages of the border area gathered to help the PLA go on the counteroffensive in the battle of northern Henan, killing five thousand Kuomintang soldiers and recovering Puyang County.[114] On 30 June 1947, one hundred thirty thousand of their counterparts left behind fields and ponds to mass at Lin Pu market in Pu*xian*, Shandong, and then assisted the PLA in striking the fifty-fifth, sixty-sixth, thirty-second, and seventieth Kuomintang armies, killing fifty-six thousand Kuomintang soldiers in the battle for southwestern Shandong.[115] Here, on the lower edge of the North China plain, the Nationalist troops suffered serious losses in the battles at Handan, Puyang, and Nanle in Hebei; Yuan Chao*xian*, Caozhou, Liangshan, and Yanggu in Shandong; Hua*xian;* and Neihuang in Henan in 1947.

The peasant saltmakers were in the thick of all these county-level battles, performing war service assignments and occasionally fighting alongside the PLA troops. They came to them as militia men with machine guns slung over their shoulders, as armed escorts of horse-drawn carts full of PLA artillery, machine guns, and explosives. These tough rural people cleared the narrow, barely navigable dirt roads and shouted directions to the horse-cart drivers following the PLA in its advances and retreats, to make sure arms and ammunition were readily available.[116] A hellacious fight took place at Wu Lu village in Hua County in the spring of 1947. Braving heavy Kuomintang artillery fire, the peasant saltmakers maintained the logistic support for the PLA to defeat the New Fifth Army under Zhou Qingchuan.[117] Although this PLA victory was not reported in Nationalist government newspapers or on major world news wires, such skirmishes were the precursors of the downfall of the Chiang Kai-shek center. Zhou Qingchuan was later killed in the battle of Huaihai by PLA forces under the command of Liu Bocheng, whose army was filled with semipeasant lads drawn from the saline villages of this remote border region.

In the larger North China region, too, these semipeasants played a critical part in turning the tide against the Kuomintang, serving as soldiers in two decisive battles: the battle of Qi Ganzhang in Handan, in which the central government commander Ma Fawu went down to defeat, and the battle for Anyang, the Beijing-Hankow rail city from which the Kuomintang, the Japanese, and now again the Kuomintang had dispatched troops into the border area. The latter battle was one of the fiercest armed struggles of the civil war in the North China plain. Tens of thousands of rural people moved constantly back and forth from the villages along the Nanle-Wei county border in Hebei Province to Anyang city, a distance of 120 *li*, carrying grain, stretchers, and grenades to PLA troops pushing into the city. Bloodied by Kuomintang air force bombs and beaten back on three separate occasions, the PLA suffered many casualties in this savage encounter. Alongside the fallen soldiers in the streets of Anyang were scores of peasant saltmakers from the villages of the border area. Yao Lishen, Yao Zheng, and Yao Yiliang fought in this battle with sixty people from Qian Foji village.[118]

In 1947, CCP-led peasant associations in the salt land villages kicked off a massive PLA recruitment drive and convened sending-off ceremonies for thousands of villagers between the ages of eighteen and forty-five, joining the armies of Zhu De, Liu Bocheng, Chen Yi, and Lin Piao. Qian Foji sent 120 men into the PLA; Qian Kou and Qi Ji each sent 50; Fanzhuang sent 20. Twenty-five Qian Foji men and 20 Qian Kou men lost their lives. As many Western scholars have pointed out, the causes of the Nationalist debacle were mainly *internal:*[119] the Kuomintang tax increases, factional splits within the Kuomintang and its military, the tactical stupidity of Chiang Kai-shek and his favorite generals. The central government did not just "fall" or "disintegrate," however. It was *pushed down* and *pulled apart.* And the peasant saltmakers were part of the popular armed collective force doing the pushing and pulling in national war theaters.

All 120 of Qian Foji's PLA recruits, for instance, were in one of the ten crack PLA regiments sent from the Hebei-Shandong-Henan liberated base to join with Lin Piao in the decisive Liaoshen campaign to liberate Northeast China from Nationalist control in the autumn of 1948.[120] Buoyed by this victory, many of them went on to fight with Liu Bocheng and Chen Yi in the battle of Huaihai, the outcome of which left Nanjing, the capital of the central government's salt affairs empire, within PLA gun sights. Six of Qian Foji's PLA warriors lost their lives in the Huaihai campaign.[121] Yao Yichang, who survived this campaign, describes the process whereby these semipeasant warriors jolted the Kuomintang state:[122]

> In late 1947, I helped defeat the Kuomintang. I shared a cart with Yao Jingsheng to carry grain, ammunition, and grenades to the PLA in Xin county, across the border in Shandong. I was there for one month.
>
> Later, in the September army recruitment campaign, I joined Chen Yi's New Fourth Army. My unit went to fight at Ma Ling, Dao Kou town, and then on to the banks of the Yellow River. We crossed the Yellow River and fought in the Battle of Xuzhou. Thereafter, I participated in the Battle of Huaihai, which took place east of Xuzhou, in Jiangsu. We then prepared to cross the Yangtse to capture Nanjing. We gathered in small boats hidden in the river inlets, and then made the crossing at night. There were lanterns on the boats and the shoreline, and there were a lot of fireworks over the water that evening. This was a spectacular sight.
>
> If Chiang Kai-shek had come back, we would have lost our good life. [But] we knew if we united, as we had in the period of the saltmakers' struggle, we could become a powerful force and defeat Chiang Kai-shek's government. So many of us joined the PLA because we knew we could win the civil war in the end.

With the capture of Nanjing, the Nationalist government salt bureau, which had extended the central state drive for revenue deep into the inland village world, suddenly was in the hands of those who had suffered from state making. There is little doubt that the modest semipeasants of the market came marching with the PLA into the cities of Kuomintang China to take over the institutions of state power—including the salt administration in Beijing, Tianjin, and Nanjing. The modern political dilemma of these rural people, grounded in their previously imperceptible relationship with the gargantuan revenue goals of Kuomintang fiscal oligarchy, compelled them to go with the CCP and to collectively support the party in the critical engagements of the civil war, thrusting the PLA to victory after victory on distant battlefronts. Thus did the violent attacks on the market rights of these quasi peasants dialectically produce the worst of all political effects for Kuomintang state makers, as they suddenly moved with the PLA to make certain that the Kuomintang fiscal center did not return to challenge their community.

By now it should be clear that these quasi peasants of the salt lands were not hard-line Communists. They taught some of the local CCP leaders the importance of the market in popular livelihood and also of a strategy of institution building grounded in popular collective antistate action. If the mandate of the CCP was based on the politics of eliminating the suffocating connection between state and society, then perhaps the October 1 revolution carried with it the hope, if not the promise, for a world with righteous government. This hope, though repeatedly dashed by the ultraleftist impulses of the postliberation Maoist party, is still alive in the villages of the Hebei-Shandong-Henan border area.

TABLE 5   Qian Foji Village Land Revolution Survey

Name	Number of People	Pre-1947 Landholding in Mu	Earth Salt Making	Post-1947 Landholding in Mu	Earth Salt Making
Yao Ran	2	5	yes	7	yes
Yao Yu	4	5	yes	15	yes
Yao Zhi	4	5	yes	18	yes
Yao Dai	3	4	no	22	no
Yao Zheng	7	18	yes	18	no
Yao Zhenxiang	5	20	no	27	no
Yao Zhimin	10	0	yes	23	no
Yao Zhenyu	4	18	no	18	no
Yao Zehnyue	4	18	no	18	no
Yao Zehmin	5	11	no	24	no
Yao Jiming	4	17	no	18	no
Yao Wuxi	3	7	yes	15	yes
Yao Zhengang	4	10	no	15	no
Yao Lancheng	3	7	yes	15	yes
Yao Zhigang	5	18	no	18	no
Yao Guanjun	3	12	no	12	no
Yao Weizheng	3	5	no	12	no
Yao Lishen	6	7	yes	27	yes
Yao Zhangjen	6	1	yes	10	yes
Yao Peiling	3	9	yes	12	yes
Yao Peifu	5	7	yes	18	yes
Yao Quanxi	5	15	yes	18	yes
Yao Baoyin	4	4	yes	21	yes
Yao Lao	6	18	yes	8	yes
Yao Zhangyin	4	3	yes	12	yes
Yao Zhenbian	5	4.5	yes	22	no
Yao Peiji	6	20	yes	13	yes
Yao Yichang	7	2.5	yes	21	yes
Yao Yiliang	5	5	yes	20	yes
Yao Xijan	6	4	yes	22	yes
Yao Yixin	4	2	yes	15	yes
Yao Famin	4	2	yes	10	yes
Sang Fang	4	5	yes	13	yes
Sang Qingxin	7	7	yes	17	yes
Sang Fuping	3	3	yes	9	yes
Sang Quan Li	6	10	yes	?	yes
Sang Wenli	7	6	yes	18	yes
Sang Faliang	3	5	yes	14	yes
Sang Chen	5	4	yes	14	yes

(Continued on next page)

TABLE 5 — *Continued*

Name	Number of People	Pre-1947 Landholding in Mu	Earth Salt Making	Post-1947 Landholding in Mu	Earth Salt Making
Sang Chunsheng	5	4	yes	?	yes
Sang Qingrui	6	10	yes	18	yes
Sang Chunyuan	5	7	yes	17	yes
Sang Zhangling	6	13	yes	?	yes
Sang Guiling	6	8	yes	18	yes
Sang Zhaorui	4	4	yes	14	yes
Sang Zhaolin	4	4	yes	14	yes
Sang Wenlin	4	8	yes	13	yes
Sang Guigun	5	7	yes	15	yes
Sang Yunzhen	2	7	yes	?	yes
Sang Xi	2	5	yes	?	yes
Sang Chunguang	5	7	yes	19	yes
Sang Mingzhai	2	4	yes	2	no
Sang Chunhai	6	10	yes	16	no
Sang Qinglin	2	3	yes	6	yes
Sang Daoying	4	3	yes	11	yes
Sang Mingli	2	2	yes	7	yes
Sang Hauqing	2	2	yes	2	yes
Sang Zhanlin	3	4	yes	10	yes
Sang Zhanren	1	2	yes	5	yes
Sang Chunxue	3	4	yes	10	yes
Sang Puke	4	4	yes	12	yes
Sang Bingwen	5	10	yes	13	yes
Sang Puyi	8	30	yes	30	no
Feng Tianhua	5	6	yes	5	yes
Feng Da	3	2	yes	6	yes
Feng Jinyong	5	10	yes	?	?
Feng Xun	7	15	no	20	yes
Feng Cunshan	7	2	yes	22	yes
Feng Lijiu	7	18	yes	18	yes
Feng Quankui	1	0	no	3	?
Wang Han	6	6	yes	15.5	no
Wang Fa	5	6	yes	15	yes
Wang Huai	6	2.5	yes	13.2	yes
Wang Guohua	4	3	yes	10	yes
Wang Hai	5	4	yes	9	yes
Wang Guoli	6	2	yes	17	yes
Wang Shilin	4	3	yes	10	yes
Wang Guozhi	6	2	yes	17	yes
Wang Qing	5	11	yes	11	yes

Conclusion

The involvement of China's rural people in the revolutionary process remains unparalleled, yet the question remains: did the Communists win the countryside, or did the Nationalists lose it?[1]

The Kuomintang debacle is still a dramatic, widely misunderstood instance of state failure: the Nationalist government failed partly because its mode of state strengthening was fundamentally incompatible with the way in which rural people made their livelihood. This book demonstrates that the pre-1949 CCP-led revolution was, to a significant extent, a broad popular struggle to preserve the market against the aggrandizement of the Kuomintang state. It was a struggle against modern state making, that is, against "the growing intrusion of state power into societal processes."[2] The marginalized peasants who marketed the salt of the earth for their existence were exemplars of this pattern in the Hebei-Shandong-Henan border area.

To link the microscopic analysis of the pattern of protest and CCP-led insurgency in this saline zone of the North China plain to a new general theoretical interpretation of the rise of revolution in all of pre-1949 China would be premature. Nevertheless, *Salt of the Earth* suggests a hypothesis that can be tested against the revolutionary experience of rural dwellers in other regions of China where the CCP was successful. Only future research will prove or disprove the relevance of this "hypothesis-generating" case study;[3] I make no claim that the argument works for the rural regions studied, or yet to be studied, by other scholars. Drawing from the political experience of the peasant saltmakers, I present a five-point hypothesis of the origins and development of popular participation in the CCP-led revolution in the countryside and compare the theoretical contribution of my study with several important Western social science works on rural revolution in pre-1949 China.

For years social scientists tended to locate the major precondition for peasant mobilization taking the form of revolutionary insurgency in the presence and political activity of the CCP.[4] *The case at hand, however, reveals that the protrusive fiscal apparatus of an increasingly assertive central government was a far more critical factor prompting the rural people to join together in collective protest.* As Lloyd Eastman points out,[5] the Kuomintang sowed the seeds of its own destruction, for the causes of its defeat were substantially the internal political activities of the Chiang Kai-shek–led central government. To be sure, Kuomintang state making was undertaken in an exacting international economic environment and was often undercut by internal quasi-government competitors, but the unrelenting fiscalism of Nanjing proved decisive. Whereas one school sees the failure of the Kuomintang in its efforts to extend its bureaucratic machinery down into local society and to remold peasant life to serve state interests,[6] this historical case study suggests that it was the centralized state push for deeper penetration that precipitated rebellion. The attempt of the Kuomintang fiscal elite to place state revenue machinery in the market-oriented villages of the remote countryside was a systematic factor giving rise to peasant mobilization and community-based collective protest. As Eastman, Bianco, and Duara have argued,[7] state tax pressure was a critical stimulant of peasant mobilization in the Republican period. Whereas Benjamin Schwartz is correct to point out that the Mao-led CCP won by conducting its revolutionary experiment in remote territorial sanctuaries,[8] it is too rarely noted that the Chinese Communists were able to link up with rural people in the so-called "base areas" because Kuomintang state makers in fact had penetrated such remote places with extractive revenue machinery, stimulating collective resistance and rebellion that the Nanjing government could not control. The subsequent Kuomintang police repression of this popular mobilization against increasing state extraction proved to be a major reason why rebellion fed into full-blown revolution.

This book provides several clues to the relationship between state coercion and the rise of popular collective protest taking the form of revolutionary political mobilization.[9] As the level of Kuomintang state repression increased, so did popular resistance, but clearly antifiscal protest proved to be more resilient in rural counties where the police arm of the Kuomintang revenue state was somewhat overextended and not consistently conjoined with centralized army coercion. Far from atomizing peasant society, police repression further homogenized the shared experiences local people had with central rulers, facilitating the process whereby the CCP could find a common basis for effectively calling on them to join in fighting against state power holders—not landlords. Hence the pattern of state-induced popular grievances in this geographic region became self-sustaining, providing a seed-bed for Communist-led insurgent groups to resonate with rural people who had a long history of self-initiated, community-sanctioned collective resistance and who were prepared to take revenge on Kuomintang central power holders.[10] Operating in local market communities where thousands of rural people had risen to repel the Kuomintang revenue state, the Chinese Communists found the grievances that had galvanized rural dwellers in failed central state policies—policies that signified economic ruin and family disintegration.

Weak as it was, the Kuomintang state was strong enough to severely damage the market-geared earth salt economies of marginalized peasant households. It was the collective political action of the market community formed by these country people—and not just Kuomintang factionalism, Kuomintang army ineptitude, or Kuomintang administrative paralysis—that eventually defeated central rulers. The semipeasants of the salt lands in this part of the North China plain had attacked the main vanguard of the Kuomintang state fiscal apparatus *before* the appearance of the CCP. Their rebellions not only constituted a crucial brake on Kuomintang state making, but also eventually provided local Communist leaders with the mass power to put an end to Kuomintang rule. Their contribution to the October 1 revolution was thus primarily the product of their participation in a long-term fight to defend the terrain of a regional market network, and only secondarily the product of CCP leadership, organization, and propaganda.

Elizabeth Perry's insightful study of the Anhui-Jiangsu-Henan area locates the preconditions for rural collective protest in the responses of differently endowed groups of rural people to the impact of environmental disaster and state demands,[11] showing that poorly endowed peasants coped with environmental crisis by engaging in predatory strategies of acquisition,[12] while wealthier country people pursued a protective mode of protest aimed at defending their "precarious advantage."[13] For the Huai-bei area, Perry finds neither predatory nor protective rebellions could fit with the methodology of CCP-led insurgency,[14] which eventually won by a novel revolutionary strategy independent of the inhibiting influence of "the fetters of local connections."[15] Perry's approach is laudable, for the history of rural-based rebellion in the Hebei-Shandong-Henan border area can be understood fully only in reference to how environmental changes affected the life chances of the village people and how they adjusted to such changes.

Yet the evolving position of the peasant saltmakers, and their movement into rebellion and onto Communist-led revolution, suggests a somewhat different historical pattern of rural political mobilization. The peasants of the salt lands were indeed poor, marginalized people, but they made a living via a strategy of market adaptation to long-term agricultural degradation, and in the Republican period they were able by and large to cope successfully with subsistence crises. This market-driven strategy of survival did not automatically involve the plunder of societal or state resources, and the initial collective protests to preserve it were essentially defensive and lawful. In redefining this peaceful market adaptation as unlawful and mobilizing deadly force to eliminate it, Kuomintang fiscal authorities placed themselves in a "state of war"[16] with tillers attempting to resecure their livelihood in the marketplace. The rebellious behavior of these rural people reflected not a predatory response to environmental downswing, but rather the increasingly contentious bent of long-term collective resistance to growing centralized state interference in a decentralized, trade-directed adjustment to food insecurity. Ironically, this adjustment promised a starlit alternative to poverty, so that the CCP caught on among the country people by siding with their mobilization against the state attempt to reverse recently earned prosperity.[17] *Thus, the revolution was, to a significant extent, an outgrowth of CCP involvement in a protracted community struggle against the antimarket acts of an aggrandizing Kuomintang tax state, for the Communists would gain popular support against Kuomintang rulers by trumpeting fair taxes and market forces.*

Salt of the Earth drives home the importance of sociopolitical relations between peasants and local Communist leaders in relieving the pressure of Kuomintang state making and organizing popular resistance to Japanese aggression in rural North China. The Communists, intimately connected with local country folk whose collective actions stalemated Kuomintang state making prior to WWII, borrowed from and built on a rich heritage of popular collective resistance to state expansion. CCP-led anti-Japanese guerrilla forces in the Hebei-Shandong-Henan anti-Japanese base were formed by educated rural youths, many from comparatively wealthy families;[18] but clearly, the CCP anti-Japanese army benefitted from enlisting local peasant leaders who were experienced in forming popular collective resistance to professional state forces. In the crucial first stage of war these peasant leaders answered the party's call to mobilize resistance to Japanese rule.[19] The Hebei-Shandong-Henan anti-Japanese base was created through united front tactics that stressed friendly relations between returned student Communists and protest leaders and the participation of people from different social classes in the resistance—the striking dual characteristic of the prewar antistate protest movement of the peasant saltmakers.

The CCP-led wartime resistance, therefore, was not necessarily a radical departure from the mass rebellion of the prewar period. By arming the country people and uniting them with a disciplined army that was driven by political necessity to honor the salt market nexus of local folk, the Communists only augmented their power to wage collective resistance.[20] To be sure, as Kataoka and others have argued, Communist military power was another key precondition for revolutionary growth.[21] However, the protest movement was also a decisive factor in fueling the revolution, for the rural people who joined in the violent political actions of the CCP army would take such actions as continuing a righteous struggle against state *cum* suprastate forces blocking a market adjustment to agricultural decline. Of course the Communists were members of a nationalist movement, but in this rural North China border region their wartime experiment was grounded in a historical form of popular rebellion that served the goals of resistance and revolution. *CCP success in creating a coalition supportive of its revolutionary purpose was substantially the product of a complex Kuomintang state-making process that alienated both local students who originally were eager participants in Kuomintang county-level committees and educational circles and local protest leaders who initially were predisposed to cooperate with Kuomintang county government, so that the mistaken policy of the central government, as much as the organizational prowess of the CCP, brought the party and the country people together in common pursuit of alternative government.*

The Leninist-centered paradigm of the CCP as an alien political elite foisting rebellion on passive peasants, of party leaders extending their hegemony down to the villages to organize local collective actions, of the party intervening in peasant struggles to raise peasant consciousness of "genuine insurgency" and inserting its own leaders in place of inept peasants seems a bit misplaced. The Communist leaders in the Hebei-Shandong-Henan border area were themselves part of a native local elite. To be sure, to paraphrase Schwartz, they were persuaded that "state power in the proper hands" could lead the common people to "the good society";[22] but they did not need to show peasants how to protest, for local popular struggles were erupting virtually everywhere they were operating. These struggles were started by country people who saw the "Communists" not singularly or primarily as "party cadres," but rather as members of a community with moral standards that were being threatened by Kuomintang state making. Thus, for the CCP, the movement into the popular struggle to hold on to these standards was not based simply on a preconceived political strategy for capturing a peasant base. Rather, it too was substantially the product of the faulty policies of the tiny Kuomintang fiscal oligarchy.

Disrupting a market system that was vital to community well-being and damaging effective discourse with local community leaders with whom the Communists shared ties of blood, lineage, and place, the process of Kuomintang state making, tragically, led to the victimization of esteemed, progressive students who had aspired to assume positions in the regionalized patron-client network of the Nationalist government itself, thus setting the stage for their involvement with the market-driven village people. These young student "activists" were originally part of, or connected with, the emergent local Kuomintang establishment. Driven back to the countryside, into the thick of conflicts between the peasant saltmakers and the national

Kuomintang state, they threw in with the CCP-led challenge to the central government, simultaneously discovering shared government-induced grievances with rural people and learning how the local popular struggle was connected with the national struggle for state power.

Whereas some scholars presume that the CCP deliberately and directly mobilized the peasant masses, who proved incapable of initiating collective action for a shared purpose,[23] this study indicates the role of the CCP in mass mobilization was indirect. The Communists welcomed the direct role played by local protest leaders in organizing villagers for collective political action. A focus on central party history, or on why the CCP could build a base in the village world, understates the pluralism of local political interests. This book adds to previous scholarship the vital independent contribution of the decentralized nonparty leaders who devised and directed local protest movements and eventually placed the power of those movements in the service of the regional *cum* national revolution led by the CCP.

As Stephen C. Averill points out, the growth of revolution in rural China was predicated significantly on patterns of local elite interaction with ordinary villagers, and such patterns rarely are comprehensible via macro-analyses of how nationally known Communist leaders solidified peasants to their purpose.[24] For the most part, the local protest leaders in the Hebei-Shandong-Henan border area hailed from, or were linked to, the local elite: the minor gentry; the network alliances of wealthy landlord families and affluent peasant households forming in the newly developing normal schools; the poor peasants whose offspring gravitated to the lowest of county-level government positions via market successes and new schools. Victory was achieved by relying on these local elites to focus the collective energy of the peasantry against the predatory forces of the central government elite—particularly on the marginalized peasants whose families were achieving security and small forms of prosperity by taking advantage of trade, an avenue of advancement that had always been important.[25]

CCP interaction with the market-oriented semipeasants who led villagers in collective protest was crucial for the party's expansion in the Hebei-Shandong-Henan countryside. These village leaders played a central role in making possible the triumph of Communism in rural China. Given their connections to commercial places, they could transcend village politics to organize the power of the market community to form collective opposition to fiscal injustice. Highly mobile participants in local markets, they were active in linking peasants from different villages, in drafting peasant demands, and in steering peasant collective protest toward state agents. Education was also important, for it provided some of these quasi peasants with the knowledge to articulate sensible, community-sanctioned protest strategies, plus the esteem needed to surround themselves with supporters from different peasant audiences and to enter into exchanges with local elites in higher regional educational networks under stress from Chiang-

Kai-shek's modernizing dictatorship. The political status of many of these semipeasant protest leaders raised the chances of the Communists locally. Enjoying connections to, and positions within, the lowest tier of Kuomintang local government, here were local village-based protest leaders with a transvillage life that had an official stamp of approval: Yang Jingcai of Cheng Guan was a jail attendant for the Puyang County government; Liu Chaode of Qi Ji worked for the land tax office of the Kuomintang Hua County government; Feng Yuqing of Qian Foji was a purchase agent with ties to the Nanle County Nitrate Bureau. These local protest leaders relied on their connections to local Kuomintang government to cultivate popular support, using this political resource to mobilize peasants from different villages to oppose the Kuomintang police state usurpation of community resources.

Whereas previous scholarship, perhaps wisely, has put more emphasis on the role of CCP leaders who "made" the revolution, this study places more emphasis on the historical impact of the struggles of local non-Communist, as well as Communist, leaders in helping the CCP build revolution in the deep countryside. Clearly, the CCP has hidden the contribution to the Chinese revolution of these local, often non-Communist protest leaders in bringing the Communists to power. Interfering with their market way of life, the supreme Nationalist power holders alienated these politically astute village people and split them away from their party's state-making project, leaving them to cooperate with local CCP firebrands. It was here, at the lowest tier of the Kuomintang body politic, that the Chiang Kai-shek center really lost peasant China. But the Communists who became the patrons of these local protest leaders did not win by harnessing them to a central party structure. Rather, the Communists defeated the Kuomintang state, and legitimized their own fragile political movement, by encouraging these local champions of community opposition to center rule and by incorporating the protest demand of the peasant saltmakers for decentralized market participation into the platform of the CCP.

This CCP embracement of the popular market was merely a momentary tactic, of course, for the party intended to annihilate the market as soon as possible. Nevertheless, the pre-1949 expansion of the CCP along the abandoned course of the Yellow River clearly benefitted from the "mutually conditioning interactions"[26] (to use Vivienne Shue's apt prose) between the violent elements of the Kuomintang central state and the local protest leaders who stood for peasant market aspirations. Working through these protest leaders, with connections to a marginally dominant Kuomintang and a mobilizing community of market-bound country people, the CCP was able to sustain its challenge to the Chiang Kai-shek–led center from below.

Local protest leaders were conscious of the national and international importance of the struggle against central rulers. To the Communists, in particular, they would play a role in the revolutionary struggle to take back the national state from the predatory forces of the international system. The salt administration of the Republican state had been seriously compromised by the world powers, and Kuomintang state making reflected the new internationalist pressure to transform the salt revenue system into a form of plunder. In challenging the police force of the Kuomintang salt administration, the protest leaders reminded local Communists of the logic of Li Dazhao, the party's co-founder and leading advocate of peasant-based revolution. By the 1920s, when Wang Congwu and his young college cohorts heard of Li, his opposition to imperialism was legendary. Maurice Meisner has noted: "Because of the oppression of international capitalism, he (Li) argued, the entire Chinese nation had been transformed into part of the world proletariat and China was thereby qualified to fully participate in the international proletarian revolution."[27] Thus, internal class struggle was subordinate to the national struggle of all domestic social groups being victimized by foreign predatory forces and their contacts in the fiscal wing of the Republican central state. In this script, the proletarianized victims of externally constrained Kuomintang state makers were the peasant saltmakers, whose leaders were orchestrating a local rebellion that had an important national dimension. Perhaps this was all that mattered to the CCP. The antistate consciousness of these local people, when combined with the antiimperialist proclivities of the Chinese Communists, proved to be a powerful revolutionary mixture: the rebellion of the market-driven peasants against the salt revenue police could take the form of a revolution against capital-seeking Kuomintang state makers who subordinated China's fiscal sovereignty to the demands of international aggressor states. The CCP won in part because its regional leadership grasped that the resistance of this politicized segment of rural people could serve a larger revolutionary purpose.[28]

The Japanese invasion of the Hebei-Shandong-Henan border area broke the back of Kuomintang central state power and, as Johnson has argued, permitted the CCP to fill the power vacuum of fleeing Kuomintang forces.[29] The local Communist leaders were able to accomplish this political task, however, because, as Lyman Van Slyke and others have suggested,[30] they were organizing popular resistance in poor, remote counties located beyond the major Japanese military strongholds on the North China plain that did not suffer much from Japanese army muscle during the early stage of the war.[31] In such rural places, the Chinese Communists rooted their national resistance in a movement of marginalized peasants with whom they had formed a prewar bond of political trust.

To be sure, the Japanese invasion, and the war-induced jolt to central government power, proved to be a critical necessary condition for the emergence of CCP-led insurgency, but the war also gave the Chinese Communists the chance to arm a pivotal contingent of previously mobilized country people with whom local party leaders enjoyed political credibility prior to 1937. The popular leaders of this subgroup knew the Kuomintang state makers had replaced discourse with deadly force and feared that the Kuomintang power elite was bent on obliterating their market approach to livelihood. The country people came over to the Communists during the war because the CCP and its popular army found it expedient to enforce a better market policy—indeed, they had been fighting for such a policy for decades. Joining with the Communist-led resistance allowed these quasi peasants to gain protection from Japanese force, of course, but it also attracted Japanese attacks. At the same time, linking up with the party-army also permitted them to prepare to counter yet another violent Kuomintang antimarket campaign, first by strengthening their local self-defense capabilities and second by becoming part of an extralocal insurgent army. This silent popular shift, which Johnson and others have attributed to patriotic impulses, was also motivated by the social promise of the party's pro-market policy and by the deep-seated fear of a more effective central government comeback after the war. Building on the insights of prior scholarship, this book adds factors that permit us to comprehend the peasantry and village-CCP relations in a more complex manner.

Surely Chalmers Johnson is right that "peasant nationalism" fostered by Japanese repression precipitated massive popular opposition, solidifying a patriotic struggle in villages under CCP leadership. *Salt of the Earth* takes another step, showing that Japanese repression, which peaked in the middle stage of WWII, also ripped apart peasant communities and reduced the CCP and its resistance army to near defeat and desperation: the repression of Japan's 1941 "three all" campaign set back the CCP's wartime base area experiment and correlated with the crash of party fortunes in forming popular village-based resistance to Japanese rule.[32] Operating in the minimally repressed villages of a remote border territory, the Chinese Communists did indeed appeal to patriotic sentiments, but grounded their appeals in a traditional popular culture that provided a paradigm for acting collectively to resist and retaliate against outside predators.[33] The Guangong culture of these country people legitimized community struggle against unrighteous outsiders and promoted values of fraternity, courage, and invincibility—ideals local Communist leaders could resonate with in promoting their party's national resistance message. Neither Kuomintang state enemies nor Japanese foes were successful in obliterating local culture. The CCP could enlist opera players and storytellers to elicit peasant support for its national resistance mission. Young CCP patriots, themselves carriers of a socialist, somewhat vacuous political culture, were pressed to persuade the country people to come together to resist Japanese invaders and save China from further national submission. *The hypothesis of this study is that CCP leaders were most likely able to mobilize resistance to Japanese rule within rural areas where their involvement with prewar antistate protest had underscored its mobilizational potential and where the country people, having preserved its purest forms through continuous struggle, were free to welcome its CCP sponsorship against Japanese puppet regimes, but in which neither fully understood or embraced the other, setting up a post-1949 party war on the peasantry.*

As Mark Selden has shown in reference to the land reform process in the Shen-Kan-Ning base area[34] and Yung Fa-Chen has demonstrated in reference to land redistribution in the Henan-Anhui-Jiangsu base,[35] peasants also were drawn to the party's wartime resistance by a socioeconomic program that appealed to their basic social needs. According to Chen, the Chinese Communists won by promoting campaigns of peasant radicalism against landlords and local Kuomintang regimes within "a facade of transclass unity,"[36] using class struggle to seize political power from the Kuomintang.[37] In contrast, the wartime united front in the Hebei-Shandong-Henan anti-Japanese base area was based on the politics of market reform, not on class struggle. The keys to the CCP success in forging it are obvious. On the one hand, the CCP anchored its program to improve peasant livelihood in a struggle for market justice, that is, in a fight to remove the central state hold on rural markets—not on redistributing the wealth of the rural elite. The political logic was that the poor could prosper through market participation, not through radically altering rural class relations. Such a premise enabled Communist leaders to appeal to landlords and lesser gentry to join in an anti-Japanese united front with peasants, peddlers, purchase agents, and others with whom they shared lineage, village, and market strategies of acquisition and empowerment. Eschewing class war and wooing the established subcounty elite by emphasizing the continuity and correspondence of its interests with popular and patriotic groups within a local united front,[38] the CCP won small landlord and gentry figures to the national struggle, sometimes recruiting them into the ranks of the party itself. On the other hand, the successful negotiations of the second united front with the Kuomintang army commanders in the Hebei-Shandong-Henan border area were dependent on a complex pattern of secret cooperation between CCP and Kuomintang leaders locally and on the intimate family and education connections of local Communist leaders and members of Kuomintang county regimes. These local connections, as well as CCP threats and momentary tactics, permitted the Communists to nudge their Kuomintang counterparts to bring their security forces and administrations over to the national struggle and to resist Japanese puppet army rule. One of the reasons the CCP could win these local Kuomintang regimes to national resistance was, of course, that they too were dissatisfied with the improper political conduct of the Chiang Kai-shek center and its dictatorial revenue agents. Thus, the CCP did not necessarily need to resort to replacing these local Kuomintang loyalists in order to expand its anti-Japanese base.[39] In short, during the war the CCP did not betray the subcounty elite by united front tactics, and the united front with the Kuomintang was grounded in a local CCP-Kuomintang alliance whose participants took it as a natural counterbalance to failing Kuomintang central state power. To be sure, the CCP would betray the subcounty elite and many of its members, along with local Kuomintang leaders, would be branded as rightists, but this betrayal occurred after the CCP had seized state power.

Among other means, the CCP rose to power by grounding its revolutionary experiment in the informal economy that lies in the "shadowy space"[40] below the national state and the international market and by supporting peasant expectations of uninhibited market entry—not exclusively by racing to the front of its rivalry with the Kuomintang to replace the market with state monopoly. The Kuomintang center lost, among other reasons, because its fiscal leaders could not craft a state-making strategy to accommodate this popular market economy in the short run and treated it as a threat to state monopoly before coming to grips with the specific factors that gave rise to its very existence. As Skinner's scholarship suggests, the earth salt trade in the Hebei-Shandong-Henan border area was neither the product of modern central state planning nor the result of the spread of European capitalism; it was an example of an embedded native regional market network that linked rural dwellers with a larger society. The CCP won in part by resonating with a community-based struggle to sustain the economic and cultural functions of this "nested marketing system."[41]

Of course to some scholars of power and Communist revolution this study might seem to make too much of the salt market issue in attracting rural people to the CCP during the critical post-1937 decade.[42] They would be correct to point out that the sheer force of the CCP-led army surely was a factor in accounting for the compliance of the region's village dwellers with the schemes of their Communist rulers—no doubt many of the peasants of the saline zone were highly conscious of pressure, and perhaps threats, when they decided to cooperate with the CCP. Of course, too, as pointed out in Chapter 7, the Communists, for their part, did not have much of a choice, for they had to embrace the making of local salt for the market partly out of necessity. Although containing important elements of truth, such a view must not be taken too far, for it is a view that "strip-mines" local and regional political history; furthermore, it underestimates the importance of systematically contrasting the Kuomintang antimarket attacks with the CCP defense, and even promotion, of the market in the decades when the Chinese Communists had to rely on the entrepreneurial activities of local people to construct a sustainable regional political economy supportive of resistance and revolution. This study shows that such a process was not simply, or solely, the product of CCP force, that many of the semipeasant supporters of the CCP had mobilized to defend a habitual pattern of marketing prior to WWII, and that CCP policies supportive of the market did have a mobilizing impact when it came to counting on the rural people to help resist the Japanese occupation and help defeat the Nationalist government.

Although the rebellion to preserve and pursue the market was a response to an attack from Kuomintang state makers who were, like their counterparts in Qing and early Republican years, attempting to cope with claims and constraints imposed by a draconian international fiscal regime, it was not simply a peasant reaction to the global expansion of North Atlantic capitalism, as Wolf's model of "peasant wars" would predict.[43] Rather, this was a popular struggle to pursue a form of domestic petty trade that was significantly dependent on a complexly sequenced combination of Republican central state policy mistakes and, intermittently, a breakdown in the local enforcement of centrist monopoly.

If the Nationalist fiscal leadership had settled for less revenue and respected its existence, this peasant economy might perhaps have fit with Kuomintang state-making designs. In rushing to improve the efficiency of revenue collection, however, the Kuomintang sought to destroy a market network that marginal rural dwellers had come to equate with survival, without completing land rehabilitation programs that would have allowed the poor to return to agriculture or forming patron-client networks to assist those who could not make it in the global market sector or the state economy. The country people in this part of rural North China faced an unusually irrational and savage form of state making. By pressing its own definition of state economic development on the peasants of the saline earth sector, the Kuomintang fiscal elite created a burst of even greater economic opportunity for the practitioners of this embedded peasant market system, then attempted to smash it. The CCP could appeal to these marginal semipeasants to join in a "people's war" to stop both the Kuomintang state and the Japanese from destroying their newfound market prosperity.[44]

This book maintains that the local Communist leaders mainly coached, and strengthened, a popular movement against Kuomintang officials and that the CCP went back to the popular movement in order to help organize its anti-Japanese resistance during WWII and help its armed forces defeat the Kuomintang government during the civil war. That the CCP came to lead these market-bound semipeasants into the politics of antistate insurgency requires us to rethink the Scott-Popkin debate[45] over the nature of peasant economy: was the CCP-led revolutionary process anchored in the "moral economy" of local nonmarket forces, as Scott's model would imply, or in the "rational economy" of peasant market choice, à la Popkin? There is no question that the semipeasants in the Hebei-Shandong-Henan border area were pursuing core social values linked to local subsistence rights, survival, and the struggle for autonomy. But whereas for Scott moral economy seems to mean the antithesis of the market, this book illustrates that for the country people the market equalled subsistence, life, and even prosperity. What was moral was rational, and what was rational was the pursuit of the socially enhancing rewards of the marketplace. Hence the great irony: the rural poor took the CCP's pledge to support their struggle for survival as a commitment to help them move from rags to riches through the mechanism of the market—which some have equated with the source of social dislocation and peasant suffering.[46]

The testable hypothesis of my case, therefore, reads like this: the CCP's revolutionary experiment flowered profusely in base areas where the party was best able to align with marginalized rural people whose adaptations to agricultural distress had involved them in similar forms of informal marketing activities comparable to the earth salt trade of the Hebei-Shandong-Henan border area, which in turn drew them into similar types of market struggle with monopoly-seeking Kuomintang state makers.[47] Poppy cultivation, alcohol production, and tobacco leaf production come to mind, and all beg the question: did Chiang Kai-shek's central government also attempt to tax, or suppress, the village people who grew poppies, brewed a part of their grain, or prepared tobacco for domestic petty trade—as it had done to those who decocted salt—in order to improve its revenue position via monopoly?

Some evidence suggests that the struggle between the Kuomintang state and the market community incorporating the peasant saltmakers in the Hebei-Shandong-Henan border area was an exemplary case illustrating processes operating in other similar types of struggle across rural China. The popular struggle over state taxation of opium, to take one example, seems analogous to the salt making case. Kuomintang-trained police force efforts to eradicate poppy cultivation for the domestic market provoked popular antistate protest in Jiangxi and facilitated CCP growth in the Kung River area during the late 1920s.[48] In this case as well as that of the peasant saltmakers, the specific rural locations of popular struggles to defend the market from Kuomintang state making correlated with the places where the CCP formed its base area. Whether the geographical expansion of the violent Kuomintang tax state ultimately proved as crucial to the CCP's revolutionary victory as other factors illuminated by scholarship on the CCP "base areas" is now an important question for academic inquiry.

Popular collective struggle inspired by intrusive Kuomintang state making is of course only one factor in the complex local socioeconomic environments in which the CCP rose to national power. The broader explanatory value of this hypothesis-generating case must be evaluated against the usefulness of approaches that stress different factors, such as the state of the rural economy, the cultural predisposition of peasant subgroups, the institutional rivalry of Kuomintang and CCP forces interacting with the rural populace, and the divergent protest movements in different regions. It may be that the CCP rose to power through different types of popular movements in different regions, so that the legacy of antistate struggle proved decisive in one region, an important active ingredient in the CCP-led insurgent coalition in another, and simply irrelevant in yet other regions. Perhaps, as Bianco's work would suggest, the CCP was able to win national power by wooing the leaders of "disparate local protest movements,"[49] linking their political strengths from point to point and lifting them onto a plane of sustained national revolutionary struggle through the institution of its popular army.[50] But one point is unequivocally clear: in the Hebei-Shandong-Henan border area the CCP and its army moved from point to plane by resonating with semipeasants involved in a long-standing war for a market threatened by the Kuomintang state.

Of course, the CCP also was involved in a competitive parallel war with the Kuomintang state to swallow up the private sector so as to replace the commerce of the country people with state monopoly. The CCP undoubtedly attempted to do this in different base areas, by forming companies to control trade in salt, opium, and other important durables and by demanding that its lower units comply with the goals of this state-run commercial sector—and Yung Fa-chen has documented the ascendance of this anti-market strategy in CCP base–area policy.[51] Surely, too, the party's commitment to the natural petty trade of rural people was tempered by protostate impulses to establish centralized administrative controls over the market-geared economy of the peasant saltmakers. Although CCP concessions to "folk capitalism" in the short span of pre-1949 party-peasant interaction contributed to the rise of a popular market-driven revolutionary political economy, the promise of "people's war" gave way to an elite-led, centralized CCP dictatorship in which the popular market "became a target for postwar class struggle."[52] Indeed, the Communists were to become even more powerful state makers and to continue the centralized political assault on the private sector, subordinating the market liberty of the semipeasants who helped lift them to victory to the involuntary production of grain "surpluses" for state accumulation.

Nevertheless, the pre-1949 local CCP leaders in the Hebei-Shandong-Henan border area derived a great deal of political legitimacy from leading the country people to pursue this matrix of market opportunity, allowing popular market networks to coexist with limited forms of protostate commerce. While Kuomintang state leaders lost sight of such a strategy of governance, the CCP seized on it, creating a broad coalition of country people who knew how to utilize the "tactical space"[53] of their semiperipheral regional market system, and the power of its collective defenses, to wage a protracted war against a self-defeating Kuomintang political order. The Communists proved to be better students of the political and cultural dynamics of this market issue than their Kuomintang foes, taking full advantage of the failure of the narrowly based, fragile Chiang Kai-shek fiscal center to establish a nonpredatory, non-violent political economy supported by local elites and semipeasants.[54]

NOTES

PEASANT MEMORY AND ORAL HISTORY

1. Craig, *The First Agraristas*, 14–15.
2. Connerton, *How Societies Remember*, 4, 17, 22–23, 30.
3. For two seminal and stimulating works on folk politics, see Scott, "Protest and Profanation," 1–38; I, 11–46; Burns, *The Poverty of Progress*, especially chap. 6.
4. Halbwachs, *On Collective Memory*, 52–53.
5. Connerton, *How Societies Remember*, 20.
6. Ibid., 20–21.
7. Babbie, *The Practice of Social Research*, 214–215.
8. Halbwachs, *On Collective Memory*, 54–59, 62–65, 71.
9. Cf. Sabean, *Power in the Blood*, introduction, conclusion.
10. Halbwachs, *On Collective Memory*, 82–83.

CHAPTER 1. BUREAUCRATIC CAPITALISM AND THE EMERGENCE OF POPULAR ANTISTATE PROTEST

1. Moore, *Social Origins of Dictatorship and Democracy*, 496.
2. See Susan Naquin, *Millenarian Rebellion in China* and *Shantung Rebellion;* Esherick, *The Origins of the Boxer Uprising;* Perry, *Rebels and Revolutionaries in North China, 1845–1945;* and Bernhardt, *Rents, Taxes, and Peasant Resistance.*
3. Cf. Pomeranz, *The Making of a Hinterland*, 116–118.
4. Johnson, *Peasant Nationalism and Communist Power.*
5. Selden, *The Yenan Way in Revolutionary China.*
6. Wou, *Mobilizing the Masses*, 379.
7. For this view, see Johnson, *Peasant Nationalism and Communist Power*, 1–14.
8. Wei Hongyun, ed., *Huabei Kangri Genjudi Jishi*, 552.

9. Wou, "The Impact of Differential Economic Change on Society in Honan in the 1920s and 1930s," 3–4. Cf. Wou, *Mobilizing the Masses,* 15.

10. On this point, see Pomeranz, *The Making of a Hinterland,* 16, 153, especially chaps. 4 and 5.

11. Cressey, *China's Geographical Foundations,* 171; Duara, *Culture, Power, and the State,* 11. According to Huang, the picture was far more complex: by the twentieth century, peasant households in parts of the North China plain averaged 11.6 *mu* (or little more than 2 *mu* per person), and one-quarter of them were landless. *The Peasant Economy and Social Change in North China,* 103.

12. Myers, *The Chinese Peasant Economy.*

13. Huang, *The Peasant Economy and Social Change in North China,* chap. 1. Although Huang's early work underplays the importance of the market, his more recent work clearly acknowledges it. See his *The Peasant Family and Rural Development in the Yangzi Delta,* 102–105. On the importance of the market also see Brandt, *Commercialization and Agricultural Development,* and Perdue, *Exhausting the Earth.*

14. Friedman, Pickowicz, and Selden, *Chinese Village, Socialist State,* xxi, xxii, and 31.

15. Pomeranz, *The Making of a Hinterland,* chaps. 1–3.

16. Skinner, "Marketing and Social Structure in Rural China," pt. 1, 3–44; pt. 2, 195–228; pt. 3, 366–399; and "Chinese Peasants and the Closed Community: An Open and Shut Case," 270–281.

17. In referring to the school of economic history that stresses growth, market competition, and better standards of living, Mann has noted that historians accepting this school's premises are prone to ask, with great frustration, "If in fact Chinese society under the Republic was not torn by class conflict, social malaise, poverty, and discontent, how was it possible to garner support for, or even acquiescence in, a revolutionary communist movement?" The answer to this question is to be found in the approach to "peasant economy" I have utilized in the chapters ahead. Cf. Mann, "Misunderstanding the Chinese Economy," 541.

18. On the importance of including the state, see Evans, Rueschemeyer, and Skocpol, eds., *Bringing the State Back In;* Bates, "Agrarian Politics"; Migdal, *Strong Societies and Weak States.* On China see Friedman et al., *Chinese Village, Socialist State;* Oi, *State and Peasant in Contemporary China.*

19. Tilly, *The Contentious French,* especially chap. 1; Ardant, "Financial Policy and Economic Infrastructure of Modern States and Nations," 164–225. A few insightful examples are Evans, Rueschemeyer, and Skocpol, eds., *Bringing the State Back In;* Bates, "Agrarian Politics," 160–195; Migdal, *Strong Societies and Weak States.* On China see Friedman et al., *Chinese Village, Socialist State;* Oi, *State and Peasant in Contemporary China.*

20. Walton, "Debt, Protest, and the State in Latin America," 301.

21. Tarrow, "Big Structures and Contentious Events: Two of Charles Tilly's Recent Writings," 194, 200–202.

22. Compare my logic with the notion that without revenue governments cannot bring about political stability. Snider, "The Political Performance of Third World Governments and Their Debt Crisis," 1269; and his other essay, "The Political Performance of Governments, External Debt Service, and Domestic Political Violence," 410.

23. Bianco, "Peasant Movements"; Duara, "State Involution: A Study of Local Finances in North China, 1911–1935."

24. For the method of history and time span see Braudel, *On History,* 25–52, 70–74. Braudel, however, is talking of even longer spans of time.

25. Scott, "Everyday Forms of Peasant Resistance," 5–35.

26. In attempting to understand why peasants move from avoidance protest to contentious antistate protest, Adas has advanced a bridge theory, in which he suggests that peasants "who engage in the protest of retribution are the most likely to become involved in direct confrontations with elite adversaries." "From Footdragging to Flight," 82.

My own position on this matter is that no one mode of protest automatically signals a prelude to contention and insurgency. Confrontation does not necessarily lead to contention, in part because the state always has to make the next move. My argument is that (1) the repeated applications of state repression followed by (2) a deflation in the institutional capabilities of the state in the context of ongoing protest signals local people they can get away with raising the stakes of the struggle to the level of contention. This, however, is a very complex matter, and Adas may be correct for some cases.

27. I agree with Scott's position on this issue, which seems to be that nonradical, everyday forms of resistance need not necessarily defuse a popular movement or deflect its cadres from effectively taking on their political enemies through open, collective acts of insurgency. See "Everyday Forms of Peasant Resistance," 24–26.

28. See Eckstein, "Introduction. Toward the Theoretical Study of Internal War," 24–25; Deutsch, "External Involvement in Internal War," 107.

29. Almond and Genco, "Clouds, Cocks, and the Study of Politics," 492.

30. Ibid., 492–493.

31. Lijphardt, "Comparative Politics and the Comparative Method," 682.

32. Ibid., 691.

33. This question has been eloquently and more systematically framed by Huang in "The Paradigmatic Crisis in Chinese Studies," 327. Also see Marks, *Rural Revolution in South China,* xv–xvii; Thaxton, *China Turned Rightside Up,* 15; Selden, *China in Revolution,* 246.

34. Cf. Verba, "Some Dilemmas in Comparative Research," 111.

35. Lijphardt, "Comparative Politics and the Comparative Method," 689–692.

36. Compare with the somewhat different, but nonetheless informative, conception of informality and its implications for societal-state conflict and why local people align with insurgents. De Soto, *The Other Path,* xvi–xix, 207–209, 231–233.

37. Cf. Zhao Jibin, "Nongcun Pochan Shenzhong Jinan Yige Fanrongde Cunzhang," 34.

38. Guo Ai, Cheng Guan, Puyang, 9/13/85.

39. Cf. Wei Hongyun, "Lun Huabei Kangri Genjudi Fanrong Jingjide Daulu," 65–71.

40. Ibid., 115.

41. For example, Wang Yuxi of Sha Wo village derived 70 percent of his household income from the earth salt market in the Republican period. Sha Wo, Puyang, 8/6/91. Gen Xinyuan of Cheng Guan village relied on salt making for 80 percent of his family income in the 1930s. Cheng Guan, Puyang, 9/14/85.

42. This figure refers to the participants in fifteen to twenty Hebei-Shandong-Henan border area counties, mainly Puyang, Daming, Nanle, and Hua. Yet another twenty counties from south central Hebei were involved, and still another thirty from Kaifeng also were enveloped by this struggle. Thus the exact number of participants is difficult to establish. The figure of one hundred thousand for Ji-Lu-Yu is from "Zhinan Nongmin Youji Zhanzhengde Shimo," in *Jinan Geming Douzheng Shiliao,* 219. The same article says the struggle impacted the lives of five hundred thousand rural people (220). Wang Congwu has put the number of struggle participants in the Hebei-Shandong-Henan border area at more than eighty thousand, but clearly he is referring to the most politically active of participants, that is, those who formally joined the Transcounty Saltmakers Association around 1932–33, right after the initial victory in Puyang. This figure is conservative for several reasons. First, it does not include the protest villages where there were no formal saltmakers' associations, places like Luo Tun in Qingfeng and Qian Foji in Nanle. Second, it does not include the growing numbers of participants and places like Daming and Nanle after 1933. See Wang Congwu, Gao Kelin, Zhang Huizhi, and Wu Baohe, "Puyang Yanmin Douzheng," 170.

43. Cf. Skinner, "Chinese Peasants and the Closed Community: An Open and Shut Case," 272–273.

44. Rankin's conception of "elite activism" differs from mine. Her argument is that the local elites of late Qing were picking up the slack of weak central state administration by actively mobilizing local resources, thereby expanding the "public sphere." By way of contrast, I think local elites in the Republican era were actively involved in thwarting state intervention in informal local economies that served the interest of the communities in which such elites resided. Cf. Rankin, *Elite Activism and Political Transformation in China,* 10–20, 303–310. For a helpful summary of Rankin's thesis, see Thompson, "Statecraft and Self-Government: Competing Visions of Community and State in Late Imperial China," 190–191.

45. Cf. Liu Qingfeng, ed., "Dongming Xian Yanmin Baodong," 209–210.

46. Cf. Lewis, "Memory, Opportunity, and Strategy in Peasant Revolutions: The Case of North China," 2. Lewis sees this tradition as being located in religious sects. He does not mention the Guandi or Guangong tradition specifically. Nonetheless, I think his point applies to the war god myths. Lewis uses the term "cultural memory" to describe the continuity of this tradition. See 4, 1–7, 30–33.

47. I have benefitted greatly from Prasenjit Duara's illuminating conceptual work on the Guandi myths in North China. Cf. *Culture, Power, and the State,* 35, 139–148, 246–250. The quote is from 144.

48. Ibid., 144–147.

49. Some of Duara's data on the war god tradition, especially pp. 141, 246–249, would support my line of analysis. I accept Duara's argument that the Imperial state attempted to transcribe its own symbolic order on these cults, thus legitimating its political presence locally in some epochs. However, I believe that at the village level the war god tradition was the product of independent popular cultural initiatives and that the Kuomintang ruling group attempted to establish total hegemony over this independent little tradition, which local people kept alive through resistance to state efforts to wipe it out. The kind of evidence Duara brings to bear on this issue in the Republican period does not permit him to fully grasp this

point. Nevertheless, Duara's more recent scholarship would point in the direction of my argument: the Kuomintang state elite forgot, and took little notice of, the importance of what Duara calls "superinscription" and undermined its legitimacy locally by attempting to directly, and forcibly, impose its culture on the same village people its revenue policy was threatening. Cf. Duara, "Superscribing Symbols: The Myth of Guandi, Chinese God of War," 782–784.

50. Scott, "Hegemony and the Peasantry," 283.

51. From talks with villagers in Luo Tun, Qingfeng County, 8/7/91; Qian Foji, Nanle County, 5/15/90; Fanzhuang, Nanle, 8/8/91.

52. Duara's brilliant work *Culture, Power, and the State* presents the Guandi cult largely as the creature of Imperial power, and as the mechanism whereby Imperial elites used official religion to bind local communities to the state (142–144, 146–147). To be sure, Duara thinks that different social groups with particular interests could bring various meanings to the myth (140–141). His basic position is that the Guandi myth integrated villages with the Imperial polity (cf. 142–147). While persuasive, Duara's work nonetheless skirts two fundamental issues, both of which he is aware of. First, it is difficult to test Duara's central thesis because he relies mainly on the myths recorded in stelae, most of which reflected the work of county officials and village elites, something Duara admits (146–147). Although Duara makes reference to "the multivocal myth of Guandi" (146), he has little, if any, evidence of voiced peasant beliefs about Guandi, so that we have no way of knowing whether the everyday beliefs and behavior of local people were stimulated and structured by Imperial versions of this myth. Second, although Duara's invaluable scholarship makes clear that Guan Yu originally was outside of the law—and hence the state— and that this folk deity appealed to marginalized rural people who had to leave their villages to scratch out a living and realize their common interests (140–141), his narrative of Guandi is not focused on the beliefs and behavior of any specific group of marginalized rural people in a specifically defined local and national political situation involving sharp conflict between them and the agents of Imperial symbolic inscription. In other words, the position from which Duara has viewed local politics, as well as his methodology, has inhibited him from testing the integrative potency of the Imperial myth of Guandi when insecure rural dwellers and government officials brought their differing interpretations of the war god's role and mission into political battles in which they were in opposition.

53. Cf. Perry, *Rebels and Revolutionaries in North China;* Esherick, *The Origins of the Boxer Uprising.*

54. Cf. Buck, *Land Utilization in China,* and *Chinese Farm Economy;* Huang, *The Peasant Economy and Social Change in North China;* Myers, *The Chinese Peasant Economy;* Duara, *Culture, Power and the State,* chaps. 1, 4, 6, 7. Also see Duara, "Elites and the Structures of Authority in the Villages of North China, 1900–1949," 261–281. Cf. David Buck's review of Huang's *The Peasant Economy and Social Change in North China,* 127.

55. Here I am following the wisdom of Huang, *The Peasant Economy and Social Change in North China,* 7.

56. Kataoka, "Communist Power in a War of National Liberation: The Case of China," 420.

57. Cf. Esherick, *The Origins of the Boxer Uprising,* 207–208.

58. For an introduction to the *chi dahu* movements, see Bianco, "Peasant Movements," 299–300.

59. On Liangmen and Yaojia, see Tian Yuan, "Wo Zai Puyang Liangmen Yidai Lingdau Nongmin Yundongde Huiyi," 71–80.

60. Wang Zaiduo and Lu Shousen, "Yijiu Sansan Nian Hua*xian* Dongbu Zaimin Fenliang Chi Dahu Douzheng," 16–18.

61. Zhang Zengjing, "Yubei Shaqu Geming Douzhengde Yixie Huiyi," 181–184.

62. For an overview of this struggle, see Thaxton, "Peasants and Porcelain: Collective Action in China's Rural Trade and Transport Sector During the Republican Period," 251–265.

63. Cf. Li Jiangang, "Huiyi 'Xiaocheshe' Douzheng," 56; "Peng Cheng Tuicihua Gongren Douzheng Gaikuang," 61–62.

64. Guo Chenpo, "Daming Yidai Hongqianghui," 4; reprinted in Chen Zhuanhai, ed., *Henan Hongqianghui Ziliao Xuanbian*, 59–60.

65. Chao Zhepu, "Zhinan Geming Ciyuandi—Daming Chishi Gemingshi," 15.

66. Guo Chenpo, "Daming Yidai Hong Qiang Hui," 60.

67. Chao Zhepu, "Zhinan Geming Ciyuandi—Daming Shifan Gemingshi," 15–16.

68. From Tai Hsuan-chih, *The Red Spear Society 1916–1949*, and from my field research in Hua County, 6/14/88.

69. See Perry, *Rebels and Revolutionaries in North China*, 177–180.

70. The most authentic source on the scope of this anti-state movement in the Hebei-Shandong-Henan border area is Liu Cun, *Liang He Yanmin Douzheng*, 154. Although I have limited the focus of this study to the core protest counties of the Hebei-Shandong-Henan border area, a similar struggle against Kuomintang state intervention in earth salt markets took place in Kaifeng, Qi*xian*, Yuancheng, Sui*xian*, and thirty other counties near Kaifeng in May of 1933. Cf. Ding Changqing, ed., *Minguo Yanwu Shi Gao*, 276.

71. Bianco, "Peasant Movements," 282–283, 287, 302–303.

72. Of course it may be that nationally or even provincially, the CCP was able to come to power through other types of popular collective movements. My claim here is only for the geographical boundaries of this border area.

73. Averill, "Local Elites and Communist Revolution in the Jiangxi Hill Country," 286–287.

74. Chao Zhepu, "Zhinan Geming Ciyuandi—Daming Chishi Gemingshi," 1–44.

75. Ibid., 1.

76. Ibid., 5.

77. Ibid., 9–10.

78. Ibid., 11.

79. Ibid., 12.

80. Ibid., 13.

81. An Ming (Liu Dafeng), "Zhinan Wu Xian Dangde Zhanli Yu Fazhan," 4–5.

82. Wang Congwu, "Zhinan Shaqu Dang Zuzhide Fazhan he Qunzhongde Geming Douzheng," 185–186.

83. Wang Congwu, "Zhongguo Gongchandong Lingdau Pu-Nei-Hua Diqu Renminde Geming Douzheng," 48.

84. Liu Yanchun, "Hongqi Piao Zai Puyang," 47–50.

85. Ibid., 51–53. Also see Wang Congwu, "Zhongguo Gongchandang Lingdau Pu-Nei-Hua Diqu," 48–49.

86. The primer on CCP leadership of this movement is Wang Congwu et al, "Puyang Yanmin Douzheng," 170–180. Also see Gao Kelin, "Zhinan Shaqu Yanmin Douzheng," 131–134. Gao Kelin was the key operative of the Hebei Province Special Committee for Southern Hebei (Zhinan Tewei) in 1931. Wang Congwu was the CCP secretary of Puyang County in 1931–32. Based in Daming, Gao informs us that, "At the time the most important activity of the Party County Committee was leading the saltmakers struggle," 131. Gao also says, "The saltmakers' struggles in the vicinity of Neihuang, Puyang, Qingfeng, Nanle, and Hua county all originally were self-initiated," 132.

87. "Wang Congwu Tongzhi Huiyilu," 27–28.

88. Liu Yanchun, "Hong Qi Piao Zai Puyang," 53–54.

89. On this point see Liu Hansheng, "Dang Lingdau Shaqu Qunzhongde Geming Douzheng," 27, 29–30. Liu Hansheng, like many CCP activists from the Daming Seventh Normal School, was a Kuomintang member and used the Kuomintang to support peasant struggles and establish village party branches. According to Liu, even after the national CCP-Kuomintang break in 1927 the local Kuomintang members actually spoke for the CCP and were united in protecting the CCP and supporting its popular legal struggles under the banner of the Kuomintang. Wang Congwu confirms this point, "Zhongguo Gongchandang Lingdau Pu-Nei-Hua Diqu Renmin Douzheng," 47, 52–53, 55. Also see Zhao Jibin, "Huiyi Puyangde Geming Douzheng," 39–41. Zhao says that after 1928 the CCP members of the Daming Seventh Normal School working in Puyang were part of the Puyang Kuomintang and used their Kuomintang labels and liaisons to infiltrate the Puyang Public Security Bureau, the local schools, and the militia, thereby facilitating work in popular mobilization.

90. See Tian Yuan's memoir, "Wo Zai Puyang Liangmen Yidai Lingdau Nongmin Yundongde Huiyi," 70.

91. Wang Zaiduo and Liu Shousen, "Yijiu Sansan Nian Hua*xian* Dongbu Zaimin Fenliang Chi Dahu Douzheng," 16.

92. Tian Yuan, "Wo Zai Puyang Liangmen Yidai Lingdau Nongmin Yundongde Huiyi," 71–73.

93. Ibid., 72–73. Also see He Linliang, "Dang Zai Yaojia Yidaide Fazhan yu Huodong," 143–144.

94. Chang Fusen, "Yijiu Wusan Nian Hua*xian* Qiangliang Chi Dahu Douzheng," 21.

95. Ibid., 19–20; separate interviews of Lui Chaoyang, Qi Ji village, Hua County, 8/9/90; Liu Chaoxun, Qi Ji village, 8/10/90.

96. Wang Zaiduo and Liu Shousen, "Yijiu Sansan Nian Hua*xian* Dongbu Zaimin Fenliang Chi Dahu Douzheng," 16–17.

97. The relief included the giving of relief grain to peasants from some of the disaster stricken villages in Puyang. The CCP enthusiasts with whom I discussed this

matter say the Kuomintang discontinued this practice after 1928–29. However, my chats with peasant saltmakers suggest that it was not discontinued; it tapered off. Zhang Youren, Cheng Guan, Puyang, 9/12/85. Furthermore, Liu Chaode, the leader of the peasant saltmakers in Hua County, praised local Kuomintang officials for their disaster relief assistance in the 1933–35 flood crisis.

98. Cf. Tian Yuan, 73.

99. He Jinze, Yaojia village, Puyang, 9/11/85.

100. Thaxton, "Peasants and Porcelain: Collective Action in China's Rural Trade and Transport Sector During the Republican Period," 251–264.

101. Li Jiangang, "Huiyi 'Xiaocheshe' Douzheng," 57.

102. Ibid., 57–58.

103. On this point, and the Kuomintang-influenced Yellow Unions, see "Zhinan Tewei Gongzuo Baogao," 8.

104. "Daming Yidai Hongqianghui Yundong Shiliao" 116–117.

105. On this point, cf. Perry's intelligent historical analysis, *Rebels and Revolutionaries in North China*, 116–117.

106. Ibid., 216–219.

107. Chao Zhepu, "Zhinan Geming Ciyuandi—Daming Chishi Gemingshi," 15.

108. Ibid., 15–16.

109. Ibid., 17.

110. The history of the CCP in this border area is complex. Liu Dafeng, for example, says that the CCP used the Red Spear Society in Fo Shan to set up the party in Nanle between 1926 and 1929. Liu Feng, "Wo Zai Nanle Xian Fo Shan Cun Geming Gongzuode Jingguo," 44.

111. Lian Enlin et al, "Jinshengdau Baodongde Shimo" 2.

112. Discussion with Nie Zhen, Beijing, 8/4/1990. The CCP, according to Nie Zhen, had little control over the Red Spears and was able to unite with them only temporarily to fight the warlords.

113. Cf. Tai Hsuan-chih, *The Red Spear Society*, 89–90.

114. Again, this interpretation is in line with Perry, *Rebels and Revolutionaries in North China*, 177–180.

115. Chao Zhepu, "Zhinan Geming Ciyuandi—Daming Chishi Gemingshi," 16–17.

116. When I use "rich landlords" here, I am referring mainly to those with several hundred *mu* of fertile agricultural cropland, not those with bad, alkaline land.

117. This pattern, according to Shi Guoqiang, prevailed in Zhang Fuqiu in Nanle County from 1928 to 1931. Nanle County town, 8/6/90.

118. Lian Enlin et al, "Jinshengdao Baodongde Shimo," 4–5.

119. From Yao Peishan of Qian Foji, in Beijing, 5/4/90.

120. Wang Peili, Sha Wo village, Puyang, 8/6/91.

121. Wang Congwu, "Zhongguo Gongchandong Lingdau Pu-Nei-Hua Diqu Renminde Geming Douzheng," 49.

122. The principal leader of this leftist faction was Gao Kelin, who is referred to as the military affairs secretary of the CCP *Zhinan Tewei*. He arrived in Daming in July of 1931 and served as the CCP Daming county secretary. He went to Puyang in the spring of 1932, where he encountered Wang Congwu. Significantly, Gao Kelin's hur-

ried departure from this border area corresponded with the failure of the impetuous leftists to develop the nonviolent struggle of the saltmakers into a guerrilla insurgency against the Kuomintang government and establish a Soviet base area. Cf. Xu Youli, "Sanshi Niandai Ji-Lu-Yu Biande Yanmin Douzheng," 61, 63–64. For the other subtle hints of conflict between the Gao Kelin–led *Zhinan Tewei* and the local Wang Congwu–led Communists, see Gao Kelin, *Gao Kelin Huiyilu*, 77–82.

123. An Ming (Liu Dafeng), "Zhinan Wu Xian Dangde Jianli Yu Fazhan," 4.

124. Wang Congwu, "Zhinan Shaqu Dang Zuzhide Fazhan he Qunzhongde Geming Douzheng, 184–185.

125. Schwartz, *Chinese Communism and the Rise of Mao,* 159–160.

126. Wang Congwu, "Zhinan Shaqu Zuzhide Fazhan he Qunzhongde Geming Douzheng," 185.

127. "Zhinan Kangri Youji Zhanzhengde Zhuanbian Jiqi Shenglide Fazhan," 79, 81–82; Shi Guoqiang, Nanle County town, 6/11/88.

128. Li Yu, "Zhonggong Zhinan Tewei Gongzuo Huiyi," 112–113.

129. "Zhinan Kangri Youji Zhanzhengde Zhuanbian Jiqi Shenglide Fazhan," 82–84.

130. Ibid., 79–88.

131. "Zhinan Tewei Liang He Yanfu Gongzuo Jue Yian," 10.

132. Ibid., 10–11.

133. Tian Yuan, "Wo Dang Lingdau Puyang Liangmen Yidaide Zaimin Douzheng," 64.

134. Ibid., 65–69. Also corroborated by my interview of He Jinze, in Yao Jia village, Puyang, 9/11/85.

135. Wang Zaiduo and Liu Shousen, "Yijiu Sansan Nian Hua*xian* Dongbu Zaimin Fenliang Chidahu Douzheng," 17.

136. Cf. "Peng Cheng Tuicihua Gongren Douzheng Gaikuang," 61–64.

137. Yao Peishan, in Beijing, 8/4/90.

138. "Ci*xian* Fadong Youji Zhanzhengde Jingguo," 67–68.

139. "Peng Cheng Tuicihua," 63; and "Ci*xian* Fazhan Youji Zhanzheng," 65–67.

140. "Cai Xiaozhuang Nongmin Baodong Shiliao," 112.

141. Lian Enlin et al, "Jinshengdao Baodongde Shimo," 1–2.

142. "Cai Xiaozhuang Nongmin Baodong Shiliao," 113–115.

143. Ibid., 111–112.

144. Lian Enlin et al, "Jinshengdao Baodongde Shimo," 5–6.

145. Yang Jiesheng, "Baodong Suiyue Suoyi," 122–123.

146. Cf. Wang Guanghua, "Zhinan Dongbu Nongmin Wuzhuang Douzheng," 54–79.

147. "Zhinan Nongmin Youji Zhanzhengde Shimo," 222–229.

148. "Zhinan Nongmin Youji Zhanzhengde Shimo," 224–229; Zhou Dongguang, "Yijiu Sanwu Nian Pingxiang Yanmin Wuzhuang Douzheng," 138–139.

149. "Zhinan Nongmin Youji Zhanzhengde Shimo," 224–227.

150. Zhang Linzhi, "Guanyu Zhinan Dangshi Zhong Jige Wentide Yijian," 211.

151. "Yijiu Saner Nian," 16–17.

152. Wang Congwu, "Zhinan Shaqu Dang Zuzhide Fazhan he Qunzhongde Geming Douzheng," 187.

153. Wang Congwu et al., "Puyang Yanmin Douzheng," 179.

154. Cf. Boorman, ed., *Biographical Dictionary of Republican China,* 189–191; Sheridan, *Chinese Warlord,* 271.

155. Chao Zhepu, "Zhinan Geming Ciyuandi—Daming Chishi Gemingshi," 35.

156. Ibid.

157. Eastman, "Fascism in Kuomintang China: The Blue Shirts," 1–4, 8–12.

158. Chao Zhepu, "Zhinan Geming Ciyuandi—Daming Chishi Gemingshi," 35–36.

159. Ibid., 38.

160. Wang Congwu, "Zhongguo Gongchandang Lingdau Pu-Nei-Hua Diqu Renminde Geming Douzheng," 52.

161. Sun Hanshang, "Geming Pinbiande Huiyi," 245.

162. Ibid.

163. Wang Zhigang, "Guanyu Qingfeng Dangshide Jidian Huiyi, 111.

164. Ibid., 110.

165. Cf. Wang Congwu, "Zhongguo Gongchandang Lingdau Pu-Nei-Hua Diqu," 55. Wang gives us only the figure for the high point of party membership, which came in 1934–35.

166. The term is from Connerton, *How Societies Remember,* 36.

167. Wang Congwu has made it diamond clear that the 1934–35 peasant salt-makers' movement in Daming was completely independent of CCP influence. "Zhongguo Gongchandang Lingdau Pu-Nei-Hua Diqu Renmin Geming Douzheng," 52.

168. For the conception, I have benefitted from Tilly, *From Mobilization to Revolution,* 205–207, 233–234.

169. See Tilly, *The Contentious French,* 5–8.

170. On state devolution, see Kuhn, "Local Self-Government Under the Republic: Problems of Control, Autonomy, and Mobilization," 257–298; Mann, *Local Merchants and the Chinese Bureaucracy,* 163–199; Barkan, "Patterns of Power: Forty Years of Elite Politics in a Chinese County," 191–215; the concluding essay in Esherick and Rankin, eds., *Chinese Local Elites and Patterns of Dominance.* According to Kuhn and Mann, since the Qing era, there had been a tendency for central rulers to extend the bureaucracy down to the county and subcounty levels and to exert fiscal authority over local societal leaders, a process of state development that pronounced itself during the Nationalist decade.

171. The term is from Ardant, "Financial Policy and Economic Infrastructures of Modern States and Nations," 173.

172. Bergere, "The Chinese Bourgeoisie, 1911–1937," 722.

173. This is where the logic of the scholarship of Tilly and Ardant would lead us. Tilly, *The Contentious French,* 131; Ardant, "Financial Policy and Economic Infrastructures of Modern States and Nations," 164–172. It is a logic also underscored, to some extent, by Chen Lifu. Cf. Chang and Myers, eds., *The Storm Clouds Clear Over China,* xxii–xxiii, 184. Chen places major blame for the failure of the Kuomintang government to gain credibility with the common people on the finance ministry under T.V. Song.

174. Cf. Gerth and Mills, eds., *From Max Weber,* 233.

175. For a view that the key to understanding Chinese history and politics is the permanence of state bureaucracy, see Balazs, *Chinese Civilization and Bureaucracy*, 13–20.

176. On the importance of looking at such intermediate institutions, see Tarrow, "Big Structures and Contentious Events," 196–203.

177. The conception of state autonomy is derived in part from Maurice Meisner, who has written of a bureaucratic apparatus that rose above society with the consolidation of the CCP in China during the 1950s. In reading Meisner, I am struck by the parallel between the early bureaucratic restoration engineered by the CCP in the post-1949 period and the quick-paced bureaucratic rejuvenation carried out by the Kuomintang Ministry of Finance officials in the 1928–37 period. Cf. *Mao's China and After*, 260–261, 272.

178. Clearly, we are discussing a revenue war being waged against country people by central state leaders. Clearly, too, as Caws has pointed out, "A lively awareness of what leaders are equipped and willing to do seems to me of great importance. . . , for war (among other things) is *a willingness to use death as an instrument of policy*—primarily and preferably the death of the enemy, but there obviously has to be a willingness to use the death of one's own people also." *The Causes of Quarrel*, 171.

179. Cf. Holcombe, *The Spirit of the Chinese Revolution*, 95–122; Wilbur, "Military Separatism and the Process of Reunification Under the Nationalist Regime, 1922–1937," 203–263.

180. Duara, "State Involution: A Study of Local Finances in North China, 1911–1935," 132–161, especially 135–137, 157.

181. Cf. Eastman, *The Abortive Revolution*, and *Seeds of Destruction*.

182. Discussion with Shi Guoqiang, Nanle County town, 5/5/90.

183. Cf. Liu Yufeng, "Zhinan Shaqu Nongmin Geming Douzheng Pianduan," 53–57; Zhao Jibin, "Huiyi Puyangde Geming Douzheng," 43–44.

184. For the evidence on this, see Chapters 4 and 5.

185. Chao Zhepu, "Zhinan Geming Ciyuandi-Daming Chishi Gemingshi," 38–40.

186. Skocpol, "France, Russia, and China: A Structural Analysis of Social Revolutions," 200.

187. Ibid., 191–192, 199.

188. As Bruce Cumings would advise. See "Interest and Ideology in the Study of Agrarian Politics," 469.

CHAPTER 2. STATE MAKING AND THE INTRUSION OF THE
SHUIJINGTUAN INTO THE PEASANTS' SALT MARKET

1. For the rich literature on state making by China scholars see Bianco, "Secret Societies and Peasant Self-Defense, 1921–1933," 213–224; Bianco, "Peasant Movements," 280–301; Duara, "State Involution: A Study of Local Finances in North China, 1911–1935," 138–140; Duara, *Culture, Power, and the State*, 66–71, 250–255; Duara, "Knowledge and Power in the Discourse of Modernity: The Campaigns Against Popular Religion in Early Twentieth Century China," 67–83, especially 76–77; Eastman, *The Abortive Revolution*, 181–243; Eastman, *Seeds of Destruction*,

45–88; Tien Hung-mao, *Government and Politics in Kuomintang China, 1927–1937,* 18–19, 25–26, 32, 43, 74–75, 77–85, 103–113; Perry, *Rebels and Revolutionaries in North China,* conclusion. The scholars of the above works do not always treat "state making" the same way, but they seem to share a common assumption with Bianco: peasants in Republican China were more likely to be aroused to spontaneous protest by the oppression of state officials than by the exploitation of class enemies. I also share this assumption.

2. Tilly, *Big Structures, Large Processes, Huge Comparisons,* chaps. 1–2.

3. Tilly, *The Contentious French,* 1–10.

4. Tien Hung-mao, *Government and Politics in Kuomintang China, 1927–1937,* 75, 77–85.

5. Although the evidence on this point for the Hebei-Shandong-Henan area is massive, I do not claim that my microscopic analysis of the villages in this border area can be extended to reach a broad macrolevel representation of the nature and origins of the Chinese revolution. Whether peasant salt making for the market was common throughout the areas where the Communist bases were formed, or whether peasants in other parts of North China were engaged in a similar struggle with the Kuomintang state, is not well established either. Still, Linda Grove has found that the issue of the earth salt market was important in local peasant support for the Gaoyang Soviet, which the CCP attempted to establish in North China during the early 1930s. Cf. "Creating a Northern Soviet," 256–257, 263; additionally, in *The Abortive Revolution,* Eastman has carefully (and astutely) noted that, "Even in Ting *hsien,* one of the relatively well-to-do *hsien* in North China, peasants could not afford salt at the official rate of Y1.00 for eight catties. They therefore soaked the soil to obtain *hsiao yen*—sometimes called "earth salt"—as a substitute for salt. Government troops stopped this practice, claiming that the peasants were obtaining salt illegally," 207.

6. Cf. Tarrow, "Big Structures and Contentious Events," 194, 200–202.

7. Xu Youli, "Sanshi Niandai Ji-Lu-Yu Biande Yanmin Douzheng," 63.

8. Wang Congwu et al., "Puyang Yanmin Douzheng," 170–180.

9. Chang Fusen, "Cong Huaxian Yannong Douzheng Kan Nongmin Yundongde Juda Weili," 1–7.

10. Liu Qingfeng, ed., "Dongming Xian Yanmin Baodong," 204–211.

11. Cf. "Daming Xiaofei," 50–53.

12. "Nanle Xian Fasheng Liuxie Canju," 3.

13. For such a view, see Gale, *Salt for the Dragon.* Gale was the American advisor to the Nationalist government's Salt Inspectorate and reportedly a professor of Chinese history at the University of California—Berkeley.

14. Cf. Myers, *The Chinese Peasant Economy,* 9.

15. Dai Qingli, "Lun Xiaoyan," 41–42.

16. Fang Qiuwei, "Jinan Xiaoyan Wenti," 45.

17. Da Jin, "Jinan Tongxun," 2b.

18. Conversation with Shi Guoqiang, Nanle County, Henan Province, 6/11/88.

19. Conversation with Xu Shirong, CCP party history historian, Puyang city, 6/13/87.

20. See Hillel, "Lash of the Dragon," 30.

21. Shi Guoqiang, Nanle County town, 6/12/88.

22. Western scholars generally associate flood alluvial deposits with soil enrichment, and indeed this is often the case over the short run. But over the centuries the enriching chemicals in these deposits were expended, whereas the salt stayed and literally "filled up" the lower and middle layers of the earth, so that it could be drawn up during periods of waterlogging.

23. Zhang Zifeng and Zhang Yingfu, *Henan Huoxiao Tuyan Zhi Diaocha*, 2–8.

24. Ibid., 39, 45.

25. Cf. *Zhongguo Shiye Zhi: Shandong Sheng*, VII, 61.

26. Xu Youli, "Sanshi Niandai Ji-Lu-Yu Biande Yanmin Douzheng," 60.

27. See, for example, the household budgets of the peasant saltmakers in Qian Kou (Chapter 4) and Qian Foji (Chapter 8). On earth salt in the border area in general, see Luo Qing, "Jinan Youjiqude Jingji Jianshe Gongzuo," 166. Also see "Tuxiao Xiaolu Ri Zeng," 13.

28. Huang, *The Peasant Family and Rural Development in the Yangzi Delta*, 102.

29. Chiang Tao-chang, "The Significance of the Salt Industry in Ch'ing China," 1–2; and Multhauf, *Neptune's Gift*, 11–13.

30. Several important studies illustrate this shift. See Adshead, *The Modernization of the Chinese Salt Administration*, 15–19, 110; Rowe, *Hankow: Commerce and Society in a Chinese City*, 90–100, 106–110; Zelin, "The Rise and Fall of the Fu-Rong Salt Yard Elite: Merchant Dominance in Late Qing China," 88.

31. Chiang Tao-chang, "The Significance of the Salt Industry in Ch'ing China," 23.

32. Cf. Multhauf, *Neptune's Gift*, 11–13.

33. Liu Cun, "Liang He Yanmin Douzheng," 153–155. Cf. Fang Qiuwei, "Jinan Xiaoyan Wenti," 40–41.

34. Liu Cun, "Liang He Yanmin Douzheng," 153–155.

35. According to Fang Qiuwei, the Qing government did decree a ban on earth salt production, and there were rebellions against this ban prior to the reign of Guangxu. "Jinan Xiaoyan Wenti," 42. Cf. Liu Cun, "Liang He Yanmin Douzheng," 153–155.

36. Li Jianchang, *Guanliao Ziben Yu Yanye*, 1–3.

37. Ibid., 2–4

38. Ibid.

39. Ibid., 4–6. I have constructed this table from data provided mainly by Li Jianchang, *Guanliao Ziben Yu Yanyue*, and partly by Young, "China's Pre-War External Obligations Under Charge of the Ministry of Finance," 5–6. Li and Young approach this issue from different perspectives, but the evidence presented by each is basically the same.

40. Li Jianchang, *Guanliao Ziben Yu Yanye*, 10–11.

41. Ibid., 10–12.

42. Ibid., 12.

43. Ibid., 11–13.

44. Ibid., 14.

45. Ibid., 14–15.

46. In synthesizing some of the literature on political elites in Mexico, Migdal has spoken of the "revolutionary family." Drawing on Kenneth F. Johnson's work,

Migdal reminds us that legitimacy in Mexico, and other Third World states, is limited to the close political clients of the "revolutionary family," to people whose "loyalty has gained them access to the most coveted posts in the state and its related political party, the PRI (Partido Revolucionario Institucional)." Those who reach the top usually are tied in with the ruling revolutionary family. Citing Hansen, Migdal stresses their access to financial means that bring them material comforts and power. Similarly, I think, we can call the Kuomintang state leaders "a fiscal family" and conceive the finance ministry as the key source of the fiscal family's budget, expanding its internal wealth-producing capabilities and its international credit and contracts. Cf. Migdal, *Strong Societies and Weak States*, 218–219. The idea of Chiang Kai-shek acting as the paternalistic head of his Nanjing government and rewarding the officials in his immediate administrative network with government largess when they, like obedient children, pleased him finds support in the memoir of Chen Lifu, who says that Chiang, when pleased with Chen's work in defeating a Hunan warlord, personally awarded Chen and his associates the equivalent of ten thousand silver dollars. Cf. Chang and Myers, eds., *The Storm Clouds Clear Over China*, 69–70.

47. Kann, "China's Salt Revenue as Security for Her Loan Obligations," 5.

48. For the 18 September 1929 correspondence form the Commission of Financial Experts recommending the refunding, see confidential letters to T. V. Song, minister of finance, Shanghai, signed by E. W. Kemmerer, Arthur N. Young, and F. B. Lynch, 6 September 1929 (and a similar letter on 23 September 1929). The story became public in "The Salt Loan," *North China Daily News*, 19 September 1929.

49. Ibid. See also *North China Daily News*, 3 January 1935.

50. *North China Daily News*, 22 October 1929.

51. See the statement issued by T. V. Song in February, 1928, and published in the *North China Daily News*, February 21. It can be found in Arthur N. Young papers, Box 14, Hoover Archives. Also see T. V. Song's statement on "Salt Revenue Loans," Nanjing, 16 November 1928 in Young papers.

52. On salt revenue deposits being placed in the Chase Bank see Arthur N. Young papers, letter of 19 July 1937 to C. S. Tsao, Director, Loan Department, Ministry of Finance, Shanghai, 1; and on the deposits in New York banks see 10 December 1937 letter from W. C. Cassels of the Hong Kong and Shanghai Banking Corp., and L. Chevretton, Representative, *Bank de l'Indochine*, to the director general of the Chinese Government Salt Administration in Shanghai.

On the squabble over where the salt tax funds were to be deposited, see (1) 18 December 1937 letter of the associate director general to M. Paul Emile Naggiar, *Ambassadeur de France*, Shanghai; (2) 21 December 1937 letter from R. E. Howe in the British Embassy to the director general of the Chinese Government Salt Administration in Shanghai; (3) 22 December 1937 letter of the associate director general to His Excellency M. Paul Emile Naggiar, Ambassadeur de France, Shanghai; and (4) director general's letter of 22 December 1937 to W. C. Cassels of the Hong Kong and Shanghai Banking Corp. and to M. L. Chevretton, *Banque de l'Indochine;* and most importantly, (5) letter of 11 December 1937 to Arthur N. Young from the ministry of finance director general of the salt administration. Hoover Archive papers of Young.

53. T. V. Song's statement of 21 February 1928. Published in the *North China Daily News*.

54. Tsao, "National Life," 10.

55. Rawski, *Economic Growth in Prewar China,* 14. Rawski has noted that Western historians have exaggerated the negative impact of warlordism on economic growth in prewar China. At best, when compared with the regime of Yuan Shikai, the warlord era saw only a slight improvement in the efficiency of salt revenue collection in the Hebei-Shandong-Henan border area, though in many counties the breakdown we associate with warlord rivalries, stalemates, and power vacuums also made an appearance. However, the important point, which lends credence to Rawski's working hypotheses, is that after 1928 the center was in the process of reemerging and regularizing its controls over salt taxation and trade. Compare the end section of this chapter with Rawski's xxviii, 32–33, 39–40.

56. I have derived this estimate by the following logic. First, according to Kann, prior to the reorganization loan, the Republican center "counted on 20 million dollars as the annual income from salt taxes." "China's Salt Revenue as Security for Her Loan Obligations," 7. Second, according to Xu Jingxing, the Changlu salt revenue in early Republican times stood between 11 and 14 percent of the national salt tax revenue. Thus the Changlu area would have contributed, at most, approximately $2,800,000 prior to 1913. Cf. Xu Jinxing, "Changlu Yanwu Yu Tianjin Yanshang," 52–53. Third, according to Ding Changqing, Changlu tax revenues stood at $29,694,000 for fiscal year 1936. Ding, *Minguo Yanwu Shigao,* 425.

57. Kann, "China's Salt Revenue as Security for Her Loan Obligations," 5; Nanjing-issued news bulletin, 7 November 1929, in Young papers, Hoover Archives.

58. "List Showing the Respective Annual Quota of Salt Funds to Be Borne by the Various Provinces for Refund of Foreign Loans." Received by Arthur N. Young from L. Chang, 6 September 1929. Young papers, Hoover Archives.

59. Kann, "China's Salt Revenue as Security for Her Loan Obligations," 6.

60. Ibid. Also see Young, Memorandum on the Position of Salt Secured Loans, 25 August 1932, 2–3. Hoover Archives.

61. Cleveland, *The Problem of Putting the Principles of the New Salt Law into Effect,* 29. Sent to Young on 18 March 1935. Hoover Archives.

62. Ibid., 18.

63. Cf. Cleveland, *Statistical Review of the Work of the Inspectorate, 1913–1933,* 54–55. According to this report, the revenue guards totaled twenty-seven thousand. Ding Changqing's figures suggest twenty-five thousand. Both sources agree that the total national salt tax army was forty-five thousand.

64. The Kuomintang salt tax police force was maintained out of salt revenue. On its combat readiness, Ruxton reported in 1934 that the revenue guards compared favorably in appearance and behavior "with other armed bodies in China," in Cleveland, *Statistical Review of the Work of the Inspectorate, 1913–1933,* 220; Liu Huheng, a graduate of Qinghua University, a banker in Kuomintang China, and a scholar of the history of the Changlu Salt Bureau, reaffirms this point when he states, "The military instrument of the *Shuijingtuan* was better than the ordinary Kuomintang Army." Tianjin, 8/2/91. According to Liu, many of the Kuomintang generals quarreled over which army unit would absorb the *Shuijingtuan* after the outbreak of the Sino-Japanese War precisely because they envied its military efficiency.

65. See Cleveland, *Statistical Review of the Work of the Inspectorate, 1913–1933,* 194. Cf. *Ministry of Finance Report for the 23rd Fiscal Year,* 7.

66. Li Pengtu, Liu Yudong, and Liu Yeting, "Changlu Yanwu Wushinian Hugu," 124–127; Kann, "China's Salt Revenue as Security for Her Loan Obligations," 7.

67. Li Pengtu, Liu Yudong, and Liu Yeting, "Changlu Yanwu Wushinian Hugu, 129–130.

68. See Chiang Tao-chang, *The Salt Industry of China, 1644–1911,* 195; Yi Shuansun, "Salt Taxation in China," 133–137.

69. Cf. Kwan Manbun, "The Merchant World of Tianjin: Society and Economy of a Chinese City," chap. 14, conclusion.

70. Adshead, *The Modernization of the Chinese Salt Administration,* 153–169; Li Pengtu, Liu Yudong, and Liu Yeting, "Changlu Yanwu Wushinian Hugu, 131–132.

71. Ding Changqing, ed., *Minguo Yanwu Shigao,* 272–273.

72. Xu Youli, "Sanshi Niandai Ji-Lu-Yu Biande Yanmin Douzheng," 61–62.

73. Liu Qingfeng, ed., "Dongming Xian Yanmin Baodong," 204.

74. Ibid., 204–208.

75. Cf. "Jiashui Gao," 2.

76. Cf. "Yanshui Jia Sanjiao" 2.

77. Cf. Eastman, *The Abortive Revolution.* In writing of peasant expenditure for salt, Eastman has noted "this represented one of their largest outlays for food." He also notes that (1) the price of salt "increased between 10 percent and 26 percent between 1931 and 1934 and was costing the consumer thirty to seventy times the cost of production" and (2) in North China many peasants "reportedly could not afford the official price of salt during the 1930s," 207.

78. Chiang Tao-chang, *The Salt Industry of China,* 203–207.

79. "Gexian Yanjia," 2.

80. Cf. Chiang Tao-chang, *The Salt Industry of China,* 193–210.

81. Wang Zhiyuan, "Bo-Li Diqude Jiandangde Nongmin Yundong," 9–10; Yin Yigang, "Huiyi Rongchengxian Jiandang Chuqide Yixie Geming Huodong," 99–100; Liu Qingfeng, ed., "Dongming Xian Yanmin Baodong," 204–207.

82. Surely, some of the rural people were indeed smuggling salt resources that legally belonged to the government, as Perry's evidence on Huai-bei suggests. *Rebels and Revolutionaries in North China,* 60–62. My point is simply that we must distinguish the peasants of the salt lands from rural elements who became habitual bandits and salt smugglers. Mr. Shi Guoqiang, the historian of Nanle County, agrees with this distinction. He points out that the peasants producing for the earth salt market in the Hebei-Shandong-Henan border area were not the people who plundered and smuggled government salt prior to the Anti-Japanese War. 8/7/90.

83. In developing this point, I have profited in talks with Shi Guoqiang, 8/7/90, and from Pitt-Rivers, *The People of the Sierra,* 33, 50–51.

84. Cleveland, *The Problem of Putting the Principles of the New Salt Law into Effect,* 7.

85. Fang Qiuwei, "Jinan Xiaoyan Wenti," 40.

86. Ibid.

87. Jiang Shouyi, "Henan Sheng Zuijin Yanwu Zhi Qingxing," 121–122.

88. Ding Changqing, ed., *Minguo Yanwu Shigao,* 424–425. And personal conversation with Ding. Tianjin, Nankai University, 8/1/91.

89. Data made available by Shi Guoqiang, Nanle County town, 11–12 June 1988. According to Shi, in the early 1920s government maritime salt reached

approximately 50 percent of the villages of Nanle and Daming. But by 1933–34 only 10 to 20 percent of the villages were purchasing sea salt because its price had soared beyond their means.

90. Discussion with Professor Ding Changqing, 8/1/91. Ding's data are essentially in line with the estimated revenue loss for Changlu reported in the *Annual Report of the Nationalist Government of China Ministry of Finance Chief Inspectorate of Salt Revenue,* 7.

91. Li Pengtu, Liu Yudong, and Liu Yeting, "Changlu Yanwu Wushinian Hugu," 136–137.

92. MacKinnon, *Power and Politics in Late Imperial China,* 35, 39–40.

93. Ibid., 58.

94. Ibid., 57–58.

95. Ibid., 58–59.

96. Li Pengtu, Liu Yudong, and Liu Yeting, "Changlu Yanwu Wushinian Hugu," 136–137.

97. Ibid.

98. Cf. "Changlu Jiwu Qinxing Jilue," 67.

99. *Zhengfu Gong Bao,* 23 August 1915.

100. Li Pengtu, Liu Yudong, and Liu Yeting, "Changlu Yanwu Wushinian Hugu," 135.

101. I do not wish to leave the impression that Chiang Kai-shek was not involved in the finance ministry's efforts to build up a modern salt revenue force. Linebarger has noted that the generalissimo was keenly interested in "state building" and that he was from a family in Fenghua County, Zhejiang Province, that "had been connected with the salt-revenue system." *The China of Chiang Kai-shek: A Political Study,* 256–257. In a 1988 interview at Harvard University, the late Hu Hua informed me that Chiang Kai-shek himself was responsible for the elimination of Yu Fangzhou and several early leaders of the saltmakers' struggles in Tianjin and other parts of China during the 1920s and 1930s. I have not been able to confirm this statement. Nonetheless, on Yu Fangzhou's involvement with popular opposition to the Republican government's taxes on alkaline lands and low-lying infertile lands, see Dou Aizhi and Liu Yuzhi, "Yu Fangzhou," 157–158, 163–164. Zhou Laifang, the leader of the peasant movement in Fenghua County, Zhejiang, led more than one thousand peasants to torch the salt bureau in Fenghua in 1927. Thereafter, he became involved in organizing a saltmakers' association of more than twenty thousand people and a saltmakers' self-defense force, all of which drew the attention of the "counterrevolutionary regime" of Chiang Kai-shek. Cf. Wang Chengfa, "Zhou Laifang," 71–72, 79–80, 83–85.

102. Ding Changqing, Nankai University, Tianjin, 8/1/91. Also see Li Pengtu, Liu Yudong, and Liu Yeting, "Changlu Yanwu Wushinian Hugu," 135. According to Liu Huheng, the *Shuijingtuan* was incorporated into the Kuomintang Ministry of Finance's Salt Tax Bureau in 1931. Tianjin, 8/2/91.

103. From Ding Changqing's unpublished manuscript, "Changlu Yanwu Shuijingde Bianzu he Yanbian," 4–5; and from a discussion with Ding, Tianjin, Nankai University, 8/1/91.

104. Ding Changqing, Nankai University, Tianjin,8/1/91.

105. *Henan Yanwu Tekan,* 4–5.

106. Ibid., 5.

107. Xu Youli, "Sanshi Niandai Ji-Lu-Yu Biande Yanmin Douzheng," 63.

108. *Henan Yanwu Tekan*, 4–5, 14–15.

109. "Heze Yanmin Yongdongshi," 84–86.

110. From "Biographical Note on T. V. Song, 1894–1971."

111. Cf. *Zhao Bao* (Morning news), 12, 19. Reissued in the *Journal of Salt Administration*, no. 60, 97–99. From the pen of a Chinese journalist writing under the pseudonym of "Sword."

112. Liu Huheng, Tianjin, 8/2/91. An eighty-one-year-old graduate of Qinghua University, Liu was a banker in Kuomintang China and a member of the Political Consultative Conference after 1949.

113. Ding Changqing, Nankai University, Tianjin, 8/1/91; and Liu Huheng, Tianjin,8/2/91. Zeng Yangfeng was T. V. Song's man in the Changlu salt area. I am not certain if he formally controlled the Changlu Salt Bureau in 1932, after which the issue is not in doubt.

114. "Guanyu Lu Situn Huodong," 1–3

115. Ibid.

116. See, for example, Ruxton's "Letter to His Excellency, Dr. H. H. Kung, Minister of Finance," which is a report on progress in remolding the revenue guards. The letter was reprinted in Cleveland, *Statistical Review of the Work of the Inspectorate, 1913–1933*, 218–223.

117. "Guanyu Lu Situn Huodong," 3.

118. Chief inspectorate of salt revenue map of earth salt production areas, printed in Cleveland, *The Problem of Putting the Principles of the New Salt Law into Effect*, 86B.

119. Tilly, *The Contentious French.* 7–8.

120. Friedman, Pickowicz, and Selden have discovered that as early as 1929 the Raoyang Kuomintang set up a salt monopoly, "so that the government could sell and tax *all* salt. . ." *Chinese Village, Socialist State*, 11.

121. *National Government of China, Ministry of Finance, Chief Inspectorate of Salt Revenue, 19th Year of the Republic of China, 1930, 4–11*, and *21st Year*, 1932, part 1, 5.

122. See *Annual Report of National Government of China Ministry of Finance, Chief Inspectorate of Salt Revenue 24th Year of the Republic of China*, 37.

123. *Changlu Yanwu Jihe Fensuo Ershisannian Jiuyuefen Gongzuo Baogao*, 60–61.

124. "Diaocha Ji-Lu-Yu Sansheng Chajin Xiaotuyan Shikuang Ji Tuijin Fangfa Baogaoshu," 97.

125. Cf. Ding Changqing, ed., *Minguo Yanwu Shigao*, 272–273, 287. Some of their opposition was triggered by the finance ministry attempt to increase the salt tax indirectly via a new weight measurement system. The Zhejiang salt merchants threatened a work stoppage over this system. Apparently their anger was echoed by merchants from all across China.

126. Cf. Yang Shaoxian, "Daming Yanmin Douzheng Jianshu,"107. According to Ding Changqing, merchants in various parts of China participated in the anti–salt police struggles of the 1930s. *Minguo Yanwu Shigao*, 291.

127. Kuhn, "Local Self-Government Under the Republic," 257–298, especially 281–288; Wei, *Counterrevolution in China*, chaps. 1–2, 7, conclusion; Huang, *The Peasant Economy and Social Change in North China*, 287–290.

128. See the example of this in Chapter 3. Cf. "Changlu Shuijing Zuzhang Diaocha Daming Yu Yanniao Chongtu Anzhi Baogao," 52.

129. *Changlu Yanwu Jihe Fensuo Ershisannian Jiuyuefen Gongzuo Baogao,* 56.

130. Cf. Pomeranz, *The Making of A Hinterland,* 104, 109–110.

131. *National Government of China, Ministry of Finance, Chief Inspectorate of Salt Revenue, 20th Year of the Republic of China,* 1931, 7–8.

132. "Changlu Jiwu Qingxing Jilue," 69–70.

133. *National Government of China, Ministry of Finance, Chief Inspectorate of Salt Revenue,* 1932, 8; and *Changlu Jiwu Qingxing Jilue,* 69.

134. Cf. *National Government of China, Ministry of Finance, Chief Inspectorate of Salt Revenue, 1932,* 29–30. These revenue guards were assisted by the military police by order of the KMT Military Council.

135. *Changlu Jiwu Qingxing Jilue,* 69–70.

136. Jiang Shouyi, "Henan Sheng Zuijin Yanwu Zhi Qingxing," 121–125.

137. Ibid., 122–123.

138. Ibid., 123–124.

139. *National Government of China, Ministry of Finance, Chief Inspectorate of Salt Revenue,* 1931, 8.

140. Ma Ruihua, a seventy-five-year-old native of Gu Chengji, interviewed in Tianjin, 8/3/91.

141. Luo Shoucheng, Luo Tun, Qingfeng, 8/7/91.

142. *Changlu Yanwu Jihe Fensuo Ershisannian Jiuyuefen Gongzuo Baogao,* 55.

143. "Heze Yanmin Yongdong Shi," in *Heze Xianzhi,* 86.

144. Ibid., 55.

145. "Lai Han Zhao Deng," 17 April 1935.

146. *National Government of China, Ministry of Finance, Chief Inspectorate of Salt Revenue, 1930,* 17; *1931,* 18; *1932,* 36.

147. Jiang Shouxi, "Henan Sheng Zuijin Yanwu Zhi Qingxing," 121–125.

148. Conversation with Shi Guoqiang, 6/1988.

149. Bu Yujie, "Yijiu Sanernian Dao Yijiu Sansannian Daming Yidai Yanmin Douzheng," 2.

150. Ibid., 3.

151. Ibid., 4–6.

152. Ibid., 6.

153. Li Shenzhi, "Da Yanbing," 1–4.

154. Bu Yujie, "Yijiu Sanernian Dao Yijiu Sansannian Daming Yidai Yanmin Douzheng, 7.

155. Yang Shaoxian, "Daming Yanmin Douzheng Jianshu," 107.

156. Ibid.

157. "Hebei Sheng Daming Xian Xiaofan Yu Shuijing Chongtu Yian Qingxing Checha," 6.

158. "Jinan Xiaoyan Zhishi," 14–19.

159. From "Yijui Sanwu Nian Shiyue Xiaoyan Jiufen," 30–33.

160. *National Government, Republic of China, Report for the 23rd Fiscal Year* (July 1934 to June 1935), 7. Young Papers, Hoover Archives.

161. *Annual Report of the National Government of China Ministry of Finance Chief Inspectorate of Salt Revenue, 24th Year of the Republic of China, 1935,* 34. Young Papers, Hoover Archives.

162. Ibid., 33.

163. *National Government, Republic of China, Report for the 23rd Fiscal Year,* 7.

164. Ibid., 7.

165. Thaxton, "State Making and State Terror," 335–376. Also see Strauss, *Bureaucratic Reconstitution,* 179.

166. See Skinner, "Marketing and Social Structure in Rural China," pt. 1, 3–44; pt. 2, 195–228; pt. 3, 366–399. Also see Mann, *Local Merchants and the Chinese Bureaucracy,* 176–177.

167. Skinner, "Chinese Peasants and the Closed Community," 270–281.

168. Pomeranz, *The Making of a Hinterland,* 114, 117.

CHAPTER 3. THE PEASANT SALTMAKERS' STRUGGLE IN PUYANG

1. Wang Congwu et al., "Puyang Yanmin Douzheng," 174–175.

2. "Sun Fuzhen Tongzhi Zai 'Puyang Diweijun Gongzuo Zuotanhui' Shangde Fayin," 20.

3. Ibid.

4. Zhao Jibin, "Nongcun Pochan Shenzhong Jinan Yige Fanrongde Cunzhuang," 33–34.

5. Wang Congwu et al., "Puyang Yanmin Douzheng," 171–172.

6. Zhang Zifeng and Zhang Yingfu, *Henan Huoxiao Tuyan Zhi Diaocha,*15.

7. Zhang Youren, Cheng Guan, Puyang, 9/11/85.

8. Lui Cun, *Liang He Yanmin Douzheng,* 155.

9. Ibid., 157–158, 168.

10. Ibid., 170–171.

11. *Puyang Xianzhi Chugao,*15–16.

12. Ibid., 16.

13. Ibid.

14. Geng Xinyuan, whose salt land provided 80 percent of his household income, reported that "the harvest was average in the years 1927–32." Cheng Guan, 9/14/85.

15. Xu Youli, "Sanshi Niandai Ji-Lu-Yu Biande Yanmin Douzheng," 60–61.

16. Wang Yuxi, Wang Choulin, and Wang Peili, Sha Wo village, 8/6/91.

17. *Yanzheng Zhazhi,* 30–33.

18. Wang Congwu et al., "Puyang Yanmin Douzheng," 172.

19. Ibid., 172–175.

20. "Jinan Tewei Liang He Yanfu Gongzuo Jueyian," 9–13.

21. Liu Cun, *Liang He Yanmin Douzheng,* 164 .

22. See Wang Congwu et al., "Puyang Yanmin Douzheng," 170–180, for the context.

23. On this form of resistance in peasant society, see Lottes, "Popular Culture and the Early Modern State in 16th Century Germany," 154.

24. Wang Choulin, Sha Wo, 8/6/91.

25. Zhang Youren, Cheng Guan, 9/11/85.

26. Yangfeng, Cheng Guan, 9/11/85.

27. Zhang Youren, Cheng Guan, 8/12/85.

28. Ren Hailong, Cheng Guan, 9/12/85.

29. Geng Xinyuan, Cheng Guan, 9/14/85.

30. Yang Feng, Cheng Guan, 9/12/85.

31. Cf. Chapter 4 on Qian Kou.

32. Yang Baozeng, Cheng Guan, 6/2/87.

33. Wang Congwu et. al., "Puyang Yanmin Douzheng," 173–174.

34. Yang Baozeng, Cheng Guan, 6/2/87.

35. Yang Laoren, Cheng Guan, 9/11/85.

36. I am indebted to Kwan Man Bun for helping me develop this point. Personal conversation, 10 January 1994.

37. *Jinan Xiaoyan Zhishi,* 14–19.

38. Zhang Youren, Cheng Guan, 9/12/85.

39. Xu Youli, "Sanshi Niandai Ji-Lu-Yu Biande Yanmin Douzheng," 60.

40. Wang Congwu et al., "Puyang Yanmin Douzheng," 174–176.

41. In developing this point, I have benefitted from Rodney's informative study of the 1905 riots in Guyana. *A History of the Guyanese Working People,* 200–201.

42. Wang Congwu, "Zhongguo Gongchandang Lingdau Pu-Nei-Hua Diqu Renminde Gemeng Douzheng," 50.

43. Cf. Wang Congwu et. al., "Puyang Yanmin Douzheng," 170–180, and interviews of Liu Xishou (see note 44).

44. Liu Xishou, Cheng Guan, 9/17/85.

45. Yang Baozeng, Cheng Guan, 6/2/87.

46. Ibid.

47. Fan Renbang, Cheng Guan, 9/14/85.

48. Li Zhaoming, Cheng Yuan, 6/3/87.

49. Yang Baozeng, Cheng Guan, 6/2/87.

50. Zhang Youren, Yang Feng, Liu Xingcheng, and Ren Hailong in Cheng Guan, 9/11/85.

51. Indeed, they tend to avoid it, and leave the impression that landlords did not support their tenants against the Republican state. Cf. Wang Congwu et. al, "Puyang Yanmin Douzheng," 170–172.

52. Zhang Youren, Cheng Guan, 9/12/85.

53. Yang Baozeng, Cheng Guan, 6/2/87.

54. Wang Congwu, "Zhongguo Gongchandang Lingdau Pu-Nei-Hua Diqu Renminde Geming Douzheng," 49.

55. Ibid., 48.

56. Wang Congwu et al., "Puyang Yanmin Douzheng," 174–178.

57. Ibid.

58. Ibid., 178.

59. Ibid.

60. Li Xuanxi, Liangmen village, Puyang, 9/18/85.

61. Ren Hailong, Cheng Guan, 9/12/85.

62. Guo Xinlai, Cheng Guan, 9/12/85.

63. Liu Cun, *Liang He Yanmin Douzheng,* 178

64. Ibid., 179

65. Xu Youli, "Sanshi Niandai Ji-Lu-Yu Biande Yanmin Douzheng," 64.

66. Zhang Youren, Cheng Guan, 9/11/85.

67. Ibid.

68. Xu Youli, "Sanshi Niandai Ji-Lu-Yu Biande Yanmin Douzheng," 63.

69. Wang Congwu et al., "Puyang Yanmin Douzheng," 179–180.

70. Ma Ruihua, a native of Gu Chengji, in Tianjin, 8/3/91.

71. Wang Congwu et al., "Puyang Yanmin Douzheng," 179–180.

72. Wang Decheng, Cheng Guan, 6/2/87.

73. In conceptualizing this issue, I have benefitted from Coleman and Davis, "Preemptive Reform and the Mexican Working Class," 3–33.

74. This popular mistrust comes through in media reports on the peasant salt-makers' attitudes toward Kuomintang government reform programs. Cf. "Nanle Xian Fasheng Liuxie Canjiu," 3.

75. On the phenomenon of successionism in peasant movements see Scott, "Revolution in the Revolution: Peasants and Commissars," 113–116.

76. Xu Jinshan, Cheng Guan, 9/13/85.

77. Guo Xinhai, Cheng Guan, 9/16/85.

78. Xu Jinshan, Cheng Guan, 9/13/85.

79. Ibid.

80. Li Fanjiu et al., "Ding Shuben Zai Pudaqu 'Kangri' Fangong Toudi Shimo," 143–144.

81. Cf. Zagorin, *Rebels and Rulers 1500–1660*,183.

82. He Jinze, Yaojia village, Puyang County, 9/11/85

83. Bailey, "Parapolitical Systems," 283.

84. Cf. Wang Dechang, Cheng Guan, 6/2/87.

85. Shi Guoqiang, Nanle town, 8/4–6/91.

86. Liu Qingfeng, ed., "Dongming Xian Yanmin Baodong," 204.

87. Liu Cun, *Xian He Yanmin Douzheng*,189.

88. Yang Baozeng, Cheng Guan, Puyang, 8/7/91.

89. Shi Guoqiang, Nanle town, 8/4–6/91.

90. Shi Guoqiang, "Oral History Notes on the Saltmakers' Struggle in Nanle, Puyang, and Neihuang."

91. Wang Yuxi, Sha Wo, Puyang, 8/6/91.

92. Ibid.

93. Ibid.

94. Liu Cun, *Liang He Yanmin Douzheng*,175.

95. Ibid., 192–193.

96. Cf. Duara's excellent study, *Culture, Power, and the State,* 139–147, 249–250. Guandi, in Duara's analysis, was both the guardian of the Imperial state and the protector of the rights of the country people. Peasants agree with this part of Duara's representation of the Guandi cult.

97. What they do not agree with, however, is the notion that their resistance to Kuomintang state campaigns against local religious institutions was effectively repressed or that local village leaders switched their allegiances from the sacred, religion-soaked subaltern universe of folk society to the Republican national state and its quasi-modern secular political order. The peasant saltmakers of Luo Tun village in Qingfeng County, for example, told me they fought a running battle with the Kuomintang to keep Guangong's statue from being destroyed between 1929 and 1932. When they were forewarned that the Kuomintang New Life Movement cadres were coming to the war god temple to smash Guangong's statue, they took the statue and hid it in piles of straw and then placed it back in the temple when the cadres had returned to Qingfeng town. Consequently, the Guangong statue was never destroyed. From a discussion with Luo Xinan, Luo Tun village, Qingfeng County, 8/7/91, with Luo Lanxue, Luo Dianchai, Luo Chaobao, and Luo Shoucheng, all former peasant saltmakers, in agreement.

98. Moreover, the peasant saltmakers still worshipped Guangong even after the statues and/or temples were pulled down by the Kuomintang, and many of them did so knowing that Guangong was a threat to the Kuomintang state. Cf. Wang Yuxi, Sha Wo, 8/6/91.

99. Bianco, "Peasant Responses to Communist Party Mobilization Policies in the Anti-Japanese Bases: Some Western Views," 2.

100. On the capacity of the market system to produce this social complexity within rural protest movements against state authorities, see Cobb, *The Police and the People,* 29.

CHAPTER 4. QIAN KOU VILLAGE

1. This is the official version of Qian Kou's history, as given to me by Xu Youli, a scholar in Zhengzhou University's history department.

2. Zhao Jibin, "Nongcun Pochan Shenzhong Jinan Yige Fanrongde Cunzhuang," 33–34.

3. *Liucun Xiang Xiangzhi Chugao,* 4.

4. Zhao Jibin, "Nongcun Pochan Shenzhong Jinan Yige Fanrongde Cunzhuang," 34.

5. Ibid.

6. Philip C. C. Huang's point that most of the surveying done by Buck and Gamble does not give us an in-depth profile of individual village or household populations and economies is well taken. Huang tells us that "by the 1930s a majority of peasant farms in the North China Plain had been driven well under the average subsistence size of fifteen *mu. The Peasant Economy and Social Change in North China,* 185. In fact, his evidence on Hebei suggests that many families had at most ten *mu* of land or, if we assume the average household to have had five persons, only two *mu* per capita. His important work is essential to our movement toward microanalysis of China's village economy, past, present, and future. *The Peasant Economy and Social Change in North China,* 103, 116, 165. That Qian Kou does not fit Huang's sense of this issue does not mean his model is irrelevant to our case. The data on Qi Ji, and in part on Fanzhuang, underscore Huang's logic.

7. Zhao Jibin, "Nongcun Pochan Shenzhong Jinan Yige Fanrongde Cunzhuang," 34–35.

8. Ibid., 34–36.

9. Liu Yufeng, Zhengzhou City, 6/14/87.

10. Liu Guoju, Qian Kou, 6/9/87.

11. Wei Jingfeng, Qian Kou, 6/9/87.

12. Zhao Yunzheng, Qian Kou, 6/11/87; Ma Xinxi, Qian Kou, 6/11/87; Liu Lanpo, Qian Kou, 6/10/87.

13. Zhao Yungzheng, Qian Kou, 6/11/87.

14. Zhao Jibin, "Nongcun Pochan Shenzhong Jinan Yige Fanrongde Cunzhuang," 35.

15. Liu Yufeng, Zhengzhou, 6/14/87.

16. Zhao Jibin, "Nongcun Pochan Shenzhong Jinan Yige Fanrongde Cunzhuang," 35–36.

17. The term "landlord" is too simple and awkward here. Even Zhao Jibin's memoir admits that Qian Kou's landlords had become merchants by 1930, mem-

bers of a suddenly rich social stratum. Zhao Jibin, "Zhinan Shaqu Dang Zuzhide Zaoqi Huodong," 173.

18. Zhao Jibin, "Nongcun Pochan Shenzhong Jinan Yige Fanrongde Cunzhuang," 35–36.

19. Zhao Sitong, the son of landlord Zhao Shaofu, Qian Kou, 6/10/87.

20. Zhao Jibin, 35–36.

21. Ma Xinxi, Qian Kou, 6/11/87.

22. Liu Lanpo, Qian Kou, 6/10/87.

23. Liu Yufeng, Zhengzhou, 6/14/87.

24. I agree with Huang, who states that falling world prices and India's peanut competition left China's peanut tillers in difficult straits from 1929 to 1934. *The Peasant Economy and Social Change in North China,* 121–124. Nevertheless, Zhao Jibin's essay, "Nongcun Pochan Shenzhong Jinan Yige Fanrongde Cunzhuang" (35–36), and my Qian Kou oral history work suggest that in this particular village the peanut producers weathered the cash export downturn until at least 1935.

25. Liu Yufeng, Zhengzhou, 6/14/87.

26. Cf. Zhao Jibin, "Nongcun Pochan Shenzhong Jinan Yige Fanrongde Cunzhuang," 36.

27. Ibid., 37.

28. Liu Gongchen, Qian Kou, 5/30/87.

29. Zhao Jibin, "Nongcun Pochan Shenzhong Jinan Yige Fanrongde Cunzhuang," 37.

30. Liu Gongchen, Qian Kou, 5/30/87.

31. Reader, *Imperial Chemical Industries: A History,* 8–15, 60–63, 97–98, 174.

32. Ibid., 175.

33. Ibid., 175, 225–227.

34. Ibid., 226–227, 335.

35. Zhao Jibin, "Nongcun Pochan Shenzhong Jinan Yige Fanrongde Cunzhuang," 37. Cf. Reader, *Imperial Chemical Industries,* 334.

36. Reader, *Imperial Chemical Industries,* 342–343.

37. Zhao Wangni, Qian Kou, 6/1/87.

38. Zhao Sitong, Qian Kou, 6/10/87.

39. Liu Yufeng, Zhengzhou, 6/14/87.

40. Zhao Jibin, "Nongcun Pochan Shenzhong Jinan Yige Fanrongde Cunzhuang," 37–38.

41. Ibid., 38.

42. Liu Shiyin, Qian Kou village, 6/12/87.

43. Liu Yufeng, Zhengzhou, 6/14/87.

44. Liu Gongchen, Qian Kou, 5/30/87.

45. Zhao Tianbao, Qian Kou, 6/1/87.

46. Liu Guoju, Qian Kou, 6/9/87; Liu Shiyin, Qian Kou, 6/12/87.

47. Zhao Jibin's characterization of the third phase as "monopoly" does not hold up against my oral history. The landlords of the village by no means monopolized earth salt production and exchange. Cf. "Nongcun Pochan Shenzhong Jinan Yige Fanrongde Cunzhuang," 38–39.

48. *Neihuang Xianzhi,* 15–16.

49. Skinner, "Marketing and Social Structure in Rural China," pt. 1, 6.

50. Liu Gongchen, Qian Kou, 5/30/87.

51. Zhao Jibin, "Nongcun Pochan Shenzhong Jinan Yige Fanrongde Cunzhuang," 39.

52. Most hired hands came from outside of the village.

53. Zhao Jibin, "Nongcun Pochan Shenzhong Jinan Yige Fanrongde Cunzhuang," 38

54. Liu Tieyu, Qian Kou, 6/12/87; Liu Shiyin, Qian Kou, 6/12/87; Zhao Yunzheng, 6/11/87.

55. Liu Yufeng, Zhengzhou, 6/14/87.

56. I use nine hundred to a thousand *jin* as the minimum grain requirement per person per year because nearly all of Qian Kou's former saltmakers said this is what they required. Whether this high figure, nearly twice that of most previous scholarly estimates for North China villages, is high because the multiple year long labor and business activities of Qian Kou's people required more grain or because they simply became accustomed to this through prosperity is uncertain. Perhaps both factors were at work in the Republican period. Cf. Liu Yufeng, Zhengzhou, 6/14/87. When I asked Liu if this was not a high figure, he told me that some people he had known consumed even more grain, as much as twelve hundred *jin* per year.

57. Liu Guoju, Qian Kou, 6/9/87.

58. Liu Futang, Qian Kou, 6/1/87. I have constructed this interpretation of how nitrate making worked from talks with Liu Futang of Qian Kou, Yao Zhenbian of Qian Foji, and with many former peasant saltmakers, and from inferences drawn from reading Multhauf's splendid study, *Neptune's Gift,* 134–135.

59. Liu Gongchen, Qian Kou, 5/30/87; Liu Guoju, Qian Kou, 6/9/87.

60. Liu Gongchen, Qian Kou, 5/30/87.

61. Ibid.

62. Wei Jingfeng, Qian Kou, 6/9/87. Cf. Zhao Jibin, "Nongcun Pochan Shenzhong Jinan Yige Fanrongde Cunzhuang," 41–42.

63. Liu Shiyin, Qian Kou, 6/12/87. Cf. Zhao Jibin, "Nongcun Pochan Shenzhong Jinan Yige Fanrongde Cunzhuang," 35–36.

64. Liu Gongchen, Qian Kou, 5/30/87.

65. Wei Jingfeng, Qian Kou, 6/9/87.

66. Liu Shiyin, Qian Kou, 6/12/87.

67. Ibid.

68. Liu Yunxing, Qian Kou, 6/12/87.

69. Liu Yufeng, Zhengzhou, 6/14/87.

70. Zhao Yungzheng, Qian Kou, 6/11/87.

71. *Liucun Xiang Xiangzhi Chugao,* 38.

72. Liu Yufeng, "Zhinan Shaqu Nongmin Geming Douzheng Pianduan," 56–57.

73. Ibid.

74. Zhao Wangni, Qian Kou, 6/1/87.

75. Liu Guoju, Qian Kou, 6/8/87.

76. Liu Shiyin, Qian Kou, 6/12/87.

77. According to Zhao Jibin, "Many peasants—almost all of the young ones—have the habit of smoking cigarettes and gambling, and there is a tendency that they will not wear anything not made of foreign cloth." "Nongcun Pochan Shenzhong Jinan Yige Fanrongde Cunzhuang," 44.

78. This was the case even for the poorest peasants.

79. *Liucun Xiang Xiangzhi Chugao*, 118.

80. I have uncovered only one exception, that of Zhao Lianqing, who died of a hunger- related health problem at the time of the 1937 flood.

81. *Liucun Xiang Xiangzhi Chugao*, 6.

82. Zhao Wangni, Qian Kou, 6/1/87.

83. Ibid.

84. Liu Yunxing, Qian Kou, 6/12/87.

85. Liu Shiyin, Qian Kou, 6/12/87.

86. Cf. Zhao Jibin, "Nongcun Pochan Shenzhong Jinan Yige Fanrongde Cunzhuang," 42–43. Prior to 1920 Qian Kou had a surplus labor force. But afterwards, with the development of peanut culture and salt making, its landlords and rich peasants had to employ at least one hundred hired hands to perform labor services for them. Ninety percent were outsiders.

87. Many peasants say they did not borrow grain or money in this period, and the only flurry of borrowing came in the face of the famine of 1942. Cf. Wei Jingfeng, Qian Kou, 6/9/87; Liu Tieyu, Qian Kou, 6/12/87; Ma Xinxi, Qian Kou, 6/11/87; Liu Yufeng, Zhengzhou, 6/14/87.

88. Liu Shiyin, Qian Kou, 6/12/87; Zhao Yunzheng, Qian Kou, 6/11/87.

89. There was, to be sure, limited indirect objective exploitation through money lending, price manipulation, and grain bank "service fee charges" such as those started by Zhao Shaofu, but few if any of Qian Kou's inhabitants were driven to desperation by landlord exploitation. Cf. Zhao Jibin, "Zhinan Shaqu Dang Zuzhide Zaoqi Huodong," 173, 179.

90. Ma Xinxi, Qian Kou, 6/11/87.

91. Cf. Zhao Jibin, "Nongcun Pochan Shenzhong Jinan Yige Fanrongde Cunzhuang," 37. Zhao's essay claims there were more than 280 households in Qian Kou at this time; local village leaders say this is too high, so that I have stayed with their estimate of 240. They agree that 90 percent of the households were involved with earth salt production.

92. For Zhao Wangni it was 55 percent, Qian Kou, 6/1/87; for Zhao Yungzheng it was 39 percent, Qian Kou, 6/11/87; for Liu Guoju it was 21 percent, though if we add nitrate it was over 50 percent, Qian Kou, 6/9/87; for Liu Shiyin it was 25 percent, Qian Kou, 6/12/87, but 43 percent if we add in nitrate income.

93. Liu Shiren, Qian Kou, 5/31/87.

94. Liu Yufeng, Zhengzhou, 6/14/87.

95. Ibid. This is corroborated in Wang Congwu et al, "Puyang Yanmin Douzheng," 171.

96. Ma Xinxi, Qian Kou, 6/11/87.

97. Zhao Tianbao, Qian Kou, 6/1/87.

98. Ibid.

99. Ibid.

100. Liu Shiren, Qian Kou, 5/31/87.
101. Wei Jingfeng, Qian Kou, 6/8/87.
102. Liu Shiren, Qian Kou, 5/31/87.
103. Liu Yufeng, Zhengzhou, 6/14/87.
104. Ibid.
105. Ma Xinxi, Qian Kou, 6/11/87.
106. Geertz, *Local Knowledge,* 53–70.
107. Liu Shiren, Qian Kou, 5/31/87.
108. Liu Yufeng, Zhengzhou, 6/14/87.
109. Zhao Yungfu, Qian Kou, 5/30/87.
110. Liu Tieyu, 6/12/87.
111. Zhao Yungfu, 5/30/87.
112. Zhao Xingzheng, 5/31/87.
113. From my talks with Liu Futang, Qian Kou, 6/9–12/87; and from my observations of the cordial relationship between Liu peasants and Liu "landlord offspring" in the alleyways of Qian Kou.
114. Zhao Yungfu, Qian Kou, 5/31/87.
115. On this point, see Liu Hansheng, "Dang Lingdau Shaqu Qunzhongde Geming Douzheng," 30–31; Wang Congwu, "Zhongguo Gongchandong Lingdau Pu-Nei-Hua Diqu Renminde Douzheng," 49. Cf. note 143 in this chapter.
116. Because the Puyang CCP leaders had infiltrated the Puyang Public Security Bureau and had the sympathy of some of its members as well as Kuomintang party activists in the Puyang County government, the Puyang magistrate had to be very careful about using force at this time. Cf. Zhao Jibin, "Huiyi Puyangde Geming Douzheng," 40.
117. Ibid., 1–2.
118. Ibid., 2.
119. Ibid., 3–4.
120. Ibid,, 3–4.
121. *Liucun Xiang Xiangzhi Chugao,* 34, 36–38.
122. Ibid.
123. Ibid., 38.
124. Ibid., 34, 36–38.
125. Ibid., 40–42.
126. My interpretation of "Wen Xinggu Shijian," 82–84.
127. Liu Yufeng, "Zhinan Shaqu Nongmin Geming Douzheng Pianduan," 53–54; *Liucun Xiang Xiangzhi Chugao,* 42–44.
128. Liu Yufeng, "Zhinan Shaqu Nongmin Geming Douzheng Pianduan," 57–58.
129. *Liucun Xiang Xiangzhi Chugao,* 44.
130. Liu Yufeng, "Zhinan Shaqu Nongmin Geming Douzheng Pianduan," 58.
131. I tend to agree with Samuel Popkin and the University of Chicago Business School in that I see peasants as rational calculators of their economic interest, as people inclined to maximize the rewards they can obtain from owning personal property and pursuing commercial exchange. Cf. Popkin, *The Rational Peasant,* 64, 69–72. This, however, does not mean that peasants do not practice moral economy.

Moreover, as I will suggest in the chapters ahead, whether peasants are "rational economists" who are getting ahead or "moral economists" at the subsistence level has little to do with *why they rebel.*

132. *Liucunxiang Xiangzhi Chugao,* 49.

133. Ibid., 50–52.

134. All of my oral histories of Qian Kou confirm this. In particular, see Zhao Tianbao, Qian Kou, 6/1/87.

135. For the original argument of "fixed scarcity" as a factor inhibiting virtually any sort of significant collective political behavior by peasants see Banfield, *The Moral Basis of a Backward Society.*

136. Compare with Lewis, "Memory, Opportunity, and Strategy in Peasant Revolutions: The Case of North China," 2, 22; cf. Lewis, "The Study of Chinese Political Culture," 503–524.

137. In every case I have investigated for Qian Kou.

138. For the concept see Bowen, "Moral Shares: Divisions of Wealth in Sumatran Societies," 5–8, 11.

139. I am indebted to Ramon H. Myers for helping me to clarify this point.

140. Liu Futang, the Qian Kou village chief, told me that Zhao Jibin was from landlord stock. Xu Shurong, the Puyang County CCP historian, also confirmed this and said it was the case for Liu Hansheng's family too. Liu Hansheng clearly had gentry connections. 6/13/87, in Puyang town.

141. Liu Yufeng, "Zhinan Shaqu Nongmin Geming Douzheng Pianduan," 54.

142. *Liucunxiang Xiangzhi Chugao,* 34–37; Zhao Jibin, "Zhinan Shaqu Dang Zuzhide Zaoqi Huodong," 177.

143. The families of Zhao Jibin and Liu Hansheng sold land to get them out of jail in 1930 and 1931.

144. Zhao Jibin, "Zhinan Shaqu Dang Zuzhide Zaoqi Huodong," 6–7.

145. Liu Yufeng, "Zhinan Shaqu Nongmin Geming Douzheng Pianduan," 54–55.

146. Ibid., 53–55.

147. Ibid.

148. Wang Congwu's memoir leaves little doubt that in discovering the salt people's indignation against the salt police the CCP discovered the necessity of uniting every force possible to resist the oppression of the ruling political class. It was through involvement with the struggles of the peasant saltmakers that the party cadres gave priority to politics and placed class concerns on a back burner. "Zhongguo Gongchandang Lingdau Pu-Nei-Hua Diqu Renminde Geming Douzheng," 49.

CHAPTER 5. THE POLICE ATTACK ON IMPOVERISHED QI JI

1. Chen Shenyi, "Yanmin Baodong," 78–79.

2. Ibid.

3. Chang Fusen, "Cong Hua*xian* Yannong Douzheng Kan Nongmin Yundongde Juda Weili," 5.

4. Ibid., 6.

5. From a discussion with Liu Jingzhao, Qi Ji, 6/14/88.

6. Duan lineage records, given by Duan Dongqing, Qi Ji village, 6/8/87.

7. Ibid.

8. Interview of Duan Dongqing, Qi Ji, 6/8/87.

9. Duan Zhouqing, Qi Ji, 6/8/87.

10. Duan lineage records, 6/8/87.

11. Popkin, *The Rational Peasant,* 28–29, 64.

12. This "submarginal peasantry" thesis is strongly implicit in Mats Lundahl's work on Haitian peasant economy. Cf. Lundahl, *Peasants and Poverty;* and *The Haitian Economy,* 23–53. Lundahl's model of Haiti has four key features, all of which recapture the pre-1949 dilemma of Qi Ji: (1) smallholding peasant villages without sharp class stratification; (2) population explosion and land scarcity; (3) low, falling, agricultural income along with great vulnerability to price increases in basic food items; (4) government neglect of agriculture. The result is a submarginal standard of living and chronic nutritional stress.

13. Liu Guoxing, Qi Ji, 6/4/87.

14. Liu Caoyang, Qi Ji, 6/5/87.

15. Liu Chaoqing, Qi Ji, 6/5/87.

16. Tawney, *Land and Labor in China,* 77.

17. Duan Aiqing tells us that the twenty *mu* of land he worked was tax exempt and that the old government taxed him only a tiny sum for five *mu* he planted to wheat. Qi Ji, 6/8/87.

18. Liu Chaodong, Qi Ji, 6/5/87.

19. Duan Fatian, Qi Ji, 6/7/87.

20. Ibid.

21. Liu Chaodong and Liu Jingzhao, Qi Ji, 6/5/87. Liu Jingzhao is the son of Liu Chaodong. He was the chief of west Qi Ji for nearly thirty years after liberation.

22. Liu Chaoyang, Qi Ji, 6/5/87.

23. Slawinski, "The Red Spears in the Late 1920s," 203–204, 210–211; Perry, *Rebels and Revolutionaries in North China,* chap. 5, 156, 163–164.

24. Liu Chaoyang, Qi Ji, 6/5/87.

25. Ibid.

26. Ibid.

27. Ibid.

28. Duan Fatian, Qi Ji, 6/7/87.

29. Wang Mingdao, Qi Ji, 6/8/87.

30. Duan Fatian, Qi Ji, 6/7/87.

31. Nie Zhen, "Guanyu Hua*xian* Geming Yundong He Jiandang Guochengde Yiduan Huiyi," 148.

32. Duan Dongqing, Qi Ji, 6/8/87.

33. Duan Fatian, Qi Ji, 6/9/87.

34. Ibid.

35. Liu Chaoyang, Duan Futain, and Liu Jingjiao all agree on this point. Qi Ji, 6/4-5/87.

36. Liu Chaodong, Qi Ji, 6/5/87 and 6/14/88.

37. Liu Chaodong, Qi Ji, 6/14/88.

38. Duan Zhouqing speaking of "landlords" Duan Baotian and Duan Jingxuan. Qi Ji, 6/8/87.

39. Xu Youli, "Sanshi Niandai Ji-Lu-Yu Biande Yanmin Douzheng," 60.

40. Xu Youli, Hua County, 6/7/87.

41. Chang Senren, "Hua*xian* Yanmin Douzheng Jishi," 21–22.

42. To this day some peasants are not clear on the difference between the "bandit police" and the police of the state-directed salt monopoly.

43. Liu Guoxing, Qi Ji village, 6/4/87.

44. Ibid.

45. "Henan Sheng Hua*xian* Ba Li Ying Xiang Shi," chap. 4, pt. 1, "Minguo Gemingqi," 1–2

46. Liu Xingquan, Qi Ji, 6/5/87.

47. Liu Chaoqing, Qi Ji, 6/5/87.

48. Liu Chaode, "Guanyu Yanmin Douzhengde Huiyi," 32.

49. Liu Jingxing, the son of Liu Chaode, in Qi Ji village, 6/14/88.

50. Chang Senren, "Hua*xian* Yanmin Douzheng Jishi," 24.

51. Liu Chaode, "Guanyu Yanmin Douzhengde Huiyi," 34; talk with Chang Fusen, local historian of Hua County, Dao Kou, 6/7/87.

52. Chang Senren, "Hua*xian* Yanmin Douzheng Jishi," 25–26.

53. Ibid., 28–29; Chang Fusen, Dao Kou, 6/7/87.

54. Chang Senren, "Hua*xian* Yanmin Douzheng Jishi, 31–32.

55. Kung-Chuan Hsiao, *Compromise in Imperial China*, 24–29.

56. Chang Senren, "Hua*xian* Yanmin Douzheng Jishi, 33–37.

57. Ibid., 32, 35–37.

58. Chang Fusen, interview in Dao Kou, 6/7/87.

59. Chang Fusen, "Yanmin Nuhuo," 26.

60. Ibid., 36.

61. Ibid., 37.

62. Liu Guoxing, Qi Ji, 6/4/87.

63. Liu Chaodong, Qi Ji, 6/4/87.

64. Liu Guoxing, Qi Ji, 6/4/87.

65. Chang Fusen, "Cong Hua*xian* Yannong Douzheng Kan Nongmin Yundongde Juda Weili," 3–4.

66. Ibid.

67. Chang Senren, "Hua*xian* Yanmin Douzheng Jishi," 46–51.

68. Chen Shenyi, "Yanmin Baodong," 82.

69. Liu Xingquan, Qi Ji, 6/5/87.

70. Chang Fusen, "Cong Hua*xian* Yannong Douzheng Kan Nongmin Yundongde Juda Weili," 4–5.

71. Ibid., 5.

72. Chang Fusen, "Yanmin Nuhuo," 34–35.

73. Ibid., 5.

74. Chen Shenyi, "Yanmin Baodong," 84.

75. Chang Fusen, "Cong Hua*xian* Yannong Douzheng Kan Nongmin Yundongde Juda Weili,"4.

76. Liu Xiaoxing, Qi Ji village, 6/7/87.

77. Liu Chaodong, Qi Ji village, 6/6/87.

78. Ibid.

79. Chang Fusen, "Cong Hua*xian* Yannong Douzheng Kan Nongmin Yundongde Juda Weili," 5–6.

80. Chang Fusen, "Yanmin Nuhuo," 39.

81. Ibid., 40.

82. Ibid., 39–40.

83. Ibid., 41.

84. Liu Chaode, "Guanyu Yanmin Douzhengde Huiyi," 31; "Wang Congwu Tongzhi Huiyilu," 29.

85. Liu Chaode, "Guanyu Yanmin Douzhengde Huiyi," 34.

86. Ibid. Cf. Wei Yinshun, Fanzhuang, 6/4/88; Shi Guoqiang, Nanle County town, 8/4/91.

87. Chang Fusen, "Yanmin Nuhuo," 33–34.

88. My inference, from Chang Lizeng, "Tianzhujiaode Youlai he Zai Wo Xiande Yanbian," 49.

89. Ibid.

90. Liu Xingquan, Qi Ji, 6/5/87.

91. Ibid.

92. Chang Fusen, "Yanmin Nuhuo," 33–34.

93. "Cong Hua Xian Yannong Douzheng," 3–4.

94. Chang Fusen, "Yanmin Nuhuo," 33–34.

95. Nie Zhen, "Guanyu Hua*xian* Geming Yundong He Jiandang Guochengde Yixie Huiyi," 148, 152.

96. Liu Jingjiao, Qi Ji; Duan Donqing, Qi Ji; and Liu Chaoyang, Qi Ji, 6/5/87. Only nine people had joined the CCP by 1949.

97. Liu Chaoyang, Qi Ji, 6/5/87.

98. Ibid.

99. Cf. Zhao Wei, *The Biography of Zhao Ziyang*, 26–28.

100. Although the case of Qi Ji warns against embracing Banfield, his hypothesis is not totally irrelevant to the political behavior of its peasants in the post-1932 period. *The Moral Basis of a Backward Society*, 85–104.

101. Lu Jingxing, Qi Ji, 6/14/88.

102. Li Yixing, Qi Ji, 6/8/87.

103. Duan Fatian, Qi Ji, 6/7/87; Wang Cishou, Qi Ji, 6/4/87.

104. Duan lineage records, related by Duan Dongqing, Qi Ji, 6/7/87.

105. Ibid.

106. Duan Fatian, Qi Ji, 6/7/87.

107. Mi Jingjiang, Qi Ji, 6/7/87.

108. Gao Tingdong remembers his aunt could not be buried in 1938 because the family could not afford a coffin. Qi Ji, 6/8/87. Peter Seybolt's interview data on Duan Jingnian confirms the point. Qi Ji village, 6/5/87.

109. Cf. J. K. Campbell's discussion of theft as an honorable undertaking in rural Greece. *Honor, Family and Patronage*, 206–207.

110. Liu Jingjiao, Qi Ji, 6/7/87.

111. Duan Fatian, Qi Ji, 6/7/87.

112. Campbell, *Honor, Family and Patronage*, 207.

113. Mi Jingjiang, Qi Ji, 6/8/87.

114. Liu Jingxing, Qi Ji, 6/14/88; Liu Chaoyang, Qi Ji, 8/9/90.

115. Ibid.

116. Ibid.

117. By way of contrast, Geertz claims that peasants in Java despised the small traders of the bazaars and looked on them as "outsiders." But Geertz also notes that the process of trade was geared to local concepts of right and wrong. *Peddlers and Princes,* 44.

118. Mi Jingjiang, Qi Ji, 6/8/87.

119. Nie Zhen, "Guanyu Hua*xian* Geming Yundong He Jiandang Guochengde Yixie Huiyi," 145.

120. Ibid.

121. Liu Chaodong, Qi Ji, 6/5/87; Liu Jingxing, Qi Ji, 6/14/88.

122. Chang Lizeng, "Tianzhujiaode Youlai he Zai Wo Xiande Yanbian," 47–48.

123. Ibid., 49–50, 64.

124. Ibid., 49, 53–54.

125. Ibid., 52–53.

126. Liu Chaodong, Qi Ji, 6/5/87; Liu Jingxing, Qi Ji, 6/14/88.

127. Chang Lizeng, "Tianzhujiaode Youlai he Zai Wo Xiande Yanbian," 53; Liu Chaodong, Qi Ji, 6/5/87.

128. Ibid.

129. Liu Jingxing, Qi Ji, 6/14/88.

130. Chang Lizeng, "Tianzhujiaode Youlai he Zai Wo Xiande Yanbian," 49–52.

131. Cf. Cohen, *China and Christianity,* 84–86, 128, 270–271; Hsu, *The Rise of Modern China,* 388; Tucker, *Patterns in the Dust,* 101–102; Esherick, *The Origins of the Boxer Uprising,* 74–75, 83, 84–86.

132. Cf. Esherick, *The Origins of the Boxer Uprising,* 267–268.

133. Wang Congwu et al., "Puyang Yanming Douzheng," 173.

134. Cf. Liu Chaode, "Guanyu Yanmin Douzhengde Huyi," 34.

135. This is in line with Hsu's logic, *The Rise of Modern China,* 90–91.

136. This is in line with Esherick's wisdom, *The Origins of the Boxer Uprising,* 90–91.

137. Nie Zhen, "Guanyu Hua*xian* Geming Yundong He Jiandang Guochengde Yiduan Huiyi," 150–152.

138. Ibid., 151.

139. Cf. Zhao Wei, *The Biography of Zhao Ziyang,* 16.

140. Liu Chaoxin, Qi Ji, 6/6/87. (Peter Seybolt)

141. Cf. Chang Lizeng, "Tianzhujiaode Youlai he Zai Wo Xiande Yanbian," 49, 51–52.

142. Ibid.

143. Liu Chaode, "Guanyu Yanmin Douzhengde Huiyi," 34.

CHAPTER 6. THE BATTLE WITH THE BICYCLE COPS
IN SUBSISTENCE-LEVEL FANZHUANG

1. *Dagong Bao,* 8 October 1935.

2. "Yijiu Sanwu Nian Shiyue Xiaoyan Jiufen," 31–33.

3. "Yijiu Sanwu Nian Wuyue Jinan Xiaoyan Douzheng," 19–20.

4. "Jinan Xiaoyan Zhishi," 14–19; Zhang Ziyou, "Nanle Xian Yanmin Douzhengde Huiyi," 199–200.

5. Zhang Ziyou, "Nanle Xian Yanmin Douzhengde Huiyi," 199–200.

6. Wu Baohe, "Dui Yanmin Douzhengde Huiyi," 229.

7. Ibid, 229–230.

8. Zhang Ziyou, "Nanle Xian Yanmin Douzhengde Huiyi," 216–217.

9. Wei Yinshun, Fanzhuang, 6/14/88.

10. Thaxton, "Fanzhuang Village Land Survey," 6/9–10/88.

11. Ibid.

12. Song Shanguan, Fanzhuang, 6/10/88.

13. Zhang Yun, Fanzhuang, 6/9/88.

14. Wang Wenxun, Fanzhuang, 6/6/88.

15. Wang Jingru, Beijing, 6/16/88.

16. Song Shanguan, Fanzhuang, 6/2/88.

17. Zhai Zhongchun, Fanzhuang, 6/3/88.

18. Ibid.

19. Wei Yinshun, Fanzhuang, 6/4/88.

20. Shi Guoqiang, Nanle County town, 6/12/88.

21. Wei Lanxi, Fanzhuang, 6/3/88.

22. Zhang Yun, Fanzhuang, 6/9/88.

23. Song Shanguan, Fanzhuang, 6/2, 10/88.

24. Wei Qingyuan, Fanzhuang, 6/5/88.

25. Zhai Zuolin, Fanzhuang, 6/3, 7/88.

26. Yao Zhixian, Fanzhuang, 6/7/88.

27. Wei Yinchun, Fanzhuang, 6/10/88.

28. Zhai Zuolin, Fanzhuang, 6/3/88.

29. Yao Zhixian, Fanzhuang, 6/6/88.

30. Wei Yinshun, Fanzhuang, 6/5/88.

31. Yao Zhixian, Fanzhuang, 6/6/88; Zhai Zuolin, 6/3, 7/88.

32. Song Shangwen, Fanzhuang, 6/2/88; Wang Linsun, 6/6/88 (one of the few households not in the seven main lineages).

33. Yao Zhixian, Zhai Zuolin, Zhang Yun, Fanzhuang, 6/6, 7, 9/88.

34. Zhang Yun, Fanzhuang, 6/9/88.

35. Ibid.

36. Zhai Zuolin, Fanzhuang, 6/3, 7/88.

37. Ibid.

38. Zhang Ke, Fanzhuang, 6/6/88.

39. The CCP documents leave the impression that Fanzhuang was one of the strongholds of a Communist-led saltmakers' protest movement from 1931 to 1934. This is not true. Cf. Zhang Ziyou, "Nanle Xian Yanmin Douzhengde Huiyi," 199–200.

40. Cf. "Changlu Jiwu Qingxing Jilue," 69–70; talks with Shi Guoqiang, Nanle town, 6/12–13/88.

41. The rumor seems to have reflected reality. Cf. "Daming Yidai Qunzhong He Yanxunde Douzheng," 121–122.

42. In developing this section, I have benefitted from reading Scott, *Weapons of the Weak*, 265–289. His thesis, which holds that peasants generally respond intelligently to situations of powerlessness and that even quiescence and deferential dissent are often conscious and calculated resistance by the powerless, seems highly plausible. I encountered few peasants in Fanzhuang who were not terrified of the police and few who said they resisted the police. Still, I was able to uncover a lively pattern of what Scott calls "routine resistance" within the framework of veiled compliance. In some ways, this resistance did such a thorough job of covering its own footprints that much of it never became common knowledge within the village as a whole, which makes it a very different affair than Qian Kou or Qi Ji.

43. Zhang Ke, Fanzhuang, 6/6/88.

44. Zhai Zuolin, Fanzhuang, 6/6/88.

45. Zhai Zhongchun, Fanzhuang, 6/8/88.

46. Ibid.

47. Wei Yinshun, Fanzhuang, 6/4/88.

48. Yao Shixuan, Fanzhuang, 6/3/88.

49. Wei Kexi, Fanzhuang, 6/9/88.

50. Yao Zhixian, Fanzhuang, 6/6–7/88.

51. Ibid., 6/6/88.

52. Ibid.

53. Zhai Zhongchun, Fanzhuang, 6/8/88.

54. Wei Yingshun, Fanzhuang, 6/4/88.

55. Zhai Fating, 6/6/88.

56. Wei Qingyuan, 6/5/88.

57. Zhai Fating, 6/6/88.

58. Zhang Yun, Fanzhuang, 6/9/88.

59. Ibid.

60. For the conceptual framework, see Scott, *Weapons of the Weak*, 274.

61. Wei Chunyun, Fanzhuang, 6/6/88.

62. Wang Wenxun, Fanzhuang, 6/6/88.

63. Ibid.

64. Wang Jingru, Beijing, 6/16/88. Wang Jian changed his name to Wang Jingru in the late 1930s after he was placed on a "wanted list" by the Kuomintang.

65. Wang Jingru, "Guanyu Zuzhi Yanmin Fan Yanxun Chajin Xiaoyande Douzheng Wenti," 6–7.

66. Cf. "Nanle Yanmin Douzheng," 229–230.

67. "Daming Yidai Qunzhong He Yanxunde Douzheng," 121–122.

68. Zhai Zuolin, Fanzhuang, 6/3/88; Wei Yinshun, Fanzhuang, 6/4/88.

69. Zhang Ke, Fanzhuang, 8/14/90.

70. On the bloody clash of 12 April 1935, see "Nanle Xian Fasheng Liuxie Canjiu," 3. Cf. "Jinan Xiaoyan Zhishi."

71. Zhai Fating, 6/6/88; Wei Qingyuan, 6/5/88.

72. Wu Baohe, "Dui Yanmin Douzhengde Huiyi," 230.

73. Wei Qingyuan, 6/5/88.

74. In 1935 the Changlu salt police sent a letter to the *Da Gong Bao* newspaper to dispute whether the saltmakers in Nanle faced a serious problem of livelihood. According to this police letter, there was no such problem. The salt people in Nanle

were said to have been stirred up by bandits in the counties along the Hebei-Shandong-Henan border area, whose plan was to use the salt people. A Kuomintang army battalion stationed in Daming and a unit of the salt tax police were said to have foiled this plan. The police letter nevertheless confirms a gathering of a thousand people in Nanle and reports that Zhang Yongheng showed up at this meeting with local notables to persuade the saltmakers they were violating the law by making salt. The leader of the saltmakers supposedly signed a document promising not to make *xiaoyan,* and thus the "riot" was peacefully resolved. According to the police, this is how the Nanle incident of the spring of 1935 started and ended.

The above letter only goes to show why we must consider events from every angle: the peasants have their version of this event; the CCP has its version; the police have their version; and the Republican newspaper reporters and editors have theirs. None of them is exactly the same. In the case of Nanle, the news stories carried by *Da Gong Bao* are pretty much in line with what I have gleaned from my talks with the older peasants. It is, therefore, very intriguing to learn that the real purpose of this police letter was to *warn* the editors of *Da Gong Bao* to check their stories with the *state authorities* in order to avoid "misunderstandings." See "Lai Han Zhao Deng."

75. Shi Guoqiang, in his home in Nanle town, 6/12/88.

76. Zhang Ziyou, "Nanle Xian Yanmin Douzhengde Huiyi," 205–206; Shi Guoqiang, 6/12/88.

77. Shi Guoqiang, Nanle town, 6/12/88; "Nanle Yanmin Douzheng," 1–3.

78. Zhang Ziyou, "Nanle Yanmin Douzhengde Huiyi," 206–207.

79. Wang Wenxun in a conversation with Wang and Wei Yinshun on 6/4/88, before I interviewed Wang individually on 6/5/88 in Fanzhuang.

80. Zhang Ziyou, "Nanle Yanmin Douzhengde Huiyi," 207.

81. Ibid, 221–222.

82. Ibid.

83. Wang Wenxun, Fanzhuang, 6/4/88.

84. Shi Guoqiang, Zhubian (Chief Editor), "Yanmin Douzheng," 266.

85. Xue Xujian, San Huang, 6/11/88.

86. Li Shengzhi, "Da Yanbing," 2.

87. Xue Xujian, San Huang, 6/11/88.

88. Zhai Zuolin first learned about the saltmakers' struggle in the years when he was forced into wage labor in the town, 1931–35. Fanzhuang, 6/3/88.

89. Xue Jianchao, San Huang, 6/11/88.

90. "Nanle Yanmin Douzheng," 2.

91. Xiao Jianchao, San Huang, 6/11/88.

92. Yang Zepu and Yang Depu (two brothers), San Huang, 6/11/88.

93. Zhang Yun, Fanzhuang, 6/9/88.

94. Wei Qingyuan, Fanzhuang, 6/15/88.

95. I have benefitted from Tilly, *The Contentious French,* 308–309, in constructing this section.

96. Shi Guoqiang, San Huang, 6/11/88.

97. Shi Guoqiang and Yang Zepu, San Huang, 6/11/88.

98. Shi Guoqiang, San Huang, 6/13/88.

99. Wang Shanzeng, "Nanle Hongqianghuide Xingqi Yu Xiaowang," 57. Also see "Jinan Xiaoyan Zhishi."

100. Wang Shangzeng, "Nanle Hongqianghuide Xingqi Yu Xiaowang," 55. Additional evidence on the Boxer–Red Spear connection, and on the Red Spear support for the saltmakers' struggle, can be found in "Gaotang Gu Guantun 'Nongmin Ziweituan' Baodong," 3–7; Jin Gulan, "Guanyu Gaotang Hongtuan Gongzuode Baogao," 12–13; Jin Weiyuan, "Jin Gulan Tongzhi Jianshi," 24–25; "Jian Zhanjia Tongzhi Zhuanlue," 27–29.

101. Shi Guoqiang, "Zhang Fuqiu 'Ba Da Jia' yu 'Xiao Ba Jia' Douzheng Shimou," 161–162.

102. Ibid., 62–63.

103. Wang Shanzeng, "Nanle Honqianghui Xingqi Yu Xiaowang," 57.

104. Shi Guoqiang, "Zhang Fuqiu 'Ba Da Jia' yu 'Xiao Ba Jia' Douzheng Shimou," 66.

105. Ibid., 63.

106. Ibid.

107. Shi Guoqiang, San Huang, 6/13/88; Shi Guoqiang, "Zhang Fuqiu 'Ba Da Jia' yu 'Xiao Ba Jia' Douzheng Shimou," 63.

108. Ibid.

109. Ibid. Yang Yan is said to have cursed the peasant saltmakers on learning, after April 12, that they had reached a peaceful settlement on the earth salt issue with the magistrate.

110. Zhang Ziyou, "Nanle Xian Yanmin Douzhengde Huiyi," 201–203.

111. Ren Zhang, San Huang, 6/12–13/88; Xue Xuqi, San Huang, 6/13/88, in separate interviews.

112. Zhou Xueming, San Huang, 6/13/88. Ren Zhang was also a witness to and participant in this collective protest. Though his published memoir makes no mention of his role in the Red Spears, Ren Zhang told me that "I joined the Red Spears when I was 22, just before the Wu Li Bei struggle. I joined the Red Spears in order to fight the salt police. All of the 50 to 60 people who joined the Red Spears in San Huang were saltmakers." 6/13/88.

113. Zhang Ziyou, "Nanle Xian Yanmin Douzhengde Huiyi," 216–217; Shi Guoqiang, Nanle town, 6/12/88.

114. Compare the logic here with Sabean, *Power in the Blood,* 3–4, 13–14, 20–24.

115. Zhang Ziyou, "Nanle Xian Yanmin Douzhengde Huiyi," 204–205, 221.

116. Shi Guoqiang, in his Nanle home, 6/12/88.

117. Shi Guoqiang, in his home, 6/13/88.

118. Shi Guoqiang, in his home, 6/13/88. For an illuminating explanation of how local sages and magistrates have aligned with peasant communities through practical actions, which, in turn, enhanced their standing locally, see Sabean, *Power in the Blood,* 193–198.

119. According to Chung-li Chang, the *gongsheng* title was Imperial acknowledgement of academic excellence and qualified the recipient as a gentry "regular," that is, as a member of the "most important sector of the gentry." *The Chinese Gentry,* 4–5.

120. Shi Guoqiang, in his home, 6/13/88.

121. See "Jinan Xiaoyan Zhishi." On the role of the gentry, also see "Nanle Canan Shanhou."

122. Shi Guoqiang, in his home, 6/13/88.

123. Zhang Yun, Fanzhuang, 6/9/88.

124. Ibid.

125. Wei Jing, Fanzhuang, 6/3/88; Zhang Yun, Fanzhuang, 6/9/88.

126. Zhai Zuolin, 6/3–7/88, Zhang Yun, 6/9/88, Wei Yinchun, 6/10/88, all in Fanzhuang.

127. Zhai Zuolin, Fanzhuang, 6/7/88.

128. Compare with Polachek's position, which is that Scott's notion of "moral economy" does not have empirical validity for Republican China. Cf. Polachek, "The Moral Economy of the Kiangsi Soviet (1928–1934)," 825–826.

129. Wei Qingyuan, Fanzhuang, 6/5/88.

130. Wang Wenxun, Fanzhuang, 6/5/88.

131. Zhai Fating, 6/6/88; Zhai Zuolin, 6/7/88; Zhang Yun, 6/9/88; Wei Yinchun, 6/10/88. In four separate household interviews, each in Fanzhuang.

132. Zhang Yun, 6/9/88; Wei Yinchun, Fanzhuang, 6/10/88.

133. On the importance of lineage relations in rural North China, see Duara, *Culture, Power, and the State,* 91–94. Duara has suggested that "there was no necessary correlation between lineage strength and wealth in North China." I suspect the strongest lineages were often the wealthiest ones. Just *how often* is, of course, the real issue.

134. I am indebted to Eastman for his survey of the issue of family structure and the inheritance process in rural China. Cf. *Family, Field, and Ancestors,* 16–18.

135. Wang Wenxun, Fanzhuang, 6/5/88.

136. As Scott's work suggests, *The Moral Economy of the Peasant,* 212–213.

137. Wei Jing, Fanzhuang, 6/10/88.

138. Wang Wenxun, Fanzhuang, 6/5/88; Wang Jingru, Beijing, 6/16/88.

139. I have profited from Scott's discussion of patronage and political activism here. Needless to say, the connection between the two does not always have to lend itself to demobilization. Cf. *The Moral Economy of the Peasant,* 222–223.

140. Wang Jingru, "Guanyu Zuzhi Yanmin Fan Yanxun Chajin Xiaoyande Douzheng Wenti," 6.

141. Wang Jingru, Beijing, 6/16/88.

142. John P. Burns has written that "before 1949 poor peasants depended on cultivating good relations with their rich peasant, landlord and merchant neighbors, who mediated between them and the state. The relations were often built on shared circumstances such as kinship, community, or village ties. In South China, in particular, the leaders of powerful lineage groups were not only the source of patronage, but acted to relay peasants' political interest to the larger community. Still, the basis of these relationships was undoubtedly self-interest: peasants accepted the protection of patrons because it was in their interest to do so." This sounds like the structure of peasant political relations in Fanzhuang, Nanle. Cf. Burns, *Political Participation in Rural China,* 7, 178.

143. Wang Jingru, 6/16/88.

144. Zhai Qingling, Fanzhuang, 6/8/88.

145. Yao Zhisan held the position of Kuomintang Party secretary for about ten years, roughly 1934 to 1944. Cao Pusheng, *Nanle Xianzhi,* 257–258.

146. Wang Jingru, Beijing, 6/16/88. This point was confirmed by several of my interviews with Fanzhuang peasants, who, after the Anti-Japanese War, requested the new CCP government to kill Yao Zhisan.

147. Ibid.

148. Zhang Yun, who says he has no religion,Fanzhuang, 6/9/88. The rich testimony on this point, however, is by Wei Jin and his son, Wei Jingbao, Fanzhuang, 6/10/ 88. I am grateful to Wei Jingbao for his thoughtful critique of my interpretation of the politics surrounding the Kuomintang destruction of the Guandi temple. After liberation, the peasants of Fanzhuang rebuilt the Guandi temple, only to see it destroyed by the Cultural Revolution radicals. In early 1988, the temple was rebuilt again, with voluntary public contributions, and peasants again are hanging little pictures of Guangong in their household altars and worshipping him during the Spring Festival.

149. Duara, *Culture, Power, and the State,* 141.

150. Wei Jing, Fanzhuang, 6/10/88.

151. I have drawn from Tarrow's helpful discussion to draw out this issue. "Big Structures and Contentious Events," 200.

152. Cf. Wei Jing and Wei Jingbao, Fanzhuang, 6/10/88.

153. Shi Guoqiang, Nanle town, 8/4/91.

154. Wang Jingru, Beijing, 6/16/88.

155. Ibid.

156. Cf. Shi Yibin, "Guanyu Sun Hanzhang Tongzhi Jianqian Zai Nanle Jianshi Jinxing Dixia Geming Houdong Qingkuangde Huiyi," 6.

157. Wang Jingru, Beijing, 6/16/88.

CHAPTER 7. PEASANT RESENTMENT, WAR,
AND NATIONAL RESISTANCE

1. The classical statement is Johnson, *Peasant Nationalism and Communist Power,* chap. 1–2.

2. Selden, *The Yenan Way in Revolutionary China,* 277–278.

3. This complex issue has been explored in a stimulating essay. See Eckstein, "Introduction. Toward the Theoretical Study of Internal War," 8–28.

4. Gu Zhike, "Yijiusanwunian Pingxiang Yanmin Wuzhuang Douzheng," 130–131.

5. Ibid., 139.

6. Cf. Chen Juanru, "Changlu Yanwu Shulue," 91–92.

7. Bates (in summarizing the work of Goran Hyden) has pointed out that one school of scholarship sees "peasant-based economies as possessing the capacity to elude the market and undermine the state and thereby forestall the transfer of resources necessary to secure development," "Agrarian Politics," 173. The case at hand underscores this possibility, but it was the peasant insistence on inclusion in the market, not exclusion, that was forestalling the transfer of money to the Republican state.

8. Li Fanjiu et al., "Ding Shuben Zai Pudaqu 'Kangri' Fangong Toudi Shimo," 143–145.

9. Xu Jinshan, Cheng Guan, 9/13/85.

10. Yao Huibin, Beijing, 8/25/89.

11. Personal correspondence with Mr. Mu, 11/28/89.

12. Interview of Jin Huayi, Tianjin, 8/2/91.

13. Ibid. Cf. Chen Juanru, "Changlu Yanwu Shulue," 91–92.

14. Ding Changqing, Tianjin, 8/1/91.

15. This is a key premise of Johnson, *Peasant Nationalism and Communist Power,* chap. 1–2. Cf. Eastman, "Nationalist China During the Sino-Japanese War, 1937–1945," 547–556; Van Slyke, "The Chinese Communist Movement During the Sino-Japanese War 1937–1945," 609–620.

16. Zong Fengming, "Guanyu Puyang Diqu Geming Lishide Huiyi," 244–255.

17. Eastman is superb on this point, "Nationalist China During the Sino-Japanese War, 1937–1945," 556.

18. An Ming (Liu Dafeng), "Ji-Lu-Yu Bianqu Diyizhi Kangri Wuzhuang," 61–62. Also see Peng Yuemei, "Wo Jihui Zongde Sizhidui," 78; Jia Juxin, "Qingfeng Xiande Yanmin Douzheng," 26.

19. Ibid.

20. Li Tiezhong, Qi Lian, and Wang Yuting, "Ji-Lu-Yu Bianqu Diyizhi Kangri Wuzhuang Minjun Sizhiduide Chungjian He Fazhan," 1–2.

21. Ibid.

22. Ibid., 16.

23. Peng Yuemei, "Wo Jihui Zongde Sizhidui," 77–78, 90–92.

24. Wang Zhijia, "Zhinan Tiewei Lingdau Xia Huangde Zhiduide Zujian he Fazhan," 95–97, 100–110.

25. He Fukui and Niu Guoqi, "Liu Yanchun Zhuanlue," 189–190.

26. Cf. Guo Chuanxi and Xu Youli, "Ji-Lu-Yu Bianqu Kangri Genjudide Chuangjian," 17. Guo and Xu do not clearly indicate that the surge in army growth was due to the saltmakers' participation per se. They refer to the new wave of recruits as "the masses who eagerly joined the resistance army." My interviews leave no doubt that the masses were the peasants of the salt lands.

27. Ibid., 34.

28. For the general progression see Li Duo, "Shaqu Kangri Genjudi Chuangjian He Jianchide Yixie Qingkuang," 35.

29. Liu Dafeng says that the Japanese first took Daming as early as October, 1937, "Zhinan Wu Xian Dangde Zhanli Yu Fazhan," 62. My other sources suggest it was in December.

30. Ping Jiesan, "Kangri Zhanzheng Chuqi Zhinan Diqu Dangde Tongzhan Gongzuo," 199–200.

31. Zong Fengming, "Guanyu Puyang Diqu Geming Lishide Huiyi," 244.

32. Eastman has emphasized the importance of distinguishing between the central army officers with binding loyalties to Chiang Kai-shek and the warlord army officers who had risen to power independently of Chiang and the center's officer academies. This is a point well made. The defections of the wartime Kuomintang warlord leaders like Ding Shuben underscore its significance. Cf. "Nationalist China During the Sino-Japanese War," 569–571.

33. Eastman, 558, 571–572. The most convincing evidence on the Kuomintang carrying out war via predatory mobilization is in Eastman, *Seeds of Destruction,* 49, 54–58, 62, 64, 67, 68, 140–142, 152.

34. Li Fanjiu, Tian Hanqing, et al., "Ding Shuben Zai Pudaqu 'Kangri' Fangong Toudi Shimo," 150–151; Zong Fengming, "Guanyu Puyang Diqu Geming Lishide Huiyi," 245.

35. Cf. Eastman, "Nationalist China During the Sino-Japanese War," 501; Eastman, *Seeds of Destruction*, 89–107.

36. For the conceptualization of this issue in general, I have borrowed from Tilly, *The Contentious French*, 85.

37. Li Fangjiu, Tian Hanqing, et al., "Ding Shuben Zai Pudaqu 'Kangri' Fangong Toudi Shimo," 130–155.

38. Ibid., 154–155.

39. Ibid.

40. White, *In Search of History*, 150–151.

41. Zong Fengming, "Guanyu Puyang Diqu Geming Lishide Huiyi," 247–249.

42. Ibid., 247.

43. Guo Chuanxi and Xu Youli, "Ji-Lu-Yu Bianqu Kangri Genjudide Chuangjian," 19; "Ji-Lu-Yu Bianqu Kangri Genjudi Henan Bufen Gaishu," 7.

44. "Ji-Lu-Yu Kangri Genjudide Chuangjian," 112; Guo Chuanxi and Xu Youli, "Ji-Lu-Yu Bianqu Kangri Genjudide Chuangjian," 17; *Henan Kangzhan Shilie*, 112.

45. "Ji-Lu-Yu Kangri Genjudide Chuangjian," 109; Guo Chuanxi and Xu Youli, "Ji-Lu-Yu Bianqu Kangri Genjudide Chuangjian," 18.

46. He Fukui and Niu Guoqi, "Liu Yanchun Zhuanlue," 181–182, 186–189.

47. Cf. "Ji-Lu-Yu Bianqu Kangri Genjudi Henan Bufen Gaishu," 3–4, 8.

48. Zong Fengming, "Guanyu Puyang Diqu Geming Lishide Huiyi," 248–249.

49. Huang Jing, "Bianqude Xingshi Yu Renwu," 367.

50. Skinner, "Social Ecology and the Forces of Repression in North China: A Regional-System Framework for Analysis," 5, 16–17, 19, 22, 24, 29, 41, 46.

51. Peng Yuemei, "Wo Jihui Zongde Sizhidui," 77–78. Cf. Skinner, "Social Ecology and the Forces of Repression in North China: A Regional-System Framework for Analysis," 16–17.

52. "Ji-Lu-Yu Bianqu Gongzuode Chubu Zongjie," 453.

53. "Ji-Lu-Yu Bianqu Kangri Genjudi Henan Bufen Gaishu," 13.

54. Zong Fengming, "Guanyu Puyang Diqu Geming Lishide Huiyi," 248–249.

55. Li Duo, "Shaqu Kangri Genjudi Chuangjian He Jianchide Yixue Qingkuang," 40–41.

56. Ibid., 40–42.

57. Yan Chaogang, ed., *Liu Cun District History*, 60–63.

58. Although one can hardly doubt the existence of Japanese atrocities, the popular tales of such are somewhat problematic. They should be checked against Japanese war records. But, of course, we first need oral history to conduct such a check. Still, I wonder if such atrocities were recorded with precision by minor Japanese field commands and if in such reports the atrocities committed by the Japanese army were distinguished from those of the Japanese puppet army.

59. Liu Fengcun, Qian Kou, 8/15/89.

60. Li Duo, "Shaqu Kangri Genjudi Chuangjian He Jianchide Yixue Qingkuang," 40.

61. Zong Fengming, "Guanyu Puyang Diqu Geming Lishide Huiyi," 250–251.

62. Li Duo, "Shaqu Kangri Genjudi Chuangjian He Jianchide Yixue Qingkuang," 42.

63. Zong Fengming, "Guanyu Puyang Diqu Geming Lishide Huiyi," 251.

64. Here I am indebted to Coser, *The Functions of Social Conflict,* 39, 74, 124–125.

65. In developing the line of analysis, I have drawn on Scott, *Weapons of the Weak,* 241–273.

66. Peng Yuemei, "Wo Jihui Zongde Sizhidui," 81–82.

67. Liu Chaoyang, Qi Ji, 8/9/90.

68. Wei Liangke, Qian Kou, 8/15/89.

69. Cf. Su Zhenghua, "Ji-Lu-Yu Qu Xiaobudui Jianshe Wenti," 431–432.

70. Ibid., 414–415.

71. Jia Zongyi, "Dui Nanle Xian Diwei Gongzuode Huiyi," 168–171.

72. Ibid.

73. Zhang Huaiwen, "Ji-Lu-Yu Kangri Genjudi Gonggu Yu Fazhande Yuanyin Chutan," 103.

74. Ibid.

75. Ibid.

76. Here I have profited from Foucault, *The Order of Things,* 344–348.

77. Shi Guoqiang, Puyang town, 8/7/90.

78. Ibid.

79. Li Huasheng, "Yijiusanwuniande Zhinan Youji Zhanzheng," 1–9.

80. Wang Guanghua, "Zhinan Dongbu Nongmin Wuzhuang Douzheng," 59, 75.

81. Ibid., 75; cf. "Zhinan Nongmin Youji Zhanzhengde Shimo," 225; Yang Shaoxian, "Baodong Suiyue Suoyi," 124.

82. Wang Guanghua, "Jinan Diqu Dongbu Nongmin Wuzhuang Douzheng Pianduan Huiyi," 48.

83. Zhou Dongguang, "Yijiu Sanwunian Pingxiang Yanmin Wuzhuang Douzheng," 130.

84. Shi Guoqiang, Nanle town, 5/5/90. Cf. Klein and Clark, *Biographic Dictionary of Chinese Communism,* 44.

85. Conversation with Wang Congwu, 5/25/88.

86. Wei Liangke, Qian Kou, 8/15/89.

87. Liu Chaoyang, Qi Ji, 8/9/90.

88. Wang Wenxun, Fanzhuang, 8/7–8/90.

89. Zhang Linzhi, "Yinian Laide Dang Yu Qunzhong Gongzuo," 71–72.

90. Liu Chaoyang, Qi Ji, 8/9/90.

91. Ma Xinxi, Liu Zhouchen, Qian Kou, 5/16/90; Liu Shiyin, Qian Kou, 5/17/90.

92. Liu Zhouchen, Qian Kou, 5/16/90.

93. Zhao Wei, *The Biography of Zhao Ziyang,* 32–33.

94. Cf. Thaxton, *China Turned Rightside Up,* 104–105.

95. Fried, *The Fabric of Chinese Society,* 104. Also see Fried, "Socioeconomic Relations in Pre-Communist China," 485–489.

96. Interviews of former tenants in Qi Ji, 6/87; Qian Fo, 8/89.

97. Gao Yuanggui, "Jianzu Zengdiao Gongzuo Zhongde Jige Juti Wenti," 492–495.

98. Ibid., 495.

99. Compare this account with Mark Selden's description of the cooperative movement in Shen-Kan-Ning, which assumes that the movement achieved success only after the Mao Zedong CCP leadership refocused on agricultural production and launched a revolution in rural labor relations. *The Yenan Way in Revolutionary China,* 237–243, especially 242.

100. "Guanyu Shaqu Choucai Gongzhuode Tongxin," 537–538.

101. Ibid., 538.

102. Cf. Xu Daben, "Caijing Gongzuo Baogao," 128–159.

103. Liu Zhouchen, Qian Kou, 5/17/90.

104. "Gongzuo Cankao: Jin-Ji-Lu-Yu Bianqu Maoyi Zongbu," 1–18.

105. "Gaishan Dui Dide Jingji Douzheng Jiaqing Genjudi Jingji Jianshe Wenti Tigang."

106. Cf. Li Chunlan, "Shengchan Yundong Xiaozongshu Zhiyi," 1–46; on the market dimension of mutual aid see "Guancheng Shengchan Yundong Zhong de Jige Wenti," 1–35.

107. *Zhonggong Ji-Lu-Yu Bianqu Dangshi Dashiji,* 201.

108. "Yan Changqing Tongzhi Huiyi," 187.

109. "Ji-Lu-Yu Bianqu Kangri Genjudi Henan Bufen Gaishu," 16.

110. Zhao Wei, *The Biography of Zhao Ziyang,* 25.

111. Ibid., 28.

112. Apparently, Wang Congwu did not venture to Yan'an until 1942, so that it was not a question of the Mao-led CCP dictating the way in which the Ji-Lu-Yu CCP leaders went about cultivating more support for the anti-Japanese struggle. Cf. Clark and Klein, *Biographic Dictionary of Chinese Communism, 1921–1965,* 935.

113. Nie Zhen, Beijing, 8/12/89.

114. Qian Foji interviews, 8/89.

115. Cf. *Zhonggong Puyang Xian Dang Zuzhi Houdong Dashiji,* 22–23; also see Crook and Crook, *Revolution in a Chinese Village,* 34.

116. Wang Jingru, Beijing, 6/16/88.

117. Correspondence with Liu Huheng of the Historical Documents Research Group of the Tianjin Political Consultative Conference, and with Mr. Mu, of the Changlu Salt Affairs Administration in Tianjin, 11/28/89. Corroborated by discussion with Professor Wei Hongyun, Beijing, 8/11/89; and "Materials on Changul Salt Flows Under Japanese Occupation," provided by Jin Huaiyi and Yan Chengzun, Tianjin, 8/2/91, 45.

118. This is not to say the Japanese did not take an interest in the issue. See, for example, "Kanasho Doen Taisaku Ni Tsuite," 1941.

119. Chen Juanru, "Changlu Yanwu Shulue," 91–92.

120. On the question of how peasants have taken advantage of weakened state controls on the countryside to accelerate production for the market and to create better terms of trade, see Robisheaux, *Rural Society and the Search for Order in Early Modern Germany,* 194–198.

121. I am indebted to Shi Guoqiang for this interpretation, which we arrived at jointly in a discussion in the Puyang Oil Field Hotel, 8/7/90.

122. Selden has shown that the CCP attempt to establish a cooperative economy anchored in "a guaranteed monopoly of the salt trade" failed to provide the impe-

tus for independent economic growth in Shen-Kan-Ning border region during the war years, *The Yenan Way in Revolutionary China,* 242.

123. Whyte, "Who Hates Bureaucracy? A Chinese Puzzle," 239.

124. Popkin, *The Rational Peasant,* 244–245, 263–264. Yung-Fa Chen has concluded that Popkin's notion of "unifying investment logic" did not apply to the context of peasant mobilization in Central China, where there was more emphasis on CCP manipulation. *Making Revolution,* 514–515.

125. Wei Hongyun, "Lun Huabei Kangri Genjudi Fanrong Jingjide Daulu," 117–118.

126. Multhauf, *Neptune's Gift,* xiv, 4–5.

127. Snow, *Red Star Over China,* 186.

128. Wilson, *The Long March 1935,* 53, 289.

129. Zhao Chunzhi, "Kaizhan Au Xiaoyan Yundong," 242–243.

130. Xiao Bianxian, Liu Gudian, 8/14/89.

131. Shi Guoqiang, Liu Gudian, 8/13–14/89.

132. Li Fanjiu, Tian Haning, et al., "Ding Shuben Zai Pudachu 'Kangri' Fangong Toudi Shimo," 156–158.

133. Shi Guoqiang, Liu Gudian, 8/14/89.

134. Yang Depu, San Huang, 6/11/88.

135. Ibid.

136. Xiao Bianxian, Liu Gudian, 8/14/89.

137. Liu Jingxiang, Qi Ji, 8/10/90.

138. Neither Liu Jingxiang nor his father was a member of the CCP during the war years.

139. The fate of many a rebel movement has hinged on its ability to obtain supplies of weapons and ammunition. For what happens when there is no such indigenous supply base and such is replaced by dependency on foreign weaponry see Fallows, "With the Rebels," 107–110.

140. Huang Jing, "Bianqude Xingshi Yu Renwu," 369.

141. Ping Jiesan, "Kangri Zhanzheng Chuqi Zhinan Diqu Dangde Tongzhan Gongzuo," 201–202.

142. Ibid.

143. Huang Jing, "Bianqude Xingshi Yu Renwu," 392–393.

144. The evidence here resonates with the wisdom of Perry, who writes, in reference to the war years, that "the Communists would look beyond the confines of predatory bands in their search for comrades-in-arms." *Rebels and Revolutionaries in North China,* 225.

145. Li Tiezhong, Qi Lian, and Wang Yuting, "Ji-Lu-Yu Bianqu Diyizhi Kangri Wuzhuang Minjun Sizhiduide Chuangjian He Fazhan," 1–58.

146. An Fagan, "Ji-Lu-Yu Kangri Genjudide Chuangjian Yu Fazhan," 206–209. The role of the gentry usually is understated in CCP sources, but also see Zhang Zengjing, "Ji-Lu-Yu Shengwei Disan Tewei Chujianshi Yixue Chingquang de Huiyi," 79–80. Cf. "Shoufu Puyang Qianhoude Jidian Gongzuo Jingyan," 153.

147. Shi Guoqiang, Nanle town, 6/11/88.

148. See Li Tiezhong, Qi Lian, and Wang Yuting, "Ji-Lu-Yu Bianqu Diyizhi Kangri Wuzhuang Minjun Sizhiduide Chuangjian He Fazhan," 57–58.

149. Benton, "The Second Wang Ming Line (1935–38)," 75–80.
150. Ibid., 61–80.
151. Li Tiezhong, Qi Lian, and Wang Yuting, "Ji-Lu-Yu Bianqu Diyizhi Kangri Wuzhuang Minjun Sizhidui de Chuangjian He Fajian," 29–36. The damage to the CCP was far greater than I have indicated, for the same pro-Wang Ming Special Committee members compelled Liu Dafeng to flee to Yan'an, where he sought protection from and was exonerated by Liu Shaoqi. They also executed two of Liu Dafeng's patriotic comrades on the charge of being Trotskyites. Liu Dafeng's party membership was restored by Liu Shaoqi, who sent him back to the Hebei-Shandong-Henan border area, 48–54.
152. Esherick, *The Origins of the Boxer Uprising,* 63–67, 218, 294, 329.
153. Yao Huibin, Beijing, 8/12/90.
154. Ibid.
155. Liu Futang, Qian Kou, 6/12/87, 5/16/90.
156. Yao Huibin, Beijing, 8/12/90.
157. This example is from Shi Guoqiang, ed., *Nanle Xianzhi,* 39–42.
158. Day, *Chinese Peasant Cults,* 54.
159. Qian Fo, 8/14–24/89.
160. Yao Huibin, Beijing, 8/12/90.
161. Cf. Edelman, "Public Policy and Political Violence, 36–37.
162. Cf. Day, *Chinese Peasant Cults,* 54, 113, 115; Duara, *Culture, Power and the State,* 143–147.
163. Esherick has uncovered a similar phenomenon at work in the relationship between popular culture and the rapid spread of the Boxer movement. Though he seems to place more emphasis on popular culture than on the variable of place, he does mention the importance of the market as a grapevine that served as a conduit for popular culture, *The Origins of the Boxer Uprising,* 65.
164. Yao Huibin, Beijing, 8/12/90.
165. Gamson, *The Strategy of Social Protest,* 132.
166. Scott makes a similar point for the persistence of peasant protest in Morelos, where nonviolent "struggles" for land reform helped to delegitimate the Mexican state and prepare the ground for the Revolution of 1910, *Weapons of the Weak,* 344.
167. Zhang Linzhi, "Yinian Laide Dang Yu Qunzhong Gongzuo," 65, 76–78.
168. Cf. Duara, *Culture, Power, and the State,* 140, 141, 147.
169. Duara's interpretation of the war god cults is sophisticated and dualistic, emphasizing (perhaps correctly) the capacity of the governing elite to bring opposing interests to its symbolism while maintaining a shared political framework that ultimately legitimated Imperial authority, ibid., 250. Although I do not doubt the plausibility of this interpretation, my reading of the data on the war god myth in the villages I have studied is that there was substantial slippage between the elite conception and the peasant conception of this myth. I also have received the impression that Republican state making radically sharpened the differences to a point where the dissenting folk version became an independent force legitimating antistate rebellion. Actually, my reading of the issue is not radically different from that of Duara, who acknowledges that the accelerated revenue demand of the modernizing

state and the state attack on religion strained relations between local people and the state and undercut the chance of the Republican elite to use the war god image to legitimate its purpose locally, ibid., 248–250. Of course if we pursue Duara's interpretation, we also can see the CCP identifying itself with the war god tradition and stepping in to superscribe its own ideological hegemony on the popular folk symbolization to which it was pandering during the Anti-Japanese War, cf. Duara, 247. Whatever the case, my point is that national resistance was mobilized within the cultural narrative of a myth that expressed the political interest of the country people.

170. Yao Huibin, Beijing, 8/12/90.

171. Edelman, "Public Policy and Political Violence," 18.

172. Yao Peishan, Beijing, 8/4–5/90. Also see Levy's informative review of the Chinese Communist interpretations of this rebellion, 613–614.

173. Liu Cun, *Liang He Yanmin Douzheng,* 154–155.

174. Yao Peishan, Beijing, 8/4–5/90.

175. Ibid.

176. Ibid.

177. Levy, book review, 612.

CHAPTER 8. COMMUNITY, CULTURE, AND THE PERSISTENCE OF RURAL COLLECTIVE ACTION

1. Xiao Bianxian, Liu Gudian, 8/13–14/89. In researching Qian Foji's wartime history, I went to great pains to discover efforts of villages to put their best face on their wartime "collaboration." The peasants here made no attempt to hide any part of their compliance with Japanese puppet army demands, which was logical because the place was a minimum security prison for much of the war. Qian Foji's inhabitants thus had little to gain or lose by "fixing up" their wartime history for me. The Nanle historian who was my host had no worry that I might uncover another hidden story about the "voluntary collaboration" of the village. Such a story does not exist. Moreover, Nanle County historians do not make any attempt to hide the names or activities of the local people who did in fact collaborate with the Japanese puppet regime; these are published in local histories.

2. Yao Huibin, "Dui Nanle Xian Kangzhan Zhong Jige Wentide Huiyi," 121.

3. Yao Zhenbian, Qian Foji, 8/4/89.

4. Ibid., 8/14–16/89.

5. Sang Mingzhai, Qian Foji, 8/16/89.

6. "Tuxiao Xiaolu Ri Zeng," 13.

7. Yao Zhenbian, Qian Foji, 8/16/89.

8. Feng Cunshan, Qian Foji, 8/19/89.

9. Yao Zhenbian, Qian Foji, 8/16/89.

10. Yao Zhenmin, Qian Foji, 8/22/89.

11. Yao Xiren, Qian Foji, 8/16/89.

12. The breakdown of Yao Xiren's income was, for example, 20 percent agricultural crops, 30 percent earth salt, and 50 percent small business income derived from the officially sanctioned market economy.

13. Sang Mingzhai, 8/16/89, Yao Xiren, 8/16, Sang Xianshi, 8/18, Yao Zhishan, 8/19, Yao Zhimin, 8/24, all in Qian Foji.

14. Sang Puyi, 8/23/89, with the former Qian Foji accountant Feng Dianchun present and registering agreement.

15. Yao Xiren, Qian Foji, 8/16/89.

16. Ibid.

17. Yao Xiren and Yao Lishen, Qian Foji, 8/16/89.

18. Yao Zhenmin,Qian Foji, 8/22/89.

19. Sang Puyi, Qian Foji, 8/21/89.

20. Yao Xiren and Yao Zhenbian, Qian Foji, 8/16/89.

21. Yao Xiren, Qian Foji, 8/16/89.

22. Huang, *The Peasant Economy and Social Change in North China,* 278–281.

23. Sang Xianshi, Qian Foji, 8/18/89. Sang was a rich peasant who held eighty *mu*of land and who had only four people in his household before 1949.

24. Yao Zhenbian, 8/16/89.

25. Sang Xianshi, 8/18/89, Yao He, 8/20/89, both in Qian Foji.

26. Yao Zhenxiang, 8/18/89, Sang Chunji, 8/24/89, both in Qian Foji.

27. Sang Chunji, 8/24/89. Sang Chunji was one of the few Protestant converts in Qian Foji. His father owned fifty *mu* of land in the early 1930s. Sang says he was from a well-to-do household. He had attended a Protestant missionary school in Nanle town around 1919. The school provided free food for poor children, a service for which he did not qualify. After 1930 Sang was involved in the earth salt economy himself.

28. Yao Zhenxiang, Qian Foji, 8/18/89.

29. Ibid.

30. White and Jacoby, *Thunder Out of China,* 172–178.

31. Sang Binwen, Qian Foji, 9/12/93.

32. According to Sang Mingzhai and Yao Zhenbian, the seven were Sang Faming, Sang Cunzhou, Feng Yushen, Sang Hetong, Zhang Mudiao, Yao Zhengong, and Yao Yinmei. Qian Foji, 8/16/89.

33. Ibid. Also supportive of this point is eighty-four-year-old Yao Zhenxiang, 8/18/89.

34. Wang Qing, Qian Foji, 8/18/89.

35. Yao Xixiang, Qian Foji, 8/19/89.

36. Sang Puyi, Qian Foji, 8/21/89.

37. Yao Zhenxiang, Qian Foji, 8/18/89.

38. Yao Huibin, Beijing, 8/25/89.

39. Sang Puyi, Qian Foji, 8/22/89.

40. Yao Huibin himself made this point when he revealed how his own landlord had stood up for his family in a lawsuit that went all the way up to Daming prefectural court. Beijing, 8/25/89.

41. Ibid.

42. On this point there is widespread agreement among the peasants of the Yao and Sang lineages. Cf. Yao Zhimin, Qian Foji, 8/24; Sang Puyi, Qian Foji, 8/21–22/89.

43. Sang Puyi, Qian Foji, 8/21–22/89.

44. Ibid.

45. Sang Mingzhai, Qian Foji, 8/20/89.

46. For a brief description of this form of rent, see Qi Wu, ed., *Yige Geming Genjudide Chengzhang*, 122–123. This *huodi* was a local version of *huomai*, which was a provisional land purchase that could become permanent if unredeemed over a stipulated period. I am indebted to Joseph W. Esherick for bringing this to my attention.

47. Sang Mingzhai, Qian Foji, 8/20/89.

48. Yao He and Sang Mingzhai, Qian Foji, 8/20/89.

49. Sang Mingzhai and Yao Zhenbian, Qian Foji, 8/20/89.

50. This account is from Yao Zhimin, Qian Foji, 8/21/89. I cross-checked it with Sang Puyi in a separate conversation. Sang agrees with it.

51. Wucunji was a rich market village, and it was here that Qian Foji's peasants often found their marriage partners in the pre-1949 period.

52. Yao Zhenbian, Qian Foji, 8/17/89.

53. Ibid.

54. Ibid.

55. Ibid., 8/14–17/89; Wang Qing, 8/18/89; Yao He, 8/20/89. Also from Feng Tianhua, 5/11/90. All in Qian Foji.

56. Yao Zhenbian, Qian Foji, 8/15/89.

57. Ibid., 8/19/89.

58. Ibid.

59. Yao Huibin, "Dui Nanle Xian Kangzhan Zhong Jige Wentide Huiyi," 126.

60. Ibid.

61. Feng Dianchun, Qian Foji, 8/23/89.

62. Sang Puyi and Yao Zhenmin, Qian Foji, 8/23/89.

63. In developing this point, I have benefitted from Scott's delightful essay, "Socialism and Small Property—Or Two Cheers for the Petty-Bourgeoisie," especially 185–189.

64. Yao Zhenbian, Qian Foji, 8/17/89.

65. Shi Guoqiang, Nanle County town, 8/13/89.

66. Yao Zhenbian, Qian Foji, 8/17/89.

67. Ibid.

68. Yao Zhenbian, 8/17/89, Yao Yichang, 8/23, Yao Zhenmin, 8/23/89, all in Qian Foji.

69. Yao Zhenbian, 8/21/89, 5/6/90.

70. Feng Tianhua, Qian Foji, 8/24/89.

71. Yao Huibin, "Dui Nanle Xian Kangzhan Zhong Jige Wentide Huiyi," 125–126.

72. Yao Zhenbian, Qian Foji, 8/17/89.

73. Yao Yichang, Qian Foji, 8/23/89. This anti-Japanese group was the same group as the Chinese Liberation Vanguards of which Wang Jian was a member.

74. Yao Huibin, Beijing, 8/25/89.

75. Sang Puyi, Qian Foji, 8/21/89.

76. Wang Qing, Qian Foji, 8/18/89.

77. Yao Zhenbian, Qian Foji, 8/14/89.

78. Yao Xiren, Qian Foji, 8/16/89.

79. Sang Puyi, Qian Foji, 8/21/89.

80. Yao Xiren, Qian Foji, 8/16/89.

81. Shi Guoqiang, ed., *Nanle Xianzhi,* 39.

82. Yao Zhenbian, Qian Foji, 8/17/89; Yao Zhenbian and Feng Tianhua, Qian Foji, 5/8/90.

83. Yao Zhangyun, Qian Foji, 8/24/89.

84. Sang Qingxing, Qian Foji, 8/18/89.

85. Yao Zhangyun, Qian Foji, 8/24/89.

86. Cf. Jia Zongyi, "Dui Nanle Xian Diwei Gongzuode Huiyi," 166. Also see *Zhonggong Ji-Lu-Yu Bianqu Dangshi Dashiji,* 174.

87. Shi Guoqiang, ed., *Nanle Xianzhi,* 39.

88. Ibid., 162–163.

89. Sang Mingzhai, Qian Foji, 8/16/89.

90. Ibid. The grain came from the Qian Foji CCP branch connection with the Eighth Route Army in Xi Tianzhou village, Wei County.

91. Yao He, Qian Foji, 8/19/89.

92. Again, I am indebted to J. Scott's *Weapons of the Weak* for its original insight into the primitive forms of resistance carried on by peasants who must comply with the rules established by power holders who can use coercion, 278–283.

93. Cf. Yao Yixian, 8/19/89, Feng Dianchun, 8/23/89, Sang Chunhai, 8/23/89, all in Qian Foji.

94. Friedman, Pickowicz, and Selden have discovered a similar collaborative "front" in the wartime politics of Wu Gong village. Cf. *Chinese Village, Socialist State,* 47–49. Yao Zheng, Qian Foji, 8/22/89.

95. Yao Zhenbian, Qian Foji, 8/16/89.

96. Yao Huibin, Beijing, 9/16/93.

97. Yao Zhenbian, Qian Foji, 8/24/89, with Sang Chunhai and Yao Zhangyun, who remember turning the lathe for cutting gun barrels, in attendance.

98. Sang Mingzhai, Qian Foji, 8/16/89.

99. Yao Zhimin and Yao Zhangyun, Qian Foji, 8/24/89.

100. Yao Zhangyun, Qian Foji, 8/24/89.

101. Yao Peiji, Qian Foji, 8/15/90.

102. Yao Yiliang, Qian Foji, 5/13/90.

103. Feng Tianhua, Qian Foji, 8/24/89.

104. Wang Qing, Qian Foji, 8/18/89.

105. Yao Zhenbian, Qian Foji, 8/14 and 17/89.

106. Sang Chunhai, Qian Foji, 8/23/89.

107. Sang Mingzhai, Qian Foji, 8/16/89.

108. Yao Zhenbian, Qian Foji, 8/14/89.

109. Jia Zongyi, "Dui Nanle Xian Diwei Gongzuode Huiyi," 161–171, especially 168–171.

110. Ibid.

111. Cf. Tilly, *The Contentious French,* 16–17.

112. Sang Qingxiang, Qian Foji, 8/18/89.

113. Sang Mingzhai, Qian Foji, 8/18/89.

114. Jia Zongyi, "Dui Nanle Xian Diwei Gongzuode Huiyi," 174; Yao Zhenmin, Qian Foji, 8/23/89.

115. "Ji-Lu-Yu Wo Jun Da Shengli Guanfu Nanle Qian Diwei Sanqian," 167. Reprinted from *Jiefang Ribao* (Liberation Daily), 5 May 1945.

116. Yao Xixian, Qian Foji, 8/19/89.

117. Yao He, Qian Foji, 8/20/89.

118. Yao Zheng, Qian Foji, 8/22/89.

119. Sang Chunhai, Qian Foji, 8/23/89.

120. Yao Zhenbian, Qian Foji, 8/21/89.

121. From Sang Puyi, the CCP secretary of Qian Foji in 1945, 8/21/89.

122. Ibid., 8/22/89.

123. Yao He, Qian Foji, 8/20/89.

124. Sang Chunji, Qian Foji, 8/24/89.

125. Yao Zhenbian, Qian Foji, 8/19/89.

126. A countervailing hypothesis might be considered here: the peasants with the least land, property, and labor were the least likely to survive, stay on in the village, and become involved in village-based resistance. This hypothesis gains some limited support in a survey I did for the period 1937–45. The majority of those who stayed and joined the CCP were from strong peasant economic positions, using the above criteria. Among the peasants who left Qian Foji in this period, 80 percent were from households with one, or less, *mu* per capita,or were landless. They averaged only four members per family, and some of them had only three members. Moreover, in interviewing a few of the peasants in these categories, I discovered that they often faced another problem: they were either widowers or unable to marry. The problem was worse for those at the lower end of the socioeconomic spectrum in the minor lineages. Interestingly, however, the underprivileged Yaos, true to their dominant lineage tradition, dealt with this crisis in family continuity not by migration but rather by joining the Eighth Route Army, which kept alive the promise of returning at a better time. Yao lineage survey, Qian Foji, 8/17–22/89.

127. Yao Zhenbian and Yao Zhimin, Qian Foji, 8/21/89.

128. Sang Chunhai, Qian Foji, 8/23/89.

129. I have relied on Tilly's discussion of issues in collective action for the interpretative slant given to my empirical data on Qian Foji in this instance. *From Mobilization to Revolution,* 233–234.

130. Yao Huibin, Beijing, 8/25/89.

131. Yao He, Qian Foji, 8/25/89.

132. Liu Shiren, Liu Shijun, and Wei Liangke, in separate interviews, Qian Kou, 8/15/89.

133. Duan Dongqing, Qi Ji, 6/8/87.

134. Zhang Ke, Fanzhuang, 8/14/90. Cf. Zhai Zuolin, 6/7/88, and Wang Wenxun, 6/7–8/90, in Fanzhuang.

135. Liu Shijun, Qian Kou, 8/15/89; Liu Chaobin, Qi Ji, 6/14/88.

136. Liu Chaoyang, Qi Ji, 6/5/87; Zhang Yun, Fanzhuang, 6/9/88; Yao Zhenbian, Qian Foji, 8/14/89.

137. Zhang Huaiwen, "Ji-Lu-Yu Kangri Genjudi Gonggu Yu Fazhande Yuanyin Chutan," 103.

138. Liu Xingquan, Qi Ji, 6/7/87.

139. Liu Peixin, Qian Kou, 8/15/89.

140. Sang Puyi, Yao Zhimin, and Yao Zheng, in Qian Foji, 8/21/89.
141. Yao Huibin, Beijing, 8/12/90.
142. Sang Puyi, Qian Foji, 8/21/89.

CHAPTER 9. THE POPULAR FEAR OF THE RETURN OF THE KUOMINTANG FISCAL CENTER AND THE OUTBREAK OF CIVIL WAR

1. This view is summarized in Skocpol, *States and Social Revolutions*, 261–262. It is also prevalent in Hinton's *Fanshen*, 149–156, 166–167, 172, 200–202, 247–250, 610–611. "The crux of the matter," writes Hinton, "lay in the land question. With land in their own hands the peasants could be counted on to volunteer for service in the regular armed forces by the hundreds of thousands, to support the front with transport columns and stretcher brigades, and to organize irregular fighting units in every corner of the Liberated areas." 200. Hinton thinks the land revolution process was entirely the product of the CCP's "land to the tiller" directive of May, 1946.

2. Pepper, *Civil War in China*, 301, 305–307.

3. Levine, *Anvil of Victory*, 239–240; cf. Eastman, *Seeds of Destruction*, 223–224, cited by Levine.

4. Levine, *Anvil of Victory*, 207.

5. Ibid, 224, 243–244.

6. Ibid., 219–220, 230, 177. My inference.

7. Cf. *Changlu Hangu Yanchangzhi*, 298; on this point, also see Li Han, *Miao Choujie Yu Minguo Yanwu Gaige*, 156.

8. Cf. Li Jianchang, *Guanliao ZibenYu Yanye*, 99–100, 108–110, 112, 114–117, 122.

9. Sang Mingzhai, Qian Foji, 5/11/90.

10. Cf. "Yanbing Zhangze." The conflict between the Kuomintang and CCP in the Tianjin area and on the east Hebei plain in 1947–48 also was a struggle for control of salt revenue. One point must be made clear. That the Kuomintang officials still considered earth salt to be illegal in this period is beyond question. There is, however, a school of thought that contends that after 1945 the Kuomintang moved away from the privileged merchant system in the Changlu area, allowing anyone to purchase government salt and sell it in any market area. Clearly, however, this was state-regulated "free trade." Moreover, the free traders were in competition with the peasant earth salt purveyors, who still were the enemies of the high Kuomintang revenue men. Some of the Chinese historians I have discussed this matter with seem to think that the peasant earth salt producers now had nothing to fear because of this Kuomintang policy change, but this simply is a misreading of the situation at both ends. This is my interpretation, and not that of Ding Changqing, who nonetheless helped me arrive at it through our Tianjin talks of 1 August 1991.

11. Lieberman, "China's Reds Press Changchun," 9.

12. Of course, as Pepper points out, there most likely were violations of the June, 1946, truce agreement on both sides. The Communists, however, felt they were not in a position to give up local administration to the central government. If

they did, where would they go? And what political forces would have checked the claims of the center? This was the real issue for the CCP's popular base in the North China base areas, one that has not been fully researched in the context of the civil war period. Cf. Pepper, "The KMT-CCP Conflict 1945–49," 732–733.

13. Yao Zhenbian, Qian Foji, 5/6/90. See, for example, Shi Xiaosheng, "Shilun Jin-Ji-Lu-Yu Jiefangqude Tudi Gaige Yundong," 59–61.

14. Liu Shiyin, Qian Kou, 5/17/90.

15. Yao Lishen, Qian Foji, 5/12/90.

16. Cf. Halbwachs, *On Collective Memory,* 54–55, 66–67, 73–74, 81–83.

17. Liu Wanli, Qi Ji, 8/13/90.

18. Spence, *The Search for Modern China,* 492–93; Thaxton, *China Turned Rightside Up,* chap. 7.

19. Whereas Pepper focused on landlords who were targeted because they had cooperated with the Japanese. *Civil War in China,*231, 246–248.

20. This interpretation of the order of the day being that of "social war" is eloquently represented in Bianco, *Origins of the Chinese Revolution 1915–1949,* 187. Nonetheless, much to his credit, Bianco does tend to downplay the early emphasis on "class war" in the factors precipitating the civil war, for he emphasizes the political and economic losses peasants anticipated they would incur with the return of the Kuomintang army and the "White Terror." Thus my downplaying of the former emphasis on "class war" in the origins of the civil war follows Bianco's great wisdom. The important points, I think, are that politics, not class action, triggered the civil war and that the CCP used what Bianco calls "social revolution" associated with its land redistribution programs only to bolster its credibility and power against troublemaking Kuomintang landlords. Cf. *Origins of the Chinese Revolution,* 187–188.

21. Sang Puyi, Qian Foji, 5/8/90.

22. Ibid.

23. Shi Xiaosheng, "Shilun Jin-Ji-Lu-Yu Jiefangqude Tudi Gaige Yundong," 59–64.

24. This interpretation is consistent with Pepper, *Civil War in China,* 248.

25. Cf. Crook and Crook, *Revolution in a Chinese Village,* 119–120, 179.

26. Ibid., 179.

27. Ibid., 120.

28. Yao Xixin, Qian Foji, 5/14/90.

29. Yao Zhimin, Qian Foji, 5/12/90.

30. Pepper makes the point nicely in *Civil War in China,* 283, 297–298, 308.

31. Shi Xiaosheng, "Shilun Jin-Ji-Lu-Yu Jiefangqude Tudi Gaige Yundong," 64; Thaxton, *China Turned Rightside Up,* 209–210.

32. Shi Xiaosheng, "Shilun Jin-Ji-Lu-Yu Jiefangqude Tudi Gaige Yundong," 64.

33. Shi Guoqiang, Nanle County town, 5/6/90.

34. Sang Puyi, Qian Foji, 5/8/90.

35. Thaxton, *China Turned Rightside Up;* Pepper, *Civil War in China.*

36. Cf. Levine, *Anvil of Victory,* 221.

37. Yao Zhenbian, Qian Foji, 5/6–7/90.

38. Liu Yunxing, Qian Kou, 5/17/90.

39. Ibid.

40. Yao Zhenbian, Qian Foji, 5/7/90.

41. Feng Tianhua and Yao Zhenbian, Qian Foji, 5/11/90.

42. Sang Chunhai, Qian Foji, 5/9/90.

43. Feng Tianhua, Qian Foji, 5/9/90.

44. Yao Zhangren, Qian Foji, 5/11/90.

45. Yao Zhenbian, Sang Puyi, Qian Foji, 5/7/90.

46. Ma Xinxi, Qian Kou, 5/16/90; Liu Shiyin, Qian Kou, 5/17/90; Liu Yunxing, Qian Kou, 5/17/90.

47. Sang Puyi, Qian Foji, 5/7/90.

48. Ma Xinxi, Qian Kou, 5/16/90.

49. He Fukui and Niu Guoqi, "Liu Yanchun Zhuanlue," 190.

50. Liu Shiyin, Qian Kou, 5/17/90.

51. Liu Wanli, Qi Ji, 8/13/90.

52. Van Slyke, *Enemies and Friends*, 188–189.

53. Yao Zhenbian, Qian Foji, 5/7/90.

54. Yao Zhangyin, Qian Foji, 5/6/90.

55. Xu Yunbei, "Canjun Yundong Jianbao," 69–74. I am indebted to Pepper for bringing this resource to my attention, *Civil War in China*, 294.

56. See Davies, "Toward a Theory of Revolution," 5–19; Cf. Gurr, *Why Men Rebel;* Muller, Finkel, and Dietz, "Relative Deprivation, Rational Action, and Rebellion," 13–14, 29, 40–41.

57. Yao Zhenbian, Qian Foji, 5/6–7/90.

58. Liu Chaoxun, Qi Ji, 8/10/90.

59. Wang Qing, Qian Foji, 5/13/90.

60. Zhang Xiaoxun, Fanzhuang, 8/9/90.

61. Surely some of the recovered counties included were those where salt production did not exist, or where the heritage of the saltmakers' struggle did not make any significant difference in the outcome of the civil war, so that other factors, such as CC-PLA strategic considerations, CCP relations with local elites and/or other protest movements, and Kuomintang state blunders were key factors in turning the tide for the CCP. However, my talks with local historians confirm that the peasant saltmakers played a major role in helping the CCP prevent a Kuomintang takeover in most of the prewar protest counties during the civil war. Shi Guoqiang, 8/9/91. Cf. Qudangwei, "Ji-Lu-Yu Wuge Yue Lai Youji Zhanzhengde Zongjie Yu Muqian Renwu," 37.

62. Liu Chaoyang, Qi Ji, 8/10/90.

63. Yao Zhenbian, Qian Foji, 5/7/90.

64. Wei Jing and Zhang Xiaoxun, Fanzhuang, 8/8/90.

65. In constructing this graph, I have relied on and benefitted greatly from Davies, "Toward a Theory of Revolution," 5–19. Also see Davies, "The Revolutionary State of Mind," 133–147. Davies says that "the majority of revolutionaries thus are likely to be poor people at loose ends who have made some progress towards a new and better life and see themselves now failing to do so," 133. This was the case for the semipeasant market leaders in most of the villages I have surveyed.

66. Yao Zhenbian, 5/7, extended to 5/13–14/90, in Qian Foji.

67. Ibid., 5/7/90.

68. Liu Chaoyang, Qi Ji, 8/8/90.

69. That the CCP attacked the market of the peasant saltmakers after winning state power does not negate my argument, which is that while out of power the party swept to victory by listening to the peasants of the marketplace. Although the market was attacked in the Great Leap Forward, there also was a silent popular struggle to preserve it, and this struggle was in part supported secretly by some of the peasant saltmakers who had joined the CCP. The Great Leap Forward attack on the market damaged the party's credibility with these semipeasants, but whether the party lost its legitimacy in these villages as a result remains to be researched.

70. Cf. Crook and Crook, *Revolution in a Chinese Village,*161–162. Nonetheless, they also mention the revival of small trade, which they claim was dependent on the mutual-aid groups and government credit, 165.

71. Yao Yiliang, Qian Foji, 5/13/90.

72. Yao Peiji, Qian Foji, 5/15/90.

73. Ibid.

74. Feng Tianhua, Qian Foji, 5/8/90.

75. Cf. Skinner, "Chinese Peasants and the Closed Community," 270–281.

76. Cf. Pepper, *Civil War in China,* 301–307.

77. Cf. Frank Miller, who reported that the trials of the people's courts in the land revolution were "not held as frequently as North China city people presumed. Miller had seen only one case in which a landlord had been punished by beating, and even then the landlord was not injured," "China Community and Small Trader," 25.

78. Cf. Shi Xiaosheng, "Shilun Jin-Ji-Lu-Yu Jiefangqude Tudi Gaige Yundong," 58–65.

79. Compare the writings of Hinton, Belden, and Strong on this point.

80. Feng Tianhua, Qian Foji, 5/8/90.

81. Yao Zhenbian, Qian Foji, 5/8/90.

82. This phase of rebel struggle to re-create openness is not part of Skinner's modeled sequence of closure and openness, but I believe it is compatible with his logic. The difference between this work and Skinner's is that Skinner sees openness as more a product of state power and closure as more a product of community mobilization, whereas I see openness as a function of community struggle as well—a struggle that can help usher in a new political order. Cf. Skinner, "Chinese Peasants and the Closed Community," 273–280.

83. Cf. Popkin, *The Rational Peasant,* 262–263.

84. Yao Zhangyin, Qian Foji, 5/11/90.

85. *Zhonggong Nanle Xian Dangshi Dashiji,* 44.

86. *Zhonggong Ji-Lu-Yu Bianqu Dangshi Dashiji,* 253.

87. Yao Zhenbian and Sang Dongchen, Qian Foji, 5/7/90.

88. Cf. Pepper, *Civil War in China,* 290.

89. *Zhonggong Nanle Xian Dangshi Dashiji,* 46–47.

90. Eastman, *Seeds of Destruction,* 220–221.

91. Wang Wenxun, Fanzhuang, 8/7–8/90.

92. Shi Guoqiang, Nanle County town, 5/5/90.

93. "We did not need to convene meetings about this matter," said Wang Wenxun. "We just talked about it among ourselves." Fanzhuang, 8/7–8/90.

94. Yao Zhenbian, Qian Foji, 5/7/90; Liu Chaoyang, Qi Ji, 8/9/90.

95. Liu Jinxiang and Liu Chaoyang, 8/9–10/90.

96. I am indebted to Joseph Esherick for helping me clarify this point.

97. Few studies treat the issue of dignity as a factor prompting rural people to rebel, and not one of the pre-1949 studies of the civil war in China adequately deals with this issue. A nice treatment of the issue as it has been played out in the rural Philippines is Kerkvliet, *Everyday Politics in the Philippines,* 256–273.

98. Liu Chaoyang, Qi Ji, 8/9/90.

99. Feng Tianhua, Qian Foji, 5/11/90.

100. Sang Chunhai, Qian Foji, 5/11/90.

101. Wang Maiji, Fanzhuang, 8/7/90.

102. Wang Wenxun and Zhang Xiaoxun, Fanzhuang, 8/8/90.

103. Liu Yunxing, Qian Kou, 5/17/90.

104. Yao Zhenbian, Qian Foji, 5/7/90.

105. This peasant rush into nitrate production is evidenced in many of my interviews. William Hinton also witnessed the same phenomenon in Lucheng and Changchih counties in Shanxi Province during this period. *Fanshen,* 593–594.

106. Cf. Multhauf, *Neptune's Gift,* 189.

107. Feng Da, Qian Foji, 5/13/90; Liu Gongchen, Qian Kou, 5/16/90. Both sold nitrate salt to the PLA through purchase agents for a profit in three different counties of the border area.

108. Liu Chaoxun, Qi Ji, 8/10/90.

109. Yao Zhenbian, Qian Foji, 5/7/90.

110. Liu Yunxing, Qian Kou, 5/17/90.

111. Yao Zhenbian, Qian Foji, 5/6/90.

112. Yao Peiji, Qian Foji, 5/15/90.

113. Bianco, *Origins of the Chinese Revolution,* 189.

114. *Zhonggong Ji-Lu-Yu Bianqu Dangshi Dashiji,* 272.

115. Ibid., 278.

116. Feng Cunshan, Qian Foji, 5/11/90.

117. Yao Lishen, Qian Foji, 5/12/90.

118. Yao Zheng, Qian Foji, 5/9/90; Yao Lishen, Qian Foji, 5/12/90; Yao Yiliang, Qian Foji, 5/13/90.

119. Bianco, *Origins of the Chinese Revolution,* 185; Eastman, *Seeds of Destruction,* 212.

120. Sang Chunhai, Qian Foji, 5/8/90; Yao Lishen, Qian Foji, 5/12/90.

121. Yao Zhenbian, Qian Foji, 5/7/90; Sang Chunhai, 5/8/90.

122. Yao Yichang, Qian Foji, 5/12/90, with Yao Zhenbian, Wang Han, Wang Fo, Feng Tianhua in agreement.

CONCLUSION

1. This point, made by many Western scholars, is too often ignored in studies of the origins of the Chinese Communist success.

2. See Wakeman, "Models of Historical Change," 68.

3. As Lijphardt would advise, "Comparative Politics and the Comparative Method," 682–692.

4. For the general party-as-mobilzer paradigm, see Huntington, *Political Order in Changing Societies*. For the application of this thesis to China, see Hofheinz, *The Broken Wave;* Wou, *Mobilizing the Masses*, 11, 379.

5. Eastman, *Seeds of Destruction*, 212–214.

6. Cf. Huang, *The Peasant Economy and Social Change in North China*, 289.

7. Eastman, *Seeds of Destruction,*chap. 2; Bianco, "Peasant Movements," 280–287, 301–302; Duara, "State Involution," 138–139, 157.

8. Schwartz, *Chinese Communism and the Rise of Mao*, 190.

9. Cf. Gurr, "A Causal Model of Civil Strife," 313.

10. I am indebted to Ramon Myers for helping me develop this point. Personal correspondence, 1991.

11. Perry, *Rebels and Revolutionaries in North China*, 47, 252–256.

12. Cf. Ibid., chap. 4.

13. Cf. Ibid., Ch. 5. The quote is from 251.

14. Ibid., 256.

15. Ibid., 255.

16. Cf. Johnson, *Revolutionary Change*, 115.

17. For a recent study that makes a similar argument, see Ch'en, *The Highlanders of Central China*, 247. Here the interventionist state is that of the warlords. Ch'en surveys a wide variety of crops, so that he is not concerned mainly with the relationship of central government attempts to take over one specific peasant economic activity.

18. 18. Friedman, "What Do Peasants Really Want," 199.

19. Cf. Johnson, *Revolutionary Change*, 162–163. I have benefitted from Johnson's description of the revolutionary process here.

20. Cf. Friedman, "Engels' Peasant War in Germany," 122; Thaxton, *China Turned Rightside Up*, chap. 6.

21. Kataoka, *Resistance and Revolution in China*, 265.

22. Cf. Schwartz, *Chinese Communism and the Rise of Mao*, 187.

23. For the CCP-as-direct-mobilizer view, see Skocpol, *States and Social Revolutions*, chap. 6; and most eloquently, Wou, *Mobilizing the Masses*, 371–372, 375–377, especially 379–380.

24. Averill, "Local Elites and Communist Revolution in the Jiangxi Hill Country," 30.

25. Cf. Esherick and Rankin, "Concluding Remarks," in *Chinese Local Elites and Patterns of Dominance*, 311.

26. Cf. Shue, *The Reach of the State*, 26–27.

27. Meisner, *Li Ta-chao and the Origins of Chinese Marxism*, 188.

28. From Friedman, "Engels' Peasant War in Germany," 120.

29. Johnson, *Peasant Nationalism and Communist Power*, chap. 1–2.

30. Van Slyke, "The Chinese Communist Movement During the Sino-Japanese War, 1937–1945," 631.

31. Cf. Thaxton, *China Turned Rightside Up*, chap. 6.

32. As Hartford also has shown, "Repression and Communist Success," 94; Selden, *China in Revolution,* 232.

33. For the general point, see Friedman, "Engels' Peasant War in Germany," 119.

34. Selden, *The Yenan Way in Revolutionary China,* chap. 3, 77–78, 121–122.

35. Yung Fa-Chen, *Making Revolution,* 99.

36. Ibid., 503.

37. The argument is Yung Fa-Chen's, 121–222, especially 204, 221, 503–507.

38. Cf. Friedman, Pickowicz, and Selden, *Chinese Village, Socialist State,* 32, 34, 36.

39. As Kataoka has implied, *Resistance and Revolution in China,* 176, 181–182, 232–233.

40. For the interpretation that follows, I am indebted first to Lemarchand, "The Political Economy of Informal Economies," 1. Wolf wisely stresses the importance of tactical freedom from the state as a precondition for rural people having a chance to fight effectively against political tyranny. *Peasant Wars of the Twentieth Century,* 290–291.

41. Cf. Skinner, "Marketing and Social Structure in Rural China," pt. 1, 30. Also see Friedman, "What Do Peasants Really Want," 199.

42. I am indebted to Lucien Bianco for stimulating this important qualification of my interpretation and hypothesis. Personal correspondence, 21 February 1996.

43. Wolf, *Peasant Wars of the Twentieth Century,*chap. 3 and conclusion. To her credit, Perry was one of the first China scholars to take up the issue of whether international capitalism was the impetus to peasant involvement in protest, showing that rebellion in rural China was recurrent and often linked to a number of embedded internal factors. *Rebels and Revolutionaries in North China,* 248–249.

44. As Selden might argue, *The Yenan Way in Revolutionary China,* 277–278; and as Ch'en has argued, *The Highlanders of Central China,* 247.

45. See Scott, *The Moral Economy of the Peasant,* chap. 1–2; . Popkin, *The Rational Peasant,* chap. 1–2, especially 6.

46. This is the position of Wolf, *Peasant Wars of the Twentieth Century,* 279–280, 285; Scott, *The Moral Economy of the Peasant,*6, 9; Scott, *Weapons of the Weak,* chap. 3. Yet, in fairness, Wolf and Scott are talking about the world capitalist market, and not about the domestic market.

47. I am indebted to Joseph Esherick for helping me develop this point. Personal correspondence, 1992.

48. Laves, "Rural Society and Modern Revolution," 154–155, 157, 188. Cf. Ch'en, who mentions the attempt of the Chiang Kai-shek's Nanjing headquarters to prohibit opium planting and trade in the parts of Sichuan and in Hunan that became CCP base areas in the early 1930s, *The Highlanders of Central China,* 79, chap. 10. Ch'en contends that "In spite of what has been said on opium prohibition, the drug was the pillar of the soviet economy," 241.

49. Bianco, "Peasant Movements," 270.

50. Mark Selden's penetrating review of the literature on rural revolution in twentieth-century China stimulated this point. *China in Revolution,* 250.

51. See Yung Fa-chen, "Between Survival and Ideology," 237–242. Cf. Selden, *The Yenan Way in Revolutionary China.* Of course, policy did not always determine

practice; and practice often tempered and sometimes reshaped policy. Furthermore, my guess is that the CCP was not powerful enough to effectively enforce an antimarket strategy in this period, and that such a strategy had serious political costs. Still, Yung Fa-chen's claims are important, and they deserve more engagement than is provided in this conclusion.

52. Yung Fa-chen, *Making Revolution*, 5.

53. On the importance of tactical space as a facilitator of agrarian revolution, see Wolf, *Peasant Wars of the Twentieth Century*, 291–293. Wolf does not fully explore the role of the market community, and its active tradition of collective protest, in creating and sustaining this space.

54. This conclusion also has benefitted from Goodwin and Skocpol, "Explaining Revolutions in the Contemporary Third World," 491–505, especially 492–499, 503–505. They stress the importance of insurgent coalitions incorporating the peasantry and the vulnerability of certain types of repressive political dictatorships as factors facilitating the overthrow of governments.

BIBLIOGRAPHY

Adas, Michael. "From Avoidance to Confrontation: Peasant Protest in Precolonial Southeast Asia." *Comparative Studies in Society and History* 23 (1981).

———. "From Footdragging to Flight: The Evasive History of Peasant Avoidance in South and Southeast Asia." *The Journal of Peasant Studies* 13, no. 2 (1986).

Adshead, S. A. M. *The Modernization of the Chinese Salt Administration.* Cambridge: Harvard University Press, 1970.

Almond, Gabriel A., and Stephen J. Genco. "Clouds, Cocks, and the Study of Politics." *World Politics* 29, no. 4 (July, 1977).

An Fagan. "Ji-Lu-Yu Kangri Genjudide Chuangjian Yu Fazhan" (The Creation and Development of the Hebei-Shandong-Henan Anti Japanese Base). In *Ji-Lu-Yu Kangri Genjudi* (The Hebei-Shandong-Henan Anti-Japanese Base Area). *Zhonggong Henan Shengwei Dangshi Ziliao Zhengji Bian* (A Collection of CCP Henan Provincial Committee Party History Materials). No. 1, *Henan Renmin Chubanshe.* 1985.

An Ming. "Ci*xian* Geming Huodong Huiyi" (Remembrances of the Revolutionary Struggle in Ci County). *Zhinan Dangshi Ziliao* [Southern Hebei Party History Materials]. *Zhonggong Handan Diwei Dangshi Ziliao Zhengji Bangongshibian.* (Published by the Editorial Office of the Chinese Communist Party Handan District Committee Party History Materials Committee.) No. 1. December, 1982.

An Ming (Liu Dafeng). "Zhinan Wu Xian Dangde Zhanli Yu Fazhan (The Establishment and Development of the Party in Five Counties of Southern Hebei)." *Zhonggong Henan Dangshi Ziliao* (CCP Henan Party History Materials). No. 4, *Henan Renmin Chubanshe.* 1985.

———. "Ji-Lu-Yu Bianqu Diyizhi Kangri Wuzhuang (The First Anti-Japanese Armed Force in the Hebei-Shandong-Henan Border Area)." In *Zhonggong Qingfeng Dangshi Ziliao Xuanbian* (A Selection of Qingfeng CCP History Materials). No. 2. 1987.

Annual Report of the National Government of China, Ministry of Finance, Chief Inspectorate of Salt Revenue, 23rd Year of the Republic of China. Nanjing, 1934–35.

Annual Report of the National Government of China, Ministry of Finance, Chief Inspectorate of Salt Revenue, 24th Year of the Republic of China, 1935.

Ardant, Gabriel. "Financial Policy and Economic Infrastructures of Modern States and Nations." In Charles Tilly, ed., *The Formation of Nation States in Western Europe.* Princeton: Princeton University Press, 1975.

Averill, Stephen C. "Local Elites and Communist Revolution in the Jiangxi Hill Country." In Joseph W. Esherick and Mary B. Rankin, eds., *Chinese Local Elites and Patterns of Dominance.* Berkeley: University of California Press, 1990.

Babbie, Earl R. *The Practice of Social Research,* 2nd ed. Belmont, CA: Wadsworth Publishing, Inc., 1979.

Bailey, F. G. "Parapolitical Systems." In Marc J. Swartz, ed., *Local Level Politics.* Chicago: Aldine Publishing Company, 1968.

Balazs, Etienne. *Chinese Civilization and Bureaucracy.* Trans. H. M. Wright. New Haven: Yale University Press, 1964.

Banfield, Edward. *The Moral Basis of a Backward Society.* New York: Free Press, 1958.

Barkan, Lenore. "Patterns of Power: Forty Years of Elite Politics in a Chinese County." In Joseph W. Esherick and Mary Backus Rankin, eds., *Chinese Local Elites and Patterns of Dominance.* Berkeley: University of California Press, 1990.

Bates, Robert H. "Agrarian Politics." In Myron Weiner and Samuel Huntington, eds., *Understanding Political Development.* Boston: Little, Brown and Company, 1987.

Belden, Jack. *China Shakes the World,* New York: Monthly Review Press, 1970.

Benton, Gregor. "The Second Wang Ming Line (1935–38)." *The China Quarterly, no.* 61 (March, 1975).

Bergere, Marie-Claire. "The Chinese Bourgeouisie, 1911–1937." In John King Fairbank and Albert Feuerwerker, eds., *The Cambridge History of China,* vol. 12, "Republican China, 1912–1949," part I. London: Cambridge University Press, 1983.

Bernhardt, Kathryn. *Rents, Taxes, and Peasant Resistance: The Lower Yangzi Region, 1840–1950.* Stanford: Standford University Press, 1992.

Bianco, Lucien. *Origins of the Chinese Revolution, 1915–1949.* Trans. Muriel Bell. Stanford: Stanford University Press, 1971.

———. "Peasant Movements." In John King Fairbank and Albert Feuerwerker, eds., *The Cambridge History of China: Republican China, 1912–1949,* vol. 13, no. 2. Cambridge: Cambridge University Press, 1986.

———. "Peasant Responses to Communist Party Mobilization Policies in the Anti-Japanese Bases: Some Western Views." Unpublished paper. Delivered to the Second International Symposium on the History of the Chinese Base Areas During World War II, Nankai University, Tianjin, China, August, 1991.

———. "Secret Societies and Peasant Self-Defense, 1921–1933," in Jean Chesneaux, ed., *Popular Movements and Secret Societies in China, 1840–1950.* Stanford: Stanford University Press, 1972.

"Biographical Note on T. V. Song, 1894–1971." Hoover Institution Archives.

Bloch, M. R. "The Social Influence of Salt." *Scientific American,* no. 209, pp. 89–98.

Boorman, Howard L., ed. *Biographical Dictionary of Republican China,* vol. 3. New York. Columbia University Press, 1970.

Bowen, John R. "Moral Shares: Divisions of Wealth in Sumatran Societies." AAS Paper, 11 April 1987.

Brandt, Loren. *Commercialization and Agricultural Development: Central and Eastern China, 1870–1937*. Cambridge: Cambridge University Press, 1989.

Braudel, Fernand. *On History*. Trans. Sarah Matthews. Chicago: University of Chicago Press, 1980.

Bu Yujie. "Yijiu Sanernian Dao Yijiu Sansannian Daming Yidai Yanmin Douzheng" (The Salt Makers' Struggle in the Vicinity of Daming from 1932 to 1933). *Daming Difang Ziliao* (Daming Local History Materials), 1987.

Buck, David D. Review of Philip C. C. Huang's *The Peasant Economy and Social Change in North China*. *The Journal of Peasant Studies* 14, no. 1 (October, 1986).

Buck, John Lossing. *Chinese Farm Economy*. Chicago: University of Chicago Press, 1930.

——— . *Land Utilization in China*. Shanghai: Nanjing University, 1937.

Bunker, Stephen G. *Peasants Against the State: The Politics of Market Control in Bugisu, Uganda 1900–1983*. Urbana: University of Illinois Press, 1987.

Burns, E. Bradford. *The Poverty of Progress: Latin America in the Nineteenth Century*. Berkeley: University of California Press, 1980.

Burns, John P. *Political Participation in Rural China*. Berkeley: University of California Press, 1988.

"Cai Xiaozhuang Nongmin Baodong Shiliao" (Materials on the History of the Peasant Rebellion in Cai Xiaozhuang). *Zhonggong Weixian Xianwei Dangshi Ziliao Zhengji Bangongshi* (CCP Wei County Party Committee Office for Collecting Party History Materials). 20 February 1982.

Campbell, J. K. *Honor, Family and Patronage: A Study of Institutions and Moral Values in a Greek Mountain Community*. Oxford: Oxford University Press, 1964.

Cao Pusheng. *Nanle Xianzhi* (Nanle County Gazetteer), 1987.

Caws, Peter, ed. *The Causes of Quarrel: Essays on Peace, War, and Thomas Hobbes*. Boston: Beacon Press, 1989.

"Chajin Xiaotuyan Zhiyiyi" (The Significance of Prohibiting Nitrate Earth Salt Production). *Yanwu Huikan* (A Compilation of Salt Affairs), no. 50 (15 September 1934).

Chang Fusen. "Cong Huaxian Yannong Douzheng Kan Nongmin Yundongde Juda Weili" (The Tremendous Power of the Peasant Movement as Illustrated by the Hua County Salt Peasants' Struggle). *Zonggong Huaxianwei Dangshi Ziliao Zhengbian Bangongtai*. (Published by the CCP Hua County Committee, Office of CCP Historical Records.) 23 July 1984.

——— . "Jingsheng Yougcunde Hu*xian* Yanmin Douzhengde Huiyi" (The Everlasting Spirit of the Hua County Salt People's Struggle). *Zhonggong Huaxian Xianwei Dangshi Ziliao Zhengbian Weiyuanhui Bangongshi Bianyin*. (Edited by the CCP County Committee Party History Compilation Committee.) Vol. 1. 1986.

——— . "Yanmin Nuhuo" (The Anger of the Salt People). No date.

——— . "Yijiu Wusan Nian Hua*xian* Qiangliang Chi Dahu Douzheng" (The 1935 Hua County Struggle to Seize the Grain and Eat in the Big Households). *Hua Xian Dangshi Ziliao Tongxin* (A Compilation of Hua County Party History Materials). Vol. 2. 1986.

Chang, L. "Letter to Arthur N. Young—List Showing the Respective Annual Quota

of Salt Funds to be Borne by the Various Provinces for Refund of Foreign Loans."
6 September 1929. Arthur N. Young papers.

Chang Lizeng. "Tian Zhujiaode Youlai He Zai Wo Xiande Yanbian" (The Origin and
Development of Catholicism in Our County). *Huaxian Zhengxie Chang Lizeng
Zengli* (Organized by Chang Lizeng of the People's Political Consultative Com-
mittee of Hua county). In *Huaxian Wenshi Ziliao* (Hua County Cultural History
Materials). No. 2. December, 1986.

Chang Senren. "Huaxian Yamin Douzheng Jishi" (Actual Events in the Struggles of
the Hua County Salt People). *Huaxian Wenshi Ziliao* (Hua County Cultural History Materials). No. 3. *Zhengxie Huaxian Weiyuanhui Wenshi Ziliao Yanjiu Wei Yuanhui*
(The Research Committee of the Cultural History Records Office of the People's
Political Consultative Committee of Hua County). No. 3. December, 1987.

Chang, Sidney H., and Ramon H. Myers, eds. *The Storm Clouds Clear Over China: The
Memoir of Ch'en Li-fu 1900–1993.* Stanford: Hoover Institution Press, 1994.

Changlu Hangu Yanchangzhi (The Annals of the Changlu Hangu Salt Fields). Tianjin: Baiwenhua Chubanshe, 1990.

"Changlu Jiwu Qingxing Jilue" (A Summary of the Conditions of Changlu Anti-Contraband Affairs). *Yanwu Huikan* (A Compilation of Salt Affairs). No. 8. 30
November 1934.

"Changlu Shuijing Zuzhang Diaocha Daming Yu Yanniao Chongtu Anzhi Baogao"
(Report on the Conflict Between the Daming Tax Police and the Private Salt
Dealers by the Changlu Tax Police Chief). *Yanwu Huikan* (A Compilation of Salt
Affairs). No. 52. 15 October 1934.

"Changlu Yanshong Fandui Feichu Yinan Zhengyanwu Shuwen" (A Formal Letter
Submitted by the Changlu Salt Merchants in Opposition to the Repeal of the Salt
Monopoly). *Jindai Zhongguo Yanwushi Ziliao* (Materials on the History of China's
Modern Salt Affairs). Nankai Daxue Chubanshe. Vol. I. 1984 (1913–1928).

Changlu Yanwu Jihe Fensuo Ershisannian Jiuyuefen Gongzuo Baogao (The Working
Report of the Changlu Branch of the Salt Affairs Investigation Institute). *Yanwu
Huikan* (A Compilation of Salt Affairs). No. 52. 15 September 1934.

"Changlu Yanwu Jihe Suo Ji Hua Jiuji Jinan Nongcun" (The Changlu Salt Police Plan
to Aid the Peasant Villages in Southern Hebei). "Chengqing Caibu Choukuan
She Nongshi Zuanke" (The Police Will Apply to the Ministry of Finance for Con-
sideration to Raise Money and Establish a Special Agricultural Department). "Jin
Xiao Zhengce Yu Minzhong Shengji Wuai" (The Anti-Salt Making Policy Does
Not Affect the People's Livelihood). *Da Gong Bao.* 8 April 1935.

"Changlu Zengyunshi Baogao Zhengli Changlu Yanwu Jingguo Zhi Qingxing" (A
Report by the Changlu Transport Officer Zeng on the Conditions Surrounding
the Reordering of Changlu Salt Affairs). *Yanwu Huikan.* No. 53. 31 October
1934.

Chao Zhepu. "Zhinan Geming Ciyuandi—Daming Chishi Gemingshi" (The Cradle
of Revolution in Southern Hebei—The Revolutionary History of the Daming
Normal School). *Zhonggong Qingfeng Dangshi Ziliao Xuanbian* (A Compilation of
CCP Qingfeng History Materials), *Zhonggong Qingfeng Xianwei Dangshi Ziliao
Zhengbian Weiyuanhui Bangongshi* (Office of the Compilation Committee of CCP
Qingfeng County Committee on Party History Materials). No. 1. 1985.

Ch'en, Jerome. *The Highlanders of Central China: A History, 1895–1937.* Armonk, New York: M.E. Sharpe, 1992.

Chen Juanru. "Changlu Yanwu Shulue" (A Brief Account of Changlu Salt Affairs). *Tianjin Wenshi Ziliao* (Tianjin Cultural History Materials). Vol. 26. *Tianjin Renmin Chubanshe.* 1 January 1984.

Chen Shenyi. "Yanmin Baodong" (The Salt People's Rebellion). In Liang Hanbing, ed., *Hua Tai Cun Qui* (Spring and Autumn in Hua county). *Huaxian Difangshi Zhizong Bianjishi* (The Office of General Editing of the Local Historical Records of Hua county). September, 1985.

Chen Zhuanhai, ed. *Henan Hongqianghui Ziliao Xuanbian* (A Collection of Materials on the Henan Red Spear Society), in *Henan Shizhi Ziliao* (Henan History Records). No. 6, *Henan Sheng Difang Shizhi Bianzuan Weiyuanhui* (Henan Province Local History Records Compilation Committee). 1985.

Chiang Tao-chang. "The Salt Industry of China, 1644–1911: A Study in Historical Geography." Ph.D. thesis, Department of Geography, University of Hawaii, 1975.

————. "The Significance of the Salt Industry in Ch'ing China." *Nanyang University Occasional Paper Series,* no. 7, January, 1976.

Chung-li Chang. *The Chinese Gentry: Studies on their Role in Nineteenth-Century Chinese Society.* Seattle: University of Washington Press, 1974.

"Ci*xian* Fadong Youji Zhanzhengde Jingguo" (The Course of Mobilization for Guerrilla Warfare in Ci County). *Zhinan Dangshi Ziliao* (Southern Hebei Party History Materials), No. 1. December, 1982.

Clark, Anne B., and Donald W. Klein. *Biographic Dictionary of Chinese Communism, 1921–1965.* Vol.2. Cambridge: Harvard University Press, 1971.

Cleveland, F. A. *The Problem of Putting the Principles of the New Salt Law into Effect: Report to Chinese National Government Ministry of Finance, Inspectorate of Salt Revenue,* 1935–36.

————. *Statistical Review of the Work of the Inspectorate, 1913–1933, with Special Attention Given to the Evaluation of Results Achieved During the Last Five Years.* Chinese National Government, Ministry of Finance, Inspectorate of Salt Revenue. Probably issued in 1934.

Cobb, R. C. *The Police and the People: French Popular Protest, 1789–1820.* London: Oxford University Press, 1970.

Cohen, Paul A. *China and Christianity.* Cambridge: Harvard University Press, 1963.

Coleman, Kenneth M., and Charles L. Davis. "Preemptive Reform and the Mexican Working Class." *Latin American Review* 18, no. 1 (1983).

Connerton, Paul. *How Societies Remember.* Cambridge: Cambridge University Press, 1989.

Coser, Lewis. *The Functions of Social Conflict.* New York: The Free Press, 1956.

Craig, Ann L. *The First Agraristas: An Oral History of a Mexican Reform Movement.* Berkeley: University of California Press, 1983.

Cressey, George B. *China's Geographical Foundations.* New York: McGraw-Hill, Inc., 1934.

Crook, David, and Isabel Crook. *Revolution in a Chinese Village: Ten Mile Inn.* London: Routledge and Kegen Paul, 1959.

Cumings, Bruce. "Interest and Ideology in the Study of Agrarian Politics." *Politics and Society* 10, no. 4 (1981).

Da Jin. "Jinan Tongxun" (Southern Hebei Correspondence). Originally published in *Anyang Dangshi Tongxun* (Anyang Party History Correspondence). No. 1. 1948.

Dagong Bao, 8 October 1935.

Dai Qingli. "Lun Xiaoyan" (On Nitrate Salt). *Yanwu Huikan* (A Compilation of Salt Affairs). 15 November 1934.

"Daming Xiaofei" (The Daming Salt Bandits). *Tianjin Da Gong Bao*. 10 October 1934.

"Daming Yidai Hongqianghui Yundong Shiliao" (History Materials on the Red Spear Movement in the Vicinity of Daming). *Zhinan Dangshi Ziliao* (Southern Hebei Party History Materials). No. 2. *Zhonggong Handan Diwei Dangshi Ziliao Zhengji Bangongshi Bian* (Compiled by the Collection Office for CCP Handan Prefectural Party History Materials). January, 1983.

"Daming Yidai Qunzhong He Yanxunde Douzheng" (The Struggle Between the Masses and the Salt Police in the Vicinity of Daming). *Zhinan Dangshi Ziliao* (Southern Hebei Party History Materials). No. 2. *Zhonggong Handan Diwei Dangshi Ziliao Zhengji Bangong Shiban* (Compiled by the Soliciting Office of the CCP Handan District Committee for Party History Materials). January, 1983.

Dane, Richard. *Report on the Reorganization of the Salt Revenue Administration, 1913–17*. Peking: Chief Inspectorte of the Central Salt Administration, 1918.

Davies, James C. "The Revolutionary State of Mind." In James Chowning Davies, ed., *When Men Revolt and Why: A Reader in Political Violence and Revolution*. New York: The Free Press, 1971.

———. "Toward a Theory of Revolution." *American Sociological Review* 27, no. 1 (February, 1962).

Day, Clarence B. *Chinese Peasant Cults*. Taipei: Ch'eng Wen Publishing, 1969.

De Soto, Hernando. *The Other Path: The Invisible Revolution in the Third World*. Trans. June Abbott. New York: Harper and Row, 1989.

Deutsch, Karl W. "External Involvement in Internal War." In Harry Eckstein, ed., *Internal War: Problems and Approaches*. London: The Free Press, 1964.

"Diaocha Ji-Lu-Yu Sansheng Chajin Xiaotuyan Shikuang Ji Tuijin Fangfa Baogaoshu" (The Investigation of the Real Situation as Regards Banning Earth Salt in the Three Provinces of Hebei, Shandong, and Henan and the Promotion of Methods). *Henan Shoushuiju Ershisinian Siwuliuchi Geyuefen Gongzuo Baogao* (Henan Tax Bureau's Working Report of April, May, June, and July, 24th year of the Republic). *Yanwu Huikan* (A Compilation of Salt Affairs). No. 78. 15 November 1935.

Ding Changqing. "Changlu Yanwu Shuijingde Bianzu He Yanbian" (The Organization and Evolution of the Changlu Salt Tax Corps). Unpublished manuscript.

———, ed. *Minguo Yanwu Shi gao* (A Historical Sketch of Republican Salt Affairs). Beijing: Renmin Chubanshe, 1990.

Dou Aizhi and Liu Yuzhi. "Yu Fangzhou." Hu Hua, ed. *Zhonggong Dangshi Renwuchuan (Biographies of CCP Figures)*. No. 10. Shaanxi Renmin Chubanshe. 1983.

Duara, Prasenjit. *Culture, Power, and the State: Rural North China 1900–1942*. Stanford: Stanford University Press, 1988.

———. "Elites and the Structures of Authority in the Villages of North China, 1900–1949." In Esherick, Joseph W., and Mary Bachus Rankin, eds. *Chinese Local Elites and Patterns of Dominance*. Berkeley: University of California Press, 1990.

———. "Knowledge and Power in the Discourse of Modernity: The Campaigns Against Popular Religion in Early Twentieth Century China." *Journal of Asian Studies* 50, no. 1 (February, 1991).

———. "State Involution: A Study of Local Finances in North China, 1911–1935." *Comparative Studies in Society and History* 29, no. 19 (January, 1987).

———. "Superscribing Symbols: The Myth of Guandi, Chinese God of War." *Journal of Asian Studies* 47, no. 4 (November, 1988).

Eastman, Lloyd E. *The Abortive Revolution: China Under Nationalist Rule, 1927–1937*. Cambridge: Harvard University Press, 1974.

———. *Family, Field, and Ancestors: Constancy and Change in China's Social and Economic History, 1550–1949*. New York: Oxford University Press, 1988.

———. "Fascism in Kuomintang China: The Blue Shirts." *China Quarterly*, no. 49 (January-March, 1972).

———. "Nationalist China During the Sino-Japanese War, 1937–1945." In John King Fairbank and Albert Feuerwerker, eds., *Cambridge History of China*, vol. 13, part 2, "Republican China 1912–1949." Cambridge: Cambridge University Press, 1986.

———. *Seeds of Destruction: Nationalist China in War and Revolution, 1937–1949*. Stanford: Stanford University Press, 1984.

Eckstein, Harry. "Introduction: Toward the Theoretical Study of Internal War." In Harry Eckstein, ed. , *Internal War: Problems and Approaches*. London: The Free Press, 1964.

Edelman, Murray. "Public Policy and Political Violence." *Institute for Research on Poverty Discussion Papers*. University of Wisconsin-Madison, 1968.

Endicott, Mary Austin. *Five Stars Over China*. Canadian Far Eastern Newsletter, 1953.

Esherick, Joseph W. *The Origins of the Boxer Uprising*. Berkeley: University of California Press, 1987.

Esherick, Joseph W., and Mary Backus Rankin, eds. *Chinese Local Elites and Patterns of Dominance*. Berkeley: University of California Press, 1990.

Evans, Peter B., Dietrick Rueschemeyer, and Theda Skocpol, eds. *Bringing the State Back In*. New York: Cambridge University Press, 1985.

Fallows, James. "With the Rebels." *Atlantic Monthly* 264, no. 3 (September, 1989).

Fang Quiwei. "Jinan Xiaoyan Wenti" (The Nitrate Problem in Southern Hebei). *Dongfang Zhazhi* (Far Eastern Magazine) 32, no. 18 (1935).

Foucault, Michel. *The Order of Things: An Archeology of the Human Sciences*. New York: Vintage, 1973.

Fried, Morton H. *The Fabric of Chinese Society: A Study of the Social Life of a Chinese County Seat*. New York: Praeger, 1953.

———. "Socioeconomic Relations in Pre-Communist China." *Modern China* 8, no. 4 (October, 1982).

Friedman, Edward. "Engels' Peasant War in Germany," *Journal of Peasant Studies* (special issue on "The German Peasant War of 1525," Jonas Bak, ed.) 3, no. 1 (October, 1975).

————. "What Do Peasants Really Want: An Exploration of Theoretical Categories and Action Consequences." *Economic Development and Cultural Change* 41, no. 1 (October, 1992).

Friedman, Edward, Paul G. Pickowicz, and Mark Selden. *Chinese Village, Socialist State*. New Haven: Yale University Press, 1991.

"Gaishan Dui Dide Jingji Douzheng Jiaqing Genjudi Jingji Jianshe Wenti Tigang" (An Outline of Problems in Unfolding the Struggle Against the Enemy and Strengthening the Economic Reconstruction of the Base Areas). *Zhanxianshe* (Frontline Press), 1943.

Gale, E. M. "Historical Evidences Relating to Early Chinese Public Finance." *American Historical Society*, Pacific Coast Branch, 1929.

————. *Salt for the Dragon*. East Lansing: Michigan State College Press, 1953.

Gamson, William A. *The Strategy of Social Protest*. Homewood, IL: The Dorsey Press, 1975.

Gao Kelin. "Yanmin Douzheng Jiankuang" (A Brief Account of the Saltmakers' Struggle). *Zhinan Dangshi Ziliao* (Southern Hebei Party History Materials). 1983.

————. "Zhinan Shaqu Yanmin Douzheng" (The Saltmakers' Struggle in the Sandy District of Southern Hebei). Transcribed in Beijing. 30 July, 1978.

Gao Kelin Huiyilu (Reminiscences of Gao Kelin). *Neimenggu Renmin Chubanshe*. 1987.

"Gao Kelin Tongzhi Huiyi Zai Hua*xian* Gongzuo Pianduan" (Gao Kelin's Recollections of His Working Days in Hua County). *Dangshi Ziliao Tongxun* (Communications on Party History Research Materials). *Zhonggong Huaxian Xianwei Dangshi Ziliao Zhengbian Weiyuanhui BangongshiBianyin(Edited by the CCP Hua County Party History Complication Committee)*. Vol. 1. 1986.

Gao Yuangui. "Jianzu Zengdiao Gongzuo Zhongde Jige Juti Wenti" (Several Concrete Problems in the Movement to Reduce Rent and Increase Salaries) 1 January 1943. *Zhonggong Ji-Lu-Yu Bianqu Dangshi Ziliao Xuanbian* (Selected Materials on Chinese Communist Party History in the Hebei-Shandong-Henan Border Region). *Henan Renmin Chubanshe*.1988.

"Gaotang Gu Guantun 'Nongmin Ziweituan' Baodong" (The Rebellion of Gaotang's Gu Guantun Peasant Self Defense Troupe). *Gaotang Dangshi Ziliao* (Materials on Gaotang Party History). *Zhonggong Gaotangxian Dangshi Ziliao Zhongji Yanjiu Weiyuanhuibian* (Compiled by the Gaotang County CCP History Soliciting and Research Committee). No. 1. 1983.

Geertz, Clifford. *Local Knowledge: Further Essays in Interpretive Anthropology*. New York: Basic Books, Inc., 1983.

————. *Peddlers and Princes: Social Development and Economic Change in Two Indonesian Towns*. Chicago: University of Chicago Press, 1963.

Gerth, H. H., and C. Wright Mills, eds. *From Max Weber: Essays in Sociology*. New York: Oxford University Press, 1946.

"Gexian Yanjia" (Each County's Salt Price). *Tianjin Da Gong Bao*. 16 July 1932.

"Gongzuo Cankao: Jin-Ji-Lu-Yu Bianqu Maoyi Zongbu" (Work References: Shanxi-Hebei-Shandong-Henan Border Region Trade Bureau Headquarters). No. 2. 20 October 1947.

Goodwin, Jeff, and Theda Skocpol. "Explaining Revolutions in the Contemporary Third World." *Politics and Society* 17, no. 4 (December, 1989).

Grove, Linda. "Creating a Northern Soviet." *Modern China.* 1, no. 3 (1975).

Gu Zhike. "Yijiusanwunian Pingxiang Yanmin Wuzhuang Douzheng" (The Pingxiang Salt Makers' Armed Struggle of 1935). The Oral Account of Zhou Dongguang, revised by Gu Zhike 2 August 1982 in *Zhinan Geming Douzheng Shiliao* (Materials on the History of the Revolutionary Struggle in Southern Hebei). No. 3. *Zhonggong Xingtai Diwei Dangshi Ziliao Zhengbian Bangongshi Bianyin (Edited by the CCP Xingtai Prefecture Committee Party History Complication Committee)* 1985.

"Guancheng Shengchan Yundong Zhong de Jige Wenti" (Several Problems in Mutual Aid Movements Around Guangcheng). *Gongzuo Tongxun* (Work Correspondence). No. 17. *Zhonggong Ji-Lu-Yuqu Dangwei Minyunbu Bian* (Civil Movement Department of the Hebei-Shandong-Henan District Bureau of the CCP). 1945.

"Guanyu Lu Situn Huodong" (On the Activities of Ruxton). No date. Unpublished private manuscript.

"*Guanyu Shaqu Choucai Gongzuode Tongxin*" (Correspondence on the Disaster Relief Work in the Sandy District). 9 March 1943 in *Zhonggong Ji-Lu-Yu Bianqu Dangshi Ziliao Xuanbian* (Selected Materials on Chinese Communist Party History in the Hebei-Shandong-Henan Border Region). No. 2. (1941–1943). *Henan Renmin Chubanshe.* 1988.

Guo Chenpo. "Daming Yidai Hongqianghui" (The Red Spear Society in the Vicinity of Daming). (Written at Beijing University.) *Morning Post.* 3–4 April 1928. Reprinted in Chen Zhuanhai, ed., *Henan Hongqianghui Ziliao Xuanbian* (A Compilation of Materials on the Henan Red Spear Society). *Henan Sheng Difang Shizhi Bianzuan Weiyuanhui* (Henan Province Local History Records Compilation Committee). No. 6. Kaifeng. 1984.

Guo Chuanxi and Xu Youli. "Ji-Lu-Yu Bianqu Kangri Genjudide Chuangjian" (The Establishment of the Hebei-Shandong-Henan Anti-Japanese Base Area). In *Zhonghua Xindaishi Xuehui Tongxun* (Correspondence of the Society of Contemporary Chinese History). No. 4. 1984.

Guo Shukui. "Nanle Yanmin Douzheng Qingkuang" (The Struggles of the Nanle Salt Makers). *Zhonggong Nanle Xianwei Dangshi Ziliao* (CCP Nanle County Committee Party History Materials). No. 1. 1984.

Gurr, Ted. "A Causal Model of Civil Strife: A Comparative Analysis Using New Indices." Reprinted from *American Political Science Review* in James Chowning Davies, ed., *When Men Revolt & Why.* New York: Free Press, 1971.

——— . *Why Men Rebel.* Princeton: Princeton University Press, 1970.

Halbwachs, Maurice. *On Collective Memory.* Ed. and Trans. Lewis A. Coser. Chicago: University of Chicago Press, 1992.

Hartford, Kathleen. "Repression and Communist Success: The Case of Jin-Cha-Ji, 1938–1943." In Hartford, Kathleen, and Steven Goldstein, eds., *Single Sparks: China's Rural Revolutions.* Armonk: M. E. Sharpe, 1989.

He Fukui and Niu Guoqi. "Liu Yanchun Zhuanlue" (A Brief Biographical Sketch of Liu Yanchun). *Zhonggong Puyang Dangshi Ziliao* (CCP Puyang Party History Materials). *Zhonggong Puyang Xianwei Dangshi Ziliao Zhengbian Weiyuanhui Bangongshi* (Office of the Compilation Committee of the Puyang County Committee Party History Materials). No. 6. 1988.

He Linliang. "Dang Zai Yaojia Yidaide Fazhan Yu Huodong" (The Development and

Activity of the Party in the Vicinity of Yao Family Village). *Zhonggong Puyang Dangshi Ziliao* (CCP Puyang Party History Materials). Vol. 1. February, 1983.

"Hebei Daming Zhongxin Wei Gongzuo Baogao—Qunzhong Zuzhi Yu Xian Weide Zuzhi Qingkuang" (The Work Report of the Daming County Central Committee of Hebei Province About Mass Organization of the County Committee). *Zhonggong Nanle Dangshi Ziliao. (CCP Nanle Party History Materials)*

"Hebei Sheng Daming Xian Xiaofan Yu Shuijing Chongtu Yian Qingxing Checha" (A Thorough Investigation into the Conflict Between the Salt People and the Salt Tax Police in Hebei's Daming County). *Yanwu Huikan* (A Compilation of Salt Affairs). No. 55. 30 November 1934.

Henan Kangzhan Shilie (A Brief History of the Anti-Japanese War of Resistance in Henan). *Zhonggong Henan Shengwei Dangshi Ziliao Zhengji* (CCP Henan Provincial Party History Materials). *Henan Renmin Chubanshe.* September, 1985.

"Henan Sheng Hua*xian* Ba Li Ying Xiang Shi" (A History of Ba Li Ying Township, Hua county, Henan Province). Chapter 4, Part 1, "Minguo Gemingqi" (The Republican Revolutionary Period). 1987.

Henan Yanwu Tekan. (Special Issue of Henan Salt Affairs). 1930.

"Heze Yanmin Yongdong Shi" (A History of the Salt Makers' Movement in Heze). *Heze Xianzhi* (Heze County Gazetteer).

Hillel, Daniel. "Lash of the Dragon." *National History,* August, 1991.

Hinton, William. *Fanshen: A Documentary of Revolution in a Chinese Village.* New York: Random House, 1966.

Hofheinz, Roy Jr. *The Broken Wave: The Chinese Communist Peasant Movement, 1922–1928.* Cambridge: Harvard University Press, 1977.

Holcombe, Arthur N. *The Spirit of the Chinese Revolution.* New York: Alfred A. Knopf, 1930.

Howe, R. E. "Letter to Director General of the Chinese Government Salt Administration in Shanghai." 21 December 1937. Also: letter of Associate Director General, "To His Excellency M. Paul Emile Naggiar, Ambassadeur de France, Shanghai. Also: letter from Director General, "To W. C. Cassels of the Hong Kong and Shanghai Banking Corp." and "To M. L. Chevretton, Banque de l'Indochine. 22 December 1937. Also: letter from Ministry of Finance Director General of the Salt Administration. "To Arthur N. Young." 11 December 1937. Hoover Archive papers of Arthur N. Young.

Hsu, Immanuel C. Y. *The Rise of Modern China ,* 4th ed. New York: Oxford University Press, 1990.

Hu Jingyi. "Wo Zai Hua*xian* Gaojian Dang Gongzuode Huiyi (My Recollections of My Role in the Founding of the Party in Hua County). *Zhonggong Huaxian Xianwei Dangshi Ziliao Zhengbian Weiyuanhui Bannggongtai Bianyin* (Published by the Office of the CCP Hua County Party History Materials Soliciting Committee). Vol. 1. 1986.

"Huabei Xingshi Ji Renwu He Shengwei Zishi" (The Situation and Task in North China and the Instructions of the Provincial Committee). "Zhinan Tewei Baogao" (A Report of the Southern Hebei Special Committee). *Hebei Sheng Danganguan* (Hebei Provincial Party Archives). 4 June 1934.

Huang Jing. "Bianqude Xingshi Yu Renwu" (The Situation in the Border Area and the Task at Hand). In *Zhonggong Ji-Lu-Yu Bianqu Dangshi Ziliao Xuanbian* (A Selection of CCP Hebei-Shandong-Henan Border Area Party History Materials). Vol. 2 (1941–1943). *Henan Renmin Chubanshe.* 1988.

Huang, Philip C. C. "The Paradigmatic Crisis in Chinese Studies." *Modern China* 17, no. 3 (July, 1991).

———. *The Peasant Economy and Social Change in North China.* Stanford: Stanford University Press, 1985.

———. *The Peasant Family and Rural Development in the Yangzi Delta, 1350–1988.* Stanford: Stanford University Press, 1990.

Huntington, Samuel P. *Political Order in Changing Societies.* New Haven: Yale University Press, 1968.

Jia Juxin. "Qingfeng Xiande Yanmin Douzheng" (The Qingfeng Saltmakers' Struggle). *Zhongzhou Guyin* (Central China Past and Present). No. 1. 1988.

Jia Zongyi. "Dui Nanle Xian Diwei Gongzuode Huiyi" (Recollections on Enemy Puppet Work in Nanle County). In *Zhonggong Nanle Dangshi Ziliao* (CCP Nanle Party History Materials). Vol. 2. 1985.

"Jian Zhanjia Tongzhi Zhuanlue" (A Biographical Sketch of Comrade Jiang Zhanjia). In *Gaotang Dangshi Ziliao* (Materials on Gaotang Party History). *Zhonggong Gaotangxian Dangshi Ziliao Zhongji Yanjiu WeiyuanhuiBian.* (Compiled by the CCP History Soliciting and Research Committee of Gaotang County). No. 1. 1983.

Jiang Shouyi. "Henan Sheng Zuijin Yanwu Zhi Qingxing" (The Recent Situation of Henan's Salt Affairs). *Yanwu Huikan* (A Compilation of Salt Affairs). No. 17. 8 July 1935.

"Jianshui Gao" (Tax Increase Announcement). *Tianjin Da Gong Bao.* 16 July 1932.

"Ji-Lu-Yu Bianqu Gongzuode Chubu Zongjie" (A Preliminary Summary of the Work of the Hebei-Shandong-Henan Border Region). *Zhonggong Ji-Lu-Yu Bianqu Dangshi Ziliao Xuanbian* (A Selection of CCP Hebei-Shandong-Henan Border Area Party History Materials). Vol. 2 (1941–1943). *Henan Renmin Chubanshe.* 1988.

"Ji-Lu-Yu Bianqu Kangri Genjudi Henan Bufen Gaishu" (A Brief Survey of the Henan Part of the Hebei-Shandong-Henan Anti-Japanese Base Area). In *Ji-Lu-Yu Kangri Genjudi.* No. 1. *Zhonggong Henan Shengwei Dangshi Ziliao Zhengji Bianzuan WeiyuanhuiBian (Edited by the CCP Henan Provincial Committee Party History Complication Committee), Henan Renmin Chubanshe.* 1985.

"Ji-Lu-Yu Kangri Genjudide Chuangjian," (The Establishment of the Hebei-Shandong-Henan Anti-Japanese Base) *Henan Kangzhan Shilie* (A Brief History of the Anti-Japanese War in Henan) *Henan Renmin Chubanshe,* 1985.

"Ji-Lu-Yu Wo Jun Da Shengli Guanfu Nanle Qian Diwei Sanqian" (The Great Victory of our Army in Hebei-Shandong-Henan and the Recovery of Nanle Town and the Annihilation of Three Thousand Japanese Puppet Forces). *Ji-Lu-Yu Kangri Genjudi.* No. 1. 1985. Reprinted from *Jiefang Ribao* (Liberation Daily), 5 May 1945

Jin Gulan. "Guanyu Gaotang Hongtuan Gongzuode Baogao" (A Report About the Work with Gaotang's Red League).

Jin Huaiyi and Yan Chengzun. "Materials on Changlu Salt Flows Under Japanese Occupation."

Jin Weiyuan. "Jin Gulan Tongzhi Jianshi" (A Brief History of Comrade Jin Gulan).

"Jinan Tewei Liang He Yanfu Gongzhuo Jueyian" (The Draft Resolution on the

Work of the Salt Farmers of Henan and Hebei, by the Southern Hebei Special Committee). Dan An Guan. Unpublished.1932.

"Jinan *Xiaoyan Zhishi*" (The Matter of Nitrate Salt in Southern Hebei). *Yanzheng Zazhi* (The Journal of Salt Administration) . No. 11. August, 1935.

Johnson, Chalmers A. *Peasant Nationalism and Communist Power: The Emergence of Revolutionary China, 1937–1945.* Stanford: Stanford University Press, 1962.

———— . *Revolutionary Change.* Boston: Little, Brown, Inc., 1966.

Journal of Salt Administration, no. 60 (May, 1935).

"Kanasho Doen Taisaku Ni Tsuite" (Counter Measures to the Problem of Earth Salt in Henan). *Mantetsu Hokushi Kezai Chosasho.* Tianjin. 1941.

Kann, E. "China's Salt Revenue as Security for Her Loan Obligations." *Financial Bulletin.* Shanghai (1937). In Arthur N. Young Papers, Box 13, Hoover Archives.

Kataoka, Tetsuya. "Communist Power in a War of National Liberation: The Case of China." *World Politics* 24, no. 3 (April, 1972).

———— . *Resistance and Revolution in China: The Communists and the Second United Front.* Berkeley: University of California Press, 1974.

Kerkvliet, Benedict J. Tria. *Everyday Politics in the Phillipines: Class and Status Relations in a Central Luzon Village.* Berkeley: University of California Press, 1990.

Klein, Donald W., and Anne B. Clark. *Biographic Dictionary of Chinese Communism, 1921–1965,* vol. 1. Cambridge: Harvard University Press, 1971.

Kuhn, Philip. "Local Self-Government Under the Republic: Problems of Control, Autonomy, and Mobilization." In Frederic Wakeman, Jr., and Carolyn Grant, eds., *Conflict and Control in Late Imperial China.* Berkeley: University of California Press, 1975.

Kung-Chuan Hsiao. *Compromise in Imperial China.* Parega Occasional Papers on China, no. 6. Seattle: University of Washington School of International Studies, 1979.

Kwan Manbun. "The Merchant World of Tianjin: Society and Economy of a Chinese City." Ph.D. thesis. Stanford University History Department, 1990.

"Lai Han Zhao Deng" (Letter to the Publisher). *Da Gong Bao* (17 April 1935).

Laves, Edward Walter. "Rural Society and Modern Revolution: The Rise of the Kiangsi Soviet." Ph.D. thesis, University of Chicago History Department, 1980.

Lemarchand, Rene. "The Political Economy of Informal Economies." Unpublished paper presented to the Yale University Program in Agrarian Studies Colloquim Series, 1991.

Levine, Steven I. *Anvil of Victory: The Communist Revolution in Manchuria, 1945–1948.* New York: Columbia University Press, 1987.

Levy, Howard S. Book Review. *Journal of Asian Studies* 16, no. 4 (August, 1957).

Lewis, John W. "The Study of Chinese Political Culture." *World Politics* 28, no. 3 (1966).

———— . "Memory, Opportunity, and Strategy in Peasant Revolutions: The Case of North China." Unpublished paper presented to the Research Conference on Communist Revolutions, Estate Carlton Beach Hotel, St. Croix, VI. 24–28 January 1973.

Li Chunlan. "Shengchan Yundong Xiaozongshu Zhiyi" (A Book in the Little Reader on the Production Movement). "Hezuo Huzhu Shengchan de Huo Yangzi" (A Living Model in Cooperative Mutual Aid). "Qian Rugui He Houshangu" (Qian

Rugui and Houshangu Village), *Ji-Lu-Yu Shudian.* (Hebei-Shandong-Henan Bookstore). May, 1946.

Li Duo. "Shaqu Kangri Genjudi Chuangjian He Jianchide Yixie Qingkuang" (The Creation and Maintenance of the Shaqu Anti-Japanese Base). In *Nanwangde Suiyue* (The Unforgettable Years), *Ji-Lu-Yu Dangshi Ziliao Xuanbian Zhiyi* (Selection of Hebei-Shandong Party History Materials). Part 1. *Zhonggong Ji-Lu-Yu Bianqu Dangshi, Yunnan Lian Luozu Bian* (The CCP Hebei-Shandong-Henan Border Region Party History from the Yunnan Province Liaison Group). July, 1987.

Li Fanjiu et al. "Ding Shuben Zai Pudaqu 'Kangri' Fangong Toudi Shimo" (Ding Shuben's Policy of "Resistance to Japan" in Puyang District was One of Opposing the Chinese Communist Party and Capitulation from Start to Finish). *Henan Wenshi Ziliao* (Henan Cultural History Materials). No. 3. *Henan Renmin Chubanshe.*1980.

Li Han. *Miao Choujie Yu Minguo Yanwu Gaige* (Miao Choujie and the Reform of Republican Salt Affairs). *Zhongguo Kexue Jishu Chubanshe* (China Technology Publishing House). 1990.

Li Huasheng. "Yijiusanwuniande Zhinan Youji Zhanzheng" (The Southern Hebei Guerilla War of 1935). *Jinan Geming Douzheng Shiliao* (Materials on the Revolutionary Struggle in Southern Hebei). 1983.

Li Jianchang. *Guanliao Ziben Yu Yanye* (Bureaucratic Capitalism and the Salt Industry). Beijing: Shenghuo Press, 1963.

Li Jiangang. "Huiyi 'Xiaocheshe' Douzheng" (Remembering the Struggle of Small Push Carters). *Zhinan Dangshi Ziliao* (Southern Hebei Party History Materials). No. 1. December, 1982.

Li Pengtu, Liu Yudong, and Liu Yeting. "Changlu Yanwu Wushinian Hugu" (Reminiscences of the Changlu Salt Company's Fifty Year History). *Wenshi Ziliao Xuanji (A Selection of Cultural History Materials).* Beijing. Vol. 44. No. 5. 1980.

Li Shengzhi. "Da Yanbing" (The Fight with the Salt Police). *Daming Difangshi Ziliao* (Daming Local History Materials). 1987.

Li Tiezhong, Qi Lian, and Wang Yuting, "Ji-Lu-Yu Bianqu Diyizhi Kangri Wuzhuang Minjun Sizhiduide Chungjian He Fazhan" (The Establishment and Expansion of the Fourth Branch of the People's Army—the First Anti-Japanese Popular Armed Force in the Hebei-Shandong-Henan Border Area). In *Zhonggong Nanle Dangshi Ziliao* (CCP Nanle Party History Materials). No. 3. April, 1986.

Li Yu. "Zhonggong Zhinan Tewei Gongzuo Huiyi" (Remembrances of CCP Special Committee Work [May , 1934-April, 1936]). *Zhonggong Ji-Lu-Yu Bianqu Dangshi Ziliao Xuanbian* (A Selection of CCP Hebei-Shandong-Henan Party History Materials). No. 1. 1985.

Lian Enlin et al. "Jinshengdao Baodongde Shimo" (The Entire History of the Golden Mean Society). *Weixian Zhengxie Wenshi Ziliao* (Political Consultative Cultural History Materials of Wei County). No. 37. 31 October 1986.

Lian Shouxian. "Daming Dang Lingdaode Ji Ci Qunzhong Douzheng" (Some Struggles of the Masses Led by the Daming Chinese Communist Party). *Zhinan Dangshi Ziliao* (Documents of Party History in Southern Hebei). No. 2. *Zhonggong Handan Diwei Dangshi Ziliao Zhengji Bangongshi Bian* (Compiled by the Soliciting Office of Party History of the CCP Handan District Committee). January, 1983.

Liang, Hanbing, ed., *Hua Tai Cun Qui* (Spring and Autumn in Hua County). 1st edition. Huaxian Difangshi Zhi Zong Bianshi (The Office of General Editing of the Local Historical Records of Hua County) September, 1985.

"Liang He Yanfu Lianhe Hui Zongzhuang Saoan" (The Draft Resolution of the Hebei-Henan Salt Workers' Alliance). *Zhonggong Nanle Dangshi Ziliao.* (CCP Nanle Party History Materials).

Lieberman, Henry R. "China's Reds Press Changchun." *New York Times,* 8 June 1948.

Lijphardt, Arend. "Comparative Politics and the Comparative Method." *American Political Science Review* 65, no. 3 (September, 1971).

Linebarger, Paul M.A. *The China of Chiang Kai-shek: A Political Study.* Boston: World Peace Foundation, 1941.

Liu Chaode. "Guanyu Yanmin Douzhengde Huiyi" (Reminiscences About the Salt-makers' Struggle). *Dangshi Ziliao Tongxun* (Communications on Party History Research Materials). *Zhonggong Huaxian Xianwei Dangshi Ziliao Zhengbian Weiyuanhui Bangongtai Bianyin.* (Published by the Office of the CCP Hua County Party History Materials Soliciting Committee) . No. 1. 1 January 1986.

Liu Cun. *Liang He Yanmin Douzheng* (The Hebei-Henan Saltmakers' Struggle). Unpublished manuscript, 1988.

Liu Dafeng (Anming). "Zhinan Wuxian Dangde Zhanli Yu Fazhan" (The Establishment and Development of the Party in Five Counties of Southern Hebei). *Zhonggong Henan Dangshi Ziliao* (CCP Henan Party History Materials). No. 4. Zhengzhou: *Henan Renmin Chubanshe.* 1985.

Liu Feng. "Wo Zai Nanle Xian Fo Shan Cun Geming Gongzuode Jingguo" (My Revolutionary Work Experience in Nanle's Fo Shan Village). *Zhonggong Nanle Xianwei Dangshi Ziliao Zhengbian Weiyuanhui.* (CCP Nanle Party History Materials). No. 1. *Zhonggong Nanle Xianwei Dang Ziliao Zhengbian Weiyuanhui Bangongtai* (Edited by the CCP Nanle County Committee Party History Complication Committee). 1986.

Liu Hansheng. "Dang Lingdau Shaqu Qunzhongde Geming Douzheng" (The Party-Led Revolutionary Struggle of the Masses in the Sandy District). In *Zhonggong Henan Dangshi Ziliao* (CCP Henan Party History Materials). No. 4. Zhengzhou: *Henan Renmin Chubanshe.* 1985.

Liu Qingfeng, ed. "Dongming Xian Yanmin Baodong" (The Dongming County Salt-makers' Rebellion). *Zhonggong Shandong Sheng Dongming Xianwei Dangshi Ziliao Zhengyuan Weiyuanhui* (CCP Shandong Province, Dongming County Party History Materials Research Collection Committee). *Zhonggong Ji-Lu-Yu Bianqu Dangshi Ziliao Xuanbian (Selected CCP Party History Materials on the Hebei-Shandong-Henan Border Area).* Shandong Daxue Chubanshe. 1985.

Liu Yanchun. "Hongqi Piao Zai Puyang" (Red Flag Fluttering Over Puyang). *Zhonggong Puyang Dangshi Ziliao* (CCP Puyang Party History Materials). No. 1. *Zhonggong Puyang Xianwei Dangshi Ziliao Zhengbian Weiyuanhui Bangongshi (Edited by the CCP Puyang County Committee Party History Compilation Committee)* 1983.

————. "Hongqi Piao Zai Puyang" (Red Flag Fluttering Over Puyang). *Zhonggong Henan Dangshi Ziliao Huibian* (A Compilation of CCP Henan Party History Materials). No. 4. 1980.

Liu Yufeng. "Zhinan Shaqu Nongmin Geming Douzheng Pianduan" (A Fragment on the Peasant Revolutionary Struggle in the Southern Hebei Sandy District). Transcribed 11 April 1981 in Zhengzhou, Henan.

Liu Zhun. "Xianjin Zhongguo Yanwu Zhizhen Tao" (An Examination of the Salt Monopoly in Present Day China). *Shehui Kexue Zazhi,* 4, 6 December 1935, pp. 572–597.

Liucunxiang Xiangzhi Chugao (The First Draft of the Liucun Village Township Rural Gazetteer). May, 1985.

Lottes, Gunther. "Popular Culture and the Early Modern State in 16th Century Germany." In Steven L. Kaplan, ed., *Understanding Popular Culture: Europe from the Middle Ages to the Nineteenth Century.* New York: Mouton, 1984.

Lu Bingcan and Shi Guoqiang, eds. *Nanle Shilue* (A Brief History of Nanle County). *Henan Sheng Nanle Xian Difang Shizhi Bianwei Hui Zong Bianshi* (The General Editorial Office of Nanle County Historical Records Editorial Committee of Henan Province). April, 1986.

Lundahl, Mats. *The Haitian Economy: Man, Land and Markets.* New York: St. Martin's Press, 1983.

———. *Peasants and Poverty, A Study of Haiti.* New York: St. Martin's Press, 1979.

Luo Qing. "Jinan Youjiqude Jingji Jianshe Gongzuo" (The Work of Founding the Economy in the Southern Hebei Guerilla Area). *Jinan Dangshi Ziliao* (Southern Hebei Party History Materials). No. 2. (1937–1949). *Jinan Geming Genjudishi Bianshen Weiyuanhui (Edited by the Southern Hebei Revolutionary Base Area History Compilation Commmittee).* Xingtai. 1986.

MacKinnon, Stephen R. *Power and Politics in Late Imperial China: Yuan Shi-Kai in Beijing and Tianjin, 1901–1908.* Berkeley: University of California Press, 1980.

Mann, Susan Jones. *Local Merchants and the Chinese Bureaucracy, 1750–1950.* Stanford: Stanford University Press, 1987.

———. "Misundestanding the Chinese Economy—A Review Article." *Journal of Asian Studies* 40, no. 3 (May, 1981).

Mao Xixue. "Kangri Shiqi Jin-Ji-Lu-Yu Bianqude Dui Di Qingji" (The Economic Struggle Toward the Enemy in the Shanxi-Hebei-Shandong-Henan Border Area in the Anti-Japanese War Period). *Zhongguo Renmin Daxue Xiaobao Ziliao Zhongxin. (Edited by the Information Center of the Chinese People's University Journal)* 1986.

Marks, Robert. *Rural Revolution in South China.* Madison: University of Wisconsin Press, 1984.

Meisner, Maurice. *Li Ta-chao and the Origins of Chinese Marxism.* Cambridge: Harvard University Press, 1967.

———. *Mao's China and After: A History of the People's Republic.* New York: Free Press, 1986.

Migdal, Joel S. *Strong Societies and Weak States: State-Society Relations and State Capabilities in the Third World.* Princeton: Princeton University Press, 1988.

Miller, Frank. "China Community and Small Trader." *New York Times* 2 May 1948.

Ministry of Finance Report for the 23rd Fiscal Year (July 1934 to June 1935). National Government, Republic of China. Nanjing.1936.

Moore, Barrington Jr. *Social Origins of Dictatorship and Democracy: Lord and Peasant in the Making of the Modern World.* Boston: Beacon Press, 1966.

Muller, Edward N., Stephen E. Finkel, and Henry A. Dietz. "Relative Deprivation, Rational Action, and Rebellion." Paper presented to annual meeting of the American Political Science Association, Atlanta, 31 August—3 September 1989.

Multhauf, Robert P. *Neptune's Gift: A History of Common Salt.* Baltimore: Johns Hopkins Press, 1978.

Myers, Ramon H. *The Chinese Peasant Economy: Agricultural Development in Hopei and Shandong, 1890–1949.* Cambridge: Harvard University Press, 1970.

"Nanle Canan Shanhou" (Dealing with the Aftermath of the Nanle Massacre). *Da Gong Bao.* 17 April 1935.

"Nanle Xian Fasheng Liuxie Canjiu" (The Bloody Tragedy that Occured in Nanle County). *Tianjin Da Gong Bao.* 16 April 1935.

"Nanle Yanmin Douzheng" (The Nanle Salt Makers' Struggle). *Nanle Xian Dangshi Ziliao* (Nanle County CCP History Materials). No date.

Naquin, Susan. *Millenarian Rebellion in China: The Eight Trigrams Uprising of 1813.* New Haven: Yale University Press, 1976.

———. *Shantung Rebellion: The Wanglun Uprising of 1774.* New Haven: Yale University Press, 1981.

National Government of China, Ministry of Finance, Chief Inspectorate of Salt Revenue, 19th Year of the Republic of China, 1930; 20th Year, 1931; 21st Year, 1932; 23rd Year, 1934; and 24th year, 1935.

"Neihuang Xian Zaiqing Quzhong" (The Extremely Serious Flood Conditions in Neihuang County). *Tianjin Da Gong Bao.* 28 August 1933.

Neihuang Xianzhi (Neihuang County Gazetter). Vols. 5, 6, 8, 15, 16 (1937).

Nie Zhen. "Guanyu Hu*xian* Geming Yundong He Jiandang Guochengde Yixie Huiyi" (Some Remembrances of the Revolutionary Movement and the Process of Establishing the Party in Hua county). *Neihuang Xian Dangshi Ziliao* (Neihuang County Party History Materials). No. 1. No date.

North China Daily News 21 February 1928, 22 October 1929, 3 January 1935.

Oi, Jean. *State and Peasant in Contemporary China: The Political Economy of Village Government.* Berkeley: University of California Press, 1989.

"Peng Cheng Tuicihua Gongren Douzheng Gaikuang" (A Brief Account of the Small Porcelain Cart Workers' Struggle in Peng Cheng). *Zhonggong Handanshiwei Dangshi Bianweihui Biande* (Published by the Editorial Committee of the Handan City Committee on Party History). 1959. Reissued in *Zhinan Dangshi Ziliao* (Southern Hebei Party History Materials). No. 1. December, 1982.

Peng Yuemei. "Wo Jihui Zongde Sizhidui" (My Memory of the Fourth Branch Army). In *Zhonggong Qingfeng Dangshi Ziliao Xuanbian (A Compliation of Qingfeng Party History Materials).* No. 2. 1987.

Pepper, Suzanne. *Civil War in China: The Political Struggle, 1945–1949.* Berkeley: University of California Press, 1978.

———. "The KMT-CCP Conflict 1945–1949." In John K. Fairbank and Albert Feuerwerker, eds., *Cambridge History of China.* Vol 13, Part 2. Cambridge: Cambridge University Press, 1986.

Perdue, Peter. *Exhausting the Earth: State and Peasant in Hunan, 1500–1850.* Cambridge: Harvard University Press, 1987.

Perry, Elizabeth J. *Rebels and Revolutionaries in North China, 1845–1945.* Stanford: Stanford University Press, 1980.

Ping Jiesan. "Kangri Zhanzheng Chuqi Zhinan Diqu Dangde Tongzhan Gongzuo" (The Party's United War Front Work in Southern Hebei During the Period of the

Anti-Japanese War). *Ji-Lu-Yu Kangri Genjudi* (The Hebei-Shandong-Henan Anti-Japanese Base Area). No. 1. *Zhonggong Henanshengwei Dangshi Ziliao Zhengji Bianzuan Weiyuanhui* (Compiled by the Collection and Compilation Committee on CCP Party History Materials of Henan Province). *Henan Renmin Chubanshe*. 1985.

Pitt-Rivers, J. A. *The People of the Sierra*. Chicago: University of Chicago Press, 1969.

Polachek, James M. "The Moral Economy of the Kiangsi Soviet (1928–1934)." *Journal of Asian Studies* 42, no. 4 (August, 1983).

Pomeranz, Kenneth. *The Making of a Hinterland: State, Society and Economy in Inland North China, 1853–1937*. Berkeley: University of California Press, 1993.

Popkin, Samuel. *The Rational Peasant: The Political Economy of Rural Society in Vietnam*. Berkeley: University of California Press, 1979.

Puyang Xianzhi Chugao (Shanju) (First Draft of the Puyang County Gazatteer) . Part 1. 1985. Qi Wu, ed. *Yige Geming Genjudide Chengzhang* (The Growth of a Revolutionary Base). Beijing: *Remnin Chubanshe* (People's Press), 1958.

Qin Senyi. "Sangcun Nongmin 'Chi Dahu'." (The Sang Village Peasants' Seizure and Eating of Food in the Homes of Landlords." In Liang Hanbing, ed., *Hua Tai Cun Qiu,* 1985.

————— . "Sangcun Nongmin Qiushou Ziyi" (The Sang Village Peasants' Autumn Harvest Uprising). In *Hua Tai Cun Qiu,* 1985.

Qin Shenyi. "Yahua Gongren Kang Kesui Douzheng (The Struggles of the Cotton Processing Workers Against the Exorbitant Taxes on Cotton Processing). In *Hua Tai Cun Qiu,* 1985.

————— . "Yanmin Baodong" (The Salt Makers' Rebellion). In *Hua Tai Cun Qui,* 1985.

Qu Dangwei (Regional Party Committee). "Ji-Lu-Yu Wuge Yue Lai Youji Zhanzhengde Zongjie Yu Muqian Renwu" (A Summary of the Past Five Months of Guerrilla Warfare in Hebei-Shandong-Henan and the Present Task). *Gongzuo Tongxun* (Work Correspondence). No. 32. 2 February 1947.

"Qunzhong Gongzuo Shi" (Instructions for Mass Movement Work). *Zhonggong Nanle Dangshi Ziliao* (CCP Nanle Party History Materials).

Rankin, Mary Backus. *Elite Activism and Political Transformation in China: Zhejiang Province, 1865–1911*. Stanford: Stanford University Press, 1986.

Rawski, Thomas G. *Economic Growth in Prewar China*. Berkeley: University of California Press, 1989.

Reader, W. J. *Imperial Chemical Industries: A History,* vol. 1: *The Forerunners 1870–1926*. London: Oxford University Press, 1970.

Register to the Arthur N. Young Collection. Hoover Archives. No date.

Ren Zhang, "Wo Dui Nanle Yanmin Douzhengde Huiyi," (My Recollections of the Struggle of the Nanle Saltmakers). *Nanle Dangzhi Ziliao* (Reference Materials on Nanle Party History), No. 1, 1986.

Rice, Edward E. *Wars of the Third Kind: Conflict in Underdeveloped Countries*. Berkeley: University of California Press, 1988.

Robisheaux, Thomas. *Rural Society and the Search for Order in Early Modern Germany*. Cambridge: Cambridge University Press, 1989.

Rodney, Walter. *A History of the Guyanese Working People, 1881–1905*. Baltimore: Johns Hopkins University Press, 1981.

Root, Hilton L. *Peasants and Kings in Burgundy: Agrarian Foundations of French Absolutism*. Berkeley: University of California Press, 1987.

Rowe, William. *Hankow: Commerce and Society in a Chinese City, 1796–1889*. Stanford: Stanford University Press, 1984.

Ruxton, R. M. C. "Letter to his Excellency, Dr. H. H. Kung, Minister of Finance." In F. A. Cleveland, *Statistical Review of the Work of the Inspectorate 1913–1933*. Chinese National Government, Minister of Finance, Inspectorate of Salt Revenue, probably 1934. Arthur N. Young Papers. Box 115, Hoover Archives.

Sabean, David Warren. *Power in the Blood: Popular Culture and Village Discourse in Early Modern Germany*. Cambridge: Cambridge University Press, 1984.

"The Salt Loan." *North China Daily News*. 19 September 1929.

Schwartz, Benjamin I. *Chinese Communism and the Rise of Mao*. New York: Harper and Row, Inc., 1967.

Scott, James C. "Everyday Forms of Peasant Resistance." James C. Scott and Benedict J. Tria Kerkvliet, eds., *Journal of Peasant Studies* 13, no. 2 (January, 1986).

——— . "Hegemony and the Peasantry." *Politics and Society* 7, no. 3 (1977).

——— . *The Moral Economy of the Peasant: Rebellion and Subsistence in Southeast Asia*. New Haven: Yale University Press, 1976.

——— . "Protest and Profanation: Agrarian Revolt and the Little Tradition." *Theory and Society* 1 and 2 (1977).

——— . "Revolution in the Revolution: Peasants and Commissars." *Theory and Society* 7, nos. 1 and 2 (January–March, 1979).

——— . "Socialism and Small Property—Or Two Cheers for the Petty-Bourgeoisie." *Peasant Studies* 12, no. 3 (Spring, 1985).

——— . *Weapons of the Weak: Everyday Forms of Peasant Resistance*. New Haven: Yale University Press, 1985.

Selden, Mark. *China in Revolution: The Yenan Way Revisited*. New York: M. E. Sharpe, 1995.

——— . *The Yenan Way in Revolutionary China*. Cambridge: Harvard University Press, 1971.

Shanin, Teodor. "Peasantry as a Political Factor." In Teodor Shanin, ed., *Peasants and Peasant Societies*. Penguin: Baltimore: Maryland, 1971.

Sheridan, James E. *Chinese Warlord: The Career of Feng Yu-hsiang*. Stanford: Stanford University Press, 1966.

Shi Guoqiang. "Oral History Notes on the Saltmakers' Struggle in Nanle, Puyang, and Neihuang." Unpublished private manuscript. September, 1979.

——— . "Zhang Fuqiu 'Ba Da Jia' yu 'Xiao Ba Jia' Douzheng Shimou" (The Whole Story of the Struggle Between the Eight Big Families and the Eight Small Families of Zhang Fuqiu). In *Nanle Wenshiziliao* (Nanle Cultural History Materials), No. 2. 1987.

——— , *Zhubian* (Chief Editor). "Yanmin Douzheng" (The Saltmakers' Struggle). *Nanle Xianzhi* (Nanle County Gazetteer). *Henan Sheng Nanle Xian Difangshi Bianzhuan Weiyuanhui* (The Compilation Committee of the Local History of Nanle County of Henan Province). October, 1987.

Shi Guoqiang, ed. *Nanle Xianzhi* (Nanle County Gazetteer), 1991–1992.

Shi Xiaosheng. "Shilun Jin-Ji-Lu-Yu Jiefangqude Tudi Gaige Yundong" (A Discussion of the Land Revolution Movement in the Shanxi-Hebei-Shandong-Henan Liberated Area).

Shi Yibin. "Guanyu Sun Hanzhang Tongzhi Jianqian Zai Nanle Jianshi Jinxing Dixia Geming Houdong Qingkuangde Huiyi" (Recollections of the Conditions of Comrade Sun Hanzhang's Underground Revolutionary Activities at the Nanle Teachers' Primary School Before the War). *Nanle Xian Difangshi Ziliao.* (Nanle County Local History Materials). No date.

"Shoufu Puyang Qianhoude Jidian Gongzhou Jingyan" (A Number of Work Experiences Before and After the Recovery of Puyang). *Jiefang Ribao.* 23 March 1945.

Shue, Vivienne. *The Reach of the State: Sketches of the Chinese Body Politic.* Stanford: Stanford University Press, 1988.

"Shunzhi Sheng Wei Gei Zhongyangde Baogao—Guanyu Youji Zhanzheng He Difang Baodong" (The Shunzhi, Provincial Committee's Report to the CCP Central Committee Concerning Guerrilla War and Local Uprisings) *Zhonggong Nanle Dangshi Ziliao* (CCP Nanle Party History Materials). No. 3, 1986.

Skinner, G. William. "Chinese Peasants and the Closed Community: An Open and Shut Case." *Comparative Studies in Society and History* 13, no. 3 (1971).

———. "Marketing and Social Structure in Rural China." *Journal of Asian Studies* 24, parts 1, 2, and 3 (1964–1965).

———. "Social Ecology and the Forces of Repression in North China: A Regional-System Framework for Analysis." Paper delivered to the ACLS Workshop on Rebellion and Revolution in North China, Harvard University, 27 July – 2 August 1979.

Skocpol, Theda. "France, Russia, and China: A Structural Analysis of Social Revolutions." *Comparative Studies in Society and History* 18, no. 2 (April, 1976).

———. *States and Social Revolutions: A Comparative Analysis of France, Russia, and China.* Cambridge: Cambridge University Press, 1979.

Slawinski, Roman. "The Red Spears in the Late 1920s." In Jean Chesneaux, ed., *Popular Movements and Secret Societies in China 1840–1950.* Stanford: Stanford University Press, 1972.

Snider, Lewis W. "The Political Performance of Governments, External Debt Service, and Domestic Political Violence." *International Political Science Review* 11, no. 4 (1990).

———. "The Political Performance of Third World Governments and their Debt Crisis." *American Political Science Review* 84, no. 4 (December, 1990).

Snow, Edgar. *Red Star Over China.* London: Victor Gallancz, Ltd., 1946.

Song, T. V. "Salt Revenue Loans." Nanjing, 16 November 1928. Arthur N. Young Papers. Stanford Hoover Archives.

Spence, Jonathan D. *The Search for Modern China.* New York: W.W. Norton, 1990.

Strauss, Julia Candace. "Bureaucratic Reconstitution and Institution Building in the Post-Imperial Chinese State: The Dynamics of Personnel Policy, 1912–1945." Ph.D. thesis, University of California, Department of Political Science, 1991.

Strong, Anna Louise. *Tomorrow's China.* New York: Committee for a Democratic Far Eastern Policy, 1948.

Su Zhenghua. "Ji-Lu-Yu Qu Xiaobudui Jianshe Wenti" (The Problems in Establishing the Small Troupe in the Hebei-Shandong-Henan District). December, 1942.

Zhonggong Ji-Lu-Yu Bianqu Dangshi Ziliao Xuanbian (A Selection of CCP Hebei-Shandong-Henan Border Area Party History Materials). Vol. 2. 1941–1943. *Henan Renmin Chubanshe.* 1988.

"Sun Fuzhen Tongzhi Zai 'Puyang Diweijun Gongzuo Zuotanhui' Shangde Fayin." *Zhonggong Puyang Shijiao Wei Dangshi Ziliao* (CCP Puyang Party History Materials). No. 5. *Zhengbian Weiyuan Hui Bangongtai* (The Editorial Office of the CCP Party History Materials Committee in the Puyang City Suburbs). December, 1986.

Sun Hanshang. "Geming Pinbiande Huiyi" (A Remembrance of a Part of the Revolution). *Zhongong Nanle Dangshi Ziliao.* (CCP Nanle Party History Materials). No. 1. *Zhonggong Nanle Xianwei Dangshi Ziliao Zhengbian Weiyuanhui Bangongtai* (Office of the CCP Nanle County Party History Materials Editorial Committee). 1986.

Tai Hsuan-chih. *The Red Spear Society, 1916–1949.* Trans. Ronald Suleski. Ann Arbor: University of Michigan, Center for Chinese Studies, 1985.

Tarrow, Sidney. "Big Structures and Contentious Events: Two of Charles Tilly's Recent Writings." *Sociological Forum* 2, no. 1 (Winter, 1987).

Tawney, R. H. *Land and Labor in China.* Boston: Beacon Press, 1966.

Thaxton, Ralph. *China Turned Rightside Up: Revolutionary Legitimacy in the Peasant World.* New Haven: Yale University Press, 1983.

———. "Fanzhuang Village Land Survey." 1988.

———. "Peasants and Porcelain: Collective Action in China's Rural Trade and Transport Sector During the Republican Period." *Peasant Studies* 16, no. 4 (Summer, 1989).

———. "State Making and State Terror: The Formation of the Revenue Police and the Origins of Collective Protest in Rural North China During the Republican Period." *Theory and Society* 19 (1990).

Thompson, Roger. "Statecraft and Self-Government: Competing Visions of Community and State in Late Imperial China." *Modern China* 14, no. 2 (April, 1988).

Tian Yuan. "Wo Dang Lingdau Puyang Liangmen Yidaide Zaimin Douzheng" (My Party's Leadership of the Calamity Victims' Struggle in the Vicinity of Puyang's Liangmen). *Zhonggong Henan Dangzhi Ziliao* (Henan Party History Materials). No. 4. Henan Renmin Chubanshe. 1985.

———. "Wo Zai Puyang Liangmen Yidai Lingdau Nongmin Yundongde Huiyi" (My Recollections of Leading the Peasant Movement in the Vicinity of Liangmen, Puyang). *Zhonggong Puyang Dangshi Ziliao* (CCP Puyang Party History Materials). No. 1. *Zhonggong Puyang Xian Wei Dangshi Ziliao Zhengbian Weiyuanhui Bangongshi* (CCP Puyang County Committee Office for Collecting and Compiling CCP History Materials). February, 1983.

Tien Hung-mao. *Government and Politics in Kuomintang China 1927–1937.* Stanford: Stanford University Press, 1972.

Tilly, Charles. *Big Structures, Large Processes, Huge Comparisons.* New York: Russel Sage Foundation, 1984.

———. *The Contentious French: Four Centuries of Popular Struggle.* Cambridge: Harvard University Press, 1986.

———. *From Mobilization to Revolution.* Reading, MA: Addison-Wesley Publishing Co., 1978.

————, ed. *The Formation of Nation States in Western Europe*. Princeton: Princeton University Press, 1975.

Tocqueville, Alex de. *The Old Regime and the French Revolution*. Trans. Stuart Gilbert. New York: Doubleday, 1955.

Trujillo, Stephen G. "Corruption and Cocaine in Peru." *New York Times* 7 April 1992.

Tsao, Y .S. "National Life." *China Christian Yearbook, 1934–35*. Shanghai: China Christian Literature Society, 1935.

Tucker, Nancy Bernkopf. *Patterns in the Dust: Chinese-American Relations and the Recognition Controversy, 1949–50*. New York: Columbia University Press, 1983.

"Tuxiao Xiaolu Ri Zeng" (The Sale of Local Nitrate Increases Day-by-Day). *Nong Shang Gongbao* (The Peasants' and Merchants' Newspaper) 4, no. 9 (15 April 1918).

Van Slyke, Lyman P. "The Chinese Communist Movement During the Sino-Japanese War, 1937–1945." In John King Fairbank and Albert Feuerwerker, eds., *The Cambridge History of China*, vol. 13, part 2. Cambridge: Cambridge University Press, 1986.

————. *Enemies and Friends: The United Front in Chinese Communist History*. Stanford: Stanford University Press, 1967.

Verba, Sidney. "Some Dilemmas in Comparative Research." *World Politics* 29, no. 1 (October, 1967).

Wakeman, Frederic Jr. "Models of Historical Change: The Chinese State and Society, 1839–1989." In Kenneth Lieberthal et al., eds., *Perspectives on Modern China: Four Anniversaries*. New York: M. E. Sharpe, 1991.

Walton, John. "Debt, Protest, and the State in Latin America." In Susan Eckstein, ed., *Power and Popular Protest: Latin American Social Movements*. Berkeley: University of California Press, 1989.

Wang Chengfa. "Zhou Laifang." Hu Hua, ed. *Zhonggong Dangshi Renwu (Communist Party Historical Figures)*. Vol. 17. Shaanxi: Renmin Chubanshe, 1984.

Wang Congwu. "Zhinan Shaqu Dang Zuzhide Fazhan He Qunzhongde Geming Douzheng (Yijiu Sanling dao Yijiu Sansan)" (The Organization and Development of the Chinese Communist Party and the Revolutionary Struggle of the Masses in the Southern Hebei Sandy District, 1930–1933). *Zhonggong Ji-Lu-Yu Bianqu Dangshi Ziliao Xuanbian* (A Compilation of CCP Hebei-Shandong-Henan Border Area Party History Materials). No. 1. *Shandong Daxue Chubanshe*. 1985.

————. "Zhongguo Gongchandang Lingdao Pu-Nei-Hua Diqu Renminde Geming Douzheng." (The CCP's Leadership of the People's Revolutionary Struggle in the Puyang-Neihuang-Hua County Area). *Zhonggong Henan Dangshi Ziliao* (CCP Henan Party History Materials). Zhengzhou: *Henan Renmin Chubanshe*. 1985.

Wang Congwu, et al. "Daming Dang Zuzhide Jian Li Qi Yanbian" (The Establishment and Development of the Daming Party Organization). *Zhinan Dangshi Ziliao* (Southern Hebei Party History Materials). 1983.

Wang Congwu, Gao Kelin, Zhang Huizhi, and Wu Baohe. "Puyang Yanmin Douzheng" (The Struggle of the Puyang Saltmakers). *Liaoyuan* (Prairie Fire). No. 3. *Henan Renmin Chubanshe*. 1981.

"Wang Congwu Tongzhi Huiyilu" (Reminiscences of Comrade Wang Congwu).

Recorded by Zhang Linnan in the Henan Province Party Committee School, 19 August 1980. *Zhonggong Puyang Dangshi Ziliao* (CCP Puyang Party History Materials). No. 1. February, 1983.

Wang Guanghua. "Jinan Diqu Dongbu Nongmin Wuzhuang Douzheng Pianduan Huiyi" (Recollections of Parts of the Peasants' Armed Struggles in the Eastern Part of Southern Hebei). *Nangong Fengyunlu* (The Stormy Years in Nangong), *Zhonggong Nangong Xianwei Dangshi Ziliao Zhengji Bangongshi* (CCP Nangong County Party History Materials Collections Office), 1983.

———. "Zhinan Dongbu Nongmin Wuzhuang Douzheng Pianduan" (A Fragment of the History of the Peasants' Armed Struggle in Eastern Part of Southern Hebei). *Jinan Geming Douzheng Shiliao (Materials on the Revolutionary Struggles in Southern Hebei).* 1983.

Wang Jiming. "Daming Lu Jia Zhai De Nongmin Douzheng" (The Peasants' Struggle in Lu Jia Village of Daming). *Zhinan Dangshi Ziliao (Southern Hebei Party History Materials).* 1983.

Wang Jingru. "Guanyu Zuzhi Yanmin Fan Yanxun Chajin Xiaoyande Douzheng Wenti" (About the Issue of Organizing the Saltmakers to Struggle Against the Salt Police Attempt to Forbid the Making of Earth Salt). *Nanle Xian Dangshi Ziliao* (Nanle County CCP History Materials). 14 January 1985.

Wang Shanzeng. "Nanle Hongqianghui De Xingqi Yu Xiaowang" (The Rise and Fall of the Nanle Red Spear Society). Wei Puzhen and Zhang Junhua, eds., *Nanle Wenshi Ziliao* (Nanle Cultural History Materials), Vol. 2, *Zhongguo Renmin Zhengzhi Xieshang Huiyi Nanle Xian Weiyuanhui Wenshi Ziliao Weiyuanhui* (The Committee of Historical Records of the Chinese People's Political Consultative Committee of Nanle County). December, 1987.

Wang Weigang. "Cixian Xiaocheshe Gongren Bagongde Shengli Yu Bailongmiao Baodongde Shibai" (The Victory of the Ci County Small Carters' Society Workers' Strike and the Failure of the White Dragon Temple Rebellion). *Zhonggong Ji-Lu-Yu Bianqu Dangshi Ziliao Xuanbian* (A Compilation of CCP Hebei-Shandong-Henan Border Area Party History Materials). No. 1. Shandong Daxue Chubanshe. 1985.

Wang Zaiduo and Liu Shousen. "Yijiu Sansan Nian Hua*xian* Dongbu Zaimin Fenliang Chidahu Douzheng" (The 1933 Struggle to Distribute and Eat the Grains of the Big Households by the Calamity Victims in the Eastern Part of Hua County). *Huaxian Dangshi Ziliao Tongxin* (Communications on Hua County Party History). Vol. 2. 1986.

Wang Zhigang. "Guanyu Qingfeng Dangshide Jidian Huiyi" (Recalling a Few Points About Qingfeng Party History). *Zhonggong Qingfeng Dangshi Ziliao Xuanbian* (A Selection of CCP Qingfeng Party History Materials). No. 1. 1985.

Wang Zhijia. "Zhinan Tewei Lingdau Xia Huangde Zhiduide Zujian He Fazhan" (The Establishment and Development of the Yellow River Detachment Under the Leadership of the Zhinan Special Committee). *Zhonggong Qingfeng Dangshi Ziliao Xuanbian* (A Selection of CCP Qingfeng Party History Materials). 1987.

Wang Zhiyuan. "Bo-Li Diqude Jiandangde Nongmin Yundong" (The Founding of the CCP and the Peasant Movement in Bo-Li District). *Hebei Geming Huiyilu* (Reminiscences of the Revolution in Hebei). No. 1, Shijiazhuang: *Hebei Renmin Chubanshe,* 1980.

Wei Bacai. "Dui Hua*xian* Dang Zuzhi Chuangjian Qingkuangde Huiyi" (Some Recollections of Founding the Party in Hua County). *Zhonggong Huaxian Xianwei Dangshi Ziliao Zhengbian Weiyuanwei Bangongshi Bianyin (Edited by the CCP Hua County Committee Party History Compilation Committee)*, Vol. 1. 1986.

Wei Hongyun. *Kangri Zhanzheng Shiqi Jin-Ji-Lu-Yu Bianqu Caizheng Jingji Shiliao Xuanbian* (Selections on the Financial and Economic History of the Shanxi-Hebei-Shandong-Henan Border Area During the Anti-Japanese War Period), Nos. 1 and 2. Beijing: *Zhongguo Caizheng Jingji Chubanshe,* 1990.

———. "Lun Huabei Kangri Genjudi Fanrong Jingjide Daulu" (The Road to Economic Prosperity in the Anti-Japanese Base Areas of North China). *Zhongguo Renmin Daxue Shubao Ziliao* (Chinese People's University Journals Publishing House). *Fuyin Baokan Ziliao.* No. 2. 1985. (Originally published in *Nankai Xuebao.* Tianjin. No. 6. 1984.)

———, ed. *Huabei Kangri Genjudi Jishi* (A Chronological History of the North China Anti-Japanese Base Areas). *Tianjin Renmin Chubanshe,* 1985.

Wei, William. *Counterrevolution in China: The Nationalists in Jiangxi During the Soviet Period.* Ann Arbor: University of Michigan Press, 1985.

"Wen Xinggu Shijian" (The Wen Xinggu Incident). *Puyang Wenshi Ziliao* (Puyang Cultural History Materials). *Puyang Weiyuanhui Wenshi Ziliao Yanjiu Weiyuanhui Bian* (Edited by Puyang City Committee Cultural History Materials Research Committee). No. 2. 1986.

White, Theodore H. *In Search of History: A Personal Adventure.* New York: Harper and Row, 1978.

White, Theodore H., and Analee Jacoby. *Thunder Out of China.* New York: William Sloane Associates, Inc., 1946.

Whyte, Martin King. "Who Hates Bureaucracy? A Chinese Puzzle." In Victor Nee and David Stark, eds., *Remaking the Economic Institutions of Socialism: China and Eastern Europe.* Stanford: Stanford University Press, 1989.

Wilbur, C. Martin. "Military Separatism and the Process of Reunification Under the Nationalist Regime, 1922–1937." In Ping-Ti-Ho and Tang Tsou, eds., *China in Crisis: China's Heritage and the Communist Political System,* vol. 1. Chicago: University of Chicago Press, 1968.

Wilson, Dick. *The Long March 1935: The Epic of Chinese Communism's Survival.* London: Hamish Hamilton, 1971.

Wolf, Eric R. *Peasant Wars of the Twentieth Century.* New York: Harper and Row, 1968.

Wou, Ordoric Y. K. "The Impact of Differential Economic Change on Society in Honan in the 1920s and 1930s." Paper presented to the Workshop on Rebellion and Revolution in North China, Harvard University, 27 July–3 August 1979.

———. *Mobilizing the Masses: Building Revolution in Henan.* Stanford: Stanford University Press, 1994.

Wu Baohe. "Dui Yanmin Douzhengde Huiyi" (Recollections of the Saltmakers' Struggle). *Zhonggong Nanle Xianwei Dangshi Ziliao* (CCP Nanle County Party History Materials). No. 1. 1986.

Xu Daben. "Caijing Gongzuo Baogao" (A Report on Financial and Economic Work). 1943. *Zhonggong Ji-Lu-Yu Bianqu Dangshi Ziliao Xuanbian* (A Selection of CCP Hebei-Shandong-Henan Border Area Party History Materials). 1943–1945. Vol. 3. *Henan Renmin Chubanshe.* 1988.

Xu Jinxing. "Changlu Yanwu Yu Tianjin Yanshang" (Changu Salt Affairs and the

Tianjin Salt Merchants). *Tianjin Shehui Kexue* (Tianjin Social Sciences). Tianjin. No. 1. 1983.

Xu Youli. "Sanshi Niandai Ji-Lu-Yu Biande Yanmin Douzheng" (The Struggles of the Saltmakers in the Hebei-Shandong-Henan Border Area in the Early Nineteen Thirties). *Henan Dangshi Yanjiu* (Henan Party History Research). No. 2. 1987.

Xu Yuanbei. "Canjun Yundong Jianbao" (A Brief Report on the Army Recruiting Movement). *Yijiu Sijiu Nian Shangbannian Lai Qu Dangwei Guanyu Tugai Yundong de Zhongyao Wenjian* (Important Documents on the Land Reform Movement During the First Half of 1947 from the Regional Party Committee). *Ji-Lu-Yu Qu Dangwei* (Hebei-Shandong-Henan Regional Committee). June, 1947.

Xu Zhanhua. "Wen Xing Gu Shijian" (The Wen Xing Gu Incident). *Puyang Wenshi Ziliao* (Puyang County Cultural History Materials). *Zhongguo Renmin Zhengzhi Xueshang Huiyi* (The Chinese People's Consultative Conference of Henan Province). *Wenshi Ziliao Yanjiu Weiyuanhui* (The Cultural History Materials Research Committee). No. 2. 1986.

"Yan Changqing Tongzhi Huiyi" (Recollections of Comrade Yan Changqing) (Recorded in 1983 in Chengdu). *Ji-Lu-Yu Bianqu Dangshi Ziliao* (Chinese Communist Party History Materials on the Hebei-Shandong-Henan Border Area). *Ji-Lu-Yu Bianqu Dangshi Ziliao Zhengji, Yanjui Gongzuo Xiaozu Bangongshi Bian* (Compiled by the Office of the Collection and Research Working Group, the Hebei-Shandong-Henan Party History) . No. 3. April, 1984.

Yan Chaogang, ed. *Liu Cun District History, 1985.*

"Yanbing Zhangze" (The Salt Police Regulations). Caizhengbu (Ministry of Finance). February, 1947.

Yang Jiesheng. "Baodong Suiyue Suoyi" (Small Memories of the Years of Rebellion). *Jinan Geming Douzheng Shiliao.* (Historical Materials on the Revolutionary Struggle in Southern Hebei). Zhonggong Xingtai Diwei Dangshi Ziliao Zhengbian Bangongshi Bianyin (Edited by the CCP Xingtai Prefectural Committee Party History Materials Committee). No. 3. 1985.

Yang Shaoxian. "Baodong Suiyue Suoyi" (Miscellaneous Recollections of the Years of Rebellion) *Zhinan Geming Douzheng Shiliao* (Materials on the History of the Revolutionary Struggle in Southern Hebei), No. 3, *Zhonggong Xingtai Diwei Dangshi Ziliao Zhengbian Bangongshi Binyin* (Compiled and Printed by the Compilation and Collection Office of the CCP Xingtai Prefectural Committee on Party History Materials), 1985.

———. "Daming Yanmin Douzheng Jianshu" (A Simple Account of the Daming Saltmakers' Struggle). *Zhinan Dangshi Ziliao* (Southern Hebei Party History Materials). *Zhonggong Handan Diwei Dangshi Ziliao* (Chinese Communist Party Handan District Committee Party History Materials). No. 2. 1983.

"Yanmin Baodong Jinan Di—Puyang Shi Laochengqu Xi Suipo" (The Locale of the Rebellion of the Salt Makers—Xi Suipo in the Old City District of Puyang Market Town). *A Local History of Puyang County. No date.*

"Yanshui Jia Sanjiao." *Tianjin Da Gong Bao.* 16 July 1932, p. 2.

Yanzheng Zhazhi (The Journal of Salt Administration). Vol. 63. February, 1936.

Yao Huibin. "Dui Nanle Xian Kangzhan Zhong Jige Wentide Huiyi" (My Recollections of Several Problems in Nanle County During the Anti-Japanese War). *Zhong-*

gong Nanle Dangshi Ziliao (CCP Nanle Party History Materials). No. 2. *Zhonggong Nanle Xian Dangshi Ziliao Zhengbian Weiyuanhui Bangongshi* (Edited by the CCP Nanle County Committee Party History Compilation Committee). 1985.

Yi Shuansun. "Salt Taxation in China." Ph.D. thesis, Department of History, University of Wisconsin, 1953.

"Yijiu Saner Nian," (1932).

"Yijiu Sanwu Nian Shiyue Xiaoyan Jiufen" (The 1935 October 10 Disputes Over Nitrate Salt). *Yanzheng Zazhi* (The Journal of Salt Administration) 63 (February, 1935).

"Yijiu Sanwu Nian Wuyue Jinan Xiaoyan Douzheng" (The May 1935 Struggle Over Nitrate Salt in Southern Hebei). *Yanzheng Zazhi* 61 (August, 1935).

Yin Yigang. "Huiyi Rongchengxian Jiandang Chuqide Yixie Geming Huodong" (Recollections of a Few Revolutionary Activities and the Early Days of Party-Building in Rongcheng county). *Hebei Wenshi Ziliao (Hebei Cultural History Materials).* No. 10. *Hebei Renmin Chubanshe.* 1983.

Young, Arthur N. "China's Pre-War External Obligations Under Charge of the Ministry of Finance." June, 1945. Hoover Archive papers of Arthur N. Young.

——— . Letters and Memos of 6 September 1929, 25 August 1932, 19 July 1937, 10–11 December 1937, 21 December 1937, 22 December 1937. Hoover Archives.

——— . "To C. S. Tao, Director, Loan Department, Ministry of Finance, Shanghai." 19 July 1937. Hoover Archive papers of Arthur N. Young.

——— . "To the Director General of the Chinese Government Salt Administration in Shanghai" from Cassels, W. C. (of the Hong Kong and Shanghai Banking Corp.) and L. Chevretton (representative of le Bank de l'Indochine). Also: letter of associate director general to M. Paul Emile Naggiar, Ambassadeur de France, Shanghai, 18 December 1937. Hoover Archive papers of Arthur N. Young.

Yung Fa-chen, "Between Survival and Ideology: The CCP Commercial Experience in Yan'an." Conference on Construction of The Party-State and State Socialism in China, 1936–1965. Colorado College, Colorado Springs, March, 1993.

——— . *Making Revolution: The Communist Movement in Eastern and Central China.* Berkeley: University of California Press, 1986.

Zagorin, Perez. *Rebels and Rulers 1500–1660,* vol. 1: *Society, States and Early Modern Revolution.* Cambridge: Cambridge University Press, 1982.

"Zai Hebei Sheng Zhengfu Minzhengting Tongling" (An Excerpt from the Hebei Provincial Government Civil Administration Department Order). *Tianjin Da Gong Bao* 16 April 1935.

Zelin, Madeleine. "The Rise and Fall of the Fu-Rong Salt Yard Elite: Merchant Dominance in late Qing China." In Joseph W. Esherick and Mary Backus Rankin, eds., *Chinese Local Elites and Patterns of Dominance.* Berkeley: University of California Press, 1990.

Zhang Huaiwen. "Ji-Lu-Yu Kangri Genjudi Gonggu Yu Fazhande Yuanyin Chutan" (An Exploration of the Reasons for the Consolidation and Development of the Hebei-Shandong-Henan Anti-Japanese Base). *Henan Dangshi Yanjiu* (Henan Party History Research). Nos. 2–3. 1987.

Zhang Linzhi, "Guanyu Ji-Lu-Yu Qunzhong Yundong Qingkuang Ji Yijian"

(Opinions on the Circumstances of the Mass Movement in Hebei-Shandong-Henan), *Zhonggong Ji-Lu-Yu Bianqu Dangshi Ziliao Xuanbian* (A Selection of CCP Hebei-Shandong-Henan Party History Materials). No. 2 (1943–1945). *Henan Renmin Chubanshe*, 1988.

——— . "Guanyu Zhinan Dangshi Zhong Jige Wentide Yijian" (Opinions on Several Problems in Southern Hebei Party History). *Jinan Geming Douzheng Shiliao* (History Materials on the Revolutionary Struggle in Southern Hebei). 1983.

——— . "Yinian Laide Dang Yu Qunzhong Gongzuo" (Party and Mass Work in the Past Year). *Zhonggong Ji-Lu-Yu Bianqu Dangshi Ziliao Xuanbian* (A Selection of CCP Hebei-Shandong- Henan Border Area Party History Materials). No. 2 (1943–1945). *Henan Renmin Chubanshe*. 1988.

Zhang Wenjie. "Jin-Ji-Lu-Yu Genjudi Chuangjian Yu Fajian Shulue" (A Brief Account of the Construction and Development of the Shanxi-Hebei-Shandong-Henan Base Area). *Henan Dangshi Yanjiu* (Henan Party History Research). Nos. 2–3. 1987.

Zhang Zengjing. "Yubei Shaqu Geming Douzhengde Yixie Huiyi" (Some Reminisces of the Revolutionary Struggle in Northern Henan's Sandy District). *Liaoyuan* (Prairie Fire). No. 3. *Henan Renmin Chubanshe*. 1981.

Zhang Zifeng and Zhang Yingfu. *Henan Huoxiao Tuyan Zhi Diaocha* (An Investigation into Saltpeter and Earth Salt in Henan). *Huanghai Huaxue Yanjiusuo* (The Yellow Seas Chemistry Research Institute), 1932.

Zhang Ziyou (Wang Zepu). "Nanle Xian Yanmin Douzhengde Huiyi" (Recollections of the Salt Makers' Struggle in Nanle County). *Zhonggong Nanle Xianwei Dangshi Ziliao* (CCP Nanle County Committee Party History Research Materials). No. 1, 1984.

Zhao Chunzhi. "Kaizhan Au Xiaoyan Yundong" (Starting the Movement to Boil Earth Salt) (7 September 1941). In Wei Hongyun, ed., *Kangri Zhanzheng Shiqi Jin-Ji-Lu-Yu Bianqu Caizheng Jingji Shiliao Xuanbian* (A Compilation of Finance and Economic History Materials on the Shanxi-Hebei-Shandong-Henan Border Area During the Anti-Japanese War Period). No. 2. Beijing: *Zhongguo Caizheng Jingji Chubanshe*. 1990.

Zhao Jibin. "Huiyi Puyangde Geming Douzheng" (Recollections of the Revolutionary Struggle in Puyang). *Zhonggong Henan Dangshi Ziliao (CCP Henan Party History Materials)*. No. 4. *Henan Renmin Chubanshe*. 1985.

——— . "Nongcun Pochan Shenzhong Jinan Yige Fanrongde Cunzhuang" (A Prosperous Village in the Disintegrating Southern Hebei Countryside), *Zhongguo Nongcun Jingji* (Chinese Peasant Economy), 1935.

——— . "Zhinan Shaqu Dang Zuzhide Zaoqi Huodong." (The Early Movements Organized by the Party in the Southern Hebei Sandy District), *Zhonggong Ji-Li-Yu Bianqu Dangshi Ziliao Xuanbian* (A Compilation of CCP Hebei-Shandong-Henan Border Area Party History Materials). No. 1. *Shandong Daxue Chubanshe*. 1985.

Zhao Wei. *The Biography of Zhao Ziyang*. Hong Kong: Educational and Cultural Press, Ltd., 1989.

Zhao Xiaomin. *Zhongguo Geming Genjudi Jingjishi, 1927–1937* (The Economic History of China's Revolutionary Base Areas, 1927–1937). *Guangdong Renmin Chubanshe*. 1983.

Zhao Ziyang. "Hua*xian* Qunzhong Shi Ruhe Fadong Qilaide" (How the Masses of Hua County Rose Up). *Zhonggong Zhongyang Ji-Lu-Yu Fenjuyin* (Printed by the Hebei-Shandong-Henan Sub Bureau of the Central Committee of the Chinese Communist Party) (written in 1944). 26 May 1946.

Zhengfu Gongbao. 23 August 1915.

"Zhinan Kangri Youji Zhanzhengde Zhuanbian Jiqi Shenglide Fazhan" (The Transformation of the Anti-Japanese Guerrilla War in Southern Hebei and Its Victorious Development) . *Huo Xian* (Firing Line). No. 44. 31 August 1935. Reprinted in *Zhonggong Ji-Lu-Yu Bianqu Dangshi Ziliao Xuanbian* (A Selection of CCP Hebei-Shandong-Henan Border Region Party History Materials). *Shandong Daxue Chubanshe.* 1985.

"Zhinan Laoku Qunzhong Wuzhuang Douzheng Kaishande Xingshi Yu Zhinan Dang Zai Lingdao Youji Yundong Zhongde Cuowo" (The Conditions of the Development of Poor People's Armed Struggle in Southern Hebei and the Mistake of the Southern Hebei Party in the Course of Leading the Guerrilla Movement). *Zhonggong Ji-Lu-Yu Bianqu Dangshi Ziliao Xuanbian* (Selected CCP History Materials on the CCP Branches in the Hebei-Shandong-Henan Border Area). *Shandong Daxue Chubanshe.* 1985.

"Zhinan Nongmin Youji Zhanzhengde Shimo" (The Whole Story of Peasant Guerilla War in Southern Hebei). *Jinan Geming Douzheng Shiliao* (Historical Materials on the Revolutionary Struggle in Southern Hebei). No. 3. *Zhonggong Xingtai Diwei Dangshi Ziliao Zhengbian Bangongshi Bianyin (Edited by the CCP Xingtai Prefectural Committee Party History Compilation Committee).* 1985.

"Zhinan Nongmin Douzheng Yu Youji Zhanzheng" (The Peasant Struggle and the Guerrilla War in Southern Hebei). From *Beifang Hongqi* (Northern Red Flag). No. 5. 5 July 1932.

"Zhinan Tewei Baogao" (The Southern Hebei Special Committee Report). *Fan Di Douzheng Gangling Tewei Wenti, Tewei Dui Yanfu Gongzuode Buzhi* (The Strategy of the Anti-Imperialist Struggle) (The Problem of the Special Committee, and the Special Committee's Assignment for Working with the Salt People). 31 January 1933. Handwritten copy from Nanle County.

"Zhinan Tewei Gongzuo Baogao" (Southern Hebei Special Committee Work Report). No. 1. "Ge Zhongxin Xianwei Qinghuang; Gongren Douzheng Wenti" (The Conditions at the Core of Each County Committee; The Workers' Struggle Problem). *Hebei Sheng Danganguan* (Hebei Provincial Archives). 5 June 1932.

"Zhinan Tewei Liang He Yanfu Gongzuo Jue Yian" (Resolution on Southern Hebei Special Committee Work with the Salt Farmers of Henan and Hebei). *Hebei Sheng Danganguan* (Hebei Provincial Party Archives). 1932.

"Zhinan Zhengzhi Jingji Yu Qunzhong Douzheng De Xiezhen" (An Authentic Portrayal of the Political Economy and the Mass Struggle in Southern Hebei). From *Honqi* (Red Flag), no. 5 (1929).

Zhonggong Ji-Lu-Yu Bianqu Dangshi Dashiji (A Chronology of Events of CCP Hebei-Shandong-Henan Border Region Party History). *Zhonggong Ji-Lu-Yu Bianqu Dangshi Bianweihu Bian* (CCP Hebei-Shandong-Henan Border Region Compilation Committee). *Shandong Daxue Chubanshe.* 1987.

Zhonggong Nanle Xian Dangshi Dashiji (A Chronicle of Nanle County Party History Events), 1988.

Zhonggong Puyang Xian Dang Zuzhi Houdong Dashiji, 1926–1949 (A Chronicle of CCP Organized Events and Activities in Puyang County, 1926–1949). *Zhonggong Puyang Xianwei Dangshi Ziliao Zhengji Bianzuan Lingdau Xiaozu Bangongshi* (Office of the Leadership Group of the Collection and Compilation of Party History Materials of the CCP Puyang County Committee). July, 1982.

Zhongguo Shiye Zhi: Shandong Sheng. (China Industrial Records: Shandong Province). *Shanghai Shiyebu Guoji Maoyizu.* 1934.

Zhou Dongguang. "Yujiu Sanwunian Pingxiang Yanmin Wuzhuang Douzheng" (The Pingxiang Saltmakers' Armed Struggle of 1935). *Jinan Geming Douzheng Shiliao* (History Materials on the Revolutionary Struggle in Southern Hebei), *Zhonggong Xingtai Diwei Dangshi Ziliao Zhengbian* (Compiled and Printed by the Compilation and Collection Office of the CCP Xingtai Prefectural Committee on Party History Materials), 1983.

Zong Fengming. "Guanyu Puyang Diqu Geming Lishide Huiyi" (Memories of the Revolutionary History of Puyang District). *Ji-Lu-Yu Kangri Genjudi.* No. 1. *Zhonggong Henan Shengwei Dangshi Ziliao Zhengji Bianzuan Weiyuanhui Bian* (Compiled by the Collection and Compilation Committee on CCP Party History Materials of Henan Province). *Henan Renmin Chubanshe.* 1985.

INDEX

Compositor: Braun-Brumfield, Inc.
Text: 10/12 Baskerville
Display: Baskerville
Printer and Binder: Braun-Brumfield, Inc.